THE CANTATAS OF
JOHANN SEBASTIAN BACH
SACRED AND SECULAR

VOLUME I

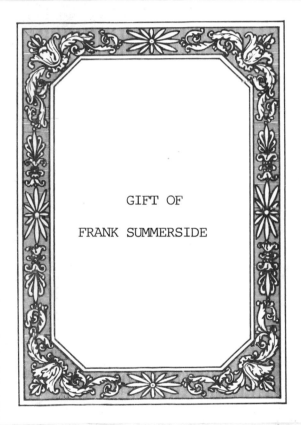

THE CANTATAS OF
JOHANN SEBASTIAN BACH

SACRED AND SECULAR

W. Gillies Whittaker

VOLUME I

LONDON
OXFORD UNIVERSITY PRESS
NEW YORK · MELBOURNE

Oxford University Press, Walton Street, Oxford OX2 6DP

OXFORD LONDON GLASGOW NEW YORK
TORONTO MELBOURNE WELLINGTON CAPE TOWN
IBADAN NAIROBI DAR ES SALAAM LUSAKA
KUALA LUMPUR SINGAPORE JAKARTA HONG KONG TOKYO
DELHI BOMBAY CALCUTTA MADRAS KARACHI

© *Oxford University Press 1959*

ISBN 0 19 315238 X

First published 1959
Reprinted 1964
Paperback re-issue 1978

PRINTED IN GREAT BRITAIN
BY THE STELLAR PRESS, HATFIELD AND
BOUND BY HENRY BROOKS (BOOKBINDERS) LTD
OXFORD

To

THREE GLASGOW FRIENDS

and associates in the production of many of these works

Percy Gordon, *Music Critic of* The Glasgow Herald

Dr. Bernard Hague, *oboe, oboe d'amore, and cor anglais*

and

Harold Thomson, *continuo*

this book is gratefully and affectionately dedicated

APOLOGIA

THE author can scarcely hope that many people will read this book in its entirety. Those who may dip into its pages will probably only do so on account of some favourite work, to discover if their impressions coincide with those of the writer, or perhaps it will be consulted by conductors who are producing this or that cantata. He has had in mind cases similar to his own when the vocal music of Bach first began to fascinate, when he had never heard any of the cantatas, when limited financial resources would not permit him to purchase more than an occasional second-hand vocal score, when he had never seen any of the full scores, and was, consequently, entirely ignorant of Bach's schemes of orchestration and subtleties of orchestral colour, and when intimate understanding of the music was denied him on account of lack of knowledge of German.

Texts and Translations: It may seem unnecessary to have quoted all the original texts of arias, duets, trios, and choruses, but few readers will be able to refer to all the German scores and may only possess English editions; without the words one cannot possibly grasp the meaning of the music, or understand Bach's methods. Also, the texts of the church cantatas indicate the religious outlook of the people of Bach's time, reveal his beliefs and faith, and help us to reconstruct his mental and spiritual life. Those of the secular works give us insight into the official ceremonies and into the home life of the burghers and Bach's relations with his friends. Most of the translations are in thoroughly bad English, but the writer's plan has been to make them as literal as possible, however crudely they may read. To see how Bach deals with individual words, to see how the music springs unerringly from the text, it is necessary to be able to follow word by word throughout. The genius of the German language is so essentially different from the English that to attempt any literary style in translation inevitably throws words in the wrong places and gives an entirely false impression of Bach's manner of treatment. It has not always been possible to carry out this plan minutely; for instance, German separable verbs completely baffle one's endeavours. But, in the majority of cases, there is sufficient correlation to enable the student who does not know German to understand every detail. In the translations of recitatives, where the original text is not quoted, the placing of marks of punctuation in corresponding places will help the student to keep his place, however strangely they may sometimes appear in English. One point to be remembered is that every German noun begins with a capital letter. Another reason for giving full translations is that much of the text is exceedingly difficult to follow, even for those who are familiar with the language, on account of turgid style, antiquated or obsolete words and expressions, and far-fetched similes and allusions. Even Germans are often puzzled by these texts. It cannot be too strongly emphasized that in Bach's vocal writings the text *is* the music. One serious handicap they have suffered from in this country is the fact that most of the translations of published vocal scores are totally inadequate; they give little or no insight into Bach's methods of dealing with verse and prose. In the writer's previous book (*Fugitive Notes on certain Cantatas and the Motets of J. S. Bach*) certain cases are dealt with at length. In this book the original texts of the recitatives are rarely quoted, because there is little repetition of words, and the translation enables the line to be followed.

It is obvious that this book will be less unendurable if analyses and descriptions are read with score (vocal or orchestral, the latter infinitely preferable) in hand, but it is realized that few readers will be able to do this. Hence the large number of musical quotations. In large centres one finds that it is not difficult to persuade a sympathetic City Librarian to add to his shelves the complete church cantatas in vocal score, 20 volumes of 10 each. An earnest student is always certain to find a personal request courteously considered.

In *Fugitive Notes* the writer collated the opinions of distinguished critics; here he has adopted the opposite course, and has recorded his personal impressions, chiefly gained by performances of the works, and has only referred to other commentators by way of comparison.

ACKNOWLEDGEMENTS

To three friends he is particularly indebted—Frau Elizabeth von Kameke, of Bach's natal town, Eisenach, and Miss Muir, of Glasgow, for supervision of the translations of the German texts, for disentanglement of their many knots, for information concerning numerous obscure allusions, and for providing interpretations of the

Italian poems; and Mr. Harold Thomson, for reading the script and for many invaluable suggestions arising out of his comprehensive and intimate knowledge of the work of Bach. In addition, warm thanks are due to other friends who have read all or part of the type-sheets and corrected many errors. Without the urgent insistence of Mr. C. Kennedy Scott, the conductor of the London Bach Cantata Club, the task would not have been begun, and without the aid of other kind helpers it could not have been completed.

However faulty the result, it has been a great joy to the writer to re-read, over and over again, the volumes of the Bach Gesellschaft, to try to put his thoughts in order and to live again through the wonderful experiences which opportunities of preliminary study, rehearsal, and performance have afforded him for over forty years. The late Sir Henry Hadow once said, 'Music is the greatest of all spiritual forces', and no more convincing proof of this article of faith can be found in the whole range of art than in the inexhaustible subject which has been dealt with so inadequately in this book.

W. GILLIES WHITTAKER

GLASGOW

PUBLISHER'S NOTE

Dr. Whittaker died after completing the typescript of this book, but before making his final revisions. These revisions were carried out by Mr. Harold Thomson, who also undertook the very considerable task of reading and correcting the proofs and seeing the book through all its stages. The Oxford University Press would like to express its deep gratitude to Mr. Thomson for all his labours.

The Press would also like to record with grateful thanks the help it has received towards the publication of the book from the Whittaker Memorial Fund, from Mr. Edward Pollitzer and the Whittaker family, and from the University of Glasgow.

In the years since the author's death, there has naturally been a great deal of research into the subject of Bach's cantatas. Most of this is not relevant to the present book. The reader should however take note of one matter of importance: the researches of Alfred Dürr have established new or revised dates for many of the cantatas. A complete list of the cantatas with these new dates will be found on pages 736-8 of Volume II, and should be consulted. This list has been compiled from Dr Dürr's *Die Kantaten von Johann Sebastian Bach* (Cassel, 1971) and his *Zur Chronologie der Leipziger Vokalwerke J. S. Bachs* (1976), by kind permission of the author and of the publishers, Bärenreiter Verlag.

CONTENTS
VOLUME I

CONTENTS

VOLUME II

NOTE

[Editions of music and books mentioned below are not necessarily in print at the present time; they may, however, be available in libraries, &c.]

WHERE cantatas are issued with English texts the following indications are used: B. = Messrs. Breitkopf & Härtel; N. = Messrs. Novello & Co.; O. = Oxford University Press; Sc. = Messrs. Schirmer, Inc. Where no such indications are added to the German titles, German texts only were available at the time of writing. All the church cantatas, except some that are incomplete, and most of the secular cantatas are issued by B., and 100 church cantatas are found in the Peters edition. (The latter are not indicated in the following pages.) A number of Sinfonias, &c., are issued in the Oxford Orchestral Series, O. They are indicated O.O.S. with number. The following issue of separate numbers with English words from the cantatas are indicated: 'Bach's Extended Chorales' Oxford University Press = B.E.C. with number; 'Oxford Choral Songs' Oxford University Press = O.C.S. with number; 'Oxford Series of Bach Arias' Oxford University Press = O.S.B.A. with number; Prout's 'Songs and Airs by J. S. Bach', Messrs. Augener & Co. = P. with number; 'Arias, Duets, &c. by J. S. Bach', Messrs. Stainer & Bell = S. & B. with title. Dates of church works and the particular Sunday of the year are stated in all cases, and it is made clear which are conjectural. It may seem that such detailed particulars are frequently unnecessary; the average layman, for instance, is not interested in the desert of Sundays which follows Trinity. On the other hand, even these occasions indicate a certain point, that the cantatas in question were not for important days in the church year, and that we need look for no special significance. When one knows that a cantata is for Christmas or New Year's Day, or for Easter, Whitsuntide, or Advent, one is aware of the qualities to be expected, one can compare the style and treatment in other works for the same festivals, and one is able to penetrate to the core of the music and its significance more readily. These facts are taken from the late Professor C. S. Terry's edition of Forkel's *Johann Sebastian Bach* (Constable), corrected by later research in his *Bach's Cantata Texts* (Cambridge University Press), and his *Bach, a Biography* (O.), together with additional matter which he generously placed at my disposal shortly before his death.

The use of Italian and English plurals to words derived from the former language, it must be admitted, is irregular. The principle has been adopted that such words as 'obbligato', 'corno', and 'flauto' where it is attached to 'traverso', retain their Italian plurals, but the common use of 'oboes', &c., is preserved, even though 'oboes d'amore' and 'oboes da caccia' be unpalatable linguistic mixtures. 'Arpeggios' and ''cellos' are ugly words, 'arpeggi' and ''celli' are therefore used. 'Bassi', to signify the orchestral 'celli and contra-basses (violone) as distinct from the choral basses, comes under a different category.

The reference *Fugitive Notes* is to the author's *Fugitive Notes on certain Cantatas and the Motets of J. S. Bach*. (O.), where a much more detailed analysis is given than is possible in a book dealing with the whole series.

Bach Gesellschaft is abbreviated to *BGS*.

References to individual numbers in a cantata are given in small Roman numerals—i, ii, iii, &c.

Where 'Gospel' or 'Epistle' is quoted, it is to be understood that it is the portion of Scripture assigned in the Leipzig services for the Sunday or Feast Day for which the particular cantata was composed.

PART I

THE CHURCH CANTATAS
FIRST PERIOD

PRELIMINARY

WE yet await a complete knowledge of the church cantatas by Bach's predecessors and contemporaries. Spitta did much research, a few examples have been published since his day, others are being gathered together in libraries, unknown except to a few scholars. Until the great mass of this material is studied in detail, we cannot estimate accurately Bach's indebtedness to other composers, how much already existing music he adapted to his own purposes (borrowings were so common in his day that we must assume that much music by other men reappears in his cantatas), how much of the advance in that branch of composition was due solely to him. We are apt to think of him as the only writer of the type of church cantata which is now inevitably associated with his name. There were many before him and many contemporary with him. Some of the church musicians of the day wrote more examples than he did. He was only one worker in the field, exerting little, if any, influence on his fellows.

We also await a comprehensive and detailed study of his church cantatas.[1] Spitta, Parry, Pirro, and Schweitzer say many pregnant things concerning them, it is true, but only as a part of their general survey of the vast field of his work, and in many cases important and interesting features are, of necessity, granted only passing references. Spitta and Parry heard few of the cantatas with orchestra; some of the latter's criticisms would, doubtless, have been revised after actual performances. Schweitzer, in his great book on Bach, the foundation of modern interpretation, complained that band parts of many had never been copied since the composer's day, a hiatus which has now been filled. The looked-for survey, to which this book is to be regarded merely as an introduction, must be based not only on a study of the scores, but must be accompanied by a practical knowledge of

[1] To avoid repetition the word 'cantata' is to be understood as signifying 'church cantata' throughout Parts I, II, and III.

the *sound* of the music itself, which, again and again, reveals matters which a silent reading of the volumes of the *BGS* leaves undiscovered. The time is ripe for such a minute examination of the entire series, for scholarship has been active. German writers, in the Bach Year Book and other publications, have contributed largely to our critical estimates. The chief honour, however, lies with a British scholar, the late Professor C. Sanford Terry, whose brilliant labours have brought order and light into our previously somewhat chaotic condition of knowledge. His three volumes on *Bach's Chorales* (Cambridge University Press) provide an encyclopedia where every known fact is marshalled. His *Bach's Orchestra* (O) contains a vast amount of information on a much-misunderstood subject, arranged in such a way that we can study in the briefest time the composer's methods of treatment of the instruments of the period, and trace every appearance of each and every variety of compass and method, in the orchestral works. *Bach's Cantata Texts, Sacred and Secular* (Constable) not only records every known historical detail, but, for the first time, reconstructs the entire services at Leipzig, so that we may see exactly what prayers, lessons, hymns, collects, &c., were used on the occasions at which the cantatas were produced, an illuminating aid to their study and interpretation. Without a knowledge of these much remains obscure, and the following pages refer to them constantly. His *J. S. Bach* (O) brings out many new facts and sets others in clearer light than in the foggy erudition of Spitta. The chronological table in his edition of Forkel's *Johann Sebastian Bach* (Constable) gives a bird's-eye view of the series, with much detailed information. No longer have we to spend untold hours in hunting through the *BGS* prefaces, through Spitta, Parry, and Schweitzer, for this or that detail. The path of study has been made easy. Schering's introductory notes in his edition of miniature scores are also most valuable.

The writer of this book makes no pretence to scholarship. No fresh knowledge relating to the cantatas is revealed in the following pages; historical facts are quarried from the authorities quoted. The utmost the author can claim is a practical acquaintance gained by rehearsing and conducting in public all the church cantatas. This experience has taken about forty years, in which many of the works have been given twice or oftener, but the rest, alas, only once. In practically all cases the writer has not accepted the expression marks and other directions given in the vocal scores, nor the bowing and tonguing in the printed orchestral parts, but has begun his pre-

paratory study for public performance with the almost naked
BGS volumes, has constructed all schemes and details of expression
afresh, and has marked practically every band part with his own
hand. Only by intimate work of this kind can one get to know a
cantata thoroughly. Yet to conduct a cantata once or twice is merely
to gain a bowing acquaintance with it and to realize how much
better one could interpret it were opportunities more frequent,
opportunities not only to perform, but to experiment time and time
again, at rehearsals, with the innumerable problems of balance and
tone-colour which arise, chiefly due to the differences between the
instruments of Bach's day and those of our own. His strings, flutes,
and brass were much less powerful than ours, his oboes more coarse
and nasal, his bassoons less suave. We cannot contrast the two types
of flute, beak and transverse, some obsolete instruments must of
necessity be replaced by modern substitutes. Players of the violino
piccolo, viola da gamba, and viola d'amore are rare, the contra-bass
does not adequately represent the violone, a harpsichord is not always
available, our organs are of a different calibre. Conditions of performance were then vastly different. Instead of a choir lined up on a
platform, with orchestra in front of it and soloists in front of that
again, with possibly a remote organ, his forces were all gathered
in the organ gallery, far from the congregation and out of sight.
Players and singers could move about, soloists could stand next the
obbligati players, performers could advance to the edge of the bal-
cony if need be, balance could be obtained by an adjustment of
positions. Performances may have been erratic, under-rehearsed, and
casual, manuscripts were hurriedly copied and were often crowded
with errors, but conditions were more plastic than those imposed by
modern conditions. Works were written for all sorts of occasions and
then forgotten; no one was sufficiently interested in them to per-
petuate any record of manner and method. Bach's church music
rapidly fell into disuse; no tradition remained. We know how in our
country, where Handel's compositions have never vanished from the
repertoire, last century showed a complete breaking away from his
own manner of performance. We rarely hear any of his music as he
intended that it should be heard. How much more, then, have we
to discover, by faithful adherence to the scores and by liberal experiment with modern forces, of the right manner of presenting Bach to
his public?

Performances of the church cantatas are so few, and often so wrong-headed, that we cannot judge of them as we do the symphonies of Beethoven and of Brahms. Life is short, and public opinion is not yet ripe for a sufficient number of performances to make the cantatas household words and to give conductors adequate opportunities for testing various methods of treatment. In a sense, the knowledge of these works has just begun. For a hundred music-lovers who know the quartets and concertos and symphonies of Beethoven thoroughly, there is possibly only one who has read through the volumes of the *BGS*. Yet we have advanced far beyond the opinion expressed by Eugène d'Albert (a member for a time of the committee of the *BGS*, by the way!) in 1906, ' There are those who can sit and listen to Bach's cantatas for two hours at a stretch, and say that they enjoy it and do not grow tired of it. They are either incorrigible pedants or unmitigated dissemblers. The manner in which the composer dealt with the words renders it impossible for us, with our modern ideas and feelings, to sit and listen to them for any length of time.' Bach's church cantatas are now being given more than ever they were; most large British cities now possess a Bach Choir, and the competitive festival movement has made some of these works familiar to the artisan, the shop-girl, and the farm-hand. We now realize that neither a large nor a technically skilled choir is necessary, and that the cantatas are mostly effective with small forces.

Even a slight acquaintance with them reveals how inexhaustible is the mine of wealth, and how infinitely varied its treasures. To quote Terry (Appendix II to his edition of Forkel, also published in the *Proceedings of the Musical Association*):

We have the statement of Carl Philipp Emmanuel Bach, confirmed by Forkel, Bach's earliest biographer, that his father composed five Cantatas for every Sunday and Festival of the ecclesiastical year. Concerted music was sung at Leipzig annually on forty-three Sundays and sixteen week-days. Bach therefore must have written at least 295 cantatas. Of this number he composed at least thirty before 1723. Hence approximately 265 were written at Leipzig. But Bach's fertility does not appear to have outlived the year 1744. We have reason, therefore, to conclude that the 265 Leipzig Cantatas were written in the course of twenty-one years, that is, between 1723 and 1744. To complete that number Bach must have composed a new Cantata every month, a surprising but demonstrable conclusion.

Of the 295 Cantatas only 202 have come down to us, three of them in an incomplete state. Of those written before 1723 the survivors are too scanty to indicate a rate of productivity. But thereafter we have fuller materials for a calculation. Bach, as Cantor, conducted his first Leipzig Cantata on May 30th, 1723, and in the following sixteen months produced twenty-four

Cantatas at the rate of more than one a month. Beginning at the New Year of 1725 he wrote eighteen Cantatas in nine months, some of which, however, may belong to the years 1726–7–8–9. But even so, his monthly average seems to have been maintained. For 1730 we have, perhaps, ten Cantatas. For 1731 about twenty survive, of which half-a-dozen may belong to 1732, a deduction which still preserves Bach's steady average. In 1735 he produced actually nineteen Cantatas between the New Year and the following November, though not all of them are positively dated. Thereafter his activity is less certainly measured. But from 1736 till the end of 1744 he composed fifty-three Cantatas, at the rate, that is, of at least six every year, without making allowance for Cantatas written and lost.

I make no apology for this long quotation, as it brings before us vividly the amazing fertility and the unceasing industriousness of the composer. Neither must we forget that many were revised and rewritten, sometimes more than once.

The three periods into which Terry divides the cantatas are those adopted here: I, The pre-Leipzig years; II, Leipzig, 1723–34; III, Leipzig, 1735–44. The classification is arbitrary; at least three of the first so-called Leipzig cantatas were written at Cöthen, there are many cases where early material appears in works produced later, there is no definite change of style between the last two periods, though certain tendencies become more marked in the third. The grouping, however, is the most satisfactory that could be made, and is convenient for the discussion of this great mass of compositions. The numerous reconstructions and the absence of many chronological details make any attempt at strict classification a matter of extreme difficulty.

The early cantatas, that is, those of the pre-Leipzig years, are not merely interesting from an historical point of view. Many of them exhibit a splendour, a virility of outlook, a richness of imagination, a speculative daring, and an experimental search for colour and diversity which are sometimes unobservable in the middle and late periods. They are all well worth considering and some of them are among his most perfect masterpieces. One factor which results in diversity at Arnstadt, Mühlhausen, Cöthen, and Weimar is the variety of the libretti. In Leipzig, when his chief duty, to provide immense quantities of music for the services, necessitated incessant and frequently hurried production, and when he had set himself the task of completing the five-year cycle, he was often compelled to rely upon stereotyped and at times poverty-stricken libretti, or, in his anxious search for texts, upon complete hymns, which severely limited his scope. He became reconciled to the constant division into separate choruses, arias, duets, and recitatives. He became reconciled, also, to the regular aria form, which, despite his boundless invention, produced too many numbers of similar quality, and which tended, at times, especially when the subject-matter was not inspiring, to lead him to rely upon set formulae.

In the early days we find a continuity and a freedom of design which make one regret the influence of so many of the middle and later libretti. In six out of the first seven cantatas he uses texts in which Biblical verses form the whole or a considerable proportion. These have not only the advantage of the high literary quality of Luther's rugged prose, but they lend themselves to a more flexible and coherent general structure than the libretti of later days. Among the cantatas which follow immediately, four out of the five libretti by Erdmann Neumeister, whose was the first *collection* of ready-made texts upon which Bach drew, contain Biblical quotations. So also do two of the ten to thirteen drawn from Salomo Franck's collection, one of them culling very liberally from Scripture. As we shall see, some of the finest of the early works are those associated with Biblical verses. Neumann's type of libretto unfortunately set the fashion for poetasters, who found it an easy matter to scribble texts for composers who had not the time to compile libretti themselves from the Bible and the chorale book.

Another interesting feature in these early works is Bach's choice of orchestral combinations. The consideration of his scoring is one which has not yet been subjected to a detailed and thoroughly practical criticism, although Terry, in his *Bach's Orchestra*, has summarized with remarkable skill and insight the methods of use of the instruments themselves. The old idea that he had no sense of orchestral colour, and that he belonged to an almost Palaeolithic era in this respect, not only dies hard, but in many quarters shows no sign of decay. It is rare to find scrupulous attention, so far as present-day instruments will allow, to Bach's intentions. To give one example—even in London, where oboes d'amore are available, the soprano recitative, 'Although our eyes with tears o'erflow' and the aria, 'Jesus, Saviour, I am Thine', in the *St. Matthew Passion*, are commonly accompanied, not by two oboes d'amore, whose tender sympathetic tones were specially chosen by Bach for these numbers, but by ordinary oboes, the character of which is lacking in the essential need of the score, and the compass of which necessitates 'cooking', or by two cors anglais, whose sombre colour is not appropriate to the text.

As the latter appear in the 'Golgotha' alto recitative and aria near the end of the work, Bach's carefully selected contrast is wantonly destroyed. What would be said of a conductor who gave the little oboe cadenza in the first movement of Beethoven's fifth symphony to a clarinet, who ordered the shepherd's lament in the third act of *Tristan* to be played on a saxophone? Times out of number his subtle combinations, written for a definite purpose, are set aside for nondescript scoring. Conductors are apt to assume that the vocal lines are all-important, and that the instruments provide mere accompaniment, to be regarded with but scant respect. One world-renowned British conductor, when questioned as to his reason for certain orchestral methods in the B Minor Mass, replied, 'But it is a *choral* work'. At a miscellaneous Bach concert attended by the writer in London, there was scarcely a single number in which the original scoring was untampered with.

Some time ago the present writer wished to give one of the small secular cantatas, scored for strings and flute only, chamber music of an intimate character. The arrival of the manuscript full score from the publisher was a shattering blow. A well-known orchestral conductor had 'arranged' it for performance. Two bassoons were added, the 'celli were frequently divided, the bowing of the bassi in one number, carefully indicated by Bach and containing much delightful phrasing across the beat, was completely altered, but, worst of all, three trumpets were added to some arias. Even if these had been treated in the style of the period they would have been utterly out of the picture, but the spoiler thought of Bach as an organist, and imagined him playing continually with his clarion stop drawn. The trumpets blazed away page after page; no singer could have been audible without bellowing himself hoarse. Where a figured bass was filled up the texture was so congested that the result was only a chaotic noise. This was foisted on the public in a stage form as Bach!

It must be stated emphatically that Bach's writing for orchestra demands much more careful attention than his writing for chorus. No doubt we sometimes find perfunctory scoring, when he was in a hurry to finish something for a pressing occasion. Other composers are not guiltless of this. No doubt he was sometimes compelled to double his vocal lines with instruments in order to pull through inefficient singers and unrehearsed soloists and choristers. Handel did the same thing; in some of his operas he seemed unable to trust his prime donne to keep on the rails without the compelling force of unisonal violins and oboes. Bach did not always have at command players of the calibre he desired or the instruments he wanted. We sometimes find alternative obbligati when a cantata was repeated; he was obliged to replace, say, an absent or inefficient flute by a solo violin. If a hornist or an oboist were indisposed on the Saturday the parts would have to be rewritten or adapted before Sunday morning, and as the work might not be given again, score and parts would be left as they were.

We must not forget the limited field of choice of his players and singers, the inadequacy of some of his orchestra, the disturbing changes that occur in every choir, even where modern organization compares favourably with the chaotic conditions at St. Thomas's which his complaints to the Council reveal. He was not an ideal diplomat with his fellow workers, his disputes were legion, his shortness of temper and his innate stubbornness would not pour oil on the troubled waters. Engrossed in his life-work of composition he would have little patience with the detailed duties of a producer. The reply made to Joachim, who, on meeting a grandson of John Sebastian who had been in the choir, asked what the cantatas were like under the composer's direction, 'Oh, he cuffed us a lot and they sounded awful', was not surprising. Works hurriedly prepared just in time for performance, parts speedily copied out by Bach himself, his wife, his family (some of them just learning to write and so prone to error), and his pupils, devoid of expression marks, full of inaccuracies, words and notes frequently almost illegible, copies shared by two or more singers or players, could scarcely have made possible a high standard. A modern choir will rehearse a chorus for weeks before allowing it to be heard in public. This could not have been the case at Leipzig. Then think of the difficulty of the music, and how it taxes the abilities of our soloists and in some cases highly skilled obbligati players today. One's wonder at the miracle of the composition of this immense mass of music is increased when one remembers the conditions of production, and one marvels that Bach should have continued, year after year, to pour out these immortal works under such circumstances.

To return to orchestral questions. That there are occasional miscalculations is not to be denied. It is not surprising considering his innumerable experiments. All important modern composers, possibly with the exception of Elgar, have made miscalculations, in spite of the unlimited opportunities today of hearing orchestras. But we cannot be *sure* that there is any defect until we have experimented in various ways. It often takes repeated trials and much patience with and on the part of orchestral players, before the desired balance can be secured. One common criticism of Bach listeners is the surplus of bass tone. 'Cellists and contra-bassists are generally apt to be too powerful when accompanying an aria or a recitative, especially as the modern contra-bass is a much heavier instrument than the silky-toned violone for which Bach wrote. Only continual insistence on the need of balance brings them to a right proportion in the scheme. 'Cellists, in particular, love to glory in their sonorous tone, and do not realize the necessity for suppression. One frequently finds that an unassertive amateur is more amenable in this respect than a hardened professional. Where recitatives are 'secco', with string bassi and continuo only, and where no organ is available, it is difficult to get just proportion with a pianoforte. Yet it is wrong to omit the string bassi. Then again, conditions alter values. Few of us, for instance, can reconcile ourselves to the horn, two bassoons, 'celli, contra-bassi, and continuo in the 'Quoniam tu solus sanctus' in the B Minor Mass. It sounds so thick and turgid, the bass soloist seems the struggling Laocoön in the coil of enveloping serpents, only there are three strangling monsters instead of the classical two. Very often one breathes a sigh of relief when the choir plunges into the succeeding number. Yet the late Dr. Frank Bates told me that the acoustics of Norwich Cathedral make this combination not only satisfactory in every way, but profoundly beautiful. One supreme advantage of performances with a small choir is that Bach's intentions can be realized without reconstructing and augmenting the orchestral scoring. One critic said that he had never understood the meaning of the orchestration of the choruses in the *St. Matthew Passion* until he heard it with a choir of forty. Sir Hugh Allen told me that of the numerous performances of the B Minor Mass he had conducted, that of the London Bach Cantata Club, with a choir of sixty, was the most overwhelming.

In small centres we cannot expect to find the rarer instruments, and it is not unforgivable to adapt what forces lie at hand, providing the composer's intentions are carefully considered. On the other hand there are many cantatas which can be performed accurately with the common instruments; it is better to choose these than to attempt those which lie outside of normal possibilities. After all, there are 200 from which to select.

The constant references to scoring which follow are not mere cataloguing, but an attempt to draw attention to the salient features of Bach's instrumental methods, especially for readers who cannot refer constantly to the volumes of the *BGS*. It may be pointed out, in passing, how much more was expected of musicians in those days in the matter of different clefs. A modern vocalist or pianist is at a loss if he encounters anything save the ordinary treble and bass clefs. The right-hand part of clavier music was usually written in the soprano clef, flutes found their G on the first line, 'cello parts were written in bass, tenor, and alto clefs, if Bach used a double line of violas the upper was written with the normal clef and the lower with the tenor, and orchestral players were expected to read the chorale from the vocal parts, whatever clef was to be found there.

Bach's orchestra was never stereotyped. I have pointed out elsewhere (*Fugitive Notes*) that in the known cantatas he uses no fewer than 153 different orchestras, and that, except for the choruses, it is rare to find the same selection of instruments repeated within a single cantata. In Leipzig, where he had a fairly regularized set of players, with the town musicians to draw upon, he experimented incessantly. In his early years, when he had to make shift with any group which chanced to be available at the moment, his combinations were all the more varied, and he exploited them with the eager enterprise and curiosity of youth.

In his solitary Arnstadt cantata, 'Denn du wirst meine Seele nicht in der Hölle lassen' ('For Thou wilt not leave my soul in Hell'), No. 15—there are two clarini, principale, timpani, and strings, with continuo. (As continuo is always implied, it will not be mentioned every time.) In the Arnstadt Solo Soprano Magnificat—flute, two solo violins, violetta, bassi.

The six Mühlhausen orchestras[1] are all different: 'Aus der Tiefe rufe ich, Herr' ('Out of the darkness call I, Lord'), No. 131—oboe, bassoon, one line of violins, two lines of violas, bassi. (The word 'bassi' will always mean 'celli and violone.) 'Gott ist mein König' ('God is my King'), No. 71—a young man's prodigal score, which will be spoken of in more detail later, and only tabulated here—three trumpets, timpani, two flutes (beak-flutes, no doubt, as the G clef is on the first line in the manuscript score), two oboes, bassoon, strings, and organ obbligato. ('Organ obbligato' always signifies an independent part.) 'Der Herr denket an uns' ('The Lord has been

---

[1] In each group the cantatas are given in the supposed order of composition.

mindful of us'), No. 196—strings only. As it was for a family wedding perhaps nothing more ambitious was forthcoming. 'Meine Seele rühmt und preist' ('My soul doth magnify'), No. 189—a chamber-music combination—flute (possibly transverse, as the normal G clef is employed), oboe, solo violin, bassi. 'Nach dir, Herr, verlanget mich' ('Lord, my soul doth thirst for Thee' B.), No. 150—bassoon, two lines of violins, bassi. 'Gottes Zeit ist die allerbeste Zeit', the Actus Tragicus ('God's time is the best' N., 'God's time is best' B.). No. 106—two beak-flutes, two gambas and bassi, no violins or violas. The combinations of the Weimar period are: 'Gleich wie der Regen und Schnee vom Himmel fällt' ('For as the rain cometh down' B.), No. 18—two beak-flutes, bassoon, four lines of violas, bassi, no violins. 'Ich weiß, daß mein Erlöser lebt' ('I know that my Redeemer liveth'), No. 160—another chamber-music combination—bassoon, solo violin, and bassi. 'Ich hatte viel Bekümmerniß' ('My spirit was in heaviness' N., 'I had great heaviness of heart' B.), No. 21—three trumpets, timpani, four trombones, oboe, bassoon, and strings 'Mein Herze schwimmt im Blut' ('My heart swims in blood'), No. 199, and 'Bereitet die Wege, bereitet die Bahn' ('Prepare the path, prepare the way'), No. 132—oboe, bassoon, and strings. 'Nun komm, der Heiden Heiland', the first of the two with that name, ('Come, Redeemer of our race' N., 'Come, Thou blessed Saviour, come' B.), No. 61—bassoon, one line of violins, except in the bass recitative, where they are divided, two lines of violas, bassi. 'Uns ist ein Kind geboren' ('Unto us a child is born'), No. 142—two beak-flutes, two oboes, and strings. 'Himmelskönig, sei willkommen' ('King of Heaven, be Thou welcome' O.), No. 182—beak-flute, one line of violins, two lines of violas, bassi. 'Der Himmel lacht, die Erde jubiliret' ('The heavens laugh' O., 'The heavens rejoice' B.), No. 31—the largest independent orchestra up to this time (in No. 21 the trombones merely double the voices), three trumpets, timpani, three oboes, taille, bassoon, two lines of violins, two lines of violas, two lines of 'cclli, violone. 'Barmherziges Herze der ewigen Liebe' ('Merciful heart of eternal love'), No. 185—trumpet, oboe, bassoon, and strings. 'Komm, du süße Todesstunde' ('Come, thou lovely hour of dying' O., 'Come thou blessed hour' B.), No. 161—two beak-flutes, strings, and organ obbligato. 'Ach, ich sehe, jetzt da ich zur Hochzeit gehe' ('Ah, I see, as I now go to the marriage'), No. 162—corno da tirarsi, bassoon, and strings. 'Nur Jedem das Seine' ('To each only his due'), No. 163—oboe d'amore (possibly a later reconstruction, as the instrument was not to be found in Weimar, so far as we know), strings, with an obbligato to the bass aria for two 'celli and continuo. 'Tritt auf die Glaubensbahn' ('O walk the heavenly way' O., 'Walk in the way of faith' B.), No. 152—beak-flute, oboe, viola d'amore, viola da gamba and bassi. 'Mein Gott, wie lang', ach lange' ('My God, how long, ah long'), No. 155—bassoon and strings. 'Wer mich liebet, der wird mein Wort halten', the first of the two with this title, ('If a man love me, he will keep my word'), No. 59—two trumpets, timpani and strings. 'Wachet, betet, seid bereit allezeit' ('Watch ye, pray ye' N.), No. 70—trumpet, oboe, bassoon, and strings. 'Herz und Mund und That und Leben' ('Heart and mouth and deed and life'), No. 147—trumpet, two oboes, oboe d'amore (again a Leipzig addition), two oboes da caccia (possibly later additions), bassoon, and strings (only two oboists are needed). 'Der Friede sei mit dir' ('Joy be with thee'), No. 158—oboe, solo violin, and bassi.

From Cöthen we have: 'Wer sich selbst erhöhet, der soll erniedriget werden' ('Whosoever exalteth himself he shall be abased'), No. 47—organ obbligato, two oboes, and strings.

It will be seen that one orchestra is used twice, but that in all other cases the combinations are different. It will also be noticed that the normal grouping of strings is frequently departed from, that he exhibits, in these early days, a fondness for a double line of violas (a common feature with his predecessors), in three cases with only a single line of violins above, and in one instance he carries his liking for violas to the extent of writing for them in four parts. In another case, 106, he does not use violins or violas at all. Two lines of 'celli appear twice. Both forms of flute are employed. At times, without doubt, as has already been pointed out, he would be compelled to write for whatever was at hand; he was not like Wagner, who scored as he desired and then forced the world to provide for him according to his needs, but in the majority of cases his choice was deliberate and for particular ends. We lose infinite variety and subtlety and the effect of the scoring is devastated if we cut and hack and add. The orchestration of his earlier cantatas is full of interest and charm, and a detailed study of that side of his work helps us to understand his aims.

There are four pre-Leipzig periods:

Arnstadt	1704–7;	age 19–22.
Mühlhausen	1707–8;	age 22–23.
Weimar	1708–17;	age 23–32.
Cöthen	1717–23;	age 32–38.

15. *Magnificat for Solo Soprano*

15. BACH must have entered into his residence at Arnstadt full of youthful hope and ardour. The charming little red-roofed town is pleasantly situated at the end of a plain which is guarded by castle-crowned low hills. Duties were light, he had a small organ of his own on which to practise, he was subordinate to the Consistory only. His troubles were brought about by himself, his inability to manage his choir-boys, his quick temper, his objection to submit to authority, his long absences caused by his insatiable desire to learn all that was possible in his art. It is strange that there are not more Arnstadt compositions in existence, for we cannot imagine that his pen was lacking in diligence. The solo Magnificat can only be placed there problematically; No. 15, for Easter Day 1704, is the only cantata. It is modelled on the works of North German composers and it is likely that it was written before his visits to Lübeck to sit at the feet of the great Danish composer and organist Buxtehude.

As the cantata was reconstructed some ten years later at Leipzig, its text is somewhat of a mixture. Spitta surmised that it was originally for the Second Day of Easter, and that the first libretto consisted of a hymn of seven stanzas, a customary practice with church composers of the period. In that case the old material is from v to the close of the quartet, x, as the final chorale is a Leipzig addition. The original form contained no chorus, the choir boys of the Neue Kirche were a poor lot. The scoring is for clarini I and II, principale, timpani, strings and, of course, continuo. The term clarino, which Bach employs in Nos. 24, 48, and 167 in addition to No. 15, is merely an Italian name for trumpet, and has no special significance, except that a slightly different mouthpiece, 'shallow and saucer-shaped' (Terry, *Bach's Orchestra*) was probably used. The principale is the third of the group, restricted to lower notes, and the mouthpiece was 'larger, deeper, more cup-shaped'. Strings begin, adagio, with solemn chords, the gloom of the sepulchre, there being four pauses in five bars. There is an interesting comparison between this opening of Bach's first cantata and the introduction to Beethoven's first symphony. Certainly, the older composer does not begin out of the key, but the chords C major, A minor, E major, and E minor (with a false relation) precede a half-close. The listener is not allowed to reflect long on the tomb, for an Allegro ensues. On the tonic chord brass and percussion thrice hammer out ♫ ♪ , strings dovetail the same idea, and a flourish of clarini I and II in thirds leads to the cadence. As the Sonata, viii, also consists of an Adagio, though different from this, and an Allegro slightly altered from the first, it may be that the original cantata began with this nine-bar orchestral prelude, which later was incorporated into the bass number (it cannot be called strictly either arioso or aria), which now became i. As in the other added portions Bach was careful to preserve his youthful style; in spite of the ten years of tremendous advance before the reconstruction, no incongruity of manner is manifest. The bass confidently announces (Ps. xvi. 10):

Ex.1

Strings repeat the phrase in the dominant. When the singer repeats *per arsin et thesin* clarino I imitates and there is a short tutti. 'Und nicht zugeben' ('and not yield') is imitated by dovetailing strings and brass plus percussion, and then there is a passage with continuo, 'daß dein Heiliger verwese' ('that thy Holy One perish'), with a long flourish on 'Heiliger'. Part of the orchestral Allegro concludes.

ii is a long soprano recitative, so-called, for the first half is arioso, with continuo. 'Mein Jesus ware todt' ('My Jesus was dead') repeats partially and wholly, in order to balance the next clause; dropping continuo phrases tell of the descent to the tomb. 'Nun aber lebt er von Ewigkeit zu Ewigkeit' ('Now however lives He from eternity to eternity') is extended to ten bars, sequentially rising semiquavers adorn 'lebet', 'Ewigkeit' has sustained notes and runs. 'His ascension delivers me from death's distress, and has for me through the grave' is pure recitative; 'den Lebensweg bereit' ('the life-way prepared') reverts to arioso and there are flourishes on 'Lebensweg'. The remainder is plain recitative: 'How could it otherwise be? A man he can indeed die, God however lives ever; dies He now as a man, so can the coffin Him not destroy, rather comes putrefaction into danger. He who me already in the flesh is like, would through the last enemy to me also alike be. I am through His burial only recovered and enters immortality into my weakness.' There is much repetition of words in 'die mich ihm einverleibet, damit mein Leib, wie er, nicht in der Erd' verbleibet' ('which me in Him embodies, that my body, as Himself, not in the earth remains'), thus stressing the message of the Resurrection.

In the S.A. duet with strings, iii, two ideas from the opening ritornello serve for vocal themes:

Ex.2
Vl.I.

is ornamented for 'Weichet, Furcht und Schrecken' ('Yield, fear and horror'), not at all apposite (an opportunity he would never have missed in later days), and

Ex.3
Vls.I.II.

is set to the last word of 'ob der schwarzen Todesnacht' ('of the black death-night'), as if to suggest wandering blindly in the darkness. Upper strings cease in Part II and the voices appear singly in tuneful phrases with effective continuo imitations: A. 'Christus wird mich auferwecken, der sie hat zum Licht gemacht' ('Christ will me awaken, Who them has to light brought'), S. 'und den Tod, im Sieg verschlungen, als er durch das Grab gedrungen' ('and death in victory swallowed when He through the grave pierced'). In iv, tenor aria, Allegro, the whole orchestra reappears, and there is a powerful tonic-and-dominant introduction, brass, percussion, and continuo leading off and upper strings imitating. The voice begins with the clarino idea (with continuo) and then plunges into quavers:[1]

Ex.4

_____
[1] Bach's continuo figuring is quoted wherever possible. Sometimes it is incomplete, or missing altogether.

clarino I entering in quavers during the run. One of the answering
ideas of the ritornello is given to the tenor, whose cries of 'entsetzet'
are replied to by brass and drums, while upper strings stress the strong
beats by mounting arpeggio-wise. It is all the chord of C only, but
Bach's meticulous care of individual lines demands nine separate
parts. The ritornello is repeated and the second clause is sung: 'Ihr
suchet Jesum von Nazareth, den Gekreuzigten' ('Ye seek Jesus of
Nazareth, the crucified'). Appropriately, the noisy orchestral elements are silent, there are simple imitations between upper strings
and voice, as if the inquirers were following each other, and the
eagerness of the quest is delightfully expressed by repetitions: 'Ihr
suchet Jesum, ihr suchet Jesum, ihr suchet Jesum von Nazareth.'
'Den Gekreuzigten' is sung twice to wailing phrases. The drama is
pursued: 'Er ist auferstanden und ist nicht hie' ('He is arisen and is
not here'). Vocal and instrumental ideas are significant of the Ascension. As if in sympathy with the searchers' desire for the person of the
Christ, 'nicht hie' is twice repeated without accompaniment and with
answering phrases in the strings. The Da Capo type of aria had not
been fully established; here Bach adopts it but writes out the old
section afresh.

We now arrive at the original material, v, verse 1 of the hymn, a
soprano aria, *Allegro, ma non presto*, with strings. The voice for
which it was written must have been exceptional, for the range is
from fiddle G to E, top space; it is better to substitute a contralto.
iv is restricted to key C on account of the brass; it is strange that the
composer did not transpose v to obtain contrast, especially as both
arias are in $\frac{6}{4}$ and have bright straightforward tunes:

Ex.5

The soloist develops this into a seven-bar phrase: 'Auf, freue dich
Seele, du bist nun getröst, dein Heiland, der hat dich vom Sterben
erlöst' ('Up, rejoice thyself soul, thou art now comforted, thy Saviour
He has thee from death redeemed'). It is a curious device that nowhere does the continuo play with the voice. The only apparent
reason is that the composer may have intended to suggest that the
command and the message are from heavenly voices. The upper

strings accompany for five bars, a solo violin with a few notes from the violas joining in at the close. The ritornello comes in the dominant, and then come two short passages for the voice, embodying (*a*)—'Es zaget die Hölle, der Satan erliegt' ('Trembles hell, Satan succumbs') and 'der Tod ist bezwungen, die Sünde besiegt' ('death is subdued, sin conquered'). The end of each of these is unaccompanied and the orchestra answers with the first half. A similar vocal idea is sung to 'Trotz sprech' ich euch allen, die ihr mich bekriegt' ('Defiance speak I to you all, who me combat'), and it is expanded, upper strings joining in the extension. Again the ritornello rounds off the aria; *p* and *f* signs abound. It is an admirable piece of early straightforward, tuneful writing.

Part II opens with the most interesting number of the cantata, verses 2, 3, and 4 of the hymn, a virile, imaginative scena for A.T.B. soli, somewhat crude, no doubt, but full of tremendous vigour and real warlike Old Testament feeling, which appealed more to Bach in his youth than the mystic cult of Christ-adoration which produced such wonderful spiritual fruits in later years. It falls into five sections, (1), (3), and (5) with continuo only, (2) and (4) with brass and percussion added. (1) The alto demands 'Wo bleibet dein Rasen' ('Where remains thy raging'). 'Rasen' tears in violent semiquavers, the bassi follow with a blustering passage:

Ex.6

The demand is repeated, 'Rasen' roaring through 3½ bars of semiquavers while the bassi play (*a*) thrice. The clause continues, 'du höllischer Hund' ('thou hellish hound') and (*b*) is played twice. During 'wer hat dir gestopfet den reißenden Schlund, wer hat dir, o Schlange, zertreten das Haupt' ('who has to you stopped up the tearing throat, who has of thee oh snake trampled upon the head') the continuo is plainer, though still vigorous. The tenor joins in four bars of duet, the time changing to ¾: 'und deine siegprangenden Schläfe entlaubt?' ('and thy victory-flaunting temples stripped?'). Returning to common-time, tenor and alto twice call out antiphonally, 'Sag Hölle' ('Say hell'), and then join to 'wer hat dich der Kräfte beraubt?' ('who has from thee strength robbed?'). (2) The answer is vouchsafed in majestic tones:

and brass and percussion repeat; the Royal Victor advances in all the pomp and circumstance of a military procession. The singer repeats the phrase with 'bei Lorbeer und Fahn' ('with laurel and banner') added, and the 'military music' answers with the complete phrase. The last four words are sung twice again, with a long dignified run, followed by a partially decorated holding note, on 'Lorbeer'; during the latter clarini I and II add a fanfare while the bassi trill. The march enters again followed by a fanfare for unaccompanied brass clenched at the cadence by drums and continuo. (3) The procession halts, and the spectators, differentiated from the martial throng by the absence of all but the continuo, address each other and the enemy in agitated tones, as if in confusion, A.—'Eilt, eilt, verrennet dem Rückgang die Bahn' ('Haste, haste, bars the retreat the road'). There are runs on 'eilt' and a stamping continuo. T.—'Tod, greife den Stachel und würge um dich' ('Death, grasp the sting and spread destruction around thee')—a stationary continuo. A.—'du giftige Natter, ver-neu're den Stich' ('thou poisonous snake, renew the sting')—a strong continuo. A.T. in imitation, afterwards in parallel motion—'ein Jedes versuche das Beste vor sich!' ('each seek the best for himself') —a moving continuo with one imitation. T.—'Seid böse, ihr Feinde, und gebet die Flucht' ('Be evil, ye enemy, and take to flight')—a slowly moving continuo. A.T. at first separately, then in parallel motion—'es ist doch vergebens was ihr hier gesucht' ('it is yet in vain, what ye here seek')—a firmly moving continuo. (4) The procession resumes its march, and the Herald sings the vocal line of (2), with modifications, to fresh words—'Der Löwe von Juda tritt prächtig hervor' ('The Lion of Judah steps splendidly forward'). The run on 'Lorbeer' is transferred to 'prächtig', broken so as to admit of a repetition of the word, and the decorated sustaining note is lengthened from eight to eleven beats, with a new flourish at the end, to make 'prächtig' more important than 'Lorbeer'. The continuo of the first two bars of the run is simplified, brass and percussion crash in on chords every two beats. The clarini flourish over the holding note is elongated. A new section is introduced, beginning as before, but break-ing into a more florid 'prächtig', joined by clarini. There are slight alterations in the final ritornello. (5) A.T. at first in imitation and then independently with cross accents: 'ihn hindert kein Riegel noch höllisches Thor' ('him hinders no bolt nor hellish gate') with a firm continuo. The movement begins in F and concludes in E minor, a bold tonal scheme. It shows how early in his career Bach had begun to understand the functions of the continuo. It is no mere support, but a vital factor in the whole; throughout this scena it is as important in the delineation of moods as the voices. After a performance of the cantata it is this trio which stands out most vividly in the memory, it is so elemental in force, the onlookers, the Herald, and the victorious procession are painted in such striking colours, a visual picture is called up before the mind.

In vi, verse 5, S.A. duet with strings (the upper ones never join the voices), the ambitious youth boldly attempts the impossible, a simultaneous presentation of joy and sorrow. The leaping quavers certainly speak of happiness and the descending semitones of grief, but they nullify each other:

both voices continue, 'ob einerlei Fall' ('over the same cause'). Terry points out that the verse runs, 'Ihr klaget mit Seufzen, ich jauchze mit Schall, Ihr weinet, ich lache: ob einerlei Fall.' He does not quote his authority. If correct, it means that Bach rearranged the words in order to contrast the two moods in different voices.

The first section consists of a seven-fold repetition, instrumental and vocal, of Ex. 8 in double counterpoint. The bassi employ (a) in almost every bar of the aria, except in the ritornelli. The voices now enter singly: A. 'euch kränket die plötzlich zerstörete Macht' ('you hurts the suddenly destroyed might'), S. 'mir hat solch Verderben viel Freude gebracht' ('to me has such destruction much joy

brought'). The two voices impressively sing short phrases with (a)
on the continuo between, and then naïvely depict a ripple of laughter:

The whole passage from 'euch kränket' is repeated with the voices
in reverse order, and Bach loves his little laugh so much that it comes
twice before the Da Capo, the second time *p*.

viii is the *Sonata*. The six-bar Adagio is not the same as the
opening; there is now no thought of the sepulchre. The Allegro
differs from that of the beginning of the cantata in a slight rescoring
only. The remainder of the work runs continuously. Verses 6 and 7
serve for a short tenor and bass arioso and recitative secco, ix, and
for a quartet, x, and a Leipzig addition closes, an extended chorale,
stanza 4 of N. Herman's 'Wenn mein Stündlein vorhanden ist'
('When my little hour (last hour) is at hand') to the poet's own
melody. The tenor elaborates for 2½ bars the second word of 'Therefore thank the Highest, the destroyer of war, the good giver of such
fortunate victory!' The bass sings simply, 'Speak, soul', and the
longish quartet begins, with continuo only. The bass leads off and
there is an admirable touch at the beginning where three names of
the Christ (the Breitkopf vocal score inaccurately prints 'Jesu' instead
of 'Helfer') stress F♯, which is also made prominent in the continuo,
as if He were penetrating every nook and corner of our being:

The same voice continues, 'die Fülle der Satzung und donnerndem Wort', ('the abundance of precepts and thundering word'), with rollings on 'donnerndem'. Bass and tenor sing 'bleib' künftig, mein Heiland, mein Beistand und Hort!' ('remain in the future, my Saviour, my standby and refuge!') in the same manner that we have noticed previously, voices separately and then in parallel motion. Soprano and alto now take up the strain for twenty bars, moving much in thirds and sixths (so often Bach's method of indicating bliss), 'Dir schenk' ich mich eigen, vertilge die Sünd', die sich noch in Geistern und Herzen befind!' ('To Thee give I my own self, wipe out the sin which itself still in spirit and heart finds!') and all voices conclude the section homophonically: 'regier' die Begierden' ('direct the desires'). The complete orchestra echoes the phrase, all unite when the phrase is sung again with the addition of 'und halte sie rein' ('and keep them pure'). With continuo only bass and tenor, followed by soprano, sing simply, 'und weil du gebüßet durch schmerzliche Pein' ('and because Thou hast atoned through grievous pain'). A more animated figure appears:

Ex.11 (a)

so   dek - ke   die   Schul - den
so   cover   the   debts

and is taken up by the other voices and the strings, concluding, 'dein Grabmal und Stein' ('Thy monument and stone'). The full orchestra enters with the 'regier'' idea, and the text from this point is sung again, homophonically at first, more elaborately when (a) is reached, clarino I partaking in the figure. An expansion of the 'regier'' theme forms the ritornello running into the chorale. The limited scope of the brass instruments does not prevent the clever young composer from making this section twenty-two bars in length. The whole movement is admirable in its tunefulness, variety, and skill.

Remembering the wonderful extended chorales in the cantatas written for Bach's first two Sundays in Leipzig, Nos. 75 and 76, one may feel a little disappointment with the concluding number (marked 'adagio', B.E.C. No. 1, O.). Yet it was the composer's sense of fitness which dictated that it should not show all the resource he had acquired since the days of Arnstadt. It fits in with the style of the rest of the cantata and makes a dignified and stirring conclusion. The violins begin with imitations on notes 1–4 of the melody, violas and bassi pulsate in repeated quavers. Lines 1–6: 'Because Thou from death arisen art, Shall I in the grave not remain, My highest comfort Thine Ascension is, Death's fear can it drive away; For where Thou art there come I thither, That I ever with Thee live and am', are delivered simply and accompanied by pulsating strings. After lines 1, 2, 3, and 4 come fanfares for brass and percussion, the strings forsaking their pulsations and moving more vigorously. Lines 5 and 6 are continuous, and just before the latter ends the strings, *f*, burst into semiquavers, which accompany line 7: 'Therefore journey I thither with joy.' During the last note there is a short fanfare. This is the last line, and Bach expands it. The choir, with continuo only, shout out the first four words— ♪♪♪♩ , another tutti fanfare answers, and before this is ended, the voices enter with lively passages containing runs on 'Freuden', the orchestra joining in the exultation.

It is a pity that there are not more performances of No. 15. It possesses many fine qualities in spite of immaturity in certain directions; the numbers are short, direct, and tuneful, it contains such striking things as i and vi, its youthful outlook makes an immediate impression on an audience. The chorale needs a chorus, a quartet would be obliterated by trumpets and drums, but it is easy to sing. The work is a worthy prelude to a series unsurpassed in the realm of church music.

Magnificat for Solo Soprano (O)

Although this is not strictly a church cantata, and although it can be placed at Arnstadt conjecturally only, it may justly be discussed in the present book and at this point.[1] Two settings of the Magnificat have been known, that in Latin and cantata No. 10, which is in the vernacular, partly paraphrased. In the preface to vol. xi (1) of the *BGS* (1862), in which the former appeared, the editor, Wilhelm Rust, wrote:

We have also to mention a one-voiced Magnificat for soprano and small orchestra, divided into several arias. The autograph referred to belonged for about six or eight years to the late Professor S. W. Dehn, and we had at the time opportunity to see for ourselves, with our own eyes, the authenticity of the work. Since then it has completely disappeared, and it is to be deplored that in spite of all endeavour one has not been able to recover possession of it.

[1] I am indebted to the proprietors of *Music and Letters* for their kind permission to quote largely from my article in the issue of October 1940.

Dehn (1799–1858), head of the music department of the Royal Library in Berlin, was an active worker in the copying of Bach manuscripts for the early volumes of the BGS, besides being a scholar of renown. Spitta (English translation, ii. 374) refers to the lost work, but in the appendix (A. no. 24, p. 685) expresses doubt as to whether Bach ever wrote another setting than those known.

In the December 1938 issue of the *Musical Times*, Mr. M. D. Calvocoressi reviewed a catalogue of the musical manuscripts in the Saltykov-Sachedrin Public Library at Leningrad, which had been prepared by Professor Andrey Rimsky-Korsakov, the composer's son. One of the items mentioned was a Magnificat for soprano solo, flute, violin, and continuo. Through the kind offices of Mr. Calvocoressi, I immediately got into touch with M. Grinev, chief of the Anglo-American department of the Society for Cultural Relations with Foreign Countries, in Moscow. M. Grinev, whose courtcous and kind assistance I wish to acknowledge warmly, instituted inquiries in Leningrad and replied that it merely numbered a few pages and was apparently only a fragment of the complete work in the Berlin State Library. The description in the catalogue did not tally with this, so I pressed the matter further. The Moscow Committee generously supplied me with a photostat. It was the missing work, complete in every particular; moreover, three paragraphs on a spare page revealed the strange story of its disappearance.

The first is in German in Dehn's writing:

The composition, the 'Magnificat' to the German translation, Luke 1, 46, for one soprano voice with flute accompaniment, one violin and continuo, is written by the hand of Johann Sebastian Bach, and originates from his younger years, believed to be before 1720. Berlin, October 1st, 1857. Professor S. W. Dehn, Custos of the Royal Library in Berlin.

Dehn's description is extraordinarily slipshod for a man of his stamp, especially considering that the manuscript had been in his possession for some years, for the first number only is scored in the manner mentioned, several subsequent movements employing two violins and one a violetta. But an even stranger circumstance is revealed in the second paragraph, in the same script (in German): 'To Herr Alexis Lvoff' (in French): 'Master at the Court, Senator & Director of the Imperial Russian Chapel in St. Petersburg'. Lvov (1798 or 1799–1870) is chiefly known to us as the composer of the national anthem of pre-Soviet Russia. Besides holding an important military position, as adjutant to Nicholas I, he was very well known in his own country and in Germany as a remarkably good violinist and quartet leader. Dehn's connexion with Russian music is familiar to us: Glinka and Anton Rubinstein studied composition with him. To give away an original manuscript of an unpublished composition by Bach, in the early days of the *BGS*, and never to breathe a word about it to people who were concerned with the monumental series, was a disgraceful and unforgivable act. The recipient was more appreciative of the treasure, as is shown in the third paragraph, which is in Russian: 'From His Excellency A. Lvoff, presented to the Royal Public Library, October 7th/19th, 1857.' There it has lain unnoticed all these years; no one in authority had the curiosity to examine it and collate it with the published work, or realized that scholars have been speculating about it for three-quarters of a century.

As the style is not that of Bach's maturity, the question naturally arises whether it may not be one of those innumerable compositions of predecessors and contemporaries which the master copied for study or performance. There are points of irrefutable evidence in the manuscript to prove that it is an original composition. Spitta, who examined every manuscript of Bach's known in his day, points out (i, Appendix A, 11, p. 625) that the composer never omitted to head a first score with the letters 'J.J.' ('Jova' or 'Jesu Juva') and to sign at the end 'S.D.G.', and that no copy or unimportant rearrangement was so inscribed. In this case at the head is 'J.J.N.H.', and at the close, in full, 'Soli Dei gloria!' This is conclusive proof. There are other hallmarks which will be detailed in discussion of the music, many signs of haste in the writing, cancellations, one fresh start, &c., as if the composer were in a hurry to prepare the score for an immediate performance. These would not have occurred had he been merely copying an existing work.

The work is probably the product of Arnstadt, written on the return from his visit to Buxtehude at Lübeck, October 1705–February 1706, for there is a distinct trace of the Danish master towards the end. But it may be Mühlhausen, or even later, because some of the arias are better than those in the first known solo cantata, No. 160 (Weimar, 1713 or 1714). The stamp, however, is clear; the general style speaks unmistakably of his younger days. There is no long development of aria, such as he revelled in in maturity and even carried to excess in the years after. The ten movements amount only to 245 bars all told. The conciseness of the arias matches with those of No. 15; the division into many movements is characteristic of

Nos. 71 and 106, which we shall examine in the next chapter. There is the frequent repetition of a little figure that one finds elsewhere in his youthful compositions, as for instance in the 'Capriccio on the Departure of a Beloved Brother', which is definitely Arnstadt. The tentative use of instruments shows that he had yet to accumulate the experience necessary to exploit their complete qualities. Yet the work exhibits thought, insight, delicate fancy, precocious maturity, much invention, a sense of unity throughout its diversity, and not a single movement is without points that command one's attention.

1. Aria, $\frac{4}{4}$, flauto traverso and violin I, 'Meine Seele erhebt den Herren, und mein Geist freuet sich Gottes, meines Heilandes' ('My soul magnifies the Lord, and my spirit rejoices in God, my Saviour'). Remembering the other two settings, one naturally expects an exuberant paean, but this begins in dreamy ecstasy, the obbligato instruments opening with an undulating figure in parallel motion:

A figure is proposed for imitation:

which is not used after the ritornello. The voice begins with continuo only, employing (a), with that type of syllabic grouping—
♪. ♫.♩ which so often is altered into the modern conventional
Mei-ne
manner by vocalists and even by editors. 'Erhebt' ('magnifies') is florid. A bar and a half for the instruments lead to a resumption of the vocal phrase, piano, with the flute and violin swaying blissfully. With 'und mein Geist freuet sich' the singer shows greater animation, there is an elaborate roulade on 'freuet', with several notes marked staccato, and the flute joins in less florid movement. After a short ritornello there is a different run on 'freuet', this time with the violin. 'Gottes, meines Heilandes' is twice sung to a firm phrase accompanied by a leaping continuo. These two ideas are developed till the end of the

vocal section and a ritornello embodying the time-pattern of (*a*) concludes.

2. Recitative, marked *Accompag*; with two violins. 'Denn er hat seine elende Magd angesehen. Siehe, von nun an werden mich selig preisen alle Kindes Kind. Denn er hat große Dinge an mir gethan, der da mächtig ist, und des Name heilig ist' ('For He has His pitiful maiden regarded. See, from now on shall me blissfully praise all children's children. For He has great things for me done, He who mighty is, and Whose name holy is'). Between 'preisen' and 'mächtig' no words are written; the singer was expected to know them. This number contains irrefutable proofs that the Magnificat is an original composition. From bar 5 to 6, Bach had written:

Ex.14

He spotted the consecutive fifths, blurred out the violin II E while the ink was still wet, possibly with his thumb, and substituted the A below. The conclusion of the vocal part was originally:

Ex.15

(The text is not written in.) Then he realized that he had missed a glorious opportunity over 'mächtig', scribbled violently through the three staves, in which violin parts had not so far been added, and substituted the following, with the text added:

Ex.16

Moreover, he first wrote a continuo ascending in crotchets, A, B, C, D, E. This did not satisfy him, so he thumbed out the D and the E, the latter of which had not had the stem added, and corrected to the above. If it be conceded that the work belongs to Arnstadt, these are the first recitatives of the master we know, and it is surprising to find how perfect they are.

3. Aria, continuo, $\frac{4}{4}$, 'Und seine Barmherzigkeit währet immer für und für bei denen, die ihn fürchten' ('And His pity endures for ever and ever with those, who Him fear'). The steady march of the continuo indicates the steadfastness of God's care for His children; 'pity' is florid:

Ex.17

This is repeated in the Scarlattian manner, slightly more ornate, and there is a repetition of a little figure to suggest continuity:

Ex.18

'Währet' has a long florid run and afterwards returns in the original way. The close is remarkable. The aria is in A minor, it moves to C major, 'fürchten' is reserved until the ante-penultimate bar of the vocal section, and when it comes in the following bar, the thought of the people's fear of the Almighty is expressed by a sudden change to C minor (with an interrupted cadence), in which key the ritornello concludes:

Ex.19

4. Aria, *Viol. all' unisono*, ⁶⁄₄, 'Er übet Gewalt mit seinem Arm, und zerstreuet die hoffärtig sind in ihres Herzens Sinn'. ('He exercises power with His arm, and scatters (those) who proud are in their hearts' mind'). It is a powerful and angry movement. The bassi stamp about, the strong opening violin theme is followed by dashing figures:

The voice adopts the chief theme for the first part of the text, with continuo only, (*a*) follows for the orchestra, and the main idea is resumed, piano, but with a persistent note for the violins, the stubbornness of the proud. This version is quoted here, to show a technical slip (on 'seinem'); the young composer was not yet immaculate in his observance of the elementary rules of harmony:

'Zerstreuet' has a vehement run which recalls those in the 'unbelief' alto aria in cantata No. 2:

Later the same word is given another vigorous passage with the violins tossing angrily underneath, the continuo being silent. The stubbornness of the proud is depicted by cross accents for the voice and by a bass which charges upwards and is then thrown down.

5. Aria, $\frac{4}{4}$, continuo, 'Er stößet die Gewaltigen vom Stuhl, und erhebet die Elenden' ('He casts down the mighty from their seat, and exalts the needy'). The movement is constructed on a splendid free basso ostinato:

Ex.23

The voice modifies the phrase for the opening words, the continuo dovetailing. 'Vom Stuhl' is sung thrice, the last two separated and hurled out vigorously. 'Erhebet', naturally, rises, and the bassi tell of the power of the Almighty:

Ex.24

The soprano note immediately following this quotation was originally D. Before the ink had dried the fifths with the continuo were noticed. As the figure of the latter was important, the D was thumbed out and B♭ substituted.

6. Recitative, marked *Accompag*; with two violins, 'Die Hungrigen füllet er mit Gütern und lässet die Reichen leer' ('The hungry fills He with good things, and leaves the rich empty'). The text is not added after 'Hungrigen'. Of five bars only, the little recitative is exquisite. The words are perfectly set, there is a compassionate drop of a diminished seventh on 'er mit', 'und lässet die Reichen leer' mounts excitedly. Then the composer feels pity for the wealthy, and repeats the words, making a break after 'lässet', and ending on the dominant with a tender phrase to 'die Reichen leer', as if full of regret. From bar 3 to 4 is the following:

Ex.25

The young composer fell into the trap that catches so many unwary students, of not examining carefully the progressions from one stave

to the next, and so the evidence of technical immaturity remains for all time!

7. Aria, $\frac{3}{4}$, with *Violetta*, 'Er denket der Barmherzigkeit, und hilft seinem Diener Israel auf' ('He remembers pity, and helps His servant Israel up'). The violetta was a type of viola, it is not found again until 1724 (No. 16) and 1727 (No. 157), and makes a fourth and last appearance in 1734 (secular cantata 'Preise dein Glücke'). The melody was obviously conceived instrumentally, because, although emotionally suited to the text, the words fit awkwardly, the only instance of a misfit in the work:

The violetta figure, allied to the opening notes of the chief theme, is the basis of a charming passage in the latter part of the introduction:

At one point there is a bold clash:

8. Recitative, with two violins, 'Wie er geredt hat unsern Vätern, Abraham und seinem Samen ewiglich' ('As He has spoken to our fathers, Abraham and his seed for ever'). Here the Magnificat proper ends, but, as in the other two settings, the customary Benediction which followed it in the Lutheran service is added.

9. The traditional plainchant in the voice, $\frac{4}{4}$, violins *all'unisono*, 'Thanks and praise be to God the Father, and to the Son and to the Holy Ghost'. The continuo moves in quavers, sometimes ceasing so that the violins are unaccompanied, and the latter play a 'moto perpetuo' of semiquavers. The counterpoint is a little stiff:

Ex.29

Not till much later came that glorious freedom and impetuous sweep which we know so well. From Bar 3 to 4 his besetting sin of consecutive fifths again ensnared him. A continuo G was responsible. He wrote a B above it and did not even trouble to thumb out the offending note.

10. Ditto, 'Wie es war im Anfang jetzt und immerdar und von Ewigkeit zu Ewigkeit, Amen' ('As it was in the beginning now and evermore and from eternity to eternity'). Here we have distinct traces of the influence of Buxtehude, chiefly in the flying phrases tossed between voice and violins:

Ex. 30

Haste caused the composer not to see that the first violini note should be a quaver and not a crotchet:

Ex.31

They foreshadow the Mühlhausen wedding cantata, No. 196. As in the other arias the chief instrumental theme is adapted for vocal purposes:

Ex.32

These ideas produce a longish and lively movement, animation being kept up to the end. At one place singer and violinists disport themselves floridly without continuo. There are three interesting personal touches. At the beginning of the seventh bar a wrong bass note was written and was thumbed out with such impatience by the impulsive young man eager to reach the end of his task, that it obscures a note on the stave below. At one point there is a N.B. referring to two bars cued near the foot of the page, suggesting that he was working from a sketch. At another, the voice is carried rather high. He writes above *N.B. si mavis vid. infra* ♭, and at ♭, at the foot of the page, he provides a less trying version with a new continuo.

Why was the work written? It is pure chamber music; violino is indicated, not the plural. That may be said of many church cantatas, of course. It cannot have been intended for one of his inefficient choir-boys, nor would Bach in that case have made such a modification as that mentioned above or added such a personal note as, 'If you prefer, see below'. Only males were allowed to sing in church except in congregational numbers. We know that on 11 November 1706 Bach was rebuked by the Arnstadt Consistory for having 'allowed a stranger maiden to show herself and make music in the choir'. This must have been when the church was empty, for it would not have been permitted during service. There seems no doubt that the 'stranger maiden' was his cousin, Maria Barbara, who had come to live in Arnstadt, to whom he became engaged some time after the rebuke from the Consistory and whom he married on 17 October 1707. May it not have been written for her and may the occasion not have been some house-festivity in connexion with the betrothal? It would be pleasant to think so.

MÜHLHAUSEN

71, 106, 131, 150, 189, 196

Order of Discussion: 131, 71, 196, 189, 150, 106

WE can only conjecture that at Arnstadt he tried his 'prentice hand at other church music, though none of it is known, because when he was appointed, at the age of twenty-two, to the magnificent Church of St. Blasius, at Mühlhausen, a few miles away, there are considerable differences in style and his increasing mastery is patent. Although the city was large and important, a fine specimen of German walled towns, containing many splendid buildings and all the marks of eighteenth-century commercial prosperity, and his church ideal for music-making, the opposition to elaborate church music by a strong sect made his position so uncomfortable and so severely limited his opportunities, that he soon sought another post. Yet the few months there certainly produced three cantatas and possibly another three which lie on the borderline between the two appointments. There is no record of any performance of any work of his in St. Blasius's. It is significant of his love of colour that, in a scheme for reconstruction of the organ, he included in the specification a device which we nowadays associate with the cinema, a set of tubular bells, 'desired by the parishioners', operated on by the pedals. Had he remained, he would undoubtedly have written something which would have anticipated Handel's Carillon in *Saul*. A Glockenspiel stop was added to the Weimar organ near the close of his service there, but by that time the day of youthful experiments was past, and so far as we know, it was not utilized in any written work.

131. The first Mühlhausen cantata, 'Aus der Tiefe rufe ich, Herr, zu dir' ('Out of the darkness call I, Lord, to Thee' B.), is a setting of the De Profundis, Psalm cxxx, with the addition of two Lenten hymn-stanzas, 2 and 5 of B. Ringwaldt's 'Herr Jesu Christ, du höchstes Gut', which are intoned by the upper voice to the chorale melody in the two duets, S.B. and A.T., while the lower voice sings verses 3 and 4 of the psalm in the first and verse 6 in the second, the earliest of the many examples of simultaneous use of two texts. The scoring is for oboe, bassoon, one line of violins, and two of violas, the latter appropriate to the form of the opening of the psalm, and a favourite practice of Bach's predecessors. The date is August 1707 for an unspecified occasion, although Terry suggests that it may have been written in commemoration of a great fire which destroyed a large part of the town in June of that year (one can still see traces of rebuilding necessitated by it at St. Blasius's), and that Eilmar, Archdeacon of Mühlhausen, compiled the libretto. The now lost original score stated that the work was composed at the request of Peter Eilmar. There are no arias nor recitatives, the numbers other than duets being choruses. No. 15 contains no fugues and no fugal writing, but its successor reveals Bach's growing interest in a style of which he was to become supreme master.

The first number opens with a lengthy symphonic description of crying from the depths ('Out of the depths call I, Lord, to Thee').

Ex.33

which is presented in various forms with the choir added, a most affecting piece of music. This leads to a Vivace (indications of tempi and dynamic marks are plentiful), in which there is much fugato. The word 'Flehens' ('Herr, höre meine Stimme, laß deine Ohren merken auf die Stimme meines Flehens', 'Lord, hear my voice, let Thine ears hearken to the voice of my supplication') is much broken up by rests:

Ex.34

Fle - - - hens,

twice the whole choir passes from *f* to *p* and *pp*, and back to *f*, with breaks between the changes, simulating gestures of despair:

Ex.35

Fle - - - - - - - - (hens,)

It is an animated scene of despair, and the frequent repeated notes for the voices suggest the clamorous appeal of a distraught crowd.

The second chorus consists of a short Adagio, 'Ich harre des Herrn' ('I await the Lord'), chord passages separated by florid runs for alto and tenor, and a long Largo fugue, in which the waiting of the soul is contrasted with a repeated expression of hope, in subject and countersubject:

Oboe and violin incessantly dovetail into each other while the violas answer each other in groups of two notes, resulting in long stretches of eight-part writing which show an early command over intricate polyphony.

The last chorus begins with cries of 'Israel', adagio, and un poc' allegro, 'hoffe auf den Herrn' ('hope on the Lord'), and then another Adagio, 'denn bei dem Herrn ist die Gnade' ('for with the Lord is mercy'), in which for the greater part the choir sustains, the upper strings pulsate, and all accompany a most beautiful oboe melody, one of the bewitching moments of the cantata. An Allegro, 'und viel Erlösung bei ihm' ('And full salvation through Him') bursts in upon this, the orchestra bustles in rapid answering passages and the chorus is carried away breathless with excitement:

Without break comes a florid double fugue. The subjects anticipate two points which are frequently found in Bach's musical language later, joyful runs on 'erlösen' and a semitone progression at the thought of sin:

Ex. 38

There is much independent writing for the orchestra and the conclusion is a bold stroke, the last two chords being a sixth on A♭ and
the root position of G major. The chorus parts are found, arranged
possibly by Bach's pupil Kittel, in the organ works.

As in the case with Schubert's boyish first Mass, the young composer did not yet fully understand vocal effect; the tessitura is frequently so low that there is a lack of clarity and brightness. The
soprano and tenor lines lie largely between C and D[1], their least
telling area. The basses are placed too low for comfort. He must have
had prodigious voices in this line at Mühlhausen; they are called
upon to sing from C below the stave to the E♭ above it, with repeated
notes on high D! Splendid though the music of the choruses be, and
delightful to rehearse, one is apt to feel some disappointment at a
first performance. One expects more choral effect than the low-lying
lines permit, there are few moments of brilliance. When one has become accustomed to this, however, and thinks less of external effect
than of the sheer beauty of the music, the cantata is a memorable
experience, with many supreme moments.

The choruses are accompanied by complete orchestra, but the first
duet employs oboe and continuo only and the second has merely
figured bass. The oboe line is elaborate and abounds in sympathetic
and expressive phrases based on:

Ex. 39

showing that at the beginning of his career he had begun to understand the special qualities of the instrument for which he afterwards wrote some of his loveliest melodies. The continuo of both duets is worked out with scrupulous conscientiousness, the initial figures being developed almost without the introduction of new matter, thus avoiding the scrappiness noticeable in No. 15, an anticipation of the wonderful power of thematic construction which makes his later scores so endlessly fascinating.

The hymn-stanza of the first duet runs, 'Pity Thou me in such a burden, Take it out of my heart, Because Thou for it atoned hast, On the cross with death-pains. And that I not with great woe In my sins be submerged, Nor eternally despair', and the commentatory text, 'If Thou wilt, Lord, iniquity mark, who shall stand? But with Thee is forgiveness, that one Thee may fear.' 'Bestehen' ('stand') is sometimes set to syncopated, twisting runs, indicative of tottering. With 'fürchte' ('fear') come long convoluting passages of semi-quavers, in which the oboe joins. By way of contrast the opening clause is frequently set to strings of repeated notes, as if sin were persisting. The stanza of the other duet is, 'And because I then in my mind, As I previously bewailed, Even a troubled sinner am, Whose conscience gnaws, And would gladly in Thy blood From sins be washed, As David and Manasseh.' The complacently flowing $\frac{12}{8}$ of the tenor and continuo does not interpret the hymn-stanza, but the psalm verse, 'My soul waiteth for the Lord more than they that watch for the morning'. It is a movement of great charm.

In spite of the frequent changes of tempo in the choruses the whole cantata is welded together in such a manner that we can see how much his assimilation and control had progressed in the three years since the first-known essay in this form. One must remember that No. 15 is known to us in a reconstructed version only, and that it may have been purged of many crudities. There we have a series of dramatic pictures; here the continuity of the text and the modifying influences of the two hymn-stanzas and the chorale melodies contribute towards a greater satisfactoriness of the whole, in spite of the fact that it is considerably less striking in performance, suitable for intimate conditions only. It is interesting to note the treatment of the bassoon in the choruses. In the first the young composer is content, with occasional exceptions, to let it double the bassi. In the second, however, he grows weary of this unenterprising dullness, and while following the outline of the continuo, it generally plays ♪ ⁊ instead of ♩. In the final bars it enjoys a fine independent flourish. The final fugue, on account of the strict writing, does not afford opportunity for independence, so the fagotto, beginning at the tenth bar, is allotted the task of aiding the vocal basses, which often pursue a line different from the continuo.

Johann Schelle, Cantor of St. Thomas's, Leipzig, from 1676 to 1701, wrote a cantata to the psalm text, without the hymns. There are certain resemblances which suggest that Bach knew this work, although it is a striking testimony to his original turn of mind that even at this youthful period he went his own way. The echo effects in both cantatas were common to the period. Schelle's little runs to 'Flehens' and 'erlösen' are far out-distanced by the novice. The most striking similarity is the repeated chords to 'Israel', but here again Bach marched farther, for Schelle's two statements are increased to three, and the rising passages between them add considerably to the effect. The mannerism of ending a chorus with a few impressive bars is common to both cantatas.

71. 'Gott ist mein König' ('God is my King', Psalm lxxiv. 12) was written for the Inauguration of the Town Council. German free cities were proud of their independence; the pompous dignity of the municipal occasion called for an unwontedly large orchestra, and resulted in a unique and particularly high distinction for the young composer, the printing of the band parts, an honour never repeated, as no other cantata ever attained to the dignity of publication in his lifetime. His own church was not the scene of its production, but the more commodious Marienkirche, where Eilmar was Pastor. The title-page of the parts, a veritable monster of grammatical distortion, reads literally as follows:

Congratulatory Church-Motett, when during solemn service in the chief church B.M.V. the blessed inauguration of the Town-Council took place, on the 4th of February of this year 1708 and of the government of the Imperial free city of Mühlhausen, the fatherly care of the new Town-Council, namely the worshipful, trusty, very-learned and most wise gentleman, Herr Adolff Strecker, and of the noble, trusty and very-wise gentleman, Herr Georg Adam Steinbach, both highly-deserving burgomasters, as also the other high and well-born members, was joyfully presented, duly returned by Joh. Seb. Bach, organist of Div. Blasii, at Mühlhausen, printed by Tobias David Brückner, printer to the worshipful Town-Council.

The printer's name is given in full, but the composer's name is abbreviated! The text, either by Archdeacon Eilmar or Bach, is a combination of Biblical quotations, a hymn-stanza, and original matter, and is interesting historically, as it contains a reference to the Emperor Joseph I and to the war of the Spanish Succession then raging, besides a prayer for the good government of the town. The orchestra is scored in a singular way, not encountered in such a complete form again, though at times there are similarities of device in later compositions. It is divided into four groups—(1) three trumpets and timpani, (2) two beak-flutes and 'celli, (3) two oboes and bassoon, (4) violins, violas, and violone, with the addition of the organ, which has an independent part and sometimes accompanies numbers alone. The four groups are often heard antiphonally, like contrasting organ manuals. Bach's intentions are clearly shown by the autograph title on the original manuscript parts: 'Mottetto, diviso in quatuor Chori. Choro 1mo â tre Trombe è Tamburi. Choro 2do â doi Violini, una Viola è Violono. Choro 3zo â doi Obboe è Bassono.' The list is incomplete, the '2 Flutti è Violoncello' of the original score are omitted. Those of us whose ears are offended by the modern American practice of speaking of the different 'choirs' of an orchestra, to us a mixture of terms, must acknowledge that it can point to a precedent! A second organ was intended to be brought into action in ii. In addition to this elaborate division, the choir is used both in full, 'coro pleno', and in part, 'senza ripieno', with numerous indications, a plan which seems to have been common at the time and which we sometimes find in his Leipzig compositions, though less meticulously detailed, and which suggests that similar treatment is legitimate in other cases. The result of this complex division of forces and a rich, imaginative handling of his material, is a brilliant and effective cantata. Sometimes the short choral phrases, answered by one or more orchestral groups, cause a feeling of scrappiness, but, generally speaking, the diversified score is unified into a satisfactory whole, and much of the development of ideas is extended and masterly.

One device common at the period, and used in other of his early cantatas, is to end a powerful chorus by a tapering-off with short and soft phrases. The last tutti chorus concludes with two quavers, s d¹, on unison oboes followed by the same notes on two flutes. It is not easy in performance to ensure a satisfactory rendering of this curious conceit. Particularly is this so in the final chorus (which is oddly termed 'Arioso', why, it is difficult to understand) where a number of varied sections lead to a fairly lengthy fugue, in which the semi-chorus, accompanied by continuo only, is added to gradually till all forces are employed. This is concluded by a diversified section, semi-chorus, Coro Pleno and groups of instruments preface a short tutti outburst, tailed off in the manner described. The young composer's ardent exploitation of the effects of contrasting large and small choral bodies leads rather to fussiness in this number, and results in some loss of weight and directness. Except in the delightful fugue this and the scrappiness of the text mar continuity; one would be grateful for more Coro Pleno and less chopping about from one idea to another. It is akin to the novice organist's love for trying this and that stop, this and that combination, instead of going ahead with his playing; he thinks of the resources of his instrument rather than of the big outlines of the music.

The opening chorus begins with two great shouts, the spaces filled up first by brass and percussion, then by two oboes, a disappointing effect with modern instruments, which are so different in calibre from those of the eighteenth century. At the fourth bar comes a vigorous shake in octaves for the strings and bassoons, which is developed in the succeeding choral bars. 'Von Alters her' ('from ages past') rises in long notes for the sopranos, through the chord of A minor, violin I doubling and trilling, while the lower voices of the semi-chorus support with short phrases. The orchestra now enters group by group, while the Coro Pleno sings the entire clause. The semi-chorus is employed for 'der alle Hülfe thut, so auf Erden geschieht' (different in the Bible, literally 'Who all help gives, that on earth happens') in joyous animation, and at the end, over a pedal, the sopranos have a naïve passage:

Ex. 40

A résumé of the first material follows. The second chorus ('senza ripieni') iii, is a fugue, accompanied by organ only, to two Biblical quotations, part of Deuteronomy xxxiii. 25, 'Thy age be as thy youth' (the German version differs slightly from the English Bible), and part of Genesis xxi. 22, 'and God is with thee in all things that thou doest'. It is again a reference to some aged and important Bürgermeister. The first clause serves for the subject:

Ex. 41

Dein Al - ter   sei wie dei - ne Ju - gend,

and the second for the countersubject:

Ex. 42

und Gott ist mit dir in Al-lem, was du thust,

It will be seen how low-lying is the delivery of the tenor theme, and this early weakness of Bach's choral writing robs the fugue of much of its vitality in spite of the many runs on 'Allem' ('all things').

The final chorus is in six sections, trumpets and drums appear in the last three only. (1) With the joy-motive prominent, the full choir cries 'Das neue Regiment' ('The new Government'). (2) 'Auf jeglichen Wegen bekröne der Segen' ('On every way (may) crown the blessing'), allegro, ³⁄₂. Above a stately continuo— ♩ ♩ ♩ | ♩ ♩ —the voices move mostly in plain minims, though the second 'bekröne' is flowing. Strings, oboes, and flutes in turn repeat the choral phrases. (3) 'Friede, Ruh' und Wohlergehen müsse stets zur Seite stehen dem neuen Regiment' ('(May) peace, rest and well-being always by the side stand of the new government'). The same plan of repeating each of the first three choral phrases by instrumental groups is followed. In the last clause wood-wind and strings reinforce the choir. The short phrases of this portion bear a resemblance to the final chorus of the cantata, 'Es erhub sich ein Streit', by his uncle, J. Christoph, but in this the two choirs dovetail into each other. (4) 'Glück, Heil und großer Sieg' (Good fortune, welfare, and great victory'), vivace, ⁴⁄₄. There are three choral phrases, Coro Pleno, Senza Ripieni, Tutti. Trumpets and drums crackle, the bassi play downward semiquaver scales, there are flourishes on 'Sieg'. The Organo is given four thick, low-placed chords which would sound odd on a modern instrument. (5) Muß täglich von Neuem dich, Joseph, erfreuen ('May (they) daily anew thee, Joseph, rejoice'), allegro, ³⁄₂, a fugue with:

Ex. 43

muß tä - glich von Neu - em dich, Jo - seph,

as subject, and:

Ex. 44

er - freu - - - - - - - - - - - - - - - - - (-en,)

as countersubject. The semi-chorus opens and the Tutti chorus enters line by line; after seventeen bars with continuo the upper instruments begin to join in and finally the whole orchestra is employed. (6) 'daß an allen Ort' und Landen ganz beständig sei vorhanden: Glück, Heil, . . .' &c. ('that in all places and lands wholly firm be at hand: good fortune, welfare, . . .' &c., $\frac{4}{4}$. The first short phrases are announced by wood-wind and the strings join in at the end. The 'Glück, Heil' section repeats (4).

There is one duet, S.T., the former intoning a highly ornate version of the anonymous chorale melody of the hymn, 'O Gott, du frommer Gott', Stanza 6 of which is employed, the latter singing verses 35 and 37 from Samuel ii. 19, 'I am now eighty years (old); wherefore shall Thy servant more be troubled? I will return, that I may die in my city, by my father's and my mother's grave.' The hymn-stanza is, 'Shall I in this world My life higher bring, Through many heavy steps Into old age press forward; So grant patience, from sin And disgrace me preserve, That I may carry with honour my grey hairs.' The venerable town councillor thus is referred to twice in the cantata. The accompaniment is for organ only, on two staves, the bass being a steady succession of quavers, the right hand, on the Positiv, punctuating with short runs, which at the end break into a long-continued florid passage. It recalls the methods of some of the early chorale preludes. In the church of St. Blasius there was a small chamber organ below the main one. Bach intended the Positiv line to be played on it, in order to produce a dreamy, remote, and un-doubtedly surprising effect, another example of his youthful desire to utilize all possible resources. As the performance, however, took place in the Church of the Holy Virgin, this plan had to be sacrificed, as only one organ was available.

A bass aria, 'Tag und Nacht ist dein' ('Day and night is Thine') employs orchestral groups (2) and (3), sometimes contrasting, some-times coalescing, a simple mode of imagery, while the organ bass divides its allegiance between the two bodies. The middle portion, for voice and continuo only, exhibits the pure Böhm style of a free basso ostinato: 'Du machest, daß beide, Sonn' und Gestirn, ihren gewissen Lauf haben' ('Thou makest that both sun and stars their ordained course have', 'ihren gewissen' circles round a point, as if to represent the orbit of the earth, but, with some inconsistency, 'Lauf' moves over a large space.) 'Du setzest einem jeglichen Lande seine Grenze' ('Thou settest to each country its boundaries'. Here the semiquaver movement is scarcely appropriate.) An alto aria, vivace, alternates ³⁄₈ with ⁴⁄₄, the quavers being of equal value in both. The ³⁄₈ sections, except for a single bar interpolated between the two groups of ⁴⁄₄, deal with the words 'Durch mächtige Kraft' ('Through mighty strength') and there are fanfares for brass and percussion, which, however, never accompany the singer. In the anti-penultimate bar are two naked consecutive seconds, major and minor, for the upper trumpets, so common in Jenkins, Young, Locke, and Purcell, though not with such penetrating instruments. The close is brass and percussion unsupported by the organ. The ⁴⁄₄ portions are with organ only: 'erhältst du unsre Grenzen, hier muß der Friede glänzen, wenn Mord und Kriegessturm sich allerorts erhebt. Wenn Kron' und Zepter bebt, hast du das Heil geschafft' ('maintainest Thou our boundaries, here must peace shine, when murder and warstorm everywhere arise. When crown and sceptre totter, hast Thou prosperity created').

One remarkable number stands out from the rest, a priceless gem. It is a setting for Coro Pleno of Psalm lxxiv. 19, 'Du wollest dem Feinde nicht geben die Seele deiner Turteltauben' ('Thou wilt to the enemy not deliver the soul of Thy turtledove', in the Lutheran Bible a statement, in the English a plea). The thought of the turtledove captured the imagination of the young composer, and the number has a Schubertian quality which is scarcely ever matched again in his writings, though there is a similar prophetic strain in No. 56. The opening almost suggests the gentle cooing of the bird:

Ex.45 (C minor with a signature of 2 flats)

The delicate choral lines are accompanied by all the orchestral groups except brass and percussion. Until nearly the end the organ bass and violone maintain the movement of detached quavers, the bassoon sways gently in a ♩ ♫ figure, with rarely an intermission. The 'celli murmur like doves in incessant semiquavers, often in a high register (written in the alto stave), the ascending group of three slurred and dropping to the fourth:

Ex. 46

At the end the chorus softly intones a six-bar unison phrase which suggests a gregorian chant:

Ex. 47

du wol-lest dem Fein-de nicht ge-ben die See-le dei-ner Tur-tel-tau-ben.

while the semiquaver figure is played simultaneously by nearly all the upper instruments, the flutes using an inverted form. The concluding harmonies are those noted in a similar place in No. 131, a sixth on the flat supertonic prefacing a tonic major common chord. The close is magical, wafting an already exquisite creation into still higher realms of transcendent beauty. Though the choral lines are easy, the orchestral part is difficult to 'pull off', it requires constant reticence on the part of the players and meticulous attention to problems of balance. With a large choir and orchestra it can only fail to achieve the long-sustained delicacy and tenderness needed to do justice to this peerless and fragile inspiration.

196. No further opportunity was forthcoming at Mühlhausen for experimenting with large orchestral forces. The wedding for which No. 196 was possibly written was no doubt a humble one, for it was celebrated in the odd little church of the tiny village of Dornheim, lying just outside Arnstadt, and the scene of his own first wedding. On 5 June 1708 an aunt of his wife, Regina Wedemann by name, was married to a clergyman, Johann Lorenz Stauber, and possibly a few members of the family provided singers and players for the ceremony. The cantata, a setting of Psalm cxv. 12–15, 'Der Herr denket an uns und segnet uns' ('The Lord remembers us and blesses us'), shows at once the varied influences of the North German Böhm and Italian masters, not yet absorbed into his composite style. The florid choral writing indicates an increasing understanding of methods of securing full effectiveness from his choir; its buoyancy and brilliance make it an exhilarating little work to perform. 'Organo' is specified in every number, and there are only strings. In the Sinfonia the bottom line is 'Organo e Continuo', while the 'cello has a special part, frequently independent of the bass. Subsequently the 'cello is not mentioned; the solitary aria has violins in unison and 'Organo e Continuo'. In the score of the duet and the choruses, the figured organ line is placed below the choir, while four lines above are allotted to violins, viola, and continuo. The continuo is often independent of the organ; the latter is employed almost incessantly, the former has frequent rests, long and short, and by not being continuous belies its name. 'Continuo' here evidently applies to violone only in the Sinfonia, and to the bassi in the remainder of the cantata. It is scarcely likely that the tiny organ gallery of this unimportant church could have contained a harpsichord, though one may have been brought by a member of the family for the occasion. The composer would direct from the organ and, naturally, would reserve the lion's share of the performance for himself.

The Sinfonia (see O.O.S. No. 023) is mostly built on ♩.♩ themes, except for the bass line, which is an almost uninterrupted succession of quavers, and some decorative triplets, so beloved by the early Bach, appear in violin I. A very short passage is indicated piano, forte being resumed immediately. A certain lack of inventive resource is shown by the continuous employment of a ♩♩♩ motive in the introduction to the fugue of the first chorus, often during the fugue itself and at the conclusion, and by a reappearance of the same figure, though differently treated, in the following number, a short soprano aria. In the unison violin passages of the latter we find the intriguing decorative triplets, which, with the florid vocal line, interpret the second word of verse 13, 'He blesses those who the Lord fear, both small and great'. A charming conceit occurs just before the dal segno. 'Both small':

Ex.48

bei-de, Klei - - - ne,

leaves out the violone (the transference of the organ and continuo part to the alto clef doubtless indicates that 8 ft. tone only is to be used), and it is resumed at 'and great':

against a combination of thirds and halves, the former having been predominant in the 'Kleine' section; thus 'small' and 'great' are indicated by simultaneous conflicting rhythms. Throughout the aria the joy-rhythm is prominent.

In the T.B. duet he spins out the text, 'Der Herr segne euch je mehr und mehr, euch, und eure Kinder' ('The Lord bless you more and more, you, and your children') to no fewer than seventy-two bars, only nine of which are concerned with the second clause, as if the nephew felt that it was scarcely discreet to emphasize the question of offspring when bride and groom were no longer young! The first clause of the opening section is a neat canon, the ritornello version of which is more ornate. The last repetitions of 'je mehr und mehr' contain further canonical treatment, of considerable charm. The second clause is set in plain sixths, an admirable device for obtaining contrast. At the end the strings drop successively in arpeggi for four octaves, as if manna were gently falling from heaven.

The two choruses are the dominating portions of the work, florid and animated, a delight to the singers. The first opens with two voices in close imitation on:

In the fugue of the first the violins have independent entries of the subject:

The counterpoints contain rushing semiquavers spread over the whole structure in a blaze of glory. At the close the imitative theme of the opening is heard again. The free double fugue of the second, which begins:

Ex. 52

contains purely instrumental interludes exploiting both subjects, showing an increasing ability to fuse both bodies into a composite structure. The choral writing exhibits an astonishing advance on No. 71. Particularly fine are the imitative Amen ideas based on the figure ♪♪♪ ♩. He evidently had good violinists, for high D's are frequent. The brilliance of the opening of this number (Verse 15) is increased by unisonal treatment of the violins in long successions of rushing semiquavers. Especially effective are chords hurled out by the choir in 'Ihr seid die gesegneten des Herren, der Himmel und Erde gemacht hat'. ('Ye are the blessed of the Lord, who heaven and earth made has') to 'der Himmel' and 'und Erde', the former placed high, the latter low. Again a powerful chorus is ended piano, in this case 1½ bars in length, more easily negotiated than the fragmentary taperings-off in No. 71. The first ideas of all movements except the last, whether intentionally or not, open with a leap from dominant to upper tonic or from tonic to dominant. While there is no depth of emotion in this cantata, its youthful freshness and boyishly healthy vigour make it full of charm, and, in spite of its complicated texture, it is quite easy to perform.

The dates of the next three cantatas are problematical. They are on the Mühlhausen-Weimar frontier, and we can be certain of little else.

189. There are certain features in 'Meine Seele rühmt und preist' ('My soul doth magnify', St. Luke i. 46) which call for consideration. If we exclude the Arnstadt No. 15, which was no doubt for soloists until reconstructed at Leipzig, this is the first solo cantata. At any rate, it is the first for a single voice. It is for the Feast of the Visitation of the B.V.M. and the date is only conjectural, possibly about 1707–10, although Schweitzer places it late in the Weimar period. I cannot help feeling that it has come down to us only in a revised form, possibly made at the time indicated, because the first aria is so very different from those in the cantatas already discussed and those in the next two. So far arias have been tentative, speaking a language which the student was busy learning from his masters. But here we have the unmistakable stamp of the style which becomes so familiar when the learner had soared high above his tutors. Its phrases are more lengthy and move with an easier stride. The texture is characteristic of more mature years, 'rühmt und preist' ('magnifies and praises') are expressed less extravagantly than they would have been earlier, and the character of the aria is reflective in spite of the inviting temptations to brilliant passage work proffered by the text. The first phrase certainly suggests that the composer had just been studying Handel, but its development is not that of Bach's great contemporary. Then, too, it is the first example of the method of aria writing which Bach made peculiarly his own, which has, so far as we know, no counterpart in the writings of his predecessors or contemporaries, the purely polyphonic treatment of all lines, whether instrumental or vocal. The solo voice is not 'accompanied' in the normal sense of the word, it takes its place on terms of absolute equality with instruments, and cannot regard them as of inferior status. The composition is a trio, quartet, or quintet, neither vocalist nor instrumentalist may claim pride of place. In the early days of the revival of Bach, when singers considered themselves as the chief stars of the musical firmament, when the public was saturated with the Italian or Handel-Italian aria, with the vocalist as supreme factor, this method stood in the way of the full acceptance of Bach's solo vocal music. The older order of singers was restive under democratic government, they thought only in terms of dictatorship. The public was puzzled because there was not a single outstanding melody to which they could give undivided attention. Critics repeated again and again the unintelligent dogmas that Bach's whole output was based upon his organ style, that he did not understand the voice as well as Handel, that he thought instrumentally and treated his singers callously and unscrupulously. It has taken generations to produce solo vocalists with the right understanding and ideals, and to educate music-lovers to a form of art which gives us something new even today, and which has bequeathed to us innumerable examples of rich beauty and almost inexhaustible emotional value. The voice is not treated as an instrument. The scrupulous care of the declamatory lines is sufficient proof that he regarded the characteristics of vocal music as of the utmost importance. The voice has its own mission to perform, its own message to deliver, its special place in a scheme which utilizes the varied qualities of voice and instruments for the purpose of a richly coloured ensemble. There are few of Bach's vocal lines which can be transferred to a solo instrument without loss, yet one may adapt many of Handel's arias in this way and not be conscious that the value of the music has been impaired. The popularity of Handel's so-called *Largo* is in part due to the fact that it sounds well on almost any combination. It is heard a thousand times instrumentally to once vocally. In spite of Handel's greatness and the stress laid by so many writers on his being more of a vocal writer than Bach, one must assert that Bach's treatment of the voice is more subtle, and that the Italianized Saxon did not explore the possibilities of the human larynx as assiduously as did his contemporary.

The opening aria of 189 is a quintet for flute, oboe, violin (possibly solo), voice, and continuo. Its texture is clear, its movement easy and gracious. The oboe phrase which begins:

Ex. 53

Cont.

and which comes successively in flute and violin, is modified for the voice:

Ex. 54

Mei - ne See - le, mei - ne See - le rühmt und preist,

Another interesting modification, with the first bar in two forms, is found in bars 7–10 of the vocal part. The semiquaver sequence which follows the oboe statement is afterwards sung to 'preist'. The aria is rich in subsidiary ideas, the swaying theme of bar 11, which in bar 14 is extended, moving blissfully in thirds, the happy chirrupings of the flute when the voice first sings 'preist':

Ex. 55

heralded by fragments in the oboe, the violin figure of ecstasy in bar 21, heard in various forms afterwards, the tender group for flute and

oboe, used sequentially in the 'senza bassi' passage beginning at
the end of bar 24. A new swaying figure comes in sixths, flute and
oboe, in bars 28 and 29, based on the  time-pattern heard
previously and is repeated by the singer to 'Gottes Huld und reiche
Güte' ('God's grace and rich goodness'), with the violin above. In
later years Bach became more economical with his material. The
middle ritornello, bars 32–46, is not a mere repetition of the introduction. Yet another swaying figure:

Ex.56

is introduced in the added violin line, bar 32, and flute and violin
entries of the chief theme use it instead of the downward slide.
Against the violin entry the oboe plays the flute chirrup of bars 16
and 17. The text of the second part is 'Und mein Geist, Herz und
Sinn und ganz Gemüthe ist in meinem Gott erfreut, der mein Heil
und Helfer heißt' ('And my spirit, heart and mind and whole being
is in my God rejoiced, Who my salvation and helper is called'). The
voice begins with a new idea, imitated by the continuo, and on
'erfreut' the violin adds a derivative. During the long run on the
word a new form of the dotted note time-pattern is heard in flute and
oboe, and then, while the continuo leaps joyful octaves flute and
oboe imitate with another form of chirruping motive:

Ex.57

The wood-wind are silent during the bars before the Da Capo, where
there are again fresh ideas.

The remainder of the cantata does not remain at the level of the
opening aria; an argument in favour of the theory that this number
was added at a later date. The text of the middle aria, with continuo
only, is, 'Gott hat sich hoch gesetzet, und sieht auf Das, was niedrig
ist; Gesetzt, daß mich die Welt gering und elend hält, doch bin ich
hoch geschätzet, weil Gott mich nicht vergißt' ('God has Himself
on high established, and looks upon that which lowly is; ordained
that me the world petty and miserable holds, yet am I highly

esteemed, because God me not forgets'). The charming continuo idea is almost an ostinato:

Ex.58

and is related to the bassi line of the previous recitative. Indeed, the time-pattern ♪·♩ or ♪·♩ penetrates the entire cantata, with the exception of iv. We found the same obsession in No. 196. There are several passages of beauty, but occasionally it sags.

The final aria, scored for the same combination as the first, is happy in feeling, with gently swaying figures:

Ex.59

and a contented, tripping idea:

Ex.60

There are many cross-rhythms for the voice, which are of interest, but its texture is not mature. The verse of the first part is 'Deine Güte, dein Erbarmen währet, Gott, zu aller Zeit' ('Thy goodness, Thy mercy endures, God, for all time') and one 'währet' is extended to nine bars. The second part is with continuo only, a plain melody except for several groups of duple time across the triple, 'Du erzeigst Barmherzigkeit denen dir ergeb'nen Armen' ('Thou showest mercy to those Thy faithful poor').

This is the earliest cantata to contain recitatives, though, if the chronological position of the solo Magnificat be accepted, they are not the earliest we possess. The first recitative opens, 'Then look I upon myself and also on my life, so must my mouth into these words break', an arioso follows, 'God, what hast Thou then to me done!' Here we again find a quasi ground-bass. Normal recitative style is resumed for, 'It is with a thousand tongues not once to be expressed how good Thou art, how friendly Thy faithfulness, how rich Thy love is. So be to Thee then laud, honour and praise sung!' The second runs, 'Oh what great things discover I in all places that God to me (has) done, for which I to Him my heart as offering bring. He does it, Whose might the heaven can confine, on Whose name's splendour the Seraphim in lowliness only meditate. He has to me body and life, He has to me also the right to blessedness, and what me here and there rejoices, from pure grace given.' Excellent as these recitatives are, one feels that those of the solo Magnificat are more apposite. This is the earliest of many solo cantatas, and there is no chorale. The libretto is a free and incomplete paraphrase, by an unknown author, of the Magnificat, a poem which, even where a fragmentary quotation is embedded in a libretto, always makes a deep appeal to him. It is the least interesting of the four, though not without qualities which, as a specimen of youthful composition, we cannot afford to neglect and which should be awarded a place in Bach performances from time to time.

150. 'Nach dir, Herr, verlanget mich' ('Lord, my soul doth thirst for Thee' B.) is for an unspecified occasion; 1712 is quoted for an approximate date. It is certainly early, as certain features of Nos. 71 and 131 recur. There are short chordal passages for the choir, brief choral passages answered by the orchestra, delight in vocal fugues wherever the text affords opportunities, frequent contrasts of style and tempo within a movement, and occasionally a resultant stiffness. The brief non-Da-Capo soprano aria is distinctly of an early type. One idea at the beginning of the first Allegro of the opening chorus strikes one today as almost comic, the quivering run on 'Ich hoffe' ('I hope') with repeated chords below:

Ex. 61 *Allegro*

In the second Andante of the next chorus there is an awkward treatment of words, the male voices sing 'denn du bist der Gott' ('For Thou art the God'), but the female voices can only fit in 'der Gott' to their notes. These inequalities are readily forgiven in view of the engaging freshness of the music. Its authenticity has been doubted, but support is not generally given to the theory that it comes from another hand. It may be a remodelled composition of some other composer, but we have no evidence, except that it is quite unlike any other cantata in the series. Constructionally it resembles No. 106 in some ways, but it is far removed emotionally.

The libretto, possibly by Bach, consists of verses 1, 2, 5, and 15 of Psalm xxv for the first three choruses, and three original stanzas for the aria, terzetto, and final chorus. The Lutheran version of the psalm differs from the English, and especially does the opening verse in the latter, 'Unto Thee, O Lord, do I lift up my soul' disagree from the mood of the first two numbers. In both of these Bach seizes on 'verlangen' ('longing') as the primary emotional content. The short Sinfonia (see O.O.S. No. 023), scored for two violins and bassoon (the sole orchestral forces of the cantata, the last-named written for as a transposing instrument) does not announce its chief motive until the fourth bar, a chromatic descent of six crotchets:

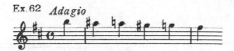

Ex. 62 *Adagio*

the suggestion of longing. This is rarely absent until the closing five bars. The continuation, or free counterpoint, is:

Ex. 63

The opening idea does not recur, except vaguely. The chromatic theme, in an altered form, beginning with an octave leap, and followed sometimes by the countersubject modified:

Ex. 64   After Thee, Lord, long   I,
           Nach dir, Herr, ver - lang - - - et mich,

Cont.

serves to build the opening section of the chorus which follows (with suggestions of the quaver idea from the beginning of the Sinfonia), where alternate choral and orchestral passages provide an impressive and poignant interpretation of the text. The young composer's growing mastery over device is shown by differing order of vocal entries in each of the three choral groups. Following the 'Ich hoffe' section (see *supra*) the chromatic descent appears in a new guise:

Ex. 65

Lass mich nicht zu Schan-den wer - den,
Let me not to shame come,

with successive entries of the voices, dovetailing upper string figures— ♪♪♪ ♪♪ and the bassoon orientating the continuo line by a moto perpetuo of semiquavers ascending scale-wise fourths, a miniature confusion of the erring world. In a short Adagio, recalling portions of No. 131, which repeats the closing words, the bassi invert the semitone progression. It dovetails into an Allegro in which the semitones, somewhat irrelevantly prefaced by hammered quavers, form the subject:

Ex. 66

dass sich mei - ne Fein - de nicht freu - - - en (über mich,)
that themselves my enemies do not rejoice (over me,)

of a lively fugue, in which, in addition to vigorous and independent violin lines, the bassoon has an ornate part containing splendid powerful leaps. Spitta thinks the F♯ minor clavier toccata to be a remodelling of this chorus: 'alike in the whole and in the details, in the feeling and in the expression.' If this be accepted, the question of authorship is beyond doubt.

In the aria we again find the ♩ ♪♪ time-pattern from which he could not rid himself at this period. The text is, 'Doch bin und bleibe ich vergnügt, obgleich hier zeitlich Toben, Kreuz, Sturm und andre Proben, Tod, Höll' und was sich fügt. Ob Unfall schlägt den treuen Knecht, Recht ist und bleibet ewig recht' ('Still am and remain I contented, though here mortal struggles, suffering, storm and other trials, death, hell and what to them belongs. If misfortune strikes the faithful servant, right is and remains eternally right'). We have pictures of 'Toben', 'Tod', 'Höll'' (twice a falling diminished seventh), and at 'Kreuz, Sturm', the violins, which are in unison, angrily repeat B E double-stopping, in semiquavers. At 'Ob Unfall' repeated quavers show the blows falling on the faithful; 'Recht ist und bleibt' rises in joyful confidence.

A charming idea opens the second chorus, 'Leite mich in deiner Wahrheit' ('Lead me in Thy truthfulness'). An ascending crotchet scale passes through all the voices and then through the violins, for a compass of over two octaves. 'Und lehre mich' ('And teach me') is set to running Allegro semiquavers, while groups of ♪ ♫ in the violins and bassoons indicate the eagerness of the believer. 'Denn du bist der Gott, der mir hilft' ('For Thou art the God Who me helps') is andante, strong and firm. 'Täglich harre ich dein' ('Daily wait I upon Thee') combines long repeated notes, the steadfastness of the Christian, with tumultuous semiquavers, the confused welter of the world.

The loveliest number is the terzetto, A.T.B., in which cedars are described as tossed by the wind, 'Cedern müssen von den Winden oft viel Ungemach empfinden, oftmals werden sie verkehrt. Rath und That auf Gott gestellet' ('Cedars must from the winds often much calamity experience, oft-times are they overturned. Thought and action on God place'). While the voices express trust in God's mercy by sustaining gently, the bassi move in rocking semiquavers throughout and the bassoon pursues independent figures. The violins are silent. There is resistance and then momentary agitation at 'achtet nicht, nicht was widerbellet' ('heed not, not what clamours'—against God's wisdom), but the close, 'denn sein Wort ganz anders lehrt' ('for His word quite otherwise teaches'), is beatifically beautiful, and there is a lovely arpeggio descent for the bassoon after the voices have finished.

Poetic qualities are predominant also in the first section of the third chorus, 'Meine Augen sehen stets zu dem Herrn' ('Mine eyes look ever towards the Lord'). The violins sway and murmur, crossing and recrossing, the bassoon sometimes rustles as the breeze and at other times maintains a decorative zigzag motion. Whenever Bach writes an obbligato for the bassoon he underlines its tender qualities, and the relatively few occasions when it is written for in this manner must be an indication that he rarely encountered a player worthy of him. In the majority of instances the fagotto is used merely as an adjunct to the bassi, as if his bassoonist at the time were worthy of nothing better. It is significant that while he often simplified 'cello parts for the violone player, the bassoon was never thus humoured.

His players must generally have been excellent technicians, but only a few of them were possessed of higher artistic qualities. His insight into the finer possibilities of this instrument is an anticipation of a much later stage in the history of orchestration. While Handel wrote for it with remarkable insight in the scene of the Witch of Endor in *Saul*, it was with him an exceptional case, although he commanded the services of the finest instrumentalists in Europe, while Bach was restricted to local players. The voice parts of this section are of exquisite tenderness; one regrets the moment when the composer changes to allegro and begins a close fugue. The first part of the subject is confident, the second, by cross-rhythms, $\frac{3}{4}$ against $\frac{6}{8}$, shows the confusion of the entanglement:

Ex. 67

and there are other symbolic syncopations later. The violins keep up an almost constant semiquaver movement. The chromatic close, where the plucking of the believer's feet out of the net is dramatically portrayed by a string of semitones and stumbling descents for violin I, is most arresting.

The cantata is concluded by a dignified and elaborately worked Ciaccona on the theme:

Ex. 68

to the text 'Meine Tage in den Leiden endet Gott dennoch zu Freuden; Christen auf den Dornenwegen führen Himmels Kraft und Segen; bleibet Gott mein treuer Schatz, achte ich nicht Menschenkreuz. Christus, der uns steht zur Seiten, hilft mir täglich sieghaft streiten' ('My days in sorrow ends God nevertheless in joy; Christians on the thorn-ways lead heaven's strength and blessing; remains God my faithful treasure, heed I not mortal suffering. Christ, Who by us stands at the side, helps me daily victoriously to strive'). Simple blocks of vocal harmony come after the announcement of the ground, 'Freuden' is lengthened by waving sixths for sopranos and altos, the basses modify and decorate the ostinato, which moves to the key of D. The next four vocal entries are in single lines, 'Dornenwegen' introduces falling semitones for the sopranos, 'Himmels' a swinging passage for the altos. In the interlude the violins express joy by curving crotchets in parallel motion. During this section the ground modulates to F♯ minor. After the tenor phrase, during which the ostinato modulates to A, the basses declare their determination by reiterating 'achte ich nicht', and the violins move doggedly in quavers, mostly repeated notes, and the ground modulates to E. A ritornello works round to the tonic, first with splendidly sweeping arpeggi for violins and bassoon and then vigorous close arpeggi quavers for violin I, crotchet movement for violin II and leaps over a wide space for bassoon. This animation ceases as sopranos and altos sing 'Christus, der uns steht zur Seiten' in sixths, as if the Saviour were walking hand-in-hand with the believer; the four voices enter in succession with 'hilft mir täglich', followed by imitation in violins II and I. 'Streiten' brings struggling passages in the voices. In the final section the warring and conquering of the Christian is expressed by rolling vocal lines and leaping runs for violins and bassoon against dogged, slow-moving vocal passages, and the strife ends in a triumphant, majestic close.

106. Interesting as all these cantatas are, there are evidences of immaturity. Suddenly, at one bound apparently (we do not know how many cantatas came between) he leaps into consummate mastery in the well-known 'Gottes Zeit ist die allerbeste Zeit' ('God's time is best' B.), at once one of the most popular and one of the most perfect of cantatas. Never again did he achieve the continuous tenderness and the elevated spiritual feeling in just the same way that it is found here; it remains unique. Written, possibly, for the funeral of an elderly man, it is a touching personal document of an already deep thinker stirred to the depths of his heart and comforted by his religion. Pirro thinks it occasioned by the death of his uncle, Tobias Lämmerhirt, September 1707. Spitta assigns it to 1711, the funeral of the Weimar Rector, Philipp Grossgebauer. Both speculations are beset with doubt. The earlier occasion certainly accounts for the intensely personal character of the music, but the cantata is so perfect that one cannot imagine it to have been written at Arnstadt. The later occasion, no doubt, brings the date within the bounds of possibility, although, in spite of certain youthful qualities, the cantata would almost seem too flawless for this stage of his career, and we know of no special relations with the Rector to call for such deep emotion. It may be that several cantatas came between No. 150 and this and enabled him to grow out of his apprenticeship. The libretto, which is exceptionally fine, both in the matter of form and of suggestiveness for musical treatment, a series of Biblical and Apocryphal quotations, with two hymn-stanzas, is of the character he began to discard at Weimar; its earlier type introduces another problem into the question of date. It would undoubtedly be compiled for the occasion, and either Archdeacon Eilmar or the composer may have constructed it. The scoring is veiled and mournful, only two beak-flutes, two violas da gamba and continuo, no violins or violas. Nowadays we are compelled to replace the gamba lines by violas and 'celli, which do not represent the delicate and wistful colouring of the older instruments, but even in this way the orchestral part is wonderfully beautiful, and so subdued that a chorus of more than eight or twelve voices is out of place. (The writer once saw a score prepared for a choral performance on a large scale, strings, clarinets, and horns!!!) The colours of the various registers of the flutes are selected with penetrating insight; the gambas contribute a quality exquisitely appropriate. The key-system is logical and unifying—Eb, C minor, F minor, Bb minor, Ab to C, Eb.

The opening Sonatina (see O.O.S., No. 013), only twenty bars in length, is one of the loveliest elegies ever penned. To the effect of flutes in unison, in middle and upper registers, above throbbing string chords, with the sympathetic 'beats' inevitable with two wind instruments of the same type playing the same notes, there is added the poignant dissonance, oft-times repeated, produced by one of the flutes sustaining a sound while the other moves a semitone away and returns to the parent note:

Ex. 69 *Molto Adagio*
Fl. I. II.
Gba. I. II.
Cont. *8ve lower*
(Key Eb, signature of 2 flats.)

After the Sonatina the music is practically continuous throughout, mostly in short sections, as we find in the earlier cantatas, but more homogeneous. A few firm chords declare trust in God's ways ('God's time is the ever-best time'), and then an Allegro contrasts our living and moving in God:

with our remaining dependent on Him, a long sustained note. ('In ihm leben, weben und sind wir so lange er will', 'In Him live, move and are we so long as He wills', Acts xvii. 28). A most poignant Adagio assai ('In ihm sterben wir zu rechter Zeit, wenn er will', 'In Him die we at the right time, when He wills') closes the chorus. Psalm xc. 12 ('Ach, Herr, lehre uns bedenken, daß wir sterben müssen, auf daß wir klug werden', 'Ah, Lord, teach us to remember that we die must, in order that we wise become') is a short tenor solo with a continuo after the style of Böhm and a persistently repeated figure for the flutes:

indicative of the impossibility of escape from the decrees of fate. The voice moves in short phrases of intense melancholy, but in the final clause, which is only sung once, there is a moment of sudden confidence.

The ritornello leads without break into vivace, a number for basses, the command of God: 'Bestelle dein Haus, denn du wirst sterben und nicht lebendig bleiben' ('Arrange thy house, for thou shalt die and not living remain', Isa. xxxviii. 1):

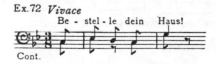

answered by a lovely staccato unison for the flutes:

the busy-ness of joyous obedience. There are fine runs on 'lebendig' and a solemn fall on 'sterben':

Ex. 74 Fl. I. II.

Bass. &
Cont. *8ve lower*
ster - - - - ben,

Unfortunately the N. and B. translations and portions in the Philharmonia miniature score do not preserve this essential imagery. The choice of flutes in unison shows Bach's unerring instinct for colour. A single instrument of this type would not produce the suggestion of a stern message from the Almighty, whereas the inevitable imperfect unisons create a feeling of impersonality. A group of basses adds to this more satisfactorily than a single voice. The voices end with the command and a long ritornello for the flutes leads into the next section. Thus early in his career, an unusual outlook for a young man, does he depict death as a beautiful and desirable state, and to the close of his days he rarely faltered. In a thousand numbers, infinitely varied though they be, he preached this Christian doctrine. Yet he never underestimated the solemnity of the last stages of human existence, and this may be seen in the succeeding number. It is a daring and successful piece of colouring. The three lower voices, poised deep, with the sole accompaniment of the continuo moving in relentless quavers, sing a fugue to 'Es ist der alte Bund: Mensch, du mußt sterben' ('It is the old covenant, Man, thou must die', Eccles. xiv. 17). The theme is awe-inspiring:

Ex. 75 *Andante* Es   ist   der   al - - te Bund:

Cont.

(F minor, signature of 2 flats.)

the countersubject stern:

Ex. 76

Mensch, du mußt ster - - - ben

and the fateful decree is further emphasized by manifold repetitions of 'du mußt'. During interludes of the fugue at first, and later combining slightly with the main idea, come exquisitely tender passages from the floating voices of the sopranos: 'Yea, come, Lord Jesus, come', Rev. xxii. 20:

Ex.77

and subsequently:

Ex.78

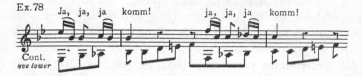

Yet a third element is added. Against the trio the flutes, in their lower register and supported by the gambas, intone the melody of Vulpius's hymn, 'Ich hab' mein Sach' Gott heimgestellt' ('I have my affairs in God reposed'), which was originally the tenor part of an anonymous four-part setting of a secular song, 'Ich weiß mir ein Röslein hübsch und fein' ('I know a little rose, pretty and fine'). It is not heard elsewhere in the work, nor indeed in all Bach; its reference to the command of the previous bass section is obvious and extraordinarily apt. The choice of the deep notes of the flutes is as masterly as that of the upper ones in the preceding number. We see how far Bach has advanced from No. 15 and its rather crude attempt to depict conflicting emotions simultaneously. The different elements are poised in perfect balance and the choice of material is miraculous and certain in its effect, the solemn fugue, with its awesome first phrase and its hammered declaration, 'Man, thou must die', the relentless continuo, the liquid hopeful tones of the sopranos, with many variations of the opening phrase, and the rich quiet sonorousness of the flutes. During the last almost despairing surge upwards of the lower voices the sopranos steal in pianissimo, and, as the instruments cease one by one, sing a marvellously lovely arabesque which tapers off in an unaccompanied, sinking cry. (The last two pianoforte chords in the N. edition are not justified; the instruments have finished, the voices must be left in mid-air.)

Another quasi-ground-bass supports a short alto solo in which the

singer commends the soul to Christ in the words of Psalm xxxi. 5:
'In deine Hände befehl' ich meinen Geist; du hast mich erlöset,
Herr, du getreuer Gott' ('Into Thy hands commit I my spirit; Thou
hast me redeemed, Lord, Thou faithful God'). The soaring of the
ostinato:

Ex. 79

(B♭ minor, signature of 2 flats.)

and like passages in the first vocal part speak of the winging of the
soul upwards; the singer's repeated notes to 'du hast mich erlöset'
her confidence in the future life. (One knows that there were no
women singers in the church choirs of the time, but we are so much
accustomed to female sopranos and contraltos that it seems natural
to use the feminine pronoun.) 'Herr, du getreuer Gott' is always
allotted phrases of its own. The number leads, again without break,
to a long development, for bass (which must be solo in this case), of
the Saviour's words to the thief dying on the cross, 'Heute wirst du
mit mir im Paradies sein' ('Today shalt thou with me in Paradise be',
St. Luke xxiii. 43), one of the loveliest ariosos the master ever penned.
Its sublime ecstasy is, in a way, incorrect; for it does not interpret
the emotion of Christ, but that of the criminal who in his death agony
sees blissful visions of the life to come. Yet the music is so wonderfully touching that few hearers will perceive the anomaly. As the endless melody proceeds, and dovetailing with the close of a rapid,
decorated, ecstatic climbing upwards on 'Paradies', the altos begin
to intone, to the Reformer's tune, the first stanza of Luther's paraphrase of the *Nunc Dimittis*, 'Mit Fried' und Freud' ich fahr' dahin',
'With peace and joy I journey thither In God's will, Comforted is
in me my heart and being, Soft and still, As God to me promised
has; Death is my sleep become'. When the chorale commences the
gambas, which have so far been silent, twine loving tendrils round
the melody. At the beginning of the antepenultimate line the solo
voice ceases. In the middle of the word 'stille' ('still') piano is marked.
Forte is resumed in the interlude. There is another curious singling-
out of one word in the last line, 'der Tod ist mein Schlaf worden'.
'Schlaf' is marked piano and 'Worden' forte. After the long final
note of the chorus the gambas waver, the upper ceases and then the
lower falls, the last flicker of the departing spirit and the relaxation
of the body in death.

The last stages of life are over; we look upwards and think of frail humanity and the earth no more. The orchestra expands to six bars the initial line of a third chorale melody—S. Calvisius's 'In dich hab' ich gehoffet, Herr' ('In Thee have I hoped, Lord'), decorates it and introduces echo effects. (It is noteworthy that all three chorales are of Thuringian origin.) Five lines of the seventh stanza of A. Reissner's hymn of this name: 'Glory, praise, honour and majesty Be to Thee, God Father and Son, given, To the Holy Ghost by name! The godlike strength Make us victorious', are sung mostly with block harmonies, the uppermost line decorated. They are accompanied in a manner unique in Bach's works, the orchestra mostly plays quavers on the second half of each crotchet, resting during the first half. The first three ritòrnelli elaborate the latter part of the lines with triplets, 'like the beating of spiritual wings' (Schering). The last line is fashioned into a brilliant double fugue:

Ex.80

Through Je - sus   Christ,
Durch Je - sum   Christ - um,   A - - - men, A - men,

A.
T.

A - - - - - - - - - men, A - men,
(Key E♭, signature of 2 flats.)

reinforced by the instruments. The last entry of the chief theme is in augmentation, the lower voices during it grow more and more animated; when the sopranos have finished with their theme they join the altos in an exciting semiquaver passage, with the lower voices shouting rapid Amens. Instead of concluding in this manner, however, after this outburst the choir sings a single Amen quietly, with continuo only, and this is repeated by the orchestra. The thought of the joy of the Resurrection is tempered by the recollection of the occasion which has brought the worshippers together, the loss of a loved friend.

Has any other composer ever compressed so much varied and exquisite beauty into the short space of eleven or twelve minutes?

WEIMAR

18, 21, 31, 59, 61, 70, 132, (142), 147, 152, 155, 158, 160, 161, 162, 163, 182, 185, 199

EIGHTEEN cantatas (another is of doubtful authenticity) possibly belong to the Weimar period and were composed between the ages of twenty-three and thirty-two. This does not seem a large output for Bach, even though it may have been considerably increased by compositions now lost, and by others, unknown to us in their first shape, which were undoubtedly rewritten at Weimar, as we shall see later. Only those which remain substantially in their Weimar form are discussed under this heading. It was here that he wrote the bulk of his organ works, so that his mind was much occupied with music for the church, and the relation between his organ and choral works is intimate. It was here that he first set texts by the cleric Neumeister, of the type which were to become predominant later. Possibly five of the Weimar libretti are by this writer, the precursors of the too regular patterns to be found in such numbers in Leipzig. Most of the remainder were penned by Salomo Franck, the Curator of the Ducal Museum of Coins and Medals in the town of Bach's residence. His schemes are more varied than Neumeister's, and although his verse is often pedestrian, his language lurid, his similes banal, and his tastes redolent of his occupation, they give rise to some of the finest of the Master's works in this period. We know little of the details of the choir at Weimar, but the number of solo cantatas is significant and leads one to comment on the popular conception of Bach's compositions. This has always been narrow, and has had two phases. The first works to steal into the horizon of musicians were his organ preludes and fugues and 'The 48', which, being also preludes and fugues, were associated in people's minds with the organ, and writer after writer stated that his work was influenced chiefly by that instrument. Even the learned Spitta repeats this doctrine *ad nauseam*. If the missing Passions and cantatas, both sacred and secular, could be discovered, the total number of *BGS* choral volumes would be well over seventy, and we may reasonably assume that relatively fewer organ works are lost. There was little inducement to copy out cantatas, as this type of service music was passing out of fashion and the labour was great, but pupils and admirers wrote out the organ works for their own use. When we consider that the organ works occupy only four-and-a-half of the forty-odd *BGS* volumes, and that Bach held posts as organist for only fourteen years in his long life, we see how absurd the idea is. These writers do not consider that his style is modelled on the harpsichord or clavichord, though he wrote as much for these as for the organ. Then his choral writings began to create interest, though in a restricted way, for few of the cantatas were performed, and public estimate veered round in that direction. We are often told that, vocally considered, he is a choral writer, and not essentially a composer for solo voice. Yet nearly 600 arias and over 100 duets exist, and recitatives are much more numerous, and his choruses, apart from simple chorales, number less than 250. Moreover, one-third of the cantatas are for solo voices without chorus other than a chorale, and sometimes not even with that. One writer of a study of Bach said, 'We need not consider' the solo cantatas! We may neglect one-third of the church cantatas!

In 1715 he wrote five or six solo cantatas and only three choral, and taking the Weimar period as a whole we find that about half are without chorus. One feature of this phase of his church music is the number of duets. These are noteworthy, generally of great beauty and mostly freer in plan than the arias. That he considered them of aria type and form is shown by his almost invariable inscription, 'Aria (Duetto)', and in the case of trios, 'Aria (Terzetto)'. All the duets sound best when sung chorally, with the exception of the two in No. 140, 'Wachet auf', which are so intimate that they must be entrusted to solo voices.

SOLO CANTATAS

59 (S.B.), 132, 152 (S.B.), 155, 158 (S.B.), 160 (T.), 162, 163, 185, 199 (S.)

Where no specification of voices is given all four are employed

Order of Discussion: 162, 160, 199, 185, 163, 132, 152, 155, 59, 158

162. The first free duet, that is, not based on a chorale, is found in 'Ach, ich sehe, jetzt da ich zur Hochzeit gehe', 20th Sunday after Trinity, 3 November 1715. The Gospel is St. Matt. xxii. 1–14, the parable of the King's invitation to the wedding of his son, and Franck's libretto skilfully compares life with a journey to a nuptial feast, speaks of fear and dread by the way and the nervous anticipation of final consequences of unworthiness. The text of the opening aria, for deep bass, bears reference to the Epistle, Eph. v. 15–21, Paul's warning against the companionship of the children of disobedience, 'Ach, ich sehe, itzt da ich zur Hochzeit gehe, wohl und wehe. Seelengift und Lebensbrod, Himmel, Hölle, Leben, Tod, Himmelsglanz und Höllenflammen sind beisammen! Jesu, hilf, daß ich bestehe!' ('Ah, I see now as I to the marriage go, weal and woe. Soul-poison and life's-bread, heaven, hell, life, death, heaven's-splendour and hell's-flames are (found) together! Jesu, help, that I endure!'). It is strongly felt and intense, appropriately grim in character. The relentless onward tread of the continuo rarely halts, the upper string parts are closely worked and carefully bowed, the continual grouping of semiquavers in twos adding to the emotional power of the texture. The chief vocal theme is derived from the opening canon:

Ex. 81

The second part opens grimly:

Ex. 82

A corno da tirarsi is employed, in a way new to Bach's treatment of the brass, and its independent movement deepens the solemnity of the aria. The singer is more concerned with the darker side of the mingled 'wohl und wehe' met with on the journey than with the brighter, and 'Höllenflammen' is more stressed than 'Himmelsglanz'. The increasing pliability of Bach's material is shown by his treatment of the several antitheses provided by the poet, beginning with 'Seelengift'. It is an unusual and striking aria. Until the final chorale-stanza 7 of J. G. Albinus's 'Alle Menschen müssen sterben', all instruments except the continuo cease. Flowing $\frac{12}{8}$ passages, the refreshment of the cooling waters by the way, are the characteristic of the soprano aria 'Jesu, Brunnquell aller Gnaden, labe mich elenden Gast, weil du mich berufen hast' ('Jesu, spring of all mercies, lave me poor guest, because Thou me called hast'). There is an interesting connexion between the first vocal phrase:

and the chief continuo idea of the second section:

In this portion, 'Ich bin matt, schwach und beladen, ach, erquicke meine Seele, ach, wie hungert mich nach dir!' ('I am faint, weak and burdened, ah, quicken my soul, ah, how hunger I after Thee!'), instead of the long placid instrumental melodies of the opening, the quoted bar occurs seven times in succession, though modified, speaking of agitation of mind. Moreover, it modulates in almost every bar; the main key of the aria is D minor, here C, D minor, E minor, A minor, the distant B minor, G major, F, G minor, B♭, and G minor follow in quick succession. With the second cadence in G minor, the initial theme is heard in a different form and is not referred to again until the dal segno, except that the dropping fifths and rising fourths of bar 4 occur. The text of the third portion is 'Lebensbrod, das ich erwähle, komm, vereine dich mit mir!' ('Life's-bread, that I choose, come, unite Thyself with me!'), and the desired quickening of the spirit is granted, for the continuo breaks into lively semiquaver runs.

The long A.T. duet, where the feast is reached and when all fears are past, contains abundant leaps of joy for the continuo while the voices move in smooth happy phrases, with many passages in parallel thirds and sixths, always a token of bliss with Bach. The opening vocal phrase:

is derived from the commencement of the continuo theme:

A striking feature of the continuation of the latter is the many derivatives of:

There are numerous lively runs to 'erfreut', which make the duet more animated than one expects from the rather sedate opening. 'Die Liebesmacht hat ihn bewogen, daß er mir in der Gnadenzeit aus lauter Huld hat angezogen' ('The love-might has Him moved, (so) that He on me in the mercy-time from pure affection has put') is a section in blissful parallel motion, with leaping bassi below. The latter continues while the next clause is sung by the voices successively 'die Kleider der Gerechtigkeit' ('the garments of righteousness'). After a statement of part of the introduction in E minor, the 'Liebesmacht' section is repeated with different tonal centres and rounded-off by the opening clause of the duet, but with new musical material, moving in thirds and sixths. 'Ich weiß, er wird nach diesem Leben' ('I know, He will after this life') opens with a strong affirmation and 'Leben' is florid. A close canon begins 'der Ehren weißes Kleid mir auch im Himmel geben' ('Honour's white robe to me also in heaven give', see Isa. lxi. 10). This ends in A minor and a shortened résumé of the previous portions, omitting the 'Liebesmacht' clause, brings us back to the tonic and a repetition of the introduction.

The alto recitative which joins the soprano aria and the duet is lengthy but textually effective, 'My Jesus, let me not to the marriage unclad come, (so) that upon me lights not Thy judgement; with fear have I indeed heard, how Thou the audacious wedding guest, who without (seemly) garb appeared, cast out and condemned hast. I know also my unworthiness; Ah, bestow on me faith's wedding garb, let Thy merit for my adornment serve, give me as marriage-garment the robe of salvation, innocence's white silk, Ah, let Thy blood the robe purple cover, the old Adam's cloak and his vice's-stains, so shall I beautiful and pure, and to Thee welcome be, so shall I worthily the feast of the Lamb taste' (see Rev. xix. 9). The two arias also are connected by a recitative, for tenor: 'Oh great wedding-feast, to which heaven's King mankind calls! Is then the poor bride, human nature, not much too base and insignificant, that Himself with her the Son of the Highest unites? Oh great wedding-feast, how is flesh to such honour come, that God's Son it has ever assumed?' (see Ps. cx. 1). 'Heaven is His throne, the earth serves as a stool for His feet, yet will He this world as bride and beloved kiss, the wedding banquet is ready, the fatted calf is slain, how gloriously is then all prepared! How blessed is he, whom here faith guides, and how cursed is indeed, he who this meal despises!' Bach's increasing mastery over recitative is evinced in this long number. Until 'How blessed' the voice never reaches a high note, the sense of human lowliness is preserved. 'Heaven is His throne' rises to F and then sinks low when the earth is spoken of as His footstool; a succession of dissonances accompanies the final clause. In 'that God's Son it has ever assumed?' the vocal phrase is flung across the bar-line and the continuo forsakes its holding-notes for a purposeful phrase:

Ex. 88

The exact melody of the concluding chorale does not appear to have been printed before the composition of the cantata. Terry, who discusses its origin at length in Volume III of his *Bach's Chorales*, is of opinion that it is Bach's variant of some melody which was familiar to him. The text is, 'Ah, I have already perceived This great glory! Now become I beautifully adorned With the white heaven's-robe,

With the golden honour-crown Stand I there before God's throne,
Contemplate such joy That no end can have!'

160. The other Weimar solo cantatas will be discussed in their
chronological order, so far as it can be ascertained. The fact that the
text of the Easter Sunday cantata, 'Ich weiß, daß mein Erlöser lebt'
('I know that my Redeemer liveth', the first clause of Job xix. 25) is
by Neumeister (with slight verbal alterations by the composer), places
it possibly on 1 April 1714. Neumeister's collection was not published
till 1716, but copies of his libretti were undoubtedly circulated before
that date. The qualities of the cantata fall below the standard of its
fellows. There is a facile tunefulness and placid contentment about it,
but it never ventures to soar. There are three arias and two recitatives,
all for tenor, with no chorale, and the arias are scored for a very
simple combination, violin, bassoon, and continuo. When one thinks
of the obbligato bassoon parts of No. 150 one is disappointed to find
that not a single note differs from the continuo line. When the violin
is silent, it is silent too. It is difficult to account for this lack of enterprise, except by the theory that sometimes his fagottists were woe-
fully inadequate. As the libretto did not appear in print till he was
thirty-one, and would scarcely have been known for many years
before, the work cannot have been a youthful effort. It may possibly
be by another hand, touched up by Bach.[1]

The treatment of the material of the first aria (see p. 2) shows some
ingenuity, however. The opening two-bar violin figure:

Ex.89

Fg Cont.
8ve lower

is expanded to four bars when the voice begins:

Ex.90 Ich   weiß, daß   mein   Er - lö - ser   lebt,

Cont.   6 6   6   6 6

but on the second entry, the soloist reverts to the violin form, as if
contemplation were giving place to eagerness. A derivative comes in
bars 7–9:   Ex.91

---
[1] Alfred Dürr attributes the cantata to Telemann.

and forms the basis of the first interlude. The bassi announce in bars
5 and 6 a running figure:

Ex. 92

which is afterwards associated with 'lebt' and is combined with the
joy-motive. In one vocal phrase it is prolonged by an idea which is
scarcely Bachian:

Ex. 93   lebt,

Another little violin figure:

Ex.94

too feeble for the now rapidly maturing composer, is not heard
vocally, but is used for a brief interlude. Elementary though the
treatment of violin and bassoon be, they are even left out of the whole
of the middle section: 'er lebt und mir zur Freude. Laß sein, daß ich
im Leide, in Arbeit, Müh' und Plage viel Stunden meiner Tage muß
auf der Welt verschmerzen; blüht doch der Trost im Herzen' ('He
lives and to me for joy. Although I in sorrow, in labour, pains and
lamentations many hours of my days must in the world endure;
blossoms yet comfort in the heart'). 'Er lebt' brings the 'lebt' motive
and 'Freude' the conventional flourish. The next portion departs
widely in style from the first, yet it fits surprisingly well into the
scheme. There are now two broken runs, typical clichés of the period:

Ex.95   Lei - - - - - - - - de,

and

Ex.96

The four bars after 'Leide' are cross-accented, producing a feeling of mental disturbance. The first part is written out again in full.

The next aria is on the same lines, a lapse which Bach would not have committed later, though some blame must be apportioned to Neumeister for his inability to get away from his previous strain. 'Gott Lob, daß mein Erlöser lebt!' ('(To) God (be) praise, that my Redeemer lives') is with violin and bassoon, the first vocal idea a modification of that of the violin, florid passages on 'lebt'. 'Er lebt, so wird sein Leben im Tode mir gegeben. D'rum will ich freudig sterben, die Freude dort zu erben, die mir im Engel-Orden von ihm vermachet worden' ('He lives, so will His life in death to me be given. Therefore will I joyfully die, joy there to inherit, which for me in the angel-order (body, fraternity) by him bequeathed was') is the middle section, with continuo only, and with frequent use of the initial violin figure:

Ex.97

The third aria is not in Da Capo form, but is in three sections, which are bound together by the fluttering angel theme of the opening:

Ex.98 *Vivace*

In the first part, 'Nun, ich halte mich bereit, meines Leibes Sterblichkeit auf der Erden abzulegen' ('Now, I hold myself ready, my body's mortality on the earth to lay down') the voice rises higher than the violin in a passage without continuo, an interesting experiment in colour. In the middle section, 'Kommt, ihr Engel, kommt entgegen, traget meine Seele hin, daß ich bald bei Jesu bin!' ('Come, ye angels, come to meet (me), carry my soul thither, that I soon with Jesus be!')

eagerness is expressed by a declamatory repetition of 'bald'. In the third, 'Ach, wie herzlich wünsch' ich mir: wär' ich heute noch bei dir!' ('Ah, how heartily wish I to myself: were I today then with Thee!') the initial phrase appears again in the voice.

Feeble as is the librettist's fancy in this aria, offering little scope for the musician, the first recitative is much worse, arid and enormously long. The picture of the believer watching the arrest of Christ and following Him to Golgotha, does not arouse any poetic powers. 'He lives and is from death arisen! Hereon rests the reason, which like a rock the fast faith carries in the hope of my blessedness. Bewailed I in the garden His bonds, which on Him the enemy's-poison and envy through the traitor (has) laid; became also my heart wounded, when men on Him so many wounds with sharp stings cut; have I so many pains with wail and woe felt, when men His head with thorns pierced and lamentably tore, followed I half-dead to Golgotha Him after, whither He the burden and shame of the cross Himself bore and on Him ferocity in such a way beat; was my soul full of misery, when men the body to the grave brought and of all mourning a mournful end made, so had then with His blood-shedding from me at the same time even joy-tears to flow, because He through His death the guilt of my misery in my place will atone.' In his later years Bach might have made something even of this dry, monstrously Brobdingnagian sentence of 122 words, utterly out of proportion with regard to the cantata as a whole, but all he was able to do at that period was to provide an oasis in the desert by a tremendous flourish on 'Freudenthränen' ('joy-tears'). A meditation on the blessings brought by the crucifixion might, in the hands of anyone but a poetaster, have given the composer some opportunity, but it does not: 'But I were ill-comforted and not quite wholly redeemed, if He were not through His own might arisen. But now is comfort at hand, and it stands fast, so that even the last mite for me is paid, and the law from me nothing more to demand has; for today becomes God my security from the grave, as from the debtors' prison, again free.'

The second recitative begins well: 'So bid I all devils defiance!' and 'Mein Held, mein Jesus ist mein Schutz' ('My Hero, my Jesus is my defence') is set as arioso. Most of the remainder is pure recitative: 'Faith will (bring) me nevermore to shame. Shall I lost go? So is then Christ not arisen!' (See Cor. xv. 13.) 'But He lives, therefore must I even through Him to life ascend, and to His kingdom of rest'; there is a brief arioso: 'der Ruh' und Ehre zieh'n' ('of rest and honour go'), a lapse from Bach's careful attention to his text. It is less unsatisfactory than its fellow, but is too much cut up into sections. One wonders what strange perversity of fate led Bach to forsake the type of such libretti as Nos. 131 and 106 and to be attracted by Neumeister, Franck and Co.

199. Much more interesting and characteristic, and possessing many of the qualities we may now look for, is 'Mein Herze schwimmt im Blut' ('My heart swims in blood'), for solo soprano, though it belongs to the same year, or to 1714, for the 11th Sunday after Trinity. The score was not found until 1911, in the Royal Library of Copenhagen, a belated discovery of one of the many missing links of the great chain, which, alas, appears to be broken for ever. Parts are also found in the Prussian State Library. The libretto is a single hymn-stanza with excellent original verses by G. C. Lehms, of Darmstadt, whose name, unfortunately, does not occur elsewhere in the series. The general drift of the text is the humility of the publican; the Gospel is St. Luke xviii. 9–14. The librettist borrowed his first line from a text by Neumeister, and, according to an article by Dr. F. Noack, Bach's music bears certain resemblances to a previous setting by Christopher Graupner, a prolific composer who was one of the three men proposed for the Cantorship of St. Thomas's, the others being Telemann and Bach. It is evidently, then, one of the numerous instances where Bach worked over the compositions of other people, not disdaining to take what good he might find in them and reshaping in his own way, a practice which seems reprehensible in these days of strict copyright laws, but which was accepted as quite permissible and honest at that time. It is this which makes Bach the most comprehensive composer of his or of any other age; all streams flow into the great river, which is sufficiently vast and powerful to absorb them all and yet retain its own unpolluted individuality. In spite of its somewhat repulsive title the work is charming. Three of the recitatives are fully scored for strings and doubling bassoon, an unusual occurrence in his early works, although there is a precedent in the German solo Magnificat, and are effective and pleasing; only a short one of three bars has merely continuo. The three arias are finely contrasted.

A recitative opens, 'My heart swims in blood, because me the sin's brood in God's holy eyes into a monster makes. And my conscience feels pain, because to me sins nothing but hell's-devils are. Hated iniquity-night! Thou, thou alone hast me to such necessity brought! And thou, thou evil Adam's-seed robst my soul of all rest, and closest to it heaven! Ah! unheard-of affliction! My withered heart will furthermore no comfort fructify; and I must myself before Him hide, before whom the angels themselves their countenances cover.' While one cannot expect at this stage of Bach's career to find the wonderful subtleties and flexibilities of later recitatives, this one possesses fine qualities. There is a tender charm of sadness, the vocal lines move gratefully, the portion beginning 'Du böser Adams-Samen' ('Thou evil Adam's seed') is intermediate betwixt recitative and arioso, after 'Höllen-henker sein' ('hell's-devils are') and 'Himmel zu' ('heaven to') the sections are neatly joined by expressive string passages, and the feeling of shame in the three bars before the close is beautifully indicated by the sinking of the continuo in semitones from C to G.

The adagio aria is of exquisite loveliness, the oboe obbligato (the upper strings are silent) is superb in its pathos. The mournfulness of the opening phrase:

sets a standard which is fully maintained throughout. Bars 5 and 6 contain bold anticipations of the next chords on the second and fourth beats of the bar:

The voice begins with a new idea:

though with the same continuo, and is answered by an oboe phrase, borrowed from bars 3 and 4:

Ex. 102

When the voice resumes it does so to (*b*) slightly altered, and (*a*) is used as counterpoint. The remainder of the text of part I is 'Ihr mögt meine Schmerzen sagen, weil der Mund geschlossen ist' ('Ye are able my afflictions to tell, because my mouth closed is'). (*d*) accompanies while the voice sinks low, struggles upwards and falls again, to 'geschlossen', as if in vain attempt to find speech. The second time this dual idea is heard, 'geschlossen' is extended, touching low B, and the upward thrust indicates an even greater struggle towards articulation. With (*b*) in the instruments the voice sings a lovely sequence:

Ex. 103

Part II begins, 'Und Ihr nassen Tränenquellen könnt ein sich'res Zeugnis stellen, wie mein sündlich Herz gebüßt' ('And ye wet tear-springs may a sure testimony produce, how my sinful heart atoned (has)'). (*a*) and (*b*) come in the oboe, the vocal material is fresh, except that the opening of (*a*) is heard. On a long decorated G to 'gebüßt' the oboe plays (*d*). Before the Da Capo is a short recitative with continuo only, an effective point of construction occasionally found in later cantatas: 'Mein Herz ist itzt ein Tränenbrunn, die Augen heiße Quellen. Ach Gott! Wer wird dich doch zufrieden stellen?' ('My heart is now a tear-well, mine eyes hot springs. Ah God! Who will Thee then to satisfy pretend?').

Upper strings and bassoon reappear in the next recitative and aria. The phrases of the first part of the recitative are short, as if in despair despite affirmations of faith: 'But God must to me gracious be, because I my head with ashes, my face with tears lave, my heart in repentance and sorrow breaks and full of melancholy say'. A firm downward arpeggio comes to 'Gott sei mir' ('God be to me'), 'Sünder gnädig!' ('Sinner gracious!') brings a diminished third for the voice and a tender phrase for the orchestra. The conclusion, 'Ah yea! His heart breaks and my soul says', leads without break into the aria. Bach expands a short text into a very long number, 144 bars to the Da Capo, 235 if the repeat is taken in full. The introduction, in itself 25 bars, begins with a flowing melody:

A leisurely sequential idea is heard in two forms:

and:

A figure from these is treated in a different manner:

and repeated by the bassi with the upper strings trilling simultaneously on dotted minims. Thirteen bars of the introductory melody are modified by the voice: 'Tief gebückt und voller Reue, lieg ich, liebster Gott, vor Dir' ('Lowly bent and full of repentance, lie I, dearest God, before Thee'). Violin II and viola are silent, violin I adds above the voice a fragment of (a) and passages formed from (c). From here to the ritornello, a repetition of the introduction, (a), (b), (c), and (d) are presented in various forms. 'Reue' is lengthened to nearly six bars, beginning at bar 43, and runs into a variant of the initial vocal melody. From bar 55 to 67 the orchestra plays bars 13–25 of the introduction, the singer adding a fifth strand. After the

voice delivers the first time the text of Part II: 'Ich bekenne meine
Schuld, aber habe doch Geduld mit mir!' ('I admit my guilt, but
have yet patience with me!') beginning with the time-pattern of bar 1
of (a), but altered melodically, the orchestral material of Part I serves
for new purposes. A halt is called on 'Geduld', which is sung thrice
Adagio. Adagio is marked again for the next five bars, with 'piu
piano' added; violin I lets us hear bar 1 of (a) twice.

Variety is secured in a happy manner by the next pair of movements, a tiny recitative of three bars—'On this painful repentance
falls to me then this comfort-word'—and a chorale. The sequence of
keys is odd, the aria finished in E♭, the recitative moves from C minor
to G minor and the chorale begins in F. Stanza 3 of J. Heermann's
'Wo soll ich fliehen hin' ('Whither shall I flee') is set to the anonymous melody 'Die Wollust dieser Welt' or 'O Gott, du frommer
Gott'. The verse is eminently suitable for a solo voice—'I, Thy
troubled child, Cast (away) all my sins, So many of them (as are)
in me fixed And me so greatly terrify, In Thy deep wounds, There I
always salvation (have) found'—and both numbers are the answer to
the last verse of the Epistle, 1 Corinthians xv. 1–10. In the German
solo Magnificat Bach exploited the violetta as an obbligato instrument, here its counterpart the viola. The chorale melody opens:

Ex. 108

and the viola treats it in diminution, following it with a demisemiquaver trilling which is an important factor in accompanying the
chorale lines:

Ex. 109

At Leipzig the obbligato was rewritten for the violoncello piccolo.
The next recitative, with strings and bassoon, falls in two sections.
'I lay myself in these wounds, as in the true rock, they must my resting place be' is plainly accompanied, with the closing portion slightly
elaborated, as we found in the first and second recitatives. 'In these
will I myself in faith soar and therein gladly and joyfully sing' begins
simply, but 'fröhlich' ('gladly') is set to a long and brilliant semiquaver run in which violin I joins.

The gigue which concludes the cantata sounds as if it had come from the Cöthen days:

Ex.110 *Allegro*

The fugal theme is not followed up completely, violin I enters with it a bar after the opening and continuo and fagotto a bar later, but the inner strings join in with other matter when the bassi commence. The singer opens with a variant, the bassi playing their figure (see above) when 'Herz' is sung:

Ex.111

Wie freu-dig ist mein Herz, wie freu-dig ist mein Herz,
How joyful is my heart,

oboe and violin I following in quick imitation, the rest of the orchestra accompanying simply. A reversal of normal procedure is found in the next idea, the decorated form first, a simple one next:

Ex.112

Wie freu - - - dig, wie freu-dig ist mein Herz,

The text of the remainder of Part I is 'da Gott versöhnet ist' ('since God reconciled is'). Part II is 'Und mir auf Reu und Leid nicht mehr die Seligkeit noch auch sein Herz verschließt' ('And to me through repentance and sorrow no longer the blessedness nor His heart closes'). None of the other themes are heard; phrases rock and flow —the anticipation of future bliss. The number is a little too short for a completely satisfactory close to the cantata, but a moderate tempo helps to remedy this and also to make the solo line more comfortable to sing. An ordinary gigue tempo can scarcely be reconciled with the vocal factor; a compromise is necessary. An alternative score without violin II exists.

185. The inequalities of Franck as a librettist and the briars of obstruction he strewed so abundantly in the path of the young composer may be seen in 'Barmherziges Herze der ewigen Liebe' ('Merciful heart of eternal love'), for all four solo voices, produced on the

Fourth Sunday after Trinity, 14 July 1715. The dryness of the words of the first recitative (ii) makes the musician hard put to find any source of inspiration. The Gospel, St. Luke vi. 36–42, beginning 'Be ye therefore merciful', sheds its poetic beauty in paraphrase and becomes a series of bald statements. The first section is a reference to the attitude of the scribes and Pharisees when Christ healed a withered hand on the Sabbath, mentioned earlier in the chapter: 'Ye hearts, which you into stone and rock have turned melt and become soft; consider what to you the Saviour teaches, exercise, exercise pity, and seek yet on earth like to the Father to become.' 'Zerfließt' ('melts') and 'Barmherzigkeit' ('pity') receive characteristic treatment, and the last clause is more arioso than recitative. The strings are marked pianissimo and the bassoon piano. The latter is treated in a curious way in this and the other recitatives; where the continuo has minims or longer notes it merely punctuates with a crotchet, allowing the bassi to sustain. The terse command of Christ, 'Judge not, and ye shall not be judged', is attenuated by being lengthened: 'Ah, presume not, through forbidden judging, against the All-Highest in His judgement, else will His zeal you annihilate.' The depths of literary dullness [are reached] in Christ's next command: 'Forgive, so will you also be forgiven; give, give in this life; make for yourself capital, so that at some time God repays with rich interest.' Bach does not know what to do with this appallingly flat statement, so irreverently livens up things with a little violin flourish. Franck's version of verse 30—'For as you mete, will man to you again measure'—at least provides some chance of symbolic treatment. Bach sets the words twice, with the second clause a third time afterwards. (See Ex. 1302.) The initial statement is a canon between singer and continuo (the other instruments are silent), a firm command for the first clause, and for the second a falling quaver scale on 'messen' ('measure') an upward rush of semiquavers with a drop of a seventh at the end, indicating the Nestorian effect of ill-doing. In the repetition each part moves by inversion, a pictorial representation of cause and effect! The third representation of the second clause is free. The second recitative (iv), with continuo and bassoon, blandly states 'so wisse, daß du auch kein Engel. Verbeß're deine Mängel!' ('So know that thou too art no angel. Improve thy deficiencies!'). Before this priceless expression the sinner is addressed: 'Self-love deceives itself. Strive, first thy beam to throw out, then mayst thou about splinters also take pains, which in thy neighbour's eyes are.' (See Ex. 1283.)

After the gem of the text comes, 'How can one blind man with the other straight and aright go? How fall they to their sorrow not in the ditch together?' At 'Gruben' ('ditch') the bassi wallow trillingly in the mud!

The text of the Vivace, non-Da Capo bass aria with continuo and unison bassoon (v) is also bald and gives rise only to pedestrian music, although there is much ingenuity of construction and a measure of brisk tunefulness, especially in the continuo introduction:

Ex. 113

There are four sections of the verse, the first three opening and closing with 'Das ist der Christen Kunst' ('That is the Christians' art'); the initial delivery of each is to the first continuo group, and the last without this preface, but concluded by the clause. After the Scarlattian start with a fragment of the chief melody, the voice sings nearly the whole of the continuo theme to the motto clause and 'nur Gott und sich erkennen, von wahrer Liebe brennen' ('only God and themselves know, with true love to burn'). The continuo idea now appears in the relative major and the next part of the text, 'nicht unzulässig richten, noch fremdes Thun vernichten' ('not inadmissibly judge, nor others' doings destroy') brings a quaint conceit; the 'nicht unzulässig' notes are inverted for 'fremdes Thun ver-', two successive fourths being answered by fifths. The continuo now mounts higher and delivers its thesis, *per arsin et thesin*, in the dominant minor, and, as in the case of the reference to 'measure' in ii, 'des Nächsten nicht vergessen, mit reichem Maße messen' (one's neighbour not to forget, with rich measure to mete') is an intriguing canon at the distance of a beat. The subdominant minor is now reached, continuo and voice give out the motto, and then the singer repeats floridly the inner sections of the first three groups of the text, while the bassi utilize the second part of the introduction, modulating through various keys. With the last vocal 'der Christen Kunst' the continuo combines with it the initial notes of its theme forte, thus stressing the message of the text. 'Das macht bei Gott und Menschen Gunst' ('That creates with God and men favour') is at first accompanied by fresh material but later the second idea reappears. It is an aria which reads better than it sounds; perhaps if we could replace the modern contrabass by a violone the conflict between bass voice and continuo would be moderated.

Where the verse is better the music is delightful. In the S.A. duet (i), based on the first verse of the Gospel, the thoughts of pity, love, and goodness are mirrored in phrases of much grace and charm. The text is 'Barmherziges Herze der ewigen Liebe, errege, bewege mein Herze durch dich; damit ich Erbarmen und Gütigkeit übe, O Flamme der Liebe, zerschmelze du mich!' ('Pitying heart of eternal love, inspire, move my heart through Thee; so that I pity and goodness exercise, Oh flame of love, melt Thou me!'). The oboe, or, as is indicated in another manuscript, the trumpet, comments on the text by playing the anonymous melody of one of the set hymns, J. Agricola's 'Ich ruf' zu dir, Herr Jesu Christ' ('I cry to Thee, Lord Jesus Christ') and the continuo, the only other accompaniment, moves with quiet, yet joyous, animation. The chief theme of two bars duration, appearing successively in continuo, soprano, and tenor, contains no fewer than four trills, indicated for the first two entries only:

Ex. 114

Doubtless it would be understood that the tenor soloist would follow suit and that the theme would be so ornamented at each appearance. Graun's *Passion* shows what was expected from solo vocalists in church music at the time, and the European influence of Italy caused trilling to be an essential part of even a boy chorister's training. An abundance of shakes was common in church music of the latter part of the seventeenth century and during part of the eighteenth. Mozart's Masses teem with flourishes. Today we are apt to regard them as means of display borrowed from the theatre rather than as emotional factors and they are generally omitted, but with Bach there was no question of association with the stage, and their deletion is a distinct loss. The employment of large choral bodies prevents the use of trills in choruses, many of which are of delightful effect. The trills in this duet are significant of burning flames of love; they enhance the beauty of the themes and contribute warmth and glow to the ensemble. The soprano entry is accompanied by its inversion in the continuo, the tenor entry by the inversion in the soprano and undulating quavers in the continuo, which, except for one set of three crotchets and references to the chief theme, persist throughout the number, an interpretation of 'bewege'. Ideas derived from these quaver undulations occur in the voice parts; 'errege', 'bewege', 'O Flamme', and 'der Liebe' are often set to pleading phrases:

Ex. 115

er - re - ge,   be - we - ge,

The leading motive is kept in evidence throughout, such ideas as:

Ex. 116

Barm - her - zi - ges Her - ze

and:

Ex. 117

da - mit ich Er - bar - men

being related to it.

The non-Da Capo alto aria (iii), oboe, bassoon (which merely doubles at times) and strings, speaks of the scattering of seed, and the contour of the melody:

Ex. 118 Adagio
Ob. Vl. I.

Cont.
8ve lower

is pure pictorial representation. 'Auszustreuen' and 'erfreuen' wing on rapid flights. The text of Part I is 'Sei bemüht in dieser Zeit, Seele, reichlich auszustreuen, soll die Ernte dich erfreuen in der reichen Ewigkeit' ('Be at pains in this time, soul, plentifully to scatter abroad, (then) will the harvest thee rejoice in abundant eternity'). During a long 'auszustreuen' the oboe begins the initial three-bar theme; there is a joyful and impulsive flourish on 'Ewigkeit' after the customary long note. Part II is 'Wo, wer Gutes ausgesäet, fröhlich nach den

Garben gehet' ('Wherever one good has sown, (he) joyously to the sheaf goes'). 'Wo' ('where' or 'in whatever place') is thrust on a high note and separated from 'wer' by a rest, one 'gehet' seems to picture gleeful hastening to the richly golden cornfield. The oboe again introduces the chief theme; except during these two portions it doubles violin I. There are many bowing and dynamic marks in this expressive aria, the upper strings and oboe are always hushed to piano or solo when the singer is engaged, an indication of Bach's habitual practice, which should be followed in a general manner in all editions. The chorale melody of the duet comes in a four-part version at the close of the cantata, violin I playing an independent line above, the other instruments doubling. The stanza of the hymn is the first; it is translated for cantata No. 177, q.v., and should be consulted in connexion with its commentary on the text of the duet.

163. Christ's injunction to the Pharisees (the Gospel is St. Matthew xxii, 15–22) to render unto Caesar that which is Caesar's, does not seem promising material for a libretto and Franck's choice is characteristic of the man's bent of mind. Yet 'Nur jedem das Seine' ('Only to each his due'), for the 23rd Sunday after Trinity, possibly of the same year, 1715, 24 November, is much more interesting than the last two and of more equal merit throughout. It must have been reconstructed at Leipzig, because the tenor aria (i) includes in the score an oboe d'amore, an instrument he did not encounter previous to his Cantorship, together with a single line of violins and violas. As the manuscript, which is in the hand of Carl Philipp, states 'Concert à 2 violini 1 viola 2 violoncello, S.A.T.B. è continuo' (the oboe d'amore is not mentioned and 'violoncello' is in the singular) it must be that solo instruments are intended. In the *BGS* score the 'cello part is printed on a separate stave, though it differs in no wise from the continuo except in the bass aria. Bach could not draw any musical inspiration from the verse of the tenor aria, with its 'duty, tax and donation', odd subjects for musical illustration, yet he wrote an engaging number which makes one forget even taxes and tax-collectors! The introduction is in two sets of four bars, each 3+1, the longer phrase forte, the shorter piano. After the continuo announces:

Ex. 119

the oboe d'amore takes it up and continues with the joy-motive. In the piano codetta:

Ex. 120

the instruments are in unison. The unattractive first clause of the text is spun out for fifteen bars. It begins in the Scarlattian manner; before the full statement the oboe d'amore begins three bars of its theme, the voice dovetails in the first idea, but proceeds independently. Variety is obtained by sometimes separating 'Nur jedem' from 'das Seine' and the piano one-bar phrase rounds off the section. The next clause is 'Muß Obrigkeit haben Zoll, Steuern und Gaben, man weig're sich nicht der schuldigen Pflicht!' ('Must authority have duty, tax and donations, one refuses not obligation's due!'). The exclamation mark is distinctly humorous. We remember how at Leipzig Bach complained of the duties levied on the gift of a cask of wine, calculated how much each draught cost him and courteously begged the donor that no gifts of this kind be sent him in future! Fragments of the chief theme appear and again the section is rounded off by the one-bar phrase. 'Man weig're sich nicht' is thrice set across the normal accents of the bar as if man *did* object! The last clause, 'Doch bleibet das Herze dem Höchsten alleine' ('but belongs the heart to the Highest alone'), introduces the chief theme from time to time and the one-bar clause prefaces the Da Capo. One marvels that Bach could rise above this mundane verse and write such interesting music. The significance of the oboe d'amore is not apparent, beautiful though its line may be.

Neither is Bach dismayed by the reference at the end of the first recitative (ii) for bass with continuo, to 'schlechtes Geld' ('bad money') and 'falsche Münz' ('false coinage'). Franck cannot get away from his museum and its contents, they had eaten into the heart of the man and corroded his imagination. The recitative is made interesting, however, by surprising modulations and chromatic chords. The text is: 'Thou art my God, the giver of all gifts, we have, what we have, alone from Thine hand. Thou, Thou hast us given spirit, soul, body and life, and goods and chattels, and honour and rank. What shall we then to Thee in gratitude therefore render, since that our whole riches only Thine and even not ours are, Yet there is one thing more, that to Thee, God, is well pleasing, the heart shall alone, Lord, Thy tribute-money be. Ah, but Ah! is that not bad money? Satan has Thine image thereon injured, the false stamp is set on it.' (See Ex. 1285.)

Both the quaver and semiquaver groups of the opening idea of the bass aria (iii):

Ex. 121
Violoncello obbligato I.

are important. It will be noticed that (a) is outlined a third lower in (b). The last three quavers of bar 1 are found in two twin figures:

Ex. 122
(c)

and:

Ex. 123
(d)

which are sometimes combined. A figure akin to these is:

Ex. 124
(e)

In bars 5 and 6 comes a crossing idea, all semiquavers, in both 'celli:

Ex. 125

'Laß mein Herz die Münze sein, die ich dir, mein Jesu, steu're' ('Let my heart the coin be, that I to Thee, my Jesu, pay') begins with a decorated form of (a); (a), (b), (c), and (e) are all heard in the 'celli and the voice often moves in derivative stepwise quavers; the last bars of the introduction close the section. (e) is heard in various forms during the earlier part of 'Ist sie gleich nicht allzurein, ach, so komm doch und erneu're, Herr, den schönen Glanz in ihr' ('Is it although not all-too-clean, Ah, so come then and renew, Lord, the beautiful lustre in it'). Near the end, 'cello I sustains a semibreve and follows with a flourish, the gleam of the newly polished coin; when the voice ceases, 'cello II repeats this with a slight modification, and its partner glistens with triplet semiquavers. Then comes a most attractive stamping portion, the swinging and striking of the busy workers' hammers:

Ex. 126

Komm, ar-bei-te, schmelz' und prä-ge, Komm, ar-bei-te, schmelz' und prä-ge,
Come, work, melt and stamp,

(again the Ducal collection!) with (c) and (d) combined. During the concluding clause—'daß dies Ebenbild in mir ganz erneuert glänzen möge' ('that this image in me quite renewed gleam may')—forms of (a) and (c) are the chief source of the obbligati lines. There would not be a spare 'cello to join the continuo line; it would be played by organ and violone. The absence of upper notes causes the texture to be disturbing at a first hearing, but the tunes are so bright, the interlacing of the obbligati instruments so intriguing, and the cross rhythms so piquant, that one is carried along from start to finish.

The splendid S.A. recitative, with continuo, is much more than it describes itself, it is even much more than recitative plus arioso, for it is developed considerably. 'Ich wollte dir, O Gott, das Herze gerne geben' ('I would to Thee, Oh God, the heart gladly give') is mostly in canon; 'der Will' ist zwar bei mir' ('the will is indeed in me') indicates unity with the Almighty by parallel motion. 'Doch Fleisch und Blut will immer widerstreben' ('Yet flesh and blood will ever against (it) strive') brings a three-part canon, the continuo participating, with conflicting accents and runs at the end. There is imitation in 'Dieweil die Welt das Herz gefangen hält' ('As long as the world the heart imprisoned holds') and the continuo moves sternly up in minims. The tempo changes, 'un poco allegro', and a closely worked threefold canon pictures an involved mesh, from which escape is impossible: 'So will sie sich den Raub nicht nehmen lassen' ('So will it from itself the prey not to be taken allow'). Adagio emphasizes the resolution of the believer, 'jedoch ich muß sie hassen' ('nevertheless I must it hate'). No change of tempo is indicated for 'Wenn ich dich lieben soll' ('If I Thee love shall') but no doubt 'poco allegro' must be resumed for the remainder: 'So mache doch mein Herz mit deiner Gnade voll, leer' es ganze aus von Welt und aller Lüsten,

und mache mich zu einem rechten Christen' ('So make then
my heart with Thy grace full, empty it completely of the world
and all desires, and make me into a real Christian'). From 'so' to
'Lüsten' is an eleven-bar canon, mostly in two parts, but with the
continuo adding a third part for a while; a trill and semiquaver runs
come on 'voll', the latter appearing also in the continuo, and a free
part for the soprano at the end, a cascade of semiquavers on 'allen'.
Bassi semiquavers roll for most of the last section, 'und mache mich'
moves in thirds and sixths and 'zu einem rechten Christen' brings
another florid canon at the distance of a beat. The ritornello is an
ecstatic upward rush of semiquavers and a quaver-crotchet cadence.
An aria-duetto for the same voices follows. The opening clause is a
quaint conceit—'Nimm mich mir und gieb mich dir' ('Take me from
myself and give me to Thee')—and the chief theme is a little caressing
figure:

Ex.127

the voices gradually draw closer together, the increasing union of the
Saviour and the heart, and then melt into parallel sixths. The next
clause:

Ex.128

is followed by 'deinen Willen zu erfüllen' ('Thy will to fulfil') and
the voices float contentedly in quavers. The continuo has been marching steadily in crotchets, but it now joins in the quaver movement,
and *violini e viola all' unisono* intone A. Hammerschmidt's melody
to C. Keimann's hymn 'Meinen Jesum laß' ich nicht' ('My Jesus
leave I not'). It is evident that Bach wished to recall to the minds of
his congregation stanza 1, which is translated for cantata No. 124.
(b) is developed till the end of line 2 of the chorale melody, and during
the latter the continuo begins a long passage of lulling quavers.
A derivative of (b) begins canonically the next gently moving idea:

Ex.129

and the text continues, 'in dir bleibe für und für' ('in Thee abide for ever and ever'). After line 3 of the chorale melody a new canonical theme is announced for this last clause:

Ex.130

and line 4 enters while the pair of believers sway in blissful quaver sixths. (*a*) with its text, is now resumed. Between lines 5 and 6 a phrase is borrowed from 'und mein Gemüthe' and fitted with words from the opening:

Ex.131

and it and (*a*) lead to line 6. This is accompanied mostly by (*a*). During the last note of the chorale melody the voices are marked piano, the soprano twice sings (*a*) and the alto twice the derivative. The last three bars are a joyful forte: 'nimm mich mir und gieb mich dir!'

No chorale is included in the score, only a figured continuo, marked 'In simplice stylo'. Caspar Stieler's (?) melody 'Wo soll ich fliehen hin' ('Whither shall I fly') fits in with the bass and the mood of the cantata. Spitta's suggestion of stanza 11 of J. Heermann's

Lenten hymn of the same melody is followed in the Breitkopf vocal
score and makes a satisfactory ending: 'Lead also my heart and mind
Through Thy Spirit thither, That I may everything avoid That me
from Thee can separate, And I of Thy body A member may ever
remain.'

132. The libretti of the next three cantatas are also by Franck and
exhibit the same mixture of flat platitudes and reasonably poetic
verses, without descending to the crudities quoted above. The Gospel
for the 4th Sunday in Advent, John i. 19–28, is the foundation of
'Bereitet die Wege, bereitet die Bahn' ('Prepare the way, prepare the
course', see Isaiah xl. 3), which was possibly produced on 22 December 1715, and the command 'Rejoice in the Lord alway' from the
Epistle, Philippians iv. 4–7, influenced the writer. It opens with a
soprano aria of happy anticipation of the coming of the Saviour. The
BGS prints two instrumental bass lines without indicating the instruments. The upper, which contains frequent forte marks, is Tacet
during the second portion of the aria, is a modification of the lower
and looks as if it were written for the bassoon. The original title-page,
however, makes no mention of fagotto; it runs, 'Concerto â 9,
1 Hautbois, 2 Violini, 1 Viola, Violoncello. S.A.T. è B. col Basso per
l'Organo'. It is difficult to understand why the 'cello is left out so
frequently; it cannot have been due to any inefficiency on the part
of the 'cellist, for the bass aria demands an excellent player. In a way
it is a reversion to the plan shown in the first Mühlhausen Cantata,
No. 71, where the 'cellist was segregated from the violinist. The title-
page indicates that Bach's forces were only one instrument to a line.
The numbering of the participants is odd—the 9 exclude violone and
organ. Eager running passages abound and the voice flourishes with
almost extravagantly long runs on 'Bahn', in one case lasting nearly
ten bars. The title of the cantata is made to serve for nearly half the
vocal line. The opening oboe theme:

which, with swirling semiquaver passages, both upward and downward, provides all the material for the introduction, is sung only
thrice in Part I, long notes in the remainder typifying the length of

the road and rapid movement the running along it of the Christian. A piquant combination appears at the opening of Part II: 'Bereitet die Wege und machet die Stege im Glauben und Leben dem Höchsten ganz eben: Messias kommt an!' ('Prepare the ways and make the paths in faith and life to the Highest quite smooth: Messiah approaches!') the voice has a repeated-note idea, the continuo plays the first theme of the aria and the oboe dance-like tunes. Later the highest and lowest parts are reversed. 'Messias kommt an!', which occurs thrice, is declamatory and unaccompanied. The oboe is often independent of the strings; one wonders why this promising treatment is not continued and why the instrument disappears from the rest of the cantata.

At the close of the first tenor recitative, with continuo, the command to roll away the heavy stones of sin from the highway—'Wälz' ab die schweren Sünden-Steine' ('Roll away the heavy sin-stones')—gives an opportunity for picturesque writing, and the remainder—'nimm deinen Heiland an, daß Er mit dir im Glauben sich vereine') ('accept thy Saviour, that He with thee in faith Himself unites')—is set to a similar passage. Preceding this lively section are recitative, arioso, and recitative. The first—'Wilt thou thyself God's child and Christ's brother call, so must heart and mouth the Saviour freely acknowledge. Yea, man, thy whole life must of faith evidence give! Shall Christ's word and teaching even through thy blood sealed be, so give thyself willingly thereto'—is not of interest. The arioso is mostly in canon: 'For this is the Christians' crown and honour.' The final portion in recitative style is much broken by rests: 'Meanwhile, my heart, prepare even today for the Lord the faith-path and clear away the hills and the heights, which to Him opposed stand.'

The bass aria (iii) begins with the priests' first question, 'Wer bist du?' ('Who art thou?'), but it is twisted round to apply not to John, but to the children of sin, and the verse ends in stern denunciations: 'frage dein Gewissen, da wirst du sonder Heuchelei, ob du, O Mensch, falsch oder treu, dein rechtes Urtheil hören müssen. Wer bist du? frage das Gesetze, das wird dir sagen; wer du bist, ein Kind des Zorns in Satans Netze, ein falscher, heuchlerischer Christ!' ('ask thy conscience, then wilt thou without hypocrisy, if thou, Oh man, false or true, thy rightful judgement hear must. Who art thou? ask the commandment, that will to thee say; who thou art, a child of anger in Satan's net, a false, hypocritical Christian!'). The ungracious text is interpreted by grim vocal phrases and an unyielding repetition of a short idea in the bassi:

Ex. 133

The low lie of the voice (there are several E's) and the absence of upper instruments are justified by the reference to stern law and unflinching judgement. 'Ein Kind des Zorns in Satans Netze' introduces chromatic passages and a striking series of downward leaps of a seventh:

Ex. 134

while 'heuchlerischer' is interpreted by a tortuous vocal line. The 'cello keeps mostly to its C and G strings, the continuo is frequently a simplified version of the line. The aria is not externally attractive, it is anything but easy to sing, but it has a certain compelling power which rivets one's attention. As in other cases, Bach, in his anxiety to express all that a text implies, is apt to seek to do so at the cost of musical beauty. Yet such numbers often possess a strange fascination and they throw the succeeding portions of the cantata into high relief. A long alto recitative (iv) is made interesting by the addition of strings and, at 'Ah! but Ah!', bold harmonies, involving a leap of a diminished third in the bassi and a daring false relation: 'I will, my God, Thee freely acknowledge; I have Thee heretofore not rightly known! Although mouth and lips even Thee Lord and Father name, has itself my heart yet from Thee turned away. I have Thee denied with my life! How canst Thou to me a good testimony give? When, Jesu, me Thy spirit and baptism cleanses from my misdeeds, have I to Thee even steadfast faithfulness promised; Ah! but Ah! the baptismal bond is broken. The falsehood repent I! Ah God, pity me, Ah! help, that I with unchanged faithfulness the mercy-bond in faith constantly renew.' (See Ex. 1309.)

The words of the final non-Da Capo alto aria speak of the cleansing power of the baptismal stream, and an obbligato—*violino solo e l'alto*—pour out floods of prismatic demisemiquavers. The opening bar:

is modified for the initial vocal phrase:

and as the obbligato plays the first five bars again and then diverges, the text continues—to a fresh melodic line—'was der Heiland euch geschenket durch der Taufe reines Bad' ('what the Saviour to you gave through baptism's pure bath'). At the close the obbligato recalls its chief idea. The voice does not borrow old material for the next sentence—'Bei der Blut- und Wasserquelle werden eure Kleider helle, die befleckt von Missethat' ('Through the blood- and water-fountain become your robes bright, those soiled by misdeeds')—but after two bars with continuo only the solo instrument repeats two bars of the original melody, *per arsin et thesin*, with an altered ending, and dovetails into the last word with (*a*). The voice takes up the variant of (*b*) to 'Christus gab zum neuen Kleide rothen Purpur, weiße Seide, diese sind der Christen Staat' ('Christ gave as new robes reddish purple, white silk, these are the Christians' adornment', see Revelation vii. 13). The obbligato imitates with (*a*), introduces new matter and then plunges again into its baptismal stream.

Franck's libretto concludes with stanza 5 of E. Cruciger's hymn 'Herr Christ, der einig Gott's Sohn', 'Ertödt uns durch dein' Güte' translated for cantata No. 96, which setting is included in the vocal score. There is no music here in the score, merely the indication *choral simplice stylo*. 'When Bach produced this work in Leipzig he probably substituted for this another chorale, which would be distributed to the choir on detached sheets, and has so been lost' (Schweitzer).

152. In 'Tritt auf die Glaubensbahn' ('O walk the heavenly way' O.

'Walk in the way of faith' B.) for the Sunday after Christmas, possibly 29 December 1715, Bach found a superior text of Franck's, and correspondingly his well of inspiration gave more abundantly. The scoring, flûte à bec, oboe, viola d'amore, viola da gamba, without other strings, singles it out as unique. All the instruments are chosen for their tender qualities. The isolated appearance of the viola d'amore must have been due to some chance player at Weimar. It does not find a place again for eight years, when the *St. John Passion* was being written at Cöthen for performance at Leipzig. There was evidently no viola d'amore player at Cöthen, for it is not heard in any cantata there. It is used twice again only, two years after this, in the secular cantata 'Der zufriedengestellte Aeolus', and the following year in another secular work 'Schwingt freudig euch empor', which in 1730 was turned into a church cantata with the same title, No. 36. The oboe part of ii of cantata 152 descends to A, so that the line cannot be played on a modern instrument. The alternatives are 'cooking' the passage, or giving the number to the oboe d'amore, whose quality is suitable to it. The preludial concerto (see O.O.S. No. 08) is an exquisitely delicate and beautiful piece of texture. After four bars of rhapsodical adagio comes a long fugue on a decorated step-motive:

Ex.137

the walking in the way of faith, and the countersubject almost suggests a child dancing happily along a woodland path:

Ex.138

The viola d'amore is especially favoured with arpeggi and some particularly decorative passages. The concerto may be interpreted as reverent honours to the Babe. The subject of the allegro was afterwards employed for the organ fugue in A. The libretto does not seem particularly apposite to the First Sunday after Christmas until one examines the Epistle and the Gospel. The former is Galatians iv. 1-7, and contains 'God sent forth His Son, made of a woman, made under

the law, To redeem them that were under the law', which is referred
to in the first aria, and the second recitative. The Gospel, St. Luke ii.
33–40, contains Simeon's prophecy: 'Behold, this child is set for the
fall and rising again of many in Israel' the stumbling of man is spoken
of in the last line of the first aria and the succeeding recitative opens
with Simeon's words. It is a duet cantata, S.B., without chorale. In
the concluding duet the male singer assumes the role of the Saviour,
but up to that time he is the preacher and the comforter, expanding
the announcement of Simeon.

The bass aria (ii), accompanied by oboe and continuo only, has a
double theme—a stepping motive for one bar and then a run (the
running on the road, as in the soprano aria of the cantata just discussed), which lasts only one bar for the oboe, but which is extended
for the voice:

Ex.139

In spite of temporary fluctuations the semiquaver groups always
show an upward tendency on 'bahn'. The continuo maintains the
step-motive whenever these words are heard and frequently introduces it elsewhere. The quoted theme is pursued by the oboe while
the bass first sings 'Gott hat den Stein geleget, der Zion hält und
träget' ('God has the stone laid, which Zion holds and carries').
'Gott hat den' and 'der Zion' move firmly in crotchets through a
common chord, the latter parts of the clauses follow the same outline,
but 'Stein' rolls and 'hält' is plainer, an example of Bach's meticulous
attention to textual detail. After a statement of the initial words to
the theme, and a modulating interlude utilizing it, there is a fresh
setting of the next clauses, with a long passage on 'träget', while the
oboe carries on a sequence derived from the semiquavers. 'Mensch,
stoße dich nicht d'ran!' ('Man, knock thyself not thereon!') brings
stumbling runs on 'stoße' and the oboe pursues a similarly erratic
path. Returning to the first clause the soloist sings a fresh version
of the quaver and semiquaver ideas and then the introduction is

repeated. This easy-going aria demands a bass who can be audible on low E (as in the last cantata), but the recitativo secco which follows is even more exacting. The opening sentence, 'The Saviour is ordained in Israel for fall and resurrection!' (see St. Luke ii. 34) is sung to a long pedal E, and 'zum Fall' drops from F♯, third line, to D♯ below the stave, and also below the continuo! (See Ex. 1323.) Even the tumbling descent to hell a few bars later is not so profound. 'The precious stone is without blemish, when itself the evil world so hard on it injures', is with slowly moving continuo; 'yea, over it to hell falls' stumbles down in semiquavers with the continuo rising a diminished fourth and falling a diminished seventh; 'because it evilly to it runs' is an upward rush of semiquavers imitated by the continuo; in 'and God's grace and mercy does not acknowledge!' 'nicht' ('not') is emphasized by a trill. Bliss is portrayed by expressive ideas to 'selig' ('blessed') and 'auserwählter' ('chosen') in 'But blessed is a chosen Christian'. During the remainder the continuo repeats the whole or portions of the figure:

Ex. 140

and the voice uses it twice, representative of the immovability of the Corner-Stone: 'who his belief, who his belief on this Corner-Stone lays, because he thereby salvation and redemption finds.' The last words are much repeated, emphasizing the culmination of the development of thought; indeed, the latter part of the number is more arioso than recitative. It shows how Bach was feeling his way to forms more flexible than those already in existence. It is known that the chief bass singer at Weimar was Hofcantor Wolfgang Christoph Alt; Bach has left a remarkable tribute to his powers.

The soprano aria (iv) 'Stein der über alle Schätze' ('Stone, which (is) above all treasures'), links up thought with the previous 'edle Stein' and 'Eckstein', and called up in Bach's imagination the image of a rich jewel shining with a soft, yet brilliant and steady light (see P. 4). The voice and the two obbligati instruments, flûte à bec (with a more penetrating, if gentler, tone than the flauto traverso), and viola d'amore, all sustain long notes in illustration of this. A remarkable feature of this entrancing aria is a passage beginning with bar 5; above a pulsating pedal bass the obbligati instruments move in sixths in strangely exotic harmonies:

a manifestly Oriental touch, achieved by the simplest means. The thought of the star guiding the Wise Men of the East was in the mind of the composer. The introduction is rich in other themes. While the flute sustains on D the viola d'amore plays a gently undulating motive:

The ending of this is modified to form one of three ideas which occur simultaneously:

A time-pattern from (b) is used for a descending sequence:

As the singer sustains 'Stein' the instruments, beginning with the continuo, take up (b) and the flute carries it to the highest register. With 'hilf, daß ich zu aller Zeit durch den Glauben auf dich setze meinen Grund der Seligkeit!' ('help (me), that I at all times through faith on Thee may set my hope of blessedness!') continuo, viola d'amore, and flute follow each other with fragments of (b), and (d) is heard in the viola d'amore. An interlude consisting of bars 1–4 of the introduction dovetails into a varied form of the first vocal section, and then the voice continues, without the upper instruments: 'und mich nicht an dir verletze' ('and myself not on Thee injure'). The initial clause reappears, with (b) in flute and viola d'amore. From 'hilf' to 'Seligkeit' recurs, with (d) in the upper instruments and (c) in the continuo, and later in the viola d'amore, the flute intoning a sustained G. The aria is non-Da Capo in form; the introduction is repeated to close. The text of the bass recitativo secco is dry. A diminished seventh chord opens: 'Let be angry the cunning world that the Son of God' and the continuo drops a diminished seventh with 'leaves the honour-throne'. At the close of 'that He in flesh and blood Himself clothes and in mankind suffers!' 'leidet' ('suffers') is set to a low-lying phrase of pathos. An expressive idea leads into the next section: 'The greatest wisdom of this earth must before the Highest's counsel greatest foolishness become!' (see 1 Cor. i. 19), 'größten' ('greatest') is stressed by an upward augmented fourth. At the end of this section is one of the few cases in Bach in which the figured bass player must wait until the vocal phrase is finished before clenching with the cadence, in contradiction to the given notation. Bach's recitatives are nearly always written exactly as they are intended to be performed. 'What God resolved has, can reason indeed not fathom'; ranges from C above the stave to E below (on the last word) and the continuo also indicates the vain attempt to plumb the depths of deep mystery of the decisions of the Almighty, by the first four notes of:

Ex. 145

the upward run being the interpretation of the last clause: 'the blind leader misleads the spiritually blind' (see St. Matt. xv. 14). This clause is repeated and the two chords before the cadence are a rich-sounding progression, successive diminished sevenths on D♯ and C♯.

In the duet between the Soul and Jesus the direction is given in the upper of the two instrumental lines, *gli stromenti all' unisono*, but one cannot think that the viola da gamba is intended to join the wind and the viola d'amore at that high pitch. Perhaps the gambist reverted to his 'cello and joined the continuo. Swaying, swinging themes are predominant. The opening of the unison melody, which is afterwards associated with the initial clause of the text, is:

Ex 146

and the introduction is based almost solely on it, with a steadily moving crotchet continuo. After the Soul has asked the question Jesus replies:

Ex. 147

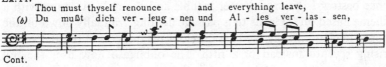

A new phrase is introduced in imitation:

Ex. 148

the obbligato plays (*a*) against short groups for the voices, the soprano takes over (*b*), and this section concludes with imitations on (*a*). The chief time-pattern of (*a*) is maintained in:

Ex. 149

and the bass replies with the same melody to 'Erkenne mich gläubig und ärg're dich nicht' ('Acknowledge me faithfully and vex thyself not') and a modified and extended repetition of the portion beginning with (*c*) comes with the new text. A variant of (*d*) serves the soprano for 'Komm, lehre mich, Heiland, die Erde verschmähen') ('Come, teach me, Saviour, the earth to disdain'), the bass answers, beginning with the same time-pattern, but resolving into quaver runs, 'Komm, Seele, durch Leiden zur Freude zu gehen' ('Come, Soul, through sorrow to joy to go'), and a canon of four bars follows. The section continues as did the previous ones. An upward stepping idea, found in the introduction, is heard to the next clause:

(the eager ninths will be noted), the bass reverses the direction of the steps to 'dir schenk' ich die Krone nach Trübsal und Schmach' ('on thee bestow I the crown after trouble and shame'). A canon with a theme based on (c) leads to a passage floating gradually down on the soprano clause, while the bass develops the quavers of (c), but with a rising seventh instead of a fifth. The obbligato now uses the full introduction form of (e), and while the soprano sings a joyous quaver run on 'folg'', a syncopated continuation of the instrumental (e), which has not been heard since the introduction:

accompanies it. The last two vocal bars, maintaining the chief time-pattern are with continuo only. The lengthy introduction is repeated. The duet is by no means easy to sing, the lower line, particularly, needs skilful handling. It is a pity that the low placing of the vocal bass passages restricts the popularity of this unique cantata. We do not meet Alts every day; the lowest line of modern choirs consists mostly of baritones.

155. The libretto of 'Mein Gott, wie lang', ach lange?' ('My God, how long, ah long?') for the Second Sunday after Epiphany, possibly 19 January 1716, again proves admirable for its purpose and provides opportunities of especial characteristics in every number. It has no bearing on the Scriptures for the Day, and neither is the hymn-stanza one of those appointed. The opening soprano lament (see P. 3) is a recitative in tempo: 'My God, how long, ah long? Of lamentation is (there) too much, I see no limit of pain and sorrows! Thy sweet mercy-glance has under night and clouds itself hidden, love's hand draws itself, Ah, wholly back! For comfort am I sorely anxious! I find, what poor me daily ails, the tears-cup is continually filled.'

Throughout this the upper strings play crotchet chords, mostly dissonances, on the fourth and first beats of the bar, the bassi pulsate
in quavers, changing from the tonic only in bar 12. Though the next
clause: 'der Freuden Wein gebricht' ('the joy-wine fails') adverts to
a state of mind before the present, Bach paints it in unmistakable
colours, the voice swirls up with a tremendous flourish of demisemiquavers, the upper strings descend in a manner which suggests
the pouring out of the refreshing nectar, a surprisingly realistic
device. The recitative concludes: 'mir sinkt fast alle Zuversicht!' ('in
me sinks almost all confidence!') and the voice curves in descent:

while the violins leap downwards in syncopation.

The altos and tenors, in a duet, assume the role of comforter, as did
the bass in No. 152: 'Du mußt glauben, du mußt hoffen, du mußt
Gott gelassen sein; Jesus weiß die rechte Stunden, dich mit Hülfe
zu erfreu'n. Wenn die trübe Zeit verschwunden, steht sein ganzes
Herz dir offen' ('Thou must believe, thou must hope, thou must to
God resigned be; Jesus knows the right hour, thee with help to rejoice. When the troublous times disappear, stands His whole heart
to thee open'). The bassoon, after having been restricted to plebeian
tasks in several cantatas, now rises in station to enjoy the luxury of
one of the finest fagotto obbligati Bach ever wrote. The many wide
leaps and runs in the tender part of its compass:

indicate a penetrating insight into the properties of an instrument
which at that time was far from the perfection we know now, and the
colour blends beautifully with the voices. G, a minor third below
modern compass, is written for. The voices move much in thirds and
sixths, a gently consoling message, there are long runs on 'gelassen',
'erfreu'n', and 'offen', but there is sufficient canonic writing to give
independent interest. It is an enchanting number.

The bass recitativo secco (iii) is saddled with the weakest part of
the libretto, but it is not permitted to lapse into dullness, there are
some lively continuo runs and one very daring false relation on 'Wer-
muth' ('wormwood'). The text is: 'So be, Oh soul, be content! When
it before thine eyes appears, as if thy dearest Friend wholly from thee
is separated, when He thee a short time leaves, heart! believe steadfastly, it will only a little while be, till He for bitter tears to thee
comfort and joy-wine and honey-sap for wormwood will vouchsafe.
Ah, think not, that He from the heart thee troubles; He proves only
through suffering thy love, he ordains, that thy heart in sad hours
weeps so that His mercy-light to thee all the more lovingly appears;
He has, what thee delights, at last to thy comfort for thee kept; therefore let Him only, oh heart, in all things govern!'

'Wirf, mein Herze, wirf dich noch in des Höchsten Liebesarme'
('Throw, my heart, throw thyself still into the Highest's loving-arms')
causes the composer to invent as the chief theme for the soprano aria
(see P. 3) a melody containing many leaps, depicting in a most extraordinary way the 'throwing' of the text:

Ex.154

Once thought of in this way, it cannot be conceived otherwise; it
gives rise to a delightfully engaging number. The figure is employed
practically throughout, both in strings and voice, and when delivered
by the bassi is led up to by a rush of demisemiquavers. The remainder
of the text is 'daß er deiner sich erbarme! Lege deiner Sorgen Joch
und was dich bisher beladen, auf die Achseln seiner Gnaden' ('that
He thee may pity! Lay thy sorrow-yoke and what thee till now
weighed down, on the shoulders of his mercy'). The 'throwing'
figure once moves steadily upwards in the continuo during the word
'beladen', as if the Christian were heaving his burdens up to the
shoulders of the Saviour. A charming variant is:

Ex.155

and at the end of the vocal part of the first and last sections the singer repeats:

Ex.156

four times, as if loving arms were twining round her. There are many triplet quavers in the vocal line with ♩.♪ in the strings; this is undoubtedly a case where the two time-values should be kept quite distinct. To treat $\frac{3}{4}\frac{1}{4}$ as $\frac{2}{3}\frac{1}{3}$ would lessen the splendid energy of the accompaniment. A four-part chorale concludes, Stanza 12 of P. Speratus's 'Es ist das Heil uns kommen her' to its anonymous melody: 'Though it appeared as would He not, Let thee it not alarm, For where He is is the best, Yet will He it not reveal; His word let to thee surer be, And though thy heart says only No, So let yet thyself not be afraid.'

59. There are considerable differences between this group and the next cantata: 'Wer mich liebet, der wird mein Wort halten' ('Who me loves, he will my word keep', St. John xiv. 23. The Gospel is verses 23–31). It was produced in the Schloss Chapel at Weimar on 31 May 1716. Neumeister is the librettist; the two original numbers he contributes are without distinction. Except for the hymn-stanza there is no reference to the origin of the Festival. It is singular also that the miracle of the tongues of fire is not referred to here or in the two other cantatas for Whit Sunday, Nos. 74 and 172; in No. 34 only is it the source of the text, and even then the cantata is an adaptation by the composer, who knew better than his librettists, naturally, where inspiration would lie. The solo cantatas up till now have been mostly on the scale of chamber music, but in this two trumpets and timpani are added to strings in i. Christ's words are set as a duet. The choice of soprano and bass is strange; a tenor would have been more appropriate than a boy treble. To sing the duet chorally makes it more impersonal and thus removes the anomaly which would be felt in a modern concert performance, the Saviour's statement delivered by a female and a male singer. Indeed, one is inclined to the opinion that it would be quite justifiable to allot the upper line to the chorus tenors, as Bach adopts the imagery with which we are familiar in the 'Et in unum Deum' of the B Minor Mass, and stresses the unity of Father and Son by making the voices sing mostly in canon. The continuo moves in unbroken quavers through the chief theme, the unyielding holding of the commandments, a point further stressed by the sustained 'halten':

At the beginning of the last vocal section the two voices indicate unity in another way, by singing in parallel motion. The remaining words— 'und mein Vater wird ihn lieben, und wir werden zu ihm kommen und Wohnung bei ihm machen' ('and my Father will him love, and we will to him come and dwelling with him make')—are set partly canonically and partly freely; there are sometimes joyous runs on 'kommen'. The trumpets and drums add majesty to the Saviour's utterance; He speaks not only as the Son of Man, but also as the King of Heaven. The strings begin with the vocal phrase, though not in canon, and brass and percussion punctuate with a grave flourish:

The trumpets throughout consider this as their characteristic motive, though sometimes the two vocal phrases are heard in the upper instrument.

Except for the chorale, interest recedes after this fine and majestic number, though the soprano recitative with strings (ii) is not negligible. The three sections are admirably contrasted. 'Oh! what are these honours to which Jesus us calls? Who us so worthy esteems, that He promises, together with the Father and the Holy Ghost, in our hearts to enter' is peaceful and happy. The first six words occur again at the beginning of the second portion, but are set differently, and the rest is gloomy: 'Man is dust, to vanity a prey, of weariness and labour the tragedy, and all misery's purpose and aim.' A false relation stresses 'Müh' ('weariness'). The mood changes again: 'How now? The All-Highest says: He will in our souls dwelling choose.' For the first time the accompaniment departs from sustained chords, and violin I mounts triumphantly while the singer declaims, 'Ah! what does God's Love not (do)? Ah, that then, as He willed'.

An arioso without upper strings concludes, a three-fold repetition of 'Him also each one should love' with tender convolutions on 'lieben' ('love').

The first stanza of the Whitsuntide hymn 'Komm, heiliger Geist, Herre Gott', Luther's expansion of 'Veni Sancte Spiritus', with the adapted plain-chant, is always stirring, but its position as third out of four numbers seems faulty. The stanza runs, 'Come, Holy Ghost, Lord God, Fill with Thy mercy's fullness Thy believers' heart, mind and being! Thy fervent love inflame within them! O Lord, through Thy light's brilliance In the faith assembled Thou hast The people of all the world's tongues, That be to Thee, Lord, praises sung. Alleluja!' Strings accompany, violin II and viola sometimes with independent lines; the same harmonization is found in cantata No. 175, to a different text.

It is strange that Bach was not stirred by the 'Königreichen' and 'Herrlichkeit' of this world to write a powerful bass number for iv. They are certainly given flourishes, the number is pleasant enough and its violin obbligato is tuneful, but that is all. That it meant nothing in particular to him is shown by the fact that when he wrote a second cantata with this title, No. 74, nineteen years later, adapting the duet as a chorus with an enlarged orchestral score, he transferred this aria to soprano, handed over the obbligato to an oboe da caccia, and fitted the vocal line with a new text which had no spiritual or pictorial connexion with the original whatsoever. Although the text is of no importance, a comparison with the substitute shows how indifferent Bach could be when not interested in his material. The two versions are shown side by side—

Bass	*Soprano*
Die Welt mit allen Königreichen,	Komm, komm, mein Herze steht
The world with all kingdoms,	*Come, come, my heart stands*
die Welt mit aller Herrlichkeit,	dir offen, ach, laß es deine
the world with all glory,	*to Thee open, ah, let it Thy*
kann dieser Herrlichkeit nicht	Wohnung sein! Ich liebe dich,
can this glory not	*dwelling be! I love Thee,*
gleichen, womit uns unser Gott	so muß ich hoffen; dein Wort
equal, wherewith us our God	*so must I hope; Thy word*
erfreut; daß er in unsern	trifft jetzo bei mir ein; denn
rejoices; that He in our	*is fulfilled now in me; for*
Herzen thronet und wie in einem	wer da sucht, fürcht't, liebt
hearts (Himself) enthrones & as in a	*who there seeks, fears, loves*
Himmel wohnet. Ach! ach Gott,	und ehrt, dem ist der Vater
heaven dwells. Ah! ah God,	*and honours, with him is the Father*

Bass	Soprano
wie selig sind wir doch, wie	zugethan. Ich zweifle nicht,
how blessed are we then, how	*well-pleased. I doubt not,*
selig werden wir erst noch, wenn	ich bin erhöret, daß ich mich
blessed become we first then, when	*I am heard, that I myself*
wir nach dieser Zeit der Erden	dein getrösten kann.
we after this time of earth	*by Thee comforted can be.*
bei Dir im Himmel wohnen werden.	
with Thee in heaven dwell shall.	

In spite of the considerable modifications of the music the superior verse of the later form is uncomfortably placed. The passage which is suitable to 'Königreichen' is quite inappropriate to 'steht', what suits 'aller Herrlichkeit' and 'dieser Herrlichkeit' is absurd to 'deine Wohnung' and 'ich liebe dich.' Instead of 'daß er in unsern Herzen' the crowd of words necessitates the pronunciation of the unwieldy 'fürcht't' on a single quaver, a task that even a German singer would fight shy of. An ecstatic flourish on 'wohnet', the joy of the believers at the thought of the Almighty dwelling in their hearts, is almost irreverent when sung to 'Vater'. The repeated, declamatory 'Ach! ach Gott' is completely altered and a run interpreting 'zweifle' is substituted, even though the clause states that the singer doubts not. The arabesque-like run to 'selig' mates indifferently with 'erhöret'. As Bach was so much attached to Marianne von Ziegler's libretti (of which No. 74 is one), one wonders why he did not think it worth while to write a fresh aria instead of forcing a relatively uninteresting one to do service. Every now and then the student is puzzled by some extraordinary lapse on the part of Bach, for instance, the mutilation of his own music in many numbers of the Short Masses. When he falls, he falls seriously, and there is no accounting for the momentary aberration.

Here the manuscript ends; one can only conjecture that it is incomplete because the aria makes such an unsatisfactory conclusion. The cantata which began so nobly peters out in undistinguished manner. On the original bass part *Chorale segue* is written, in a copyist's hand, but whether or not this is Bach's direction, or what chorale is intended, we do not know. Terry suggests the repetition of the chorale to the third stanza of Luther's hymn, and this certainly makes an appropriate close, though two verses of this powerful chorale enclosing the none-too-interesting aria are not wholly satisfactory.

158. The last Weimar solo cantata 'Der Friede sei mit dir' ('Peace be unto you', Luke xxiv. 36) is known to us in a Leipzig revision only, the dates of both being unascertainable. The texts of ii and iii, by an anonymous author, are probably the earlier and are for the Feast of the Purification, which is the occasion specified on the manuscript. The other two numbers, possibly part of a libretto by Franck, are pertinent to the Gospel for Easter Tuesday. Terry's theory is that it was written at Weimar for the first-named and revised at Leipzig for the second. The texts do not form an inevitable sequence; iii does not follow i and ii suitably, after Simeon's farewell to the world comes a prayer for direction whilst left in the world, iv leaps suddenly from the infancy of Christ to His Passion and crucifixion and the rage of the Destroyer introduces a thought strangely at variance with the Nunc Dimittis. One cannot blame this lack of continuity, however, for the neglect of this beautiful cantata, which is so easily performed. Two soloists, or bass solo and soprano chorus, a vocal quartet for the final chorale, oboe (which can be dispensed with as it merely doubles the soprano chorale), solo violin and continuo, with or without bassi, are all that are needed. Audiences are generally too mentally lethargic to apprehend the faults of the libretto (how many congregations really attempt to understand the meaning of the church music to which they listen indifferently?); we can only blame the lack of enterprise of singers.

The opening bass recitativo secco is in Bach's best manner. It is virtually a combination of recitative and arioso, for the initial sentence is set thrice, once with repeated words, and while the beginning of the last group transposes the opening phrase down a fifth, the other repetitions of the words are never allotted the same music. It refers to the incident of the appearances of the risen Lord to the disciples. On the first occasion He pronounced this blessing thrice twelve days later He repeated it. The quotation is likewise heard on three occasions, and the last time it comes thrice complete, the middle one being elongated by a thrice-repeated 'Der Friede', an interesting example of Bach's literalness. Here, however, Christ speaks not to the disciples, but to 'du ängstliches Gewissen!' ('thou fearful conscience!'). A comparison with the much more elaborated and extended treatment of the same words, in No. 67, written about thirty years after Bach had left Weimar, is interesting. The recitative portions are direct and impregnated with deep feeling—'thou fearful conscience! Thy Mediator stands here, Who has thy guilt-book and the law's curse annulled and torn up' and 'The Prince of this world, who thy soul waylays is through the Lamb's blood conquered and overthrown. My heart, why art thou so troubled, when thee then God through Christ loves! He Himself says to me.' The different sections are most skilfully blended into a continuous whole, the flowing melodies and quaver-stepping continuo differentiating the greeting of Christ from the reflections of the believer.

ii is longer than all the rest of the cantata and remarkable for its rich beauty. The bass sings one of Bach's many 'farewell' songs, a truly 'endless melody':

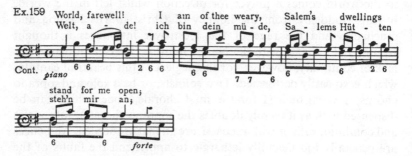

a lovely touching line which, in spite of the length of the aria, nearly 100 bars (in non-Da Capo form), is of never-failing charm. The violin solo is the finest obbligato written up to this time, sometimes winging its flight upwards to the longed-for heavenly abode, in intricate arabesques (frequently unaccompanied), at others, moving up with the two-note angel-motive:

and yet at others sinking in poignant chromatic intervals:

The remaining portions of the aria text are: (1) 'Wo ich, ich Gott, in Ruh' und Friede ewig selig schauen kann' ('Where I, I God, in rest and peace everlastingly blessed regard can'); in addition to weary passages on 'müde', 'ewig selig' floats gently down as if the soul were

swayed on light breezes, 'schauen' impulsively soars upwards; the
opening is declamatory, 'Ruh'' once has the conventional sustained
note; (2) 'Da bleib' ich, da hab' ich Vergnügen zu wohnen' ('There
remain I, there have I delight to dwell'); the first words swing blissfully:

Ex.162

and are imitated by the violin, 'bleib'' does not rest but curves with
serene delight. (3) 'Da prang' ich gezieret mit himmlischen Kronen'
('There shine I adorned with heavenly crowns'); combined with (2)
this gives rise to the longest spell of sustained singing in the aria, the
violin scintillates with light during the opening clause, near the end it
plays several bars of its initial melody. The soprano intones stanza 1
of J. G. Albinus's 'Welt ade! ich bin dein müde' to J. Rosenmüller's
melody: 'World adieu! I am of thee weary, I will to heaven; There
will be the true joy And everlasting soul-rest. World, in thee is war
and strife, Nothing other than pure vanity, In heaven to all time,
Joy, peace and blessedness.' There are few lovelier numbers in the
whole range of the solo cantatas. Sometimes when a chorale is super-
imposed length becomes inordinate; not so here, however, one is
spellbound and content to listen to its infinite beauties as if they could
well go on for ever.

iii is half recitative and half arioso, all with continuo. The recitative
portion is finely and flexibly spun: 'Now Lord, govern my mind, so
that I in the world, so long as it Thee me here to leave then pleases,
a child of peace am, and let me to Thee out of my sorrows like
Simeon in peace depart!' For the arioso the librettist repeats (2) and
(3) from the aria; Bach is not content with repetition but develops
in a fresh way the ideas which were originally associated with the
words, producing a fine climax on the first 'Kronen', modelling anew
the violin passage quoted *supra*, which has not been previously
heard vocally. It is curious that one of the other rare cases of quotation is found in another solo bass cantata, No. 56. The four-part
Easter chorale, which has no accompaniment except continuo
(though presumably violin and oboe would join in), is stanza 5 of
Luther's 'Christ lag in Todesbanden' ('Christ lay in death's bonds')

to its anonymous melody. For a translation see cantata No. 4. There are no more solo cantatas till the first or second year at Leipzig.

CHORAL CANTATAS

18, 21, 31, 61, 70, 142, 147, 161, 182

Order of Discussion: 21, 31, 70, 147, 18, 61, 182, 161, 142

21. It is difficult to understand why every now and then in this period one encounters, in the midst of solo cantatas, works with well-developed choruses and a large orchestra. One can only surmise that some special occasions, concerning which we are in ignorance, called them into being. Nos. 21 and 31 are particularly big and powerful; the former has become popular in this country as 'My spirit was in heaviness' N. ('I had great heaviness of heart' B. 'Ich hatte viel Bekümmerniß', Psalm xciv. 19). Terry, in his biography, puts forward a theory to account for this first essay on a really great scale. Shortly after 6 November 1713,

he visited Halle and was so attracted by the new instrument that he declared his willingness to undergo the customary Probe, being warmly urged to do so by Dr. Heineccius, Pastor Primarius of the church. Bach accordingly prepared a 'Stück' which he rehearsed and conducted. It can be identified as No. 21, which was also performed at Weimar on the Third Sunday after Trinity in the following year (17th June, 1714). But its introductory Sinfonia, its proportions (it is in two parts), its rich treatment of the text, and the fact that Bach inscribed the cover of the parts with the additional direction 'Per ogni tempo', all point to the conclusion that it was written for another occasion. If in fact it was performed at Halle, Bach found pleasure in associating Zachau's memory with it by its references to Zachau's greatest pupil; the cantata contains positive indication of his familiarity with Handel's 'Almira', produced in Hamburg in 1705 and in 1713 famous throughout Germany.

Much of this one cannot accept. In the *Musical Times* of May 1907 Mr. P. Robinson tried to prove that Bach had borrowed extensively in this and other cantatas from *Almira*. The essay was reprinted in his *Handel and his Orbit*. I have examined (see 'Handel, Bach, and Mr. Robinson' in my *Collected Essays*) the points of alleged resemblance, and must reject them all except one tiny similarity, between the bass of Handel's *Der Mund spricht zwar* (p. 40, German Handel Society's edition) and the fugal theme 'Ich hatte viel Bekümmerniß.'

That might well have been an unconsciously remembered phrase, but I cannot think it to have been adopted deliberately. It is an idea that anyone might have used at the period, there was no originality in the adoption of it by either Bach or Handel. The other 'coincidences' are so far-fetched that it is only with difficulty that one can see any connexion at all. Surely Bach was sufficient of a composer at this age not to need to go to another man for a little phrase and place it where it had no relationship with its original context! When Bach 'worked over' another man's composition, or rewrote it deliberately, he was testing his powers with those of another composer, seeing how much he could improve the work, how he could strengthen its weak joints, discovering what he could learn from it. That is an entirely different thing from picking out a plum, or a morsel of a plum, from one confection and popping it into another, even if Mr. Robinson's examples were to convince one that he did so. One can find resemblances between any two composers of a period; there is always a common stock of speech which no one can avoid using. Professor E. J. Dent, in his *Mozart's Operas*, speaks of the necessity for the historian to saturate himself in the second-rate works of a period in order to understand the difference between what is merely the idiom of the time and the individuality of the outstanding composer. He concludes: 'Those who have given some patient study to his [Mozart's] contemporaries begin to realize that most of those features of Mozart's music which we are apt to consider so typically Mozartian are not Mozart in the least, but are simply the common stock-in-trade of all the music-makers of the day'. Until the bulk of the manuscripts of the beginning of the eighteenth century are more fully examined, we cannot say—this is real Bach, or—this is real Handel. Supposing the cantata *was* composed for the occasion mentioned *supra*, which does not seem likely, would Bach, had he been anxious to obtain the appointment at Halle, have risked his reputation as a composer by serving up to the congregation in his Probe snippets of a popular opera, in which such an interest would have been taken by the townspeople? It would have been unlike Bach to do so and, anyhow, it would have been bad policy. Spitta (i, p. 638) is of opinion that the work was not written for Halle. He gives two reasons: (1) the date on the manuscript is 1714, the year after his visit there; (2) the Probe would undoubtedly be composed to a text provided by the authorities. These arguments outweigh Professor Terry's theories, which were evidently influenced by Mr. Robinson's mare's nest. In correspondence subsequent to the issue of Terry's book, he confessed to me that he had adopted Mr. Robinson's 'findings' without having probed the matter for himself.

It is not known who is the librettist; Franck's name is mentioned by Spitta, on account of evidences of style, but the text did not appear in print under his name. For more than one reason I am inclined to think that its present form is not what was at first designed. Part I seems to have been at one time a complete cantata in itself. It may be regarded as an exposition of the Epistle, 1 Peter v. 6–11, 'Humble yourselves—casting all care upon Him.' i–v are lamentations, vi is a longish chorus of comfort and hope, in the same key as i, C minor, with a *tierce de picardie* to conclude. It might well have closed a choral cantata of the same proportions as the majority of the Weimar products. The same orchestra begins and ends, oboe, bassoon, strings with *organo e continuo* always specified. The text of the remainder does not follow naturally on Part I. Doubt and fear seem out of place after vi. A new path is pursued, and vii and viii are dialogues between Jesus and the Soul. At the end of viii confidence is restored, but in the first verse of ix, 'What avails us heavy sorrow?', we revert to despair. x and xi speak of rejoicing and praise. The progression from sorrow to joy is, therefore, related twice. The orchestra of Part II departs from the scheme of I. Four trombones are added in ix. In xi three trumpets and timpani join with the original forces. Why do the trombones disappear after ix? Why are they not used to reinforce in xi, where they would have a magnificent effect? It is true that Bach's use of trombones, save in the exceptional case of No. 25, or where a bassi chorale is to be reinforced, is invariably to bolster up the vocal lines in motet-like choruses, but if trombones had entered into his conception of the cantata as a whole, the last chorus would have been written on a different plan. Its choral lines are more in need of help than the relatively simple ones of ix. The text of vi would welcome trumpets, but the key is C minor, which rules them out. Had the cantata been conceived as a unit, keys which preclude trumpets would not have been chosen. Another point is that there are two arias for tenor, one in each part, which is most unusual. The heterogeneous orchestration, therefore, as well as the irregularities of the libretto, points to a composite work. It is reasonable to suppose, in view of this evidence, that for some particularly important event, possibly decided upon in a hurry, the second part was tacked on to the first, either specially written or, what is more likely, wholly or partly compiled out of existing material. Part of the cantata, of course, may have come from the Halle Probe. The four choruses are fine specimens of early maturity. The first is somewhat archaic in character, but vitalized by the young master's spirit. It opens strikingly, with three detached chords, 'Ich, ich, ich,' ('I, I, I,') each answered by upper instruments and bassoon. Novello's edition substitutes 'Lord, my God', lessening the deep intensity of the personal cries. It may be more in accordance with modern taste, but no substitution can give the superbly emotional effect of the original. It is this chorus which Mattheson pilloried on account of the repetition of words, a strange condemnation in view of universal custom. It is quoted by Spitta (i. pp. 535, 536), but the English translation makes the extraordinary blunder of rendering, 'Ich, ich, ich,' by, 'Lord, Lord, Lord,', which takes the sting out of Mattheson's un-understanding attack. A free fugue follows, on almost the same theme as that of the Weimar G major organ fugue, but in the minor:

Ex.163

ich hat - te. viel Be - küm - mer - niß, ich hat - te viel Be -
I had great affliction
(C minor, with signature of 2 flats.)

- küm - mer - niß in mei - nem Her - - zen,
in my heart,

During the greater part of the fugue, oboe, bassoon, and upper strings enter for brief periods only, generally adding four fresh strands to the existing four. During the last four bars the upper strings reinforce the voices, but the oboe is independent. The text of the Psalm verse differs considerably from the English Bible. The remainder is 'aber deine Tröstungen erquicken meine Seele' ('but Thy consolations refresh my soul'). After a powerful and arresting Adagio of one bar to the single word 'aber', a rhetorical pause to call attention to the coming change of thought, comes an animated Vivace containing a tremendous passage to 'Seele', continuous semiquavers everywhere except in the continuo. It is repeated in an altered form just before the concluding Andante, where short answering phrases delineate the quickening of life.

The second chorus, Psalm xlii. 5, is a prelude and fugue. Again the

Lutheran version differs from the English. The introduction is lengthy, in four sections: (1) Adagio, 'Was betrübst du dich, meine Seele' ('Why troublest thou thyself, my soul'). A solo quartet begins, with continuo only. The four bars are then varied and extended to six, full choir and orchestra. (2) Spirituoso, 'und bist so unruhig' ('and art so unquiet'). Cross-rhythms indicate the disturbed state of the soul. The gigantic contrapuntal powers of Bach, even at this early stage of his career, are shown by ten-part writing. (3) Adagio, 'in mir?' ('in me'?). Two plain chords forming an imperfect cadence. (4) The tempo is not indicated, but it is certainly not adagio, probably moderato. 'Harre auf Gott; denn ich werde ihm noch danken' ('Wait upon God; for I shall Him yet thank'). 'Harre' is interpreted by a long soprano note and, in a brief interlude, where the oboe curves gracefully down, by a pedal bass. The last clause is homophonic. The fugue subject is:

Ex. 164

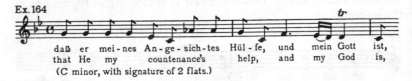

daß er mei-nes An-ge-sich-tes Hül-fe, und mein Gott ist,
that He my countenance's help, and my God is,
(C minor, with signature of 2 flats.)

That Bach had not yet completely subordinated his musical ideas to his literary material is shown by the long note and syncopated stress on 'und', finely effective as part of the fugue subject, but attaching a false importance to an unimportant word. The same rather square treatment is further shown in the counter-subject, though not to the same degree:

Ex. 165

daß er mei-nes An-ge-sich-tes Hül-fe, und mein Gott ist,

The exposition is for solo voices accompanied by continuo, with a fifth entry for the oboe. There is a counter-exposition for the upper strings and then tutti vocal lines take up the subject in turn, with again an extra entry for the oboe. As in the first fugue of 'The 48' there are no episodes.

The third chorus is on an unusual plan. The text is a combination of Psalm cxvi. 7, a message of comfort—'Sei nun wieder zufrieden, meine Seele; denn der Herr thut dir Guts' ('Be now again contented, my soul; for the Lord does to thee good things')—and two stanzas, 2 and 5, of G. Neumark's hymn, 'Wer nur den lieben den Gott läßt walten' ('Who but the beloved God allows to guide'), to the customary Neumark melody. Stanza 2 is despairing, 5 is hopeful. The hymn-stanzas are translated under the discussion on cantata No. 93. The first half is accompanied by *organo e continuo*, solo S.A.B. singing the first clause of the Psalm verse, weaving lovely counterpoints round the tenor chorale, which is not marked solo, and is therefore presumably tutti. In the second half the chorale is transferred to the sopranos and the other voices weave fresh counterpoints to both clauses of the psalm verse. All are marked Tutti. The scale passage of the first section is used inversely, and a new and lively figure appears:

Ex. 166

denn der Herr thut dir Gut's,

The running quavers are often heard in the continuo independently of the vocal bass. With stanza 5 the other instruments enter, trombone I, oboe, and violin I double the chorale, trombone II plus violin II the altos, trombone III plus viola the tenors, and trombone IV plus bassoon the basses. It is the most elaborate chorale treatment and the longest chorus up to this date, and it is the first appearance of trombones in Bach's scores. They were of lighter calibre in those days and would strengthen, not obliterate, the choral lines. In modern usage this is one of the few factors of scoring in which it is legitimate to depart entirely from Bach's practice. For one thing, we have not a complete family of trombones ranging from treble to bass. For another, the power and dominating personality of our instruments make their use for this purpose absurd, except possibly where there is a festival choir of three or four hundred. It is best to omit them.

The final chorus takes as its text Revelation v. 12, familiar to us musically in Handel's *Worthy is the Lamb*. It is again a prelude and fugue. In the former the choir hurls out rock-like chords: 'Das Lamm, das erwürget ist, ist würdig zu nehmen Kraft, und Reichthum, und Weisheit, und Stärke, und Ehre, und Preis, und Lob' ('The Lamb, which slaughtered is, is worthy to take might, and riches, and wisdom, and strength, and honour, and praise, and laud'). Oboe, bassoon, and strings form one instrumental group, trumpets, and presumably timpani a second (although *Tamburi* is stated on the

manuscript title-page the part is lost), and they answer each other
antiphonally until the last bars of the prelude, where they coalesce, the
bassoon occupying itself with a repeated semiquaver time-pattern.
The first fugal entries are for solo voices, supported by organ and
continuo, the Handelian subject stately and powerful:

Ex. 167

Lob,   und Eh - re,   und Preis,   und Ge - walt   sei
Laud,   and honour,   and praise, and might   be

un - serm Gott von E - wig - keit zu   E - wig - keit.
to   our God from everlasting   to   everlasting.

The countersubject is a florid Amen, culminating in a twenty-note
semiquaver trill:

Ex. 168

A - - - - - - - - - - - - - - - - - - -

- - - - - - - men.

As the choral lines enter one by one, the two instrumental groups
again answer each other, eleven independent parts, many of them
florid, producing a scene of the utmost animation and brilliance.
Here, as often, Bach ends, not with a pause chord, but with a quaver.
It is a difficult point to 'bring off' in a concert performance, it sounds
so abrupt. Possibly the acoustic properties of his churches produced
echoes, which would make a short fortissimo ending roll round the
building in majestic volumes of sound. Under modern secular
conditions it is advisable and certainly permissible to make a slight
pause instead.

The dialogues consist of a recitative with strings (fagotto doubling
continuo) and a duetto with continuo minus bassoon. The texts are
of the type of those naïve conversations which occur so often in
church-music of the time and which are somewhat difficult to accept
today. Violin I begins the recitative with a step-wise ascent of an
octave, interpreting, no doubt, the word 'Licht' ('light') (see Ex.
1300), as the Soul sings 'Ah Jesu, my rest, my light, where remainest

Thou?' The highest note is sustained when Jesus answers, 'Oh soul, see! I am with thee'. (The two lines are merely marked soprano and bass, but in similar duets in other cantatas the participants are definitely stated.) The strings lie low, as if the Soul were not yet consoled, while she sings, 'With me? here is yea only night!' and the Saviour assures her, 'I am thy faithful friend, Who even in darkness watches', and there is a comforting curving of the strings as He concludes, 'where only evil-doers are'. Strings and voice are thrown higher as the Soul sings, 'Break then with Thy splendour and light of comfort in!' and in the Saviour's final clause, 'The hour comes already when thy war-crown to thee will a sweet refreshment be'. Strings and voice sway ecstatically. The text of the Duetto is given below in parallel columns, so that the curious methods of the religious poets of the time may be understood thoroughly:

Soprano	*Bass*
I $\frac{4}{4}$	I $\frac{4}{4}$
Komm, mein Jesu, und erquicke	Ja, ich komme und erquicke
Come, my Jesus, and revive	*Yea, I come and revive*
und erfreu' mit deinem Blicke!	dich mit meinem Gnadenblicke,
and rejoice with Thy countenance!	*thee with My mercy-look,*
Diese Seele, die soll sterben	Deine Seele, die soll leben
This soul, which shall die	*Thy soul, which shall live*
und nicht leben,	und nicht sterben,
and not live,	*and not die,*
und in ihrer Unglückshöhle ganz verderben?	hier aus dieser wunden Höhle sollst du erben.
and in its misfortune's-pit wholly decay?	*here from this wounds-pit shalt thou inherit.*
Ich muß stets in Kummer schweben,	Heil! durch diesen Saft der Reben,
I must ever in grief hover,	*Hail! thro' this juice of the grape,*
ja, ach ja! ich bin verloren,	nein, ach nein! du bist erkoren,
yea, ah yea! I am lost,	*nay, ah nay! thou art chosen,*
nein, ach nein! du haßest mich.	ja, ach ja! ich liebe dich.
nay, ah nay! Thou hatest me.	*yea, ah yea! I love thee.*
II $\frac{3}{8}$	II $\frac{3}{8}$
Ach Jesu, durch-süße	Entweichet, ihr Sorgen,
Ah Jesus, throughout-sweeten	*Yield, ye sorrows,*
mir Seele und Herze.	verschwinde, du Schmerze.
my soul and heart.	*disappear, thou pain.*

As has been pointed out elsewhere (*Fugitive Notes*), the singers in Bach's churches were unseen, and the part of the Soul, or, as it is in other cases, the Church, would be sung, not by a woman, but by a boy soprano. This would lessen the feeling we have today that such numbers are little removed from love duets. The Protestant religion was more personal than the Roman Catholic; one of its chief tenets was that man went straight to his Maker without any intervening medium, and in the early days of a struggle for freedom in matters of faith, this element was undoubtedly more prominent than at later periods. Thus the idea of intimate conversation with the Saviour in duets such as this was not only accepted, but popular, in religious poetry. Here the dialogue is carried on mostly in the first and last sections (the latter a shortened remodelling of I) by short phrases answering one another rapidly, with at other times passages together. II affords a contrast of time-signature as well as of longer answering phrases, and there is a larger proportion of simultaneous singing. Theoretically, of course, the latter is wrong. If Christ and the Soul were conversing, they would not speak at the same time, especially for long stretches. But one must not view these scenes strictly, otherwise one could not accept the same musical phrase to 'die soll sterben' and 'die soll leben', which Bach gives to the two participants in quick sequence, consideration for melodic outline prevailing over literalness of expression, even in a supremely literal conception.

The tenor recitative with strings, prefacing the aria in Part I, is masterly in every device, its advanced character contrasting vividly with the older-fashioned choruses. Bars 1–4 are a passionate complaint that God has forsaken him: 'Why, hast Thou Thyself, my God, in my need, in my fear and trembling, then completely from me turned?' After a break comes a cry, 'Ah, knowest Thou not Thy child?' Suddenly, on the second beat of the bar, is an impassioned 'Ah!' followed by 'hearest Thou not the laments of those, who to Thee are with covenant and faithfulness bound?', a diminished seventh chord on C moving to one on D, and violin I poignantly stepping from F♯ to A♭. (See Ex. 1310.) During the last part of the sentence violin I indicates the covenant by moving stepwise in crotchets up to G, the reverse of Wagner's leit-motiv in *The Ring*. After a rest the sustaining of a peaceful chord of E♭ tells of previous happiness: 'Thou wert my delight', the 'wert' ('warest') being stressed—changes of harmony occur to 'and art to me cruel become!' A series of much broken-up sobbing passages follows: 'I seek Thee in all places, / I call, / I cry to Thee, / but, / my woe / and agony / appear now, as were they to Thee completely unknown', one of the most heart-rending passages in the whole range of the cantatas.

Each of the three arias is distinctive in character. The soprano, in
a particularly lovely number, (iii) (see P. 2) interprets 'Seufzer,
Thränen, Kummer, Noth' ('Sighing, weeping, trouble, need') by
many delayed resolutions of auxiliary notes; the oboe obbligato adds
its wailing tones in similar devices:

(C minor, with signature of 2 flats)

The remainder of the text merely stresses human misery without
introducing any fresh thought: 'ängstlich's Sehnen, Furcht und Tod
nagen mein beklemmtes Herz, ich empfinde Jammer, Schmerz'
('anxious longing, fear and death gnaw my downcast heart, I experience mourning, pain').

It is an error of the libretto to follow this number with a tenor
recitative and aria in the same vein (see P. 4), but Bach's boundless
invention provides fresh commentaries on his text. The aria is scored
for strings with *organo e continuo* doubled by bassoon. The first part
is built up on a weary, sighing two-note figure, heard incessantly:

(F minor, with signature of 3 flats)

In the allegro middle section—'Sturm und Wellen mich verschren'
('Storm and waves me overwhelm')—the voice whirls and twists, as
if a drowning man were struggling against overwhelming waters, the
violins alternately toss up and down with wild leaps, and the bassi
rock and roll till they are eventually dragged into the depths. Adagio
and the same ideas (the use of both largo and adagio is curious) recur
in the final section before the Da Capo: 'Und dies trübsalvolle Meer
will mir Geist und Leben schwächen, Mast und Anker wollen brechen! Hier versink' ich in den Grund, dort seh' ich der Hölle
Schlund' ('And this trouble-full sea will to me spirit and life weaken,
mast and anchor will break! Here I sink in the earth, there see I the
abyss of hell'). 'Hier versink' ich' precipitates down to low C, then

there is an agonized leap to high G♮ as the singer catches sight of the terrifying chasm.

The other tenor aria, x, with continuo, is more cheerful: 'Erfreue dich Seele, erfreue dich Herze, entweiche nun Kummer, verschwinde du Schmerze!' ('Rejoice thee soul, rejoice thee heart, yield now sorrows, disappear thou pain!'). It will be noticed that two clauses are quoted from the dialogue. It continues, 'Verwandle dich Weinen in lauteren Wein, es wird nun mein Ächzen ein Jauchzen nur sein? Es brennet und flammet die reineste Kerze der Liebe, des Trostes in Seele und Brust, weil Jesus mich tröstet mit himmlischer Lust' ('Transform thyself tears into pure wine, will now my sighs an exultation only be? There burns and flames the purest candle of love, of comfort in soul and breast, because Jesus me comforts with heavenly delight'). The punning clause about tears and wine is the source of swiftly flowing semiquavers for the chief continuo phrase:

Ex.171

and for the accompaniment to the main vocal idea, almost a bubbling of liquid:

Ex.172

The connexion between the opening of the chief continuo theme and the close of the vocal will be noticed. These ideas are kept up nearly all the way through, the vocal melodies of Part II are free modifications of those of Part I.

One of the most interesting numbers is the beautiful Sinfonia (see O.O.S. No. 010) 'Adagio assai'; oboe and violin I vie with each other in emotional arabesques or wailing passages of falling seconds, while the rest of the orchestra accompanies, the inner parts slow-moving, the lowest line a steady progression of quavers. The chromatic harmonies of the penultimate bar add a special intensity, and the oboe is left alone on a pause-shake, followed by a flickering upwards, as if the troubled spirit were making a rapid flight from the body which confined it to weary earth. In spite of the chaotic libretto

and the varied periods of much of the music, the cantata justifies its
popularity and represents Weimar worthily.

31. The other large-scale cantata is 'Der Himmel lacht, die Erde
jubiliret' ('The heavens laugh' O. 'The heavens rejoice!' B.). It is
the composer's first association with Salomo Franck, and was produced on Easter Day, 21 April 1715. In 1731 it was given for the same
Festival at Leipzig, the libretto amended by Bach, and, no doubt, the
music revised. It is in this form that we know it. With the exception
of the chorale the libretto is original. The laughing of the heavens is
realistically pictured in the Sinfonia (see O.O.S. No. 053), which has
an astonishing score—three trumpets, timpani, three oboes, taille,
bassoon, two lines each of violins, violas and 'celli, the lower of the
latter identical with the continuo. Circumstances must indeed have
been favourable to permit the composer to indulge in such forces.
The fifteen lines unite for a tremendous unison passage at the opening
and close:

Ex.173
Allegro

and the rest of the movement is appropriately vigorous. One feature
is short crackling explosions for groups of instruments— —
while the others are actively engaged in lively contrapuntal lines, outbursts of Olympic laughter breaking in upon the mêlée. The same
scoring and imagery are found in the succeeding chorus, which has
five vocal lines, a division he employs only twice elsewhere in the
cantatas, in his adaptation of the *Gloria* of the B Minor Mass, No.
191, and in the closing chorale of No. 27. There are four sections.
In (a) a florid fugal subject:

Allegro
The heaven   laughs,
·Der Him-mel   lacht,
Ex.174

is developed, with an equally florid countersubject to 'die Erde jubiliret' ('the earth jubilates'), the whole orchestra bursting in thrice during the exposition and then gradually partaking in the subsequent development, a glorious maze of sound. After a short florid treatment of 'und was sie trägt in ihrem Schoos' ('and what it bears in its bosom'), a short fanfare for brass, percussion, and continuo heralds (b), a repetition of all material with fresh words: 'der Schöpfer lebt, der Höchste triumphiret und ist von Todesbanden los' ('the Creator lives, the Highest triumphs and is from death's-bonds loose'). (c), an Adagio, speaks of Christ in the tomb, and brass and percussion are silent: 'Der sich das Grab zur Ruh' erlesen, der Heiligste kann nicht verwesen' ('Who for Himself the grave for rest (has) chosen, the Holiest cannot decay'). They are silent also when the Allegro is resumed, (d), in a short fugal section to the second clause:

Ex.175

der Hei - lig-ste kann nicht ver - we - - - - - sen,

The voices are then silenced and trumpets I and II and violin I reiterate the theme of (a), the rest of the orchestra entering twice with short masses of sound and then in the closing bars.

Bass, tenor, and soprano each have a short recitativo secco and an aria. The bass begins with a combination of recitative and arioso ('cello II and continuo), with many changes of tempo and style. (See O.S.B.A. No. 5.) Recitative, tempo unmarked—'Desired day! Be, soul, again glad'; Allegro—the last clause repeated, without 'soul', with quaver and semiquaver imitations; 'Desired day!' leads to an Adagio, in which clause 2 is sung again, with a break in the middle; Allegro—'the Alpha and Omega, the first and also the last, Whom our heavy guilt in death's prison placed', a long pedal A indicates the immortality of the Saviour, 'und O' ('and Omega') and 'der Letzte' ('the last') both solemnly drop a seventh, the last clause sinks to the depths; Allegro—'is now drawn out of distress'—ascending semiquavers for the voice and a run for continuo finally falling to G♯, which is sustained for most of an Adagio—'The Lord was dead, and see! He lives again'; andante, arioso—'lives our head, so live also the limbs'; adagio, recitative with chromatic harmonies—'The Lord has in His hand death's and Hell's key! (He) Who His raiment blood-red besprinkles in His bitter sorrows, will today Himself with adornment'; andante, arioso—'and honour clothe', the continuo moves up stepwise, the voice sings a graceful and tender phrase. The text of the aria is, 'Fürst des Lebens, starker Streiter, hochgelobter Gottes-sohn, hebet dich des Kreuzes Leiter auf den höchsten Ehrenthron? wird, was dich zuvor gebunden, nun dein Schmuck und Edelstein? müssen deine Purpurwunden deiner Klarheit Strahlen sein?' ('Prince of life, strong champion, highly-praised God's-son, raises Thee the Cross's ladder to the highest honour-throne? will what Thee previously bound now Thine adornment and jewel be? must Thy crimson-wounds of Thy clearness rays be?'). The continuo gravely announces the rhythm of solemnity:

another figure suggests the bursting of the bonds of death:

The voice also employs largely the dotted note time-pattern, though never with the melodic outline of the continuo. There are majestic rising scales, convolutions on 'Leben', struggling movement on 'starker Streiter', brilliant ascents on 'höchsten' and a twisted, syncopated melody on 'gebunden'. While the combination of bass voice and continuo provides no relief from a dark colour, the aria is powerful and imposing. In view of the question of Handel's influence at this period, it may be noted that *Almira* contains an aria (for *Emilia*, p. 82, German Handel Society's Edition) which is also accompanied by a dotted time-pattern continuo, a similarity overlooked by Mr. Robinson.

The opening of the tenor recitative (see O.S.B.A. No. 6) ascends gradually, 'So arise then, thou God-devoted soul, with Christ spiritually', and stepwise movement is heard, naturally, on 'enter into the new life's way'; 'up! from death's works' is picturesquely expressed. The normal recitative style is continued for, 'Let that thy Saviour in the world, in thy life be seen! The vine-stock that now

blooms, carries no dead grapes; the life-tree lets its branches live.'
Rapid upward and downward scales characterize 'A Christian flees
right quickly from the grave'; and the remainder is in recitative: 'he
leaves the stone, he leaves the cloth of sins behind, and will with
Christ living be.' The aria is scored richly for strings, with two viola
lines which rarely move contrapuntally. Violin I is given mostly
decorative figures, the open G string being frequently heard:

Ex.178

and violin II generally moves in quavers, parallel with the melodic
outline above. 'Cello I joins 'cello II and continuo from time to time,
but is often silent. The soloist begins with a fresh theme—'Adam
muß in uns verwesen, soll der neue Mensch genesen, der nach Gott
geschaffen ist' ('Adam must in us decay, shall the new man recover,
who in the image of God created is')—and one feels the extraordinary
aptness of the vigorously pulsating full-blooded string themes. With
the latter half of the text—'Du mußt geistlich auferstehen und aus
Sündengräbern gehen, wenn du Christi Gliedmaß bist' ('Thou must
spiritually arise and out of sins'-graves go, when thou Christ's
member art')—the voice acts towards violin I as violin II did earlier,
but with a decorated line. There is no Da Capo, the orchestra merely
repeats the ritornello.

The soprano recitative (see O.S.B.A. No. 7) turns the progression
of thought from the new life to its close: 'Because then the head its
limb naturally after itself draws, so can me nothing from Jesus
separate. Must I with Christ suffer, so shall I also, after this time,
with Christ again arise to honour and glory, and God in my flesh see.'
The aria is the outstanding solo number of the cantata, a beautiful
song of the last hour of life and a prayer to attendant angels. Above
a continuo in which the 'cello is marked pizzicato the oboe is given an
important obbligato, phrased frequently in groups of two notes, the
customary angel-motive, bending low and soaring, as if Bach visualized celestial beings floating above the bed of the departing believer:

Ex.179   *piano*   *forte*

Indications of forte and piano are uncommonly numerous in this line, there being frequent alternate bars of contrasting strength. The voice begins with a beautiful variant:

Ex.180

Letz - te   Stun - de,   brich her - ein,
Last   hour,   break herein,

and the continuation is graceful and tender: 'mir die Augen zuzu-drücken!' ('to me the eyes to close!'). There is more animation with, 'Laß mich Jesu Freudenschein und sein helles Licht erblicken' ('Let me Jesu's joys'-glory and His bright light descry') with runs on 'schein' and 'erblicken'. The last clause, 'laß mich Engeln ähnlich sein' ('Let me unto angels like be'), begins tentatively, but gains confidence. Except at the end 'Engeln' is decorated. Violins and violas in unison gently intone a ¾ version of the melody of N. Herman's chorale, 'Wenn mein Stündlein vorhanden ist' ('When my last hour at hand is'). It is an exquisite picture of faith and confident anticipation during the hushed passage from this life to the next.

The same chorale is heard to close, stanza 5: 'So journey I thither to Jesus Christ, Mine arms do I outstretch; So sleep I and rest sweetly, No man can me awaken; For Jesus Christ, God's Son, Who will the heavens' door open, Me guides to eternal life', an anonymous addition to Herman's hymn. Tromba I (II, III and timpani are tacet) and violin I soar, in unison, in an independent line above the chorus and doubling instruments, touching a great altitude, high E; the immortal spirit has now left its binding clay and hovers over the final scene we have just witnessed. The progression from the riotous laughter of heaven and earth to the intimate and affecting close provides a varied dramatic scheme of arresting significance and human interest, and Bach's magical touch has endowed every phase of it with immortal art.

70. Less resounding than these two cantatas, yet containing large-scale choral writing, is 'Wachet, betet, seid bereit' ('Watch ye, pray ye' N.). It also was possibly revised at Leipzig, where it was produced after 1722. The earlier date is not known, it is only conjectured as 6 December 1716. Franck is the author of i, iii, v, viii, and x, which were published by him for use on the Second Sunday of Advent. The text of the remainder is from another hand, supposedly Bach's, and the cantata in its present form is for the 26th Sunday after Trinity.

The original may be reconstructed by omitting the recitatives and the first chorale. Except for the two hymn-stanzas the libretto is original. Both the Gospel, St. Matthew xxv. 31–46, and the Epistle, 2 Peter iii. 3–13, deal with the Day of Resurrection, but Christ's prophecy of the judging of the King is less taken into account than Peter's warning. Although the orchestra employed is relatively small, trumpet, oboe, bassoon (with the continuo in every movement and never independent), and strings, the first chorus plunges us into a world of tumult which is astonishingly powerful and descriptive. 'bis der Herr der Herrlichkeit dieser Welt ein Ende machet' ('till the Lord of glory of this world an end makes') which one does not hear until the number is well under way, is the key-note of the text. The opening is startling; twice the trumpet rings out the dread summons, oboe and strings accompany with impulsive arpeggi:

A second theme soon follows, tromba and oboe answer each other at close quarters:

Incidentally, this shows that in Bach's time the strength of the two instruments was about the same, very different from today. During the imitations violin I maintains an agitated succession of semiquavers:

and the lower strings throb tensely. The orchestra has given us a picture of the world thrown into confusion, the voices add the cries of the faithful. The opening choral bar is unaccompanied, an unusual device with Bach, rushing upward scales call out the injunction to watch ('Wachet'), then come sustained chords to 'betet' ('pray'), and then again involved passages to 'wachet', the orchestra pursuing its own motives. The cries of 'wachet, betet' are heard on every side, an excited medley. Suddenly all instruments except the continuo cease, and hurriedly and nervously, tossing from side to side, comes an unforgettable time-pattern:

Ex.184

seid be‑reit   al‑le‑zeit, al‑le‑zeit, seid be‑reit,
be prepared   always,

Pulsating strings enter and work up to a resumption of the first material while the chorus proclaims the coming of the Lord of glory. One notable passage is where the summoned are depicted as praying in trembling terror:

Ex.185.
be -   - tet,

be -   - tet,

The remainder of this thrilling chorus, one of the most tensely nervous and exciting scenes of the Last Judgement ever penned, is derived from the material already heard.

A bass accompanied recitative contrasts the state of sinners with that of believers when separated by the King. It is marked *Siebenstimmig* (seven-part) for all instruments participate and are given distinct lines. The warning to the guilty is punctuated with threatening semiquaver chords: 'Tremble, ye hardened sinners! A day breaks, from which himself no one hide can. It hastens with thee to stern justice, Oh! sinful generation, to everlasting heart-sorrow.' The declamation is superb. Semiquavers change to quavers when the children of God are addressed, and the mood merges from sternness into peace and then into riotous joy, the solo voice indulges in tremendous flourishes in which oboe and violin I join: 'but to you, elected God's children, is it a beginning of true joy, The Saviour comes for you, when all falls and breaks.' When the faithful are admonished not to be afraid—'before His exalted countenance: therefore, tremble not!'—the threatening chords reappear, a reminder of the condition of the unwise.

An alto aria has a 'cello obbligato, with bassoon and continuo (presumably joined by 'cello II); sometimes the two are identical, sometimes quite distinct. It is clear that $\frac{3}{4}$ must be treated as $\frac{9}{8}$ and that all divisions of a pulse must be in thirds and sixths. The day of judgement is compared, in mixed metaphor, with the flight from Egypt for the believer; the wicked suffer the fate of Sodom (Gospel v. 41, Epistle v. 7)—'Wenn kommt der Tag, an dem wir ziehen aus dem Egypten dieser Welt, ach! laßt uns bald aus Sodom fliehen, eh' uns das Feuer überfällt. Wacht, Seelen, auf von Sicherheit und glaubt, es ist die letzte Zeit' ('When comes the day, on which we go out of the Egypt of this world, ah! let us soon from Sodom flee, before on us the fire falls. Awake, souls, from security and believe, it is the last hour'). 'Feuer' and 'fliehen' are depicted realistically. It is the least interesting number in the cantata, in spite of the pleasing obbligato and such themes as:

Wenn kommt der Tag, an dem wir zie - hen

and:

Wacht, See - len, auf von Sich - er - heit

The fault must be laid on the uninspiring text.

A short tenor recitativo secco is plainly set: 'Even in our heavenly longing holds our body the spirit imprisoned; lays the world through its cunning for the pious nets and snares.' The next is happier—'The spirit is willing but the flesh is weak' (see Matt. xxvi. 41)—and there is a cry of despair—'this forces from us a lamentable Ah!' (See Ex. 1287.)

Imagery is conspicuous in the soprano aria also. The librettists of the day luxuriated in references to mocking tongues, envy, ridicule, spite, and v. 3 of the Epistle gives Franck his opportunity. There is no mistaking the meaning of the initial unison figure for upper strings:

and later ones such as:

Ex.189

It is curious that this idea should have been borrowed from an aria in Handel's *Almira*, the bass solo 'Gönne nach den Thränengüssen' (p. 84, German Handel Society's Edition), both vocal and instrumental lines being practically identical. Here is a genuine case of adoption and adaptation, though Bach's treatment is wholly his own. The voice opens with a modification of the string figure:

Ex.190

Let the mockers' tongues   jeer,   it will yet, and must happen,
Laß.der Spöt-ter Zun-gen schmä-hen,es wird doch,und muß ge - sche-hen,

Cont.

and as the voice continues—'daß wir Jesum werden sehen auf den Wolken, in den Höhen' ('that we Jesus shall see on the clouds, in the heights')—the mocking of the world persists in the orchestra. The strings are more slurred in the ritornello which introduces, 'Welt und Himmel mag vergehen, Christi Wort muß fest bestehen' ('World and heaven may disappear, Christ's word must fast hold'), betokening a temporary defeat of the revilers. Most of this clause is sung with continuo only, with sustained notes on 'bestehen', the spiteful tongues disturb now and then, but with the resumption of the opening of the text they reappear in full force.

There is another brief tenor recitativo secco: 'Yet! in this wicked generation thinks God of his servants, that this evil manner them further does not corrupt, while He them in His hand preserves, and in a heavenly Eden sets.' Part I of the cantata ends with a simple chorale, strengthened by the whole orchestra. It is stanza 10 of the anonymous funerary hymn 'Freu' dich sehr, O meine Seele', to L. Bourgeois's melody 'Ainsi qu'on oit le cerf': 'Rejoice thee greatly, Oh my soul, And forget all need and torment, Because to thee now Christ, thy Lord, Calls out of this lamentation-valley. His joy and majesty Shalt thou see in eternity, With the angels jubilate, In eternity triumph.'

A cheerful Handelian tenor aria (see P. 2), with oboe and strings,

opens the second part of the cantata. The oboe only thrice desists
from doubling violin I, and one cannot see the reason for the changes
at these points. Normally it would have been a question of compass,
but as fiddle G is touched elsewhere that cannot have been the reason.
The continuo moves steadily in quavers almost from end to end.
The inner strings have little of importance. Attention is concentrated
on the top line, which contains three main ideas, a bright, straightforward melody:

a bustling figure:

and:

with a variant:

The voice begins with a form of (*a*):

with detached chords for the upper instruments. Charming repetitions of 'seid getrost' are accompanied by fragments of (*a*) and by

(*b*). The significance of (*c*) is seen when it accompanies 'zu eurer Seelen Flor' ('to thy soul's blossoming') with 'Flor' shooting up in semiquavers like a rapidly growing plant. The variant of (*c*) is used aptly to 'Ihr sollt in Eden grünen' ('Thou shalt in Eden flourish') and (*b*) returns with 'Gott ewiglich zu dienen' ('God eternally to serve'). At the close of the vocal portion there is an exhilarating semiquaver upward rush of a twelfth to the opening clause. Bach omits line 3 of Franck's stanza.

The succeeding two numbers expand v. 12 of the Epistle and provide the composer with the opportunity of raising the close of the work to the level of the opening. The scheme of many of the cantatas, a great chorus to open with, followed by a string of arias, often dealing with mere platitudes and scored as chamber music (and as often as not sung indifferently by unintelligent solo vocalists), resulting in a considerable change of scale, weighs against a commanding effect in a concert room today. An audience is not assembled in the same frame of mind as a congregation, it is not interested in the niceties of religious thought, in theological reasoning, it has not been prepared for the cantata by a service, with its appropriate Scripture readings, collects, prayers, and hymns, it is not gathered to celebrate some Feast Day of the church year, some reason of rejoicing or of mourning. It is a haphazard collection of people, some having come for one purpose, some for another, few with the intention of putting themselves in the composer's position and of trying to grasp his meaning and message. The cantata to them is an isolated and perhaps not a particularly interesting event, a piece of music, a mere item in a mixed programme. The final chorale is frequently unfamiliar, whereas in Bach's day it appealed to even the humblest member of his congregation, more, perhaps, than the elaborate portions of the Hauptmusik. Conductors venturing these works on untried audiences should choose examples where something striking comes at or near the close, as here, as the fugal choruses in Nos. 21 and 68, or where choral interest is kept up throughout, such as Nos. 4, 106, or 150, or where some familiar chorale comes at the end, as, 'How brightly shines the Morning Star' in Nos. 1 and 61, 'A stronghold sure' in No. 80, 'Sleepers Wake' in No. 140 (English editions only are quoted).

To return to No. 70, the bass recitative (see P. 41) is one of the additions, and a magnificent piece of work. It speaks of dread and fear and thoughts of Hell on the last day: 'Ah, shall not this great day, the world's fall, and the trumpet call, the unheard-of last knell, the

Judge's pronounced words, Hell's jaws' open gate, in my spirit much doubt, fear and trembling, as I who a child of sin am, awaken? Yet, there arises in my soul a joy-gleam, a light of comfort. The Saviour can His heart not dissemble.' As in ii the declamation is superb; a dramatic bass of great quality and range is needed, the compass covers nearly two octaves. The bassi maintain an agitated repeated semiquaver movement, the upper strings mount on repeated-note semiquaver arpeggi and tear down in violent demisemiquavers, but when belief in the pity and mercy of the Saviour is realized—'therefore for pity breaks, His mercy-arm leaves me not'—the upper strings play confident arpeggi and short passages of an appealing nature. The vocal part of the close is jubilantly confident: 'Well then! well then! so end I with joy my course'; for three bars there are sweeping semiquavers on the last five words, but the strings paint the failing powers of man, a ♪ ♪♩ figure slowly struggles up and then gradually sinks exhausted. During the scene the trumpet rings out the melody of B. Ringwaldt's Advent hymn, 'Es ist gewißlich an der Zeit' ('It is sure at the time'), also associated with Luther's hymn 'Nun freut euch, lieben Christen, g'mein' ('Now rejoice, beloved Christians'). Either text would call up in the minds of the hearers thoughts of the day of judgement, adding great intensity to the already powerful number.

The succeeding bass aria is one of Bach's most supreme creations in this form. It begins adagio, with bassoon and continuo only, a joyous welcome of the day of resurrection. The vocal line is of unwonted simplicity:

Ex.196

an ecstatic confession of sublime Christian faith. One is reminded of the original chorale-arias written so long after for Schemelli's collection. But the believer has not yet left the world, for he draws a picture of the destruction of the world—'Schalle, knalle, letzter Schlag! Welt und Himmel geht zu Trümmern!' ('Peal, sound, last knell! World and heaven fall in ruins!'). The strings play incessant semiquavers in octaves, the trumpet peals almost solely in monotone, with grim time-patterns, and the voice matches the strings in the vigour of its runs, which include huge leaps of tenths in the middle of a florid passage to 'Trümmern'. The closing bars revert to the style and accompaniment of the opening; Jesus guides the singer to complete peace. At the end the voice slowly scales the heights, but not without an extraordinary drop of a twelfth:

Ex.197   Jesus leads   me to   calm, to the place,where of delight the abundance.
         Je-sus füh-ret mich zur Stil-le, an den Ort, da Lust die Fül -   - le.

It is one of the most ecstatic moments in the cantatas and the number is another tribute to the powers of Hofcantor Alt.

In the closing chorale, stanza 5 of C. Keimann's 'Meinen Jesum laß' ich nicht' to A. Hammerschmidt's melody—'Not after the world, after heaven not My soul desires and longs, Jesus desire I and His light, Who me has with God reconciled, Who me free makes from judgement, My Jesus leave I not'—trumpet, oboe, and continuo double the voices. These sink lower and lower in the last four bars, the body is laid to rest. The three upper lines of strings are independent throughout, violin I poised higher than the sopranos; at the end they are all higher than the voices and ascend as the latter descend. While the mortal frame of man sinks to its bed of rest, the soul wings its way upwards. It is a beautiful piece of imagery, and a fitting end to a fine cantata. With the exception of the alto aria, which does not make a ready appeal, the work is an excellent one for audiences not familiar with Bach. (See *Fugitive Notes*.)

Mr. Robinson propounds the theory that No. 70 was based on Handel's *Almira*. The connexion of the soprano aria with the opera is acknowledged *supra*. None of the other 'coincidences', however, will hold water. He finds the opening choral passage of i in Handel's sinfonias, overlooking the fact that anyone can write an upward semiquaver scale. It did not require Handel's youthful opera to teach Bach this, nor to give him the trouble to turn an instrumental idea into a vocal, to change it from bass to treble and to write it in thirds instead of in unison. A Handel tenor aria (P. 17 of the G.H.S. edition) and Bach's alto aria are supposed to be identical. They are certainly both in A minor, and both vocal lines begin with m l t d¹, a common enough progression which a child could write. Mr. Robinson points out that Handel's number has a $\frac{4}{4}$ voice part and a $\frac{12}{8}$ bassi, and argues that Bach's combination of $\frac{3}{4}$ and $\frac{9}{8}$ is derived therefrom. This suggests that Bach was hard put to it to invent themes when he needed to distort existing music in this way. As a matter of fact, Bach's aria does *not* contrast $\frac{3}{4}$ and $\frac{9}{8}$; it has been pointed out that the aria is purely in compound time and that the notation of $\frac{3}{4}$ was the ordinary method of writing at the period. Handel's aria is on a different footing. While it is clear that Bach modelled one number on Handel, and while the tenor aria is distinctly in a style which we call Handelian, which was not uncommon at the time, we may take it quite definitely that the cantata as a whole is *not* based on the opera.

147. Though 'Herz und Mund und That und Leben' (Heart and mouth and deed and life') is very different in character from No. 70, there are points of resemblance historically and in general structure. It was written for the 4th Sunday in Advent, possibly 20 December 1716, and afterwards expanded in Leipzig, *c.* 1727, for a different Feast Day, the Visitation of Mary. i, iii, v, and vii are probably all that remain of the original, as the texts are by Franck, scarcely apposite to the new occasion. The remaining verses are added by an unknown writer, probably the composer himself, and are based on the Gospel, St. Luke i. 39–56, the conception of Elizabeth, Mary's visit to her, and the Magnificat. Except for the two chorales, neither of which is in Franck's scheme, the libretto is original and, on account of its composite nature and the two Feasts, somewhat lacking in definite purpose. The cantata is long, consisting of ten numbers, and is in two parts, each ending with an extended chorale. The original orchestration was probably the same as No. 70, but was expanded later; a second oboe is added in the bass aria, an oboe d'amore in the alto aria and two oboes da caccia in a recitative. The latter instrument, like the oboe d'amore, was not available at Weimar. The greater part of the cantata, therefore, dates from Leipzig, and might possibly have been more conveniently discussed later under the group of reconstructed works. As a link with No. 70, however, it is included here, and the Weimar numbers will be dealt with first.

The opening chorus is extensive and a magnificent example of Bach's genius. It is so mature that one may wonder if it was not

completely re-written for the later production. There are many
indications of forte, piano, and pianissimo; the trumpet part is
virtuosic (we shall see later how Bach revelled in the capabilities of
his Leipzig trombists), the bassoon mostly doubles continuo or the
choral basses, but is sometimes independent of both, and the oboe,
save for an occasional note, is identical with violin I. There is much
independent orchestral counterpoint, seven- and eight-part writing
occurring for long stretches. The musical material consists of four
ideas. The trumpet, accompanied by continuo and bassoon only,
leads off with a subject which is repeated immediately by violin I:

It does not recur in the ritornello, though the arpeggio with which it
begins is utilized and there are semiquaver passages which recall the
end of it. When the voices enter:

it is seen that the semiquavers are associated with 'Leben'; these are
developed prolifically, in one case filling five bars of $\frac{6}{4}$ time with
one word. In the introduction comes an idea used several times later,
alternating *p* and *pp* phrases accompanied by continuous semiquavers. The extra entry of the vocal exposition is overlapped by the
instrumental form of the subject in the trumpet, and then comes, still
to the first clause of the text, a series of athletic leaps and bounds, the
voices acting in pairs. All the while the other motives are heard, the
quaver arpeggio, the semiquavers, and a ♪♪♪ ♩ figure, also consisting of leaps, which is first found in the continuo of bar 2. The last
contribution to the material appears just at the end of the first choral
section, after the words, 'muß von Christo Zeugniss geben' ('must
of Christ testimony give'). It is always sung with continuo only,
and interprets 'ohne Furcht und Heuchelei' ('without fear and

hypocrisy'), or, rather, the last word only, by cross accents which thwart the normal march of the bars. Later it is developed into a passage of four bars and rounded off by 'daß er Gott und Heiland sei' ('that He God and Saviour be'). This ends in F and there is another fugal exposition on the lines of the first, with voices in reversed order. With the bass entry, the bassoon plays a passage which is akin to the trumpet theme. Upper strings double the next three entries, but ornament the quavers of 'That und' by semiquavers.

The tenor recitative (ii) with strings, is finely wrought. The first section is straightforward, beginning in F, and is marked off by a cadence in G minor: 'Blessed mouth! Mary makes her innermost soul through thanks and praises known; she begins in herself, the Saviour's wonder to proclaim, what He in her, as His maid has done.' (See the Magnificat.) As the key changes to A minor and to E, violin I slowly wends its way higher by a curving line, and the upper strings play with 'Christi', a tender group of semiquavers: 'Oh! human race, Satan's and sins' bondsman, thou art freed through Christ's comforting appearance from this load and servitude!' Less placid is the next, 'Yet, thy mouth and thine obdurate spirit remain silent', while violin I covers the wide compass of a twelfth, 'denies such favour, but know, that thee according to the Gospel, an all-too sharp judgement befalls!', and a diminished third in the continuo adds a feeling of awe to the thought of the 'scharfes Urtheil' ('sharp judgement').

The text of the alto aria (iii) belongs to the older scheme, but there is an oboe d'amore obbligato, which indicates either that the music was written for the revised version, or that the obbligato instrument was changed. The oboe d'amore part is carefully tongued throughout, affording a useful example of Bach's methods. The opening phrase:

Ex.200

Cont.
8ve lower

is modified for the voice:

Ex.201   Be ashamed,   oh   soul,   not,
         Schä-me   dich,   o   See-le   nicht,

Cont.

and as the singer proceeds—'deinen Heiland zu bekennen, soll Er dich die Seine nennen vor des Vaters Angesicht' ('thy Saviour to confess, shall He His own name before the Father's countenance') the oboe gambols in slurred quavers. A sweeping run of semiquavers on 'vor des Vaters' includes a group on 'vor', which points to an early period of composition. (The *BGS* has 'Deine'; as it does not make sense the vocal score suggests 'Seine'.) The remainder of the text is scarcely a stimulus to the composer—'doch wer Ihn auf dieser Erden zu verleugen sich nicht scheut, soll voll Ihm verleugnet werden, wenn Er kömmt zur Herrlichkeit' ('but whoever Him on this earth to disown is not afraid, shall by Him disowned be when He comes to glory')—but Bach's skill in developing his themes prevents a lapse. During the first clause he reminds the Christian to confess his Lord on earth by making the oboe play the first theme. In the first 'wenn Er kömmt zur Herrlichkeit' the voice ascends in quavers; during the last, semiquavers climb successively in continuo, voice, and obbligato.

The violin solo and continuo of the soprano aria (v)—'Bereite dir, Jesu, noch itzo die Bahn, mein Heiland, erwähle die glaubende Seele, und siehe mit Augen der Gnade mich an!' ('Prepare Thee, Jesus, then now the way, my Saviour, choose the believing soul, and look with eyes of grace me on!')—are almost like a preliminary study for the D minor prelude in Book I of 'The 48'. The $\frac{24}{16}$ movement is rarely departed from by the obbligato violin:

Ex.202

Cont.

(D minor, no key signature)

The voice employs no triplets, but moves independently, mostly in the joy-rhythm, and once sustains lengthily on 'bereite'. Wide sweeps are common, as in the two following quotations:

Ex.203

mein Hei - land, er - wäh - le   die glaub - en - de See - le,

Cont. as above

and:

Ex.204

The singer is light-heartedly tripping along the road which the Saviour is asked to prepare.

Florid triplets and contrasts of halves and thirds are features of the tenor aria (vii) also, in which the continuo line, moving mostly in quavers, is ornamented by the 'cello, nearly always by the simple device of beginning on the foundational note and moving up a third by two steps:

Ex.205

At first one thinks this to be merely decorative, but when the sentence 'daß stets mein Herz von deiner Liebe brenne' ('that ever my heart for Thy love burns') is heard, and the voice flickers upwards in semiquaver triplets, we see that the last word of this clause determined the style of the instrumental ideas. The voice begins with a cry:

Ex.206   Help, Je-sus, help,
          Hilf, Je - su, hilf,

and this appears incessantly in the continuo, stressing the appeal to the Saviour. The cry opens and closes the vocal line, and the remainder of the text is 'daß ich auch dich bekenne, in Wohl und Weh, in Freud' und Leid, daß ich dich meinen Heiland nenne in Glauben und Gelassenheit' ('that I even Thee acknowledge, in weal and woe, in joy and sorrow, that I Thee my Saviour name in faith and calmness'). Variety is secured in 'Wohl und Weh' by a series of short instrumental phrases; 'Freud'' is always ornamented. The last clause utilizes the scale theme quoted above and 'Heiland' is set to a run of immense length.

Three recitatives (ii has already been dealt with), one aria and two chorales are the new matter. iv, for bass and continuo, contrives to pack an astonishing amount of variety into a few bars. 'Obstinacy can the mighty delude, till them the Highest's arm from their seat hurls', the continuo dashes down a semiquaver arpeggio; 'that this arm upraises',—a reverse movement in the continuo; 'Although before it the earth's round quakes'—repeated bassi semiquavers; 'on the other hand, the wretched, whom He redeems'—'Elenden' ('wretched') has an expressive melisma, the continuo a diminished third. From reflection we pass to admonishment—'Oh highly-fortunate Christians, up, make you ready, now is the appointed time, now is the day of salvation'—the continuo marches up through quaver arpeggi, the believer is girding up his loins. The remainder— 'the Saviour calls upon you body and spirit with faith's-gifts to harness, up, cry to Him in burning desire, in order Him in faith to receive'—is pure recitative, save for a decorated 'ruft zu ihm' ('cry to Him').

The third recitative (viii) for alto, chooses a subject which to us seems extraordinary, the visit of Mary to Elizabeth, as recorded in St. Luke i. It is very long, twenty-seven bars of slow tempo; two oboes da caccia play placid figures in thirds and sixths:

Ex.207

the conversation of the two women; 'The highest Almighty's wonder-hand works in the secrecy of the earth. John must with the Spirit filled be, him draws the love-bond already in his mother's body, so that he the Saviour knows, although he Him not yet with his mouth names.' Where the text speaks of the unborn John leaping in the womb of Elizabeth—'er wird bewegt, er hüpft und springet', ('He becomes stirred, he leaps and springs')—the obbligati instruments play detached ascending arpeggi, a diminution of the vocal line. The remainder of the text is: 'whilst Elizabeth the wonder-work declares, whilst Mary's mouth the lip-offering brings; when to you, oh believers, flesh's weakness will come, when your heart in love burns, and yet the mouth the Saviour does not own, God is it, Who us powerfully strengthens, He will in you the Spirit's might inspire, yea, thanks and praise on your tongues lay.' It is a number which, naturally, is banned by public taste today.

ix is a magnificent bravura bass song of praise, with much illustration of 'heil'ges Feuer' ('holy fire'), a penetrating trumpet part and energetic string lines, oboes doubling violin I and II. The opening trumpet fanfare, slightly modified, serves for the first clause:

and it is imitated by unison violins, tromba, and continuo in quick succession. 'Und ihm der Lippen Opfer bringen' ('And to Him the lips' offering bring'), is accompanied by the vigorous semiquaver passages which follow the trumpet opening. Next comes a tremendous flourish on 'Opfer'. The text borrows ideas from the recitative 'er wird nach seiner Liebe Bund das schwache Fleisch, den ird'schen Mund durch heil'ges Feuer kräftig zwingen' ('He will according to His love-bond the weak flesh, the earthly mouth by holy fire mightily compel'). 'Kräftig' has a run equal in length to 'Opfer', semiquavers abound in every part of the orchestra. Eleven bars before the dal segno the trumpet twice rings out quaver arpeggi, and then seven bars of the introduction are repeated with modifications and with the voice added. The text certainly provides ample opportunities for the composer, despite crudities and a redundancy of references to the 'Mund' of the believer.

The two parts of the cantata close with an extended chorale, the same music in both cases—J. Schop's melody 'Werde munter, mein Gemüthe'—but with different stanzas, 6 and 17 of J. Rist's hymn of that name. 6—'Well for me that I Jesus have, O how fast hold I Him, that He may my heart refresh When I ill and mournful am. Jesus have I, Who me loves And Himself to me for my own gives, Ah therefore leave I Jesus not, If to me even my heart breaks.' 17—'Jesus remains my joy, Of my heart comfort and sap, Jesus checks all sorrow, He is my life's strength, My eyes' desire and sun, My soul's treasure and bliss, Therefore let I Jesus not Out of the heart and sight.' Recently this number suddenly attained an enormous popularity in this country under the title, 'Jesu, joy of man's desiring' (B.E.C. No. 14, O), and is published under nearly as many guises as was a certain Humoresque by Dvořák a few years back. It is so often played and sung with sickly sentimentality, with exaggerated pianissimos and gushing stresses, that one wishes that all performers would take the trouble to consult the full score and study the orchestration. Here there is no soft-breathing emotion; the trumpet doubles the tune, the oboes double violin I, and the strings sweep majestically along in flowing motion like a mighty river. Bach marks his pianos and pianissimos in the first chorus and in the trumpet aria, but there are none here. The chorus does not need to be bellowed in the Victorian tradition of the Hallelujah Chorus, but a vast difference separates that from the maudlin 'crooning' one sometimes hears applied to this extended chorale. Neither is it a 'chorale prelude', as one often sees it described on programmes; it is a chorale and not a prelude to one. Nor is it a 'motet', a term applied in sheer ignorance of Bach's church music.

18. The remaining Weimar choral cantatas are not on a large scale but all are of interest. The particular point concerning, 'Gleich wie der Regen und Schnee vom Himmel fällt' ('For as the rain cometh down' B.), is its unique scoring, two beak-flutes, bassoon, four lines of violas, 'cello, and continuo, without violins. The employment of four lines of violas was by no means uncommon among Bach's predecessors; they experimented ceaselessly with all manner of combinations of strings. The Gospel for Sexagesima, St. Luke viii. 4–15, for which it was written, is the parable of the sower, and Neumeister, in the first libretto of his set by Bach, begins his text with an appropriate quotation from Isaiah, and, in his contributed matter, brings in allusions to fruit, seed, soil, and harvest. The probable date of performance was 4 February 1714, a month before the composer was raised to the office of Konzertmeister. The opening Sinfonia (see O.O.S. No. 015) is a lovely pastoral, with gently descending passages depicting the quiet fall of rain and snow:

Ex.209

and:

Ex.210

The function of the flutes, as throughout the cantata except in the chorale, is invariable, they supply the first overtones to violas I and II, thus not only adding to the charm of the colour, but obviating the monotony that would have resulted from the absence of upper registers and from the uncovered tone of the viola, less pliable and more satiating than that of the violin. The type of flute is not specified, but the use of the clef on the first line and the transposition up a tone preclude the traverso. The quality of the flûte à bec is more appropriate to the colour scheme. The Sinfonia is mostly founded on a ground-bass:

Ex.211

which is announced in unison by all instruments except the flutes, with continuo 'tasto solo' (without chords). It should be heard in concert rooms apart from the cantata.

The Biblical extract, Isaiah iv. 10, 11, is set as a recitative and arioso for bass, with continuo and bassoon, the sustained notes of the bassi being only reinforced for a crotchet by the fagotto. The Lutheran version differs from the English. Recitative—'Even as the rain and snow from heaven falls'—the voice descends by leaps and bounds, with broken phrases, not the gentle movement of the Sinfonia, where we seem to see the erratic courses of snowflakes, sometimes overtaken by their upper companions, but as if rain-drops were pattering from rock to rock; 'and not again thither comes'—it is as if the rain tried to defeat the law of gravitation but tumbled in the attempt; 'but fructifies the earth'—a swirling run down on 'fruchtet'; Arioso, andante—'and makes it fertile and growing, (so) that it gives seeds to sow and bread to eat'—the continuo quickens into life; Recitative—'thus shall the word, which from my mouth goes, even be; it shall not again to me empty come'—'auch sei' ('even be')

is curiously set— 𝄻 —the trill possibly signifying fruitfulness;
Arioso, andante—'but do, what me pleases, and shall in that succeed,
whereto I it send'—a canon between voice and continuo, indicating cause and effect, a quaint conceit. The editor of the B. vocal
score works in a line of the concluding chorale over the closing bars
of the continuo, a piece of misguided ingenuity. Under modern
conditions, it is difficult to know whether to follow Bach's instruc-
tions and add a bassoon to numbers which have no support but
continuo. The fagotto of his day must have been heavier in tone than
our instrument, and yet even with the latter the lowest line is apt to
sound too heavy. It does not matter here so much, as the long notes
are not sustained by the bassoon, but in many other instances a just
proportion is not easy to obtain. Possibly in a large church the effect
would be modified.

iii is a recitative and chorus, or rather scena, incongruous in the
scheme of the libretto. Passages from Luther's militant Litany, praying for delivery from Satan, from the cruel murder and blasphemy
of Turks and Papists, disturb the idyllic peace of the rural scene.
They were probably included in reference to the persecution and
sufferings of Paul, narrated in the Epistle, 2 Corinthians xi. 19–xii. 9.
They are sung chorally to the intonation in Leipzig use, a single line
always beginning and the full choir entering with, 'Hear us, good
Lord God'. The introductory lines are accompanied by continuo
only—(1) 'Thou wilt Thy Spirit and strength to the word give', (2)
'Satan under our feet tread', (3) 'and us from the Turks' and Pope's
gruesome murder and blasphemies, fury and raging paternally protect', (4) 'all wandering ones and those led astray again bring'. The
orchestra joins in the four-part choruses. In the monotone sections
the continuo moves severely in heavy quavers, except in the 'murder'
part, where it tosses angrily in semiquavers. The interleaved recitatives are generally accompanied by all instruments except bassoon,
though some passages are with continuo only. The texts of the recitatives, here numbered to agree with the Litany clauses they preface,
are extremely varied. All begin with sustained orchestral chords.
(1) is a picture of a spiritually peaceful country: 'My God, here will
my heart be, I open it to Thee in my Jesu's name; so scatter Thy seed,
as into good soil. My God, here will my heart be, let such (i.e. my
heart) fruit and hundredfold bring. Oh Lord, Lord, help! Oh Lord,
let it succeed well.' The second 'My God' moves in quiet animation,

as if in excitement that the seed were beginning to germinate. 'O Lord, help!' is tense. (2) 'Now grant, faithful Father, grant that neither me nor any Christian may the devil's deceit lead astray.' 'des Teufels Trug' ('the devil's deceit') is repeated and flung across the normal accentuation of the bar and against a series of orchestral chords, betokening terror. Minim chords accompany most of 'His being is completely therein set, us of Thy counsel to rob'—with 'zu berauben' the tempo changes to allegro and furious passages for voice and orchestra tell of the violence of the plunderer. 'Mit aller Selig-keit' ('with all blessedness'), alters to adagio, and felicitous phrases depict the state of the Christian who is now not endangered by the Evil One. (3) 'Ah! many disown word and faith and fall away' (the latter descends in a tumbling phrase), 'like rotten fruit' brings a decorated orchestral phrase, fluttering down. The continuo is now left alone with the voice and develops a stubborn motive:

Ex.212

during 'whenever they persecution shall suffer'. Bach picks out 'Verfolgung' and allots to it the most extraordinary run found in all his church music. The knowledge of the life-long persecution suffered by Luther led the composer to match the violence of the language of the Litany of his spiritual father in musical speech. Flutes and violas now re-enter and calm confidence pervades: 'Thus, thus, thus fall they into everlasting heart-affliction, when they a temporary woe elude.' (4) is a catalogue of sinners: 'Another cares only for his belly, meantime will the soul wholly forgotten (be). Mammon also has many hearts possessed. So can the word to no strength attain. And how many souls holds voluptuousness not imprisoned! So greatly leads astray it the world.' These changes almost always have some significance, analysis finds it difficult to say why. Calm chords are resumed for 'the world, which for them must instead of heaven stand, besides they from heaven go astray'. 'irre' ('astray') is twice set to long runs, with vacillating syncopations, only the continuo accompanying. This lengthy number, extending to nearly ninety bars, is a bold and interesting early experiment, and its like is not met with elsewhere in the cantatas.

There is only one aria, for soprano (see P. 1), scored for all violas in unison, with flutes an octave above, and by it we are removed far from scenes of strife, contemplating man's iniquities from afar. The graceful obbligato for all six instruments is most carefully phrased:

Ex.213

(Key E♭, signature of 2 flats)

The chief vocal phrases are allied to this, the stepwise fourth in:

Ex.214

Mein See-lenschatz ist Got-tes Wort;
My soul-treasure is God's word;

and an even more close outline in the next:

Ex.215 mein See-lenschatz ist Got-tes Wort;

The continuation does not disturb the serenity of the pastoral scene: 'außerdem sind alle Schätze solche Netze, welche Welt und Satan stricken, schnöde Seelen zu berücken' ('beyond (that) are all treasures such snares, which world and Satan entwine, worthless souls to beguile'). An engaging phrase is sung to the remaining clause, almost a physical gesture of throwing something to one side:

Ex.216 Away with all things, away, only away,
Fort mit al - len, fort, nur fort, fort mit al-len, fort, nur fort,

which is imitated immediately by the upper instruments. It is sung again in a modified form and the line of flutes and violas introduces a new phrase of similar pictorial suggestion.

In the closing four-part chorale, stanza 8 of L. Spengler's 'Durch Adams Fall ist ganz verderbt', to its anonymous melody, flutes and violas I and II double the sopranos, but presumably the former should follow the plan of the remainder of the cantata and play an octave higher. The verse is a petition: 'I pray, Oh Lord, from heart's depth, Thou wilt not from me take Thy holy word from my mouth; So will me not shame My sin and guilt, for in Thy favour Set I all my confidence. Who himself only fast thereon relies, He will death not behold.' It is a pity that the unusual number of violas required prevents frequent performances of this delightful little work. Yet its difficulties can be easily overcome and a double quartet is ample for the choruses. The passage offensive to the Church of Rome can readily be altered.

61. Short and almost perfect is the first of the two cantatas bearing the title, 'Nun komm, der Heiden Heiland ('Now come, the heathen's Saviour'. 'Come, Redeemer of our race.' N. 'Come, Thou blessed Saviour, come.' B.). Two performances are known; its initial production was on the First Sunday in Advent, 2 December 1714, at Weimar, and the other at Leipzig. A note on the manuscript in Bach's handwriting details the order of the Leipzig service. Spitta suggests 1714. Professor Richter, in the Bach Jahrbuch, proposes 1722. Terry, however, points out (in his biography) that at this stage of the vacancy of the Cantorship Bach was not a candidate. He dates the Leipzig performance on Advent Sunday (either in St. Thomas's or St. Nicholas's) in 1717, in the December of which year the composer was invited by the university authorities to present a report on the organ in their church. The cantata possesses all the freshness of youth, its outlook is entirely different from what we find in the next period, and there is something so winningly attractive about it that we can always turn to it with delight, however the later monumental masterpieces may impress us. Neumeister's libretto is quite satisfactory, it is concise, reasonably well expressed, and there are two hymn-stanzas and a Biblical quotation, raising the general level of the text higher than is wont with this writer. The first chorus is modelled on a plan which we shall encounter several times later, a choral version of the French 'Ouverture', as it is called in the score, combining with a chorale. The Advent melody, Luther's hymn with the title of the cantata, encountered frequently in the series, is short, only four-lined, the first and last clauses being identical. The opening four notes—l l s d¹—are here altered, and in other cases as well, to l l s e d¹, producing the poignant interval of a diminished fourth, significant of the sufferings on the Cross foreshadowed by the coming of the

Saviour. The *Ouverture* opens with a solemn procession, violins in unison, two lines of violas and *fagotto, organo e continuo*, the double viola line deepening its sonorousness. The prevailing time-pattern— ♩. ♪ — must always be played as ♩ ⅎ. ♪, and the three rushing semiquavers which often follow a crotchet tied to a semiquaver should be halved in value and preceded by a rest, the traditional method of playing these time-divisions in a French overture. Only so can the full dignity of the movement be attained.

Ex. 217

A decorated form of line 1 supports this and the next bar, overlapping the soprano chorale entry. It also heralds the tenor. The figure of Christ moves slowly past, the entry into Jerusalem (the Gospel is St. Matthew xxi. 1–9, the Epistle Romans xiii. 11–14: 'Now is our salvation nearer than we believed') typified by the chorale in minims, the first line of stanza 1 in all voices singly in turn, the second—'As the Virgin's child recognized'—in four-part harmony. Line 3—'Of Whom wonders all the world'—in a quick version serves as theme for the fugal second movement, $\frac{3}{4}$, marked *Gai* (another link with the French model), animated passages indicating 'alle Welt' ('all the world') wondering at the marvel of the divine descent from heaven. In the short concluding section the procession is resumed, and the last line—'(That) God such birth to Him ordained is heard in block harmony. It is one of those pictures which once witnessed are stamped on the memory for ever.

The tenor recitative, arioso (ii) and aria (iii) were evidently for some singer of limited upward compass, possibly a choir man growing old in the service of the church, to whom Bach was kindly. The recitativo secco tells of the coming of Christ—'The Saviour has come, has our poor flesh and blood to Himself taken, and accepts us as blood-relations. Ah! All-Highest Good, what hast Thou not for us done? What doest Thou not still daily for Thy servants?' It is set unwontedly simply; just at the end it merges into arioso style. In the arioso itself—'Thou comest and allowest Thy light with full blessings to shine'—the voice moves in graceful curves. *Organo e continuo* imitate and the semiquavers are bowed in twos, almost suggesting the Angel-motive, divine beings hovering round the manger. The aria is a slow gigue, in which the chief melody:

Ex.218

Cont.
8ve lower

is played by the rich combination of violins and violas in unison. The bowing is detailed, probably on account of his unknown Leipzig players, and is an excellent guide to similar movements. The brief text sets forth the blessings desired for the coming year: 'Komm, Jesu, komm zu deiner Kirche, und gieb ein selig neues Jahr. Befördre deines Namens Ehre, erhalte die gesunde Lehre, und segne Kanzel und Altar' ('Come, Jesu, come to Thy church, and grant a blessed New Year. Promote Thy name's honour, confirm the true doctrine, and bless pulpit and altar'). A delightful device is the isolated cries of 'komm' on the second beat of the bar, which tell effectively against the flowing melodies. Possibly the singer was not only lacking in compass but short of wind, for less than half the number is vocal.

The gem of the cantata, indeed one of the most priceless treasures in them all, is the ten-bar bass recitative: 'Siehe, siehe! Ich stehe vor der Thür' und klopfe an. So Jemand meine Stimme hören wird und die Thür' aufthun; zu dem werde ich eingehen, und das Abendmahl mit ihm halten, und er mit Mir' ('Behold, behold! I stand at the door and knock. If (then) anyone My voice hear will and the door open; to him will I enter, and the evening-meal (Communion) with him hold, and he with Me'—Revelation iii. 20). Violins (divisi), violas, and continuo maintain a steady progression of pizzicato chords, the gentle knocking of the Christ (see Ex. 1321), beginning with a strong yet soft dissonance, $\frac{3}{4}$, and the voice, in a miracle of declamatory appositeness, speaks gently. One can never think of the words without their association with the music. The picturesque treatment of 'klopfe' is infinitely daring, a succession of staccato notes:

Ex.219

klo - pfe an

Org. e pizz.
Cont.

yet it is a reverent and perfect limning of the Saviour. No Italian masterpiece of painting brings Jesus so clearly before our eyes as these few bars of simple music.

It is followed by an aria in which a soprano addresses her heart and commands it to open and rejoice in the blessedness of being possessed: 'Öffne dich, mein ganzes Herze, Jesus kommt und ziehet ein' ('Open thyself, my whole heart, Jesus comes and enters therein'). 'Celli and organ form the sole accompaniment to this engaging song. 'Öffne dich', with its upward steps, almost an eager running towards the Saviour, forms a kind of motto:

Ex.220

The middle section is adagio:'Bin ich gleich nur Staub und Erde, will er mich doch nicht verschmähn, seine Lust an mir zu sehen, daß ich seine Wohnung werde. O, wie selig werd' ich sein!' ('Am I even only dust and earth, will He me yet not disdain, His joy in me to see, that I His dwelling become. Oh, how blessed shall I be!'). During the last clause the 'celli move blissfully in carefully bowed semiquavers, and the ending is of rapturous expectation.

One factor which contributes greatly to the success and popularity of this cantata is the brevity of its verses. There is no temptation to expand any number to undue length. Yet this results in its one weakness, the closing chorus is too short to balance the rest. Only part of stanza 7 of P. Nicolai's hymn, 'Wie schön leuchtet der Morgenstern' ('How beautifully shines the Morning Star'), is quoted: 'Amen, Amen! Come thou lovely joy-crown, come, and delay not long, For Thee wait I with longing.' The whole of Nicolai's melody would have made a magnificent conclusion. The treatment, brief though it be, is splendid. The basses begin with the Amen, but after that the sopranos alone sing the tune. The lower lines are animated and are doubled by all the instruments except the violins, which, in unison again, throw a brilliant light over the structure, scaling, at the end, to the unwonted pitch of G above the treble stave. This cantata, like

No. 70, is an excellent one for introducing Bach to choirs and
audiences. The chorales are familiar, the choruses are effective, contrasted, and relatively simple, the solos are short and make an instant
appeal, and as the bassoon merely doubles, strings only are required.
The sole obstacle is the double line of violas, and the solemn opening
procession loses much of its richness if the upper of these two parts
is played by violins, though the compass makes it possible. Where
forces are limited the procedure is justifiable. (See *Fugitive Notes*.)

182. The same grouping of upper strings is to be found in 'Himmelskönig, sei willkommen' ('King of heaven, be Thou welcome' O.)
and it also opens with a processional, as it is for Palm Sunday. The
date is 1714 or 1715, and the libretto may be by Franck. A flûte à bec
and a *violino concertante* are added to the two lines of violas in the
introductory Concerto (see O.O.S. No. 013) which is marked Grave.
Adagio., the former evidently referring to style and the latter to speed.
(There is no tutti violin I line, the *BGS* score adds one in italics.)
Until near the end all the tutti strings are pizzicato, a steady march
of crotchets. The two solo instruments move mostly in dotted time-
pattern, the motive of solemnity, which must be played as ♩ ♪ ♩ :

Ex.221

In this case they are slight in character and not pompous and powerful as in No. 61. The existence of an extra part makes it probable that
the concertante line may have been played at times by an oboe.

The welcome song of the crowd is light in character, matching the
Concerto, of a colour rarely found in Bach's choruses. The people
are regarding the Saviour not as a great monarch, but as a welcome
friend coming among them. The construction is interesting. The opening fugal subject soon slips into semiquavers:

Ex.222

which are used decoratively by the flute, always pitched high, and a
second and shorter fugal theme is announced:

The thin tone of the flûte à bec makes for a lighter touch than our
modern instrument. After some development of the new theme the
crowd shouts welcomes, answered by violas and 'celli, while flute
and violins carry on above with figures derived from the first subject,
suggestive of the waving of branches. After the *Fine* the crowd cries
'Komm herein!' ('Come hither!'), flute and violin imitate the first
subject, and there are some delightful short canons at the octave:

with seven successive entries at various distances of time, the instrumental ones being decorated. A short phrase is now imitated:

and before the dal segno the section is repeated in various forms. In
all the choruses the 'celli are favoured with a line to themselves, and
are often independent of the continuo, which would be doubled by
a violone. It would be in accordance with Bach's custom, as indicated
in other cases, to allot the first fugal entries to solo voices, the tutti
joining in with the second.

The only recitative (see O.S.B.A. No. 19), for bass with continuo,
is the voice of the Saviour surrendering Himself to His coming
Passion, Psalm xl. 7 and part of 8: 'Siehe, siehe, ich komme. Im Buch
ist von mir geschrieben; Deinen Willen, mein Gott, thu' ich gerne'
('Behold, behold, I come. In the book is of me written; Thy will, My
God, do I gladly'). 'Siehe, siehe, ich komme' is sung to the step-
motive in the joy-motive time-pattern. 'Deinen Willen' is an arioso,
andante, beginning with three crotchet C's, the unalterableness of the

Divine ordinance. The continuo repeats the 'Siehe' motive, indicating the joy of the Saviour in obeying the commands of His Father. At the close of its 1st, 3rd, 5th, 7th, 9th, and 10th appearance it drops a seventh instead of a fifth, a version suggesting inevitability and power. 'Thu' ich', also, by means of the motive, tells of the gladness of the Sufferer.

The bass aria (see O.S.B.A. No. 19) is low-lying, an early trait. It is dignified and the chief melodic interest lies in the elaborate violin part, which is supported by the other strings:

Ex.226

Cont.
8ve lower

The singer begins with the initial five violin notes: 'Starkes Lieben, das dich, großer Gottes-Sohn, von dem Thron deiner Herrlichkeit getrieben' ('Mighty love, that Thee, great God's-Son, from the throne of Thy glory (has) driven'). Although it stands in the key of C it modulates, after 'daß du dich zum Heil der Welt als ein Opfer fürgestellt' ('that Thou Thyself for the salvation of the world as an offering (hast) presented') to the remote centre of B minor, and later to the still more distant F♯ minor, at the words 'daß du dich mit Blut verschrieben' ('that Thou Thyself with blood (hast) sealed').

The idea of bending or surrendering to the Saviour is the reason why so many curving, descending passages in the obbligato flute and voice are found in the alto aria (see O.S.B.A. No. 20), which is a little heavy in character and, through the slow tempo, rather long:

Ex.227   Put   thyself   the Saviour   under,
           Le - get   euch dem Hei - land un - ter,

Cont.
8ve lower

and:

Ex.228
Fl.

Cont.
8ve lower

The text continues, 'Herzen, die ihr christlich seid' ('hearts, ye who Christlike are'). Part II is andante: 'Tragt ein unbeflecktes Kleid eures Glaubens ihm entgegen' ('Wear an unspotted robe of thy faith Him to meet'). After singing with continuo only, the voice is again joined by the flute, which fashions the first phrase anew. The same procedure is followed with 'Leib und Leben und Vermögen sei dem König itzt geweiht' (Body and life and possessions be to the King now dedicated'). While 'Tragt ein unbeflecktes Kleid' is ornate, suggestive of flowing robes, 'Leib und Leben' is at first straightforward and confident. After the flute enters there are runs on 'Leben' and the vocal line becomes more and more florid. At the end the flute again bends low, covering nearly two octaves.

The waving of the 'Kreuz-Panier' no doubt dictated the opening phrase:

Ex.229   Vc. col Cont.

of the striking and intensely felt tenor aria (see O.S.B.A. No. 21). Contrasted with this is a passage which struggles painfully upwards:

Ex.230

mich   auch   mit   dir
me   also   with Thee

When this occurs in the continuo it produces extremely sharp dissonances:

Ex.231   zie - hen

Cont.

and:

Ex.232   zie - hen

Cont.

The cry of the world—'Kreuzige' ('crucify')—is expressed in poignant passages, one, beginning at b. 41, being particularly long and

tortuous. The harmonic scheme is at times extraordinarily daring, so
much so that the addition of a keyboard part above the sparsely
figured bass is a matter of considerable difficulty. The boldest stroke
is in b. 44:

The complete text is 'Jesu, laß durch Wohl und Weh mich auch mit
dir ziehen. Schreit die Welt nur "Kreuzige!", so laß mich nicht fliehen.
Herr, vor deinem Kreuz-Panier Kron' und Palmen find' ich hier'
('Jesus, let through weal and woe me also with Thee go. Cries the
world only "Crucify!", so let me not flee. Lord, before Thy cross-
banner crown and palms find I here'). It need scarcely be pointed
out that the contrabass should be *tacet* in this number.

Few cantatas end on a gloomy note; after the mental anguish of vi
it is necessary to bring us back to the rejoicing of Palm Sunday. One
of the hymns authorized for the Sunday is P. Stockmann's Passion-
tide poem 'Jesu Leiden, Pein, und Tod' ('Jesu's suffering, pain, and
death'). It bears on the Epistle—Philippians ii. 5–11—'He humbled
Himself and became obedient unto death'. A choral fantasia on M.
Vulpius's melody is based on stanza 33. Lines 1–4 set in antithesis the
pains endured by Christ and the benefits brought by His agony to
the believer: 'Jesus, Thy Passion is for me pure joy, Thy wounds,
crown and shame My heart's pasture.' Bach lays stress on lines 2 and
4 by many joyful runs, thus preparing the mind for the close of the
cantata. Lines 5–8 are: 'My soul on roses walks, If I thereon think;
In heaven an abode For us therefore prepare.' Lines 5 and 6 give
rise to a graceful syncopated figure:

a happy, lilting walk, and further semiquavers lead to a confident
ending. The form is modified Pachelbel; instead of the lines being
dealt with separately they are grouped in twos, one contrapuntal
derivative serving for both, until the close, where the last two lines
are treated individually so as to broaden out the finale. Violin and

flute double the soprano chorale at the unison and the octave respectively, and the other instruments double the lower parts at the unison. In spite of its fine qualities, it is perhaps the least interesting number to the listener, although to the singers it is deeply affecting.

It is unusual to find two consecutive choruses, so Bach especially marks the next number *Schlußchor* (closing chorus). It is the gayest of dancing processions. We see the strewing of garments and branches and hear the welcome of the crowd innocent of the approaching tragedy. The opening clause has the usual step-motive, with light airy feet:

Ex.235

So let us go in the Salem of joy,
So las-set uns ge - hen im Sa - len der Freu - den,

Cont.

The colour of the instrumental opening (the above for flute, 8va, and 'cello), sets the mood for the whole. The instruments enter as follows with the theme—flute, 'cello, violin, and then violas and continuo together. A passing cloud darkens the sky at the end of the sentence, 'Begleitet den König in Lieben und Leiden' ('Accompany the King in love and sorrow'), but on its repetition the change from G minor to G major brings again the blue heavens of Palestine. Novel and very charming is the second section.

Ex.236

He goes before and opens the way,
Er ge - het vor - an und öff - net die Bahn,

is formed into a series of canons, the passing of many believers, and below are lengthy pedal notes, which, no doubt, are illustrative of the long road.

The cantata is a delightful one and the buoyancy of the *Schlußchor* leaves one with the happiest of impressions. It would be most effective in the original service, providing relief from the severity of the plainsong recitation of the Passion which took the place of the Gospel. If it has a weakness, it is due to the arrangement of the libretto, which brings in succession three slow-tempo arias. The only recitative, to the one Biblical text, comes after the first chorus. The librettist would have been wiser had he chosen another Scriptural quotation, placed it between iv and v, or between v and vi, and separated the last two choruses. These flaws of planning suggest that the scheme of the whole was not the work of a single hand, but that additions were made. The score is inscribed 'Tempore Passionis aut Festo Marie Annunciationis'. The Feast of the Annunciation fell in Holy Week thrice in Bach's cantorate, 1739, 1744, and 1750, which would preclude music, while in 1725 and 1736 Palm Sunday and the Annunciation coincided. On one or more of these occasions the cantata may have been performed at Leipzig. (Terry.) Probably there was some reconstruction; the first and last choruses are definitely early, the bass aria seems likewise, but the alto and tenor arias may have been touched up or rewritten for later performances. According to notes on the original violin copy, the opening chorus was at one time repeated after the tenor aria to close the work. Possibly the *Schlußchor* was added in later Weimar days in place of this Da Capo, and the chorale fantasia may have been written and inserted at Leipzig, the composer being unwilling to sacrifice the delightful final number, and yet desiring to change the mood less abruptly.

161. Two beak-flutes and strings provide the simple orchestral palette for the mournfully-happy 'Komm, du süße Todesstunde' ('Come, thou lovely hour of dying' O. 'Come, thou blessed hour' B.). It has no particular appropriateness for the indeterminate 16th Sunday after Trinity, possibly 6 October 1715, except that the Gospel, St. Luke vii. 11–17, relates the raising of the widow's son, not for the Sunday named on a later copy of the score, the Purification. It is just one of Bach's many sermons on the hour of death, preaching in words of exquisite beauty the Christian doctrine of a welcome passing to a happier life, but with sufficient sympathy with human relationships and pleasures not to forget that we cannot bid farewell to our living associations without pangs of regret. There is not the poignancy of the opening of No. 106, for that mourns the loss of a loved one; this cantata is purely a matter of a single person; the relationship of a Christian and Christ, brought so close at the 'Todesstunde' ('death-hour') is the sole theme of Franck's libretto. The cantata is interesting to British music-lovers in one way—it is the first to contain the German hymn-melody which is best known in this country, the so-called Passion Chorale, H. L. Hassler's 'Herzlich thut mich verlangen'. It occurs in the first number, played by the organist's right hand on the *sesquialtera ad organo*, a rare treatment of a chorale in the cantatas. It is as if the dying soul were comforted by the strains of the hymn heard from some neighbouring church. To the pedals is assigned the line marked *organo e continuo*, a direction not given elsewhere in the cantata; the left hand would fill in according to the figures. The flutes move mostly in the tender two-note 'tear' motive:

and both are frequently in the bottom octave, breathing soft tender tones. A surprising chromatic treatment of the motive occurs in the eighth bar:

and also closes two of the subsequent sections. The alto voice employs the same fragment and once depicts the raging of the lion—'da mein Geist Honig speist aus des Löwen Munde' ('when my spirit honey eats out of the lion's mouth')—by triplet semiquavers. The reference of course, is to the incident in Samson's life. 'Honig' is always decorated. The same instrumental motives are employed in Part II: 'Mache meinen Abschied süße, säume nicht, letztes Licht, daß ich meinen Heiland küsse' ('Make my departure sweet, delay not, last light, that I my Saviour (may) kiss'). The vocal line is new, 'küsse' is elaborated and the chromatic passage is heard again in the penultimate vocal bar.

A charming effect is found in the arioso at the close of the beautiful recitativo secco; the world, from which the singer wishes to be freed ('I have desire with Christ to pasture') is suggested by an implied pedal point, the other semiquavers reaching upward, till in the penultimate bar, after the singer ends, comes a slowly descending, curving, chromatically decorated arpeggio of C minor, changing suddenly from the major, and sinking to rest: 'I have desire from this world to depart.' As it is marked 'tasto solo' voice and bassi are left alone in stark solitude during the arioso, a most affecting passage, unique in Bach's works. The recitative portion is of haunting beauty, 'Freudenlicht' ('joylight') is melismatic in 'World, thy pleasure is burden, thy sugar is for me as a poison hated, thy joy-light is my comet'). Franck's far-fetched imagery evidently intends to convey the thought that the world's joy is merely a passing feature of life. In 'And where man thy roses breaks, ∧ are thorns, ∧ without number, ∧ to my soul's torment' there are rests at the points indicated, productive of a feeling of intense poignancy. 'Pale death' is accompanied by falling semitones and 'is my morning-redness (dawn)' is contrasted by a tender vocal passage. The text continues, 'with such rises for me the sun of glory and heaven's bliss. Therefore sigh I right from heart's depth only for the last death-hour.' At the close the bassi discontinue their sostenuto and as 'der letzten Todesstunde' ('the last death-hour') sinks to almost inaudible notes in the singer's compass, they play solemn detached quavers. 'Seelen Qual', 'blasse Tod', 'Morgenröthe', 'Himmelswonne', 'Herzensgrunde', and 'Todesstunde' ('soul's torture', 'pale death', 'morning-redness', 'heaven's bliss', 'heart's depth', and 'death's hour') are also all melismatic, 'Himmelswonne' and 'Herzensgrunde', which lie near each other, being placed high and low respectively.

The tenor aria, with strings, speaking of longing, dust and earth, and death, is singularly undescriptive, though 'mutilated' and 'prangen' (literally 'to make a show', here evidently meaning the 'appearing' of the angels) are appropriately treated. The compass is low-lying, involving no effort on the part of the singer; the lovely music suggests that the forces of the body are swiftly diminishing. The text is 'Mein Verlangen ist, den Heiland zu umfangen und bei Christo bald sein. Ob ich sterblich' Asch' und Erde durch den Tod zermalmet werde, wird der Seele reiner Schein dennoch den Engeln prangen' ('My longing is, the Saviour to embrace and with Christ soon to be. Though I, mortal ashes and earth, through death mutilated become, will the soul's pure brightness yet like the angels shine'). The alto voice is again heard, in an extraordinary scena (though merely termed recitative) accompanied by all the small orchestra. 'The ending is already made' is heralded by a single chord and sung confidently to an arpeggio; 'World, good night!' is accompanied by soft chords. 'And can I only comfort win, in Jesu's arms soon to die', brings detached chords and at the end the bassi descend by semiquavers to low D♯. While the upper strings sustain, the voice sings a lovely slumber-phrase and continuo and flutes imitate:

The words are repeated with a pause on 'Schlaf' and the composer
is so possessed with the thought of

> Sleep after toyle, port after stormie seas,
> Ease after warre, death after life,

that he repeats them twice again with a fresh melodic line, including
two diminished thirds, with continuo only. Plain, detached chords
accompany 'The cool grave will me with roses cover, till Jesus me
will awaken', and the final word brings an animated vocal and
orchestral passage. Only one piano chord steals in during 'till He
His sheep leads to the sweet heaven's pasture, (so) that me death from
Him (may) not separate', and 'Himmelsweide' ('heaven's-pasture')
sways like grasses in a gentle breeze. Semiquaver chords and arpeggi
come at 'So break, thou glad death's-day'. At 'So schlage doch, du
letzter Stundenschlag' (So strike then, thou last hour-knell') the first
flute reiterates, in semiquavers, the highest C, the second imitates a
lower bell in quavers, the upper strings, pizzicato, beat out in unison the
G below the treble stave, and the bassi swing up and down, the clanging of larger bells, and the repeated 'schlage doch' suggests the stroke
of clappers. It is interesting to compare this section with the more
developed recitative on the same lines in the much later Trauerode.
   A lovely chorus follows, the voices flow along quietly in placid
counterpoint, the flutes let us hear the tear-motive in a less solemn
manner than in the opening aria, play joyous passages of demisemiquavers in thirds, like the fluttering of the departing soul, and depict
the joys of heaven in high-placed staccato figures. The strings mostly
provide a background, though sometimes they use the two-note

motive. At the line 'Jesu, komm und nimm mich fort!' the upper
instruments sustain, the bassi swing to the lower bell theme, a beautiful interlude. Vocally, it is one of Bach's simplest choruses, with
themes of charming unpretentiousness:

Ex.240

Wenn es   mei - nes Got - tes Wil - le
If   it   my   God's   will (is)

and:

Ex.241

und   der Geist, des Lei - bes Gast,
and   the spirit, the body's   guest,

The complete text is: 'Wenn es meines Gottes Wille, wünsch' ich,
daß des Leibes Last heute noch die Erde fülle, und der Geist, des Leibes
Gast, mit Unsterblichkeit sich kleide in der süßen Himmelsfreude.
Jesu, komm und nimm mich fort! Dieses sei mein letztes Wort' ('If
it (be) my God's will, wish I, that the body's burden today even the
earth fill, and the spirit, the body's guest, with immortality itself
clothes in the sweet heaven's-joy. Jesus, come and take me away!
This be my last word').

The chorale reappears to close the cantata, stanza 4 of C. Knoll's
funerary hymn commonly associated with the melody, 'The body
indeed in the earth By worms is destroyed; But awakened shall be
Through Christ beautifully transfigured; Will shine as the sun And
live without distress In heavenly joy and bliss. How can hurt me then
death?' The flutes play in unison a beautiful counterpoint above the
voices and a surprising harmonic change, major to minor, is heard
at both double bars. At the final question the flutes curve upwards
and sink backwards after the voices and doubling strings have come
to rest on the dominant chord; no answer is vouchsafed, but the bliss
of the music tells us that none is needed.

142. Various years, 1712, 1713, and 1720, have been named by
commentators for the only remaining work assigned to Weimar, the
Christmas Day cantata 'Uns ist ein Kind geboren' (Neumeister
altered) ('For unto us a Child is born', Isaiah ix. 6). Wherever and
whenever Bach produced it, however, it was, without doubt, only as
an adaptation, for it is extremely unlikely that he was the composer.

Arnold Schering, in the Bach Year Book for 1912, suggests the preceding Leipzig Cantor, Johann Kuhnau, a worthy musician and in
some ways an adventurous composer, whose reputation today is
solely based on his odd yet interesting 'Bible Sonatas'. His vocal
technique was deficient, his choruses halting and often guilty of
technical blunders; he may well have been responsible for the first
version. If Bach took a hand in it at all, it may have been in remodelling the arias, which are all short and not without charm. There
is one for bass, with two violins and continuo, containing some pleasing movement for the upper strings and a gracious vocal melody.
That for tenor is accompanied by two oboes. After a recitative the
aria comes again, with different words and transposed for alto from
A minor to D minor, and with beak-flutes instead of oboes. This
curious procedure is not found in genuine Bach cantatas, but a repetition of an aria to a fresh text is not unknown in their predecessors.
The opening concerto, in which flutes and oboes join with complete
strings, is pleasant and animated, without being possessed of any
features of note. It is in the choruses where one feels the lack of kin-
ship with such cantatas as Nos. 21, 31, 70, or 106; they are stiff and
angular, particularly the second. The fugal writing of the first:

Ex.242

in spite of some effective passages, is somewhat halting. Both choruses
are accompanied by normal strings. In the last number, a chorale—
stanza 5 of C. Fuger's 'Wir Christenleut', to C. Fuger, Jnr,'s melody,
'Allelujah, praised be God!'—is simply harmonized for voices, the
viola is independent, the wood-wind and the two lines of violins unite
in a unison 'moto perpetuo' of semiquavers. (B.E.C., No. 13, O.) i is
a simple 'concerto' for two flutes, two oboes, and strings. (See O.O.S.
No. 024.)

The author of *Handel and his Orbit* tries to prove that *Almira* is the
source of this cantata also. His arguments, however, are again quite
unconvincing, and his illustrations prove nothing whatsoever. It would
be quite easy to construct such a thesis on any opera of Handel
and point out phrases which have something vaguely in common.

CÖTHEN
47, 141

Order of Discussion: 141, 47

THE six Cöthen years, when he was chamber composer to the Court, were almost fallow so far as our particular subject is concerned. The severely Calvinistic principles of the Prince, so different from Luther's art-loving conceptions of divine service, did not sanction church music of any degree of elaboration. Nos. 134 and 173 in their original secular form were written at Cöthen, but they will be discussed according to the time of their adaptation.

141. Only one church cantata, No. 47, can be attributed definitely to this period, until Leipzig loomed ahead. It is almost certain that the other, No. 141, 'Das ist je gewißlich wahr' ('This thou knowest', 1 Timothy i. 15), to a libretto by J. F. Helbig, for the Third Sunday in Advent, 1721 or 1722, is not by Bach. The fugue subject of the chorus, with its nine solid G's in succession:

Ex. 243

Das ist je ge-wiß-lich wahr, und ein theu-er werth-es Wort,
That is always assuredly true, and a precious honoured word,

the attempt of the composer to express dogged belief, is incredibly stiff; fugal writing, so beloved of Bach, soon weakens into homophony and frequently the inner parts are perfunctory. Neither of the arias has the charm of the other doubtful cantata, No. 142, and the syncopated melody of the second stresses the second syllables of 'Jesu' and 'uns're' and throws into relief such an unimportant word as 'der'. There is also to be found 'kein falsches, kein falsches Wort' ('no false, no false word') an absurd repetition which, so far as I know, has no counterpart in the writings of the master. Two copies of the work in the Prussian Staatsbibliothek, Berlin, do not name Bach as the composer. This fact and the quality of the music itself may be considered as disposing definitely of the question of authenticity.[1]

47. If we consider the church cantatas written at the close of the Cöthen period in preparation for Leipzig as belonging more correctly

---

[1] Alfred Dürr attributes the cantata to Telemann.

to the latter, only one example can be attributed to those years so fruitful in immortal orchestral and chamber music. 'Wer sich selbst erhöhet, der soll erniedriget werden', for the 17th Sunday after Trinity, cannot have been performed at the court chapel, but must have been composed for some journey as organ virtuoso. Spitta surmises that it was written when he visited Carlsbad in May 1720, for his journey later in the year to Hamburg. There is no direct evidence, and Terry scouts the theory, pointing out that the particular Sunday came before his visit to the mouth of the Elbe. It is a remarkable work, in his ripest early maturity. J. F. Helbig's text begins with the last verse of the Gospel, St. Luke xiv. 1–11, 'For whosoever exalteth himself shall be abased, and he that humbleth himself shall be exalted', a text which roused Bach to his highest powers, stirring him as did corresponding passages in his settings of the Magnificat. Thematically the chorus shows affinities with the magnificent concert-like prelude to the Weimar organ fugue in C minor (Peters, Bk. II, No. 6). The opening phrase is the same in both compositions:

Ex. 244

The descending two-note figure in the eighth bar of the prelude:

Ex. 245

is identical with the second limb of the vocal fugue subject (see first six crotchets of (*b*) below). The figure which occurs first in the fourteenth bar of the former:

Ex. 246

is the foundation of the quavers of the first limb of the latter (see bar 2 of (*a*)). These resemblances are too close to be merely accidental. The chorus is so monumental that it demands a detailed analysis.

Two oboes and strings are almost too modest forces for his tremendous ideas, yet the writing is so masterly that one scarcely feels aware of the smallness of the orchestra. The number falls into seven sections. The instrumental introduction begins with the concerto theme, strings answered by oboes. Soon a short rising and falling idea appears in violin I:

imitated at close quarters by the oboes in thirds, the bassi hurling down the proud. The rising sequential figure referred to makes its first appearance in the oboes, but its chief development is given to the bassi, foreshadowing a more extended treatment later. Otherwise the vocal fugue is not referred to in the introduction. Accompanied by the concerto theme, the nine-bar fugue subject is announced by the tenors. It is a vivid piece of imagery; the first clause, following four strong crotchets, climbs upwards by a sequential figure:

After it reaches a climax, the second clause falls to the depths, beginning with the two-note figure used chromatically:

This picturesque ascent and descent are found everywhere in the chorus, the countersubject falling while the subject rises, rushing scale-wise up the distance of a twelfth (Ex. 250). All the free counterpoints carry out the same pictorial delineation in a tumultuous scene of ordered confusion. With an extra entry on the oboes the second

Ex.250

section ends. Throughout the third the bassi pursue the sequential figure, the concerto theme on the other instruments alternating with short passages for the voices. The fourth section is a second exposition, with the voices entering in a different order, except that the basses come last, and the oboes again clench with the subject. The fifth section is another presentation of the third. The voices now enter in pairs with subject and countersubject, the concerto theme being absent and the instruments doubling the voices. The fugue subjects are heard no more in their entirety after this, though the sequential figure is often in evidence. The sixth section closes with a reference to the episodical material, and after a heralding of the concerto theme by the orchestra, all unite in a magnificent passage where the voices for the first time sing the opening instrumental bars. The seventh section develops this and the sequential figure to the end. Halfway through there is a tremendous effect, where the voices excitedly hurl out a great chord on 'und' ('and') as if to clench the argument. Bach wrote few choruses so mighty and forceful as this.

A soprano aria speaks of the necessity for humility on the part of a true Christian, and the obbligato follows the same imagery as the chorus, rising and falling. It is always fascinating to see how flexible Bach's ideas were and how he shaped them according to his needs. The chief theme is stated in three ways, the upward and downward movement clearly outlined in each:

Ex.251

Ex.252

and:

Ex.253

There is yet a fourth:

Ex.254

where the upward and downward movement comes in diminution in the first two bars of the continuo. The text continues, 'Muß der De-muth sich befleißen, Demuth stammt aus Jesu Reich' ('Must to humility himself apply, humility springs from Jesu's kingdom'). One 'Demuth' sinks to the bottom of the compass, there are many vocal phrases suggestive of genuflexions. One 'stammt' climbs slowly through a decorated scale while the obbligato, pivoting on C, repeats the figure of the third example above, and there are other ascents on the word. The *BGS* score assigns the obbligato to an organ manual, but Spitta and Schweitzer rightly point out that this is a mistake, that the instrument intended is a solo violin. This is demonstrated by the double stopping in the second part, where organ chords would be meaningless, but where the crunching two-string groups, occurring nearly forty times, form a striking element in the varied picture. Moreover, Bach's meticulous markings demand string technique. The vocalist twice sings 'Hoffahrt ist dem Teufel gleich' ('Arrogance is to the Devil akin') with a stubbornly long note on 'Hoffahrt' and flaring trills to the remainder. The bassi alternate the climbing figure which opens the aria with a staccato leaping figure indicative of stubbornness. In the remainder of Part II the sentence 'Gott pflegt alle die zu hassen, die den Stolz nicht fahren lassen' ('God is wont all those to hate, who pride will not (to) go let') is given extended treatment. A hurried series of notes throws 'hassen' into high relief, the two syllables being marked staccato, 'fahren' has a wild and confused run, the bassi refer no more to the mounting figure, but paint 'stubbornness' in increasingly forceful tones.

The crudely extravagant language of the bass recitative did not deter the composer from writing a chromatic Wagnerian texture for the strings, with a fine melodic line for violin I, and it calls up splendid declamatory passages for the singer. The opening is agitated: 'Man is dirt, dust, ashes and earth. Is it possible, that by arrogance, as (by) a devil's brood, he yet bewitched is?' Sustained chords calm the next section: 'Ah! Jesus, God's Son, the creator of all things, became for our sakes lowly and humble, He suffered shame and derision'. (See Ex. 1269.) Agitation is resumed: 'and thou, thou poor worm, seekest thou to boast? appertains that to a Christian? Go, be ashamed, thou proud creature, do penance and follow Christ's footsteps'. Violin I now climbs to high C and the rest is peaceful: 'cast thyself before God in spirit believing down, in His time raises He thee also again.' Modern ears are apt to be offended at such texts as this and modern taste to censure Bach for setting them. We must remember, however, the difference between our religious outlook and his. Luther was the keystone of his earthly temple, and the Reformation was not merely a matter of conflicting opinions, but of warring states, persecution, and bitter enmities. Luther had to fight not only the spiritual Rome but all the earthly principalities which owed it allegiance. Men found in the Old Testament scenes of strife and slaughter which seemed to them to reflect their own position, and in the contest for life and death passions and language became hot and violent. We have only to compare modern religious expression with that of the English Puritans or the Scottish Covenanters to realize that our world is not theirs, and that we must try to understand the conditions under which they fought for the continuance of their faith. The battle that Luther had waged against unscrupulous enemies was used as a model by himself and his followers when considering the opposing elements within their own hearts, and the evil elements of the mixture of good and bad which is found in every one of us are addressed in the same terms as hostile powers, sacred or secular. We find side by side the most tender worship of Christ and vehement hatred of all that seems opposed to Him, and we must accept, in our study of the master, the latter as an essential factor in his outlook. We do not permit our veneration for the Psalms to be disturbed because the writer of LIX begs the Almighty that his personal enemies may 'make a noise like a dog and go round about the city' as scavengers.

The bass aria contains both phases of Lutheran thought. 'Wie der erste Höllenbrand' ('As the first hell-fire') gives rise to chromatic harmonies in an otherwise diatonic section. 'Laß mich deine Demuth suchen und den Hochmuth ganz verfluchen' ('Let me Thy humility seek and haughtiness completely execrate') would revolt most composers, but Bach thoroughly enjoys dealing with it. The semiquaver run on 'Hochmuth' contains a detached note every two beats:

Ex. 255

which is striking enough, but the most startling passage is reserved for the final 'verfluchen', where a series of semiquaver leaps is slurred in twos, across the accent, the second note of each group being marked staccato:

Ex. 256

It is an effect more instrumental than vocal and an unusually difficult passage to sing. The charm of the aria lies in the treatment of the opening words 'Jesu, beuge doch mein Herze' ('Jesus, bend then my heart'). There is an obbligato for violin (solo) and oboe; the former begins with a sinking down and then comes a quaver idea which curves round a central note:

Ex. 257

When the oboe takes up the theme the violin sustains the central note while the other instrument circles round it, sometimes in sharp dissonance. It suggests actually the bending of the character (not the fleshly heart) round the divine stem. In bar 9 the theme comes in another way, simultaneously in quavers and semiquavers. It is a quaint conceit on the part of the composer, yet it is productive of delightful music. The voice enters with the violin theme, against it are the sustained note and the semiquaver version, both forms being present together. The connecting words between 'Herze' and 'der erste Höllenbrand' are 'unter deine starke Hand, daß ich nicht mein Heil verscherze' ('under Thy strong hand, that I not my salvation through folly lose'). The turn motive is heard in the orchestra during the second clause and 'verscherze' is allotted picturesque runs. During the 'Laß mich' section the semiquavers of the quotation *supra* are imitated between oboe and violin, later the other semiquaver group from the introduction:

Ex. 258

occurs in all instrumental lines, and the last repetition of 'Laß mich deine Demuth' combines it with the twin motive. A canon for oboe and violin springing from the semiquaver stepwise fifth is heard at the beginning of the last vocal section—'Gieb mir einen niedern Sinn, daß ich dir gefällig bin' ('Give me a lowly mind, that I to Thee pleasing be')—the run also comes in the continuo and 'Gieb mir' is a ♩♪ ♩ skeleton of it. The quaver portion of the chief theme in the continuo supports imitations of the last example quoted, which continues while the voice takes over the quavers, forming the real bass, the continuo being silent. The descending group gives rise to a new and placid imitative passage for the obbligato instruments, while the voice borrows from it and quotes the seven semiquavers in a long roulade on 'gefällig'. The texture of the aria sums up a development which had been progressing for years. The close and intricate weaving, the fascinating freedom of every line, the richness of the harmonic counterpoint and the contrapuntal harmony, the bold clashings, the flowering of the whole from a few phrases so that every part is intimately connected with every other, these are the technical essence of the three-part sinfonias and Part I of Das Wohltemperirte Klavier, both of which belong to Cöthen, a superb art evolved by the assimilation of the art of his predecessors and contemporaries, and transmuted by the fires of his own colossal mind into an art not equalled, let alone surpassed, by anything before or since. The student saturated in Bach finds his delight in the silent reading of the scores increased as the years pass onwards, he discovers more and more to admire, and in performance the possibilities are infinite, the varieties of shading, of balance, of tempo rubato, which may be experimented with are so boundless, that he feels that here is an everlasting stimulus and inspiration.

A whole book, too, could be filled with a study of the four-part chorales alone. These should always be examined with the particular hymn-stanzas set, and not considered merely as examples of clever and beautiful harmonization. Every surprising progression and every unusual line of counterpoint is determined by the text and by no other consideration. The closing chorale of this cantata is stanza 11 of 'Warum betrübst du dich, mein Herz', supposedly by Hans Sachs, the melody of which is supposed to be descended from the Meistersinger themselves: 'Temporal honour will I gladly forego, (If) Thou wilt me only the eternal grant, That Thou acquired hast Through Thy harsh, bitter death. That ask I Thee, My Lord and God!' One has only to look at the last two lines to see how aptly the harmonies heighten the colour of the poem. The melody has little to do with it, for that is a fixed element. Over and over again, by some magical transmutation, a chorale acquires qualities which fit it perfectly for its situation in the emotional scheme. Often one cannot divine by what subtle process the result has been obtained; if one examines the melody by itself one can see no attributes likely to make it appropriate, an analysis of the harmonic and contrapuntal devices employed does not reveal the secrets of Bach's alchemy. One astonishing thing is the way in which the same melody is transfigured so as to serve different purposes. Some tunes, apart from their harmonization, seem merely dull, but when clothed by the composer they shine with radiant beauty. Several melodies are so well known to us, such as 'Ein' feste Burg' or 'Wie schön leuchtet der Morgenstern', that we recognize them immediately under any guise. But with some that are less familiar, whose melodic outlines have not sunk deep into one's mind, one is often astonished to find that one which has been heard with one setting does not appear to be the same when heard with another. Two endless sources of variety and transmutability are decoration of the line and rhythmic alterations. There are few of the four-part settings in which the melody is not ornamented in some way or other, by the addition of passing notes, by the introduction of embellishments. Bach elaborated the simple hymn tune till it became plastic, rich, and glowing. His tendencies in that direction may be realized by an examination of his contributions to the Schemelli chorale book, where one or two are almost of the type of a small aria. Indeed, he marks one with that title. But it is never mere baroque with him, the profusion of detail often covering the stern old melodies is not an end in itself, but a means of intensifying the emotional contents. When Handel wished to be most effective, he was most simple; Bach's mind worked in the opposite direction, and he generally touches one's heart-strings most profoundly when his harmony, texture, and ornamentation are most complex. In the Passions, cantatas, and organ chorale preludes these melodies are subjected to an infinite number of rhythmic changes. A given musical theme did not tie him down to any prescribed manner of treatment, but his unerring instinct moulded it anew, cast it into any desired shape, so that the meaning of the text could be intensified and expanded to an almost unbelievable degree. Perhaps some day a scholar of insight will write a treatise covering the whole ground of Bach's transformation of the melodies of his church.

Johann Kuhnau, Cantor at Leipzig, died on 5 June 1722. Negotiations for a successor were protracted and it was not until the following May that Bach entered upon his new duties. The interim, however, was not unconcerned with composition for Leipzig. He was asked to provide a Passion, and that according to St. John was the result. He wrote church cantata No. 22 for his Probe on 7 February, possibly No. 23 with a view to the same purpose, and Nos. 75 and 76 for the first two Sundays of his last long office. These four works are links between the few Cöthen and the many Leipzig cantatas, and are more conveniently discussable in the next section. He was growing dissatisfied with Cöthen; the Prince's bride, Friederica Henrietta, had caused a change in the attitude of the court towards music, he had almost exhausted the possibilities of the chamber music of his time, he was evidently anxious to expand his growing powers in more extensive forms, and his strongest inclinations were towards church music. Leipzig brought him new visions and a new impulse, and the transference from the narrow limitations of a ceremonial, princely court in a tiny town to the wider outlook of a great commercial city where the services of the four churches were of considerable importance, destined this prosperous community of proud, self-governing merchants to become the birth-place of the greatest religious music of all time.

PART II

THE CHURCH CANTATAS OF THE MIDDLE PERIOD

CÖTHEN AND LEIPZIG, 1723-34

FROM henceforth there is no clear dividing line in the production of cantatas, but some classification is necessary for purposes of discussion. In following the grouping of the complete Leipzig period into the two portions adopted in Terry's chronological table, one is not implying any marked difference, but merely adopting a convenient arrangement for the examination of a great mass of works. There is one point, however, which helps to differentiate the closing from the middle years, the increased number of paraphrased hymn-texts, and that in itself, which will be considered in due time, is sufficient reason for establishing a boundary, even though it be not an entirely decisive line of demarcation. In the eleven years during which the age of Bach moved from thirty-eight to forty-nine, cantatas flowed from his pen with supernatural rapidity, and no fewer than 100 are still in existence, complete or incomplete. Their study is complicated by the fact that the order of production, so far as can be ascertained (whatever chronological sequence is adopted contains many conjectural dates), is not always the order of composition, as we find earlier works given either intact or remodelled, early fragments incorporated into later works, and previous compositions adapted in a variety of ways to new purposes. We shall consider the cantatas of the middle period under the following headings: (1) those prepared at Cöthen for Leipzig; (2) those which are probably founded on Weimar material, but concerning the origin of which we have no information; (3) cantatas containing borrowed material; and the remainder grouped as follows: (4) solo cantatas; (5) hymn cantatas; (6) miscellaneous choral cantatas.

Cöthen–Leipzig, 1723
Nos. 22, 23, 75, 76

22. On 7 February 1723, Quinquagesima, Bach undertook his Probe at Leipzig, and submitted as a specimen of his powers of composition 'Jesus nahm zu sich die Zwölfe' ('Jesus called to Him the twelve' O. St. Luke xviii. 31). The texts of ii, iii, and iv are probably by himself and v is a chorale. Possibly he was anxious to woo the reluctant Leipzigers, who were not particularly disposed to appoint him, and who considered his name seriously only after the two favoured candidates, Telemann and Graupner, had used the vacancy to advance their own interests in their present appointments. As he was desirous of leaving Cöthen he diplomatically presented himself as a composer on quite modest lines. Oboe and strings are the sole forces, there are no daring and disturbing flights of imagination. The first part of the text of the opening number, which is from the Gospel, 'Jesus took unto Him the twelve, and said: 'Behold, we go up to Jerusalem, and it will all accomplished be that written is of the man- kind's Son', is set as an arioso, the tenor taking the part of the Nar- rator and the bass singing the words of Christ. In the first two bars all the upper instruments move by step upwards:

Ex. 259

the journey to Jerusalem, in the third and fourth, oboe and violin I alternate a phrase of pathos:

Ex. 260

referring to verses 32 and 33, speaking of his sufferings, which are omitted from the text. The inner instruments forsake their previous movement and undulate gently over a stationary bass, and then the bassi take up the tale of suffering. Out of these motives the whole of the introduction to the chorus is constructed. The bass voice uses the step motive, in varied forms, to 'wir gehen hinauf' (Ex. 261) and there are emotional phrases indicative of the human side of the Saviour, especially to 'Menschen' ('men', the plural is used in the German). The English Scripture version of the chorus reads: 'And they understood none of these things, neither knew they the things which were spoken' (the central clause of the Biblical verse is omitted). The German runs rather differently: 'Sie aber vernahmen der Keines, und wüßten nicht, was das gesaget war' ('They however

Ex. 261

understood of it nothing, and knew not, that which said was').
A vocal fugue leads off supported only by continuo, the first five
words being employed for the subject:

Ex. 262

The countersubject utilizes the next three words twice over. So far
treatment is normal, but the free counterpoints make of the last four
words dramatic ejaculations, 'was' being separated from 'das' by a
rest and 'das' from 'gesaget', 'das', and 'was' usually being thrust
on unaccented beats. The picture, therefore, is of turmoil and confusion, implying scorn at the lack of understanding of the disciples,
and the setting of the text is an interesting example of Bach's subtle
methods of dealing with words. When the upper instruments enter
they merely double the voices, but they increase the animation and
lead to a forceful climax.

The alto soloist (see O.S.B.A. No. 3) pleads that she may be
allowed to accompany the Saviour and share in His sufferings:
'Mein Jesu, ziehe mich nach dir, ich bin bereit, ich will von hier und
nach Jerusalem, zu deinen Leiden gehen. Wohl mir! wenn ich die
Wichtigkeit, von dieser Leid und Sterbenszeit zu meinem Troste
kann durchgehends wohl verstehn' ('My Jesus, draw me after Thee,
I am ready, I will from here and to Jerusalem, to Thy Passion go.
Well for me! when I the significance of this sorrow and death-time
to my comfort can right well understand'). The oboe begins with a
melody laden with heavy grief:

Ex. 263

(Key C minor, signature of 2 flats.)

which is not sung in complete form; only occasional phrases from
it are allotted to the voice. The singer also uses the step motive when
speaking of accompanying the Christ to His scene of woe:

Ex. 264

The bass follows with a recitative accompanied by strings. Again
we have the step motive, 'laufen' ('run') has a roulade, the penultimate word 'Freuden' ('joys') uses the step motive in elaborated form
and the final bars are florid, violin I breaking into a short arabesque.
The text is lengthy: 'My Jesus, draw me, so shall I run, for flesh and
blood understand utterly along with Thy disciples not, that which
said was. It longs them (they long) for the world and after the greatest
multitude, they want both, when Thou transfigured art, certainly a
strong citadel on Tabor's mount (to) build; whereas (on) Golgotha'
(see Ex. 1267) '(which) so full (of) suffering is, in Thy humiliation
with no eye (to) look. Ah! crucify in me, in the corrupted breast,
first of all this world, and the forbidden desire; so shall I, what Thou
sayest, fully well understand, and to Jerusalem with a thousand joys
go.' Again, 'to Jerusalem' is stepwise. Terry points out that the first
two vocal phrases are inspired by the chorale melody 'O Gott, du
frommer Gott' ('Oh God, Thou holy God').
    The tenor has a song of praise (see O.S.B.A. No. 4) accompanied
by strings, the chief melody lilting and swinging:

Ex. 265

and winging florid passages, embodying the joy motive, for violin I.
The quoted melody is repeated a tone higher to 'verbessre das
Herze, verändre den Muth;' ('reform the heart, change the dis-

position') and continues—'schlag' Alles darnieder, was dieser Ent-
sagung des Fleisches zuwider' ('strike everything down, which to this
renunciation of the flesh (is) contrary'). Florid movement ceases
temporarily with 'Doch wenn ich nun geistlich ertödet da bin' ('Yet
when I now spiritually put to death am'), but the voice mounts in
semiquavers to 'so ziehe mich nach dir in Friede dahin'. ('so draw
me after Thee in peace thither'), and while the voice sustains on
'Friede' we hear the opening melody on violin I. Later this is sung
to 'so ziehe', &c.

The extended chorale (B.E.C. No. 2, O.) is stanza 5 of E. Cruciger's
Christmas hymn 'Herr Christ, der einig' Gott's Sohn'—'Mortify us
by Thy grace, Awaken us by Thy mercy, The old man chastise That
he anew live may Well here on this earth, Mind and all desires And
thoughts have to Thee'—to its anonymous melody. The vocal harmonies are plain, but oboe and violin I decorate with an uninterrupted flow of legato semiquavers, called up by 'neu' Leben' ('anew
live'), while the bassi move steadily in quavers from start to finish,
the journey of the disciples to the fulfilment of the prophecy.

23. It is practically certain that 'Du wahrer Gott und Davids Sohn'
('Thou very God and David's Son' B.) was composed at Cöthen in
1723, possibly with the Probe in view, that it was set aside in favour
of No. 22, and not performed until Quinquagesima of the next year.
The libretto is again possibly by the composer. The final chorale
formed the conclusion of the *Passion according to St. John*. It may
be that in the haste of production of the latter this number was
borrowed from the already completed cantata, and that Bach thought
it wise not to offer as his test a work containing a number he intended
incorporating in the Passion which he was probably invited to provide during the vacancy. The chorale is equally appropriate to both
places, because Quinquagesima is not far removed from Passion-tide
and a foreshadowing of the Crucifixion is legitimate; and besides, as
has already been pointed out, the Gospel narrates the story of the
journey to Jerusalem and prophesies the tragedy there. 'Christe, du
Lamm Gottes' is a prose translation of the Agnus Dei and the melody
is the three-limbed plain-chant with which it was associated. The
treatment is unique, all three verses are heard in the soprano and
each is presented in a different manner. Two oboes begin with a
supplicating passage in thirds and sixths and the strings fill the intervening spaces with short groups of chords:

This is continued through most of the first verse—'Christ, Thou Lamb of God, Thou Who bearest the sins of the world, Pity Thou us!'—though another oboe figure occurs against a series of chromatically descending crotchets:

The choral harmonies are fairly simple; cornetto and three trombones double the choir. Verse 2, with the same text as the first, changes to andante, the lower voices, instrumentally doubled, become more animated, unison oboes and violin I imitate each of the chorale lines. The oboes play the interludes, based on:

tender, mournful duets, and the first phrase finds its way into the voice parts. Verse 3, in which the last line is 'gieb uns dein'n Frieden' ('Give us Thy peace'), enters without change of tempo, the lower voices still more animated, the only independent instrumental line being a syncopated melody for oboes in unison poised above the chorus. A florid Amen concludes this hauntingly beautiful and deeply felt number.

The S.A. duetto, 'adagio molto', which opens the cantata, is a prayer for compassion in the midst of misery: 'Du wahrer Gott und Davids Sohn, der du von Ewigkeit, in der Entfernung schon, mein Herzeleid und meine Leibespein umständlich angesehen, erbarm' dich mein!' ('Thou very God and David's Son, Thou Who from eternity, in the distance already, my heart's grief and my body's pain minutely (hast) seen, pity Thou me!'). There is much chromatic harmony, there are many ascending and descending semitones. Both instrumental and vocal themes move much in canon, significant of the dual personality spoken of in the title. It is curious that the theme for the two obbligato oboes and the first vocal idea both circle round the dominant, the same notes being used in different time-patterns:

Ex. 269 *Adagio molto*

Ob. I.

Cont.

(Key C minor, signature of 2 flats.)

and

Ex. 270 S.

Du   wah - rer Gott

The extremely ornate oboe parts and the expressive vocal lines produce an effect of great richness. The second part is 'Und laß durch deine Wunderhand, die so viel Böses abgewandt, mir gleichfalls Hilf' und Trost geschehen' ('And let by Thy wonderhand, which so much evil turned away (has), for me likewise help and comfort come to pass'). The vocal parts begin much more simply, but in the closing bars, when the oboes are silent, they are ornate and decorated with trills.

During ii, a tenor recitative with oboes and strings, unison oboes and violin I intone the Agnus Dei. Unusually for a recitative, the opening cry of despair, 'Ach! gehe nicht vorüber' ('Ah! pass not over'), is repeated. The remaining portion associated with line 1, 'Thou, of all men salvation, hast yea appeared, the sick and not the healthy to serve', is closed with a tender instrumental cadence. The second is 'Therefore I take likewise in Thine omnipotence part, I see Thee on these paths, on which one me has wished to lay, even in my blindness'. Melismata vary the otherwise plain style on 'fasse' ('recover') and 'lasse' ('leave') in 'I recover myself, and leave Thee not without Thy blessing' (see Gen. xxxii. 26), and the cadence from bar 4 closes. It is a question whether the last note of the chorale should be sustained to the full length or cut off when the voice sings the otherwise unaccompanied two final notes. Certainly the effect of the long drawn-out ending against the dissonant vocal E♭, resolved by violin II, is striking. The cantata is very short and its four numbers present an unusual plan. In iii, original lines are added to part of Psalm cxlv. 15:

Ex. 271

(Key E♭, signature of 2 flats.)

The complete chorus confines itself to this text. There are seven appearances of this idea, the chief subject of a free rondo form. The second and last entries only are identical, the others exhibiting differences, fresh keys, transference of the melody from the sopranos to other parts. The original lines are sung as episodes by tenors and basses with oboes: (1) 'und die meinen sonderlich' ('and mine particularly'), there are two short canons, and with that love of infinite change of detail characteristic of Bach, the second is a modification of the first, reversed voices, quavers on 'meinen' altered to crotchets, and quaver thirds on 'und die' inverted. Part of the 'Aller' idea is borrowed, inverted, for the instrumental lines. (2) 'Gieb denselben Kraft und Licht, laß' sie nicht immerdar in Finsternissen' ('Give to the same strength and light, leave them not always in darkness'), with strings and oboes. Though this begins with imitations, there is parallel motion in the middle by way of contrast, and the seven-note 'Aller' is played piano by unison oboes. (3) 'Künftig soll dein Wink allein der geliebte Mittelpunkt aller ihrer Werke sein' ('In the future shall Thy sign alone the beloved middle-point of all their works be') with continuo—this odd expression begins in canon, the lower part ornamented with leaning tones and trills, the upper plain. There is probably some hidden symbolic meaning. The bassi move in quavers and the scale passage is frequent. (4) 'bis du sie einst durch den Tod wiederum gedenkst zu schließen.' ('till Thou them one day through death again designest to close.')—this, the longest of the episodes, begins with continuo, the later part is with oboes, the upper playing the opening theme of the chorus, but with five bars condensed to four, and a solitary entry of unison violins, the six-note quavers. Six bars of the vocal lines are in canon; after a free part there are imitations on a fresh idea. There are three purely instrumental episodes as well, restatements of the chief theme in different keys. It is difficult to see the reason for this unusual form, unless it be that a full chorus throughout would have caused a lack of contrast and that the important S.A. duet at the beginning was to be balanced by one for T.B. The original score concluded with this number, but as the customary letters 'S.D.G.' were not added, it is clear that Bach intended it to be followed by something else. Possibly the present ending of the cantata was in his mind. As some of the orchestral parts were written out at Cöthen and others at Leipzig, it overlaps the two periods.

75, 76. Forkel tells us that Bach was inducted into his office at 9 o'clock on the morning of Monday, 31 May 1723. He would no doubt officiate at St. Nicholas's on the previous day. (Cantatas were given alternately in the two chief churches.) With what enthusiasm he entered upon his duties and how he set himself out to impress his congregation, may be seen from the compositions he had prepared for his first two Sundays. They open a new chapter in the story of the cantatas by reason of their expansiveness, and it seems as if the prospect of a life devoted to church music in a large centre had given a mighty impetus to his powers. Fine as are the choruses of Nos. 22 and 23, they are in a different category from those of Nos. 75 and 76, which are superb, overpowering, glowing with a wonderful vitality. Both of the cantatas are on a great scale, in two parts, divided by the sermon. Terry points out that this was an innovation in Leipzig use, and that all subsequent cantatas for the First Sunday after Trinity (the day before the induction) are written on these lines. Part I in each case opens with a magnificent chorus, in form a prelude and fugue, the fugues being brilliant and florid, the second of the two working up from solo to tutti, in the manner noted in No. 71. Part II of each work begins with an instrumental Sinfonia. That in No. 75 is a chorale on the trumpet, accompanied by rushing string passages, the only purely orchestral work in all his compositions in which a chorale is introduced. (See O.S.S. No. 019. O.C.S. 'What God doth' arranges the chorale melody for voices.) Was it a piece of unconscious humour on Bach's part which made him choose, after the many months of vacillation by the Council and their almost reluctant appointment, the anonymous melody of S. Rodigast's 'Was Gott thut, das ist wohlgethan' ('What God does, that is well done')? The sinfonia in No. 76 (see O.O.S. No. 020) is a delicate piece of chamber music for oboe d'amore, viola da gamba and continuo, afterwards incorporated into the fourth of his pedal clavicembalo sonatas, now generally classified as organ works. This is his first use of the oboe d'amore, which evidently he had not been able to command before. He eagerly seized the opportunity to explore its possibilities, and we find it in sixty other church cantatas, to say nothing of secular and larger church works, sometimes singly, sometimes paired, but never with a third.

Another point of similarity between the two cantatas is that Part I concludes with a remarkably fine extended chorale, which is repeated to close Part II. In No. 75 is employed stanza 5 of the hymn which is used in the Sinfonia 'What God does, that is well done! Must I the cup immediately taste Which bitter is after my delusion; Let me yet not fear: Because then at the last I shall delight With sweet comfort of heart; Then vanish all pains'. The violin I line, doubled by oboe I, is very active, and is based on notes 1–4 of the melody, possibly an interpretation of 'With sweet comfort of heart' looking beyond lines 2–4. Oboe II doubles violin II. The orchestral sinfonia must have had a thrilling effect when it came after the sermon, with the recollection of the choral setting still in the minds of the worshippers. At the end of the cantata, a note directs the repetition of the extended chorale. It is likely, however, that another verse would be sung. A reconstructed version is found in No. 100. (B.E.C. No. 9, O.)

In No. 76 Luther's versification of Psalms lxvii is used, 'Es woll uns Gott genädig sein', with its anonymous melody. (B.E.C. No. 6, O.) Stanza 1 concludes Part I: 'May to us God gracious be And His blessing give; His countenance us with bright splendour Lighten to eternal Life; That we (may) know His works And what to Him (is) dear on earth, And Jesus Christ's salvation and strength Known to the heathen may be, And them to God convert!' The tender chamber music sinfonia after the sermon would recall line 1. Stanza 3, a song of thanksgiving, ends the cantata: 'Let thank, God, and praise Thee The people with good deeds; The land brings fruit and multiplies, Thy word is well proved. (May) us bless Father and Son, (May) us bless God, the Holy Ghost, To Whom all the world honour do, Before Him fear greatly And say from the heart: Amen!' The texture is amazingly complicated. Trumpet and strings play incessantly throughout, filling the spaces between the choral lines, and the tromba anticipates partly or wholly each limb of the melody. Violin I maintains a syncopated movement all through, a noteworthy feat, but the astounding thing is the continuo part. The alto recitative

which leads *attacca* into verse I speaks of bowing in prayer. The
bassi continue the thought and play:

Ex. 272

symbolic of genuflexions. This figure is repeated nearly fifty times,
and on five occasions only is the composer compelled to forego a
seventh as the falling interval.

Among Bach's new acquaintances at Leipzig must have been a particularly able trumpeter, for both cantatas contain bass arias with
brilliant 'tromba obbligati'. In both cases strings participate. In
No. 75 practically the whole of the thematic material is found in the
opening bar:

Ex. 273

In bar 2 the tromba plays (*a*) and (*c*); in bar 3 the violins do likewise,
in bar 4 the tromba begins a series of brilliant triplet semiquavers
which are continued, with the aid of violin I, to the Fine bar. (*a*) and
(*b*) serve for the opening vocal clause, 'Mein Herze glaubt und liebt'
('My heart believes and loves'), and as it continues the trumpet
repeats its own second bar slightly altered. (*b*) is heard in unison
upper strings and in continuo, and the tromba glitters piercingly
above. The three themes are fashioned into a ritornello, and then the
singer, at first with continuo and then with unison violins added,
playing (*b*) and (*c*), reveals the meaning of the triplets: 'Denn Jesus'
süße Flammen, aus den'n die meinen stammen, gehn über mich
zusammen' ('For Jesus' sweet flames, out of which mine spring, go
over me together'). A roulade on 'zusammen' is indicative of licking
flames. 'Weil er sich mir ergiebt' ('because He Himself to me gives')
completes the text. The molten fire of the tromba triplets remains the
chief memory of this splendid aria.

The corresponding number in No. 76 is a tirade against idolatry.
Repeated notes for the strings:

Ex. 274

reiterated notes and repeated fragments for the trumpet:

Ex. 275

tell of the stubbornness of unbelievers. The vocal opening, with its scattering run:

Ex. 276   Away,   away,   idolatrous   tribe!
            Fahr'_____ hin, fahr' hin, ab-göt-tis-che Zunft!

Cont.

contains in the middle a melodic fragment which is of the utmost importance:

Ex. 277

fahr' hin,

a commanding and impetuous gesture. The continuo begins with it, in bars 2–4 of the introduction the bassi and viola answer with it, and it is heard dozens of times throughout the aria. During the next part of the text, with continuo only—'Sollt' sich die Welt gleich verkehren, will ich doch Christum verehren' ('Should itself the world even pervert, will I yet Christ honour')—it persists in the bassi. It is a lapse on Bach's part that he repeats the 'verkehren' run to 'verehren'. With 'er ist das Licht der Vernunft' ('He is the light of reason') the trumpet joins in, beginning with the fragment.

The orchestra required for the two cantatas is trumpet, two oboes, one oboe d'amore (this implies two oboists only, each man was expected to play oboe, oboe d'amore, oboe da caccia, and possibly taille as required), and strings, and the bassoon is included in No. 75 for doubling purposes, but not in No. 76, though it would be understood. In No. 76 one of the 'cellists would transfer to viola da gamba. The opening choruses may be considered together. They are both to Biblical texts and both on the same plan. 'Die Elenden sollen essen' (Ps. xxii. 27) opens with a scene of deep pathos (the present condition of the miserable), tottering chords and oboe wailings forming the introduction:

and the orchestral basis of intense choral passages. Altos and tenors imitate with a wailing phrase:

The introduction is repeated in a lengthened form, with voices added; 'daß sie satt werden' ('(so) that they satisfied become') is accompanied by the tottering chords, 'satt' is stressed on the weak parts of the bar and the basses roll contentedly on the same word. An interlude leads to 'und die nach dem Herrn fragen, werden ihn preisen' ('and (those) who after the Lord ask, shall Him praise'. The Lutheran version differs from the English bible.) The voices climb, the ascent of prayer; both 'fragen' and 'preisen' are to involved choral writing, the latter joyous, yet with the tottering chords. The introduction rounds off the prelude to the brilliant fugue. The vocal entries begin over continuo and bassoon:

The answer enters at $2\frac{1}{2}$ bars, the remainder of the above tenor line is countersubject; the oboes enter in stretto with part of the subject after the statutory vocal entries. After a two-bar interlude of oboe imitations and a fine leaping continuo, vocal entries are resumed, from bass upwards. The oboes continue independently and, beginning with the tenor entry, the strings join in gradually, doubling the choir. At the close of this section the oboes again play part of the subject in stretto and there is another two-bar interlude in six parts. The closing section, tremendously animated, is built on the subject, though treated freely.

The text of the introduction and fugue of No. 76, Psalm xix. 1, is familiar to all by reason of Haydn's setting in *The Creation*. Two portions are in the same tempo but the division is clearly marked by other means. In the prelude the trumpet leads off:

Ex. 281

Cont. *8ve lower*

Oboes and upper strings answer and combined treatment leads to a bass solo:

Ex. 282

Cont.

and a four-bar interlude founded on the trumpet figure, but excluding that instrument, is followed by the tutti chorus, the theme in the basses, the trumpet figure in the orchestra. The latter continues during the next verbal clause, 'und die Veste verkündiget seiner Hände Werk' ('and the firmament proclaims His handiwork'), a splendidly animated section in which the everlasting endurance of the firmament is depicted by holding notes. A longer interlude, a restatement of the previous choral section, but with different keys, and a ritornello conclude the prelude. Dovetailing with the final chord, a solo tenor announces the fugue subject, verse 3 of the psalm (Ex. 283). The answer enters at five bars, the remainder of the tenor line is countersubject. It is interesting to compare the rhythmical spring of the repeated note with the similar fugue theme in the spurious No. 141. There is all the difference in the world. The succeeding entries are solo bass, solo soprano, solo alto, tutti soprano plus

Ex. 283

oboe I and violin I, tutti alto plus oboe II and violin II, tutti tenor plus viola, tutti bass, trumpet. The complete forces produce a climax of tremendous exhilaration with the first limb of the subject, torrents of semiquavers dashing themselves on the rock of hammered repeated notes. It is as if all nature were dancing in ecstasy.

If Bach had been careful not to shock the Leipzigers with his Probe Stück, he was not afraid of startling them when his position was secure. Some of the passages in the bass recitative, with strings, of No. 75, surprising chromatic changes, two sets of false relations in hard succession, must have made them wonder what manner of man was this who had come among them. The text is 'What avails purple majesty since it passes? What helps the greatest abundance, because all, that we see, disappear must? What avails the gratification of vain senses, for our body must itself from here (go)? Ah! how speedily is it come to pass that riches, voluptuousness, splendour, the spirit to hell turns!'

The sweetness of the following tenor aria (oboe and strings) would make amends; its principal melody has a leisurely sweep:

Ex. 284

and after reaching its zenith it descends by fascinatingly graceful curves:

The first vocal clause—'Mein Jesus soll mein Alles sein!' ('My Jesus shall my all be!')—is set to a fresh melody, but part of the climbing idea comes in the continuo, prefaced by a phrase borrowed from bar 2 of that part. The interlude develops this twin idea, and then the singer applies the original instrumental melody to the words. These few ideas, divided between voice and orchestra, suffice for nearly sixty bars. The middle section of the text—'Mein Purpur ist sein theures Blut, er selbst mein allerhöchstes Gut, und seines Geistes Liebesgluth' ('My purple is His precious blood, He Himself my all-highest good, and His spirit's love-glow')—does not offer much to stimulate. 'Mein allersüß'ster Freudenwein' ('My all-sweetest joy-wine'), however, produces leaping string arpeggi and vocal runs, and fragments of the gracious opening melody are heard in the various sections of the orchestra.

Another lovely tune comes in v, soprano aria (see P. 39), the first oboe d'amore obbligato he wrote. The vocal equivalent is:

The bassi figure is most engaging, and besides the principal tune the soloist has long flourishes, one of them semiquaver triplets, the other demisemiquavers, to 'Freuden' and a soaring one to 'Engel'. The first three words of 'Wer Lazarus' Plagen geduldig ertragen, den nehmen die Engel zu sich' ('Who Lazarus's torments patiently bears, him take the angels to themselves') bear a melody founded on the above, but moving generally downward, contrasting the Christian's sufferings with the heavier ones of Lazarus. The almost stationary vocal line on the first 'geduldig ertragen' is accompanied by the chief oboe d'amore theme, and after it part of the theme is given to the continuo, where it has not been heard before. 'Col. accomp.' is written under the continuo of the score. This may possibly mean, Spitta points out, that the obbligatist is to be allowed liberty in the ritornelli, a principle of universal application. The alto is provided with an aria of contentment (x) with violins in unison. The economy is remarkable. The ritornello is constructed out of two ideas:

and

which, it will be seen, flower from a single bud. (*a*) is now freely inverted, a shortened form of (*b*) brings us to a repetition of the second form of (*a*). The continuo, too, partakes in these ideas, three and four notes of (*a*), the bud of (*b*), and charming octave leaps ♪ ♩ . 'Jesus macht mich geistlich reich' ('Jesus makes me spiritually rich') is sung to (*a*), continuo and obbligato imitate; the vocal melody is repeated while the bassi concern themselves with (*b*). 'Kann ich seinen Geist empfangen, will ich weiter nichts verlangen, denn mein Leben wächst zugleich' ('Can I His spirit receive, will I further nothing long for, for my life grows at the same time') brings a new vocal melody, during which the violins play (*b*) and the bassi hint at (*a*). An interlude introduces (*a*) in imitation, (*b*) follows in the violins. The first clause is repeated to the inverted form of (*a*), but with a delightful upward leap of a seventh to 'geistlich', (*b*) is in the obbligato, (*a*) in the continuo. 'Kann ich' produces a fresh melody, 'will ich' recalls its previous one, 'denn mein Leben' reverts to (*a*), (*b*) and fragments of (*a*) are heard in the continuo, (*b*) in the violins. In a short interlude the inverted (*a*) fits against (*b*) in the continuo. The 'denn mein Leben' clause comes first to (*a*), incorporating the bud at the end, and then to the inverted form, while the octave leaps and one reference to (*b*) support, and the violins introduce a new form of (*b*). The introduction is repeated. Even that does not satisfy the delight of the composer in his themes. Eight bars of the beginning of the vocal section come again, with 'reich' prolonged, during which the bassi contentedly play their octaves and the obbligato expands (*b*). Against (*b*) in the continuo, the singer begins the most highly placed version of the inverted (*a*), commencing on top E, and introduces a tiny decoration of 'geistlich'. Then we must needs listen for the third time to the introduction.

Another recitative with strings and four short recitatives with continuo help to make an admirably balanced scheme, the latter being well chosen and well planned and placed by the librettist in order to secure variety. The four are models of beauty. iv, tenor—'God casts down and exalts in time and eternity!'—there are breaks after the verbs. 'Who in the world heaven seeks, is there accursed.' 'Heaven' is melismatic, 'accursed' is flung downwards. 'Who but here hell endures will be there rejoiced.' vi, soprano—'Meanwhile gives God a good conscience, by which a Christian can a little possession with great delight enjoy.' After 'Ja' ('yea') is thrust out separately, there is a rather curious speeding upwards to 'leads He also through long suffering' and the voice falls—'to death'. The number concludes: 'so is it yet at the end well-done.' xi, bass—at first without incident, 'Who only in Jesus remains, the self-denial practises that he in God's love himself believingly exercises', then a rise and a quick fall to 'has, when the earthly disappears', and impressive breaks, 'himself—and God—found'. Short as the recitative is, only seven bars, it modulates from D through B minor, E minor, and A minor to the confident C major at the clenching of the argument. xiii, tenor, begins on a diminished seventh, 'Oh poverty, that no riches equals! when out of the heart the whole world disappears'; the latter group drops from high A–F♯, D♯, B, G. 'And Jesus only alone reigns' is broken into fragments (see Ex. 1303). 'So is a Christian to God led!' ascends stepwise. Confidence gives place to dread in the last clause, again broken twice—'Grant, God, that we it do not lose (by folly)' curves down to low D, and an ominous diminished third is heard in the bassi. In spite of the splendidly confident Sinfonia, viii, affirming that all that God does is good, ix, alto recitative with strings, bewails human frailty—'Only one thing ails a Christian mind; when it of its spirit's poverty thinks. It believes indeed God's goodness, which all things anew creates'—here the singer gains courage and ascends to the highest point of the compass, but sinks again with 'yet lacks to it the strength'. This weakness of spirit is only temporary, the close looks cheerfully towards the aria of hope which follows: 'to the heavenly life the growth and the fruit to give.'

It is the least distinguished of the recitatives; Bach's librettist failed him here.

No. 76 is equally rich in varied solo material. ii, tenor with strings, is neatly constructed and contrasted. With plain chords the voice declaims in recitative: 'So lets Himself God not be untestified! Nature and mercy address all mankind.' Then we have a picture in miniature of the creation, 'andante ed arioso', 'this all, all has yea God done, that themselves the heavens stir, and spirit and body themselves move'. The flowings and crossings of the violins are the stirring of the face of the waters, the dovetailing ♪♫♫ of bassi and violas speaks of the moving of the depths below, the voice waves to 'regen' ('stir') and to 'bewegen' ('move'). Then in plain recitative, 'God Himself has Himself to you inclined, and cries through messengers without number', and in declamation, with commanding chords: 'up, up, up! come to My lovefeast!'

A soprano voice, in an aria with violin solo, iii, calls upon all men to obey the summons: 'Hört, ihr Völker, Gottes Stimme, eilt zu seinem Gnadenthron!' ('Hear, ye people, God's voice, hasten to His mercy-throne!'). The musical conception is simple, almost as if instead of 'people' the text has said 'children'. Violin and continuo mostly play antiphonally, a little figure is tossed from part to part:

Ex. 289

and other themes are akin to it:

Ex. 290

'Eilt zu seinem Gnadenthron' is, of course, stepwise, and both instrumental lines have scales to the dotted-note time-pattern. The continuo moves in plain quavers when the next words begin: 'Aller Dinge Grund und Ende ist sein eingebor'ner Sohn' ('Of all things (the) foundation and end is His only begotten Son'), but the new material is not allowed to remain and soon the old takes possession of the field. The stepwise idea is useful for 'wende': 'daß sich Alles zu ihm wende' ('(so) that itself all to Him turns').

From this engaging picture we must look away, to the disturbing power of evil. In the bass recitativo secco, iv, which prefaces the fierce trumpet aria, the continuo awesomely drops E, B, F♮: 'Who but hears, when themselves the greatest crowds to other gods turn?' (See Ex. 1272.) After 'The oldest idol of selfish desire reigns over mankind's breast. The wise give birth to folly, and Belial sits firm in God's house', comes brief and free canonical symbolic writing to 'because also the Christians themselves from Christ run'.

The alto recitativo secco preparatory to the first chorale speaks again of the summons: 'Thou hast us, Lord, from all ways to Thee called, as we in darkness of the heathen sat, and, as the light the air enlivens and quickens, (Thou hast) us also enlightened and animated, yea, with Thee Thyself (hast given) to eat and drink, with Thy Spirit endowed, which continually in our mind floats.' The arioso, 'Therefore be to Thee this prayer most submissively made', is accompanied by repeated quavers, a leit-motiv frequently employed when prayer is mentioned. The connexion between this arioso and the extended chorale has already been mentioned.

Having introduced the viola da gamba into the Sinfonia, viii, he employs it in the next four numbers. A bass recitative with strings indicates that the gamba is to join the continuo. This suggests that the gambist was the chief 'cellist and that solo strings only accompanied. Bach seemed to lay great stress on clear outlines, on what in modern parlance would be called 'elocutionary delivery'; the important point in recitatives was to get the meaning through distinctly to the congregation, as a well-speaking cleric would do. He did not study rhetoric at school in vain. The opening of ix is not important, yet how much care is spent over it and how effective the breaks!: 'God bless still the faithful host,—so that it His honour— through belief,—love,—holiness,—show and increase.' 'It is the heaven on the earth', rises and then falls, 'and must through continual strife' rises boldly, 'with hate—and with danger' brings a diminished third in the continuo on the last word, 'in this world—purified be'. (See Ex. 1288.) 'Haß' ('hate') occupies the central point of the antepenultimate bar, and forms the basis of the tenor aria, more than the basis, indeed, for it almost becomes the whole structure. 'Hasse nur, hasse mich recht, feindlich's Geschlecht!' ('Hate only, hate me well, hostile race!') positively revels in being detested by the opposite side, and 'Hasse' is heard seventeen times in twenty-two vocal bars, sometimes on runs, often thrust on the weaker parts of the bar, a stronger stress being obtained thereby. *Viola da gamba e continuo*, the only accompaniment, contribute their quota to the orgy, two related figures from which the whole of the line is created:

Ex. 291

and

Ex. 292

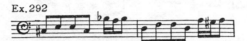

Needless to say, all quavers and crotchets should be played staccato. Even during the middle section—'Christum gläubig zu umfassen, will ich alle Freude lassen' ('Christ believingly to embrace, will I all joy abandon')—with its extravagant runs on 'umfassen' and more reasonable ones on 'Freude', the enemy raging without is indicated by the persistence of the continuo 'Hasse' themes.

The same combination supports the alto in a recitative and arioso, in which we turn to more pleasant thoughts: 'I feel already in (my) spirit, how Christ to me the love-sweetness grants', and in the arioso the bassi depict the falling of celestial food while the voice moves gracefully: 'and me with manna feeds; in order that among us here brotherly faithfulness may be continually strengthened and renewed.' In the alto aria, xii (see O.C.S. 'Come, ye faithful'), Bach reverted to the combination of the Sinfonia and wrote music of the charm one would expect from such a colour-scheme, a grateful contrast to the 'Hasse' aria. In doing so he rose above his text, which is deadly dull: 'Liebt, ihr Christen, in der That, Jesus stirbet für die Brüder, und sie sterben für sich wieder, weil er sie verbunden hat' ('Love, ye Christians, in the reality, Jesus dies for the brethren, and they die for each-other again, because He them united has'). (The Epistle, 1 John iii. 13–18, speaks of Christian brotherly love.) It may be that the general intention is to indicate a blissfully loving state of mind. Gamba and oboe d'amore begin with a tender duet:

Ex. 293

Although the continuo utilizes and expands some of the ideas, it never partakes in the inversions or development of either (a) or (b) and remains modestly a less important partner. The voice, except in the penultimate bar, remains entirely independent of (a) and (b). Its own theme:

Ex. 294

occurs four times, once slightly modified. One attractive phrase is:

Ex. 295

with a curling derivative of notes 1–4 in the obbligati; it will be noticed that part of the continuo figure is derived from notes 4–6 of (b). A short tenor recitative and arioso with continuo (the gamba is not mentioned) connects the aria with the final chorale—'So shall Christendom the love of God praise and it in itself prove; till in eternity the heavens to pious souls'—followed by a canon at the distance of a crotchet—'God and His praise tell', God and His praise separate entities yet united.

Terry thinks that both libretti were written by Christian Weiss, Senr., pastor of St. Thomas's from 1714 to 1734. It is evident that relations with Bach became intimate, his daughter was godmother to one of Bach's sons, a son sponsor to a daughter, and the choice of names from the Weiss family for other daughters of Bach strengthens the supposition of a close domestic connexion. The pastor may have offered the new Cantor his poems to inaugurate his period of service, and so have begun one of the few friendships to cheer the composer through his long years of non-appreciation and bitter conflicts. Christian Weiss, Jnr., also one of the pastors, followed in his father's footsteps as librettist for Bach. No. 75, abridged and altered, beginning with the first recitative, was subsequently known as 'Was hilft des Purpurs Majestät'. Part II of No. 76 was afterwards used for a Reformation Festival: 'Gott segne noch die treue Schaar.' The choruses must have been beyond the capabilities of the singers.

One wonders what the choristers thought when they were confronted with the opening numbers of these two cantatas. Kuhnau's choral writing was simplicity itself; this would plunge them into a new and bewildering world with unheard-of difficulties, baffling counterpoint and disturbing harmonies. One wonders, too, what the Leipzigers thought of these two magnificent cantatas on Bach's opening Sundays, the first of a long and unbroken line which was destined to make their church the most musically famous in Europe, the hallowed shrine of pilgrimage for many generations, and the present centre of the cult of their most famous citizen. We have no record, but it is significant that the plan of the cantatas was not followed often during the succeeding years. Did his newly fired enthusiasm receive a sudden damping through cold indifference on the part of his congregation or even rebukes from the proud merchants who ruled the destinies of his church? One can imagine the rueful shaking of heads and the adverse comments of the worshippers as they strolled through the narrow streets and under the lindens on the banks of the Pleisse after service. 'If only we had secured Graupner or Telemann we wouldn't have had to listen to such harsh, involved, inharmonious Hauptmusik! So terribly long too! Kuhnau's was always short and tuneful. But this man's! Whatever have we let ourselves in for?' The history of the musical profession is strewn with the wrecks of ardent men shattered, bruised, and crushed by the misunderstanding and pigheaded opposition of ignoramuses in authority, who ought to have been only too grateful for the opportunity to sit at the feet of their temporal servant and learn something about his art. That is the way of the world.

LEIPZIG 1723-1734
Reconstructed Weimar Cantatas
4, 12, (21), (31), (70), 80, (147), (158), 164, 168, 186, (189)

Those with brackets have already been dealt with.

Order of discussion: 164, 186, 4, 12, 168, 80

THE reconstructed cantatas which can be dated definitely during the period of his third appointment as organist have already been considered under the section dealing with Weimar. There are six others concerning which we have no particulars, relating to Weimar, but which were no doubt written there and afterwards produced during the first seven years at Leipzig.

164. 'Ihr, die ihr euch von Christo nennet' was given on the Thirteenth Sunday after Trinity in 1723 or 1724, but was perhaps composed in 1715, as Franck's libretto was published in that year. The Gospel, St. Luke x. 23-37, includes the parable of the Good Samaritan; the text is a sermon on the virtue of pity for one's neighbour's sufferings, and incidents from the parable are referred to. It is a solo cantata, all four voices being employed, with a chorale to conclude. The opening tenor aria complains of the want of mercy among professing Christians and of the hardness of heart of those who passed on the other side of the road. 'Ihr, die ihr euch von Christo nennet, wo bleibet die Barmherzigkeit, daran man Christi Glieder kennet? Sie ist von euch, ach, allzu weit. Die Herzen sollten liebreich sein, so sind sie härter als ein Stein' ('You, who you yourselves after Christ call, where abides pity, whereby one Christ's members knows? It is from you, ah, all too distant. The hearts should rich in love be, but are they harder than a stone'). It is not a subject suitable for musical treatment, so Bach conceives it as a pastorale, picturing the country highway along which the wayfarers travelled. A swinging $\frac{9}{8}$ movement is kept up throughout, but the main theme is in dotted crotchets—m l_1 se$_1$ l_1—and is subjected to much canonical device, the stream of the passers-by. The question 'Wo bleibet die Barmherzigkeit' is contrasted with 'härter als ein Stein' by pitting soft chromatic harmonies against passages of a stubborn character, and 'Stein' is four times elongated. There is a lengthy run on 'kennet', of which one fails to see the meaning.

The bass recitativo secco contains a paraphrase of the fifth Beatitude (St. Matt. v. 7): 'Blessed are the merciful' ('They who with mercy the neighbour here embrace, they shall before the judgement seat mercy obtain'), set in arioso. It is preceded by 'We hear verily what itself love says;' and is succeeded by 'Yet' with a sharp false relation, to differentiate between Christ's attitude to the wayfarer and ours, 'We heed such not, we hear still the neighbour's sighs!' and another false relation adds a touch of poignancy. In 'He knocks at our heart; yet is it not opened!' the first idea is possibly an unconscious remembrance of the 'knock' in the wonderful bass recitative of No. 61. 'We see indeed his hand-wringing'; 'Händeringen' is melismatic. The voice falls low with 'his eye, that with tears flows'; and there is a forceful protest with 'yet lets the heart itself not to love be constrained'. The proud measured steps of the two unfeeling travellers is shown by a slow ascent of the continuo during 'The priest and Levite, who here to the side step, are indeed a picture of loveless Christians, they act as if they nothing of others' misery knew; they pour neither oil nor wine into neighbours' wounds'. 'Wein' is thrown to the top of the compass, as if the neglected traveller were crying out in his agony.

This leads to an alto aria which speaks of the love and pity of Good Samaritans: 'Nur durch Lieb' und durch Erbarmen werden wir Gott selber gleich. Samaritergleiche Herzen lassen fremden Schmerz sich schmerzen und sind an Erbarmung reich' ('Only through love and through pity become we (to) God Himself like. Samaritan-like hearts allow others' pains themselves to pain and are in pity rich'). Two flutes provide an obbligato of melting beauty:

Ex. 296
Fl. tr. I.

Cont.
8ve lower

and the two-note tear-motive permeates all parts, in one case descending step by step in the vocal line for the distance of a whole octave. The bassi generally play it in ascending versions. The singer begins with the above phrase ornamented by a slide. 'Samaritergleiche' introduce a new form of the motive:

Ex. 297
Sa - ma - ri - (-tergleiche)

which is copied by the flutes. A prayer that the cold heart may be melted into compassion is set as a recitative for tenor, with many chromatic harmonies for strings: 'Ah, melt then through Thy love-beam the cold heart's steel! that I true Christian love, my Saviour, (may) daily exercise, that my neighbour's woe, be he who he may, friend or foe, heathen or Christian, to me as mine own suffering to my heart always (may) go! (May) my heart be rich in love, gentle and mild, so will in me be transfigured Thine image.'

A device met with in another Weimar cantata, No. 152, is found in the S.B. duet which follows. *Gli stromenti all' unisono* (The instruments in unison) is indicated—in this case two flutes, two oboes, and violins. Violas are *tacet*, no doubt on account of the pitch. The oboes make their first appearance here and also play in the final chorale. The construction is most ingenious. The text contains three clauses: (*a*) Händen, die sich nicht verschließen, wird der Himmel aufgethan' ('To the hands, which themselves do not close up, is the heaven opened'), (*b*) 'Augen, die mitleidend fließen, sieht der Heiland gnädig an' ('(on the) eyes, which compassionately flow, looks the Saviour mercifully'), (*c*) 'Herzen, die nach Liebe streben, will Gott selbst sein Herze geben' ('To the hearts, which after love strive, will God Himself His heart give'). Each of these has its characteristic theme. (*a*) shows a strange piece of imagery. The two instrumental lines open with an inverse canon, the two hands separating, moving away from each other, the converse of the action described by the text:

Ex. 298

Then the voices take up the theme:

Ex. 299

The bass enters in canon at the octave in bar 2. Though the remainder of the section, in which the unisono joins, is not in strict canon, there are many imitations by inversion. The theme instrumentally stated, in B♭, leads to (b), in which a tender melody above gently rocking bassi quavers is announced by the bass and imitated by the soprano:

Ex. 300

While the voices proceed, the upper instruments play the 'Händen' theme and the continuo follows with it inverted. The remainder of the section is free, the unisono ceasing and leaving the voices alone with the continuo, which introduces a fragmentary and varied form of (a):

Ex. 301

An interlude brings a new form in the unisono and a variant of the variant in the bassi. (c) calls for a stronger theme:

Ex. 302

the syncopations illustrative of striving. The time-pattern of bar 2 of (a) reappears, the bassi thrice let us hear (a) inverted. The voices now develop a joyous section with the remainder of the text, partially canonical, partly freely imitative, with vigorous leaps of a sixth and an octave to the word 'Gott'. (The *BGS* score omits seven prolongation dots which ought to come after bar-lines.) (The unisono enters with a free inversion of (a) and later the bassi follow suit. An interlude is formed from it and then the complete text is repeated, but the 'Händen' and 'wird der Himmel' themes only are employed, the former ten times, once inverted and sometimes fragmentarily. It is a splendid number, unhampered by its curious imagery.

Flutes are not mentioned in the score of the final chorale, but would doubtless play from the oboe or violin copies. Stanza 5 of E. Cruciger's Christmas 'Herr Christ, der einig' Gott's Sohn' ('Lord Christ, Thou only Son of God') is sung to its original melody. (For a translation, see No. 22, p. 177.) The strings double the voices, the two oboes join the top line. It would be interesting to know why sometimes oboes divide in four-part chorales and sometimes concentrate on the highest part. There seems to be no reason why one method should be found at one time and the other at another. The second oboe part of the cantata provides a delightful peep into the home-life of the Bach household. Anna Magdalena prepared it, writing in directions, clefs, key and time signatures, *volti* and *fine*, and the thirteen-year old Wilhelm Friedemann laboriously copied in the notes.

186. The libretto of 'Ärg're dich, o Seele, nicht' is somewhat of a mixture. As we know it now it is for the Seventh Sunday after Trinity, and as the Gospel, St. Mark viii. 1–9, is the narrative of the miracle of the loaves and fishes, there are references in the two recitatives to hunger and want, in the tenor aria to deeds of mercy, and in the soprano aria to rescue of the faithful from poverty by the Saviour. The text of the opening chorus has nothing to do with these; it has bearing on the doubts expressed by John the Baptist, when in prison, concerning the divinity of Christ, as narrated in the Gospel for the Third Sunday in Advent, St. Matthew xi. 3–10. The discrepancies may be explained by the supposition that Franck's libretto, which Bach set in 1716, was written for the latter occasion, and that when the cantata was adapted for 11 July 1723, alterations were made, possibly by the composer. Franck's libretti never contained recitatives. The autograph score is so clean and neat that it suggests a rewriting of an earlier work. As the first form has not come to light we cannot tell how much apart from the recitatives is old and how much new. One must conclude that the original cantata was much shorter than the present version, as large-scale works divided into two parts did not appear before Leipzig.

In the orchestral introduction of the opening chorus the upper strings, doubled by two oboes and taille (the latter must have been a Leipzig addition), propose two themes, one never heard in this form vocally, one, in imitation at a bar's distance:

the other a canon at the distance of a crotchet:

which, in an altered form, becomes the second choral theme to the opening words:

During the fifth and sixth bars the two top lines and the bassi are marked piano, while the violas and taille play the opening idea, evidently continuing forte so as to make it stand out. Both of the themes are used contrapuntally during the later tutti sections. The bassi do not participate in these throughout the whole number, but develop the rising quaver arpeggi. A bassoon reinforces, but is silent when the voices sing with continuo only, and is only independent once. The chorus enters with a remarkable passage indicative of doubt, the voices beginning with sustained tones, entering from top to bottom with a striking series of notes—D, E♭, F♯, B♭, the second, third, and fourth as strangely unexpected dissonances. Below, the bassi move in the rising arpeggi. A more arresting choral passage cannot be conceived; even after repeated hearings the chain of dissonances, each entry almost seeming wrong, holds one in breathless suspense. The upper instruments re-enter with the same progression, which occurs once again later, in a modified form, but with choir and continuo only. The voices now enter severally with the second instrumental theme, the text being articulated more rapidly and the first instrumental subject used as counterpoint. The other is also heard in

a freely inverted form. The second clause of the text, 'daß das aller-
höchste Licht, Gottes Glanz und Ebenbild, sich in Knechtsgestalt
verhüllt' ('that the all-highest light, God's splendour and image,
itself in servant-form veils'), is sung twice, in both cases supported
by the continuo arpeggi. The phrases are powerful, the sopranos preceding the lower voices. 'Verhüllt' climbs in the sopranos to a ♫
time-pattern, but, curiously enough, this attractive feature is omitted
when the passage is repeated. One instrumental idea in the violin lines
of the latter part of the number is widely leaping quaver arpeggi, a
development of the continuo motive. This extremely fine chorus
demands the utmost freedom of tempo and the second theme must
needs be treated almost as recitative.

The next three numbers are with continuo only. The flatness of the
text of the bass recitative does not permit of much musical interest
until at the end, in a short arioso, the voice sings sinking phrases as
the soloist asks—'Ah, Lord, how long wilt Thou me forget?'—with
the often-used prayer-motive in the bassi. The lengthy recitative portion is: 'Servitude, distress, want affect Christ's members not alone,
will your head Himself poor and miserable be. And is not riches, is
not abundance Satan's mantrap, that one with care avoid must?
Becomes to thee on the contrary the load too much to bear, if
poverty thee encumbers, if hunger thee consumes, and (thou) wilt
forthwith lose courage, if thinkest thou not on Jesus, on thy salvation.
Hast thou, like that people, not soon to eat, so sighest thou.' It is
not to be wondered that in spite of Bach's chromaticisms the number
falls far below the high level of the chorus.

Doubt is again expressed in the succeeding bass aria in which the
text is a development of that of the arioso: (1) 'Bist du, der mir
helfen soll, eilst du nicht mir beizustehen?' ('Art Thou He Who me
help shall, hurriest Thou not me to stand by?'). The swinging $\frac{9}{8}$
continuo theme (written as $\frac{3}{4}$) expresses the desire for the hastening
of the Saviour:

Ex. 306

It acts as a connecting-link between the vocal sections. (2) 'Mein
Gemüth ist zweifelsvoll, du verwirfst vielleicht mein Flehen' ('My
mind is full of doubt, Thou rejectest perhaps my supplication').

'Zweifelsvoll' is allotted a tortuous run, and in twelve bars the singer has to negotiate three diminished and two augmented fourths, a diminished fifth, and a minor ninth. (2) 'Doch, O Seele, zweifle nicht, laß Vernunft dich nicht bestricken' ('Yet, Oh soul, doubt not, let reason thee not ensnare'). The continuo mounts and leaps and confidently asserts its first melody, the singer depicts doubt, once by a diminished third; 'bestricken' has another tortuous passage including three diminished fourths and the same number of minor sevenths. Bach never spares his vocalists. (4) 'Deinen Helfer, Jacobs Licht, kannst du in der Schrift erblicken' ('Thy helper, Jacob's light, canst thou in the scriptures behold'). The voice now moves wholly diatonically and 'erblicken' is elongated in a fine rolling passage. The continuo remodels phrases found in (3) and introduces its initial theme. With consummate skill Bach passes through these varied emotional phases by transformation of a bare minimum of musical ideas.

The tenor recitative is more interesting than the bass because the text is better, opportunities for sharply rising and falling passages occur: 'Ah, that a Christian so much for his body cares! What is it besides? A building of earth, which again must earth become, a garment, so merely borrowed. He could indeed the best part choose so (that) his hope never deceives; the salvation of souls, thus in Jesus lies.' There is an ecstatic melisma on 'Oh blessed'; the text of the previous aria is referred to in 'Who Him in the scripture perceives how He through His teaching to all, who Him hear, a spiritual manna sends!' In the 'arioso. andante' the continuo repeats:

Ex. 307

ten times, falling a step on each occasion and introducing diminished thirds, while the voice sings 'Therefore, if grief even the heart gnaws and devours' to an ornate line. The bassi continue in quavers but completely changed in mood while the soloist advises 'So taste and see then how friendly Jesus is' with a soaring passage to 'freundlich' ('friendly') and hints of the joy-motive below.

The first oboe da caccia obbligato in the cantatas (endorsing the theory of a recast of the work at Leipzig) is found in the tenor aria. The ritornello contains two contrasting motives, neither of which is

heard in full in the vocal line. The first is a dual idea which is of no
special significance:

Ex. 308

because the text is void of suggestive ideas: 'Mein Heiland läßt sich
merken in seinen Gnadenwerken' ('My Saviour lets Himself be seen
in His mercy-works'). The two themes are subjected to ingenious
inversions, and the ascending quavers are heard in the voice part.
The second is florid, based on the time-pattern  and makes
considerable demands on the technique of the obbligatist. It is the
vivifying influence of the Saviour. The text states crudely: 'Da er
sich kräftig weist, den schwachen Geist zu lehren, den matten Leib
zu nähren, dies sättigt Leib und Geist' ('As He Himself powerful
shows, the weak spirit to teach, the tired body to nourish, this satisfies
body and spirit'). The first clause is set to firm repeated notes; 'Leib'
is given a meaningless upward rush at the close. It is clear that Bach
found himself in difficulties with such unsatisfactory verse.

A fine extended chorale—stanza 12 of P. Speratus's 'Es ist das
Heil uns kommen her' ('Salvation comes to us') with its anonymous melody—closes Part I (B.E.C., No. 17, O.), speaking of the
comfort that can be brought by God. The oboes play a distinctive
phrase in thirds and sixths:

Ex. 309

which is answered by a streaming down from heaven of gracious
mercy, violins also in thirds and sixths:

Ex. 310
VI. I. II.

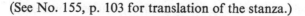

(See No. 155, p. 103 for translation of the stanza.)

Part II opens with another bass recitative, this time accompanied by strings, a picture of the world as a desert and the starving people being nourished by Christ's word. The text is as arid as the waste of sand itself: 'The world is the great wilderness; heaven becomes as brass, the earth becomes as iron, when Christians through faith show that Christ's word their greatest riches is; nourishment-blessing seems from them almost to fly, a constant want is bewailed, wherewith they only from the world themselves the more retire; then finds first the Saviour's word, the highest treasure, in their hearts' place; yea, laments (He) Him about the people there, so must also here His heart break.' Bach seeks relief from these deadening lines in an arioso— 'and over them blessing speak'—with gracious semiquaver groups in the upper strings, pulsating quavers in the continuo and convolutions on 'Segen'. It is a relief to pass to the soprano aria—'Die Armen will der Herr umarmen' ('The poor will the Lord embrace')—where for the third time in the cantata the instrumental introduction presents two contrasting themes. The violins in unison begin with a chromatically descending melody:

Ex. 311

the pangs of the needy, and in antithesis is heard a series of upward and downward semiquavers, also chromatic, bowed in twos, the compassion of the Almighty, at the end rising to a passionate climax. In order to emphasize the difference between the present and the future state of the poor, Bach makes a break between the first three words and the last three when the voice enters. This phrase is independent of the orchestral ideas. The violins are silent, the continuo accompanies with a variant of its arpeggi. After the violins have restated their second theme, the voice re-enters with a modification of its first melody against the principal violin theme and yet another form of that of the bassi. It continues—'mit Gnaden hier und dort' ('with mercy here and there')—with continuo. The remainder of the text—'er schenket ihnen aus Erbarmen den höchsten Schatz, das Lebenswort' ('He gives them out of pity the highest treasure, the life-word')—is accompanied both times at first by the arpeggi, differently stated in each case, and during a florid 'Erbarmen' the violins play their second idea, a solacing flood of divine pity welling up and down.

The text of the alto recitativo secco is, mercifully, vastly better than the others, and Bach seizes the opportunity of frequent use of the step-motive. 'Now may the world with its pleasures pass away, breaks immediately the want in, still can the soul joyful be' passes from a pedal C, the continuance of the world, to a phrase of contentment. 'Becomes through this lamentation-vale the way too heavy, too long', brings a painful climbing, and mournful 'too long'. In the middle of 'In Jesus' word lies salvation and blessing' an adagio arioso begins. The continuo slowly moves down to low B♭, the fate of the people that walk in darkness, and the contrasting state of believers is shown simultaneously by a stepwise movement upwards: 'It is their feet's lantern and a light on their ways.' (See Ps. cxix. 105.) A vigorous recitative follows: 'Who believingly through the desert journeys, will through this word be given drink, and food; the Saviour opens Himself, according to this word'—the steps come again with 'to him one day Paradise's portals'. After 'and after the accomplished course' it breaks again into arioso: 'sets He on the believing the crown.'

The concluding number of this unequal cantata is a splendid S.A. duet, no doubt a Weimar product, though certainly remodelled, as the presence of the taille indicates. The two oboes and taille are never independent of the strings, but they are frequently silent, only reinforcing from time to time. 'Laß, Seele, kein Leiden von Jesu dich scheiden, sei, Seele getreu!' ('Let, soul, no sorrow from Jesus thee separate, be, soul, faithful!') is set to the swinging tune of the long introduction:

Ex. 312

(C minor, with 2 flats)

The vocal version of this is in sixths, the bassi are silent and unison upper strings leap joyfully over widespread arpeggi. There is much blissful singing in thirds and sixths, then as a relief from parallel motion the voices pursue a derivative in imitation, with continuo only, and while the soprano repeats the idea the alto personifies steadfastness by a sustained note. 'Dir bleibet die Krone aus Gnaden zu Lohne' ('For thee abides the crown through mercy as reward') after an initial entry in thirds with an idea formed from the first by inversion, gives rise to trilling and florid exuberant phrases. 'Wenn du von Banden des Leibes nun frei' ('When thou from the bonds of the body now (art) free') calls forth many joyous leaps in both instruments and voices. Upward and downward forms of the motive are used simultaneously and then the words are sung in canon while the continuo uses a form of it in sequence. At one place the soprano sings the first clause of the latter part of the text while the alto sings the second, an unusual procedure for a passage which is not fugal. There are more than 200 bars of this engaging duet, and one would not have it shortened by a single beat. The score ends here, but probably the extended chorale would be repeated with a different stanza.

4. The first hymn-cantata Bach wrote was 'Christ lag in Todesbanden' ('Christ lay in death's dark prison' N., 'Christ lay fast bound in death's harsh chain' B.) to Luther's seven-stanza poem. The earlier manner of portions of it suggests a pre-Leipzig date, possibly Weimar, and it is the only cantata in the manner of Buxtehude, Pachelbel, and Kuhnau. It was produced in its present form at Leipzig on Easter Day, 9 April 1724. The chorale melody proper to the hymn and sung at the service appears in full, plain, or varied, in all the vocal numbers, and the opening downward semitone is the foundation of the short sinfonia which opens. It is a reconstruction of an old tune and was published by Johann Walther in 1524. The diversified treatment of the canto, the plasticity given to it in the various numbers, the rich resource of treatment, and the variety obtained in spite of the facts that all eight numbers are in the same key, E minor, that the first two lines of the tune are repeated, that all eight cadential notes are either tonic or dominant, constitute one of the miracles of Bach's genius. One has only to compare it with Kuhnau's cantata to the same text to see the tremendous advance made in the art of composition in a short time. The cantata is a succession of beauties, with many strikingly dramatic features, and presents a unity rarely attained in the series, even though we see in it traces of Böhm, Pachelbel, and Buxtehude.

The opening two lines speak of Christ in the tomb: 'Christ lag in Todesbanden, für unser Sünd' gegeben' ('Christ lay in death's bonds, for our sins delivered'). The sinfonia, only fourteen bars in length,

scored for two lines of violins, two of violas and continuo, paints the
gloom of the sepulchre. The falling semitone occurs in the first six
bars of violin I and in the two opening bars of the continuo:

Ex. 313

Schering aptly terms it 'The emblem of death' and points out its
association with 'den Tod' ('death') in verse 2. During bars 5–7,
line 1 is quoted in violin I and at the tenth and eleventh bars the
violins climb slowly, the ascent from the tomb. Spitta thinks the sinfonia to be a very early and independent piece, but the thematic connexion with the chorale and its appositeness as an introduction to
stanza I negative this supposition. The first chorus is a magnificent
chorale fantasia, with the melody in the sopranos, doubled by cornetto, the other voices doubled by three trombones, the violins
generally independent and the violas usually strengthening the middle
voices. By a poetic licence the message of the close of the sinfonia is
forgotten, and gloom again prevails. The lower voices and strings,
in succession, enter with the falling idea, the second line is accompanied by descending semitones, the sins which have committed
Christ to the grave, but the violins, in antiphonal groups—
—speak of the pulsating of life which leads to freedom from the tomb
and redemption for mankind. The third and fourth lines—'Er ist
wieder erstanden und hat uns bracht das Leben' ('He is again arisen
and has to us brought life')—are each prefaced by vigorous passages
founded on the first (third) line, 'Leben' being set to runs based on
the joy-rhythm, and the violins becoming more and more animated.
Lines 5, 6, and 7—'deß wir sollen fröhlich sein, Gott lobet und ihm
dankbar sein, und singen Hallelujah' ('therefore we shall joyful be,
God praise and to Him thankful be, and sing Hallelujah')—are all
heralded by the lower voices in a free Pachelbel manner, line 6, for
instance, utilizing a counter-subject as well as the material of the tune,
and line 7 broken groups of quavers to 'Hallelujah'. Gloom has now
completely given place to rejoicing, 'fröhlich' is set to tumbling semiquavers. The last line, a scale-wise descent of a fifth to 'Hallelujah',
is extended to twenty-seven bars of 'alla breve'. The sopranos had
already in line 7 reduced their minims to crotchets and in the last

two bars had departed from the strict Pachelbel manner by partaking in the broken Hallelujahs. In the 'alla breve', after delivering the final line in the syncopated version which runs through that section, they join in the general rejoicing, at one point repeating the figure six times in succession. The broken Hallelujah quavers which are found in a section of line 7 and rising groups of four quavers, to the same word, complete the musical material. Six bars before the end comes a dominant pedal in the continuo, and as the voices utter wild cries of joy, the two violins alternately play a dropping octave— ⌐ ♪ ♪ — the tumultuous ringing of bells, and the second violas busily ring bells of their own. The 'alla breve' almost oversteps the bounds of church decorum in its breathless, whirling, excited exhilaration.

Luther's poem is singularly rich in suggestions for musical treatment and in dramatic indications; consequently this is the most uniformly successful of all the pure hymn-cantatas. Verse 2 opens: 'Den Tod Niemand zwingen kunnt bei allen Menschenkindern' ('The Death no-one force could among all men's-children'). The idea of a continued effort to force, to compel, is illustrated by giving the sopranos the first two words twice over as crotchets to the descending semitone, and by answering each group a third lower with the altos, creating a sense of dogged persistence. The voices are doubled by cornetto and trombone I, and the line of continuo, the only accompaniment, is almost solely constructed out of the falling second, but moving in quavers:

Ex. 314

the long-continued repetition of the figure adding to the feeling of relentless perseverance. The sopranos sing right through the tune in varied form—'That makes everything our sin, No innocence was to be found. Therefrom came death so quickly, and took over us power, Held us in his kingdom imprisoned'—the altos imitate, and the closing Hallelujah is extended.

The opening of verse 3 speaks of the coming of Christ—'Jesus Christ, God's Son, In our stead has come'—the freeing from sin— 'And has the sin taken away'—the dissipation of the might of the

grave—'In order from death to take All his claim and his power'.
During these lines the tenors sing the tune in plain style (see P. 11),
on a crotchet basis, while violins in unison play a brilliant counterpoint of semiquavers, the figuration being derived from the falling
semitone:

Ex. 315

Line 6 reads: 'Da bleibet nichts denn Tod'sgestalt' ('There remains
nothing but death's shape'). Immediately before it is sung the violins
play crashing chords in double, triple, and quadruple stopping, while
the bassi, the only other accompaniment, which have previously
moved in crotchets and quavers only, tumble down in semiquavers
for the space of an octave and a half, a Miltonic thrusting below of
the rebellious angel. The voice enters with 'denn Tod's' unaccompanied, adagio, and violins and continuo employ new material. The
original manner is now resumed for the remainder of the verse—
'The sting has he lost'—the tenor Hallelujah line being decorated
and the bassi joining in the rapid runs.

Verse 4 is treated as a motet-like chorale fantasia, free Pachelbel
in form save for the last two lines, the canto in the alto and continuo
the only accompaniment. The texture is lively and brilliant. Lines 1 and
2 of the verse—'Es war ein wunderlicher Krieg, da Tod und Leben
rungen' ('It was a wonderful fight, When death and life struggled')—
are employed against line 1 of the canto, though the first chorale line
only is used as counterpoint. The derivative is aggressive, in plain
quavers, which should be sung non-legato. The first countersubject
has an impulsive flourish on 'wunderlicher', contributing to the
splendid animation of the scene, and the free second countersubject
is in whirling semiquavers. The derivative introducing line 2, though
based on the appropriate melody, is free; the three voices enter in
close canon, at the octave and the fourth, tumbling and rising again
in the throes of mortal combat. Lines 3 and 4—'Das Leben behielt
den Sieg, Es hat den Tod verschlungen' ('Life won the victory, It has
death swallowed')—are a repetition of 1 and 2, the 'wunderlicher'
flourish falling appropriately on 'Leben'. The introductory derivative of line 5—'Die Schrift hat verkündiget das' ('The scripture has
proclaimed this')—announces the joy-motive on 'verkündiget' and

firm crotchets in the middle of the phrase tell of the inevitability of the decree. Line 6 reads—'Wie ein Tod den andern fraß' ('How one death the other devoured')—and the preliminary figure is in a curious cross-rhythm:

Ex. 316

the voices entering hastily after one another, as if in hot pursuit. Line 7 declares 'Ein Spott aus dem Tod ist worden' ('A mockery of death has become') and the accompanying voices reiterate antiphonally 'Ein Spott' to detached quavers, an arresting break in the florid movement of the chorus, leading to a less ornate, though by no means lacking in power, Hallelujah section. A majestic bass line, descending sequentially a distance of nearly two octaves, commands the closing bars.

The strings re-enter for the next stanza, which is set for bass solo. There are few solo voices, however, which can deliver this remarkable number adequately; it must have been written for the exceptional Hofcantor Alt at Weimar (see p. 96). If the choir is not too large the number is better performed by basses in unison. Not only is it enormously effective so, but the cantata can thereby be given without soloists, a financial consideration which weighs with small societies. The consummate art with which Bach evolved this aria from the chorale melody, already submitted to four methods of elaboration, deserves especial study. Line 1—'Hier ist das rechte Osterlamm' ('Here is the true Easter Lamb')—is prefaced by a descent in semitones of the continuo, from tonic to dominant, reminding us of the sins of mankind which brought the Saviour to His Calvary. The voice enters with line 1 on the last two notes:

Ex. 317

while the continuo moves in quavers. It will be seen that the time is changed from quadruple to triple. The voice continues in a free line as the upper strings enter, violin I playing line 1 a fifth higher. Line 2—'Davon Gott hat geboten' ('Thereof God has commanded') —the soloist sings the line and continues in free counterpoint while violin I repeats the melody an octave higher. Now come two bars of interlude, the continuo descending by semitones while the upper strings resume the type of passage with which they accompanied the vocal delivery of line 2. Line 3—'Das ist hoch an des Kreuzes Stamm' ('Who is high on the Cross's stem')—vocal line as in 1, but all strings playing. Violin I begins to repeat as before, but the antepenultimate bar is extended to three, while the voice poises on 'des Kreuzes, des Kreuzes Stamm', the hanging on the Cross. The repetition of the possessive is unusual with Bach, and is employed here to deepen intensity. Though possibly in later days he would have adopted other means, it is an effective device, and, moreover, prevents the monotony which would have resulted from a rigid adherence to scheme. Line 4—'In heißer Lieb' gebraten' ('In hot love burned')—identical treatment with 2. Line 5—'Das Blut zeichnet unser Thür' ('The blood marks our door')—the previous mode of treatment now ends; the flowing quavers cease. Notes 1–3 of the line come as crotchets in the continuo, unaccompanied, the soloist repeats them and continues, the upper strings play them, evidently non-legato. The bass repeats his four-note phrase and rounds it off with an idea which sweeps vigorously aloft. The crotchet theme is resumed by soloist and orchestra, leading to line 6: 'Das halt der Glaub' dem Tode für' ('That holds faith death away'). Vocal style as in 1, quavers in continuo, upper strings sustain chords and there are imitations in violin I. The latter begins its repetition of the line, but prolongs D for three bars, during which the voice drops the astonishing distance of a diminished twelfth. The continuo is marked tasto ('without chords'), the middle strings sway in gentle crossing arpeggi:

Ex. 318

dem   To - - - - de   für,

It is one of those moments when, as at the close of the Crucifixus of the *B Minor Mass*, one listens breathlessly, gripped by some mysterious power. After a string cadence line 7—'Der Würger kann uns nicht mehr schaden' ('The destroyer can us no more harm')—is extended to fifteen bars. Here again are new and astounding devices. 'Der Würger' is thrust from G to an unaccompanied high D (the soloist has just been singing nearly two octaves lower) and then, as the D is sustained for nearly four bars, violin I moves in brilliant zigzag arpeggi, the rest of the orchestra stamping in heavy chords.

For the remainder of the vocal line the continuo only accompanies in quaver runs. The voice eludes the expected final note of the phrase in order to bring about a repetition, which drives home in defiant, detached crotchets 'nicht, nicht, nicht, nicht'. The upper strings now repeat the melody of the line, in plain form, while the soloist begins quick Hallelujahs, which continue for twelve bars. One may discern the much-disguised closing line of the melody in this final section. In the last two vocal bars the soloist has an amazing passage ranging over two octaves in three beats, and dropping a twelfth at one point

Ex. 319

hal - le - lu - jah!

Sopranos and tenors now sing a duet, with continuo. It is the disappearance of sin and the celebration of the greatest of days: 'So celebrate we the High Festival With heart's joy and bliss, Which to us the Lord to shine causes, He is Himself the sun, Who through His mercy-beam Enlightens our hearts wholly. The sin-night has disappeared. Hallelujah.' The lines are introduced in imitation, sometimes plain, often ornamented. 'Wonne' ('bliss'), 'Sonne' ('sun'), 'Gnaden' ('mercy'), and 'Herzen' ('hearts') are expanded into waving triplets in thirds and sixths. One thinks of the Sanctus of the *B Minor Mass*. The voices in part of line 6 are left unsupported, but otherwise the continuo never departs from its dancing ⌐⌐⌐ time-pattern, which, of course, should be played ♪♪. The imitative triplet version of the close is startlingly like the duet 'Turn, turn your eyes' in Purcell's *Fairy Queen*:

Ex. 320

Brass and strings reappear in the plain final chorale: 'We eat and live well In the true Passover; The old leaven not shall Exist in the promise of mercy, Christ will the food be And feed the soul alone, Faith will not otherwise live. Hallelujah.' (See *Fugitive Notes*.)

12. While the Third Sunday after Easter is entitled 'Jubilate' and the prescribed motet is 'Jubilate Deo', the three cantatas we possess

for that day have titles that speak of suffering and sorrow—No. 12,
'Weinen, Klagen, Sorgen, Zagen' ('Wailing, crying, mourning,
sighing' N., 'Weeping, wailing, mourning, fearing' B.), No. 103,
which begins with St. John xvi. 20, 'Ye shall weep and lament', and
No. 146, the chorus of which is based on Acts xiv. 22, 'We must
through much tribulation'. The reason for this apparent contradiction is that the Gospel, St. John xvi. 16–23, deals with the prophesied return of the Saviour and sorrow which shall be turned into joy.
Each of the three libretti, therefore, progresses from lamentation to
rejoicing, and the titles create a false impression of their contents.
No. 12 was produced in 1724 or 1725, but there are tokens that much
of the music was composed at Weimar some ten years earlier and the
text is probably by Franck. The double viola line also points to an
early date. A Sinfonia (see O.O.S. No. 010), 'adagio assai', F minor
with a signature of three flats, anticipates the mood of the first
chorus. It is scored for oboe and strings, with bassoon doubling the
continuo, and for the most part four distinct ideas are maintained.
The bassi have a regular │♩ ♩ ♩ ♩│, the two lines of violas throb
gently—♪♪♪♪, the two lines of violins play in thirds and sixths a
figure almost indicative of the lapping of water:

Ex. 321

and the oboe soars above in lengthy arabesques. Near the end the
violins play descending passages suggesting a rain of tears. The first
part of the opening chorus is chiefly famous as the precursor of the
Crucifixus of the *B Minor Mass*, remodelled some ten years after the
production of the cantata at Leipzig. A comparison of the two versions is interesting. The Crucifixus begins with a short introduction,
not so the earlier form. We miss in the first version the striking entry
of the altos, unexpectedly a minor third above the continuo. It was
at first a major third, although it is changed to minor at the ninth
entry of the ground-bass. For some thirty-five bars the voice parts of
the two versions are identical, except for the disposition of the words.
Fine though the Weimar chorus is, the Crucifixus version is superior
in three most important factors. In the latter flutes and upper strings
answer each other continuously, in groups of two minims, one of the
most fascinating elements in the number. In the cantata, though the
minim figure is maintained, the chords, in the double violin and viola

lines, are always simultaneous. In the cantata the continuo moves in
minims; in the Crucifixus always in repeated crotchets, the throbbing
thus produced having a deep emotional effect. The earlier form ends
with a plain tonic cadence, whereas the later leads to the Et resurrexit
by a simple passage containing one of the most wonderful modulations in the whole of music. There may be a literal significance in the
fact that in the cantata the ostinato figure is heard twelve times, seeing that the libretto is based on Christ's farewell to His disciples.
The text after 'Weeping, complaining, sorrowing, fearing' is 'Angst
und Noth sind der Christen Thränenbrod' ('Anxiety and need are
the Christian's tears-bread'). The second portion, 'un poco allegro',
supported by continuo only and with a Da Capo to the ostinato, is
less noteworthy. It begins with a free imitation by inversion:

Ex. 322

there are long passages on 'tragen' and the last few bars are andante,
solemn imitations on:

Ex. 323

A seven-bar recitative for alto is accompanied by strings, the continuo doubled by fagotto. It had not appeared in the chorus, it does
not come again till the final chorale, also merely doubling. One must
assume that it played in ii. The text is that which is set in the first
chorus of the third cantata for this Sunday: 'Wir müssen durch viel
Trübsal in das Reich Gottes eingehen' ('We must through much
tribulation into the kingdom of God enter', Acts xiv. 22). The
heavenly journey is illustrated by violin I slowly mounting the scale
of C major and by a quaver vocal ascent at the close. 'Trübsal' is
thrice sung to the same falling phrase, at different pitches, and the
fourth time is set to a lovely melisma. The alto aria is undoubtedly a
product of Weimar; the slow shake on 'Kampf' is early in type. The
text of Part I is 'Kreuz und Krone sind verbunden, Kampf und

Kleinod sind vereint' ('Cross and crown are bound together, conflict and jewel are united'). The oboe obbligato is based on two ideas:

Ex. 324

and a descending sequence embodying the seventh:

Ex. 325

Cont.
8ve lower

The initial three notes of (*a*) are heard in various ways in the continuo and in the vocal line.

Part II is 'Christen haben alle Stunden ihre Qual und ihren Feind, doch ihr Trost sind Christi Wunden' ('Christians have (in) all hours their torment and their enemy, yet their comfort is Christ's wounds'). The same motives are employed.

A low-lying bass aria speaks of following Christ: 'Ich folge Christo nach, von ihm will ich nicht lassen' ('I follow Christ after, from Him will I not leave'). It opens with a happy form of the step-motive:

Ex. 326
VI.I.II.

Cont.
8ve lower

which often appears in four-fold imitation. While the singer sustains on 'im Wohl' ('im Wohl und Ungemach, im Leben und Erblassen' ('in well-being and adversity, in living and dying'), the two violins (violas are absent from the score) trip merrily above the voice and the bassi step upwards. Part II consists of the crude sentence 'Ich küsse Christi Schmach, ich will sein Kreuz umfassen' ('I kiss Christ's shame, I will His cross embrace') and a short figure is associated in Bach's mind with 'kiss':

Ex. 327

Ich küs - se,   ich küs - se Chri - sti   Schmach,

Cont.

for it occurs plentifully wherever that word and 'Schmach' come. The sombre fall on the last two words contrasts the adoration of the believer with the ignominy of his Saviour. At the end the singer begins on E♭ below the stave, majestically ascends a twelfth and then sinks back again.

The tenor aria is on lines not previously found. The listener is admonished to be true and thereby all pain will be for a short while only. The persistent continuo figure:

Ex. 328

is probably intended to remind the believer of the necessity for steadfast faithfulness. The trumpet plays a slightly elaborate version of the chorale 'Jesu, meine Freude' ('Jesus, my joy'). We see the benign figure of the Saviour confronting the sufferer. The apparently odd combination of voice, trumpet, and continuo is surprisingly effective. The text begins 'Sei getreu' ('Be faithful'). 'Pein' in 'alle Pein' ('all pain') is suitably set to chromatic passages, 'alle' is appropriately allotted a run. Yet a four-bar florid passage on 'Kleines' ('wird doch nur ein Kleines sein') ('will then only a trifle be') is completely out of place; indeed, according to Bach's methods, it is opposed to the meaning of the word. 'Nach dem Regen blüht der Segen, alles Wetter geht vorbei' ('After the rain blossoms the blessing, all bad weather passes by') is luxuriant with florid passages on the three nouns. But why is there a long run on the second syllable of 'vorbei'? It is quite nonsensical, though it would have matched 'geht' happily. One can only surmise that the aria passed through two or more stages, that Bach rewrote the text, not to advantage in certain parts, or that some previously written number was adapted to new words, some lines being appropriate, others not. In the final chorale—stanza 6 of S. Rodigast's 'Was Gott thut, das ist wohlgethan' ('What God does, that is well done') with its anonymous melody—the trumpet is again independent, save that the oboe joins in its contrapuntal line. The verse is translated for Cantata No. 99, p. 510. The Eulenberg miniature score should be consulted before a performance, as it contains many corrections of the *BGS* score.

168. It is difficult to see why Bach should have rewritten 'Thue Rechnung! Donnerwort' ('Make a reckoning! Thunder-word') (a solo cantata, S.A.T.B. *c.* 1725), unless, indeed, it was for the sake of

the splendid opening bass aria. Salomo Franck was led by the Gospel
for the Ninth Sunday after Trinity, St. Luke xvi. 1–9, which relates
the parable of the unjust steward, to speculate in terms of money,
payment, and business calculations, scarcely inspiring topics for the
sacred Muse! Bach wrote the first version, no doubt, when the libretto
appeared in print, 1715. Spitta, however, is of opinion that the composer from time to time harked back to Franck and did not write
this cantata at Weimar. He conceived the parable as concerning God
and man, for the rushing triplet semiquavers, three bars of $\frac{24}{16}$ in
the bassi followed by four bars of similar movement in violin I, the
dotted-note passages for the upper strings at the beginning:

Ex. 329

and the continuo idea repeated by unison strings at the *fine*, tell of
the Almighty speaking through the thunder and the lightning. 'Thue
Rechnung!' is a stern command, 'Donnerwort' always appears in
triplet runs. 'Das die Felsen selbst zerspaltet' ('that the rocks themselves (may be) split'), brings vigorous passages and a scattering run
on the verb; 'Wort, wovon mein Blut erkaltet' ('Word, at which my
blood chills'), throws its verb on a low note while violin I sways
above and the bassi mutter the 'Thue Rechnung' idea below.
Part I concludes with the command, 'Seele, fort!' ('Soul, away!').
Even where the sinner is admonished to render back to God His
gifts—'Ach, du mußt Gott wiedergeben seine Güter, Leib und Leben'
'(Ah, thou must to God give back His favours, body and life'), the
awful mutterings of the angry Omnipotent are heard in the bassi.

After this the interest of the cantata sags for a while. The tenor
sings of the lament of the unjust steward, but the text contains
nothing of note until the plea that the mountains fall and the hills
cover him from God's judgement of anger, when the accompaniment
appropriately descends in leaps, and the reference to lightning, where
it springs upwards. Why Bach should choose oboes to play sustained
chords in recitatives is one of the puzzles that one has not yet been
able to solve. Two or three oboes are commonly employed and in
No. 183 he demands for that purpose two oboes d'amore and two
oboes da caccia. These combinations are difficult to handle techni-

cally; unanimity is rarely achieved, even with good players, some of
the sustained notes are so long as to be barely possible, the quality
of tone, even with modern instruments, so different from the coarse
reeds of that day, is insistent and does not yield sympathetically to
the voice. There are cases where an aria is scored for three oboes
which are remarkably effective, but it is not the same with sustained
chords in recitatives. The accompaniment to this number is for two
oboes d'amore, so it must have been rewritten at Leipzig, and one
sees no reason for the choice. The complete text is: 'It is only
borrowed property, that I in this life have' (see Ex. 1278) 'spirit, life,
courage and blood, and place and position is my God's gift; it is to
me for cultivation and faithfully therewith house to keep, from high
hands entrusted. Ah! but ah! I shudder, when I into my conscience
go and my reckonings so full of defects see: I have day and night the
possessions, which to me God lent, callously dissipated!' An expressive
oboe phrase heralds 'How can I from Thee, righteous God, flee? I cry
pleadingly; ye mountains, fall, ye hills, cover me from God's righteous
anger and from the lightning of His countenance.' (See St. Luke
xxiii. 30.)

The oboes d'amore in unison play the obbligato in the succeeding
tenor aria, though doubtless one would be *tacet* during the vocal
portions. What composer could write good music to a text beginning
'Capital und Interessen meiner Schulden groß und klein müssen
einst verrechnet sein.' ('Capital and interest of my debts great and
small must some day reckoned be')? Why should the tender tones
of the oboe d'amore be used with these words? Yet the long-enduring
composer contrives to pen not uninteresting music. The opening
phrase, modified for the voice:

Ex. 330

Cont.
8ve lower

is not without charm, and semiquaver groups in voice and continuo
waft a certain naïvety into the spiritual counting-house. Part II is
not so crude: 'Alles, was ich schuldig blieben, ist in Gottes Buch
geschrieben, als mit Stahl und Demantstein' ('All, of which I owing was,
is in God's book written, as with steel and diamond-stone'). The
customary run is allotted to 'Alles', beginning with the semiquaver

group, 'steel' and 'stone' are appropriately to long notes, there are interesting variants of the first phrase and many graceful semi-quaver passages for the instruments.

The words of a bass recitativo secco, in which the erring and con-trite steward is comforted (the character of the man is not that indi-cated in Holy Writ!) are uninspiring, though not so guilty of exe-crable taste. Franck's texts certainly do not err on the side of brevity, scriptural incidents are productive of compound interest: 'Yet, terrified heart, live and despair not, step joyfully before judgement! and convict thee thy conscience, thou wilt here to keep silent be obliged, so contemplate the Security, who all debts has remitted; it is paid and fully discharged; what thou, Oh man, in computation owed, the Lamb's blood, Oh great love! has thy debt cancelled and thee with God reconciled. It is paid, thou art acquitted. Meanwhile, because thou knowest, that thou householder art, so be striving and unforgetting, worldly riches prudently to employ, the poor to treat well, so wilt thou, when for thee time and life end, in heaven's dwellings securely rest.'

The composer must have breathed a sigh of relief when he turned from this dreary admonition to the S.A. duet: 'Herz, zerreiß' des Mammons Kette, Hände, streuet Gutes aus!' ('Heart, rend Mam-mon's chains, hands, spread goodness around!'). Three character-istic ideas present themselves, a rushing up of the continuo (the only accompaniment):

Ex. 331

to represent the breaking of the iron, a snapping off of 'zerreiß'':

Ex.332

and an involved run to 'Kette'. The vocal parts rush towards each other on 'streuet'. The chains continue to be broken even when 'Machet sanft mein Sterbebette' ('Make soft my death-bed') is sung, although the voices sway gently down and up. The outlined melody of the continuo sinks step by step, until the lowest depths are reached with 'bauet mir ein festes Haus' ('build me a firm house'). Neither does symbolic breaking cease during 'das im Himmel ewig bleibet, wenn der Erden Gut zerstäubet' ('that in heaven everlastingly remains when earthly possessions turn to dust'). The voices begin this with yet another idea, all three being unrelated to the continuo theme, with a trill on 'im' and swimming blissfully on 'ewig, ewig'; there are holding notes on 'bleibet' and long convolutions on 'zerstäubet', and, at the end, a semiquaver rest between the last two words, the snapping off of all relations between here and the hereafter. With this attractive duet and the closing four-part chorale the work recovers from the artistically devastating influence of the usurer's office. The anonymous melody of B. Ringwaldt's 'Herr Jesu Christ, du höchstes Gut' ('Lord Jesus Christ, Thou highest good') is sung to stanza 8: 'Strengthen me with Thy joy-spirit, Heal me with Thy wounds, Wash me with Thy deathsweat. In my last hours; And take me one day, when Thee it pleases, In true faith from the world to Thine elect.'

80. The celebration of the Reformation Festival was, naturally, a highly important one in the year of the Saxon Lutheran Church, a national occasion as well as a religious, and a panoply of splendour was displayed in the services. The Kyrie was sung to concerted music, the Gloria was intoned, the Te Deum was ordered to be sung with trumpets and drums. The lessons were 2 Thessalonians ii. 3–8 (concluding 'And then shall that Wicked be revealed, whom the Lord shall consume with the spirit of His mouth, and shall destroy with the brightness of His coming') and Revelation xiv. 6–8, 'Babylon is fallen, is fallen, that great city' Such stirring hymns as Luther's 'Erhalt uns, Herr, bei deinem Wort' ('Sustain us, Lord, by Thy word'), 'Wir glauben all' an einen Gott' ('We believe all in one God'), and 'Ein' feste Burg ist unser Gott' ('A strong citadel is our God'), the last the great Reformation battle-cry, a national paean, and Rinkart's 'Nun danket alle Gott' ('Now thank we all God') were sung. For the Third Sunday in Lent, possibly 15 March 1716, Bach set a libretto by Franck—'Alles, was von Gott geboren' ('All, that from God is born.')—which begins with stanza 2 of the hymn 'Ein' feste Burg', and which concludes with the final verse. In 1730, for the Festival, the 200th Anniversary of the Augsburg Confession, stanzas 1 and 3 were added, thus including the entire hymn. The new libretto of No. 80 ('A stronghold sure', N., B.) thus consists of i—stanza 1 (new), ii—stanza 2 in the soprano with added matter by Franck in the bass, iii, iv—Franck, v—stanza 3 (new), vi, vii—Franck, viii—stanza 4. Luther's vigorous and strongly worded poem stirred Franck deeply, and he based his verse on the casting out of a devil by Christ, St. Luke xi. 14–28, but he wisely affords relief from what might otherwise have been too prolonged a series of scenes of spiritual and physical warfare. The well-contrived utterances of the individual Christian, standing prayerfully apart from fields of strife, make the libretto as a whole admirable in spite of an occasional crudity unpalatable to modern taste. Franck's contribution was altered, no doubt, by the composer, to fit the new circumstances.

The fantasia on stanza 1 is one of the most colossal and monumental of Bach's choruses. The importance of the Festival in the church year and the significance of its coincidence in 1730 (c. 31 October) with the centenary of the Augsburg Confession, the splendid tune, its association with a text by the founder of his religion (it is notable that Bach was always richly inspired by Luther's hymns), all combined to stimulate him to put forth his fullest powers. The plan is almost strict Pachelbel and no independent orchestral treatment, except a free continuo, is allowed to interfere with the presentation of the well-known lines of the melody. They are always unmistakably prominent; to his congregation it must have been like meeting a bewilderingly large crowd in which every face is known. The chief entries of the lines are in canon at the octave, at the distance of a bar. The melody has to be refashioned somewhat to permit of this unbending rule, but one scarcely notices the alterations. The voices do not partake in the foundational presentation; each line is delivered by Tromba I, doubled an octave lower by two oboes, and imitated by the violone and organ pedal—*Posaune 16 Fuss*. No part is marked continuo, but there are two staves for the *organo*, both bass, the upper marked manual, the lower pedal. Except for the pedal entries of the chorale, with prolongations of the final notes, the chorus is always supported by 8 ft. tone only. The manual generally, though not always, doubles the vocal bass, and when the latter is not employed, keeps moving below the other voices. The upper strings double soprano, alto, and tenor. Trumpet I joins II, III, and timpani in short fanfares when not delivering the canto, and in the last five bars only do the oboes strengthen the vocal lines. Apart from the choral lines and the canto fermo, therefore, there is little elaboration, the stupendous rock stands bare to the winds and the storms, with its bluntness of outline unsoftened and its hardness unmellowed by the gentle influence of foliage. As each of the nine lines is provided with generous prologues and epilogues, the fantasia runs to great length, no fewer than 228 bars. Canonic devices abound; technically the movement is a superb example of the master's command of musical resources. In the preface to line 1, line 2—'ein' gute Wehr und Waffen' ('a good defence and weapon')—is used as countersubject, and the two clauses serve for the development of lines 1–4, thus not adhering strictly to the Pachelbel principle. Lines 3 and 4 are 'er hilft uns frei aus aller Noth, die uns jetzt hat betroffen' ('He helps us free from all distress, which us now has befallen'). When the basses lead off the prologue to line 5—'Der alte böse Feind' ('The old evil enemy')—the organ manual stealthily creeps upwards by semitones. 'Mit Ernst er's jetzt meint' ('With sternness he it now purposes') is diatònic. There are chromatics in line 8—'Sein' grausam' Rüstung ist' ('His cruel armament is')—but the rest of the chorus is magnificently diatonic, a defiant and invincible front facing the world of a thousand devils. Especially stirring are the vigorous leaping of the manual theme in line 7—'groß' Macht und viel List' ('great might and much cunning') the upward leaps on 'Gleichen' ('auf Erd' ist nicht sein's Gleichen', 'On earth is not his equal'), in the ninth section, and the magnificent final entry of the basses, the descending scale of line 9, with trumpet cracklings answered by drum beats. One can never look at the score without feeling a sense of awe at the thought of the mighty brain which conceived and worked out in such faultless detail this paean of Lutheran faith and of rugged, unshakable strength. It is one of the few cantata choruses which justify the employment of a large number of voices.

Stanza 2 occurs in the upper voice of ii, a S.B. duet: 'By our might is nothing done, We are soon all lost. There strives for us the right Man, Whom God Himself has chosen. Askest thou, Who is He? He is called Jesus Christ, The Lord of Sabaoth, And (there) is no other God, The field must He retain.' Additional lines by Franck are sung by the lower voice—'Alles, was von Gott geboren, ist zum Siegen auserkoren' ('All that of God born is, is to victory chosen')—there are spacious runs to 'Alles' and 'auserkoren', warring being interpreted by this word in preference to 'Siegen' on account of the closed vowel of the latter: 'Wer bei Christi Blutpanier in der Taufe Treu' geschworen, siegt im Geiste für und für' ('Who by Christ's bloodbanner in baptismal faith pledged (is), conquers in spirit ever and ever'). A fine militant figure opens, but the remainder is florid. As has been pointed out, this is the first number of the original version, in which the oboe alone maintains the chorale, and the earlier style

is patent. The tune is decorated in the Böhm manner and doubled
by the oboe in an even more ornate version. Apart from the chorale
the chief musical interest lies in the splendid theme announced by
violins and violas in unison, the turmoil of battle:

Ex. 333

This persists until the end; the upper strings are allowed no other
material. 'At the mention of the blood-stained banner of Christ in
the second half the chorale melody hovers over the rest as a symbol
of perfect protection and safety.' (See Arnold Schering's excellent
essay in the Eulenburg score.)

To deal with the other appearances of the canto:—verse 3, v, a
Leipzig addition, is given to all voices in octaves, a device unique in
Bach's works, and strikingly appropriate to Luther's bellicose sum-
mary of his conflicts with the mighty powers of the earth: 'And if
the world full (of) devils were, And would us entangle, So fear we not
so much (that) It shall against us then succeed. The Prince of this world,
However bitterly he takes his stand, Does he to us yet nothing, That
is because he is condemned; A little word can him fell.' As the choir
hurls out the mighty tune, three trumpets, timpani, two oboes
d'amore and taille (mostly doubling violins and violas) and strings
paint another battle scene. As a contrast to the common-time
settings of the other three stanzas, the tune is changed into $\frac{6}{8}$.
Strings and reeds in unison announce a quaver version of line 1
against a rising passage for trumpets:

Ex. 334
Tpts. I. II. III.

with vigorous battering of drums. This form of the first limb of the
canto accompanies lines 1 and 3 and part of 7, and furnishes material
for much of the continuo besides portions of the string lines. A long
struggling of upward semiquavers leads to a short descent with
powerful repeated notes in the upper strings; practically no other

instrumental ideas are heard during this long fresco of the Church Militant. i exists with a Latin translation—'Gaudete omnes populi' —in the script of Wilhelm Friedemann, minus oboes, and this number, also with Latin translation—'Manebit verbum Domini'—was found among Kirnberger's manuscripts. Both are printed in the appendix to *BGS*, xviii. As trumpets and drums are found in no early version of i, B. F. Richter (*Bach Year Book*, 1906) argues that these were additions by Friedemann, and it is thought by some scholars that the scoring of v is not wholly authentic. It is difficult to think of *additions* to i, the conception seems to be a complete unity. The closing chorale is more direct and simple than is usual with Bach, and there is no indication of the orchestration: 'The word they shall leave standing And no praise thereto have. It is for us well according to design With His spirits and gifts. Take they from us body, Possessions, honour, child and wife; Let them go, They have from it no profit; The kingdom must for us yet remain.'

The non-chorale numbers are four, grouped in twos, iii, iv and vi, vii. The texts of iii, bass recitativo secco, and iv are somewhat out of place in the general scheme, except for the opening of the former, though certainly the latter provides relief in the series of powerful numbers. The recitative is picturesque. At the close of 'Consider then, child of God, the so great love, since Jesus Himself with His blood seals', both voice and continuo drop like the falling of blood. Hurried and yet powerful is 'Wherewith He thee as a victory against Satan's army and against world and sin won has'. Declamation is splendid in 'Give not in thy soul to Satan and to evil place, Let not thy heart, the heaven of God on the earth, a desert become! Repent thy guilt and pain'. 'So that Christ's spirit with thee itself firmly may unite' is developed into an arioso:

Ex. 335

becomes a motto in voice and continuo; there are fine sequential quaver sixths in the latter and strong cross-rhythms for the former on 'verbinde'.

The frequent use of the tenor clef and the positions where changes of clef occur in the soprano aria (see P. 35) point to the use of 'cello as sole accompaniment. It is an invitation to Christ to enter the

'Herzens-Haus' ('Komm in mein Herzens-Haus, Herr Jesu, mein Verlangen!' 'Come into my heart's-house, Lord Jesus, my desire!') and one is reminded of the setting of similar words in another Weimar cantata, No. 61, also for this same combination. The lovely 'cello phrase:

Ex. 386

is associated with the invitation to the Saviour and there is a long pleading phrase on 'Verlangen'. The second clause—'Treib' Welt und Satan aus' ('Drive world and Satan out')—concludes with an upward gesture, the throwing out of evil:

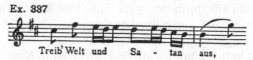

Ex. 337

Treib' Welt und Sa - tan aus,

The 'Verlangen' passage is balanced in this section by a joyous run on 'erneuert' ('und laß dein Bild in mir erneuert prangen' 'and let Thine image in me renewed shine') while the 'cello figure is heard almost uninterruptedly. The accompaniment becomes more active during 'Weg, schnöder Sünden Graus!' ('Away, evil sins' fear!') and the singer repeats 'Weg' with gestures of contempt.

The tenor recitativo secco and arioso, vi, is very much in the early manner, with sudden outbursts of demisemiquavers, in the voice part to 'freudig' ('joyfully'), in 'Step joyfully to the war!', in the continuo where the singer dramatically exclaims 'So will the enemy be forced to depart', and in the arioso, 'thy Saviour remains thy refuge'. A long A♯ in the continuo supports the opening words—'So stand then by Christ's blood-stained banner, Oh soul, fast' and there is a melisma on 'Seele' ('soul'). The connecting clauses are 'and believe, that thy Head thee (does) not leave, yea that His victory also to thee the way to thy crown prepares', and 'Wilt thou only God's word hear as well as keep'.

The succeeding A.T. duet, while included in the original libretto, must have been re-composed at Leipzig. The obbligati are violin and oboe da caccia, the latter an instrument not in use at Weimar. Also, the subtle reflectiveness of the duet and its easy command of technical resource assuredly place it in a mature period. It falls into five sections. There is much canonical writing and the ritornello (1) contains two canons, one of seven bars, the other of six. In (2) the voices begin with 'Wie selig sind doch die, die Gott im Munde tragen' ('How blessed are then they who God in their mouths carry' or 'speak of God'), the theme of the first canon in blissful thirds:

Ex. 338

Wie   se - lig sind doch   die,

As the text is repeated, a modified version of the canon is transformed into one of four in two, leaping figures from the second canon telling of the clamour of tongues, and 'tragen' is extended to eight bars. (2) is rounded off instrumentally by another version of canon II. (3)—'doch sel'ger ist das Herz, das ihn im Glauben trägt' ('for more blessed is the heart, that Him in faith carries')—again begins with sixths (it is fascinating to notice how the master rarely permits two successive entries to be alike, except in rondo form, when he will repeat long sections without change) and then voices and obbligati instruments enter in succession with the theme, the violin and oboe da caccia winding up with yet another version of canon II. The joy-motive takes possession of 'Glauben' and 'trägt' is sustained. (4)— 'Es bleibet unbesiegt und kann die Feinde schlagen' ('it remains un-conquered and can the enemies slay')—is very different. Long notes to 'bleibet' contrast with vigorous leaps and semiquavers, the bassi being busily engaged. (5) is short and without obbligati. 'Und wird zuletzt gekrönt' ('and is at last crowned') is diatonic, but 'wenn es den Tod erlegt' ('when it death overcomes') brings unexpected chro-matics, a bass descending to the depths and two diminished thirds coming in the alto line within the space of a bar. In the exultation of battle and victory, the warrior is not allowed to forget that the final hour must be faced.

The band-parts of No. 71 were printed by the Mühlhausen Council in 1708; no other cantata was published for 113 years, when No. 80 was issued, in 1821. Its appearance caused little interest. In 1826 Spohr's *Last Judgement* proved so popular at a Düsseldorf Festival that it had to be repeated a few days later, while in 1829 'Ein' feste Burg' was reported to be still a drug on the market! We may smile at the artistic blindness of our forefathers, but are we ourselves guilt-less? Are there not a hundred performances of Stainer's *Crucifixion* in British churches in Holy Week to one of Bach's appropriate cantatas?

INTERLUDE I

Bach's Borrowings

ANY attempt to arrive at some reasonable idea of the development of Bach's powers during the early Leipzig years is complicated not only by the number of speculative dates which must be assigned, but by his astonishing addiction to the habit of borrowing, and it may be well to survey the subject before considering the cantatas of this period which contain arrangements. No composer ever adapted so many works, both his own and other people's, as he did. At least a dozen of his predecessors and contemporaries furnished him with material, and his own writings were laid under contribution time after time. Apart from the reconstructed cantatas already discussed, quite a fifth of those of the first Leipzig period contain numbers from earlier instrumental compositions and from sacred and secular vocal works. Instrumental works are revived in their original form, or rescored, or made to serve as vocal-orchestral numbers. Vocal works appear in new guise, changed from one voice to another, fitted to fresh texts, rescored, and so on. It is understandable why he scraped together earlier music to serve for a wedding. Haste and lack of interest in the celebrants would not incline him to prepare new music. The fees were welcome additions to his meagre income; so long as he produced music that was all that mattered. A funeral ode would mean even more desperate hurry. But why did he borrow for so many other occasions? Was his well of inspiration denied him when some new cantata was needed? Did the text fail to call up in his mind suitable musical images? Did such spates of original composition as the first ten months of 1735, when he produced nineteen church cantatas, exhaust his inspiration temporarily, causing his mind to lie fallow for a while? Did his inventive powers prove sterile at certain times? That was the case with Hugo Wolf; and one of the most prolific of modern British composers told me that for a year and a half he could not create a single musical idea.

There was certainly no shirking; think of the labour of rewriting the first movement of the third Brandenburg Concerto, with its nine lines of score and its figuring, in order to add horns and oboes to form the Sinfonia to the tiny solo cantata No. 174, resulting in a movement occupying forty pages, of fifteen staves each, in the *BGS*, out of all proportion to what follows. In the second Leipzig period we find a similar reconstruction of a long movement, the first of the D minor clavier concerto, the solo part rewritten, with numberless alterations of details, for organ, and with two oboes and taille added, to become the introduction to No. 146. The argument may be advanced that he wished to hear again favourite compositions, but in some cases the music is not of supreme interest. The first chorus of No. 136, for instance, is interesting up to a certain point, but not of the highest quality. It must have come from some earlier work, as the text and the music have no particular qualities which bind them together. He used it again as the 'Cum Sancto Spiritu' of the short Mass in A major, where the text is as little appropriate as in the cantata, although many more suitable and interesting numbers lay in his cupboards. Another puzzling point is that whereas in original compositions Bach was scrupulously careful as to the relation of words to music, setting his text with faultless scanning, bringing every important word on important notes, defining musically idea after idea, detailing single words, besides making the music as a whole a fitting mate to the thought of the author, yet in many of his adapted numbers such matters are wholly neglected, indeed often resulting in absurd associations. It is an axiom that wherever faulty accentuation exists and that wherever there is not absolute unity of purpose between text and music, there has been adaptation. It is not a case of the occasional nodding of Homer, but of cynical callousness in matters which elsewhere are vital principles with him. It is one of the inscrutable problems connected with the study of the master, and no commentator has been able to offer any explanation except that of haste and temporary indifference. The adaptation of absurdly inappropriate music to form much of his four short masses (all of which are borrowed) may be attributed to a positive distaste for that side of his duties, but it seems a strange way of exhibiting resentment to destroy deliberately the results of his high ideals of composition.

Bach's instrumental and vocal writings are so much bound together that the following tables of his borrowings include all branches of his composition. It would have been inadequate to have listed the examples of adapted numbers in the church cantatas without tabulating the others as well. The survey of the whole indicates some measure of the problems involved in the consideration of the church cantatas alone, and helps to link up one department of his work with the others.

TABLE OF BACH'S BORROWINGS

Abbreviations:

A. = Alto; B. = Bass; C.C. = Church Cantata; Chle. = Chorale; Chs. = Chorus; Cl. = Clavier; Con. = Concerto; Mov. = Movement; N. = Novello's Edition; Or. = Organ; P. = Peters' Edition; Rec. = Reconstructed; Recit. = Recitative; S. = Soprano; S.C. = Secular Cantata; T. = Tenor; V. = Violin; Vc. = Violoncello; V.S. = Violin Solo.

In the clavier and organ lists no mention is made of earlier versions for the same instrument; that is too large a subject to be dealt with here, and, moreover, is not relevant to our subject.

Chorale Melodies and Plain Chants are not tabulated. Terry's *Bach's Chorals* gives full particulars of these.

1. INSTRUMENTAL WORKS

LUTE

Present form	*Source*
1st Mov., Suite in E (known only in Cl. arrangement. *BGS.* xlii, p. 16)·	Prelude of V.S. Partita, No. 3, in C
Fugue in G minor. (Existing only in tablature)	Fugue from V.S. Sonata, No. 1, in G minor
Suite in C minor. (Existing only in tablature)	Vc. Solo Suite, No. 5, in C minor

CLAVIER SOLO

Present form	*Source*
Adagio in G minor (unfinished) P. 214	V. Sonata No. 3, in C

Concertos, P. 217

No. 1, in D	Vivaldi, V. Con., Op. 3, No. 7
No. 2, in G	Vivaldi, V. Con., Op. 7, No. 2
No. 3, in D minor	Benedetto Marcello, Oboe Con.
No. 4, in G minor	Vivaldi, V. Con., Op. 4, No. 6
No. 5, in C	Vivaldi, V. Con., Op. 3, No. 12
No. 6, in C	Unknown
No. 7, in F	Vivaldi, V. Con., Op. 3, No. 3
No. 8, in B minor	Unknown
No. 9, in G	Vivaldi, V. Con., Op. 4, No. 1
No. 10, in C minor	Unknown
No. 11, in B♭	Duke Johann Ernst of Sachsen-Weimar, V. Con.
No. 12, in G minor	Unknown
No. 13, in C	Possibly Con. by Duke Johann Ernst of Sachsen-Weimar
No. 14, in G minor	Telemann, V. Con.

CLAVIER SOLO (*continued*)

Present form	*Source*
No. 15, in G	Unknown
No. 16, in D minor	V. Con. by Duke Johann Ernst of Sachsen-Weimar
Fugue in B♭, P. 1959, p. 75	Reinken. ('Hortus Musicus')
Fugue in B♭, P. 1959, p. 90	J. C. Erselius
Subjects of Fugues in A, P. 13, No. 10, and B minor, P. 3, No. 5	Albinoni
Fugue in A minor, Bk. 1, 'Das Wohltemperirte Klavier'	Fugue for Pedal-Clavicembalo
1st Mov. Italian Concerto	Muffat. Final Mov. of Symphony in 'Florilegium Primum'
Prelude in C Minor, No. 3 of Twelve Little Preludes, P. 214	Lost Lute work
Prelude in E♭, P. 214	Lost Lute work
Sonatas in A minor and C, P. 213, Nos. 1 and 2	Reinken. (Suites for 3 strings, 'Hortus Musicus')
Sonata in A minor. *BGS*, xlv, i, p. 168. Not in P	Lost orchestral work (?)
Sonata in D minor, P. 213, No. 3	V.S. No. 2, A minor
Suite in E, *BGS*, xlii, p. 16. Not in P	V. Partita No. 3, in E
Suites in E minor, P. 214, and C Minor, *BGS*, xlv, p. 156. Not in P	Lost Lute works
Prelude of English Suite No. 1, in A	Dieupart (Gigue from Suite No. 1)
Quodlibet of Goldberg Variations	Folk-tunes

ORGAN

Present form	*Source*
Schübler Chorales. N. xvi	
No. 1, 'Wachet auf'	C.C. 140, iv
No. 2, 'Wo soll ich fliehen hin' or 'Auf meinem lieben Gott'	Lost C.C.
No. 3, 'Wer nur den lieben Gott läßt walten'	C.C. 93, vi
No. 4, 'Meine Seele erhebt den Herren'	C.C. 10, v
No. 5, 'Ach, bleib bei uns, Herr Jesu Christ'	C.C. 6, iii
No. 6, 'Kommst du nun, Jesu, vom Himmel herunter'	C.C. 137, ii
Concertos:	
No. 1, in G	Possibly V. Con. by Duke Johann Ernst of Sachsen-Weimar
No. 2, in A minor	V. Con., Vivaldi
No. 3, in C	V. Con., Vivaldi

ORGAN (*continued*)

Present form	Source
Concertos (contd.):	
No. 4, in C	Possibly 1st Mov. of V. Con. by Duke Johann Ernst of Sachsen-Weimar
Fantasia and Fugue in G minor, N. viii, p. 127. Subject of Fugue	Reinken. 5th Suite. ('Hortus Musicus')
Fugue in G minor, N. ii, p. 141	C.C. 131, v. Possibly arr. by J. C. Kittel
Subject of Fugue in C minor, N.x. p. 230	Legrenzi
Subject and Countersubject of Fugue in B minor, N. iii, p. 60	Corelli. 3-part string sonata
Passacaglia	Theme by André Raison. Possibly orig. a pedal-clavichord work
Eight short Preludes and Fugues. N.i.	Several are founded on other composers' works
Prelude and Fugue in G, N. viii, p. 112. Subject of Fugue	C.C. 21, ii
Prelude and Fugue in A, N. iii, p. 64.	
Prelude	Based on Purcell's Harpsichord Toccata.
Subject of Fugue	C.C. 152. 2nd Mov. of i, Sinfonia
Prelude and Fugue in D minor. N. ix, p. 156	V.S. Sonata No 1, in G minor
Prelude and Fugue in A minor. N. vii, p. 42. Subject of Fugue	Cl. Fugue in 3 parts

PEDAL-CLAVICEMBALO

1st Mov. Sonata No. 3, in D minor, and possibly other sonata movements	Cl. Works
1st Mov. Sonata No. 4, in E minor	C.C. 75, Sinfonia, No. 4

SOLO VIOLIN

Fugue from Sonata 1 in G minor „ „ 3 in C	Possibly Or. Fugues

VIOLA DA GAMBA AND CLAVIER

Sonata No. 1	Sonata for 2 Flutes and Cl.

CONCERTOS FOR CLAVIER AND STRINGS

Present form	Source
No. 1. D minor	Lost V. Con.
No. 2. E major	Possibly lost V. Con. though it *may* be in its first form

CONCERTOS FOR CLAVIER AND STRINGS (*continued*)

Present form	*Source*
No. 3. D major	V. Con. in E major
No. 4. A major	Lost Oboe d'amore Con.
No. 5. F minor	Lost V. Con. in G minor
No. 6. F major	Brandenburg Con. No. 4, in G
No. 7. G minor	V. Con. in A minor

CONCERTOS FOR TWO CLAVIERS AND STRINGS

No. 1. C minor	Lost V. and Oboe Con.
No. 3. C minor	Con. for 2 violins, in D minor

CONCERTO FOR FOUR CLAVIERS AND STRINGS

A minor	Vivaldi. Con. for 4 violins and strings

OTHER CONCERTOS, ETC.

Flute, violin, clavier, and strings.
A minor

1st Mov.	Prelude of Cl. Prelude and Fugue in A minor. P. 211, p. 14
2nd Mov.	Pedal Clavicembalo Sonata No. 3, in D minor
3rd Mov.	Fugue of Cl. Prelude and Fugue in A minor. P. 211, p. 14
2 Flutes, clavier, and strings, in F. *BGS*, xviii, p. 153	Brandenburg Con. No. 4, in G
Sinfonia in F. *BGS*, xxxi, i, p. 96	Brandenburg Con. No. 1, in F

'MUSICAL OFFERING'

Theme of six-part cl. fugue and two canons	Frederick the Great, King of Prussia
Sonata for Flute, V. Cl.	Based on above

2. CHORAL WORKS

THE PASSIONS. MOURNING ODES

Present (or latest recorded) form	*Source*
Passion according to St. Matthew. Closing Chorus of Pt. I	Opening number of the orig. version of the Passion according to St. John
Trauerode. 'Laß, Fürstin'	Wholly from lost Passion according to St. Mark
Lost Trauermusik for Prince Leopold—'Klagt, Kinder' i	Lost Passion according to St. Mark. (Identical with i of Trauerode, above)
ii, iv, v, vi, vii, viii, ix, xi	Passion according to St. Matthew

MASS IN B MINOR

Present form	Source
'Gratias agimus.' Chs. vi	C.C. 29. Chs. ii. (Possibly itself borrowed from an unknown work)
'Qui tollis.' Chs. viii	C.C. 46. Chs. i. 1st Mov.
'Patrem omnipotentem.' Chs. xiii	C.C. 171. Chs. i. (Possibly itself borrowed from an unknown work)
'Crucifixus.' Chs. xvi	C.C. 12. Chs. ii. 1st Mov.
Vivace ed Allegro of 'Confiteor', Chs. xix	C.C. 120. Chs. ii
'Osanna.' Chs. xxi	Lost work
'Benedictus.' T. Aria. xxii	Lost work
'Agnus Dei.' A. Aria. xxiii	C.C. 11. A. Aria. iv
'Dona nobis pacem.' Chs. xxiv	Same as vi, above

SHORT MASSES (wholly borrowed)

Present form	Source
No. 1, in F	
'Kyrie.' Chs.	Five-part 'Kyrie' combined with 'Agnus Dei.' (See 'Lamb of God' O.)
'Gloria.' Chs. 'Laudamus.' Chs.	
'Gratias.' Chs.	} Lost works
'Domine Deus.' B. Aria	
'Qui tollis.' S. Aria	C.C. 102. A. Aria, iii
'Quoniam.' A. Aria	Ibid. T. Aria, v
'Cum sancto.' Chs.	C.C. 40. Chs. 1
No. 2, in A	
'Kyrie.' Chs.	Lost work
'Gloria.' Chs.	
'Laudamus.' Chs.	C.C. 67. B. solo and Chs. vi
'Gratias.' Chs.	
'Domine Deus.' B. Aria	Lost work
'Qui tollis.' S. Aria	C.C. 179. S. Aria, v
'Quoniam.' A. Aria	C.C. 79. A. Aria, ii
'Cum sancto.' Chs.	C.C. 136. Chs. i. (Possibly itself derived from a lost work)
No. 3, in G minor	
'Kyrie.' Chs.	C.C. 102. Chs. i
'Gloria' Chs. 'Laudamus' Chs.	C.C. 72. Chs. i
'Gratias' B. Aria	C.C. 187. B. Aria, iv
'Domine Fili' A. Aria	Ibid. A. Aria, iii
'Qui tollis' T. Aria	Ibid. S. Aria, v
'Cum sancto' Chs.	Ibid. Chs. i
No. 4, in G major	
'Kyrie' Chs.	C.C. 179. Chs. i
'Gloria' Chs.	C.C. 79. Chs. i
'Gratias' B. Aria	C.C. 138. B. Aria, v
'Domine Deus' S.A. Duet	C.C. 19. S.B. Duet, v
'Quoniam' T. Aria	C.C. 179. T. Aria, iii
'Cum sancto' Chs.	C.C. 17. Chs. i

MAGNIFICAT

In D, without chorales   In E♭, with chorales

MOTET

ix, S.S.A.T. Chorus from 'Jesu,   ⅜ section of Or. Chle. Fantasia of
meine Freude'   same title. N. xviii. No. 64

CHRISTMAS ORATORIO

For discussion as to which numbers of this work are borrowed, see Part
IV. The numbers without brackets refer to the Part, those in brackets to
Messrs. Novello's edition.

Part III
    A. Aria, viii (xxxi)   Possibly lost work
Part IV
    T. Aria. vi (xli)   Possibly lost instrumental work
Part V
    Chs. i (xliii)   Possibly lost work
    S.A.T. Terzett. ix (li)   Ditto
Part VI
    Chs. i (liv), S. Aria, iv (lvii)
    T. Aria, ix (lxii)   Possibly lost works

CHURCH CANTATAS

The initial figure of the left-hand column is the number of the cantata.
Reconstructed cantatas are included.

Present form	*Source*
1. T. Aria, vi	Possibly lost C.C.
2. T. Aria, v	Ditto
4.	Rec. Weimar (?) C.C.
6. A. Aria, ii	Possibly lost S.C. 'Thomana saß annoch betrübt'
8. B. Aria, iv	Possibly unknown instrumental work
11. Chs. i	Unknown S.C.
12.	Rec. Weimar C.C.
15.	Rec. Arnstadt C.C.
20.	Rec. Weimar (?) C.C.
26. Chs. i	Or. Chle. Prelude 'Ach wie Flüchtig.' Orgelbüchlein
27. A. Aria, iii	Possibly unknown gamba and cembalo sonata
Chle. v	J. Rosenmüller's harmonies, slightly altered
29. Sinfonia, i	1st Mov. of 6th V.S. Sonata in E
Chs. ii	Possibly lost work
All Arias	Possibly lost instrumental works
30. All except Recits. and Chles.	S.C. 'Angenehmes Wiederau'
31.	Rec. Weimar C.C.
34. All except Recits.	Incomplete Wedding Cantata of the same title

CHURCH CANTATAS (continued)

Present form	Source
35. All except Recits.	Lost Cöthen (?) instrumental work. A fragment of a Cl. Con. in D minor (possibly itself derived from a V. Con.) reveals the source of the first Sinfonia
36. Chs. i. T.B.S. Arias, iii, v, vii	Lost Cöthen (?) S.C. 'Steigt freudig in die Luft.' found in S.C.'s 'Die Freude reget sich' and 'Schwingt freudig euch empor'
38. T. Aria, iii	Possibly lost work
41. Chle. vi	C.C. 171
42. Sinfonia, i	Possibly lost instrumental work
A. Aria, iii	Possibly lost work
49. Sinfonia, i	Lost V. Con. now 3rd Mov. of Cl. Con. in E, No. 2
B. Aria, S.B. Duet, ii, vi	Possibly lost instrumental work
51.	Text revised, musical material identical
52. Sinfonia, i	1st Mov. of Brandenburg Con. No. 1, in F
58. Duet, v	Possibly lost Con. movement
66. Chs. B. Aria, Dialogus, Aria, i, iii, iv, v	Lost cantata or cantatas
68. Vc. piccolo obbligato to S. Aria, ii	Vc. obbligato to S. Aria, xiii, S.C. 208, 'Was mir behagt'
Final instrumental ritornello. Ibid.	MS. sketch on the back of above S.C.
B. Aria, iv	B. Aria, vii. of above S.C.
69.	Rec. C.C. of same title
70.	Rec. C.C. of same title
Theme of S. Aria, v	Opening instrumental ritornello of Bellante's Aria, p. 45, Handel Society's edition of opera 'Almira'
74. Chs. i	S.B. Duet, i, C.C. 59, of same title
S. Aria, ii	B. Aria, iv. Ibid.
78. B. Aria, vi	Possibly lost instrumental work
80.	Rec. and enlarged Weimar C.C. of same title
91. Chle. vi	C.C. 64, ii
97.	Lost work
100. Chs. i	C.C. 99, Chs. i, of same title
Chle. vi	C.C. 75, vii
110. Chs. i	1st Mov. of Orchestral Overture (or Suite) No. 4, in D
S.T. Duet, v	'Virga Jesse floruit' E♭ Magnificat
120. A. Aria, i	Possibly from an unknown instrumental work
S. Aria, iii	3rd Mov. of Sonata No. 6 for V. and Cl.

CHURCH CANTATAS (*continued*)

Present form	Source
121. T. Aria, ii	Lost work
127. The vocal melody in 2nd $\frac{6}{8}$ section of B. Recit. and Aria, iv	Passion according to St. Matthew. 2nd Chs. of xxxiii
132. Chle. vi	C.C. 99, vi
134. T. Aria, S.A. Duet, Chs. ii, iv, vi	T. Aria, S.A. Duet, Chs. i, iii, vii, of S.C. 'Mit Gnaden bekröne.' later an earlier form of C.C. 134
Recitatives	Earlier form of C.C. 134
135. T. Aria, iii	Lost work
136. Chs. i	Lost work
Possibly whole cantata, except Recits. and Chle.	Lost work
141.	Lost work of unknown composer, possibly touched up
142.	Possibly by Kuhnau, touched up
144.	Possibly lost work
Chs. i	Possibly an instrumental fugue
146. Sinfonia, i	1st Mov. of lost V. Con. now 1st Mov. of Cl. Con. No. 1, in D minor
Chs. ii	2nd Mov. Ibid.
T.B. Duet, vii	Possibly lost instrumental work
147.	Rec. Weimar C.C. of same title
149. Chs. i	S.C. 208, 'Was mir behagt.' Chs. xv
153.	Possibly a composite work
156. Sinfonia, i	2nd Mov. of lost V. Con., now 2nd Mov. of Cl. Con. No. 5, in F minor
158.	Rec. Weimar C.C. of same title
166. T. Aria, ii	Or. Trio, published in 1842, reprinted in Bach Jahrbuch, 1909, p. 35
168.	Rec. Weimar C.C. of same title
169. Sinfonia, i	Possibly 1st Mov. of lost V. Con. now 1st Mov. of No. 2, in E
A. Aria, iii	Lost instrumental (?) work
A. Aria, v	2nd Mov. of lost V. Con., now 2nd Mov. of Cl. Con. No. 2, in E
170. A. Aria, v	Possibly lost instrumental work
Later version	Chs. i from C.C. 174 included
171. Chs. i	Possibly earlier work
S. Aria, iv	S.C. 205, 'Der zufriedengestellte Aeolus.' S. Aria, vii
172. Chs. i	Possibly from lost S.C.
173. All numbers	S.C. 'Durchlaucht'ster Leopold.' i, ii, iii, iv, v, vii
174. Sinfonia, i	1st Mov. of Brandenburg Con. No. 3, in G
175. T. Aria, iv	S.C. 'Durchlaucht'ster Leopold.' vii
Chle. vii	C.C. 59, iii

CHURCH CANTATAS (continued)

Present form	Source
181. Chs. v	Possibly from a lost S.C.
184.	Possibly lost S.C.
186.	Rec. Weimar C.C. of same title
187. A. Aria, iii	Possibly from lost S.C.
188. Sinfonia, i (not included in the score, but a note is added that this arrangement (C.C. 146, i) is to be played)	1st Mov. of lost V. Con. now 1st Mov. of Cl. Con. No. 1, in D minor
191. All three numbers	B Minor Mass, iv, vii, xi
194. All except Recits. and Chles.	Possibly lost orchestral suite
195. Chs. B. Aria, Chs. i, iii, v	Possibly from a lost work
197. B. Aria, S. Aria, vi, viii	Incomplete C.C. 'Ehre sei Gott in der Höhe.' iv, vi
A. Aria, iii	Possibly from a lost Christmas C.C.
'Mein Herze schwimmt im Blut.' (Unnumbered)	Modelled on C.C. of same title by Christoph Graupner
'Herr Gott, Beherrscher aller Dinge.' (Incomplete)	
Chs. S. Aria, i, iii	C.C. 120, ii, iv
Sinfonia, iv	C.C. 29, i. (Itself a re-written version of the 1st Mov. of V. S. Suite No. 6, in E)
Ritornelli of A.T. Duet, vi	C.C. 120, i. (Possibly itself borrowed)
Chle. viii	C.C. 137, v
'O Ewiges Feuer. (Incomplete and un-numbered Wedding Cantata)	
A. Aria, v	Possibly from lost Christmas Cantata
'Gaudete, omnes populi'	Latin version of C.C. 80, i. in W. F. Bach's script. Whether arranged by the composer or not is not known
'Manebit verbum Domini'	Latin version of C.C. 80, v., found in Kirnberger's MSS. Whether arranged by the composer or not is not known

SECULAR CANTATAS
(Arranged alphabetically)

Latest form	Source
207. 'Auf, schmetternde Töne.' Chs., T. Arias, S.B. Duet, A. Aria, S.A.T.B. Recit., Chs. i, iii, v, vii, viii, ix	S.C. 'Vereinigte Zwietracht.' ii, iv, vi, ix, x, xi
'Angenehmes Wiederau.' S. Aria, xi	Possibly from lost work
'Blast Lärmen, ihr Feinde'	S.C. 205, 'Der zufriedengestellte Aeolus'

SECULAR CANTATAS (*continued*)

Latest form	*Source*
205. 'Der zufriedengestellte Aeolus'	
Recit. xii, last 11 bars	Folk-song
'Die Freude reget sich'	Lost Cöthen S.C. 'Steigt freudig in die Luft'
213. 'Die Wahl des Herkules'	Christmas Oratorio
Chs. i	Chs. Part IV, i. (xxxvi)
S. Aria, iii	A. Aria, Part II, x. (xix)
A. Aria with Echo A, v	S. Aria with Echo S. Part IV, iv. (xxxix)
T. Aria, vii	T. Aria, Part IV, vi. (xli). Possibly itself adapted from an instrumental work
A. Aria, ix	A. Aria, Part I, iv. (iv)
A.T. Duet, xi	S.B. Duet, Part III, vi. (xxix)
Chs. 1st part. xiii	C.C. 184, vi. Possibly itself borrowed from a lost S.C.
'Erwählte Pleißen-Stadt.' (Lost)	S.C. 'Vergnügte Pleißen-Stadt.' i, iii, v, vii
204. 'Ich bin in mir vergnügt'	
S. Aria, viii	S.C. 'Vergnügte Pleißen-Stadt.' iii
212. 'Mer hahn en neue Oberkeet.' ('Peasant' cantata)	
B. Aria, xx	S.C. 201, 'Phoebus und Pan.' vii
Sinfonia, S.B. Recit., S. Aria, B. Aria, S. Aria, i, iii, viii, xvi, xviii, and possibly others	Folk-songs and dances
'Mit Gnaden bekröne'	
A. Aria, v	Possibly from lost work
'O, angenehme Melodei'	
S. Recit., Aria, Aria, Aria, Recit., Aria, i, ii, iv, vi, viii, ix, x	S.C. 210, 'O holder Tag.' i, ii, iv (possibly itself borrowed), vi, viii (possibly itself borrowed), ix, x
210. 'O holder Tag'	
S. Aria, iv	Possibly from lost Christmas Cantata
S. Aria, vi	Possibly from lost S.C.
S. Aria, viii	S.C. 'Angenehmes Wiederau.' xi. Possibly itself borrowed from unknown work
'Preise dein Glücke, gesegnetes Sachsen'	
Chs. i	Possibly from unknown work
S. Aria, vii	Christmas Oratorio. B. Aria, Part V, v. (xlviii)
206. 'Schleicht, spielende Wellen'	
B. Aria, iii	Possibly from lost C.C.
A. Aria, vii	Possibly from lost work

SECULAR CANTATAS (*continued*)

Latest form	Source
'Schwingt freudig euch empor'	Possibly lost Cöthen S.C. 'Steigt freudig in die Luft'
'Tönet, ihr Pauken'	
Chs. i	Christmas Oratorio, Chs. i
S. Aria, iii	Possibly lost work
A. Aria, v	Christmas Oratorio, T. Aria, Part II, vi. (xiv)
B. Aria, vii	Ibid. B. Aria, Part I, viii. (viii)
Chs. ix	Ibid. Chs. Part III, i. (xxiv)
Trauerode	
Chs. vii	Possibly from lost work
'Vereinigte Zwietracht der wechselnden Saiten'	
Chs. ii	3rd Mov. of Brandenburg Con. No. 1, in F
Ritornello, vii	Ibid. Concluding Trio
A. Aria, ix	Possibly from lost work
'Vergnügte Pleißen-Stadt	
S.A. Duet, vi	S.C. 205. 'Der zufriedengestellte Aeolus.' A.T. Duet, xiii
A. Aria, ix	Possibly from lost work
'Verlockender Götterstreit' (Lost)	Rec. of S.C. 208. 'Was mir behagt'
'Was mir behagt'	
Version 2, same title	S.C. 208, 'Was mir behagt.' (Original version) with 'Christian' changed to 'Ernst August'
Version 3, same title	Ibid. With other alterations of text
202. 'Weichet nur, betrübte Schatten'	
Continuo subject of S. Aria, iii	V. and Cl. Sonata, No. 6. Allegro

CANTATAS UTILIZING BORROWED MATERIAL

THESE will be discussed under the following headings:

(A) Those with organ obbligati, including borrowed instrumental material;

(B) Other cantatas with borrowed instrumental material; and

(C) Cantatas with borrowed vocal material—(C1) Secular, (C2) Sacred.

(A) ORGAN OBBLIGATO CANTATAS UTILIZING BORROWED INSTRUMENTAL MATERIAL

27, 29, 35, 49, 169, 170, 188

Order of Discussion: 170, 35, 169, 49, 29, 27, 188

Bach never wrote out a figured bass part realized for the organ except fifteen bars of the bass aria of No. 3, evidently by way of example to a pupil or assistant. As it is very simple, clearly on lines which would be suitable for an immature player, we can only surmise what his own amplification would be from panegyrics on his skill by contemporaries, from Kirnberger's clavier working-out of the figured bass of the trios in *The Musical Offering*, and from Bach's corrections, given in the Appendix to Spitta, vol. iii, of Gerber's expansion of the bass of a violin sonata by Albinoni. Nor did he ever employ in his choral-orchestral works organ music of the type of his independent compositions for that instrument. The organ obbligati in the cantatas are scored for one manual and pedal or occasionally for two manuals, but in all cases each of the manuals plays only a single melodic line. Chords are never filled in but are left to the player. Twelve cantatas employ organ obbligati. No. 47 belongs to Cöthen, 1720, No. 73 to early Leipzig, possibly about 1725. In both cases the manual part is merely a substitute for some inefficent or absent member of the orchestra, flute, or oboe obbligato in the first, and horn, mostly sustaining the chorale melody, in the second, just temporary expedients. The last two date from the second Leipzig period and are concertos for organ and orchestra, in the incomplete and un-numbered wedding cantata 'Herr Gott, Beherrscher aller Dinge', the number being borrowed from No. 29, and in 146. The remaining eight, Nos. 172, 170, 35, 29, 27, 169, 49, and 188, all belong possibly to 1731, between

May and October, during which period the Positiv organ of the school was temporarily housed in the church, thus affording an additional and independent instrument. Of these, only No. 172 is wholly original, the other seven make use of old material.

Nos. 170, 35, and 169 fall into a group by themselves and will be considered first. They are all for alto solo, implying the presence of some singer in whom Bach was particularly interested. The inclusion of much borrowed material and the fact that, as is often the case where adaptations are present, the libretti are possibly by the composer, are further links.

170. 'Vergnügte Ruh', beliebte Seelenlust' ('Pleasant rest, beloved soul-desire'), for the Sixth Sunday after Trinity, contains more original matter than the others; possibly the final aria only is derived. The title-page of the score, in the handwriting of Carl Philip, states the instrumentation, but absence of further indications leaves details to conjecture. The organ part is determined because it exists separately, transposed a tone lower. There are three arias and two recitatives (one secco, the other with strings) which come alternately. The opening aria (strings, with possibly oboe d'amore doubling Vl. I) is a $\frac{12}{8}$ slumber song of considerable charm, with the accustomed features, gently pulsating notes in the accompaniment, sinking bassi and placidly swinging figures:

Ex. 339

and

Ex. 340

The 'Rest' desired is that referred to in the Epistle, Romans vi. 3–11, to be found in 'the newness of life'. The voice begins with a peaceful phrase of great beauty, against the opening bars from the introduction:

Ex. 341

Ver - gnüg - te Ruh', be - lieb - te See - len-lust,

Passages alternating continuo only with full orchestra accompany 'dich kann man nicht bei Höllen-Sünden, wohl aber Himmels-Eintracht finden, du stärkst allein die schwache Brust' ('Thee can one not in hell's-sins, but (in) heaven's-concord find, Thou strengthenest alone the weak breast'). The remainder of the text—'Drum sollen lauter Tugendgaben in meinem Herzen Wohnung haben' ('Therefore shall pure virtue-offerings in my heart dwelling have')—is almost all without the upper instruments.

There is a remarkable progression in the recitative, an upward continuo A, D♯, G, during which the latter part of 'The world, the sin-house, breaks only in hell-songs out and seeks through hatred and envy Satan's image upon itself to bear'. The Gospel, St. Matthew v. 20-26, is drawn upon for the remainder: 'Her mouth is full of viper-poison, which often the guiltless mortally strikes, and will only Raca say. Righteous God, how far is then mankind from Thee separated; Thou lovest, nevertheless his mouth proclaims curse and enmity and (he) will his neighbour only with (the) feet trample. Ah! this guilt is difficult to pardon.'

iii is a lamentation over the perversities of mankind. It is scored in a curious way; the 'organo obligato' is for two claviers without pedal, both in treble compass, the left hand not reaching below A, second ledger line below the stave, except for five notes. Violins and violas play in unison a theme of sobbing and sighing, virtually an ostinato. There are neither bassi nor continuo. The chief idea in the opening bars of the organ manuals is another wailing theme, which continually drops to the auxiliary note a semitone below the constituent of the chord:

Ex. 342

Adagio
Organ, upper manual

Unis. Vl. & Va.

thus producing a texture which becomes even more chromatic when the soloist uses the string theme in semitones. The whole structure is constructed with the greatest elaboration. The tear-motive presaged in the first ritornello is developed in the opening vocal phrase:

Ex. 343

How grieve   me   then the   perverted   hearts,
Wie jam-mern mich doch die   ver - kehr - - - ten Her-zen,

unis. Vl. & Va.

The text continues, 'die dir, mein Gott, so sehr zuwider sein' ('which to Thee, my God, so much opposed are'). The voice is provided with a very expressive line. The chromatic passage to 'Ich zitt're recht' ('I tremble truly') is broken with a rest in the middle of the verb, 'und fühle tausend Schmerzen' ('and feel (a) thousand pains') has tortuous phrases, 'Rach'', in 'wenn sie sich nur an Rach' und Haß erfreu'n' ('when they themselves only in revenge and hatred rejoice') is set to furious demisemiquaver runs, while the organist's hands tear alternately up and down the keyboards. When the singer enjoys a brilliant run to 'erfreu'n' the manuals indulge in little rippling laughs, and these reappear when a similar run, moving in the opposite direction, occurs to 'verlacht' ('Gerechter Gott, was magst du doch gedenken, wenn sie allein mit rechten Satans-Ränken dein scharfes Strafgebot so frech verlacht. Ach! ohne Zweifel hast du so gedacht'—'Righteous God, what mayst Thou then think, when they alone with (the) very Satan's wiles Thy sharp punishment-command so insolently deride. Ah! without doubt hast Thou so thought'). 'Frech' is given the same treatment as 'Rach'' and 'verlacht' is realistically portrayed as the voice trills for thirteen beats and tumbling runs chase one another on the manuals. It is an aria that demands exceptional intelligence on the part of the singer.

The singer now affirms, in recitative, that she will obey the commands of Christ; long string chords speak of the rest of the soul: 'Who should accordingly well here to live desire, when one only hatred and evil for His love sees? Yet because I even the enemy as my best friend, according to God's behest, should love, so flies my heart (from) anger and ill will, and wishes alone with God to live, Who Himself Love is called. Ah, wholly-united spirit, when will He to thee then only His heaven's Zion give?' Bach cannot resist setting 'flieht' flies) to a flourish.

v, an aria of rejoicing, suggests an instrumental origin. While one is never surprised at anything Bach does, it would seem unlikely that he would begin a purely vocal line with an upward leap of an augmented fourth, changing abruptly from the tonic chord to the last inversion of the chromatic supertonic seventh, especially to the word 'ekelt' (Ex. 344). (The complete phrase is here quoted, not the fragmentary opening.) The demisemiquaver figuration in the organ part just before the voice enters, which is developed considerably in the second part of the aria, is of a type often employed in concertos. Violin I and oboe d'amore, in unison, frequently double the upper manual, but they and violin II and viola at other times have mere chords, accompany-ing the principal melody. The organ part is for manual and pedal. The latter line consists solely of occasional octave leaps. It suggests that the arranger was at a loss as to what to do with the pedals. The idea of Bach being devoid of resource in this particular is too humorous to contemplate. Did some junior of the family make the arrangement as a task assigned by his father in haste of production? Bach himself

Ex. 344

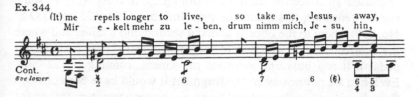

wrote out the manual line on another sheet for flauto traverso, no doubt as an alternative, with certain changes of pitch. The number of repetitions of the above sentence, occupying the whole of a lengthy Part I, is also evidence that the text was fitted to existing music. Part II—'Mir graut vor allen Sünden, laß mich dies Wohnhaus finden, woselbst ich ruhig bin' ('I shudder because of all sins, let me this dwelling find, wherein only I restful am')—certainly links up with i, but the organ figuration is quite out of place with Bach's methods. At the close he tries to accommodate matters, with a long descending vocal passage to 'ruhig', followed by a descent in the bassi. The dance-like themes and the brilliant concerto-like passage make this number a delightful conclusion to the cantata. There is no chorale.

Spitta places the work in 1732, but Professor B. F. Richter (Bach-jahrbuch, 1908) proves that the organ obbligato dates it a year earlier. i, transposed into C, and followed by a new recitative and the chorus from No. 147, formed a composite cantata, which may have been performed on the Feast of the Visitation, 2 July 1742 (Spitta).

35. Six weeks later, for the Twelfth Sunday after Trinity, 25 Septem-ber, came 'Geist und Seele wird verwirret' ('Spirit and soul become disordered'). As the two Sinfonias and the three arias are adapted from instrumental material, and the two recitativi secchi only are original, it is not to be expected that there should be any intimate connexion between words and music, except in the recitatives. But the librettist (the composer, no doubt) found a useful subject in the Gospel, St. Mark vii. 31–37, the incident of the curing of the deaf

man who had an impediment in his speech. The first aria and both recitatives refer to the miracle, the second quoting the healing word 'Ephphatha'. The second aria develops the idea of v. 37—'He hath done all things well'—and the last speaks of the future condition of the blest. Bach could preach his sermon as well as the clergy. In *BGS*, xvii, p. xx, is given a fragment of nine bars of a cembalo concerto in D minor (not the well-known one) with strings, and, what is unusual in concertos, an oboe doubling violin I. Apart from some small alterations, this opens the first Sinfonia of No. 35 (see O.O.S. No. 059) where to the oboe is added a second and a taille, and where the cembalo solo is assigned to 'organo obligato' (one manual and pedals). It is a busy and vigorous movement, running to 132 bars. Even had we not possessed the fragment it would have been obvious that oboe II and taille were additions, as they can vaunt no reason for their place in the score except to strengthen the string tone in order to counterbalance the organ. Occasional string passages must have been reconstructed to allow them to stake small claims of their own.

The first aria was no doubt the slow movement of this concerto, a siciliano:

with many long-continued decorative passages for the organ manual, which may have been derived from an earlier violin form. The scoring is the same as in the Sinfonia, save that the reeds are frequently independent, string and wind acting antiphonally. It is a heavy accompaniment for the voice to battle against, and as the same disproportion occurs again later, we must conclude that the favourite alto of 1731 was powerful as well as artistically gifted. The text is short (making adaptation easier), continuing after the initial clause:— 'wenn sie dich, mein Gott, betracht. Denn die Wunder, so sie kennet und das Volk mit Jauchzen nennet, hat sie taub und stumm gemacht' ('when it Thee, my God, contemplates. For the wonder, which it knows and the people with exultation names, has it deaf and dumb made'). Music and verse are on the whole not ill mated; the soothing rhythms of a siciliano are elsewhere employed for vastly different words in Bach's compositions for the church. In spite of the pre-ordained music, Bach cleverly manages to secure some characteristic word-treatment, a tortuous passage on 'verwirret', an adaptation of an instrumental phrase to serve for 'Jauchzen'; later there are rapid arpeggi flinging upwards, possibly an addition to the siciliano, as the figure does not come elsewhere, and, finally, a contrast of position for 'taub' and 'stumm'. The third movement of the concerto is doubtless the Sinfonia which opens Part II (see O.O.S. No. 060), and which stands fifth in the scheme. Thus the whole work is preserved. v is a Presto, in the customary $\frac{3}{8}$ time, slighter in every way than i, passage work being mostly accompanied by detached chords and octave leaps. Oboes and taille do nothing but double the upper strings.

The other arias are iv and vii. iv has a curious accompaniment; continuo and organ pedal are identical, and for seventy-one bars (all but the last) they play on every beat of the 4/4 bars: | ♪ ♪ ♪ ♪ |. The right hand has an obbligato which ranges from F below the bass stave two octaves upward, a shrunken 'cello compass. The figuration:

Ex. 346

suggests a string instrument. The number may have been derived from a gamba or 'cello sonata movement. The general character of the music fits quite well with the text—'Gott hat Alles wohl gemacht! seine Liebe, seine Treu' wird uns alle Tage neu' ('God has all well made! His love, His faithfulness becomes to us every day new')—with long passages on 'Alles' and 'Tage' matching the virtuosity of the original string soloist. The remainder is 'Wenn uns Angst und Kummer drücket, hat er reichen Trost geschicket, weil er täglich für uns wacht: Gott hat Alles wohl gemacht!' ('When us anguish and grief afflict, has He rich comfort sent, because He daily for us watches: God has all well made!'). Bach's contrapuntal skill enables the first clause of the latter sentence to be set suitably, in spite of the merry instrumental solo, an augmented fourth introducing 'Kummer' and cross accents when the words are repeated.

In vii the full scoring reappears and we evidently possess in this number the finale from yet another lost violin concerto, as all the passage work, with its numerous triplets:

Ex 347

Cont.
8ve lower

is given to the manual and the pedals merely support their brilliant partner. These triplet runs come in handy when the composer wants to set 'fröhliches': 'Ich wünsche mir bei Gott zu leben, ach! wäre doch die Zeit schon da, ein fröhliches Hallelujah mit allen Engeln anzuheben' (I desire with God to live, ah, would then (that) the time (were) already here, a gladsome Hallelujah with all the angels to raise'). In the flourish on the last word the singer impulsively leaps up a major ninth. Again, in spite of the contrary character of the concerto movement, Bach contrives to write a suitable vocal line for 'Mein liebster Jesu, löse doch das jammerreiche Schmerzensjoch, und laß mich bald in deinen Händen mein martervolles Leben enden!' ('My dearest Jesus, loosen then the lamentation-rich sorrow-yoke, and let me soon in Thy hands my torment-full life end!'). The passage to 'deinen' is inappropriate, but the second 'martervolles Leben', with a diminished third and an augmented fifth, preceded by an agonized high note on 'mein', and the third treatment of these words, introducing the tear-motive, are splendidly effective, and an upward rush of triplets on 'enden', following the second 'martervolles Leben', pictures the soul's flight when released from the mortal body.

Although Bach develops his train of thought admirably in the first recitative, iii, it is more an intellectual exercise than a stimulus to musical imagination: 'I marvel, for all that one sees, must us astonishing give. Contemplate I Thee, Thou dear God's Son, then flees reason, and also understanding away. Thou showest it even that what otherwise a wonder-work (is) before Thee mere baseness is. Thou art according to name, deeds and office solely wonder-rich, to Thee is no wonder-thing on this earth equal. To the deaf givest Thou hearing, to the dumb their speech again; yea, what (is) even more, Thou openest at a word the blind eyelids. These, these are wonder-works, and their power is even the angel choir not mighty (enough) to utter.' During the sentences about the deaf, dumb, and blind, the continuo ascends slowly and the voice moves higher and higher, as if in glowing excitement at the marvellous works of God. Bach must have credited his congregation with retentive memories, because after the second Sinfonia, v, the other recitative, vi, comments on the previous aria, iv—'Ah, powerful God, let me then this ever remember, then can I Thee delightedly in my soul receive. Let Thy sweet "Ephphatha" my completely hardened heart soften' (see St. Mark vii. 34) 'ah! lay only the mercy-finger in my ears, otherwise am I immediately lost. Touch also my tongue-string with Thy strong hand

that I (may) these wonder-signs in holy devotion praise, and myself
as child and heir prove.' At the end is one of those rare cases in Bach
where the penultimate chord must needs be played after the voice,
and not with it, though not so indicated. The production of this scrap-
album cantata led the composer into inconsistency of key, it begins
in D minor and ends in C. Here again there is no chorale.

169. After another six weeks, for the Eighteenth Sunday after
Trinity, 23 September, came a partner to this: 'Gott soll allein mein
Herze haben' ('God shall alone my heart have'). The same instruments are employed, though not in such a troublesome way for the
singer, as oboes and taille are not heard save in the opening Sinfonia
and the closing four-part chorale. The Sinfonia and the second aria,
v, are the first and second movements of the E major clavier concerto,
originally for violin. The treatment of the reeds in the Sinfonia is on
the lines adopted in the last cantata, another proof of the connexion
between these works. The harpsichord part is transferred to the
organ, one manual and pedals. The siciliano is fitting to the mood of
the text of v, a farewell to the world: 'Stirb in mir, Welt und alle
deine Liebe, daß die Brust sich auf Erden für und für in der Liebe
Gottes übe! Stirb in mir, Hoffart, Reichtum, Augenlust, ihr verworf'nen Fleischestriebe' ('Die in me, world and all thy love, that
the breast itself on earth for ever and ever in the love of God disciplines! Die in me, arrogance, wealth, eye-lust, you worthless flesh-
impulses'). Although the aria is heavy to sing, the soloist has an
interesting line, sustained notes and one expressive sinking to
'Stirb', leaping passages to 'verworf'nen', a tumultuous run on
'Welt', but there are closed vowels on the long wanderings on 'übe'
and 'triebe', a flaw practically unknown in original compositions.

Bach's (?) libretto is a skilful blend of ideas found in the Epistle,
1 Corinthians i. 4–8, and the Gospel, St. Matthew xxii. 34–36, Paul's
thanks for the virtue of the Corinthians and Christ's answer when the
Pharisees ask which was the greatest commandment. After the Sinfonia an arioso and recitative (three sections of each) with continuo
speaks of surrender to God. A falling phrase delivered by the continuo:

Ex. 348

becomes the motto for 'Gott soll allein mein Herze haben' and is used in each of the arioso sections. The first recitative portion is unwontedly plain: 'Truly perceive I in the world, Which its filth valueless holds, because it so friendly towards me acts, it would willingly alone the beloved of my soul be. But no!' The second arioso adds to the original words: 'ich find' in ihm das höchste Gut' ('I find in Him the highest good'). There is more incident in the second recitative portion. At the end of 'We see truly on earth, here and there, a brooklet of joyfulness, that from the Highest Good wells' is an ascending continuo semiquaver scale; 'Strömen' ('streams') rushes upward in 'God however is the source, with streams filled'; at the end of 'there draw I, (that) which me always can sufficiently and truly refresh', is another upward scale. Although the third arioso is derived from the same material as the others, the treatment is entirely different— 'Gott' had previously been stressed, here the first syllable of 'allein' is thrown at different times on high notes. The final two bars of recitative repeat 'Gott soll allein mein Herze haben' but with a new melody, 'soll' being made prominent this time.

The same words open the first aria, iii, and they continue, 'ich find' in ihm das höchste Gut. Er liebt mich in der bösen Zeit, und will mich in der Seligkeit mit Gütern seines Hauses laben' ('I find in Him the highest good. He loves me in the evil time, and will me in blessedness with the bounty of his house refresh'). The accompaniment is for a single organ manual and continuo, the latter presumably doubled by the pedals. It is undoubtedly derived from some lost instrumental work, possibly an Andante for clavier; in spite of the interest of much of the obbligato, one can never forget that one is listening to an arrangement.

Recitatives with continuo follow both arias. iv is 'What is the love of God? The spirit's repose, the senses' delight-enjoyment, the soul's Paradise. It closes hell, but the heaven opens, it is Elijah's chariot, so shall we (up) into heaven into Abraham's bosom carried be.' vi, without much relevance, quotes the two great commandments: 'Then be ye therein to your neighbour faithful, for so stands (it) in the Scripture written; thou shalt God and thy neighbour love.' A plainly harmonized version of Walther's reconstruction of the pre-Reformation melody 'Nun bitten wir den heiligen Geist' ('Now pray we to the Holy Ghost') concludes. The stanza is the third of three which Luther added to the thirteenth-century vernacular verse associated with the tune: 'Thou sweet love, give us Thy grace, Let us experience love's ardour, That we from our hearts One another love And in peace in one mind dwell. Kyrie eleison.'

49. These two cantatas are more closely allied to each other than
to No. 170, and are also similar to a S.B. duet-cantata or dialogus
which followed a fortnight later, on the Twentieth Sunday after
Trinity, 7 October, 'Ich geh' und suche mit Verlangen' ('I go and
seek with longing'). Having plundered the E major clavier concerto
(or its source) of its first and second movements, Bach now com-
mandeers the third and makes it into the Sinfonia. An oboe d'amore
is added, which, except for one solo passage, is not independent of
violin I. The parable of the marriage of the king's son is related in
the Gospel, St. Matthew xxii. 1–14, and the libretto, possibly by the
composer, is a conversation between the Heavenly Bridegroom and
the Church, the Bride. The first aria, for bass, is borrowed from some
lost work. There is probably some reconstruction, as the initial vocal
phrase moves by an appropriate step-motive:

Ex. 349

which never fits in with the manual theme but is always supported
by the instrumental bass only. The accompaniment is for one organ
manual and continuo. The freedom of the latter points to a keyboard
composition. The repetitions of 'dich' in the continuation—'dich,
meine Taube, schönste Braut!' ('thee, my dove, most beautiful
bride!')—are happy. 'Verlangen' is once set appropriately to chromatics, but there is an awkward accent on 'und', and a long passage
to 'Taube', derived from the manual part, is quite meaningless. The
next portion of the text—'Sag' an, wo bist du hingegangen, daß dich
mein Auge nicht mehr schaut?' ('Say, whither art thou gone, that
thee mine eye no more beholds?')—is set more satisfactorily. The
exigencies of adaptation compel the composer to arrange the sections
of text in the order A B A B A.

In the first section of iii—(a) recitative, (b) arioso, (c) recitative,
(d) arioso, with strings: the Bridegroom invites the Bride to the feast
—'My meal is prepared, and my marriage-table ready, only my Bride
is yet not present'—and the Bride answers joyously—'My Jesus
speaks of me, O voice, which me gladdens!' In (b) the Bridegroom
repeats the first words of the aria, with the same melody for five bars,
a rare instance of quotation. (c) consists of two bars only, an ecstatic

'My Bridegroom! I fall at Thy feet'. The voice descends gracefully and upper strings follow suit. (*d*) is a frank love-duet, which may well take a place on the boards of an Italian opera house, and is developed at length. The tender instrumental figure:

Ex.350

of (*b*) is borrowed by both voice and instruments and there are hints of the 'Ich geh' und suche' idea in the continuo. Bride and Bridegroom sing almost identical words: 'Come, most beautiful (one), come, and let Thyself be kissed, let me Thy (Thou shalt My) rich meal enjoy. My Bridegroom! I (Come, beloved Bride, and) hasten the wedding garments to don.' 'Eilen' ('hasten') is, naturally, allotted runs, 'Hochzeitkleider' ('wedding-garments') moves in parallel motion as if Bride and Bridegroom were walking hand in hand. It is an enchanting number.

The soprano now has an exquisite aria, with delicate obbligati for oboe d'amore and violoncello piccolo:

Ex.351   Vc. picc.

Cont.
8ve lower

and

Ex.352   Vc. picc.

Cont.

The text begins 'Ich bin herrlich, ich bin schön' ('I am glorious, I am beautiful') with (*a*), and the obbligato instruments call to each other with the initial four notes of (*b*) and a derivative. Later (*a*) and (*b*) are combined. When the singer continues—'meinen Heiland zu entzünden' ('my Saviour to inflame')—the voice wings its way heavenward in a rising sequence derived from (*b*), while the obbligati repeat it in another form and then play (*a*) in canon. No new themes are introduced into the remainder; both 'Seines Heils Gerechtigkeit ist mein Schmuck und Ehrenkleid' ('His salvation's justice is my ornament and honour-garment') and 'und damit will ich bestehn,

wenn ich werd' in Himmel gehn' ('and therewith will I endure, when
I shall to heaven go') begin with (*a*). 'Bestehn' is sustained and there
is another, though different, winging upwards on 'Himmel'.

The mood is sustained in the ensuing duetto-recitativo secco, the
text mostly paraphrases from the Scriptures, the librettist making a
felicitous selection. The Bride: 'My faith has me myself so clothed!'
The Bridegroom: 'So remains my heart to Thee affectionate, so shall
I with Thee in eternity (be) wedded and affianced.' (see Hos. ii. 19.)
The Bride: 'How well is it with me!' (these words are sostenuto)
'heaven is for me opened, the Almighty calls Himself and sends His
servants, that the fallen race, in heaven's hall, at the sacramental
meal as guests may be', the remainder is in arioso—'here come I,
Jesu, admit me!' The Bridegroom: 'Be till death faithful, so place I
on Thee the life-crown.' The close of this quotation from Revelation
(ii. 10) is striking:

The dialogus concludes with a long duet. In further paraphrases
the Bridegroom sings of love: 'Dich hab' ich je und je geliebet, und
darum zieh' ich dich zu mir' (see Jer. xxxi. 3) 'ich komme bald, ich
stehe vor der Thür' (see Rev. iii. 20) 'mach' auf, mein Aufenthalt'
('Thee have I ever and ever loved, and therefore draw I Thee to Me,
I come soon, I stand before the door, open, mine abode.') The Bride
intones stanza 7 of P. Nicolai's 'Wie schön leuchtet der Morgenstern' ('How brightly shines the Morning-Star') to the well-known
tune of the author, 'How am I then so heartily glad, That my Treasure is the A and O' ('Alpha and Omega') 'The beginning and the
ending. He will me then as His prize Receive in Paradise, For this
clap I My hands! Amen, Amen. Come, thou beautiful joy-crown,
delay not long! For thee wait I with longing.' The scoring is the same
as in i, though the oboe d'amore is never independent. The organ
obbligato:

is clearly an instrumental composition, charmingly engaging in quality, possibly refashioned to allow for the chorale. The tuneful bass line:

Ex. 355

Dich hab'   ich je   und je   ge - lie - bet,

(Same continuo as above)

modifies the ideas of the organ part, and faulty accentuation suggests that other themes were part of the original structure. In spite of this flaw the duet provides a fascinating conclusion to an attractive cantata.

29. On 27 August of this year, only fifteen days after No. 35 was produced, a cantata was necessary for the Election of the Town Council. With the fever of transcription upon him, he compiled a bulky work by scissors-and-paste methods: 'Wir danken dir, Gott, wir danken dir' ('We thank Thee, God, we thank Thee'). The text of the first chorus, ii, is Psalm lxxv. 1. The remainder of the words are 'und verkündigen deine Wunder' ('and proclaim Thy wonders'). Possibly every number except the two short recitatives with continuo, iv and vi, is derived from earlier material, although only in the case of the Sinfonia, i (see O.O.S. No. 042) do we possess the first form. That number is an extraordinary expansion, the first movement of the violin solo suite in E, No. 6, transposed into D and transformed from a single line to a concerto-like movement for 'organo obligato' of two manuals, three trumpets, timpani, two oboes (which merely double the violins), and strings. The high-pitched detached trumpet chords add to the brillance of the passage-work of the solo instrument. The hurry of providing the cantata did not deter Bach from writing out this ten-staved score of 138 bars. One cannot help imagining how majestic would have been the result had he ever orchestrated the violin solo chaconne. Perhaps he did and it is lost to us! At a later date this Sinfonia was inserted into the incomplete and unnumbered wedding cantata, 'Herr Gott, Beherrscher aller Dinge.'

While no earlier version is known of ii, one cannot help feeling that its archaic style and severity are so unlike what is usually met with in the church cantatas that it must be borrowed from some other work. The trumpets are used with the utmost reticence, the first not entering till bar 30, and another fifteen bars of rest intervening between its first delivery of the subject and its second. Trumpets and

drums are heard for seventeen bars only. Possibly brass and percussion were additions to the original score on account of the splendour of the municipal festival. Its powerful and dignified character
fits it well to become the 'Gratias agimus' and 'Dona nobis pacem'
of the *B Minor Mass,* although its architecture is somewhat Gothic-
ized in the process. A comparison of the two versions shows interesting features of Bach's methods of transcription, which rarely allowed
a work to be reproduced unaltered.

iii is a bright tenor aria with violin solo obbligato. Evidently Bach
had not much opinion of the literary acumen of the solid Burgomasters and concluded that in this adaptation (for it is certainly not
an original aria, possibly it is derived from a movement of a sonata
for violin and clavier) there would be things which they would never
notice! One wonders why he did not rectify them when the cantata was
repeated in 1739 and 1749, seeing that he was such an inveterate re-
viser of his own compositions, and seeing that he was himself the
librettist. The flying figures and the strong bass make it attractive.
A clear indication of arrangement is the fact that the opening violin
idea:

Ex. 356

is altered considerably when the beginning of the text is announced:
'Halleluja, Stärk', und Macht sei des Allerhöchsten Namen!'
('Hallelujah, power and might be to the All-Highest's name!'). It
disappears entirely in Part II, which, instrumentally, is based wholly
upon the three ideas of the second section of the introduction, quaver
runs, a delightful figure:

Ex. 357

and a leaping motive:

Ex. 358

Most of Part I is also devoted to these. Lively runs decorate the
Hallelujahs, but the vocal line of Part II: 'Zion ist noch seine Stadt,

da er seine Wohnung hat, da er noch bei unserm Saamen an der
Väter Bund gedacht' ('Zion is still His city, where He His dwelling
has, there He still with our seed our fathers covenant remembers')
[moves largely in crotchets,] though the latter part grows more ornate.

The soprano aria, v (see P. 21) is evidently a siciliano from some
lost violin composition:

Ex. 359

thus making three adapted movements of this type in adjacent cantatas, a curious obsession of these months. The arrangement is
peculiar. The first seven sections alternate tutti (oboe and strings)
with the voice plus this combination minus continuo, the organ, a
pedal line only, distinct from the continuo, being marked 'tasto
solo'. In 'Gedenk' an uns mit deiner Liebe, schleuß' uns in dein
Erbarmen ein' ('Think on us with Thy love, enclose us in Thy pity')
the passage on 'Erbarmen' is appropriate, but that on 'deiner':

Ex. 360

is quite nonsensical, charming though it be instrumentally. Eleven
bars before the Da Capo the voice is heard for the first time with
the continuo—'Segne die, so uns regieren, die uns leiten, schützen,
führen, segne die gehorsam sein' ('Bless those, who us govern, who
us direct, protect, lead, bless those who dutiful are')—this time with
oboe alone, the upper strings not entering until the last four bars.
The association of the pompous burgomasters with a siciliano is quite
humorous.

A short alto recitative—'Forget it further not, with Thy hand to
us good to show; so shall Thee our town and our land, that of Thine
honour (is) full, with offerings and with thanks praise, and all people
shall say'—concludes with an 'Amen' for all voices, and then without a break the first aria is reintroduced, or, rather, the first part of it
without the ritornello. It is transposed from A to D, the vocal line
is transferred to the alto, and, a most singular thing, the violin solo
now becomes organ obbligato, the only changes being transposition

and addition of mordents at various points. As the new obbligato is well within the compass of the violin one cannot see why the trans- ference was made. The cold, unyielding line of the organ stop comes as ungratefully after the warm, living tone of the violin, as does the repetition of the melody at the beginning of Beethoven's violin and pianoforte sonata in F. Perhaps again it may be reasoned that Coun- cil cantatas, like the Short Masses, did not matter. But if so, why did he take the trouble to write the splendid Sinfonia when more im- portant cantatas were denied one?

The cantor-librettist assures the masters of Leipzig, in the bass recitative, iv, that their citizens are fortunate: 'Praise be to God! it is well with us! God is still our confidence, His protection, His com- fort, His light protects the city and the palaces, His wing holds the walls firm. He causes us on all sides to be blest, faithfulness, which peace kisses' (see Ps. lxxxv. 10) 'must for ever and ever righteousness meet. Where is there such a people, as we, to whom God so near and gracious is?' This is lip-service which Bach cannot possibly have felt in his heart.

A curious point in key-planning suggests that the succeeding aria was dragged in by the hair of its head, for the recitative ends with a half-close on a B major chord, and the siciliano is in B minor.

A chorale setting closes the cantata, the complete orchestra re- appearing, oboes and strings doubling the voices, trumpets and drums reserved for clenching the cadences of the first two (repeated) and the last two lines, tromba I, and sometimes the others, being independent. The stanza is an anonymous addition to J. Graumann's four-versed 'Nun lob', mein Seel', den Herren' (see cantata No. 51, p. 362 for translation) with the associated melody supposedly by J. Kugelmann.

27. There is only one adapted number in 'Wer weiß, wie nahe mir mein Ende' ('O teach me, Lord, my days to number' N. 'Who knows how near my latter ending' B.). Again it is the alto voice which is favoured with a transcription, and the scoring is odd, 'organo obligato' for manual or manuals without pedal:

Ex. 361   Organo obligato

L.H.
8ve lower

continuo, which doubles the left-hand of the organ, and oboe da caccia. In the score is written 'Aria a Hautb. dà Caccia e Cembalo obligato', whereas Bach's own organ part states 'Organo obligato', and on the cover he writes 'Organo oblig'. It seems as if this number were derived from a sonata movement for gamba and cembalo, although Spitta thinks it original. The line assigned to the oboe da caccia is not particularly suitable to it. Vocal accentuation is not always happy, and in bars 28–30 there is an awkward disposition of words, which would not have occurred had the aria been original. The text is 'Willkommen! will ich sagen, wenn der Tod an's Bette tritt. Fröhlich will ich folgen, wenn er ruft, in die Gruft. Alle meine Plagen nehm' ich mit' ('Welcome! will I say, when death to my bed steps. Joyfully will I follow, when He calls, into the grave. All my burdens take I with (me)'). In spite of the vocal line being superimposed upon a settled texture, there are many happily devised points, the tumbling groups:

Ex.362 will - kom-men, will ich sa - gen,

the ascending passages on 'fröhlich', the almost merry phrase:

Ex.363 wenn er ruft, in die Gruft,

with its high-pitched 'ruft' and the drop of a seventh to 'Gruft', and chromatics to 'Plagen'.

The rest of the cantata is of superb quality. The Gospel for the Sixteenth Sunday after Trinity relates the story of the raising of the widow's son (St. Luke vii. 11–17), and all the four cantatas written by Bach for that day deal with the call of death. A hymn-stanza, interleaved with recitatives, is the text of the opening number, a vocally simple choral fantasia, placing the cantata on the borderline between solo (S.A.T.B.) and choral. A double quartet is ample for i. Stanza 1 of Emilie Juliane, Countess of Schwarzburg-Rudolstadt's funerary hymn 'Wer weiß, wie nahe mir mein Ende', is employed: 'Who knows, how near me (is) my end? Departs the time, arrives the death. Ah, how fast and nimbly Can come my death-peril! My God, I beg through Christ's blood, Make it only with my ending good.' The melody, which is strengthened by a horn, is G. Neumark's 'Wer nur den lieben Gott läßt walten' ('Who only the loving God allows to rule'). The inevitable passing of time is adumbrated by a pendulum-like figure in the continuo, while the upper strings fall in arpeggi:

(C minor, signature of 2 flats)

the sinking to death, and, combining with these, the two oboes sing a duet of lamentation:

The picture is deeply moving. The two-note tear-motive occurs in various transmutations throughout:

even decorating the continuo amplification of the vocal bass. A questioning idea, derived from bar 2 of oboe I, is frequently heard:

and

the first group of four notes is repeated over and over again, subjected to many alterations, a series of cries of lamentation, and the persistent falling diminished fourth, (a), never allows the sounds of sorrow to be absent from our ears. Lines 1 and 3 of the chorale are not prolonged, 2, 4, and 5 are lengthened with exquisitely beautiful passages for the lower voices against holding notes, line 6 is introduced by imitations, and also prolonged. The three upper voices interleave the chorale lines with recitatives; soprano (after 1)—'That knows the loving God alone, if my pilgrimage on earth short or longer may be' (the penultimate quotation *supra* in canon between the oboes); alto (after 2)—'and finally, comes it then so far, that they together meet will' (the last quotation as an oboe canon); tenor (after 4)—'Who knows, if today not my mouth the last words speaks?' (treatment as in the alto section), 'therefore pray I at all times' (while 'bet'' ('pray') is sustained, five bars of the introduction begin).

An expressive recitativo secco for tenor joins the chorus with the borrowed number: 'My life has no other aim, than that I may blessed die, and my faith's portion inherit. Therefore live I always for the grave ready and prepared, and what the work of the hands does, is as it were (as) if I surely knew, that I even today die must? for an ending good makes all good.' The continuo must be *tacet* at the beginning of bar 4, and take up again when the singer has finished his word, a rare instance in Bach. A charming little conceit occurs in the soprano recitative with strings, iv; at the words 'Flügel her!' ('Wings hither!') violin I twice scurries upwards in demisemiquavers, in contrast to the sober and restrained character of the remainder of the number: 'Ah, who then already in heaven were! I have desire to depart' (see Phil. i. 23) 'and with the Lamb, the devout one's Bridegroom, myself in blessedness to pasture.' After 'Flügel her!' the opening clause is repeated. The first is an affirmation, this is an exclamation of wonder, ending on the dominant chord of the key.

The bass aria, with strings, v (see P. 55) sets out two ideas only, a slow-moving 'Gute Nacht' ('Good night' or 'Farewell').

Ex. 369

and a bustling one associated with 'du Weltgetümmel' ('thou world-confusion'):

Ex. 370

They are the same as those used in the bass scena of No. 70; there a Presto comes between two Adagios, but here there is no change of tempo, and the two ideas are alternated and blended, sometimes combined. 'Gute Nacht' is twice set to a beautifully expressive phrase, 'Weltgetümmel' sometimes to quaver arpeggi, sometimes to tumbling semiquavers. The middle section—'Jetzt mach' ich mit dir Beschluß; ich steh' schon mit einem Fuß bei dem lieben Gott im Himmel' ('Now make I with thee conclusion; I stand already with one foot with the beloved God in heaven')—begins with continuo only, the bassi playing short ♩♫♩ | ♩ groups derived from the 'Gute Nacht' idea; with 'ich steh'', &c., which poises on 'Fuß', violin I slowly curves downwards, the thought of the 'lieben Gott' brings soaring passages. With the repetition of the second clause, where both 'steh'' and 'Fuß' are sustained, the 'Gute Nacht' idea is heard in the orchestra, newly harmonized.[1] Few arias are so simple and straightforward, few make such a direct impression. The closing chorale has two features of interest. It is the only chorale in five parts in the cantatas (the motet 'Jesu, meine Freude' contains one), and the only other five-part choral writing is to be found in Nos. 31 and 191, the latter merely an adaptation. The other point is that for the only time in the cantatas Bach introduces a chorale harmonization not his own. The version by the composer, Johann Rosenmüller, published in 1682, is reproduced with slight alterations. Perhaps Bach felt that so recent a composition did not need to be treated afresh. Stanza 1 of J. G. Albinus's 'Welt ade! ich bin dein müde', for which the music was written, is 'World adieu! I am of thee weary, I will to (the) heaven go, There will be the true peace And the eternal, superb repose. World, in thee is war and strife, Nothing but pure vanity; In heaven always Peace, joy and bliss.' It is not known who is the librettist of the cantata.

188. 'Ich habe meine Zuversicht' ('I have my confidence'), for the Twenty-first Sunday after Trinity, 28 October 1730, brings a matter for speculation. A note to the score indicates that as a Sinfonia the organ version of the first movement of the D minor clavier concerto is to be played. In this arrangement the keyboard part is altered in detail and two oboes and taille added. It is found in the score of No. 146, which, however, was not produced until 1740, and there the second movement of the concerto is transformed into the succeeding

[1] Cf. the opening of the last chorus in the *St. Matthew Passion*.

chorus. It is probable that the spate of concerto arrangements occurred in 1731, but if the version was written then why was it not included in the manuscript? Only a copy of the original of No. 188 is known. Spitta thinks that the whole concerto acted as a prelude, to show off the reconstructed Rückpositiv. Did Bach, finding that No. 188, a solo cantata for S.A.T.B., was rather short and lacking in weight, indicate this addition at some subsequent performance for which something more imposing was needed? On account of there being two movements of the concerto in No. 146, it is more likely that they were both arranged at the same time than that nine years should separate them. Nor can one see why the same Sinfonia should preface two such contrasting texts, Picander's No. 188 speaks of confidence in God, in His uprightness and everlasting strength, while No. 146 begins with Acts xiv. 22, 'We must through much tribulation enter the kingdom of God'. The character of the first movement fits the mood of No. 188 better, but it seems more appropriate musically, if not emotionally, when the two movements are brought together in No. 146.

Scheyer attributes part of the cantata to Wilhelm Friedemann, but one can scarcely credit him with the opening tenor aria (oboe and strings), which is a number of outstanding beauty and one of the most grateful pieces of writing for that voice in the cantatas. The chief melody is winning in its graciousness:

Ex. 371 I have my confidence on the faithful God placed,
Ich ha - be mei-ne Zu - ver-sicht auf den ge-treu-en Gott ge-richt,

Cont.

There is a felicitous touch in one portion to 'da ruhet meine Hoffnung feste' ('there rests my hope secure'), where a waving figure enters in imitation:

Ex. 372 Ob.

The section 'Wenn alles bricht, wenn alles fällt, wenn niemand Treu' und Glauben hält' ('When all breaks, when all falls, when nobody faithfulness and belief holds') has leaping figures in voice and continuo, dropping staccato passages for oboe, and the upper strings, massed into unison, picture the confusion of the world. 'So ist doch Gott der allerbeste' ('So is yet God the best of all') recalls the opening idea, and in five and four bars from the Da Capo are splendid leaps for violin, expressing exuberance at the thought that God is the best of all.

A long and distinguished bass recitativo secco separates the two arias of the work: 'God means it well with everyman even in the all-greatest need. Conceals He although His love, so thinks His heart yet secretly thereon; that can He never not take away, and were me the Lord even to kill, so hope I yet on Him. For His angry countenance is otherwise not than a cloud heavy, which hinders only the sunshine, that through a soft rain the heaven's blessing so much the richer may be. The Lord transforms Himself into a cruel (one), as (the) more comforting to appear; He will, He can not evil purpose.' A $\frac{6}{8}$ arioso at the end livens up interest with a paraphrased scriptural quotation, Genesis xxxii. 26: 'Therefore leave I Him not (that), He bless me then.'

The number for alto, iii, recalls the first aria of No. 169; it is an instrumental movement given to organ obbligato (written a tone lower) and a voice part adapted. In this case a 'cello doubles the left hand of the organist:

Ex. 373

for which there is no indication as to 8 or 16 ft. and no figuring. There is no continuo part proper; perhaps 8 ft. tone was intended in all these obbligati. The organ part sounds better without the vocal addition; the latter makes the number sound laboured. The first part of the text is devoid of suggestions for musical treatment—'Unerforschlich ist die Weise, wie der Herr die Seine führt' ('Unfathomable is the way (in) which the Lord His own guides')—and the elaborations mean nothing. The previously composed music does not prevent the remainder—'Selber unser Kreuz und Pein muß zu unserm Besten sein, und zu seines Namens Preise' ('Even our cross and pain must to our best (interest) be, and to His name's glory')—from being admirably expressed in the vocal line, there are leaning tones on 'Kreuz' and 'Pein', 'Preise' rejoices in lengthy flourishes and the final words of this section are set in coruscating trills and leaps. 'Unserm Besten', however, does not mate comfortably with coloratura. The penultimate number is a fine little recitative for soprano. 'Die Macht der Welt verlieret sich' ('The might of the world loses itself') is heralded with crashing chords for strings, both lines of violins and violas being in double stopping, and followed by an arpeggio descent. 'Wer kann auf Stand und Hoheit bauen?' ('Who can on rank and position build?') is accompanied by detached chords. After a sustained chord to 'God but abides eternally', the strings pulsate in gentle repeated quavers, the prayer-motive, during '(It is) well for all who in Him trust'.

The melody of the final chorale is one of those secular tunes which curiously came to serve for hymns, 'Venus du und dein Kind' ('Venus thou and thy child'). Another instance is H. Isaak's 'O Welt, ich muß dich lassen' ('O World, I must thee leave'), which was originally 'Innspruck, I must thee leave'. The melody of the song about the goddess of love came to be associated with two hymns— J. Hermann's 'Wo soll ich fliehen hin' and S. Weingärtner's(?) 'Auf meinen lieben Gott', and it is the first stanza of the latter which is set here: 'On my beloved God, Rely I in anguish and need; He can me always deliver From trouble, anguish and needs, My misfortune can He turn, Stands everything in His hands.'

The numerous borrowings in these cantatas should not prejudice one against their use. There are many attractive numbers. Cantatas 29 and 49, for instance, are full of good things. That the composer selected for transcription certain instrumental works from the great mass he had written argues some merit in them. Audiences and students of Bach, however, should be fully acquainted with the circumstances of these cantatas, otherwise there will be misunderstanding as to the relation between words and music and as to Bach's methods of composition.

(B) OTHER CANTATAS CONTAINING BORROWED INSTRUMENTAL MATERIAL
42, 52, 58, 83, 120, 156, 166, 174, 194

These will be discussed in their chronological order: 194, 83, 156, 174, 52, 166, 120, 42, 58

194. 'Höchsterwünschtes Freudenfest' is singular in several respects. We know that Bach was much in demand as an adviser in matters of organ-building, in which he possessed unique knowledge and insight, and as recitalist at opening ceremonies. Doubtless he often composed music for these occasions, but this is the solitary remaining example. A new church and organ were dedicated on 2 November 1723, the year he went to Leipzig, at Störmthal, a near-by village. The instrument has been recently restored at the instance of the National Socialist Kulturgemeinde Kreis; see *Musical Times*, July 1936, which contains a photograph. The manuscript of the score associates this work with the service and Anna Magdalena was soprano soloist. The text, possibly Bach's own, was printed and contains a dedication to Herr Statz Hilmor von Fullen, Knight of the Holy Roman Empire, of Störmthal, Marck-Klebern and Liebert-Wolckwitz, gentleman-in-waiting to the King of Poland and worshipful honorary Chamberlain to the Princely House of Saxony and Assessor at the Supreme Court of Justice, who had provided the funds for the building of the instrument. The work was subsequently used for Trinity Sunday, 1731, although the text has nothing to do with that occasion except that the first and second recitatives of Part II may be references to the Gospel, St. John iii. 1–15, the discussion between Christ and Nicodemus. The second of these, for S.B., is modelled freely on the dialogue. He would, naturally, write his original libretto with an eye to future service at St. Thomas's. That he concocted the cantata from previous instrumental material is obvious; it looks as if a lost Cöthen orchestral suite was commandeered. The opening number is in overture form, two of the arias and the duet are dance measures. It is amazing that he should have gone to such trouble and have written such a long work, twelve numbers in all, for a ceremony in such an obscure place, although the dedication suggests that he may have had some reason for winning the favour of the dedicatee. Another curious feature is the exceedingly high tessitura of the vocal lines. The organ must have been of a very low pitch, and one wonders what happened when the work was given at Leipzig. For performance today one must transfer some of the vocal lines to singers other than those indicated. The writer found it necessary to write out the orchestral parts of the chorus a tone lower, in order to make it more comfortable for the choir and to avoid such terrifying trials for the sopranos as entries on high C. The scoring is for three oboes, bassoons (the plural is indicated, but there is a single line only), strings, and continuo. The *grave* is replete with dotted notes, oboes, bassoons, and continuo maintaining the chief idea:

Ex. 374

and the upper strings enter from time to time in unison:

Ex. 375

What was no doubt the chief theme of the Allegro was well served by the composer-librettist with an appropriate text:

Ex. 376

After a short development, including a quasi-stretto, a new theme is treated as a trio of upper voices and strings:

Ex. 377

The violin version may have been a subsidiary idea of the original movement. (c) is resumed, with voices in a different order. Then comes another trio, of twelve bars, of the character we find in the overtures, possibly originally for two oboes and bassoon; the latter line is now for organ solo and choral basses in unison:

Ex. 378

The remainder of this portion of the text is 'im erbauten Heiligthume uns vergnügt begehen läßt' ('in the erected sanctuary us delightedly to celebrate allows'). A section for full chorus ensues, recapitulating the text. The first five notes of (d) appear in various ways, unison oboes, oboes in sixths, in the upper voices and in the bassi, there is a triple trill for sopranos, altos, and tenors, the basses sing broad melodies, in which one finds traces of (*e*). Then comes a final fugal section based on (*a*), with a quasi-stretto over a dominant pedal and an eight-bar run for the basses on 'Freudenfest'. In a shortened form of the *grave*, upper strings and fagotti take over (*a*) and the oboes (*b*). In the last three bars the chorus joins the orchestra with a shout of 'Höchsterwünschtes Freudenfest', a thrilling conclusion.

The bass aria, iii, is better sung by a tenor (see P. 9 for the latter voice). It is a $\frac{12}{8}$ movement somewhat of the siciliano type, although the usual ♪.♫ of that dance is not present. The scoring is for strings and oboe, the latter, except for a few downward running passages, doubling violin I. Bowing and tonguing are unusually full and directions of forte and piano are common. These again suggest an instrumental origin. The opening melody is adapted for the voice:

Ex.379   what the Highest's lustre fills,   is in no   night veiled,
         was des Höchsten Glanz er - füllt,   wird in kei - ne Nacht ver-hüllt,

Cont.

In bar 6 the semiquavers on 'in' are an example of meaningless mating of music and verse. Another proof of adaptation is that the only other words are an alternative to the first clause: 'Was des Höchsten heil'ges Wesen sich zur Wohnung auserlesen' ('What the Highest's holy Being Himself as dwelling (has) chosen'). Even the most unimaginative poetaster would not have allowed his stanza to fizzle out in this ineffective way had he been inventing independent verse. It is, however, a gracious number musically, and one may well forget that it is an arrangement. There are some fine runs to 'erfüllt' and to 'auserlesen', and the four semiquavers allotted to 'in' are more important instrumentally than their appearance in the vocal line would suggest. The tempo must be leisurely, on account of the flourishes of semiquaver triplets.

v is a fully developed gavotte, in which, apparently, the melodic interest was originally confined to violin I, a continuously flowing line:

Ex.380

(E♭, with signature of 2 flats)

and the lower strings restricted to crotchets and a ♩ ♩ | ♩ time-pattern. The chief theme is modified for the voice:

Ex.381 Help, God, that it (to) us succeeds and Thy fire   in us   pierces;
Hilf, Gott, dass es uns ge-lingt und dein Feu-er   in uns   dringt;

Cont. 8ve lower   4♭   6   6   6   4   3
                         2   5♭

Bach is here more successful as composer than as poet. Anything more incongruous with the idea of divine fire urging through one's veins than the happy music of the gavotte could scarcely be imagined, although there is evident attempt at pictorial treatment in the run which commences in the last bar of the above quotation. During Part II—'Daß es auch in dieser Stunde wie in Esaiae Munde seiner Wirkung Kraft erhält, und uns heilig vor dich stellt' ('That it also in this hour as in Isaiah's mouth of his working strength receives' (the reference is to Isaiah vi. 6 and 7), 'and us holy before Thee places')—the voice maintains the gavotte movement above the continuo and violin I indulges in delicious flourishes illustrative of the flight of the seraphim. There are again liberal directions, even including pianissimo, indicative of a previously conceived scheme.

The least interesting number is the tenor aria with continuo, viii. The movement is almost throughout in the style of the opening:

Ex.382
(a)

♯ 6   6   ♭   6
  ♯
  2

but numerous triplets indicate that the real time-signature is $\frac{12}{8}$ and that its origin was possibly a slow gigue. 'Des Höchsten Gegenwart allein' ('The Highest's presence alone') is set to (a) and 'kann unsrer Freuden Ursprung sein' ('can of our joys (the) source be') slips into trills and triplets. A strange passage comes later, 'allein' reposes upon an F♯, and then suddenly bursts into a rapid, brilliant flourish, quite at variance with the rest of the aria and totally uncalled for by the word. Part II is 'Vergehe, Welt, mit deiner Pracht, in Gott ist, was uns glücklich macht' ('Vanish, world, with thy pomp, in God is what us happy makes'). Declamatory passages make a contrast from the previously flowing melody.

x is an enormously long S.B. duet with two oboes, 324 bars in all
if one repeats in full. It is a development of what was probably a
minuet in the original orchestral suite. The ritornello falls into four
sections:

(the connexion between this and (*aa*) and (*aaa*) will be noticed)

and (*d*), in which the scalic passages of (*c*) are decorated with (*aa*);
(*aaa*) frequently occurs in the continuo. There is very little other
material in the number, although (*d*) does not appear again in its
entirety save in the middle ritornello. Every vocal section begins with
the voices in parallel motion, happily illustrative of the blissful contentment of those who assemble in the new house of God. The opening words—'O wie wohl ist uns gescheh'n, daß sich Gott ein Haus
erseh'n' ('Oh how well has to us happened, that Himself God a home
(has) chosen')—are sung to (*a*) and (*b*); (*c*), with a pedal instead of a
moving bass, affords the opportunity of adding two vocal counterpoints moving against each other instead of in parallel motion.
Part II—'Schmeckt und sehet doch zugleich, Gott sei freundlich
gegen euch' ('Taste and see yet together, God is friendly towards
you')—introduces a vocal variant of (*a*):

most of the other lines for the singers are new, though the orchestra
keeps to the old themes. On account of the compass it is well to

replace the basses by tenors after the Fine pause, allowing the original voices to return at the closing sentence: 'Schüttet eure Herzen aus hier vor Gottes Thron und Haus' ('Pour your hearts out here before God's throne and house').

The recitatives, all with continuo, contain little of musical interest. The texts, however, are indications of Bach's reverence for the House of God, his facility for spinning sermonettes on an equality with those of his clergy, and of his tireless industry. They are thus of interest to all students of his ways of thought and are worth quoting for these reasons. ii (B., better sung by T.): 'Infinitely great God, ah, turn Thyself to us, to the chosen race, and to the prayer of Thy servants, ah, let (us) before Thee through a fervent singing of the lips offerings bring. We consecrate our heart to Thee publicly as a thanks-altar. Thou, Whom no house, no temple holds; as Thou no limit nor boundary hast, let to Thee this house pleasing be, be Thy countenance a true mercy-stool, a joy-light.' iv, S.: 'How could to Thee, Thou Highest countenance, as Thy infinitely bright light in hidden sources penetrates, a house pleasing be? Insinuates itself vanity everywhere on all sides. Where Thy glory enters in, there must the dwelling pure and of this Guest worthy be. Here avails nothing human-power, therefore let Thine eye open remain, and mercifully on us look; so lay we in holy joy to Thee the aims and the offerings of our songs before Thy throne down, and bear to Thee the wish in devotion ever.' vii, T.: 'Ye holy ones, rejoice ye, hasten, hasten your God to praise; the heart be uplifted to God's honour-kingdom, from whence He on thee, thou holy dwelling, looks down, and a purified heart to Himself from this vain earth draws. A state, so fairly blessed called; one beholds here Father, Son and Spirit. Well then, ye God-filled souls! You will now the best part choose; the world can you no comfort give, you can in God alone delighted and blessed live.' ix, B.: 'Can possibly a man to God towards heaven climb?' S.: 'Faith can the Creator to him bring down.' B.: 'It is often a too weak bond.' S.: 'God guides Himself and strengthens of faith (the) hand, the ordained declaration to achieve.' B.: 'How though, if the flesh's weakness would waver?' S.: 'The Highest's strength becomes mighty in the weak.' B.: 'The world will at them laugh.' S.: 'Who God's grace possesses, despises such mockery.' B.: 'What will they except this lack?' S.: 'Their every wish, their all is in God.' B.: 'God is invisible and afar;' S.: 'Well for us, that our faith learns, in spirit its God to behold.' B.: 'Their flesh holds them imprisoned.' S.: 'The Highest's grace furthers their longing, for He builds the place, wherein one Him gloriously beholds.' Andante, S.B.: 'There He the faith now rewards and with us dwells, with us as His children, so can the world and mortality' (arioso) 'the joy not prevent.' xi, B. (may be sung by T.): 'Boldly therefore, thou saintly congregation, prepare yourself for holy delight! God dwells not only in every single heart, He builds Himself here a house. Boldly, so array yourselves with spirit and gifts, that Him as well thy heart as even this house (may) please!' (Possibly the text refers to the Collection and the Communion which would follow.)

The tutti chorales which close both parts have two verses each, no doubt to give the large congregation, which would assemble from far and near, a vocal part in the ceremony, even if the gifts asked for in xi were not forthcoming. (Terry chronicles that at a similar service in Dresden 1,000 people contributed only 837 coins, totalling in value 9 thaler, 22 groschen, $2\frac{1}{2}$ pfennig. History repeats itself. Then, as now, congregations at special musical occasions in church considered it as their privilege to show their appreciation of the endless labours of willing and self-sacrificing musicians with the widow's mite, and less!) The first melody is Bourgeois's 'Ainsi qu'on oit le cerf' and the hymn drawn on is Hermann's 'Treuer Gott, ich muß dich klagen.' Stanza 6: 'Holy Ghost on heaven's throne, An equal God from eternity With the Father and the Son, The afflicted's comfort and joy! All faith that I find Hast Thou in me kindled, Over me in grace govern, Further Thy mercy hold.' Stanza 7—'Thy help to me send, O Thou noble heart's-guest! And the good work accomplish That Thou begun hast. Blow in me the tiny spark up Till that after the accomplished course I to the elect glide And faith's goal reach.' The other is N. Selnecker's(?) melody 'Nun laßt uns Gott dem Herren' with verses from Gerhardt's morning hymn 'Wach auf, mein Herz, und singe.' Stanza 7: 'Say Yea to my doings, Help even the best to advise; The beginning, middle and the end, Ah Lord, to the best turn.' Stanza 8: 'With blessings me cover, My heart be Thy house, Thy word be my meat, Till I towards heaven journey.'

83. The next four cantatas in this group assayed some of their gold from concerto-ore, quarrying one unknown and three known works. 'Erfreute Zeit im neuen Bunde' was composed for the Feast of the Purification of the Blessed Virgin Mary, 2 February 1724. It is a solo cantata, with a chorale to conclude. i and iii, arias for alto and tenor,

are adaptations from the first and last movements of a lost concerto.
If the violin solo, tutti strings and continuo of i are taken from the
score as they stand, they may be played as a first movement. The
opening tutti:

Ex.387   Vl. Solo. Tutti Vl.I.

and the figuration which succeeds:

Ex.388   Vl. Solo.

and the favourite device of alternating stopped and open strings:

Ex.389

indicate clearly its origin. (c) is used in the soprano aria of No. 133
to illustrate the words 'Wie lieblich klingt es in den Ohren!' ('How
lovingly rings it in the ears!'), here it is but a factor in violin virtuosity
and has no relation to the text. On the stirring score Bach has super-
imposed the vocal part and lines for two oboes and two horns, sometimes weaving ten strands in all. A powerful singer is needed to battle
with the orchestral forces, which are employed in full almost throughout. It may have been the same alto for whom the organ obbligato
cantatas were written. Except for a few notes here and there, the vocal
line is completely independent. 'Erfreute Zeit' ('Joyful time') opens
with (a) and continues with flourishes; 'im neuen Bunde,' ('in the
new dispensation') incorporates (bb), 'da unser Glaube Jesum hält'
('when our faith Jesus holds') begins with a time-pattern found in
the added parts of the introduction— ♪ | ♪ ♫ ♪ . 'Erfreute',
naturally, is associated with extensive runs and trills, and 'hält'
brings holding notes. It is after the *fine* pause that (c) comes into play.
'Wie freudig wird zur letzten Stunde' ('How joyfully will be at the
last hour') is not at all appropriate, but when the middle strings sustain and the voice sings waving passages to 'die Ruhestatt, das Grab,

bestellt!' ('the resting-place, the grave, prepared!') it is much more in keeping. A downward scale to the last clause as far as 'Grab', which then leaps suddenly upwards, and a flourish on 'bestellt', are as apt as if the vocal line had been composed first. There is now a ritornello, developing figures akin to (b), and introducing part of (a). The voice flourishes on 'freudig', and then there is a rescored version of the opening of Part II.

The violin solo line of iii is almost a moto perpetuo of triplets, the lower strings are staccato, violin I tutti mostly in unison with the first of each triplet. Three quotations show the principal material:

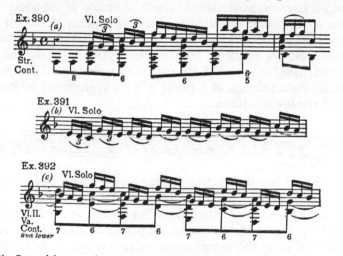

Violin I tutti is not shown in (c), it follows the plan of the rest. It is clear that staccato will not apply to crotchets and to the tied notes of (c). Occasionally the upper strings cease, to allow the voice to be heard with continuo only. One may take it that in these cases the solo violin is deprived of its original matter. Bach was possibly his own librettist, for the text—'Eile, Herz, voll Freudigkeit vor den Gnadenstuhl zu treten' ('Hasten, heart, full of joyfulness before the mercy-stool to step')—suits the movement admirably. 'Eile' begins with a fragment of (a), re-enters with a longer portion, 'treten' has enormously long runs, mostly of triplets. Against (c) is fitted 'vor den Gnadenstuhl', a happy choice; against an ascending and descending form of (b) there is a long and varied run on 'treten'. The triplets appear occasionally in the continuo. Part II—'Du sollst deinen Trost empfangen und Barmherzigkeit erlangen, ja, bei kummervoller Zeit, stark am Geiste, kräftig beten' ('Thou shalt thy comfort receive and pity obtain, yea, in trouble-full time, strong in spirit, mightily pray') —departs from the earlier style. The winging triplets are there, sometimes in short flights for the solo instrument, inappropriately to 'sollst' and in a long, meaningless run on 'erlangen', and a cascade of them is still less suitable to the penultimate word 'kräftig'. The tutti strings mostly move in a different manner. In spite of these misfits, the aria is most charming.

ii, *Intonazione* (*Nunc dimittis*) *e Recitativo*, for bass, is almost in the style of the chorale with recitatives of which we shall meet many examples later on, particularly in the third section of the book. 'The verses of the 'Nunc Dimittis' used are the Collect Verses for this Festival' (T.). In the following analysis, the Collect is printed in normal type, the recitative texts in italics. The latter sections are common time, as is always the case with recitatives. The form is peculiar. Four sections of $\frac{6}{8}$ (these will be represented by capital letters) employ this theme:

Ex. 393

in canon or in imitation between upper unison strings and continuo. The scheme is—(A), canon of six bars at the octave below, in B♭; plainchant, 'Lord, now lettest Thou Thy servant in peace depart'— against it part of the (*a*) canon; on the penultimate note of the voice, two bars of (*a*) in the upper strings, on the second bar of the latter (*a*) begins in the continuo, C minor, upper strings answering by two entries of the first limb, after these finish bar 3 of (*a*) combines with an inversion of bar 1 in the continuo, G minor; plainchant—'as Thou said hast', continuation of the canon, the upper strings in the direct form; at the fourth bar the first limb of (*a*) in the upper strings, F, at the fifth bar the bassi begin (*a*) in B♭, and the complete canon, reversed order of entries, rounds off the section. '*What to us as men terrible appears, is for us an entrance to the life.*' Dovetailing with 'Leben' ('life') (*B*) begins, three bars of the (*a*) canon, commencing with continuo in B♭. '*It is the death (that is) an end of this time and suffering, a pledge, that to us the Lord given (has) as sign, that He it sincerely means, and us will after completed struggling into peace bring*' (the close is arioso). (*C*) dovetails two bars of the canon, beginning in the upper strings, B♭, answered by the continuo at the fifth below, E♭ moving to F minor. '*And because the Saviour now the eyes' comfort, the heart's refreshment is, what wonder? that a heart the death-fear forgets! It can joyfully the declaration make.*' This modulates from F minor to C minor; at 'der Todesfurcht' ('death-fear'), bar 1 of (*a*) appears in the continuo, followed by a drop of a diminished seventh. It may be that (*a*) is intended to symbolize Simeon's calm welcome of death, and the canonical treatment the inevitability of departure from this world. Bach does not make quotations without definite purpose. (*D*), again dovetailing, thirty-seven bars. The key is now A♭ and the intonation a tone lower than before. 'For mine eyes', four bars, is accompanied by the canon modified. The continuo begins, but after two bars plays the first group of semiquavers in inversion and then modified. The answer is a sixth higher and only three bars of (*a*) are used. On the last vocal note, dovetailing with bar 3 of (*a*), the bassi play 2 bars of (*a*) in F minor. With its second bar the upper strings begin three bars of (*a*) in B♭ minor, and then we have the combination of bar 1 and the inverted form of bar 3 that we found in (*A*). 'Have thy Saviour seen,' is sung to the second part of the plainchant, five bars. The upper strings finish the two-bar quotation of (*a*), repeat it a tone higher and a second lower, modulation to E♭. The bassi, beginning in the first vocal bar, play all (*a*) except the closing notes, and an interlude is formed by the complete canon, the continuo leading, there being a change at one point. 'Which Thou prepared hast' is sung to the first limb of the intonation, four bars, a fifth lower than the original, E♭. The accompaniment is the same as that to 'Then mine eyes'. The corresponding interlude follows. With 'before all peoples', five bars, the continuo plays bars 2–4 of (*a*) with a leap to the semiquavers, followed by the inversion of bar 3, the upper strings play three bars, making a canon at the sixth. We are now back to the key of B♭. When the last vocal note commences, the upper strings begin a recapitulation of the introduction, the bassi taking up the theme in the next bar. In spite of all this ingenuity and symbolism, the effective sinking of the intonation in pitch, as if Simeon were growing weaker and weaker, and beauty at certain places, the number is not wholly satisfactory. It is too much of a mixture, as we shall find in similar instances later. One wishes that Bach had paraphrased the slow movement of the concerto, so that we might have been able to reconstruct it in its entirety.

A fine little alto recitativo secco, iv, colours 'Nacht' ('Night'), 'Tode' ('death') and the last syllable of 'Finsterniß' ('darkness'):

'Yea, observes thy faith yet much darkness, thy Saviour can doubt's shadows dissipate, yea, when the grave's night the last hour terrible makes, so wilt thou yet certainly His bright light in death itself recognize.' A beautifully harmonized tutti chorale ends, stanza 4 of Luther's paraphrase of the 'Nunc Dimittis', 'Mit Fried' und Freud' ich fahr' dahin', to his own tune: 'He is the salvation and blessed light For the heathen, To enlighten Those who Thee know not, And to lead. He is of Thy people Israel The praise, honour, joy and bliss.'

Spitta holds that there is no adaptation in this cantata. He puts forward a theory that as No. 194 (2 November 1723) is in the form of an orchestral suite, and the first chorus of the Latin Magnificat (Christmas, 1723) virtually an opening movement of a concerto, the alto aria of No. 83 (2 February 1724) is intended to be a pendant to No. 194, and that the composer, desiring to impress this on the consciousness of his hearers, introduced a violin solo into the first and third movements of the cantata. It is a far-fetched theory, especially as No. 194 was produced, not at Leipzig, but at Störmthal. If Bach had wished to write a sequence of movements based on instrumental forms he would have used a third type and not repeated the second. Spitta says that No. 83 'has assumed the form of a complete Italian concerto'. This ignores the facts that the recitative with plainchant is very far removed in character from the slow movement of a concerto and that the concluding recitative and chorale are quite redundant to that kind of composition. He also argues that the ritornelli of No. 83, 'though worked out on the same method as those in the Magnificat, prove that it is an original composition'. One does not see any force in this argument. Had Bach desired to enshrine the Italian concerto in a church cantata he could have ended with a true finale, minus chorale, as he has done in other cases. Besides, the period abounds in cases of borrowing from instrumental works.

156. The title of this truly lovely solo cantata, 'Ich steh' mit einem Fuß im Grabe', is a hindrance to its popularity. Anyone with a knowledge of Bach, however, knows that such a vein of lamentation could not last very long, that the composer's Christian belief would soon find cause for quiet, if solemn, happiness, or even rejoicing. While Picander's libretto opens with a note of despair, and does not hesitate to speak of sick-beds and devouring worms, its message is of calm resignation and of hope for ultimate peace. The poem was printed in 1728, the music was composed in the next year or 1730, for the

Third Sunday after Epiphany, 22 January. The clavier concerto in F minor is a reconstruction of a lost violin concerto. (The supposed original form of the latter, in G minor, is published by O.) The slow movement became, in a second transcription, the sinfonia to this cantata (see O.O.S. No. 010), solo oboe with strings. Its haunting melancholy is a fitting prelude to the tenor aria. In this violins and violas (which are all in unison throughout) begin with a holding note and there is a syncopated descent below for the continuo:

Ex. 394

one foot clings to earth, the other unsteadily falls into the abyss. Another sinking figure comes first in the continuo:

Ex. 395

and is repeated in a four-fold descending sequence by the unison strings, the last two phrases piano and pianissimo. On the last a passionate chromatic theme begins in the bassi, and its full form comes in the upper line:

Ex. 396

The voice sings 'I stand with one foot in the grave', to the opening violin-viola idea, (a) is divided between the instrumental parts. As the singer ends his phrase the soprano (or sopranos) commences a chorale—'Do with me, God, according to Thy goodness, Help me in my sorrows, What I Thee ask, deny me not! When my soul shall depart, So take it, Lord, into Thy hands; Is all good, when good the end.' It is stanza 1 of J. H. Schein's 'Mach's mit mir, Gott, nach deiner Güt'', to his own melody (1628). 'Bald fällt der kranke Leib hinein' ('Soon falls my sick body therein') is associated with (b). Later these words are sung to (c). With (b) in the instrumental lines and later in the vocal part, comes the next part of the text: 'Komm, lieber Gott, wenn dir's gefällt, ich habe schon mein Haus bestellt'

('Come, dear God, when Thee it pleases, I have already my house arranged'). At first the voice sings in detached notes and groups, there is a long, gradually sinking 'gefällt', while both instrumental lines imitate with (b). After a long treatment of these words, twenty-six bars are devoted to 'nur laß mein Ende selig sein' ('only let my end blessed be'); (b), (c), the holding note, and a modification of (a) are all heard in the vocal line. On the last note a reprise of the introduction begins in the subdominant, adding yet another factor to the sombreness of the scene. The line-by-line use of the chorale produces a long movement, the themes are few, and repeated incessantly, yet the music grips one from start to finish.

After the opening chord, the bass recitativo secco plunges at once into a ♯7/5/4/2 on D, which continues for 1½-bars, with 5 moving to 6 in the second, and 'Angst' ('anguish') a semitone below the continuo pedal[1]—'My anguish and need, my life and my death.' The dissonance resolves on a ♯6/4/2 on C, with a false relation, on the last word quoted, and there is a rest before 'steht,' ('stands,'). Although the rest of the recitative is not so adventurous, it is of fine quality—'dearest God, in Thy hands; so wilt Thou also on me Thy gracious eye turn. Wilt Thou me my sins because (of) in the sickbed lay, my God, so pray I Thee, let Thy goodness greater be than the justice! Yet hast Thou me thereto ordained, that me my sorrows shall consume, I am ready; Thy will shall in me be fulfilled, spare not and continue; let my distress not long endure,', Arioso—'the longer here, the later there!' and as the continuo climbs slowly and painfully upwards, 'länger' ('longer') falls a sixth and 'später' ('later') rises through a like interval. This thought inspires confidence and a bustling alto aria (see P. 54) ensues, with oboe and violin solo. The continuo borrows the initial figure of the oboe:

Ex. 397 *(a)* Ob.

Cont.
8ve lower

The semiquavers of bar 2 become a waving idea:

Ex. 398 *(b)*

Ob.
Vl.

Cont.
8ve lower

---

[1] i.e. below the written continuo note, not of course below the pitch of the double basses.

and the next bar reverses the obbligati instruments. The opening notes of (a) constitute a leitmotiv, the singer nearly always employs them to the first three words of the text: 'Herr, was du willst soll mir gefallen, weil doch dein Rath am besten gilt' ('Lord, what Thou willst shall me please, because yet Thy counsel of the best (value) is'). Semiquavers abound in all four lines, everything pulsates with the life of the new birth. The ritornello, in the dominant, reverses the upper lines. The text of Part II is 'In der Freude, in dem Leide, im Sterben, im Bitten und im Fleh'n laß mir allemal gescheh'n, Herr, wie du willst!' ('In the joy, in the sorrow, in the death, in the prayer and in the pleading let to me always happen, Lord, as Thou willst!'). Joyous flourishes to 'Freude' are left to make their full effect without the obbligati, 'im Sterben' brings a solemn hush, the bassi throb, the upper instruments sigh and then play a modified form of (b), 'Bitten' ascends a diminished seventh. But it is soon over, the motto is heard in all orchestral lines, the singer flourishes to 'allemal'. A new counterpoint is supplied to the semiquavers in the ritornello, (b) and (a) are heard again. In the next vocal section these themes recur, the voice laments on 'Leide', there is another form of the 'im Sterben' passage. The second ritornello is repeated with reversed upper parts and then Part I is recapitulated. To mention even a tithe of the points of interest which abound in Bach's church music would expand this book into many volumes; two others in this aria must suffice. The initial four quavers of (a) give rise to many bassi figures. The complete idea is heard with 'In der Freude, in dem Leide', but the upward leap is changed from a sixth to a tenth, in order to make it even more joyous.

v is a bass recitativo secco: 'And willst Thou, that I not shall ill be, so will I Thee from the heart thank; yet but grant to me moreover, that even in my restored body the soul without illness (may) be and always healthy remain. Take it through spirit and word in (Thy) care, for this is my salvation, and when in me body and soul languish, so art Thou, God, my comfort and my heart's portion!'

Stanza 1 of C. Bienemann's 'Herr, wie du willt, so schick's mit mir' (1582) to its customary anonymous tune, found nowhere else in Bach's vocal music, concludes: 'Lord, as Thou willst, so ordain it with me, In life and in death; Alone towards Thee stands my desire, Lord, let me not be destroyed! Keep me only in Thy favour, Otherwise, as Thou willst, grant me patience; Thy will it is the best.'

174. One cannot see why Bach took the trouble to rescore the first movement of the third Brandenburg concerto to stand as sinfonia to this little solo cantata, unless the Epistle for Whit Monday, the descent of the Holy Ghost on Cornelius and his associates, stirred him to find something of tremendous vigour to compensate for the quiet opening of Picander's libretto (from the same collection as the last), and the passing into oblivion during his lifetime of the immortal concerti of his Cöthen days caused him to desire to hear his music again. As a preface to the cantata it is not particularly happy, as a celebration of the Whitsun feast it is wonderfully appropriate. Another matter of surprise is that this task should have been undertaken when the provision of three cantatas for three successive days meant a congestion of work, which his frequent adaptations for this period of the year attests. It may have been written in this form for some other purpose, but one cannot conjecture what that could be. Thirty-nine pages of the Gesellschaft score are occupied by this great transcription; to the original triple lines of violins, violas, and 'celli, plus violone and continuo, are added independent parts for two corni da caccia, two oboes and taille, and a bassoon is directed to double the continuo-violone. We are so much accustomed to this concerto being a battle-horse for the fifty or sixty or more string players of a modern orchestra, or, rather, a display of cavalry tactics, mass after mass prancing to the foreground and exhibiting their prowess, that it is a surprise to realize that Bach must have had only one player to each string part, and that even then the amount of tone produced by each instrument would be much smaller than now, on account of the more arched bow. That he could have had six 'celli is inconceivable, and the number of violins and violas is clearly shown by the indications in iii, a tenor recitative: '3 violini all' unisono' and '3 Viole all' unisono'. The writer has given the cantata with the same number of instruments that Bach employed, and found the Sinfonia quite overwhelming, so much so that during performances of the concerto under customary modern conditions he is always haunted by the memory of the gorgeous splendour produced by his little company of seventeen, mostly amateurs and students.

The Gospel for Whit Monday, St. John iii. 16–21, tells of the love of God; Picander develops, per contra, the theme of the love a Christian should bear to his Maker. The alto aria, ii (two oboes)—'Ich liebe den Höchsten von ganzem Gemüthe, er hat mich auch am höchsten lieb' ('I love the Highest with my whole mind, He holds me also in the highest dear')—is a kind of pastoral, one thinks instinctively of the 23rd Psalm. Oboe II announces the chief theme, which is afterwards sung to the opening words, and the continuo quavers speak of the lulling of the soul to blissful rest:

Ex. 399

When oboe I takes up the theme, the other adds a lovely phrase which is much in evidence throughout the number:

Ex. 400

(*b*) being afterwards used in imitation and (*bbb*) in tender descending sequence. (*bb*) is found in the continuo, the oboes sometimes answer each other with it. Up to a few bars before the end of the first vocal section, all is based upon these ideas; then there is a sudden quickening of emotion:

Ex. 401

in which the oboes reply to the voice with (*c*). The next vocal section modifies (*a*), the singer uses the (*bbb*) sequence, sinking to a long low note while the oboes carry it on. Just after this we have an example of the shortening of ideas commonly practised by Beethoven; a form of (*c*) occurs with notes 1 and 2 omitted, and this is imitated by the oboes, there being frequent appearances of (*bbb*). 'Gott allein soll der Schatz der Seelen sein,' ('God alone shall the treasure of souls be,'), after the Fine pause, is vigorous, opposed to the former portion, although (*bb*) and (*bbb*) are still heard in the obbligati. There is a striking phrase (Ex. 402), in which the repeated notes, so different from what has gone before, and the drop of a seventh, imply strong confidence. Later we have (*a*), (*b*), (*bbb*), (*c*) modified, and (*d*) is heard in the final bars. The manuscript of this number (in the Peters collection) fixes the year of the cantata; it is inscribed 'Fine d. 5 Junii, 1729. Lipsiae'.

Ex. 402

Though the string parts of iii, tenor recitative, are slow-moving, modulation during its fifteen bars is incessant—B minor to C♯ minor, 'O love, of which (is) no equal! Oh inestimable ransom!'; C♯ minor to F♯ minor, 'The Father has the child's life for sinners in death given, and all, who the heavenly kingdom squandered and lost (have), to blessedness chosen'; F♯ minor to D, 'For God so loved the world!' (the beginning of the Gospel); D to E minor, 'My heart, that mark you, and strengthen thyself with these words'. The close is striking. To illustrate the penultimate word of 'before this mighty banner tremble even' the strings shudder and introduce a harsh false relation:

Ex. 403

The last words—'the hell-portals'—are unaccompanied.

Long and leisurely is the bass aria, in which the three violins and the three violas are massed in unison. One figure, always confined to the upper line:

Ex. 404

dominates the number; its corollary:

Ex. 405

is sometimes heard in the bassi also. The opening theme is of blissful
complacency:

forms of (*a*) are heard above. The continuo mostly moves in steady
crotchets, the firmness of faith. Especially arresting are later settings
of the initial words:

and

Part of the chief theme and many repetitions of the 'hold fast' idea
are heard in the orchestra during 'Jesus giebt sein Himmelreich und
verlangt nur das von euch: gläubt getreu bis an das Ende' ('Jesus
gives His heavenly-kingdom and desires only that from you; believe
faithfully up to the end'), which, in two long sections, is provided
with two quite distinct melodies, both profoundly beautiful. One may
be quoted:

Before the initial words are resumed, part of (*b*) comes to 'gläubt getreu'. With that infinite resource so characteristic of the master, before (*b*) is heard again in full, this time in canon with the upper strings, 'Greifet zu, faßt das Heil,' is delivered as a prelude, to the time-pattern of Ex. 407, but with leaps instead of steps and on a different part of the bar. Later Ex. 407 is repeated, the second time a tone higher, intensifying the command.

Stanza 1 of M. Schalling's 'Herzlich lieb hab' ich dich, O Herr' (1571), with its original tune, concludes this delightful cantata: 'Heartily dear have I Thee, Oh Lord, I pray: (that Thou) wilt be from me not far With Thy help and grace. The entire world joys me not, After heaven and earth ask I not, If I Thee only can have. Lord, if in me my heart breaks, So art Thou yet my confidence, My salvation and my heart's comfort, Who me through His blood hast redeemed. Lord Jesus Christ, My God and Lord, my God and Lord, In shame leave me nevermore!' The corni are silent, oboe I plus violins I and II doubles the sopranos, oboe II plus violin III the altos, taille and the three violas the tenors.

52. There can have been no reason, other than a wish to hear the music again, or to make the cantata longer, to justify the adaptation of the opening movement of Brandenburg Concerto No. 1 as a sinfonia to 'Falsche Welt, dir trau' ich nicht.' (Twenty-third Sunday after Trinity, *c.* 1730. Soprano solo). There is no connexion with the text of the despairing recitativo secco which follows: 'False world, thee trust I not! here must I among scorpions and among false serpents dwell. Thy countenance, that yet so friendly is, plots a secret ruin; when Joab kisses, then must an upright poor man die. Honesty is from the world banished, falsehood has it driven away, now is hypocrisy in its place enduring. The best friend is faithless: oh miserable condition!' The original scoring is two horns, three oboes, bassoon, violino piccolo, and strings. The function of the small violin is to add brightness to the top line of the strings; it has nothing independent. It is omitted from the sinfonia; perhaps a player was not available at the time. In bars 8–13, beat 1, and 79–84, the horns, which at these places play a triplet figure not found elsewhere in the movement, are reversed. There are no other changes.

The music of the recitative is not so vehement as one might have expected from the text. The modulations, however, are striking, D minor, G minor, E♭, D♭, B♭ minor, D minor. Terry points out that in one sentence the *BGS* score and the Breitkopf vocal score do not follow the original. The latter reads: 'wenn Joab küßt, so muß ein frommer Abner sterben' ('when Joab kisses, then must an upright Abner die'). The incident referred to is Joab's treacherous murder of the son of Saul's captain, 2 Samuel iii. 'Abner' is replaced by 'Armer' ('poor man'). We turn suddenly from this depressing condemnation of the world to the Christian's delight in God. iii abounds in joy; an idea is announced which is the kernel of almost everything which follows, all life is derived from one supreme thought:

(The violas are not employed in the aria.) The fifth bar commences a new treatment:

the seventh yet another:

(*aa*) is the basis of an important continuo run which supports another version of (*c*):

With (*d*) below, (not quoted here), voice and violins alternate:

As it continues—'wenn ich gleich verstoßen bin' ('when I even repudiated am')—(*aa*) is in unison violins, and then the introduction is recapitulated, with change of keys, the voice ceasing just before the (*d*) clause, which acts as a ritornello. 'Verstoßen' is allotted different and picturesque runs, the longest of them combined with (*b*) and ending with (*aa*). 'Ist die falsche Welt mein Feind, o, so bleibt doch Gott mein Freund, der es redlich mit mir meint' ('Is the false world mine enemy, oh, yet remains then God my friend, Who it honestly with me purposes') brings two fresh melodies for the voice. (*aa*) is present in the violins during the earlier, a new type of accompaniment begins with the later, but both motives soon join in. During a long run to 'Freund' (*a*) is heard twice in the bassi, a form of (*aa*) in the violins, followed by a fragment from (*c*). 'O' is thrust on high, both it and 'der' occur on syncopated notes. In the reprise of Part I there are fresh ideas, an intriguing version of 'immerhin':

Ex.415

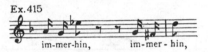

im-mer-hin,   im-mer-hin,

and an entirely new coloratura passage to 'verstoßen', combined with (*b*). Ingenuity of construction could scarcely go farther, yet the music is childlike in its simple innocence.

iv is a recitativo secco; 'Gott ist getreu!' ('God is faithful!') is melismatic, it comes a second time to a different phrase and a third time is developed into a three-bar arioso, based on the first. 'He will, He can me not leave. Will me the world in its madness in its snares grasp, then stands by me His help. God is faithful! on His friendship will I build, and my soul, spirit and mind, and all that I am, to Him commend. God is faithful!'

The scoring of the following aria is three oboes, with fagotto doubling *organo e continuo*. This is the earliest example in the series of this apparently formidable combination. However contrary the practice to modern ideas, experience shows that most beautiful results are obtainable from it, especially with the sensitive instruments of today. It is true that not every soloist is capable of cleaving a mass of tone which is much less resisting than strings, but arias in this class often possess a unique charm. This one is most attractive. The text begins—'Ich halt' es mit dem lieben Gott, die Welt mag nur alleine bleiben' ('I hold to the loving God, the world may merely alone remain')—and the lovely orchestral theme reflects its serenity:

Equally charming is the opening vocal phrase:

during the latter part of which the oboes play a form of (b). 'Halt'' is sustained against (a), and while the oboes develop this theme the voice moves in bewitching counterpoint:

Except for the portions without oboes the continuo either moves in placid quavers or reiterates drops of an octave— ♩ ♪ ♩ —a delightful feature of this fascinating aria.

Part II opens 'Also kann ich selber Spott' ('Therefore can I even the mockery') and there is a twisting run to 'Spott', during which five bars of (a) indicate the calm of the Christian who in supreme confidence views the railing unbelievers. The repetition of the clause and its continuation—'mit den falschen Zungen treiben' ('with the false tongues drive (away)')—are with continuo only, a canon at the distance of a beat, introducing thus cross accents to tell of the conflicting ways of those who trust God and those who do not. This section is repeated with key-changes and with the continuo section extended, the singer becoming more and more angry. At the twelfth bar of the reprise of Part I, the key changes, and near the end oboes II and III cease, leaving oboe I to illustrate 'die Welt mag nur alleine'.

The full orchestra returns for the closing chorale—stanza 1 of A. Reissner's 'In dich hab' ich gehoffet, Herr' (1533) set to S. Calvisius's melody (1581). The tune lies within the natural notes of corno

I, but its associate has to dodge certain passages in the alto line. The text is 'In Thee have I hoped, Lord, Help, that I not to shame come, nor eternally to mockery. This pray I Thee, Sustain me in Thy faithfulness, Lord God.' There is no reason why Nos. 52 and 174 should not be given without their Sinfonias where instrumental forces are few, or in church with organ only. The preludes are extraneous numbers, quite unessential.

166. The derived number, ii, in 'Wo gehest du hin?' is adapted from a previously unknown organ trio in G minor, published by G. W. Körner in 1842 in his 'Orgelfreund'. The oboe and continuo parts of thirty bars of this aria are, with slight changes, the same as the top and bottom lines of the organ composition, which may be consulted in the Bachjahrbuch for 1909. The discoverer concludes that the trio preceded the aria. The number may be conveniently studied in six sections. (1) There is a five-fold presentation of the chief theme, oboe and continuo sharing the honours:

Ex. 419

This is followed by two subsidiary themes, both containing (*aa*) and both used in different forms during the vocal sections—

Ex. 420

and

Ex. 421

(2) (*a*), modified in the later part, is set to 'Ich will an den Himmel denken, und der Welt mein Herz nicht schenken' ('I will on the heaven think, and on the world my heart not bestow'). Bach separates 'ich' from 'will', in all cases but one, by a semiquaver rest,

thus creating a tense emotional atmosphere and stressing the personal pronoun. (3) (*a*) begins in the oboe, the voice enters in the next bar in counterpoint, with a long run on 'schenken'. (4) After a short ritornello the voice takes up (*a*) again, there is new matter for the oboe, as well as part of (*a*), it modifies the previous 'schenken' run, the voice introduces a form of (*a*) and the concluding 'schenken' run is based upon (*c*). (5) Ritornello, (*a*). (6) Part II, 'Wenn ich gehe oder stehe, so liegt mir die Frag' im Sinn: Mensch, ach Mensch! wo gehst du hin?' ('Whether I go or stay, so lies to me the question in the mind: man, oh man! where goest thou hither?') does not belong to the trio, and is mainly based on the step-motive, with sustained notes on 'stehe'. Two fragments of (*a*) appear in the oboe, and, with 'Mensch', the obbligato instrument combines the step-motive with (*a*), an effective questioning:

Ex.422

One 'wo gehst du hin?' utilizes (*aa*). After this, Bach suggests an indeterminate wandering through the world by making one 'wenn ich gehe' move downwards and the next upwards. When 'Mensch, ach Mensch!' comes the second time, the continuo adds its question by playing (*c*). Altogether, the aria is a particularly happy specimen of adaptation.

The cantata was written for the Fourth Sunday after Easter, *c.* 1725. The libretto, possibly by Christian Weiss, Senr., is in a rather gloomy vein, the uncertainty of man's destiny, yet Bach's music is always full of hope. The first aria, for bass and strings, is wholly concerned with the question which Christ lamented that none of His disciples would ask, 'Whither goest thou?' (The Gospel is St. John xvi. 5–15.) The simple introduction suggests rather the erring steps of mortals than the departure of the Son of Man:

Ex.423
Ob. Vl.I (*a*)
Vl.II
Va.

Cont.

This three-bar phrase is presented thrice, the second considerably altered, and is answered by a six-bar idea of graceful sequential descent, dovetailing into the vocal entry:

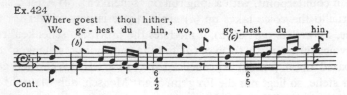

Ex.424

Where goest   thou hither,
Wo ge - hest du   hin, wo, wo ge - hest du   hin,

Cont.

(The bold clashes in bar 4 are worth noting.) (*a*) occurs ten times, the answer comes once at the close, when the introduction is repeated entire, and once in the middle, the sequence being extended. In no other aria is the accompaniment so simple. (*b*) and (*c*) are at times developed into runs, there is much repetition of 'wo' and 'wohin'. This childlike and transparent aria makes an exquisite opening to the cantata.

iii is a soprano chorale (see O.C.S. 'Lord Christ above'), with upper strings in unison, stanza 3 of B. Ringwaldt's 'Herr Jesu Christ, ich weiß gar wohl' (1582), set to the melody of 'Herr Jesu Christ, du höchstes Gut' (1593), which was usually associated with it: 'I pray Thee, Lord Jesus Christ, Keep me in Thy thoughts And let me yea at no time From this resolve stray, But thereby continue fast, Till that the soul from its nest Will to heaven come.' There is possibly no symbolic significance in the obbligato, but line 1 of the melody:

Ex.425

Ich   bit - te dich, Herr Je - su   Christ,
(C minor, signature of 2 flats)

can be clearly discerned in the opening unison passage and in notes 2–5 of the continuo:

Ex. 426
Vl.I.II. Va.

Cont.

Spitta thinks that the composition of the pedal clavicembalo sonatas at this period induced Bach to exploit three-part writing in this manner. The derivation of ii, not known to Spitta, supports this interesting theory.

The opening of the bass recitativo secco is picturesque, the close of 'Even as the rainwaters soon flow away' runs quickly down, there is a soft diminished chord on the last word of 'and many colours easily fade', and a soaring run on 'Freude' ('joy') in 'so goes it also with joy in the world, on which many a man so much stress lays'. The remainder is 'for though one sometimes sees that his wished-for good-fortune blooms, so can yet indeed in the best days wholly un-expectedly the last hour strike'.

The alto aria, v, is also simple in character and is scored like i; it is rare to find two numbers with an identical orchestral combination in the same cantata. The text of Part I is 'Man nehme sich in Acht, wenn das Gelücke lacht' ('(Let) one take himself in care when the fortune laughs'); instead of painting the mistrust of the believer Bach depicts the hilariousness of those who enjoy the good things of the world! The orchestra begins:

Ex. 427 Ob. Vl. I

Cont. *8ve lower*

the semiquavers running in 6/3 chords. When the voice enters the introduction is repeated, slightly modified, the first six notes are selected for the opening clause of the text (except that the initial note is altered), the semiquavers of bar 2 are omitted, bar 4 launches forth into three bars of semiquavers on 'lacht'. A new figure arises later, stepwise quavers, which combines with the rippling cascades of laughter, and the final 'lacht' is expanded to seven bars. The composer does not allow the rest of the verse—'Denn es kann leicht auf Erden vor Abends anders werden, als man am Morgen nicht ge-dacht' ('For it can easily on earth before evening otherwise become, than one in the morning not thought')—to disturb him with any fleeting thought of unhappiness. The same motives continue, voice and upper instruments being mostly used alternately; at one place the bassi roll and tumble in riotous merriment, and there is a fine expansion of the opening orchestral idea before voice and continuo approach the Da Capo. The simplicity of the closing chorale is in keeping with i and v. The verse is stanza 1 of Countess Emilie Juliane of Schwarzburg-Rudolstadt's(?) 'Wer weiß, wie nahe mir mein Ende' (1695), and the tune to which it was written, G. Neumark's

'Wer nur den lieben Gott läßt walten' (1657)—'Who knows how near to me mine end, Away goes time, hither comes death. Ah, how quickly and nimbly Can come my death-agony! My God, I entreat through Christ's blood; Make it only with mine end good!'

120. The Town Council cantata 'Gott, man lobet dich in der Stille zu Zion' (the German version of Psalm lxv. l, 'God, one praises Thee in the stillness of Zion', is different from the English Bible—'Praise waiteth for Thee, O God, in Sion'), dates possibly to 1730 (towards the end of August was the customary time), and may have been sung also on Augsburg Centenary Festival, 26 June, of the same year. The libretto is probably by Picander. It begins, most unusually for a choral cantata, with an aria, for alto, with verse 1 of the Psalm as text, the remainder being 'und dir bezahlet man Gelübde' ('and to Thee pays one vows'). The number is long, nearly one hundred bars of slow $\frac{6}{8}$ time; in spite of its great charm, one feels incongruity between text and music. It is true that there are characteristic touches in the vocal line, immense runs to 'lobet', sustained notes to 'Stille', but we have seen how Bach could superimpose anything he desired on music previously composed, and these features are confined to the vocal line. Except for the siciliano-like theme:

commentaries of:

and a few references to the two-note semiquaver figure:

Ex. 430

the upper strings have little of importance to do compared with the two oboes d'amore, they have much filling in of the harmonies by chords on the second and third parts of each half-bar, and pulsating in unison semiquavers. The oboe d'amore parts demand virtuosi. Some of the demisemiquaver flourishes in the difficult solo line are more instrumental than vocal. Is the aria borrowed from some instrumental work? In the incomplete and un-numbered wedding cantata 'Herr Gott, Beherrscher aller Dinge' this number appears in a curious form. So far as can be judged from the remnant of a score (only viola and continuo are known), the opening ritornello is the same and there are resemblances in the others. But the vocal lines (it is an A.T. duet), which are complete, are totally different in style, much simpler, more like a siciliano, and harmonic connexion with the alto aria is very slight. Why should Bach take the ritornello from one work to open an entirely different one?

In ii the oboes d'amore merely double violins I and II, an unsuitable task for them, and three trumpets and timpani are added. In this brilliant chorus the voices fling out rising arpeggi:

Ex. 431

sing excited syncopated passages:

Ex. 432

and ascend by glittering steps:

Ex. 433

This breathless chorus, shorn of some of its vocal exuberance and with the second section partly rewritten, became i of the incomplete cantata rewritten. We are familiar with the first part in another version, almost completely rewritten, the 'Vivace ed Allegro' from the 'Confiteor' of the *B Minor Mass*. Other arresting features are the tossing of short groups— ♫ ♪ —between tromba I and upper

strings, the breaking up of 'Jauchzet' into detached arpeggi with this
time-pattern, exciting imitations:

Ex. 434

the 'Jauchzet' idea used instrumentally and inverted, and tromba I
mounting on the 'steiget' theme to high C♯. The middle section—
'Lobet Gott im Heiligthum und erhebet seinen Ruhm; seine Güte,
sein erbarmendes Gemüthe hört zu keinen Zeiten auf' ('Praise God
in the sanctuary and exalt His fame; His goodness, His pitying feelings cease at no time')—begins more homophonically, with continuo,
but the figure soon appears arpeggio-wise in the strings and monotoned in brass and percussion. After the initial announcement of these
sentences an interlude introduces, most unusually, a new idea not
used elsewhere, possibly indicative of God's pity. Trumpets, drums,
and bassi monotone the joy-rhythm. With the re-entry of the choir
movement becomes more animated, there are imitations on a figure
akin to that in Ex. 434, and a highly placed bass trill on 'erhebet'.
Brass and percussion cease after two bars. If this cantata borrowed,
it also lent, and attained to more universal glory thereby.

The bass recitativo secco is formal and concludes with a reference
to the newly elected Council, the first direct allusion to the occasion:
'Up, thou beloved linden-town!' (Leipzig was proud of its linden
groves). 'Come, fall before the Highest down; know, how He thee
in thy adornment and splendour so fatherly maintains, protects,
guards, and His loving hand still over thee continually has. Well then,
fulfil the vows which thou to the Highest hast made, and sing thanks-
and humility-songs; come, ask, that He town and land unendingly will
more quicken, and (that) this worthy Council, which today position
and choice renews, with many blessings shall adorn.'

On page 252, vol. ix of the *BGS* is to be found a *Cantabile, ma un
poco Adagio* for Violino, Cembalo, and Fundamento, which formed
the third movement of the first-known version of the sixth violin and
clavier sonata, in G, but was eventually discarded. The soprano aria
of this cantata is the movement in new guise. The violin line is given
to a violino concertante, and support provided by normal strings.

Tutti violins and violas do little but represent the figuring, in a very simple manner. The right-hand part of the cembalo:

Ex. 435

is given to the voice, modified to suit its new medium:

Ex. 436

At bar 42 the first divergence occurs; where the violin was silent before, it now has florid passages. At bar 47 two fresh bars are introduced, but after that it proceeds as in the original except for the vocal alterations and a few modifications in the continuo line. The text continues 'sich auf unsre Obrigkeit in erwünschter Fülle legen, daß sich Recht und Treue müssen mit einander freundlich küssen' ('itself upon our government in desired fulness lay, that righteousness and truth must with one another friendly kiss') (see Ps. lxxxv. 10).

Another formal recitative, this time for tenor with strings, follows: 'Now, Lord, so consecrate Thyself Thy government with Thy blessing, that all evil from us fly, and the justice in our houses bloom, that Thy Father's pure seed and Thy blessed name with us glorified may be!' Clauses 22 and 23 of Luther's Te Deum, 'Herr Gott, dich loben wir', corresponding with the four portions of the English version beginning with 'We therefore pray Thee', are plainly set to the plainsong attached to the German hymn. The orchestration is not stated, merely vocal lines and continuo are given in the score.

42. It may be questioned whether Bach ever wrote an original Sinfonia to open any Leipzig cantata. In his earlier days they were common, but after Cöthen he apparently relied solely on adaptations. Evidence with regard to that of 'Am Abend aber desselbigen Sabbaths' ('Then the same day at evening, being the first day of the week', St. John xx. 19) (solo cantata, S.A.T.B.) is not sufficiently strong to determine its definite inclusion in the category of borrowings, yet there are points which it is difficult to understand otherwise.

(See O.O.S. No. 011.) Why, for instance, do violin I and II play almost all passage-work in unison? It does not conduce to good balance, indeed it creates problems for the conductor. iii employs the same orchestral group, two oboes, bassoon and strings, *organo e continuo* being specified throughout the cantata, but the treatment of the violins is quite different. It is easy to understand why Bach wished to rescue this introductory number from oblivion, for it is worthy to be ranked with the greatest orchestral literature since his time. Why this Sinfonia has never been placed among the world's concert masterpieces is a mystery. Perhaps some day a fortunate conductor will discover it! It is a heavenly picture of evening. The throbbing chords remind one of the first chorus of No. 6, 'Abide with us, for the evening is far spent.' Indeed, the present writer always feels that this Sinfonia must have been written for a cantata which dealt with the walk to Emmaus; the lovely phrases for oboe and bassoon:

Ex. 437

with unison violins and violas pulsating on quaver D's, suggest a conversation between three companions walking in cool twilight, and the opening is a leisurely, thoughtful pacing of wayfarers:

Ex. 438

The Sinfonia is not necessary to create 'atmosphere', because although the time of day is evening (the libretto is based on the Gospel, St. John xx. 19–31, the first appearance of the risen Christ to the apostles) the disciples were assembled in a house. A solemn and beautiful recitative for tenor narrates the appearance of Jesus: 'On the evening but of the same Sabbath, when the disciples gathered and the doors closed were, from fear of the Jews, came Jesus and stepped into their midst.' 'Furcht' ('fear') is melismatic, and the last clause, with 'Jesus' thrown high to indicate the surprise of the apostles, is infinitely tender. The continuo pulsates throughout in sostenuto semiquavers, organ and bassoon sustain.

The words of Christ (not in the Gospel for the day)—'Where two or three are gathered together in My name'—are paraphrased in the alto aria: 'Wo Zwei und Drei versammlet sind in Jesu theurem Namen, da stellt sich Jesus mitten ein und spricht dazu das Amen' ('Where two and three gathered are in Jesu's dear name, there places Himself Jesus in the midst and speaks thereto the Amen'). The declamation of the initial clause is most effective, there are breaks after the second, fourth, and sixth words, each of which is approached from below by leap. Yet one feels much of the vocal line to be artificial. Why should 'ein' be given a brilliant run? Why should 'theuren' be sometimes a long note and sometimes moving passages? The lovely oboe duet:

Ex. 439

certainly suggests the conversing of the faithful, and the accompaniment, slow-moving upper strings, detached bassi notes, the bassoon always dovetailing into the latter with a monotoned ♪♪♪ , helps to produce a touching piece of music. One wonders if it is an adaptation, possibly of a slow movement from a two-violin sonata or concerto, and if Bach considered it appropriate here on account of the conversational upper lines. A second section 'un poco andante', ¹²⁄₈, continuo and unison bassoon only, seems to have little relation to the first, and the text is not such as to demand any particular style: 'Denn was aus Lieb' und Noth geschieht, das bricht des Höchsten Ordnung nicht' ('For what from love and distress happens, that breaks of the Highest (the) decree not'). A long flourish on 'Ordnung' is without relevance. While Part I of this adapted instrumental composition partially justifies the added text, Part II certainly does not.

iv is headed *Chorale. Duetto.*, but there is no hymn-melody. The words are stanza 1 of J. M. Altenburg's(?) 'Verzage nicht, o Häuflein klein' (1632), and Terry points out that this is a solitary instance of separation of a hymn-stanza from its tune, and thinks that 'the melody' (the anonymous 'Kommt her zu mir, spricht Gottes Sohn' (1530)) 'seems to be implied and its closing cadence is introduced'. The accompaniment to the solo voices, S.T., is remarkable. The lower line is *organo e continuo* and either moves in crotchets or—

$$| \; \downarrow \quad \downarrow \quad \neg \quad \flat \; | \; \downarrow \quad \downarrow \quad \neg \quad \flat \; |$$

—the crotchets nearly always dropping an octave. The upper instrumental line is *fagotto e violoncello*, and it almost wholly consists of two figures which produce a large number of chromatic notes:

Ex.440
Bsn.Vc.

and

Ex.441

Although the first words are 'Verzage nicht', it is the initial word only with which Bach concerns himself in the opening vocal passages:

Ex. 442

Despair   not,
Ver-za - - - - - - - - - - - - ge nicht,
S.

T.
Ver - za - - - - - - - - - - - ge nicht,

'O Häuflein klein' (literally 'Oh little flock small'—the multitude, the populace), is set pityingly in parallel motion; 'obgleich die Feinde willens sein dich gänzlich zu verstören' ('although the enemies disposed are thee wholly to destroy') is set stormily in imitation, with violent passages on 'verstören', and at the close 'gänzlich' is repeated in leaping figures. 'Und suchen deinen Untergang' ('and seek thy downfall') is the source of the imagery of Ex. 441, which descends to chromatic auxiliary notes of the chord and then plunges to a deep note. The voices move for eight bars in canon, as if the enemy were relentlessly pursuing the misguided multitude; 'davon dir wird recht angst und bang' ('therefrom to thee will be veritable anxiety and fear') is agitated, the tenor thrice dropping a seventh. 'Es wird nicht lange währen' ('it will not long endure') is set to confident repeated notes, and later reintroduces the soprano 'recht angst und bang' idea for the tenor. The Duetto is unusual but of fine quality throughout.

v is a short bass recitativo secco with all the orchestral bass forces, which plunge down in semiquavers during the closing arioso: 'D'rum laßt die Feinde wüthen' ('Therefore let the enemies rage'). The recitative portion comments again on the main incident of the libretto: 'One can here of a good example see from that which in Jerusalem happened; for when the disciples themselves gathered had in dark shadows, from fear of the Jews, then came my Saviour in their midst as a token that He of His church protection will be.'

This leads to an almost extravagantly joyful aria for the same voice: 'Jesus ist ein Schild der Seinen, wenn sie die Verfolgung trifft' ('Jesus is a shield of His own, when them the persecution befalls'). A persistent figure in the heavy instrumental bass indicates strength:

Ex. 443

Far-flung semiquaver arpeggios, and the following figures:

Ex. 444

and

Ex. 445

are features of the lowest line, and the bassi are taken to the unwonted height of A above the bass stave. A curious point of the scoring is that the first violins are divided; perhaps the second violins were unreliable, they and the violas are omitted. The former have many

rushing passages, semiquaver arpeggi leapings like the continuo, they
use Ex. 445:

and arpeggi with the time-pattern ♪ ♪♪♪ are frequent, often dovetailing in contrary motion. The voice begins with a fine sweep:

There are mighty runs to 'Verfolgung', one of them lasting for six
bars, chiefly semiquavers. The remainder of the text is: 'Ihnen muß
die Sonne scheinen mit der goldnen Überschrift' ('On them must the
sun shine with the golden superscription'). Here Ex. 445, with a drop
of a seventh afterwards, is the source of much of the continuo line,
and it is heard gleaming in thirds in the violins.

To the stanza of the four-part chorale, No. 1 of Luther's 'Verleih'
uns Frieden gnädiglich' (1529)—'Grant us peace graciously, Lord
God, in our time, There is verily yet no other not, Who for us could
fight, Than Thou, our God alone'—a translation of the Antiphon
'Da pacem, Domine', with its anonymous melody, is added a prose
prayer—'Give to our princes and the authority Peace and good
government, That we under them A restful and quiet life lead may
In all divine blessedness and honour' (1566). The concluding Amen
is found in association with the melody in 1573. The title 'Concerto
da Chiesa' is given to the cantata in the score.

58. There are two cantatas bearing the title 'Ach Gott, wie
manches Herzeleid' ('Ah God, how many a heart-pang'), this solo
work and No. 3, a choral composition. The libretto of the Dialogus,
S.B. No. 58, possibly by Bach, contrasts two ideas to be found in the
Gospel and the Epistle for the Sunday after the Circumcision. The
date is 4 January 1733. St. Matthew ii. 13–15 relates the narrative

of the flight into Egypt and the soprano pictures herself in like situation, surrounded by foes, and pursuing a long, dangerous journey. Paul's declaration, in Titus iii. 4–7, that all justification is by faith and not by works (a frequent theological proposition in the libretti and one of Luther's fundamental doctrines), is the message delivered by the bass. The plan of the cantata is unusual, both first and last numbers are chorale fantasias, stanzas of different hymns, the canto in the soprano, a free part for bass, strings with the three upper parts doubled by two oboes and taille. The opening Duetto is adagio, there is a prevalence of dotted-note passages in the orchestra:

and as one long passage of this kind occurs set to 'Gang' ('way'), the reference to the wearisome journey of life is obvious. The bass exhorts to patience—'Nur Geduld, mein Herze' ('Only patience, my heart')—speaks of the evil time—'es ist eine böse Zeit!' ('it is an evil time!')—and of the way to heaven—'Doch der Gang zur Seligkeit, führt zur Freude nach dem Schmerze' ('But the way to blessedness leads to the joy after the pain')—in flexible musical language, while the orchestra and chorale pursue their paths undisturbed. There is a long run on 'Freude' and there are sinking chromatics on 'Schmerze'. The anonymous melody is that associated with the hymn and also with 'O Jesu Christ, mein's Lebens Licht' and 'Hilf mir, Herr Jesu, weil ich leb''. For a translation of the stanza see cantata No. 3, i, p. 346, Vol. II. The oboes are tacet except in the ritornelli, and during the chorale lines the taille is directed to play *col Soprano, ma piano*, an unusual example of solicitude for the singer!

In a recitativo secco the bass, in a rapid flow of words, points the lesson of the safety achieved by the flight into Egypt and preaches the doctrine of Paul. It is a fine specimen of declamation and of bold harmonies—'Persecutes thee even now the evil world' (a diminished seventh on G♯ moves to one on D♯ with a false relation) 'so hast thou nevertheless God as friend, Who against thine enemies to thee always the rear holds'. (At 'Feinde' ('enemies' a $\frac{6}{2}$ on D falls to another on G, the latter note producing an ominous false relation.) 'And if the raging Herod,' (on 'wüthende' ('raging') comes another false relation) 'the judgment of a shameful death even over our Saviour pronounces;' (a $\frac{6}{2}$ on C is followed by a diminished seventh on A♭, the bass creating a false relation) 'so comes an angel in the night' (a drop of a major seventh):

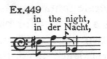

Ex.449
in the night,
in der Nacht,

'who causes Joseph to dream, that he from the slaughterer shall flee, and to Egypt hie' (an agitated phrase culminating in 'entfliehen' ('flee') and a sinking into secrecy at the close). 'God has a word,' (a break after 'Gott') 'that thee confident makes'. 'He says' rings out commandingly, 'if mountain and hill down sink' is a vigorous arpeggio, 'if thou in waterfloods wilt drown,' (a dark chord, $\frac{♭6}{4}$ on G for 'Fluth des Wassers' ('flood of water') and the voice pitched low) 'so will I thee yet not leave, nor delay' (an upward leap of a minor ninth on 'doch nicht' ('yet not')). From 'if mountain' the text is Isaiah liv. 10.

The soprano declares contentedness amid sorrow in a very flexible aria-line (with violin obbligato), which contrasts sorrow with delight, the latter expressed by decorative passages. 'Denn Gott ist meine Zuversicht' ('For God is my confidence') is treated declamatorily, 'Ich habe sichern Brief und Siegel, und dieses ist der feste Riegel, den bricht die Hölle selber nicht'. ('I have sure warrant and seal, and this is the firm bar, which breaks the Hell itself not') introduces new syncopations:

Ex.450 Ich ha - be si - chern Brief und Sie-gel,
Cont.
8ve lower

chromaticism, diminished thirds and defiant, broken phrases. 'bricht' and 'die Hölle' are separated by rests, 'Hölle' is set to tortuous runs. The caressing opening violin phrases serve for the beginning of the vocal line:

which is accompanied by an obbligato figure culminating in a laughing upward flash of semiquavers. A delightful feature of the introduction, afterwards developed considerably, is a rippling cross-bowed idea:

In v, a recitative and arioso with continuo, the soprano longs for a sight of Eden. In the recitative portion the continuo mostly punctuates the bars, 'Can it the world not leave, me to persecute and to hate, so points for me God's hand another land', as if to indicate relentless enmity. The arioso is eager, with impetuous scale passages over a quietly moving bass: 'Ah, might it today even happen, that I my Eden might see!' As so often in Bach, various words are stressed at different times to emphasize different points, 'könnt'', 'heute', 'geschehen', 'ich', 'Eden', 'möchte', 'sehen', ('might', 'today', 'happen', 'I', 'Eden', 'might', 'see'). There is a like instance with a similar text in No. 56, iii.

Although the hymn of the concluding Duetto speaks of a long and heavy way, the music recks little of it. The bass contrasts present anguish and sorrow with joy, though the musical references to the former are but in passing, the animated sections being predominant. The number begins with a vigorous ritornello:

and its character is so concerto-like that one is led to the conclusion that Bach constructed it as he did the finale to the other S.B.

Dialogue, No. 49, and fitted chorale and bass into some existing movement. The opening three notes are the same as in the E major violin
concerto, and much of the passage work suggests that instrument as
soloist. The chorale melody is the same as in i, though cast into $\frac{2}{4}$
time, and the verse is stanza 2 of M. Behm's funerary hymn 'O Jesu
Christ, mein's Lebens Licht': 'I have before me a heavy journey;
To Thee, in heaven's Paradise; There is my rightful fatherland, For
which Thou Thy blood hast given.' The bass opens with a modification of the chief instrumental theme: 'Nur getrost, ihr Herzen, hier
ist Angst, dort Herrlichkeit!' ('Only trust, ye hearts, here is anguish,
there glory!'). Sometimes the chordal leaps of the voice are accompanied by syncopated continuo arpeggi, 'hier ist Angst' is chromatic,
'Herrlichkeit' florid, 'Und die Freude jener Zeit überwieget alle
Schmerzen' ('And the joy of that time outweighs all sorrows')
begins again with the chief theme, 'Freude' is tremendously florid
and 'alle Schmerzen' is tender. The scoring is as in i. Except for the
final entry of the chief theme, the oboes are silent during the vocal
sections, and the taille, besides participating in the tuttis, lends aid to
the soprano chorale.

CANTATAS CONTAINING BORROWED VOCAL MATERIAL

(C.1.) FROM SECULAR SOURCES

36, 134, 149, 171, 173, 184, 195

Order of Discussion: 36, 149, 171, 173, 134, 184, 195

While at all times Bach was prone to make use of previous material, it almost seems that at certain periods his mind ran on the possibilities of the richness of certain mines, and that in several cantatas of the same months or years he borrowed from similar sources. We must not forget that our data are necessarily faulty and that so many of the cantatas have been lost that we are arguing from only a scanty treasury. We have seen two groups, however, concertos used for organ obbligato cantatas, and concertos used for a set of solo cantatas. Nos. 36, 149, 171, and 184 possibly belong to the years 1729 and 1730-1, are choral, and contain vocal material from secular works. As they cannot be dated precisely, they may be considered in their numerical order, except Nos. 134 and 173 which are definitely known to belong to 1731. No. 195 is placed conjecturally *c*. 1726, but as there is no definite evidence it can be discussed conveniently after the others.

36. i, iii, v, and vii of No. 36 appear in four different cantatas, the main columns of their edifices:

(*a*) Secular Cantata—'Steigt freudig in die Luft' ('Mount joyfully in the air')—for the birthday of the Princess of Anhalt-Cöthen, 30 November 1726. This version of the music has been lost, but Picander's libretto is known and establishes the relation with the other three.

(*b*) Church Cantata No. 36—'Schwingt freudig euch empor' ('Swing joyfully yourselves on high')—for the First Sunday of Advent, possibly 1730. The four chorales take the place of the recitatives of the secular work.

(*c*) Secular Cantata—'Schwingt freudig euch empor'. Perhaps in honour of Johann Matthias Gessner, Rector of the Thomasschule 1730-4. The manuscript score is in existence. The exact date is not known, but it must have been during the Rector's term of office.

(*d*) Secular Cantata: 'Die Freude reget sich' ('The joy stirs itself'). Performed on the birthday of Johann Florens Rivinus, Professor in the University of Leipzig, possibly about 1733. The orchestral parts, with the exception of violin I, are in existence. The Gospel for the First Sunday of Advent, St. Matthew xxi. 1–9, relates the entry of Christ into Jerusalem, and the cries of the multitude—'Hosanna to the Son of David; Blessed is he that cometh in the name of the Lord; Hosanna in the highest'—are the foundation of the libretto of the church cantata, which possibly Bach himself modelled, in the chorus and arias, on Picander's secular text. The similarity of the first word of each—'Steigt' and 'Schwingt'—enabled the imagery of the opening chorus to be preserved. The scores of (*c*) and (*d*) are printed one above the other in the *BGS* edition, so that comparison is easy. (*b*) employs, in addition to strings, two oboes d'amore in unison, (*c*) one oboe d'amore, (*d*) flauto traverso, the only differences in the lines being that in (*d*) the part is sometimes an octave higher and that a few grace notes are added in (*d*). Except for a note or two here and there, and the presence of new grace notes for voices and strings in (*d*), the three scores are identical, though (*c*) is devoid of many bowing, tonguing, and staccato marks which occur in (*b*) and (*d*).

The opening bar of i contains two ideas which contribute largely, a theme afterwards used in imitation:

Ex.454

(the flinging up is to be noted) and a germ of triplets in violin I:

Ex.455

which develops afterwards into many soaring runs. The chorus is full of splendid energy and the mass of sound brilliant and exciting. The voices enter successively with a modification of Ex. 454:

Ex.456

mass together for 'zu den erhab'nen Sternen' ('to the sublime stars'). Another series of entries, in a different order, employs a second modification of the theme, approximating much more to the original, but more exultant on account of the leap of a seventh instead of a sixth:

Ex.457

schwingt freu - dig euch em - por,

The semiquaver descent is incorporated into another theme for imitation:

Ex.458

zu den er - hab'- nen Ster - nen,

but the altos depart from the strict order of succession and sing a florid bar related to one of the oboe d'amore phrases. This choral portion culminates in 'ihr Zungen, die ihr jetzt in Zion fröhlich seid' ('ye tongues, you who now in Zion joyful are'). After a rush of semiquaver triplets, violin I now for the first time takes over Ex. 454, and the flying figures are allotted to the oboes d'amore. At the end the upward triplet-semiquaver rush comes again, and the choir shouts, unaccompanied, 'Doch, haltet ein!' ('Then, pause!'). The twin instrumental themes are resumed in B minor and in the second bar the choir shouts again 'haltet ein!', like a lightning flash. Vigorous, almost homophonic groups—'der Schall darf sich nicht weit entfernen, es naht sich selbst zu euch der Herr der Herrlichkeit' ('the peal may itself not far remove, there approaches Himself to you the Lord of glory')—are joined by the various themes of the introduction and a brilliant climax is reached. After a brief interlude comes a condensation of the first vocal section, in different key order and a varied succession of voices. Even this is not sufficient development for the vivid imagination of the composer, set on fire by the splendour of his subject. There is another interlude in which violin I has a more florid and exciting passage than before, the second vocal section comes again, with the short shout twice instead of once, and close and brilliant imitations on 'es naht' form an exultant finish.

The borrowed arias, standing iii, v, and vii in the sacred work, appear in the same order in (c) and (d), though they are separated

by different numbers. iii is for tenor, and the opening of the text—
'Die Liebe zieht mit sanften Schritten'—is almost the parallel of (c)
(the libretto of all of (d) is an entirely new poem and not related as
are (b) and (c)), and calls up a winsome melody (with a gracefully
curving continuo):

which in the second section is used as an episode to more florid
writing. There are a few differences between the three versions, and
while oboe d'amore is specified as the obbligato instrument in (b),
it is only conjectural in (c); the line is missing in (d) and would therefore be played by violin I. The oboe d'amore melody is 8+8 bars.
The voice delivers half of it as above and there are four bars of an
interlude based on a semiquaver figure for the obbligato taken from
the second half of the introduction:

the continuo pursuing a rising stepwise motive, as if the believer were
being drawn inevitably upward. The voice now repeats its four bars,
with a counterpoint above, the oboe d'amore takes up the answering
four bars while the voice sings 'sein Treugeliebtes allgemach' ('His
true-beloved gently'). Voice and obbligato climb gently to the first
clause. A delightful passage is where 'allgemach' is used for a very
gradual ascent of seven bars and the obbligato sways up and down
alluringly:

and the bassi move in gentle motion. The text of Part II is 'Gleich
wie es eine Braut entzücket, wenn sie den Bräutigam erblicket, so

folgt ein Herz auch Jesu nach' ('Even as it a bride enchants, when she the bridegroom perceives, so follows a heart also Jesus after'). A lovely vocal melody, decorated with trills, is supported by a rich continuo alone; the oboe d'amore eight bars form an interlude, voice, and continuo begin again, but the obbligato soon joins in. With 'wenn sie den Bräutigam erblicket' the oboe d'amore borrows its previous gently climbing phrase from Part I, the bassi softly pace upwards, the approach of the bridegroom, repetitions of 'so folgt' are sung to a modification of the slowly ascending 'allgemach' sequence, and although the obbligato sways as before the bassi move upwards with a new figure.

The text of v is different in (b) and (c); in the sacred work it is a welcome to the Babe Who is coming—'Willkommen, werther Schatz' ('Welcome, precious treasure')—while in the secular it is in praise of the day of the celebration. The healthy and vigorous character of the song suits both verses. It is given to a bass in (b) and (c), and to an alto in (d). The chief motto—  —tossed between bassi or voice and upper strings, is attached to 'Willkommen', the gradual ascent which follows, first plain:

then florid:

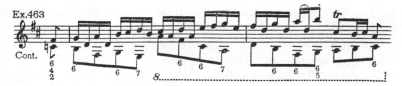

is, in the vocal section, divided between voice and violin I. In bar 5 of the introduction is a scintillating sequence on the figure

in 6 an ascent in triplet semiquavers, and during the remaining bars ejaculations of the motto in the bassi support a florid violin line. All these elements take part in the development. In the next vocal section —'Die Lieb' und Glaube machet Platz für dich in meinem Herzen rein; zieh' bei mir ein!' ('The love and faith make (a) place for Thee in my heart pure; come unto me in!')—the upper strings are mostly tacet; 'Die Lieb'', 'Glaube' and 'zieh' bei mir ein' all use the motto, which, with the first rising idea, also appears in the upper strings. The opening vocal sentence is now repeated and the remainder of the vocal portion is devoted to an enlargement of the two sections. There is an arresting passage where the singer cries 'zieh' bei mir ein!' and with sustained notes for the middle strings, violin I soars aloft in an ecstatic arabesque. Instead of 'Die Lieb'—rein' in (b), 'als jener, da der Schöpfer spricht; es werde Licht' ('as that one, when the Creator speaks; it shall be light') is substituted in (c), and wherever this occurs, the music, while not differing greatly in style, is altered considerably in detail, the portions before and after being skilfully fitted in. There are also minor textual differences. In (d) a flute is added; if violin I is the same as in (b) and (c), it merely doubles.

The obbligato instrument of vii is different in all three, *violino con sordino*, viola d'amore (one of the rare appearances of this instrument in Bach's scores), and flauto traverso respectively. A comparison of the three lines is an interesting study of Bach's methods. At times the flute is dropped, presumably where it would be less effective than the other instruments. Bowing and tonguing are carefully marked. There are many slight alterations of bowing when the part is transferred from violin to viola d'amore, though it is fundamentally the same. The flute shows many new groupings, for instance six semiquavers ((b) and (c) are in $\frac{12}{8}$, (d) in $\frac{6}{8}$) are sometimes indicated as ♪♪♪♪♪♪ in the first two and as ♪♪♪♪♪♪ in the last. The dividing line between sacred and secular texts is very thin; 'Auch mit gedämpften, schwachen Stimmen wird Gottes Majestät verehrt' ('Also with subdued, weak voices is God's majesty revered') and 'Auch mit gedämpften, schwachen Stimmen verkündigt man des Lehrers Preis' ('Also with subdued, weak voices announces one the teacher's praise'), but the essence is the same, and the aria is beautifully reverent and intimate. The obbligato figuration of Part I is pure string music, lovely floating passages, fascinating in their delicacy:

A comparison of the opening of violin and vocal lines shows Bach's infinite care in securing variety of detail:

Ex.465

and

Ex.466

With the second section comes a change, 'Denn schallet nur der Geist dabei' ('For resounds only the spirit thereby')—in (c) 'Es schallet kräftig in der Brust' ('It resounds strongly in the breast') —and broken, flying passages, with frequent staccato indications, in one case on five successive vocal quavers, occur in both voice and obbligato, while the bassi leap in detached quavers. This vocal passage must be quoted to show how realistic Bach can be:

Ex.467

Yet the present writer has been pilloried in the press for making Bach's church music sound dramatic! The remainder of the text is 'so ist ihm solches ein Geschrei, das er im Himmel selber hört' ('so is to Him such a cry, that He in the heaven itself hears'). The violin joins in all these striking passages in canon, plays fragments of Ex. 465 as interludes, and adds florid counterpoints to the more sustained vocal lines. It is a noteworthy aria in every way. G is the key of (b), A of (c) and (d).

The remaining numbers of the sacred work are chorales; ii, vi, and viii are settings of Luther's Christmas hymn 'Nun komm, der Heiden Heiland' ('Now come, of the heathen (the) Saviour') and iv is a splendid, direct four-part harmonization of stanza 6 of P. Nicolai's 'Wie schön leuchtet der Morgenstern' ('How brightly shines the

Morning Star'), the former, but not the latter, prescribed in the very elaborate service for the day. The verse from the Nicolai hymn, written as an affirmation of confidence during the horrors of plague, is an admirable choice wherewith to end Part I of this stirring cantata: 'Pluck the strings in Cythara And let the sweet music Completely overjoyed resound, That I may with child Jesus, The wonderful Bridegroom of mine, In steadfast love wander. Sing, leap, jubilate, triumph, thank the Lord! Great is the King of honour.'

ii is an S.A. duet with continuo (see S. & B. 'Oh come, the people's Saviour'), the oboes d'amore doubling the voices. As in cantata No. 61, the third note of the melody is sharpened in order to produce the poignant interval of a diminished fourth. The tune is short, four lines only, the first and fourth identical:

Ex.468

Bach's ingenuity and prolific invention make out of it a long movement. (See No. 61, pp. 146–7 for translation of the verse. A version in English is published by S. & B.: 'Come now, Saviour of Mankind.') Though the lines are sometimes reduced to a duration of one bar by being sung in diminution, the resultant number of bars in each section is as follows: I 9; II 10; III 11; IV 16; with a continuo coda of $3\frac{1}{2}$ bars. Each vocal line is prefaced by line I in the continuo, quavers, and there are references to it while the voices deal with all four lines. Line II:

Ex.469

is not referred to by the continuo, but line III is:

Ex.470

A florid passage in bar 3 of the introduction:

Ex.471

illustrative of the ecstasy roused by the coming of the Saviour, is developed into a great profusion of runs, in which, however, the voices never participate. Yet their lines are very elaborate and full of cross-rhythms, and the number, with its numerous imitations, its animated runs on 'alle' ('all'), its eager spirit and the florid continuo, is exceedingly fine.

vi (see S. & B. 'Thou that art God's Son'), *Allegro molto*, stanza 6 —'Thou Who art to the Father equal, Lead forth the victory in the flesh, That Thine eternal God's-power In us the sick flesh (may) maintain'—is uninspired. The melody is allotted to the tenor, in dotted minims, $\frac{3}{4}$ time, and the two oboes d'amore are added. There are no references to the chorale in the instrumental parts, except that perhaps notes 1 and 2 and the rising fourth, here left perfect, are found in the repeated-note figure:

which is heard persistently in the bassi and sometimes in the oboes d'amore, and the variant with which the obbligati open:

Bach is merciless towards the oboes d'amore, they are allowed scarcely any time for breathing. The last version of the chorale is plain, 'Praise be to God the Father given, Praise be to God His only Son, Praise be to God the Holy Ghost, Always and in eternity' (stanza 8). Except for a single continuo note the orchestra doubles the voices.

149. The charming hunting cantata, produced on 23 February 1716, 'Was mir behagt', written in honour of Duke Christian of Sachsen-Weissenfels, who was entertained by Duke Wilhelm Ernst of Weimar, was useful in providing game for other occasions. It made three subsequent appearances as occasional music for princely celebrations (with alterations of text), and three of the numbers, vii, xiii, and xv were utilized for church purposes, vii and xiii in No. 68, and xv in No. 149. The year of the latter can be fairly well determined, as Bach sketched out a setting of the text of i on paper which he used in 1731

for 'Phoebus and Pan'. That evidence supports the placing of the cantata in the period of borrowing from secular works. The sketch was discarded, and the text, Psalm cxviii. 15–16, was fitted to a modified version of the concluding chorus of the Tafelsmusik. The reconstruction must surely have caused as much labour as an original composition; one must assume that Bach desired to hear his old chorus once again. In the hunting cantata it stands in F, in $\frac{6}{8}$, the scoring two corni, two oboes, taille, fagotti, violin I, II, viola and violoncello on separate staves, and violone plus continuo grouped together. In 'Man singet mit Freuden vom Sieg' ('Let songs of rejoicing be raised' N.) it is in D, three trumpets, timpani, three oboes, bassoon, and strings in the normal manner. While the ritornelli are transferred bodily, the vocal parts are almost completely rewritten. The same general ideas are employed for the choir, but there is more imitative treatment and there is less squareness of phrase. One passage is reproduced intact, where the voices rise one after the other in long rolling phrases, to 'besieget' ('conquer', to conquer sorrow) in the old, and 'erhöhet' ('exalted') in the new. The German version of the Psalm verses differs from the English. Fifteen is 'Man singet mit Freuden vom Sieg in den Hütten der Gerechten' ('One sings with joy of the victory in the abodes of the righteous') and sixteen 'Die Rechte des Herrn behält den Sieg; die Rechte des Herrn ist erhöhet' ('The right-hand of the Lord maintains the victory; the right-hand of the Lord is exalted').

The rest of the libretto is original. As the Epistle describes the victory of St. Michael and his angels over the dragon (Rev. xii. 7–12), it is only natural that such a tempting subject should be seized upon by writers of libretti for St. Michael's Day (in this case 29 September), and the four cantatas which Bach wrote for this Feast (the others are 19, 50, and 130) contain opportunities to exploit musically the spectacle of conflict and victory. The tumultuous continuo of the bass aria is a splendid picture of the struggle, and a powerful voice is needed to do justice to the inspiring vocal line, even although there is nothing to battle against but continuo and violone. Bach's violonist at that time was evidently none too agile, for a simplified version of the continuo is provided for him:

Ex.474

becomes:

Ex.475

and

Ex.476

becomes:

Ex.477

The simplifications are made in the ritornelli only; perhaps the incompetent one was instructed verbally to be silent during the remainder. Bach's indifference to dissonant clashes is shown by the fact that the violone plays the essential note of the melody when the continuo decorates it from above or below by an auxiliary note of a tone or semitone, as may be seen above. The fine continuo idea is altered to provide the vocal material:

Ex.478

When the singer continues 'Gott, dem Lamme, das bezwungen und den Satanas verjagt' ('(to) God, to the Lamb, Who subdued and the Satan drives away'), the continuo resumes its theme and the voice adds new ideas, 'Kraft' being isolated on high notes and a mighty run occurring on 'Stärke'. 'Der uns Tag und Nacht verklagt' ('who us day and night accuses') is leaping, with chromatics on 'verklagt'. In the interlude semiquavers 9–16 of Ex. 476 are developed, and play an important role during the remainder of the text: 'Ehr' und Sieg ist auf die Frommen durch des Lammes Blut gekommen' ('Honour and victory is upon the pious through the Lamb's blood come'). It is obvious that this is the outpouring from Christ's wounds, for similar figures are used in other works where the rushing of waters is mentioned. The singer's first five notes are an inversion of notes 1–5 in Ex. 474, and they occur elsewhere. Otherwise the line is new, splendidly vigorous, with syncopations and joyful leaps. The three ideas quoted *supra*, together with another from the introduction and a run rolling to the depths, form almost the whole material for the bassi, the 'outpouring' motive being given especial prominence.

A short recitativo secco turns from the fallen angel to those who in heaven watch over mankind. The text is a versification of passages from the Psalms and Kings ii: 'I fear me of a thousand enemies not, for God's angels encamp themselves by my side: when all falls, when all breaks, then am I yet at rest. How were it possible to despair? God sends me fiery steeds and chariots and whole hosts of angels.' The remainder of the cantata is praise of the divine beings and prayers to them. One of the loveliest of 'angel' arias comes next; (see P. 20) the strings suggest gentle undulations of their wings (see (a) in Ex. 479) and ecstatic peace prevails. The hovering of the heavenly protectors above the bed of the sleeping believer is limned by the undulating motion set against sustained notes or chords. It is curious that this characteristic motive is practically identical with that indicative of tears, but Bach's treatment makes its effect totally different. Vocalists hesitate to separate these two-note groups, as a violinist would do, but there should always be a distinct break between them. Examples have already been given which prove that the idea that Bach should be invariably sung smoothly is quite false. The chief melody is exquisite:

The two clauses—'Wenn ich schlafe' ('When I sleep') and 'wachen sie' ('watch they')—are set in antithesis; there is movement, naturally, to 'wenn ich gehe' ('when I go') and a sustained note to 'wenn ich stehe' ('when I stand') and the angel-motive appears for the first time vocally on the last word of 'tragen sie mich auf den Händen' ('bear they me on the hands').

The low tessitura of most of the tenor recitativo secco suggests that Bach thought of the singer as lowly before the glory of these beings

'I thank Thee, my beloved God, therefor; thereby grant to me, that I my sinful deeds repent, that himself my angel thereat rejoices, that he me on my death-day into Thy bosom to the heaven (may) carry.'

One of the all-too-rare bassoon obbligati is heard in the arresting A.T. duet. (There is evidence that a good fagottist resided in Leipzig at that time. See Terry's *Bach's Orchestra*.) It is a poetic picture, the approach of darkness, the restlessness of the longing Christian and a plea to the 'holy watchers' to be vigilant, 'Seid wachsam, ihr heiligen Wächter, die Nacht ist schier dahin' ('Be wakeful, you holy watchers, the night is almost past'). The opening bassoon melody:

Ex.480

Cont.

serves, slightly modified, for the above text; the waving figures:

Ex.481

Cont.

and

Ex.482

wach - - - - - sam,

typify the floating of the divine beings in the aether. Bassi and obbligato continue in the same strain during the next clauses: 'Ich sehne mich und ruhe nicht, bis ich vor dem Angesicht meines lieben Vaters bin' ('I long and rest not, till I before the countenance of my dear Father am'). 'Sehne' is expressed by long-drawn syncopations, 'meines Vaters' is ecstatic. The colour of the fagotto tone gives a feeling of loneliness, almost of awesomeness; the choice of obbligato instrument is not fortuitous. It is as apt as Gluck's use of the flute in the Elysian scene in 'Orpheus'.

The treatment of the concluding chorale is unique. Strings, oboes, bassoon double the voices, trumpets and timpani are silent until the final bar-and-a-half, when they thunder out a few notes on the word 'ewiglich' ('eternally'). This unexpected blaze of glory is particularly thrilling. Stanza 3 of M. Schalling's hymn for the dying—'Herzlich lieb hab' ich dich, O Herr'—to its anonymous melody, is set: 'Ah, Lord, let Thy beloved angels At the latter end my soul Into Abraham's bosom bear; The body in its little sleep-chamber, Quite softly, without any torture and pain, Rest till the last day! When then from death awake I, That my eyes (may) see Thee In all joy, Oh God's Son, My Saviour and my mercy-seat! Lord Jesus Christ, Hear me, hear me, I will Thee praise eternally!' The librettist of this fine cantata, so varied and so well-balanced in interest, is not known.

171. One number in 'Gott, wie dein Name, so ist auch dein Ruhm' ('According to Thy name, O God, so is Thy praise unto the ends of the earth', Ps. xlviii. 10) is known to be borrowed, the soprano aria, iv (see P. 19). It comes from the secular cantata, No. 205 'Der zufriedengestellte Aeolus', performed on 3 August 1725, for the birthday of August Friedrich Müller, one of the university professors, and reproduced on 17 January 1734, as 'Blast Lärmen, ihr Feinde', in honour of the coronation of the Saxon monarch, Augustus III, as king of Poland. The first text begins 'Angenehmer Zephyrus' ('Pleasant Zephyr'), and the gentle breeze is depicted in graceful and incessantly soaring and falling phrases of a beautiful violin obbligato. Picander's new text does not utilize this imagery, but is a New Year's song (the cantata is for this occasion), saying that 'Jesus' is the first word uttered—'Jesus soll mein erstes Wort in dem neuen Jahre heißen' ('Jesus shall my first word in the New Year be')—and will also be the close of life: 'und in meiner letzten Stunde ist Jesus auch mein letztes Wort' ('and in my last hour is Jesus also my last word'). Consequently, wonderfully beautiful though the aria be, the obbligato is of no special significance. The long notes of the singer originally on 'Kühlen' ('coolness'), with a pulsating bass not heard elsewhere in the aria, mean nothing when allotted to 'Jahre', the soaring passages to 'Höhen' ('height') are strangely misplaced to 'Jesus', and the first vigorous phrase to 'Großer König' ('Great King', addressed to Aeolus) has nothing to do with 'fort und fort' ('continually'), though the second is more appropriately set to 'lacht Sein Nam' in meinem Munde' ('laughs His name in my mouth') with the high note for 'Nam''. The sacred version stands a tone lower than the secular.

A bad mis-accentuation at the end of the fugue subject of the opening chorus:

Ex.483

| God, | as | Thy | name, | so | | is | also | Thy |
| Gott, | wie | dein | Na - me, | so | | ist | auch | dein |

T.

Cont.

| fame | to | | the | world's | end, | | | |
| Ruhm | bis | an | der | Welt | En - | de, | | |

points here also to adaptation, although the source has been lost. The number is familiar to concert-goers in the form of a readaptation, the second 'Credo' of the *B Minor Mass*. The orchestration is preserved, three trumpets, timpani, two oboes and strings, but there is much rewriting of the choral parts. Fine though the fugue-subject sounds in the cantata, it is much more compelling in the Mass. One new feature there is the three-fold hurling out of 'Credo in unum Deum' by the voices not for the moment occupied with the subject. The unforgettable closing sixteen bars, beginning with the tonic pedal, are reproduced almost faithfully, although the later version contains a new exciting point, the exhilarating leap of the sopranos to high B. Spitta thinks that after this chorus was written the cantata lay long unfinished, in spite of the propitious opening, and that the remainder was not added for a considerable time.

The chief theme of the tenor aria, ii (two violins and continuo), a climb upwards, appears in two forms, the semiquaver version with which the violins begin:

Ex.484

VI.II

Cont.
8ve lower

and a skeleton version for the voice:

Ex.485

| Lord, | as | far as | the | clouds | go, | (goes Thy name's renown.) |
| Herr, | so | weit | die | Wol - | ken ge-hen, | (gehet deines Namens Ruhm.) |

Cont.

which the singer is allowed to use in the more ornate form later to 'erhöhen'—'Alles, was die Lippen rührt, alles was nur Odem führt, wird dich in der Macht erhöhen' ('All that the lips touches, all that only breath draws, will Thee in the might elevate'). It is a companion nature-picture to the Zephyr aria, sweeping arpeggi descend, scale passages cross and recross each other while the voice scurries along to 'gehen'. Between the arias comes a recitativo secco for alto: 'Thou sweet Jesus-name Thou, in Thee is my rest, Thou art my comfort on earth, how can then to me the Cross anxious become? Thou art my impregnable castle and my banner, thither hasten I, when I persecuted am. Thou art my life and my light, my honour, my confidence, my standby in danger and my gift for the New Year.' (See Ex. 1279.)

There is a curious recitative-arioso for bass, v. After a single bar of recitative—'And as Thou, Lord, (hast) said;'—comes a ten-bar arioso, in $\frac{3}{8}$, the words of Christ—'If ye shall ask anything in my name, I will do it' (St. John xiv. 14)—paraphrased as 'Ask only in my name, so is all Yea! and Amen!' The oboes now join the continuo while the singer, in recitative, reflects on this promise;—'so implore we, Thou Saviour of all the world, to Thee; drive us farther not away, guard us this year from fire'. 'Pest, und Kriegsgefahr!' ('Pestilence and war-danger!') brings an ominous diminished third in the bassi (see Ex. 1314). It continues placidly, with sustained notes of such length as to tax the oboists considerably: 'Let for us Thy word, the bright light, still clearly and brightly burn: grant to our Government and to the whole land the happiness of Thy blessing to know; give always good-fortune and salvation to all ranks.' This suggests the presence of the Municipal Council at the service. The last few bars, reverting to prayer, are again arioso, with an accompaniment in the repeated-note prayer-motive (more string music than reed): 'We ask, Lord, in Thy name, say: "Yea!" also say: "Amen, Amen". Amen.'

The concluding chorale presents a problem. Oboes and strings double the voices, and the cadences of lines 1, 2, 3, 4, and 11 are punctuated with fanfares for the three trumpets and timpani, in all cases the last four beats of these being unaccompanied; thus the cantata ends with ringing brass and percussion. The same number is found, a tone lower, in another New Year's cantata, No. 41, based on the hymn and probably written in 1736. There the fanfares are also among the thematic material of the first chorus, which is based on the chorale. Picander's libretto of No. 171 was published in 1728, so that cantata would probably be given in 1729 or 1730. There are two possibilities; (1) that the number was borrowed from No. 41 for a later performance of No. 171 to replace one already there; and (2) the fanfares in No. 171 pleased the composer so much that when he came to write No. 41 he adopted them for the long chorale fantasia which opens that cantata, and developed them with evident delight. The stanza is No. 3 of J. Hermann's 'Jesu, nun sei gepreiset' to its anonymous melody: 'Thine is alone the honour, Thine is alone the glory. Patience in suffering us teach, Govern all our doings, Till we comforted depart Into the everlasting heavenly kingdom, To true peace and joy, To the saints of God equal. Meanwhile do it with us all After Thy pleasure. Such sings today without grief The Christ-believing host, And wishes with mouth and heart A blessed New Year.' The text of the last two lines is repeated.

173. In 1717 Bach wrote a Serenata at Cöthen for the Prince's birthday—'Durchlaucht'ster Leopold' ('Most serene Leopold')—possibly to words of his own. Six out of eight numbers were commandeered to make a Whit-Monday cantata for 1731, eight years after he had settled in Leipzig, 'Erhöhtes Fleisch und Blut' ('Exalted flesh and blood'). One of the two other numbers appears in No. 175. It may have been pressure of work caused by the need of cantatas for the three successive Feast Days of Whitsuntide, coming so soon after the same number at Easter, that caused him to indulge his passion for borrowing so much at this season. Of the three we possess for the Sunday, two, Nos. 34 and 74, of the three for the Monday, two also, Nos. 68 and 173, and both of those for the Tuesday, Nos. 175 and 184, contain adapted material. The new text of No. 173 runs parallel to the old for the most part, new lines being inserted only to delete direct reference to Leopold. The imagery is ingeniously preserved, so that association between words and music is unharmed. It is likely, therefore, that Bach himself undertook the task. He deftly worked in references to the Epistle, Acts x. 42–48, the descent of the Holy Ghost upon Cornelius and his company, vi, and their magnifying God, ii and iii, and to the Gospel, St. John iii. 16–21, beginning iv with part of the opening verse, 'For God so loved the world that He gave His only begotten Son.' The original score includes two flauti traversi, the earliest occasion, as has been pointed out, on which these are definitely specified. A bassoon introduced into one number is not transferred; there are strings and two voices only, both lying high, the soprano touching B and the baritone frequently singing top G. There must have been some male vocalist of peculiar character attached to the court. In the new version there is no change in the instrumental score, although the vocal lines are altered from time to time. Much of the music is in Bach's most gracious manner; one wishes it had been rescued in some other form, for its odours are not of incense, but of the perfumes of the court, strangely unsuited to the rather severe Thomaskirche. A tenor replaces the soprano in i and ii. i is a short recitative with strings; the later version alters a few notes in bars 3, 4, and 5, and the original tremendous flourish in the penultimate bar on 'Durchlaucht'ster' is neatly accommodated to 'Erhöhtes'. The two texts are:

Serenata	Cantata
Most serene Leopold,	Exalted flesh and blood,
sings Anhalt's world	that God Himself on Him takes,
anew with delight,	to which He already here on earth
thy Cöthen itself before thee places.	a heavenly salvation determines,
in order before thee to bow,	of the Highest Child to become,
most serene Leopold.	exalted flesh and blood!

ii is an engaging aria with strings and two flutes doubling violin I—

Serenata	Cantata
Güldner Sonnen frohe Stunden,	Ein geheiligtes Gemüthe
(Golden suns' joyous hours,)	(A sanctified mind)
die der Himmel selbst gebunden,	sieht und schmecket Gottes Güte,
(which the heaven itself (has) bound,)	(sees and tastes God's goodness,)
sich von Neuem eingefunden,	
(anew appeared,)	
rühmet, singet, stimmt die Saiten,	rühmet, singet, stimmt die Saiten,
(praise, sing, tune the strings,)	(praise, sing, tune the strings,)
seinen Nachruhm auszubreiten.	Gottes Güte auszubreiten.
(his posthumous glory to spread abroad.)	(God's goodness to spread abroad.)

The opening melodic fragment:

Ex.486
Fl.I.II.Vl.I

is transformed twice:

Ex.487   Ein ge-hei - lig-tes   Ge-mü - the,

and:

Ex.488 ein ge - hei - lig-tes Ge-mü-the,

(same continuo)

not to the advantage of the accentuation, as will be seen. The remainder of the first half of the introduction places florid semiquaver
triplets in the top line and accompanies for a while with a variant of
the initial figure. A deft alteration of the opening, with a new bass,
begins the second clause, and a new version of the triplets, circling
round G and its peaks rising gradually, is accompanied in the inner
strings by a criss-crossing of ♩ ♫ . An altered form of the first
triplets to 'sieht', &c., is supported by the bassi figure, and fresh
ideas appear above. A fascinating development of all these themes
brings us to a delightful treatment of the remainder of the text.
Triplet arpeggi are bandied about between the voice ('rühmet, singet')
and the upper strings, and a florid ascending passage related to the
latter part of the introduction:

Ex.489 rüh-met,sin - get,stimmt die Sai-ten,Got-tes Gu - te aus - zu - brei - - ten,

Cont.

is answered by violin I. This opulent character continues till the Da
Capo. The movement must be treated as $\frac{24}{16}$ time.

The next aria, vivace, with originally a high bass tessitura, is transferred to alto, with a few changes in the vocal line to accommodate
the new voice. Praise of the Almighty is unblushingly substituted for
encomiums on the Prince:

Serenata	*Cantata*
Leopolds Vortrefflichkeiten	Gott will, o ihr Menschenkinder,
(Leopold's excellences)	(God will, oh ye men's-children,)
machen uns itzt viel zu thun.	an euch große Dinge thun.
(give us now much to do.)	(in you great things do.)
Mund und Herze, Ohr und Blicke	Mund und Herze, Ohr und Blicke
(mouth and heart, ear & sight)	(mouth and heart, ear & sight)
können nicht bei seinem Glücke,	können nicht bei diesem Glücke
(can not in his good-fortune,)	(can not in this good-fortune)
das ihm billig folget, ruh'n.	und so heil'ger Freude ruh'n.
(that on him justly waits, rest.)	(and such holy joy rest.)

The accompaniment is curious; for the greater part the violins are in unison, playing decorated arpeggi in staccato semiquavers. The violas are much occupied with octave quaver leaps, and until 'Mund und Herze' is reached the bassi move mostly in quavers with occasional excursions into the joy-motive. With these words, which, as also 'Ohr und Blicke', have effective rests after the initial notes, the bassi become more active. The penultimate 'und so heil'gen Freude ruh'n' sweeps down to a sustained 'ruh'n', over which the violin figure is played piano; the final one moves in the opposite direction during a bar of adagio. The chief theme is attractive:

Ex.490

The flutes are absent from this number but return in the S.B. duet. The serenata indicates *Al Tempo di Menuetto*; out of deference to sacred surroundings this is omitted in the cantata. It should nevertheless be played as a dance measure. The lengthy ritornelli seem to indicate that some action took place during them, some dignified ceremonial. Long as it is, and unbroken as is the style, interest is maintained by the diversity of treatment to which the lovely themes are submitted. A complete analysis is called for. (*a*) strings, twelve bars moving from G to D—

Ex.491

(*b*) repeated with a modification of the melody for the bass:

Serenata	Cantata
Unter seinem Purpursaum	So hat Gott die Welt geliebt,
(Under his purple-edge)	(So has God the world loved,)
ist die Freude nach dem Leide,	sein Erbarmen hilft uns Armen,
(is joy after sorrow,)	(His pity helps us poor (ones),)
Jeden schenkt er weiten Raum,	daß er seinen Sohn uns giebt,
(to all bestows he ample place,)	(that He His Son us gives,)

(*c*) strings and bass, twelve bars, moving from D to G, a modification of the first melody. Serenata and cantata texts are here identical:

'Gnaden-Gaben zu genießen, die wie reiche Ströme fließen'
('Mercy-gifts to enjoy, which like rich streams flow'). (*d*) repetition
of (*c*) with strings only. A connecting link of less than a bar leads to
(*e*), with a double bar and an addition of a sharp to the signature.
Twelve bars, modulating from D to A. Flauto I plays the melody of
(*a*), decorated at first, but afterwards normal, flauto II has independent counterpoint, the continuo is silent, unison violins and violas
make a trio with the flutes. Bach's strings would be few, otherwise
the flutes, which do not rise high, would be drowned. (*f*)Twelve bars,
D to A; the melody of (*b*), slightly altered, is assigned to the soprano:

Serenata	*Cantata*
Nach landesväterlicher Art	Sein verneuter Gnadenbund
(In sovereign-like manner)	(His renewed mercy-bond)
er ernähret, Unfall wehret;	ist geschäftig, und wird kräftig
(he nourishes, misfortune drives back;)	(is active, and becomes powerful)
drum sich nun die Hoffnung paart,	in der Menschen Herz und Mund,
(therefore itself now the hope unites,)	(in the men's heart and mouth,)

Flauto II doubles the voice, flauto I and unison upper strings add
counterpoints, the former decorative at first, the latter crotchets and
quavers. (*g*) Twelve bars, D. The same scoring and manner. The
soprano sings the melody of (*c*), slightly altered, to:

Serenata	*Cantata*
daß er werde Anhalts Lande	daß sein Geist zu seiner Ehre
(that he will Anhalt's land)	(that his spirit to his honour)
setzen in beglücktem Stande.	gläubig zu ihm rufen lehre.
(set in favoured condition.)	(believingly to Him to call teaches.)

(*h*) Twelve bars, A to D. An instrumental modification of (*c*), flauto
I decorating the melody, unison upper strings providing a new bass,
flauto II adding a counterpoint. During the last bar the bassi re-enter,
flauto I trills, violin I breaks into semiquavers. (*i*) The signature
changes to three sharps. The twelve-bar melody of (*d*), altered in
bars 1 and 2 so as to modulate from D to A, is repeated by low-
lying unison flutes, finishing in E. Violin I continues in semiquavers,
which, with one slight break, do not cease till the final bar of the
movement. Sometimes they are independent of the melody, sometimes they decorate it, indulging in sharp clashes, consecutive
seconds and the like. As the violin line often lies above the flutes,
balance can only be secured in modern performances, with our more
powerful strings, if one violin only is employed. Once the opening

modulation is accomplished, the continuo plays as in (d); there are slight alterations in the middle parts. (j) Twelve bars, A to E. The bass sings the melody of (b).

Serenata	Cantata
Doch wir lassen unsre Pflicht	Nun wir lassen unsre Pflicht
(Yet we let our duty)	(Now we let our duty)
froher Sinnen itzt nicht rinnen	Opfer bringen, dankend singen,
(of glad minds now not trickle)	(offerings bring, thankfully sing,)
heute da des Himmels Licht	da sein offenbartes Licht
(today there the heaven's light)	(as His revealed light)

The voices join for the first time, the soprano singing a counterpoint, doubled and sometimes decorated by unison flutes. Violin II performs the same office for the bass, an octave higher; the continuo is mostly new. (k) The bass sings the melody of (c):

Serenata	Cantata
seine Knechte fröhlich machet	sich zu seinen Kindern neiget,
(his servants joyful makes)	(Himself to His children inclines,)
und auf seinem Scepter lachet.	und sich ihnen kräftig zeiget.
(and on his sceptre smiles.)	(and itself to them powerfully shows.)

The 'moto perpetuo' of violin I is clearly an interpretation of the last line of the serenata text; it loses its meaning when allied to the substituted verse. The other orchestral strands follow the procedure of (j), though the continuo is more closely related to (c). A florid soprano passage to 'lachet' is not happily mated to 'zeiget' in the new version. (l) ritornello. The melody of (c) is assigned to the flutes and decorated, the low register producing a feeling of sensuous warmth. The continuo is altered only where accommodation to the new pitch is compulsory, the inner parts are almost the same. The movement exhibits an unwonted key-scheme, beginning in G and concluding in A, and is an interesting set of free decorative variations, not met with elsewhere in the church cantatas. We find a similar type of structure, though on a much lesser scale, in several numbers of the 'Peasant' cantata.

New recitatives are usually provided when a secular work dons clerical vestments, but here the duet-recitative which follows remains. The serenata text begins—'Durchlauchtigster, den Anhalt Vater nennt' ('Most serene, whom Anhalt father calls'); the substitution is 'Unendlichster, den man doch Vater nennt' ('Most eternal, whom one yet Father calls'); the remainder agrees: 'wir wollen dann das Herz zum Opfer bringen; aus unsrer Brust, die ganz vor Andacht brennt, soll sich der Seufzer Gluth zum Himmel schwingen' ('we will then the heart as offering bring; from our breast, which wholly in devotion burns, shall itself the sighs' passion to heaven swing'). For four bars the voices move together *in stilo recitativo*; the remainder is arioso, mainly canonical, with swirling passages on 'schwingen', in which the baritone climbs to the giddy height of G, more comfortable for the tenor who in the sacred work replaces him. The continuo also scales aloft, to B, the alto clef being used. There is no indication where the violone may rejoin; entry where the bass clef is resumed would sound crude.

The next two secular numbers are omitted (the second of these was reserved for No. 175) and the final duet is transformed into a four-part chorus with strings and unison flutes. The latter sometimes double the principal melody and sometimes decorate it, and at other times are independent. It is another graceful minuet, though not marked so, with again much repetition of material. Soprano and bass retain their original parts, though the latter line is modified to suit normal voices; the sopranos are considered less and not excused their high B's. To have two minuets separated by a brief recitative only is a flaw in the design of the latter part of the sacred work, though the entry of chorus altos and tenors, silent up to this point, helps to modify the lack of contrast. (*a*) Sixteen bars, D–A, instrumental:

Ex.492

(*b*) repetition with voices added, introduced with an upward glide for flutes and violin I in the serenata, but for flutes only in the cantata:

Serenata	*Cantata*
Nimm auch, großer Fürst, uns auf	Rühre, Höchster, unsern Geist,
(Take also, great Prince, us up)	(Touch, Highest, our spirit,)
und die sich zu deinen Ehren	daß des höchsten Geistes Gaben
(and who to thine honour)	(that the highest Spirit's gifts)
unterthänigst lassen hören.	ihre Wirkung in uns haben.
(submissively sing.)	(their results in us have.)

For eight bars the voices move together, the sopranos singing a plain version of the melody. For the next four the sopranos introduce a fresh melody, imitated by the basses. In the last four the voices unite.

(c) Thirty-two bars, instrumental. A development of the themes of (a), the flutes running in quavers almost all the time. (d) Repetition of (c) with voices added:

Serenata	Cantata
Glücklich sei dein Lebenslauf,	Da dein Sohn uns beten heißt,
(Fortunate be thy life's-course,)	(As Thy son us to pray bids,)
sei dem Volke solcher Segen,	wird es durch die Wolken dringen,
(be to the people such (a) blessing,)	(will it through the clouds penetrate,)
den auf deinem Haupt wir legen.	und Erhörung auf uns bringen.
(as on thy head we lay.)	(and (a favourable) hearing to us bring.)

As in the case of several of Bach's adapted secular cantatas, one longs for the co-operation of some poet of understanding who could fit fresh words which would dissipate the feeling of incongruity and enable the cantata to be given as a concert-work. The original text is of so little interest that it can scarcely be used today. The repeated 'Leopold, Leopold, Leopold', in one of the omitted arias, would upset the gravity of a modern audience.

134. A congratulatory ode to the Prince of Cöthen, 'Mit Gnaden bekröne' (*Gratulations-Cantate*, hereafter referred to as 'G.C.'), dating 1721, was also produced as a church cantata (hereafter referred to as 'C.C.') at Leipzig on Easter Tuesday, 1731, as 'Ein Herz, das seinen Jesum lebend weiß' ('A heart that its Jesus living knows'). Spitta argues in favour of 1735, but recent research has discovered the libretto in a printed 'Text of the Leipzig church music for the Holy Festival of Easter and the two following Sundays, 1731'. Of the six numbers in C.C., three recitatives, i, iii, and v, are new, but the plan of the three in G.C., which the later ones replace, is retained; they are A.T. duets with continuo only. An alto aria is not transferred. Possibly both libretti are by the composer; the new text does not follow the old so closely as in the last case discussed. There is no connexion with the appointed readings except references to the risen Christ. The instrumental portions are unaltered, save for the addition of an occasional trill, and there are only trifling emendations of the vocal lines, long notes being sometimes split up by repetitions so as to accommodate the words better. The single aria, tenor, ii, and the closing chorus are alike in style, in $\frac{3}{8}$ time, scored for two oboes and strings, heroic in character and abounding in vivacious runs.

ii, of which the first 144 bars are missing from the manuscript of
G.C., is long and calls for a tenore robusto. The splendidly vigorous
introduction begins with imitations:

There are three other fine ideas:

and

(*a*) gives rise to the rousing opening call:

Bars 1–9 of the introduction follow and the voice joins in during (*b*)
with a melody related to (*c*)—'singet die lieblichen Lieder' ('sing the
glad songs'). While the singer revels in a roulade on 'Lieder' the
whole of the introduction begins again in the dominant, though
scored differently and with many impetuous leaps for the inside parts.
The voice adds a fresh line, and continues 'euch scheinet ein herrlich

erneuetes Licht' ('to you appears a gloriously renewed light'). In this
section and elsewhere the singer excitedly cries 'auf, auf!' on upward
octave leaps, and rises on the same word— ♪ | ♪ ⁷ ♪ | ♪ —to
high B♭. Developments of all four ideas take place during the
remainder of Part I, the leaping passages dovetail between oboes
and upper strings while the voice swirls on 'scheinet'. Contrary to the
usual practice, when the ritornello is repeated before the *fine* pause,
the singer continues during the imitations, a thrilling ascent:

Ex.498
auf, auf, auf, auf, auf, auf, auf, auf!

Cont.

'Der lebende Heiland giebt selige Zeiten, auf, Seelen, ihr müsset ein
Opfer bereiten, bezahlet dem Höchsten mit Danken die Pflicht'
('The living Saviour gives blessed times, up, souls, you must an
offering prepare, pay to the Highest with thanks the obligation')
brings new flowing themes, with imitations between pairs of upper
instruments. 'Auf, auf, auf!' breaks through the smoothness,
'Höchsten' is flung on high B♭, approached by a slide. (*c*) and (*d*),
followed by running semiquavers, form an interlude for strings. It is
during this that the incomplete manuscript of G.C. begins. (The text of
the latter agrees with C.C. except that the initial clause is 'Mit Gnaden
bekröne der Himmel die Zeiten', 'With gifts (may) crown the heaven
the times'). When the words are repeated the flowing passages are
given to the oboes and are more continuous. Later (*b*) is heard from
unison violins, and during a long flourish on 'bereiten' imitations on
(*a*), in the relative minor, are resumed. The flowing runs for oboes
come in a different form, with interlacing quaver groups in the upper
strings and joyous bassi octave leaps. The remainder exploits (*a*) and
(*b*) and introduces a new repeated-note idea, an unusual procedure
so late in an aria.

The secular manner of the chorus, vi, is not unbefitting to the call
to the heavens to praise the Almighty, and is effective as church
music.

G.C.	*C.C.*
Ergötzet auf Erden, erfreuet von oben,	Erschallet, ihr Himmel, erfreue dich, Erde,
(Delight upon earth, rejoice from above,)	(Resound, ye heavens, rejoice thee, earth,)

G.C.

glückselige Zeiten, vergnüget dies Haus.

(blessed times, make happy this house.)

Es müsse bei diesen durchlauchtigsten Seelen

(Must with these serenest souls)

{die Gnade } des Himmels die
{der Segen } Wohnung erwählen.

({the grace   } of heaven the dwell-
  {the blessing} ing choose.)

Sie blühen, sie leben, ruft Jedermann aus.

(They bloom, they live, calls everyone out.)

C.C.

lobsinge dem Höchsten, du glaubende Schaar,

(sing praise to the Highest, thou believing host,)

Es schauet und schmecket ein jedes Gemüthe

(There sees and tastes an every mind)

des lebenden Heilands unendliche Güte,

(the living Saviour's unending goodness,)

er tröstet und stellet als Sieger sich dar.

(He comforts and places as victor himself there.)

The invigorating introduction is rich in material:

Ex.499
Ob.I.Vl.I
(a)
Cont.
8ve lower

Ex.500
Ob.I.Vl.I
(b)
Cont.
8ve lower

Ex.501
Ob.I.II
(c)
Cont.
8ve lower

which springs from (*b*), and a direct descent:

Ex.502
Ob.I.Vl.I
(d)
Cont.
8ve lower

answered by a more lengthy descent (*e*), incorporating the syncopation of (*b*). The development of these in the choral sections exhibits

Bach's consummate skill, while all is as merry as a marriage bell. At
the outset oboes and violin I play (*a*) pianissimo, and tenor and alto
enter with the latter part of (*d*). When the full chorus enters, forte
is marked in the orchestra, an unusually violent contrast for Bach.
The (*b*) section is given with altos, tenors, and continuo only, full
forces being reserved for the conclusion of the idea. (*a*), with choral
passages based on (*b*), and imitations based on the latter, leads to (*e*),
tutti, in F, the voices moving mostly homophonically. After the
first sentence of the introduction in F, the whole of the vocal section is repeated, but working from dominant to tonic. The introduction comes again. Part II falls into three divisions, each a miniature prelude for A.T., lightly accompanied, and a fugato, the latter
always on the same subject and with full orchestra. The first two are
separated by (*e*) in the orchestra. To discuss these preludes: (1) the
voices sing in thirds a freely inverted form of (*d*), the altos sing (*d*)
against a tenor sustained note, the tenors sing the free inversion
against a fresh alto idea. Rolling and leaping passages are in the
continuo. Oboe I commences (*a*) and continues in semiquavers overlapping with the fugato. (2) tenors and altos imitate with part of (*d*)
and continue for ten bars with florid passages and holding notes
alternately. An abbreviated (*e*) is hinted at by the altos and then the
conclusion of (1) comes with reversed voices. The upper strings stress
eleven bars with detached quavers, after which the continuo sways
up and down. Violin I borrows the oboe passage of (1). (3) is with
continuo only. The voices imitate with the (*b*) figure and merge into
florid passages. A fragment of (*d*), ending with an upward leap of a
sixth, forms a six-bar canon and also merges into roulades, into
which the fugato breaks. The fugatos also show great variety of
detail. The theme is:

Ex.503

Er trös-tet und   stel -   -   -   - (-let)

In (1) the entries are B., T. at one bar, A. at three bars, S. at one bar.
In (2) S., A. at one bar, T. at two bars, B. at one bar. In (3) the keys
are different, though the entries are in the same order and at the same
distances as in (1). The runs are now amplified, the basses enjoying
one of eight bars on 'stellet'. At the end are six homophonic bars,
with the last 'als' dramatically flung on an isolated high-pitched
chord. Bach often chooses novel forms for his secular choruses.

The finest number is a lengthy A.T. duet with strings, iv. The texts are:

G.C.	C.C.
A.	**A.**
Es streiten, es siegen die künftigen Zeiten	Wir danken, wir preisen dein brünstiges Lieben
(There strive, there conquer the future times)	(We thank, we praise Thy fervent love)
T.	**T.**
Es streiten, es prangen die vorigen Zeiten	und bringen ein Opfer der Lippen für dich.
(There strive, there shine the former times)	(and bring an offering of the lips for Thee.)
Both.	**Both.**
im Segen für dieses durchlauchtigste Haus,	Der Sieger erwecket die freudigen Lieder,
(in blessing for this serenest house,)	(The Victor awakens the joyful songs,)
Dies liebliche Streiten beweget die Herzen,	
(This glad striving moves the hearts,)	
die Saiten zu rühren, zu streiten, zu scherzen,	der Heiland erscheinet und tröstet uns wieder,
(the strings to touch, to strive, to play,)	(the Saviour appears and comforts us again,)
es schläget zum Preise des Höchsten hinaus.	und stärket die streitende Kirche durch sich.
(it strikes to the praise of the highest out.)	(and strengthens the fighting church through Himself.)

It is an unusual plan for two voices to sing in parallel motion with different words. It seems as if the librettist of G.C. had wished to speak at once both of the past and present and yet failed to do so within the limits of his verse, and, in consequence, Bach supplied the deficiency by putting them together. There are six lines in the G.C. (the versions given in *BGS* vols. 28 and 29 are different in some particulars) and five in C.C. The simultaneous words could scarcely have been disentangled by his hearers. The fine opening theme:

Ex. 504

simply accompanied by (*a*) in the inner strings, is remarkably fertile in offspring; there is scarcely a bar of the vocal sections in which it does not appear in one form or another. After Ex. 504 violin I breaks into a long series of figurated semiquavers, of the type of decorations in a concerto. About seventy bars of the number are devoted in all to this. The bassi play the opening idea, and then violin II and viola play a long quaver melody:

Ex.505

with (*a*) and its time-pattern in the continuo.

During the last four bars of the introduction violin I outlines a melody against alternate E♭'s or D's:

Ex.506

dovetailing into the vocal entry of Ex. 504. The arrangement of the words according to the cross-bowing produces an engaging effect and this is maintained every time the idea occurs. Twice, in the tonic and in the dominant, seven bars of the introduction, with an additional bar of wide-sweeping arpeggi, an anticipation of later passages, come with voices superimposed, partly new florid ideas, partly the cross-bowed theme, partly with sustained notes in one voice against melodious progressions in the other. Both these sections conclude with voices and continuo only, derivatives of the chief melody being prominent. After the seven bars, with a new ending, as interlude, a long vocal section begins, with the same material for the voices, but in the orchestra two bars of a development of Ex. 504, two of the inverted pedal-note, then the first six bars of the seven, violin II swinging up and down with the cross-bowing, and a continuation of semiquavers. Even yet Bach is not tired of his themes, for he repeats the introduction. Nor does Part II bring much that is new. The voices exploit a derivative of Ex. 504 in parallel motion, construct a short canon from it, toss it about from one to the other. Roulades are more suitable to the G.C. 'streiten' than to the C.C. 'tröstet'. Notes are held against other derivatives of Ex. 504. The orchestra is allowed more latitude. There is a new set of octave leaps in the bassi, fragments in the upper strings present the chief theme in new guise, a variant of the seven bars comes in F minor, and there are some detached quaver passages. In G.C. Bach adopts the old plan of writing one fewer flat in the signature than the key requires, but the years which separate the two versions convert him to the more modern method.

On account of the incompleteness of the manuscript of G.C. we do not know whether it began with a recitative, but the close connexion with C.C. suggests that it did. i of the latter is—T. 'A heart, that its Jesus living knows, feels Jesu's new goodness, and meditates only on its Saviour's worth.' The alto portion is arioso, semiquaver triplets for the voice answered by semiquavers in the continuo to begin with—'How joys itself a believing mind!' Only the last seven bars of the second recitative in G.C., iii, are preserved—A. 'house by time's Lord chosen.' T. 'What lacks to me of mercy-gifts?' A. 'Still greater things have I raised up.' T. 'My fame is now already not trifling.' A. 'In God's praise will such greater be.' It is evidently a dialogue between two symbolic characters. As there are similarities between this fragment and the close of the corresponding number in C.C., there was probably some adaptation. The C.C. recitative is very long —T. 'Well for thee, God has on thee thought, Oh God-consecrated possession; the Saviour lives and conquers with might, for thy salvation, for His fame must here Satan fearfully tremble and itself hell even shudder.' (This is finely dramatic, 'zittern' ('tremble') is placed low, there is an upward leap of a minor ninth to 'Hölle' ('hell').) 'Dies the Saviour thee to benefit, and journeys for thee to hell, even pours out He His precious blood, that thou in His blood conquerest, for this can the enemies overcome, and, when strife to thee to the soul penetrates, that thou then not overcome liest.' (The personal equation is stressed by 'du' ('thou') on high A, which is nowhere else reached.) A. 'The love-might is for me a banner to heroism, for strength in the strife; for me victory-crowns to prepare, tookest Thou the thorns-crown to Thyself, my Lord, my God, my arisen Salvation, so has no enemy in me for harm a portion.' T. 'The enemies indeed are not to be numbered!' A. 'God protects the to Him faithful souls.' T. 'The last enemy is the grave and death.' (See 1 Cor. xv. 26.) A. 'God makes even that as an end to our distress.'

Except for proportion, the tenor lengthy, the alto short, the other recitatives, v, have no similarity. In C.C. the tenor section moves rapidly vocally, but slowly instrumentally: 'Then bring forth Thyself

thanks in our mouth, although it too earthly is; yea ordain that at no
hour, Thee, and Thy work no human heart forgets; yea, let in Thee
the refreshment of our breast, and all heart's comfort and desire (for)
those who through Thy mercy trust, fulfilled and unending be. Let
enclose Thy hand us, that we the effect mightily see, what for us Thy
death and victory wins, and that one now after Thy resurrection not
dies, if one indeed temporarily dies, and we thereby to Thy glory
go.' A. 'What in us is, exalts Thee, great God, and praises Thy
greatness and faithfulness; Thy resurrection makes them again new,
Thy great victory makes us from enemies free, and brings us to life;'.
The close is arioso: 'therefore be to Thee praise and thanks given!'
An earlier version of C.C., standing midway between G.C. and
No. 134, contains differences in the recitatives. The opening tenor
line of i is slightly remodelled and the alto bars are not so florid as in
No. 134. The intermediate version of iii has the same text as the third,
but the music is entirely different, except for the opening two notes for
the voice and some similarity of harmony at the end. The seven
closing bars of this number in G.C. agree with the second version; the
whole of the music may have been adapted to the new text. While v
in the last version is entirely new, in the second the sacred words are
adapted to the music of G.C. The only numbers of the latter, therefore, which are not used in either of the church cantatas are a long
recitative, rich in extreme modulations, and the alto aria. Evidently
Bach was not satisfied with this aria, which was itself apparently
adapted (see the discussion of G.C. in Part IV of this book) and
in consequence left it out when remodelling the work for church
purposes. The three versions of the cantata are an interesting
example of the ceaseless industry and perpetual self-criticism of the
composer.

184. The date of 'Erwünschtes Freudenlicht' ('Desired joy-light')
is definitely fixed for Whit Tuesday, 1731, on account of the printed
text in the Leipzig Town Library. The character of the final chorus
no less definitely fixes a secular origin. The measure is that of a
gavotte. Four-part singing is confined to a few bars, in homophonic
style, and for the rest soprano and bass only are employed, for no
apparent reason whatever. In this long duet section the orchestral
ritornelli are short and scrappy and the length of the portion accompanied by continuo only is out of proportion to the remainder. The
adaptation was evidently made hurriedly. The charming dance mea-

sure is played by strings, with two unison flauti decorating the melody:

Ex.507

The theme is sung to 'Guter Hirte, Trost der Deinen, laß uns nur dein heilsam Wort!' ('Good Shepherd, comfort of Thy people, grant to us only Thy healing word!'). The gavotte continues:

Ex.508

and this is repeated with the text sung twice. The duet section begins with a two-bar phrase—'Laß dein gnädig Antlitz scheinen,' ('Let Thy merciful countenance shine,')—answered by two bars in the orchestra. Fifteen bars with continuo follow—'bleibe unser Gott und Hort, der durch allmachtsvolle Hände unsern Gang zum Leben wende' ('remain our God and refuge, Who through all-powerful hands our way to life turns')—with 3¾ bars of High E and an F♯ for the unfortunate basses (scarcely a refuge!) and a long passage on 'wende' for the sopranos. A series of short alternating passages, orchestra and voices, leads to a repetition of the long duet portion, altered in key and with voices reversed. There is a distinct resemblance in style to the Cöthen Birthday Serenade 'Durchlaucht'ster Leopold', which, it will be remembered, was dished up again in No. 173, and the duet for soprano and high baritone is another connexion with that period. This indicates a lost Cöthen secular work. The initial twenty-four bars of this chorus were incorporated, in 1733, into the final chorus of the secular cantata 'Die Wahl des Hercules'.

ii, a S.A. duet (see S. & B. 'The sun is descending'. The text is not a translation), with the same scoring, may have come from the same

source. The charming and leisurely melodies and the general innocence of the music agree well with the 'Shepherd and sheep' text
fitted by the nameless librettist, who was perhaps the composer himself. The alternate forte and piano bars, with flying violins and flutes:

have no origin in the words, and it is not likely that Bach would have
set 'schmeichelnden Erde' (flattering world') to a guileless wandering passage in thirds. Like the final chorus, it is intriguing music, but
not of the church. The principal melody is

The introduction begins with this, four bars of flying demisemiquavers follow, without contrasts of strength, and lapse into a plainer
melody; there are then sixteen bars on a similar plan with the forte
and piano alternations as shown in Ex. 509. The opening sixteen bars
are now repeated, but with the vocal form, Ex. 510; the upper strings
are tacet, the flutes wander peacefully. The second half of this section
is purely instrumental. The eight vocal bars are repeated, followed
by eight in which the voices move independently, violin I alternates
demisemiquavers with quavers, flutes, violin II and viola being silent.
The first sixteen bars are repeated in the dominant as interlude. The
voices enter with a variant, accompanied by violin I and continuo,
pass through a tutti section founded on the flying passages, with
'gesegnete' sustained, continue in thirds, repeat the contrapuntal section with reversed parts and end with a fresh figure in imitation, with
continuo only. The introduction comes again, leading to the *fine*

pause. 'Verachtet das Locken der schmeichelnden Erde, daß euer Vergnügen vollkommen kann sein' ('Despise the allurement of flattering earth, that your delight accomplished can be') begins with the principal melody in the minor, 'schmeichelnden' ambles pleasantly in thirds at great length, the final clause harks back to the imitations which closed the vocal section of Part I. At first the flutes are divided, for the only time in the cantata, playing the demisemiquaver groups four times in thirds, the last twice adding a tail-piece of leaping quavers, violins in unison follow with a derivative of Ex. 510, and the remainder is with continuo only. A condensation of the introduction serves as interlude, and then the voices resume, beginning in imitation, but soon slipping into parallel sixths, this time to 'Locken'; and the world's allurement lasts for more than eleven bars, accompanied by short groups of demisemiquavers for violin I, and then by the forte-piano section of the introduction, tutti, and during this the singers sustain. The imitative idea which in Part I was associated with 'kommt, stellt euch bei Jesu' serves for 'daß euer Vergnügen kann sein' with the same accompaniment. This indifference to the significance of the words, the repetition of the imitative figure, bringing the unimportant 'daß' where 'kommt' lay, and even decorating it with a new trill, together with the obvious makeshifts of the instrumental lines of the score, are additional evidences that some secular composition must have been pressed into service, not as successfully as usual.

The libretto of the cantata neatly combines the visitation of the Holy Ghost in Samaria (Epistle, Acts viii. 14–17) with the thought of Christ as Shepherd (Gospel, St. John x. 1–10), and the long tenor recitative and arioso, i, is a pastoral idyll. The flutes, mostly moving in thirds and sixths, repeat endlessly a five-note figure:

Ex. 511

conjuring up a picture of a shepherd wandering among his flock and trilling on his 'Doppel-flöte'. Recitative—'Longed-for joy-light, that with the new covenant dawns through Jesus, our Shepherd; we, who otherwise in death's valleys wandered, perceive fully now, how God to us the long-desired Shepherd sends, Who our souls feeds and our going by word and spirit to the right way turns; we, His chosen people, feel His strength; in His hand alone is, what for us refreshment creates, what our heart mightily strengthens. He loves us, His flock, who His comfort and assistance observes; He draws them from vanity, from the earth, on Him to gaze and all time in His grace to trust. Oh Shepherd, Who Himself for the flock gives, Who till the grave and till in death them loves! His arm can against enemies defend, His care can us sheep spiritually nourish; yea, (when) comes the time, through the dark vale to go, then helps and comforts us His gentle staff' (see Psalm xxiii. 4). The bassi move slowly and gently, except that once they play two sextuplets. The flutes cease during the arioso, which exploits 'Freuden' ('joy') in running passages ('Therefore follow we with joy to the grave'), but the figure returns, both in flutes and continuo, for the brief recitative-coda: 'Up! hasten to Him, transfigured before Him to stand.'

The tenor has another recitativo-arioso, this time secco. The text is 'So rejoice, ye chosen souls! The joy establishes itself in Jesu's heart. This refreshment can no man relate. The joy moves even downwards' ('Freuden' is melismatic, indicating the descent of the Holy Ghost) 'to those, who in sin's bonds lay. These has the Hero of Judah already smitten. A David helps us, a hero-arm makes us from enemies free. When God with might the flock protects, when He in anger on its enemies flashes, when He the bitter cross's death for you not shuns, so bears it further no distress, so lives it in its God gladdened. Here tastes it the noble pasture and hopes there (for) complete heaven's-joy.' 'Labsal' ('refreshment') is melismatic, 'auf ihre Feinde blitzt' ('on its enemies flashes') is tense with high notes, and the clause about Christ's death on the cross falls as if in shame. The treatment of 'Himmelsfreude' ('heaven's-joy'), the arioso section, is exceedingly florid.

The prevailing tunefulness also pervades the solitary aria for tenor. The chief obbligato violino solo theme:

Ex. 512

and the principal vocal melody:

Ex.513

(the faulty accent on 'die' is a sure sign of adaptation) are equally attractive. There are ingenious devices of construction. Ex. 512 lasts ten bars, Ex. 513 four, the first four violin bars are repeated, and then both come simultaneously for four bars, the initial bar of the vocal theme altered. The voice begins a modification of Ex. 512 and the obbligato follows in canon for four bars. The violin now modifies and extends its second sentence and the voice provides a counterpoint. Ex. 513 is restored complete in the dominant. The voice incorporates some of the violin figures in:

Ex.514

(Wustmann, in his edition of the texts, New *BGS*, suggests 'Wenn wir uns zu ihm gewöhnen' ('If we ourselves to Him accustom') instead of the ununderstandable second clause) and the violin decorates with its initial bar followed by a two-bar 'golden time' figure. An episode is formed by a four-bar condensation of the introduction. The voice begins a new melody, the violin enters a bar later with a new version of its opening two bars, solo and obbligato move together in animation. After six violin bars using the material of the introduction to modulate from relative major to tonic, a condensation of Part I and Ex. 512 round off the aria. It may well have come from the same lost cantata; the long run on 'krönen' may have been to the same word in the original text, a common one in congratulatory cantatas.

A four-part chorale precedes the closing chorus, an unusual order. It is stanza 8 of Anark von Wildenfels'(?) 'O Herre Gott, dein göttlich Wort'—'Lord, I hope ever, (that) Thou wilt those In no distress leave, Who Thy word rightly as true servants In heart and faith hold; (That Thou) givest to those prepared The blessedness And lettest them not be destroyed. O Lord, through Thee beg I, let me Joyful and blest die.' The anonymous melody is not used elsewhere by Bach.

195. Whatever may be the unknown sources of the wedding cantata 'Dem Gerechten muß das Licht' ('For the righteous' B.), it is certain that the bass aria, which Spitta considers to be 'in the Lombardic style', must have come from a secular composition, indeed possibly from a comic work. Its jerky rhythms and the jauntiness of its melody are more allied to the bass aria in No. 30 (which was adapted from a secular cantata) than to music befitting a solemn ceremony:

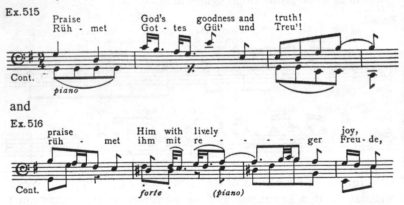

and

'Preiset Gott, verlobten Beide' ('Praise God, betrothed couple') is accompanied by:

'Denn eu'r heutiges Verbinden läßt euch lauter Segen finden' ('For your today's union let you pure blessing find') is accompanied by the same idea, and 'Freude' in 'Licht und Freude werden neu' ('light and joy become new') exploits the jerks even further:

Ex. 518

Not content with this, Bach accompanies the return of the first clause with a fresh treatment of the ubiquitous time-pattern, and in the second part of the concluding ritornello forms a long sinking and soaring passage out of it for two oboes d'amore and violins in unison:

Ex. 519

The indication in the Breitkopf edition, andante religioso, is a silly attempt to cloak the jester's motley with a monk's cowl, and the aria treated in this way is insufferably dull. Only when dealt with as Schlendrian's arias in the 'Coffee' cantata does the music sound attractive, and then it is false to the words. Through the disappearance of the original text we are denied one of Bach's best secular songs. One cannot see why he chose to add two oboes d'amore to the strings in this anything-but-tender aria, and one can only wonder how it could have come about that the master who wrote the finest of all sacred music could be guilty of such deplorable taste as to adapt such a number for performance in a church.

Large-scale wedding cantatas are usually in two parts, placed respectively before and after the ceremony. In this case the text of an aria, recitative and chorus designed for the second part (Part I is headed 'Vor der Trauung', 'Before the wedding') and possibly by Bach, are in existence, but no music; their place is taken by a simple chorale. Perhaps he had embarked on too immense a scheme, which time did not permit him to complete, and the chorale was made to serve. It shows some interesting points. The first two notes are unaccompanied, a rare occurrence. The two flauti traversi double the melody at the octave above, except in line 2, where they break away. Corno I (there are no horns elsewhere), oboe I and violin I double the tune, oboe II and violin II the alto, and viola the tenor, while the continuo has a slightly ornate version of the bass. Corno II and timpani are independent. The melody is that of N. Herman's Christmas hymn 'Lobt Gott, ihr Christen alle gleich' and the words stanza 1 of P. Gerhardt's 'Nun danket all' und bringet Ehr''—'Now thank all and bring honour, You men in the world, To them whose praise the angel host In heaven continually announces'. Line 1 only is written in the score; the Breitkopf vocal edition gives three verses.

Many errors in the manuscript suggest that the cantata was produced in a hurry. If so, why did Bach take the trouble to begin with such a huge chorus, which occupies thirty pages of eighteen staves each in the BGS? The text is Psalm xcvii. 11, 12:—'Dem Gerechten muß das Licht immer wieder aufgehen, und Freude den frommen Herzen. Ihr Gerechten, freuet euch des Herrn, und danket ihm und preiset seine Heiligkeit' ('On the righteous must the light always again break, and joy in pious hearts. Ye righteous, rejoice ye in the Lord, and thank Him and praise His holiness'). It is fitted so badly that haste to provide for a mortal marriage must have made the composer reckless concerning the marriage of words and music. Whether a secular or a sacred work was plundered to provide a wedding gift it is not possible to say, but the prize was worth the crime, even if it suffered in the violence of the raid. There are three trumpets and timpani, a flauto traverso doubles oboe I, another doubles II, strings are normal, and the chorus is divided into solo and ripieno, the choral scheme treated with great elaboration. The form is that of a prelude and fugue. The prelude itself contains a kind of fugue, the elaborate theme (Ex. 520) being presented in turn by soloists, S.A.T.B., then tutti, B.T.A.S. The entries are not continuous; there are tutti outbursts (not always with brass and percussion, however) between each pair of entries. The introduction is based on Ex. 520. Oboes and flutes

announce its last bar, ending differently, with repeated-note arpeggi in
the upper strings, octave leaps in the bassi and a short fanfare for brass
and percussion. The wood-wind play the complete subject in parallel
motion, the bassi leaping and running, the upper strings punctuating

Ex. 520

in unison with the time-pattern ♫ ♪. The concluding bar is
treated like the opening, but made more resplendent by an ascent
of tromba I to high E. Violins and wood-wind change places in the
dominant. In the last bar trumpets I and II begin a shining passage
in thirds, later the upper strings reverse the direction of their arpeggi.
The tutti outbursts in the preludial fugue are derived from the opening
bar. The overwhelming final 6½ bars are based on the opening bar,
and the first part of Ex. 520 is fitted in the basses wholly to 'und
Freude'. The score is wonderfully brilliant, Italian in its imposing
external splendour.

The $\frac{6}{8}$ fugue consists of a double exposition:

Ex. 521

solo voices and tromba I, the latter continuing also with the countersubject:

Ex. 522

(und danket ihm, und preiset seine Heiligkeit,)

followed by ripieni, two episodes based on an idea from the 'freuet'

of the subject, with an abundance of flaring vocal and instrumental
trills:

Ex. 523

freu - - - - - - - - - (-et)

three further vocal entries and one for tromba I. During the first exposition the upper strings mark the half-bars with quaver chords;
during the second they, together with the wood-wind, double the
entries. During the episodes trumpet I participates in the theme and
adds independent matter. Trumpets II and III and timpani do not
enter till the trumpet tutti subject. Prior to the final tromba subject
the voices excitedly cry:

Ex. 524

und   dan - ket ihm,   und   dan - ket ihm

The recitatives, ii and iv, are addressed to the happy pair in terms
which would have made them feel uncomfortable if they were not
endowed with the saving grace of humour. ii, bass, is probably
original; it has continuo only, but an active one, revelling in many
semiquaver triplet embellishments: 'To the joy-light of the righteous
pious (ones) must always a new increase come, which well-being and
fortune with them multiplies. Also for this new couple, in whom one
as much righteousness as virtue honours, is today a joy-light prepared, that establishes new well-being there.' The bassi triplets have
been indicative of the light of joy; a new figure enters:

Ex. 525

'Oh! a desired union! So may two their good-fortune, one in the
other find!' The bridal pair would doubtless understand the billing
and cooing in the bassi. iv, soprano, is accompanied by two flutes and
two oboes d'amore. The former indulge in many chasing scale passages in demisemiquavers, moderating their exuberance in the centre
portion by more demure descending scales at half-speed. The oboes
d'amore behave sedately. One fails to see the reason for this un-

wontedly elaborate accompaniment to a recitative, for the text affords no clue; one is driven to the conclusion that Bach liked the number in the secular cantata and adopted it for the new text: 'Well, so join them a bond, that so much well-being prophesies. The priests' hand will now the blessing on your marriage-state, on your steps lay. And, when the blessing-strength in you thrives, so praise the Highest's Father-hand. He joins Himself your love-bond, and permits that, which he began, also a desired end to reach.'

It is unlikely that Bach, in his haste, would have had time to compose the second chorus, which closes Part I; we must assume that it also is an adaptation, though there are no injustices to the text, which would probably be a mere modification. The manner of the music is undoubtedly secular. Scoring and lay-out of choir and orchestra are the same as in i, but the music is more direct and less ornate, the chief elaboration being the often-broken runs to 'preisen'. The frequent cross accents, two bars of $\frac{3}{4}$ sounding as three of $\frac{2}{4}$, in the quaver stepwise passages, constitute a feature of rhythmical interest. The four chief motives are announced in the introduction— (a) an ascending scale idea, the upper strings, violin I and II doubled respectively by flauto I and oboe I, and flauto II and oboe II, entering successively, the rest of the orchestra punctuating the bars with crotchet chords:

Ex. 526

(b) a florid theme in tromba I:

accompanied by a version of (a) in the bassi and staccato crotchet chords for wood-wind and upper strings, trumpets II and III and timpani continuing as before; (c) the joy-motive:

Ex.528

(*b*) is now developed for eight bars by wood-wind and strings, with fragments of (*c*) for trumpets I and II. Wood-wind and strings call a two-bar halt on sustained chords during which the bassi play a form of (*b*) and the trumpets give out (*d*):

Ex. 529

With continuo only, the chorus sings 'Wir kommen, deine Heiligkeit, unendlich großer Gott, zu preisen' ('We come, Thy holiness, everlastingly great God, to praise') beginning with (*a*) and continuing with the aforementioned cross-accents. (*a*), (*b*), and (*c*) are utilized in an interlude and twenty-two bars of chorus follow. The first eight reproduce the opening of the introduction; the lower voices shout 'Wir' on the first beats of the bar before they take up (*a*), the basses expand (*a*) to eleven bars. The remainder is without brass and percussion. (*b*) and (*c*) are developed; for twelve bars sopranos and altos sing the single word 'preisen', first to (*b*) and then to detached groups from (*c*). A version of (*d*) ascending an octave appropriately to 'unendlich großer Gott', is given to the voices, with the same accompaniment as before. Dovetailing with an orchestral (*a*) in the dominant, a short double fugue is opened by the solo voices. Both subjects begin with (*a*) and the soprano theme adds (*b*):

Ex. 530

The awkward textual lead-off in the soprano is a sure sign of adaptation. After the male solo voices enter the scheme is unusual. The soprano sings part of (*f*); so far the continuo only has been present, reiterating the time-pattern ♩♩♩ | ♩ ♪. When the soprano reaches the top note, flute II, oboe II and violin II play the whole of (*f*), the upper voices continuing till it finishes. This instrumental unison now plays (e), (f) is added by flute I, oboe I and violin I, during which the basses flourish on 'preisen'. Except for two bars the continuo maintains its time-pattern. The bass roulade dovetails into eight bars of the vocal-instrumental form of (a), exactly repeated. The ten bars which followed this are now expanded to eleven, with key changes, and the last five bars of the introduction are repeated with all forces. After the *fine* pause there are twelve bars for the solo quartet with continuo—'Der Anfang rührt von deinen Händen, durch Allmacht kannst du es vollenden und deinen Segen kräftig weisen' ('The beginning springs from Thy hands, through omnipotence canst Thou it accomplish and Thy blessing mightily show'), an expansion of the concluding sentence of the soprano recitative. Several of the vocal and continuo passages are derived from (d), the bassi open with an inversion of (a) and a bar of (b). An interlude for strings and woodwind (brass and percussion are silent in Part II) exploits (a) and then (d), though, except in the bassi, the melodic outline is different. During the latter inner strings and bassi accompany with | r ♩ ♩ |, which is used by wood-wind and upper strings through most of the twelve tutti choral bars which lead to the Da Capo. Here the (d) grouping is used, the continuo decorating the bass line with it.

Terry thinks the date of the reconstruction to be about 1726.

(C.2.) FROM SACRED SOURCES
136, 144, 191

136. The tender prayer 'Search me, O God, and know my heart; try me, and know my thoughts' Psalm cxxxix. 23, is not akin to the confident chorus which opens 'Erforsche mich, Gott, und erfahre mein Herz'. Another text must have been the first cause of this number. Nor is the music particularly interesting in this guise; there are fine moments, without doubt, it is difficult to imagine Bach without them, but in spite of the splendid and animated counterpoint it fails to grip. A horn delivers the principal tune (Ex. 531) at the beginning, an oboe and an oboe d'amore are added to strings. Rushing semiquaver scales, sometimes answering each other by contrary motion, and florid passages for the corno, oboe, and violin I conclude the introduction. A partial delivery by the sopranos, constituting the formal fugue subject, is clenched by a repetition of the close of the introduction, and then the regular exposition unfolds itself. An extra entry for sopranos, doubled by corno and wood-wind, is followed by six bars of an involved episode. With the horn repeating a C♯ in quavers, and violin I extending its semiquaver runs, comes a cunningly planned four-part stretto in the relative minor, the voices

Ex.531

entering at increasing distances, 1 beat, 2 and 4 beats. A conclusion of the choral section and an episode taken from the introduction proceed to two sequential presentations of the subject in the basses, the other voices accompanying in a new manner. There is a fresh stretto with the voices entering from below, 2 beats, 2 and 4 beats. Five bars of episode, during which the corno mounts an arpeggio to high A, lead to two from the sequential entries in the bass, the second accompanied as before. The finest portion comes after this, three homophonic shouts of 'prüfe mich'. The final vocal entry is for the sopranos, and then violin I dashes down nearly two octaves. One cannot help being moved at times by the stirring polyphony and attracted by the superb craftsmanship even though inspiration sometimes lags. Bach's adaptation of this number as the 'Cum Sancto Spiritu' of the Short Mass in A does less violence than is the case of other rearrangements in these odd pasticci. As a matter of fact it sounds very much finer in the Latin version than in the German, and one is less conscious of its occasional defects.

The two recitativi secchi are not distinguished in any way, though they are not without attractive features. ii, for tenor, runs: 'Ah, that the curse' (see Gen. iii. 17) 'which there the earth strikes, also men's hearts smote! Who can for good fruit hope, where this curse in the soul penetrates, so that it sin's thorns brings (forth), and vice'sthistles bears. Yet will themselves often the children of hell as angels of light disguise; one shall from the corrupted nature of these thorns grapes gather. A wolf will itself with pure wool clothe' (see Ex. 1305) 'yet dawns a day which will, ye hypocrites, to you a terror, yea, intolerable be.' iv, for bass, is 'The heavens themselves are not pure, how shall (it) then a man before this Judge be? Yet, who through Jesu's blood (is) cleansed, in faith himself with Him united, knows, that He to him no hard judgement speaks. Burdens him the sin still the inadequacy of his doings, he has in Christ however righteousness and strength.' 'Christo' is melismatic; the remainder is arioso, a fine roulade on 'Stärke' ('strength') is answered by a powerful descending passage for continuo.

The solitary aria, for alto, is full of interest, in spite of the fact that the text, which speaks of the trembling of the hypocrites and the disclosure of secrets (the Gospel for the Eighth Sunday after Trinity, St. Matthew vii. 15–23, is a warning against false prophets, ravening wolves in sheep's clothing), promises little: 'Es kommt ein Tag, so das Verborg'ne richtet, vor dem die Heuchelei erzittern mag;' ('There comes a day, which the hidden (things) judges, before which the hypocrisy tremble may;'). The oboe d'amore obbligato is based almost wholly upon the beautiful first phrase:

and a figure running to notes 2–5 of the above:

The voice has its own melodies:

and

Ex. 535

The brief $\frac{12}{8}$ presto section, of nine bars only, with continuo, matches the fierce vehemence of the words—'Denn seines Eifers Grimm vernichtet, was Heuchelei und List erdichtet' ('For its zeal's fury annihilates what hypocrisy and cunning fabricates')—with flaming trills and runs on the two verbs. Mention of hypocrisy always stirs Bach to righteous wrath. The reprise of the first ideas is more concentrated, and the trembling of the hypocrites calls up a running passage in which the voice has to negotiate a diminished third followed by a diminished fifth. In spite of these appropriate features, one cannot help feeling, from the use of the words in the $\frac{4}{4}$ sections, that it is an adaptation.

The T.B. duet is not devoid of charm, but it is not a success as a whole and is evidently patched-up from some previous work. The principal instrumental theme, for violins in unison (there are no violas):

Ex. 536

seems to be an unconscious reminiscence of the B minor three-part invention, and promises more than the later portions fulfil. The voice parts in time grow to be somewhat monotonous; the lively runs to 'Gnaden-Strom' certainly introduce an element of brightness, but also an element of difficulty. A tempo adopted to make these comfortable for the singers causes the rest to drag, an appropriately rapid movement of the remainder causes these runs to be confused. The contrasting violin figure is attractive:

Ex. 537

The voices open in canon—'Uns treffen zwar der Sünden Flecken' ('On us fall indeed the sin's stains')—with a long run on 'Flecken'. Possibly Ex. 537 is an interpretation of this clause. At the close the violins enter with bar 2 of the introduction, as a message of hope, and during bars 4–6 the voices sing simultaneously phrases akin to their first, proceeding to the next part of the text: 'so Adams Fall auf uns gebracht' ('which Adam's fall on us brought'). The most interesting portion of Part I follows, a short canon depicting the descent from the first estate:

Ex. 538

so A - dams Fall auf uns ge - bracht;

so A - dams Fall auf uns ge - bracht,

with further canons, the violins pursuing Ex. 537 in long descending scales, the bassi following in like manner. Ex. 536 re-enters, super-imposed upon vocal imitations and parallel ideas. The 'Uns treffen' canon reappears with reversed voices, but instead of a plain continuo, fragments of Ex. 537 come in both instrumental lines. This idea forms an interlude, then Ex. 536 holds sway for five bars, while the voices, after a simultaneous 'Allein' ('But') pursue a long canon on 'wer sich zu Jesu Wunden, dem Gnaden-Strom' ('who himself in Jesu's wounds, the mercy-stream'). The passage passes through minor keys, F♯, B, E, A, and D, 'Jesu' moves in semitones and the bassi well up and down, in a phrase which incorporates the semiquaver slide:

Ex. 539

7   6 7
♯   4

The remainder of the verbal sentence—'voll Blut, gefunden, wird dadurch wieder rein gemacht' ('full of blood, (has) found, will there-through again clean (be) made')—is with continuo. As in Part I Ex. 536 is dovetailed, with semiquaver slides in the continuo, and then a long run in parallel motion to 'Gnaden-Strom' brings a new feature, monotoned quaver throbbings, for violins and bassi. After another brief canon the section is repeated. One's reaction to this cleverly constructed number is much the same as to the chorus.

In the final chorale violin I plays an independent line. The melody
is the secularly derived 'Auf meinen lieben Gott' (see p. 264) and the
words the ninth stanza of J. Heermann's Lenten hymn 'Wo soll ich
fliehen hin', 'Thy blood, the honoured essence, Has such strength
and might, That even a droplet small The whole world can cleanse,
Yea, even from the devil's jaws release, Free and untrammelled
make'. The date of the cantata is possibly about 1725, the librettist
is unknown, as is also the reason for an adaptation so unequal.

144. A casual glance at the small cantata, 'Nimm, was dein ist,
und gehe hin' ('Take what thine is, and go thy way' O., St. Matthew
xx. 14) is sufficient to show that it is quite different in style from
other works of the period, possibly about 1725. The plain movement
of the chorus, the simplicity of the first aria and the lack of spon-
taneity of the second, are indicative of some deflexion from the normal.
So much is this so that its authorship has been doubted, though the
case is not proven. If by Bach, it is assuredly a compilation. The
opening chorus is a plain fugue, in motet style:

Ex. 540

Take   what   thine is, and   go   hence,
Nimm,   was   dein ist, und   ge - he   hin,

Cont.

with continuo only, though doubtless strings and oboe would double
the upper voices. It is sufficiently interesting to make one think that
Bach wrote it: indeed, it is full of quiet charm. The numerous repetitions of 'depart';

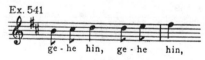

Ex. 541

ge - he hin, ge - he hin,

show that the composer was in difficulties with his diminutive text,
seven words only. There are other cases in Bach; composers then
were not so sensitive to the effect caused by immoderate repetition
of words as we are today. Purcell could write such magnificent music
that we forget that the poetaster has provided him with next to
nothing; Samuel Wesley thought it quite congruous to arrange the F♯
major fugue in Part I of 'the 48' for four-part choir, using the word
Hallelujah only, every semiquaver of the counter-subject being provided with a syllable! It would be joyous to hear choir-boys mounting

step by step to high B at the end! Bach builds up an interesting episode from a long succession of the 'gehe hin' motive in the bassi, while the voices pursue imitations on a slow-moving phrase:

It may be that this number is an adaptation of an instrumental fugue. The Gospel for Septuagesima was the parable of the labourers in the vineyard, St. Matthew xx. 1–16; doubtless the manifold reiterations of the master's command would not come amiss to the worshippers at St. Thomas's.

The alto aria, with strings (see O.S.B.A. No. 30 & P. 50), in which the librettist (possibly Picander) contrasts content and discontent, is in popular style, in directness recalling the alto aria-cantata No. 53, 'Schlage doch'. It is often taken too slowly; it needs to move at rather a rapid pace to prevent monotony and a heaviness of the pulsating bassi notes. It was no doubt originally a slumber song; evidences of awkwardness in fitting the new words are noticeable in bars 88 and 89, besides other places. The sixteen-bar introduction provides a sustained melody of great beauty, much more simply accompanied than is Bach's wont. The master hand shows its cunning by the finely effective free inversion of bars 1–4:

in bars 9–12:

Ten bars of the melody are sung to 'Murre nicht, lieber Christ, wenn was nicht nach Wunsch geschieht' ('Murmur not, beloved Christian, when anything not according to desire happens'). At bar 11 Bach avoids what the ordinary composer would have written, a repetition of the lovely tune, and switches off so as to end the sentence in the dominant. Eight bars of ritornello bring one to an enchanting derivative:

Ex. 545

A derivative of bars 6 and 7 of the introduction is heard vocally:

Ex. 546

Violin I inserts part of Ex. 544 and alternates with low repeated notes. Murmuring is further symbolized by deeply placed waving quavers for the violins; twice the voice sings passages of much eagerness against continuo only. Part II is 'sondern sei mit dem zufrieden was dir dein Gott hat beschieden, er weiß, was dir nützlich ist' ('but be with that contented which to thee thy God has ordained, He knows, what for thee necessary is'). The vocal melody is wholly new, mostly accompanied by continuo, except that fragments come in the upper strings, twice bar 1 of Ex. 543, with murmurings, and twice a scale passage derived from bar 6, and that for five bars violin I plays an independent counterpoint. In the middle is an interlude based on Ex. 544.

The soprano aria, with oboe d'amore obbligato (see O.S.B.A. No. 31), is much less interesting; if it is borrowed it is not because of outstanding merit. The opening phrase:

Ex. 547

is much used by the obbligato and by the singer in—'Genügsamkeit ist ein Schatz in diesem Leben, welcher kann Vergnügung geben in der größten Traurigkeit' ('Contentedness is a treasure in this life, which can satisfaction give in the greatest mourning')—the first group of notes being nearly always associated with 'Genügsamkeit'. 'Denn es lässet sich in Allem Gottes Fügung wohl gefallen' ('For it allows itself in all with God's providence (to be) well pleased') is not distinguished, save for some runs on 'Allem' and 'gefallen'. An unusual plan is adopted for the final ritornello. The melody begins before the voice is finished; there are two new vocal phrases, the obbligato tune is broken to allow the voice to end, and then resumes, *per arsin et thesin*.

Between the arias are a richly harmonized chorale and a tenor recitativo secco, the latter: 'Where contentment reigns and over all the rudder guides, there is the man contented with that, which God sends. But, where the discontent the judgement speaks, there appear grief and sorrow, the heart will not be contented be, and one thinks not thereon.' A version of line 1 of the preceding chorale ends: 'What God does, that is well done.'

The chorale is stanza 1 of S. Rodigast's hymn of that name, to its anonymous melody: 'What God does, that is well done, Remains just His will; However He does with my affairs, Will I to Him hold contentedly. He is my God, Who in the distress Me well knows to hold; Therefore let I Him alone govern.'

The final chorale is more elaborately set. The melody is another of those of secular origin—a French song—'Il me souffit de tous mes maulx', associated with Markgraf Albrecht of Brandenburg-Culmbach's 'Was mein Gott will, das g'scheh allzeit', of which stanza 1 is used—'What my God wills, (may) that happen alway, His will is the best. To help those He is prepared Who on Him believe steadfastly. He helps out of distress, the righteous God, And disciplines with moderation. Who God trusts, fast on Him builds, Him will He not abandon.' The connexion with the parable is obvious. There is no indication of orchestration in either chorale.

191. No 191 is an exceptional case and the only cantata not in the vernacular. No year of the Christmas Day for which it was prepared is ascertainable, and no reason for this departure from the normal. There are three numbers. i is the opening chorus of the Gloria in excelsis Deo of the *B Minor Mass*. Text and score are practically identical, although the bassoons are omitted from the cantata. Latin is retained in the direction before the other two—Post orationem. The S.T. duet Domine Deus, vii in the Mass, appears with the text of the first part of the Doxology: 'Gloria Patri, et Filio, et Spiritu Sancto.' The original scoring is flauto traverso and muted strings.

Here two flutes in unison replace the single instrument, and the last twenty-one bars are omitted. The 'Cum Sancto Spiritu', xi of the Mass, becomes iii in the cantata, set to the remainder of the Doxology, and with interesting differences. There are two clauses in 'Cum Sancto Spiritu in gloria Dei Patris' while there are three in 'Sicut erat in principio, et nunc et semper, et in saecula saeculorum'. The sentence in the Mass first occupies two bars of tonic chord and a beat on the dominant, S. II, T. and B. It is repeated, S. I and A., dovetailing with the first, two bars dominant, with 'Patri' long sustained, beginning with the tonic chord. This is impossible with the more extended sentence of the Doxology, and the opening groups therefore fall into three-bar rhythm, bars 2 and 3 being 1 and 2 of the original version, the vocal theme slightly altered, while bar 1 of the cantata is new. A fresh figure also appears in the flutes in bar 1. These changes occur each time the idea is heard, whether vocal-orchestral or purely instrumental, thus causing important rhythmical changes. The bassoons of the original score are omitted, and while there flauto I doubles oboe I, and flauto II oboe II, in the cantata all four have separate lines, sometimes coalescing, but often independent. In the Mass the first vocal fugal section is accompanied by continuo only, in the cantata strings and woodwind participate. During the long choral chords just before the first fugal section, tromba I plays, in the Mass, a series of arpeggio quavers, five in each bar; in the cantata all except the initial one are allotted to flutes in unison. In the corresponding portion after the first fugal section, trumpets I and II play, in the Mass, brilliant groups of semiquavers, but in the cantata they are relegated to the flutes. It was pointed out in the discussion on No. 70 that Bach evidently considered a single oboe as equivalent to a trumpet; here two unison flutes are looked upon as satisfactory, and later two flutes as equal to two trumpets, a striking example of differences in strength as compared with those of our modern instruments. Here again one wonders why Bach took such immense trouble over rearrangement and why he did not write original music, in this case to an inviting text. Think of the enormous labour of writing out this score for a single cantata, 56 pages of 17 staves and 6 pages of 21 staves in the *BGS*!

CANTATAS APPERTAINING WHOLLY TO THE MIDDLE LEIPZIG PERIOD

SOLO CANTATAS

COMMENT has already been made on the common view that the solo cantatas are merely incidents and of relatively little importance in the general output. How false is this impression may be seen from the fact that thirty-three cantatas of the middle period, nearly one-third of the total number, are without chorus other than a simple chorale. Many of them, too, are of outstanding beauty, remarkable examples of his genius. In seven of them no four-part chorale appears, although in two of these a hymn-verse with its melody is introduced into a solo line. In one case the chorale is extended, thus bringing the work on the border-line between solo and choral. It is, however, included in this section. There is one five-part chorale. They will be classified according to the voices employed, and in the lists given at the head of each section cantatas already discussed will be noted in parentheses, in order that a complete survey may be made. An asterisk indicates that a four-part chorale is included.

Soprano Alone
51, (52*), 84*

51. 'Jauchzet Gott in allen Landen' ('Praise God in all lands'), one of the best known of solo cantatas, was written possibly about 1731 or 1732 and designed for general use. Some time later it was produced again and the revision of the text points to the coincidence (1737) of the Feast of St. Michael with the Fifteenth Sunday after Trinity. Bach is presumably the librettist. Trumpet and voice vie with each other in bravura passages in i, and while violin II and viola are relatively unimportant, violin I shares in the honours. It is this number which stands out most vividly in one's memory after a performance. A mighty unison opens, almost too great for a solo cantata:

Ex.548

and tromba and violin I continue:

The leaping bassi figure is crystallized for violin I in bar 6:

during which the trumpet trills and the continuo plays (b). The voice
begins with an idea which is foreshadowed by the tromba at the end
of bar 5:

and the orchestra dovetails with 3½ bars of the introduction, switching
off suddenly to complete the phrase in the dominant. The remainder
of the introduction is reproduced in the new key, tromba and violin I
reversing. In the working-out, new melodies spring from (d), which
appears twice in the bassi, once concluding with (a); the latter occurs
thrice, (b) and (c) are absent, voice and trumpet compete with each
other in flourishes. 'Was der Himmel und die Welt an Geschöpfen
in sich hält, müße deßen Ruhm erhöhen' ('What the heaven and the
world of creatures in itself holds, must His fame upraise'), brings at
first new ideas, but (a) and (b) soon reappear, the voice pitting against
the latter impulsive syncopations. Fresh ideas come again with 'und
wir wollen unserm Gott gleichfalls jetzt ein Opfer bringen, daß er
uns in Kreuz und Noth allezeit hat beigestanden' ('and we will to
our God likewise now an offering bring, because He us in suffering
and want ever has stood by'); (a) comes twice, (b) once, and part of
(d) is incorporated into vocal, violin I, and continuo lines. Bassi leaps
akin to (c) add to the general animation. The singer begins clause I
again, and a new combination of (a) and (d) brings the Dal Segno,
the voice dovetailing and returning to bar 10, thus cutting into the
introduction.

The single recitative adopts rather a curious procedure: it begins
with a section for strings, with repeated quavers, the prayer-
motive: 'We adore in the temple, where God's honour dwells' (see
Ps. cxxxviii. 2; xxvi. 8) 'as His goodness, daily new, with pure
blessings rewards. We praise, what He for us has done.' Then comes a
very varied arioso secco. It is more common to find a tutti concluding
a combination of recitative and arioso. A continuo figure persists
almost throughout:

Ex.552

'Muß gleich der schwache Mund' ('Must even the weak mouth') is
set plainly twice, 'von seinen Wundern lallen' ('of His wonders
stammer'), brings a wriggling, hesitating run on 'lallen'. 'So kann
ein schlechtes Lob' ('so can a feeble praise') shows a quaint conceit,
the vocal phrase is imitated by the continuo in inversion! The conclusion of the text is 'ihm dennoch wohl gefallen' ('Him yet well
please'). The section is repeated ('mein' ('my') being substituted for
'der'), *per arsin et thesin,* and with variety of detail as well as of key.
The first 'muß gleich mein schwacher Mund' is slightly different, in
the second 'schwacher' is a faltering melisma; the next clause,
though the previous style is adhered to, is reconstructed, the vocal
phrase of 'so kann ein schlechtes Lob' is altered and decorated,
though its perverse imitation is plain. In the ritornello the bassi soar
confidently, the mouth no longer stammers.

A second aria follows, in flowing $\frac{12}{8}$ time, with continuo. While the
voice begins independently, with a commanding octave drop on
'Höchster', never repeated, the scalic sixth of the bassi theme, (*a*),
finds its way into the middle of the succeeding vocal phrase:

Ex.553

and may be traced several times subsequently in the upper line.
Part II opens with a fragment of (*a*) for the voice—'So soll für die
Vatertreu'' ('So shall for the Father-faithfulness')—and the com-
plete phrase follows in the bassi, in C, during 'auch ein dankbares

Gemüthe durch ein frommes Leben weisen' ('also a thankful spirit through a pious life show') and in G with 'daß wir deine Kinder heißen' ('that we Thy children may be called'). Thus (*a*) is associated with every section of the text; it continues to dominate the rest of the aria. The vocal line contains many new ideas and there are roulades to 'heißen'.

A chorale is now introduced for the solo voice, iv, with extensive ritornelli based upon a merry leaping figure:

Ex.554

which, with a swirling semiquaver figure, is developed into a complex three-part texture for two violins (violas are silent) and continuo. There are many close imitations on a six-note derivative. The verse is stanza 5 of J. Graumann's (Poliander) 'Nun lob', mein' Seel', den Herren', a song of joyful praise to the Trinity, set to J. Kugelmann's (?) melody: 'Be laud and praise with honour To God Father, Son, Holy Ghost! Who will in us increase What He to us through mercy promises, That we (may) in Him steadfast trust, Wholly rely upon Him, From the heart on Him build, That our heart, spirit and mind To Him closely cling; Therefore sing we immediately: Amen! we shall it attain, If believe we from the heart's depth.' The figured chorale, in itself nearly 120 bars, runs without break into a concluding Allelujah of almost the same length, in which the orchestra of i returns. It is of the same brilliant Italian type and is a free six-part fugue on the subject:

Ex.555

The bassi are allotted the theme once only, but by way of compensation they maintain a connexion with the previous number by the frequent use of the figure: ♪♪♪ | ♪ . In the middle a repeated-quaver arpeggio idea becomes important and an 'allelujah' is sung twice, beginning with a fourfold repetition of a note, which is developed later by the tromba. Near the close the trumpet mounts to

high D and then descends— | ♪ ♩ ♪ ♩ | —for more than two octaves.
Bach revelled in the powers of his soprano; one passage is:

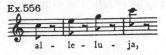

and another:

While the cantata plumbs no depths, it is externally attractive, and
this has caused it to be a favourite battlehorse of coloratura singers.

84. The same year (21 January 1731 or 10 February 1732) and
possibly the same singer accounted for 'Ich bin vergnügt mit meinem
Glücke' ('I am happy in my good-fortune'), but it is vastly different
in character, and although it, too, touches no sorrow and utters no
complaint, it is more intimate and possesses deeper qualities. Spitta
thinks that it was written for domestic purposes but Terry scouts the
theory. As in the case of No. 144, the libretto (by Picander, revised
no doubt by Bach) is based on the parable of the workers in the vineyard, the day being Septuagesima and the Gospel St. Matthew xx.
1–16. There is no reference to the dissatisfied labourers, however; the
singer is content with whatever the master provides. In the first of the
two arias violin II and viola move in detached quaver arpeggi;
the oboe has the chief melody:

although violin I and continuo borrow its phrases. The falling scale
is always tongued and bowed in twos, but when the voice takes it up
the grouping is: | ♪ ♫. ♫. ♪ | ♩. How often do we find singers
ignoring this characteristic of the methods of the time, so productive
of delightful sublety of phrasing! Editors are often guilty in the same

way; certain popular songs of Bach are frequently printed incorrectly in this particular. Such passages are undoubtedly easier to sing in the modern method, but, after all, the composer knew what he was about, and it is a crime to act contrary to his wishes. The same practice is followed extensively by Tudor madrigalists and lutenist composers. All through the vocal line are similar groupings, more than in almost any other aria, and it forms one of the most charming features of this delicious number. Although the aria is very long the text consists of five lines only, the others being: 'daß mir der liebe Gott beschert. Soll ich nicht reiche Fülle haben, so dank' ich ihm für kleine Gaben, und bin auch nicht derselben werth' ('which to me the dear God gives. Shall I not rich fullness have, then thank I Him for small gifts, and am even not of the same worthy').

The other aria is equally attractive. 'Ich esse mit Freuden mein weniges Brot und gönne dem Nächsten von Herzen das Seine' ('I eat with joy my scanty bread, and grant to my neighbour from my heart his') is the quaintly happy theme; oboe, solo violin, voice, and continuo furnish a fascinating texture. The opening vocal phrase—

Ex.559 Ich' es-se mit Freu-den mein we-ni-ges Brot
Cont.

is first delivered by the violin in semiquavers, the melodic outline alternating with the dominant on an open string, while the oboe picks out the chief notes staccato, a piquant device:

Ex.560 Ob.
Vl.

The upward and downward leap of a sixth is almost like a quiet laugh of contentment; merry rapid scale passages in imitation abound. Part II begins with continuo: 'Ein ruhig Gewissen, ein fröhlicher Geist, ein dankbares Herze, das lobet und preist, vermehret den Segen, versüsset die Noth' ('A quiet conscience, a joyful spirit, a thankful heart, that lauds and praises, multiplies the blessing, sweetens the woe'). A downward sixth opens, the bassi borrow semiquavers from Part I: ♫♫ | ♪ . At 'Noth' is one of Bach's delightful little homilies; the voice, despite semiquaver groups, strikes a mournful note, but oboe and violin enter with the semiquaver group, the comforting in need by belief. The oboe now presents a variant of Ex. 559, with a bass including the semiquavers, and the violin adds a counterpoint of leaps and arpeggi. The words are repeated, with a sustained note on 'ruhig' and a flourish on 'fröhlicher', the oboe climbs on a figure containing six semiquavers, also borrowed from Part I. 'Noth' is expanded into nine bars, culminating in a pause; oboe and violin add to the wailing, but the bassi cheer the Christian with lively phrases.

The two recitatives are charming. i, secco, unites in mood the two arias, and simple chromatic chords produce a wistful effect in the last sentence: 'daß ich nicht hungrig darf zu Bette geh'n' ('that I not hungry may to bed go'), one of Picander's most felicitous touches. The text is: 'God is to me yea nothing owing, and when He to me something gives, so shows He to me that He me loves; I can to myself nothing by Him merit, for what I do is my duty. Yea! if my doing even then so good appear, so have I yet nothing right performed. Yet is the man so impatient, that he himself often afflicts, if to him the dear God not abundantly gives. Has He us not such a long time vainly nourished and clothed, and will us in the future blessedly in His glory exalt? It is enough for me, that I not hungry may to bed go.'

iv, with strings, is more solemn in mood, a contemplation of death, yet breathing complete contentment: 'In the seat of my countenance will I meanwhile my bread enjoy, and, when my life's course, my life's evening will close, then apportions to me God the penny, then stands the heaven afterwards. Oh! if I this gift as my wages have, so need I further nothing.'

The chorale, while referring again to the last hour, is a song of a simple-minded child of faith: 'I live meanwhile in Thee contented, And die without all anxiety, For me suffices, how it my God ordains, I believe and am of it wholly certain: Through Thy grace and Christ's blood Makest Thou it with mine end good.' It is stanza 12 of Emilie Juliane, Countess of Schwarzburg-Rudolstadt's funerary hymn 'Wer weiß, wie nahe mir mein Ende' to G. Neumark's tune 'Wer nur den lieben Gott läßt walten'. The variety of these three cantatas for soprano (No. 52 may well belong to the same year as the others) causes one to marvel once more at the infinite scope of the imagination and art of the composer.

Contralto Alone
(35), 53, 54, (169), (170)

53. The authorship of 'Schlage doch, gewünschte Stunde' ('Strike, O Bell' O., 'Strike thou hour' N., 'Sound your knell' B., P. 59) has been doubted. It must be acknowledged that the style is somewhat unusual, that nowhere in the cantatas do we find a similar aria (for it is merely an aria and not a cantata), that frequently the composer does not seem to know what to do with his violas. Yet the main theme—

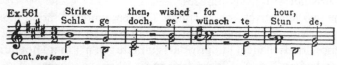

Ex.561

is so lovely and the charm of the whole is so great that one questions whether any other composer of the day could have written it. The attitude to death is that which one finds in a hundred cases in the series. It may, of course, be Bach's version of some other composer's work which attracted him. The violins imitate the ringing of small bells:

Ex.562

but realism goes farther, and for the only time in Bach's scoring a line is given to *Campanella*. There are two bells, B and E, written for in the bass stave as transposing instruments, D and G being the indicated notes. There is nothing to tell whether deep or high bells are required, though the string bell effects suggest that a contrast of pitch is needed. It will be remembered that when Bach drew up a specification for the reconstruction of the Mühlhausen organ he inserted a set of bells to be operated by the pedals. This was in youthful days, yet one also remembers that his great contemporary became infatuated with a keyboard carillon quite late in life. 'Mr. Handel's head is more full of maggots than ever. I found yesterday in his room a very queer instrument which he calls carillon (Anglice, a bell) and says some call it a Tubalcain,—'Tis played upon with keys like a Harpsichord and with this Cyclopean instrument he designs to make poor Saul stark mad.' So wrote Charles Jennens, his censorious librettist. Although the libretto is perhaps by Franck, no date can be ascribed to the music, only the possibility of its coming somewhere in this period.

The remainder of the text is 'brich doch an, $\left\{ \begin{matrix} \text{du schöner} \\ \text{gewünschter} \end{matrix} \right\}$ Tag! Kommt, ihr Engel, auf mich zu, öffnet mir die Himmels-Auen, meinen Jesum bald zu schauen in vergnügter Seelen-Ruh'. Ich begehr' von Herzens Grunde nur den letzten Seigerschlag' ('dawn then, $\left\{ \begin{matrix} \text{thou lovely} \\ \text{wished-for} \end{matrix} \right\}$ day! Come, ye angels, to me, open for me the heavens'-meadows, my Jesus soon to behold in contented soul-peace. I desire from (my) heart's-depth only the last tolling'). 'Trauer-Aria' is written on the manuscript, and that it was for a child's funeral is surmised. The tempo must not be slow; the aria seems interminable if it does not move fairly quickly, and it must be sung happily. The sound of the bell is a welcome one, the call to an ideal life.

54. The same uncertainty of date applies to 'Widerstehe doch der Sünde' ('Watch and pray when trials beset thee', B.). Even the occasion is unspecified. One thing is certain, however, that a voice of remarkable strength and with powerful low notes must have been available at the time. The tessitura of no other contralto music of Bach is so deep. The compass is from E below the stave to B♭ within it, and not only are the lower notes employed largely but the orchestral accompaniment is heavy; only an exceptional voice can make itself felt. The cantata is splendidly effective when performed by a group of altos. Several factors are employed in the first aria (see P. 60) to support a text which is unsparingly stern: 'Widerstehe doch der Sünde, sonst ergreifet dich ihr Gift. Laß dich nicht den Satan blenden, denn die Gottes Ehre schänden, trifft ein Fluch, der tödlich ist' ('Resist then the sin, otherwise seizes thee its poison. Let thee not the Satan blind, for God's honour to violate, falls a curse which deadly is'). The lower strings have mostly repeated chords, strong and stubborn; the chief motive, a struggling motive, associated with the opening clause, which is announced by violin II and which constitutes almost the sole thematic material, employs also dogged repeated notes:

Ex.563   Wi - der-ste-he doch der Sün-de,

Cont.
8ve lower

The theme is used suggestively by the bassi in the second section, where new vocal lines are sung against it. The low notes of the soloist, the dark colour obtained by a double line of violas (which suggests an early date of composition), contribute to the severity of outlook. The opening is startling, an uncompromising chord, $\frac{7}{4}$ on Eb, eight times over. The thirty-two continuo quavers of the initial four bars support four consonances only, all the rest are dissonances, twelve of them being chords containing five different notes. It is a remarkable picture of desperate and unflinching resistance of the Christian to the fell powers of evil. The third syllable of 'widerstehe' is twice held stubbornly against the orchestra, 'ergreifet' bends and twists like a poisoned creature.

The text of the one recitative, secco, is even more grim: 'The nature of infamous sins is indeed from without wonderfully beautiful, but one must afterwards with sorrow and vexation much hardship experience. From outside is it gold, yet if one deeper goes, so shows itself only an empty shadow and whitewashed tomb.' 'Leerer' ('empty') is melismatic, a continuo diminished third marks the hideousness of the whitened sepulchre. 'It is Sodom's apples like, and who themselves with the same consort arrive not in God's kingdom. It is like a sharp sword,'. The continuo now gloomily urges upwards in forceful semiquavers: 'that us through body and soul goes.'

The concluding aria (there are only three numbers) tells us that he who commits sin is of the Devil, and is by him destroyed: 'Wer Sünde thut, der ist vom Teufel, denn dieser hat sie aufgebracht; doch wenn man ihren schnöden Banden mit rechter Andacht widerstanden, hat sie sich gleich davon gemacht' ('Who sin commits, he is of the devil, for he has them reared; but when one its base hosts with rightful devotion (has) withstood, has it immediately fled'). Above the continuo is a three-part fugue, violins in unison, violas in unison, and voice; the singer must of necessity be equal in strength to each instrumental line. The voice descends first in semitones, indicative of sin:

Ex. 564

The countersubject is the devil twisting in convulsive semiquavers:

The heavy quaver movement of the continuo in Ex. 564 we see afterwards, when the voice takes it over—

to be significant of the raising of a brood of evil. Thus there are two countersubjects, though the quaver one is never heard in the upper strings. The clause 'doch wenn', &c., is set to a rugged and powerful phrase which is worked into the fugal texture:

'Davon' is set to repeated leaps, sometimes of a downward seventh, while the upper strings have flying upward phrases and the writhing of the devil continues underneath. There are tense stretti of the 'sin' progression in violins and violas; the bassi play it once only, in the final ritornello, when it is thrust out in the upper compass, reaching to high F, an unwonted pitch for the violone, and followed by a portion of the semiquaver countersubject. The bassi plunge downward and the strongly syncopated leaping figure associated with 'der ist vom Teufel' mounts in stretto in the upper strings. Although the aria is on a smaller scale and more gloomy, it reminds one of the vivid chorus in No. 19, for St. Michael's Day.

Tenor Alone
55*

55. While the alto is the most favoured voice so far as number of cantatas is concerned, the tenor is the least. Moreover, the solitary work, 'Ich armer Mensch, ich Sündenknecht', is much less attractive externally than any of the others for a single voice, although it possesses extraordinarily deep and moving qualities. The libretto, by an unknown writer, suffers from lack of contrast; only towards the end of the second recitative and in the chorale do we find relief from the tenseness of its general mood. Few tenors desire to perform it, as it lies high, touching B♭ constantly, and the scoring of i is somewhat overpowering. Only a tenor who is a musician before he is a singer is likely to measure his intelligence and artistry with this fine cantata. The occasion is the Twenty-Second Sunday after Trinity (possibly 21 October 1731, or 9 November 1732), and the Gospel unfolds the story of the unforgiving servant, St. Matthew xviii. 23–35. The librettist transforms the flint-hearted creditor into a penitent, and the development may be stated briefly as follows—i, aria, lamentation; ii, recitativo secco, fear of God's wrath; iii, aria with flauto traverso obbligato, pleading for mercy; iv, recitative with strings, gradual finding of comfort; v, chorale, renunciation of sin and faith in the mercy of the Almighty.

The scoring of i is curious, flauto traverso, oboe d'amore, violin I and II and continuo, no violas. The wind generally act together and the two violins together. Four important ideas occur in the opening ritornello. (*a*) is a four-bar weary wood-wind passage in sixths, expressive of utter wretchedness:

Ex.568

(*b*) is a derived waving figure in thirds, heavy-laden with woe:

Ex.569

It is heard during the sustained notes of Ex. 568 and then during (*c*)

sinks slowly and despairingly. (*a*) is not found in the vocal line; (*b*) is heard later as (*d*). (*c*) is a slowly climbing phrase for wood-wind,

Ex.570

afterwards set to 'ich geh' vor Gottes Angesichte' ('I go before God's countenance'). Bach seems here to have in his mind the summoning of the servant before his Master, approaching with guilty conscience and painful steps. (*d*) is founded on (*b*), a waving idea creeping up by semitones,

Ex.571

which we afterwards find associated with 'Zittern' ('trembling'). Instruments and voice rarely double each other, so that six-part writing is common. The opening vocal phrase is weighed down with deep anguish:

Ex.572

'Mit Furcht und Zittern zum Gerichte' ('with fear and trembling to judgement') comes above continuo only, in falling semitones and with a diminished third in which both notes are dissonant with the bassi, a passage of great intensity. 'Er ist gerecht, ich ungerecht' ('He is righteous, I unrighteous') are always contrasted; if one clause moves up the other moves down, and vice versa. Few solo numbers by Bach are so consistently intense and despairing.

ii, based appropriately upon the part of Ps. cxxxix which begins 'Whither shall I go from Thy spirit?', continues the chromaticism, but in a milder way. The lamentation is no less poignant, and musically it is on as high a level as i. The continuo sustains a C through most of 'I have against God acted, and have that path, which He for me prescribed has, not followed' to indicate the persistence of sin. After 'Wohin?' ('Whither?') the voice climbs to 'shall I the dawn's wings for my flight choose', and falls to the bottom of its compass to ' which me to the last sea direct' (see Ps. cxxxix. 7), as if the wings of faith had failed the aspiring sinner. It continues: 'so will me yet the hand of the All-Highest find, and to me the sin-rod bind. Ah yea! If even hell a bed for me and my sins had, so would be then the anger of the Highest there.' 'The earth protects me not, it threatens me, horrid monster, to swallow up', is dramatically set. 'And desire I to heaven to soar, there dwells God, Who to me the judgement speaks' rises to high B♭ and then sinks despairingly.

iii is another of the numerous 'Have mercy' arias; its first words— 'Erbarme dich!' ('Have mercy!')—identical with the opening of the well-known alto aria in the *St. Matthew Passion*, also begin with a rising minor sixth. The next note surprises one, it is the flat supertonic:

The pleading-motive abounds, the flute has many arabesques; these features are frequently found elsewhere, yet with endless resource Bach always creates something fresh from them. Age cannot wither them nor custom stale their infinite variety. Both sections of the text begin with the quoted clause; the first continues—'laß die Thränen dich erweichen, laß sie dir zu Herzen reichen' ('let the tears Thee soften, let them to Thy heart reach') to downward-running passages, the sinner's tears coursing down his cheeks. The second: 'laß, um Jesu Christi Willen, deinen Zorn des Eifers stillen' ('let, for Jesus Christ's sake, thy anger of jealousy quieten'). The major part of the vocal line, however, is concerned with 'erbarme dich!'

iv opens with the same words, to a tender melisma based on the two-note figure, and continues: 'Yet now comfort I myself, I shall not before judgement stand, and rather before the mercy-throne to my righteous Father go.' An expressive figure for violin I, based on the 'Erbarme dich!' of the opening, tells of the infinite mercy of God and joins up the next section: 'I represent to Him His Son, His suffering, His salvation, as He for my sin paid (has) and enough done, and pray Him for patience: henceforth will I it no more do.' 'So receives me God' is again melismatic, yet another form of the two-note figure, and 'into grace again' concludes.

Over and over again one realizes that a chorale is harmonized in such a way that the setting is perfect for its position, and that no other harmonization would have been apposite. One cannot analyse the cause, it lies beyond analysis, in the regions of art where only the imagination of the creator can penetrate. The concluding chorale conveys the assurance that the penitent has found peace; one cannot say why this is so, but the effect is indisputably there. It is the delicate and sensitive stanza 6 of J. Rist's evening hymn, 'Werde munter, mein Gemüthe', with J. Schop's associated tune: 'Have I even from Thee wavered, Return I myself then again; Has us yet Thy Son reconciled Through His anguish and death-pain. I deny not the guilt, But Thy grace and clemency Is much greater than the sin, which I ever in me find.'

Bass Alone

56*, 82

56. Both of these are of superb quality. They must have been written for the same sympathetic singer and they may conjecturally be attributed to 1731–2. The texts may be by the composer, although Wustmann thinks that of No. 56, which is exceptionally fine, to be founded on a Neumeister libretto. The cantata in question is an example of how Bach students without a knowledge of German have been wickedly misled by so-called translators. The title, 'Ich will den Kreuzstab gerne tragen', is literally 'I will the cross-staff gladly carry'. In the B. edition it is falsely given as 'I with my cross-staff gladly wander', while the music clearly indicates a weary, sin-laden pilgrim, labouring heavily and with infinite pain towards his ultimate goal. The rest of this English translation (?) is no less destructive of the meaning of the original. The text is one of the most cohesive in the whole series, a description of a Pilgrim's Progress, each number indicating a stage on the journey. Well-varied similes and imagery suitable for musical treatment abound. The Epistle and Gospel for the Nineteenth Sunday after Trinity (7 October 1731 or 26 October 1732), are skilfully combined. The former is Ephesians iv. 22–28, 'That ye put off . . . the old man . . . and be renewed in the spirit of your mind'; the latter St. Matthew ix. 1–8, the healing of the palsied man. Verse 1: 'And he entered into a ship, and passed over, and came into his own city' gives rise to comparisons between life and a sea voyage.

The scoring of the first aria (see P. 57) is heavy, two oboes and taille doubling the upper strings throughout save for a few notes. Bach does not interpret the words as meaning that trials are over; he legitimately pictures the Pilgrim as being more heavily laden than the text would suggest. The spirit indeed is willing but the flesh is weak. Not only is this a subtle point in interpretation but it affords opportunity for a more gradual progress through the cantata, and the scoring is a factor in the situation; strings alone would have been insufficient to provide the effect he wished for. The heaviness of the struggle is shown in the chief vocal theme, with which violin II opens the introduction, a weary climbing upwards, partially by an augmented second, and a sinking down:

Ex.574

(a) Ich will den Kreuz-stab ger - ne tra - - - - (-gen)

Cont. (b)

'Tragen' is carried on for six further bars. Violin I begins the sub-dominant reply at the fifth bar of Ex. 574, but already in the second they and the violas have anticipated (a), expressive of utter weariness, which becomes tremendously important, dominating the entire scene and colouring it with passionate intensity. It must always be treated as ♩♪ ♩♪ ♩♪, whether it is vocal or instrumental. Only so can the scene be made consistent throughout. There is a striking resemblance in character between (a) and (b) and the subject and countersubject of the F♯ minor fugue in Book I of 'The 48'. In bars 8–10 violas and taille, which should here be brought out strongly, play an extremely beautiful version of (b):

Ex.575
Tai.Va.

Cont.

A sinking figure is heard in the upper strings during (a), beginning at the end of bar 17:

Ex.576

These various ideas are woven into the texture with consummate skill. 'Er kommt von Gottes lieber Hand' ('it comes from God's dear hand') brings phrases of infinite tenderness, punctuated by upper-string phrases formed out of (*b*). Bars 91–98, 'der führet mich nach meinen Plagen zu Gott, in das gelobte Land' ('which leads me after my troubles to God, in the promised land'), are a slow climbing to the desired heaven. 'Der führet mich' is a quaver version of (*a*); it comes thrice again, rising each time, and then in a crotchet form. The comment is obvious, that only by bearing the Cross can one ascend to the Promised Land. The style changes completely in the section before the Da Capo; it is almost arioso. The Pilgrim speaks of laying sorrow in the grave, his Saviour will wipe all tears away. The vocal phrases are Schubertian in their romantic tenderness:

Ex.577

(See Rev. vii. 17, for the latter part of the text). The upper instruments play (*b*) and Ex. 577. At the close comes a passage of extraordinary beauty:

Ex.578

Few pages of the cantatas are so wonderfully moving as this.

The succeeding recitative employs the imagery of a sea voyage, the billows, the raging foam; Christ is the Pilgrim's anchor. Against a pulsating continuo the 'cello undulates in semiquaver arpeggi, the gentle motion of the boat, the voice moves in marvellously expressive 'endless melody', every idea of the text—'Betrübniß', 'Wellen', 'hält', 'Barmherzigkeit' ('affliction', 'waves', 'hold', 'pity'), being faithfully mirrored—'My wandering in the world is to a ship-journey like; affliction, cross and distress are waves which me cover and to death me daily affright. My anchor though, which me holds, is the pity wherewith my God me often rejoices. Who cries thus to me: I am with thee, I will thee not forsake, nor neglect!' (See Heb. xiii. 5.) After 'And when the raging foam its end has', the 'cello sinks in arpeggio to join the continuo, the motion of the boat has ceased and it is moored. A stately passage begins at this moment, 'So step I out of the ship into my city, which is the heavenly kingdom, whither I with the righteous'; and a joyful upward rush of semiquavers on 'vieler' ('many') and a melisma on 'Trübsal' ('trouble') ('out of much trouble shall come') proclaim that the woes of this world have been left behind. The picturesqueness of this recitative was never equalled until Wagner, whether consciously or not, wrote on identical lines.

The Pilgrim's burden has fallen from his shoulders and he surrenders himself to joy in a splendid aria with oboe obbligato: 'Endlich wird mein Joch' ('At last will my yoke'). The Lord has bestowed on him the nature of an eagle, he ascends far from the earth, the winging of voice and obbligato are strong and buoyant:

Ex.579

Two other figures are a fluttering

Ex.580

(it will be noticed that notes 3–5 from bar 2 of (a) are incorporated) and a poising:

Ex.581

Cont. *8ve lower*

(here notes 5–8 of the same bar are found) before a soaring of nearly two octaves (with notes 1–3 of bar 3 of (*a*)) and a fall to the tonic, in which notes 5–8 of bar 1 and 1–8 of bar 2 of (*a*) are heard. Economy of material is so severe that notes 1–3 of bar 3 of (*a*) are turned into quavers for the bassi. The voice opens with bar 1, and while the oboe imitates, the singer sweeps up impulsively:

Ex.582

wird   mein Joch,

The joy of the Pilgrim is so overwhelming that even 'Joch' is set to brilliant runs, incorporating part of bar 2 of the ubiquitous (*a*); the yoke of sin bounds away. 'Wieder von mir weichen müssen' ('again from me fall must') begins with notes 1–3 of bar 3 of (*a*), with altered accents. 'Weichen' is later set in brilliant coloratura. Imitations on bar 1 of (*a*) come at the distance of a beat. One delightful point is bar 1 of (*a*) for the voice, the run of the latter part of the bar inverted, pitted against (*c*). Later the upper lines reverse the procedure of the opening of the vocal section. Part II begins with four clauses: 'Da krieg' ich in dem Herren Kraft, da hab' ich Adlers Eigenschaft, da fahr' ich auf von dieser Erden in Laufe, sonder matt zu werden' ('So obtain I in the Lord strength, there have I (an) eagle's nature, there ascend I from this earth in the course (flight), without weary to become'). These are sung once only, the first two incorporating notes 5–8, bar 1, and notes 1–3, bar 3, of (*a*), the third and fourth employing notes 5–8 in inverse and direct motion. Each phrase is answered by bar 1 in the oboe. This unwonted lack of repetition is to allow for an expanded and delightful section before the Da Capo. The exclamation, 'Oh', is repeatedly thrust out separately from the succeeding words, ('gescheh' es heute noch') ('happen it today again'), and three of these words, 'gescheh'', 'heute', and 'noch', at times receive the principal accent, thus creating different shades of meaning: 'Oh that it might happen THIS day, this DAY, that it might HAPPEN.' Fragments of the chief theme are heard in the oboe.

In iv, during a few bars of recitative with sustained strings, the Pilgrim views the promised land: 'I stand ready and prepared, the inheritance of my blessedness with longing and yearning from Jesu's hands to receive.' (See Ex. 1261.) A rapid modulation from G minor to A♭ occurs as he exclaims: 'How well will (it) to me happen,when I the port of rest shall see.' Then comes a remarkable stroke of genius and an unusual point in form for the period. The quasi-arioso of i is resumed, marked 'Adagio', a memory of the days, now happily past, when the Pilgrim saw the promised land only from afar, and when tears of sorrow were loading him down. An extraordinary change in the quotation thrusts at the end, in a moment of tremendous exaltation, the word 'Heiland' on a high note:

mein Hei-land selbst ab.

Above a pulsating bassi C, the tear-motive in the upper strings sinks slowly to the depths.

The imagery of the sea returns in the exquisite hymn-stanza, No. 6 of J. Franck's 'Du, o schönes Weltgebäude': 'Come, oh death, thou sleep's brother, Come, and lead me only away; Loose my little ship's rudder, Bring me to safe port. Let him, who will, thee fear, Thou canst me greatly rejoice; For through thee come I therein To the fairest Jesus.' ('Jesulein', literally 'little Jesus', a diminutive of endearment; 'Schifflein' ('little ship') is used in line 3.) J. Crüger's tune is not found elsewhere in Bach's church works. The voices are low-lying, the harmonies are richly solemn; it makes a hushed and magical close to a wonderful cantata. To sing this chorale unaccompanied is a mistake; sonorousness of the pianissimo tutti orchestra is needed to secure fully its 'softened splendour'. (See *Fugitive Notes*.)

82. Anna Magdalena's 1725 Notenbuch contains a recitative for soprano and unfigured continuo, 'Ich habe genug', and the melody only of an aria for the same voice, 'Schlummert ein', without accompaniment. Later in the book the aria comes again, with twenty-eight bars of unfigured continuo. From the twenty-ninth bar the voice part only is written, and it ends abruptly 7½ bars short of the other. Except for omission of grace notes, the two musical texts are identical. All are in E minor. They are the same as ii and iii of the cantata, 'Ich habe genug' ('It is enough' B.), though there they stand in

C minor. Which came first, the soprano or the bass version? If the conjectural date of the cantata is correct, there is a gap of six years, and it would seem that the two numbers were written first for Anna Magdalena and afterwards incorporated into the cantata. But the text of the recitative is more suitable as a cantata number than as a separate composition. The opening words come at the beginning of both i in the cantata and this recitative, and the repetition in the aria makes the latter more striking. The cantata is for the Purification, the Gospel for which (St. Luke ii. 22–32) contains the Song of Simeon. This is referred to in the Recitativo, and the stepwise movement of bars 7 (marked 'Arioso. Andante' in the cantata, but with no indication of change in the Notenbuch) to 'Laßt uns mit diesem Manne ziehen!' ('Let us with this man go!'), thus calling especial attention to it, is more appropriate after i than in its isolated soprano version. The text before this passage is, 'I have enough!' (or 'what suffices!') 'My comfort is this solely, that Jesus mine and I His own might be. In faith hold I Him, there see I also with Simeon the joy of that life already.' After it comes 'Ah! may me from my body's chains the Lord deliver. Ah! were only my departure here, with joy would I say, world, to thee: I have enough!'

Spitta points out that the autograph score of the cantata shows the vocal line of i in the alto clef, and that at the foot of the page is written: 'The voice part must be transposed into the bass.' He judges from this that Bach first intended the cantata for mezzo-soprano or alto and then changed his mind. The soprano version of the aria begins without ritornello, and except where the long notes to 'schlummert ein' ('fall asleep') are followed by short rests, all intermediate ritornelli are omitted. If Bach had written the aria first for soprano it is scarcely likely that he would have been content with a mere transposition for bass; following his inevitable practice he would have touched it up at point after point. Consideration of this evidence leads one to conclude that the Notenbuch version is a copy of an existing and complete composition, although a contradictory fact is the existence of the obbligato to i for flute, in E minor, instead of oboe, C minor. It is remarkable that no other extracts from the church cantatas are found in these delightful collections for home use. Possibly the loving wife was particularly charmed by this most beautiful of all 'slumber' arias, with its rocking initial melody, its murmuring bassi, its gently dropping phrases to 'fallet sanft' ('fall softly'), its magical atmosphere of somnolent contentment, and,

some years after the Notenbuch was begun, copied it into a suitable
key for herself. The chief melody (see P. 58) is one of Bach's divinest
inspirations:

It forms the first half of the introduction (strings); in the vocal section it is stated first as above, then repeated with bar 1 thrice at
different pitches, the voice sustaining during 1 and 2 and joining
violin I at 3, when the original form of the melody is resumed. The
second half of the introduction consists of a modified (*a*) twice, followed by a form of (*b*). This is heard after Ex. 584, the two bars of
(*a*) in thirds in the violins, the voice sustaining low B♭ and then
decorating. (*b*) comes in octaves, singer and violin I. Where the final
cadence fell in the introduction, violin I now sinks to the flattened
seventh and elongates the sentence in the key of the subdominant,
with a pause on which the voice now sinks also to the flattened
seventh, a magical touch. Then, with continuo only, a most beautiful
slumbrous passage is sung before the introduction is resumed:

The aria is unique in being in rondo form. Episode I is with continuo
only: 'Welt, ich bleibe nicht mehr hier, hab' ich doch kein Theil an
dir, das der Seele könnte taugen' ('World, I remain no longer here,
have I indeed no share in thee, that (to) the soul could serve'). The
motion is more lively and the ideas new. The vocal expansion of the
chief theme is repeated, with the difference that after the first
'Schlummert ein' the voice allows violin I to carry on the melody,
joining in again with its sustained notes. The section is rounded off
by a new two-bar form of the chief idea. Episode II is 'Hier muß ich
das Elend bauen, aber dort, dort werd' ich schauen süßen Frieden,
stille Ruh'' ('Here must I the misery build, but there, there shall I
behold sweet peace, quiet rest'). The bassi move as in Ex. 584, the
vocal line is new, the upper strings recall (*a*) and introduce fresh
material. Before the Da Capo there are two bars of adagio, the

orchestra pianissimo, the voice piano, repeating the melody from the end of the introduction. The aria must not be taken slowly, it must move at an easy pace. A part for oboe da caccia, doubling violin I, exists in Bach's handwriting, though there is no mention of it in the score.

First and last arias add an oboe to the strings. The organ part in i is separate from the continuo. The latter moves almost throughout in repeated bowed quavers, changing every bar. The organ plays on the first of each three only. On the rare occasions when the continuo departs from the normal the organ is in unison with it. Violins I and II play an accompaniment figure in thirds, interesting in itself, as Bach's accompaniments always are, syncopated and murmuring in blissful drowsiness:

and support an oboe melody which is as important as the vocal line. The opening phrase, the motto of the aria,

is identical with the beginning of the 'Have mercy' alto aria in the *St. Matthew Passion*. The introduction is long, thirty-three bars. After two statements of the motto the oboe indulges in arabesques and later has sostenuto melodic ideas. For twenty bars the violins rarely depart from Ex. 586, but later become more independent. Thirteen bars of the introduction are now repeated, the voice taking over the motto to 'Ich habe genug'. The oboe borrows from its ecstatic arabesque and adds a figure and grouping ((*a*) below) which are given to the voice in i, cantata No. 84:

'Ich habe den Heiland, das Hoffen der Frommen auf meine begierigen Arme genommen' ('I have the saviour, the hope of the pious into

my longing arms taken') is set to phrases akin to ideas in the introduction; the upper strings sigh, the oboe shows the eagerness of the
believer by the use of (*a*). After a development of these themes the
voice sings a new idea against a graceful oboe melody, with the upper
strings merely stressing the bars. The whole of the introduction is
repeated in the dominant. The remainder, up to the Da Capo, contains a larger proportion for the voice than Part I and is in two sections, with a fifteen-bar interlude. 'Ich hab' ihn erblickt' ('I have
Him seen') is set to a variant of the motto; 'mein Glaube hat Jesum
an's Herze gedrückt, nun wünsch' ich noch heute mit Freuden von
hinnen zu scheiden: Ich habe genug!' ('My faith has Jesus to the
heart pressed, now desire I even today with joy from hence to depart:
I have enough!'), introduces nothing new except flourishes on 'Freuden', and all the instrumental material has been heard previously.
Yet Bach's magic skill in handling his themes and presenting them
in ever new guises keeps our attention unerringly focused throughout
this lengthy number—over 200 bars of slow tempo.

A short recitativo secco divides the slumber song from the final
aria: 'My God! when comes the beautiful "Now" when I in peace
journey shall, and in the dust of cool earth, and there, with Thee, in
Thy bosom rest? The departure is made.' There are two bars of
arioso, adagio—'World! goodnight'—and the continuo gently sinks
down two octaves to the lowest C.

The concluding aria is vivace and abundantly marked with bowing,
tonguing, and dynamic signs. The oboe is completely independent
in the vocal portions only; in the tuttis it generally doubles violin I.
The relation between the introduction and the first vocal section is
interesting. The former begins with flying scale passages:

Ex.589 *Vivace*

follows these up with detached groups based on bars 4 and 5:

Ex.590

((*b*) is never heard except in the ritornelli), and the concluding cadence is preceded by the upward run extended to an octave and a half. The voice opens with a totally new theme:

Ex.591

I rejoice (me in my death)
Ich freu — — — — — — e (mich auf meinen Tod)

Cont.
8ve higher piano

6 6 ("freue mich auf" is idiomatically "look forward to")

accompanied by | ♪♫ ♩ | chords in the strings and a chirruping little figure for the oboe:

Ex.592

The 'freue' idea is never heard elsewhere except in the corresponding portion of the reprise. The voice immediately repeats these words, freshly set, with a low G on 'Tod'; and at the beginning of the repetition of the text the orchestra commences a repeat of the introduction, with C minor as the chief key instead of modulating to the dominant, and with two bars inserted after the short group. Dovetailing into the close of this the voice starts again, using a modified form of (*a*), and continues: 'ach! hätt' er sich schon eingefunden' ('Ah! had it itself already presented'), mostly with continuo, although fragments of previous matter appear in the orchestra, and mostly with new ideas, although (*c*) is found near the close. The introduction is repeated and then the voice takes up the remainder of the text: 'Da entkomm' ich aller Noth, die mich noch auf der Welt gebunden) ('There escape I from all suffering, which me still to the world (has) bound'). Here we see the significance of the flying scale passages, the escape from the world, although they are never used by the voice. They are heard, however, in violin I and oboe, and during the initial presentation of the second verbal clause the bassi pursue them in an inverted form. At first the upper instruments utter the staccato chords only; later, to a longish, sinking 'gebunden', these are maintained solely by the upper strings, while the oboe forms a new melody out of bar 4 of (*a*). After that the flying passages predominate. (*a*) in the orchestra leads to the reprise, which for thirty-nine bars is an exact repetition. After a variant for purposes of modulation, the voice joyfully proclaims:

Ex.593

and the original matter is resumed.

Once more one is compelled to ask, 'Why do not vocalists include these splendid works in their recitals, instead of contenting themselves with conventional strings of hackneyed Lieder?'

For Two Voices

S.B. (49), (58)   T.B. 157*

157. Picander's text—'Ich lasse dich nicht, du segnest mich denn' —was published in his 'Satyrische Gedichte', 1727, and inscribed 'Trauermusik beim Grabe des Herrn J. C. von P., 31 Okt. 1726' ('Funeral music at the grave of Herr J. C. von P., October 31st 1726'). The initials stand for Johann Christoph von Ponickau. The music would be hurriedly written for that date. A memorial service was held at Pomssen, where Ponickau was buried, on 6 February 1727. As the score indicates the Feast of the Purification as the Leipzig occasion, and as this occurred four days before the memorial service, we may assume that the cantata was performed again twice. The text, which suffers from lack of progression, has little to do with Candlemas, if we except the beautiful and extremely long bass scena, which speaks of holding fast to Christ on the heavenly journey, and which may be associated with the Nunc Dimittis in the Gospel lesson. The cantata is a piece of chamber music with prominent wood-wind.

The opening duet—'I will not let thee go, except thou bless me' (Gen. xxxii. 26)—consists of three distinct strata—flute, oboe and violin solo, the two voices, and the continuo. The voices borrow from the upper layer the opening notes only:

Ex.594

and use them merely in parentheses; there is no other connexion between the two upper strata, and the continuo has no rhythmical relation with either, though notes 1–3 of the flute theme above, mostly in quavers and sometimes in crotchets, and notes 2–5 of bar 2, in quavers, are the basis of most of its passages. The voices sing mostly in canon, the interlocking of the wrestlers:

Ex.595

The initial flute figure is maintained almost incessantly in the topmost stratum. The duet is rather long for its short text, as is so often the case with Bach's settings of Biblical words for opening numbers, and while interesting as absolute music and as a piece of texture, it fails as an interpretation of the words and suffers from a want of climax.

The opening obbligato of the tenor aria, ii:

Ex.596

is altered to fit the first clause—'Ich halte meinen Jesum feste' ('I hold my Jesus fast')—and the oboe d'amore adds a counterpoint partly based upon a caressing two-note figure found in bar 27. The music now deviates from a strict recapitulation of the introduction, the voice developing the initial idea, the oboe borrowing phrases from its opening solo and the continuo repeating descending passages, in both quavers and semiquavers. 'Ich laß' ihn nun und ewig nicht' ('I leave Him now and evermore not') completes the text of Part I. The remainder of the verse is 'Er ist allein mein Aufenthalt, d'rum faßt mein Glaube mit Gewalt sein segenreiches Angesicht, denn dieser Trost ist doch der beste' ('He is alone my sojourn, therefore holds my faith with power His blessing-rich countenance, for this comfort is yet the best'). The voice incorporates into its line the caressing figure, a sweep of oboe d'amore demisemiquavers from near the end of the introduction is borrowed for 'Gewalt', the obbligato exploits most of the ideas of the introduction, developing the two-note figure during the long note to 'Aufenthalt'.

In the tenor recitative with strings, iii, and final chorale a violetta is specified instead of the ordinary instrument, for what reason it is impossible to say. It is used only thrice elsewhere, the earliest example being the solo soprano Magnificat. (See p. 30.) iii begins with an arioso phrase—'My dear Jesus Thou', and continues in stilo recitativo—'when I vexation and affliction suffer, then art Thou my joy, in unrest my rest and in anxiety my soft bed!' As the voice sinks low on 'Bette' ('bed') the violins play in thirds a passage derived from the arioso bar. With expressive harmonies the singer continues—'The false world is not faithful, the heaven must grow old, the desire of the world disappears like spray; if I Thee not, my Jesus, had, to whom should I otherwise cling? Therefore leave I nevermore (hold) of Thee, Thy blessing remain then with me!'—and the violins soar aloft in blissful confidence.

The bass aria, with violin and flauto traverso, is virtually a scena: (1) aria, (2) recitativo secco, (3) arioso, (4) recitativo secco, (5) arioso. (1) the violin leads off with a lovely theme of two limbs:

Ex.597

The flute repeats (without the appoggiatura, which is sometimes included and sometimes not), while the violin accompanies with semiquavers, the rocking figure of beat 1 of bar 4 being frequent. After an episode in which the figure is heard twice, and in which leaping quavers and a new figure appear:

Ex.598

the voice takes up (a): 'Ja, ja, ich halte Jesum feste' ('Yea, yea, I hold Jesus fast'). The episodical matter returns and then the voice states the complete theme, adding, 'so geh' ich auch zum Himmel ein' ('so go I also to heaven in') to (b) with the rocking figure and a

derivative of (c) above. Two bars of tutti lead to another vocal statement of the theme, in A. Syncopated treatment of the first clause
leads to an orchestral restatement of (a), (b), and (c), in A. A modified
version of (a) and (b) is sung to 'wo Gott und seines Lammes Gäste in
Kronen zu der Hochzeit sein' ('where God and His Lamb's guests in
crowns at the wedding are') and a new accompaniment figure appears:

which is derived from the countersubject. An interlude based upon
(c), (d), and the two-note figure brings yet another version of (a) and
(b) to 'Da laß' ich nicht, mein Heil, von dir, da bleibt dein Segen
auch bei mir' ('There leave I not, my Saviour, (hold) of Thee, then
remains Thy blessing also with me'). (d) the quaver leaps and the
semiquaver figure are features of the accompaniment. An interlude
formed from (b) leads to a two-fold statement of (a) to the latter part
of the text; the countersubject, the quavers, and (c) occupy the
obbligato instruments. (c) and (d) join up (2): 'Ah, how pleasant is
to me my death-casket, because Jesus to me in (the) arms lies! So
can my spirit right joyfully repose!' Though (3) and (5) are marked
'Arioso', only the central portion of the former justifies the title.
Here the instruments pulsate in repeated bowed quavers, Adagio, the
prayer-motive, while the voice exclaims, 'Oh beautiful place! Come,
gentle death, and lead me away'. Before it are (a) and (b) to 'Yea, yea',
&c., with the countersubject and the quavers above; after it 'where
God', &c., with a fresh opening, the latter part of (a) and a new run
to 'Kronen'. (d) appears in flute and violin. (4) 'I am overjoyed'
(with a flourish), 'the misery of this time even from me this day to
lay aside, for Jesus awaits me in heaven with the blessing.' (5) is a
repetition, with key-changes, of the portion from 'Da laß' ich nicht'
to the end of (1). The scena is attractive by reason of its tunefulness
and the frequent repetition of (a), but one cannot help feeling that it
is an adaptation; to assign the same melody, even though it be varied,
to three different clauses is unusual.

   Stanza 6 of C. Keimann's 'Meinen Jesum laß' ich nicht' ends the
cantata, with A. Hammerschmidt's melody: 'My Jesus leave I not,
Go with Him ever by his side; Christ lets me forever and ever To the
life's-streamlet (be) led; Blessed who with me thus says: "My Jesus
leave I not!"'

For Three Voices
S.A.B. 89*
A.T.B. 60*, 81*, (83*), 153***, 154**, (174*)
Order of discussion: 89, 154, 81, 153, 60

Solo cantatas would be written for one of two reasons, the presence of exceptional voices, which accounts for those for one or two soloists only, or during periods when his choir was in bad condition. His complaints to the authorities show how serious was this at times and how burdensome the upkeep of the musical part of the services. The proportion of one cantata with soprano to six without is, no doubt, due to the same cause, the indifferent standard of his boys.

89. The only cantata in this group which includes a soprano is a remarkable one. It belongs possibly to the years round about 1730, for the Twenty-Second Sunday after Trinity, and is based upon the same theme as the solitary cantata for tenor solo, discussed supra, the parable of the unmerciful servant, from the Gospel, St. Matthew xviii. 23–35. In No. 55 it is the sinner, placing himself in the position of the hard-hearted servant, who speaks; in No. 89 the personal element does not come until iv; i, ii, and iii are addressed to him. A splendid verse from Hosea (xi. 8) opens, 'Was soll ich aus dir machen, Ephraim? Soll ich dich schützen, Israel?' ('What shall I of thee make, Ephraim? Shall I thee protect, Israel?'), an inviting text for musical setting. But the unknown librettist overlooked one point. The unmerciful servant was 'delivered to the tormentors, till he should pay all that was due', whereas in Hosea, in spite of the fierce anger of the Lord against Ephraim, the verse concludes 'My repentings are kindled together' and the next begins 'I will not execute the fierceness of mine anger, I will not return to destroy Ephraim; for I am God, and not man'. Thus i does not tally with ii and iii, as will be seen later. However, the text from Hosea results in a remarkable bass aria, unique in Bach's writings, and one is content to overlook the irregularity of the libretto for the sake of the music. In bars 1 and 2 four distinct motives are announced, a grim muttering in the bassi, the anger of God:

Ex.600

(C minor, signature of 2 flats)

a rising and falling questioning idea in the strings:

a sighing phrase for the two oboes:

while the corno relentlessly intones a repeated-note figure—(*d*)
| ♪♪♪ ♩ A forbidding, dark-clouded atmosphere is thus thrown
at once on the canvas. In bar 4 (*c*) is quickened into quavers and a
powerful leaping figure appears in violin I:

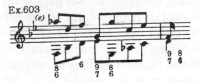

At the end of the bar an ominous melody in thirds begins in the
oboes:

which continues with (*a*). When the thirds begin (*a*) is heard in the
violins and then (*c*) in the bassi. The texture of the aria is rich, eight-
part counterpoint being frequent. The vocal line is superbly declamatory and descriptive. The voice sings, 'Was soll ich aus dir
machen' four times, using a derivative of (*b*) and ending each set of
two with 'Ephraim', the second with a pause. (*a*), (*c*), (*d*), and (*e*) are
heard in the orchestra. Six and a half bars of the introduction now
come in the instruments, in E♭ instead of C minor, and the soloist
sings the second clause, with first a holding note and then a vigorous
run, partly based on (*b*), to 'schützen', and concludes with a pause
on 'Israel'. Another impressive pause is at the end of 'Soll ich nicht
billig ein Adama aus dir machen, und dich wie Zeboim zurichten?'

('Shall I not cheaply an Admah of thee make, and thee as Zeboim punish?'); the fate which befell the two wicked cities and the sternness of the 'zurichten' are grimly depicted by runs. (*a*), (*b*) in part and complete, (*c*), (*e*), and (*f*) come in the orchestra, (*b*) for the first time in the continuo. After these terrible warnings, forbidding in their pauses, the Judge reveals His leaning towards forgiveness—'Aber mein Herz ist anders Sinnes' ('But my heart is of other mind')—and as the singer delivers the words seven times, omitting the conjunction in the later repetitions, the vocal melody is less angry. There is a long trill on 'Sinnes' and runs on 'Sinnes' and 'anders', and (*a*) is found in the vocal line. The horn is silent until the Dal Segno; all the motives associated with the other instruments are there; beginning with bar 3 of this section the whole of the introduction is introduced, different in key and in scoring. Dovetailing with the end of the section the introduction is inserted again identical in key, but with many alterations—not only is the horn absent but (*f*) is in sixths instead of in thirds, the lower notes of oboe II producing an even more sinister effect. The vocal line—'meine Barmherzigkeit ist zu brünstig' (the magnificent Biblical clause, 'My repentings are kindled together' suffers lamentably in a literal translation, 'my compassion is too ardent')—is new, except that (*a*) appears in it and becomes more and more florid. All the orchestra save the continuo ceases, to allow a wonderful coloratura on 'brünstig' and an impassioned close. As in Wagner, the vocal line of this extraordinary aria moves in free independent melody, though borrowing occasionally from the symphonic orchestral texture. A dramatic bass can find a superb opportunity here.

ii, an alto recitativo secco, speaks of judgement and vengeance, and culminates in a fine succession of chromatic chords in the penultimate bar: 'Yea, verily should God a word of judgement speak and His name-mocking on His enemies avenge. Uncountable is the reckoning of thy sins, and had God even equal patience, rejects then thy hostile mind the offered goodness, and oppresses the neighbour for his debt; and therefore must vengeance itself kindle.' An aria for the same voice and accompaniment begins: 'Ein unbarmherziges Gerichte wird über dich gewiß ergehn' ('An unpitying judgement will on thee surely fall'). In 'Die Rache fängt bei denen an, die nicht Barmherzigkeit gethan' ('The vengeance begins with those, who not compassion (have) done'—see James ii. 13), 'Die Rache' is set to fierce and fiery trills; 'und machet sie wie Sodom ganz zu nichte' ('and brings them as Sodom wholly to nought'), is vehemently dramatic, with a run on 'Sodom' which matches those on 'Admah' and 'Zeboim' in i. The continuo line is constructed completely out of the 'judgement' theme (a), and scales tearing upward and downward (b):

Ex.605

The inevitability of divine judgement is indicated by canons at a beat distance on (a); (b) storms with fine effect during 'die Rache' and 'Sodom'. This aria almost negates musical beauty; its gloom, relentlessness, and intensity sacrifice art to Old Testament realism. There is no denying its truthfulness and its appositeness to the grim first part of the cantata, but one wonders if Bach did not go a step too far in his passionate denunciation of the sinning creditor.

A soprano recitativo secco now brings us back to a more human state of mind; evil things are cast out of the heart, the culprit shudders at the realization of the consequences of a sinful life, and at the close, when Jesus is approached in faith, an Adagio wandering passage gradually sinks down in contrition: 'Well then! my heart puts anger, quarrel, and discord away; it is ready the neighbour to pardon. But, how affrights me my sinful life, that I before God in guilt am! Yet Jesu's blood makes this account good, if I to Him, as the law's end, myself faithfully turn.' (See Rom. x. 4.)

The succeeding soprano aria, with oboe obbligato, is confident in the results of the mercy of Christ. The oboe opens with a lovely melody of upward ripples and joyful leaps:

Ex.606 (a)

Cont.
8ve lower

the vocal melody outlines the first oboe phrases without filling in intermediate details:

Ex.607 (b)

Ge - rech - ter Gott, ach, rech - nest du?
Righteous God, ah, reckonest Thou?
(Same continuo as in (a).)

After the Scarlattian statement of (a) oboe and voice give out (a) and (b) in canon (if it can be called technically a canon when the two melodies are not exactly the same!) and the singer continues with an expansion of the answering oboe clause:

Ex.608 so shall I for the salvation of souls the drops of blood from Jesus count,
(c) so wer-de ich zum Heil der See-len die Tro-pfen Blut von Je-su zäh-len,

A version of (a) now appears in the continuo. After an interlude in which (a) is followed by a free inversion of (c), the soloist pleads, 'Ach! rechne mir die Summe zu!' ('Ah, count to me the total up!'), using a new version of (b), while the run of (a) comes in oboe and continuo. (a) in the oboe leads to: 'Ja, weil sie Niemand kann ergründen, bedeckt sie meine Schuld und Sünden' ('Yea, because it nobody can fathom, covers it my guilt and sins'). The vocal melody is new, the upward flight of (a) is heard in oboe and continuo, the falling of the cleansing drops of blood is indicated by downward scales in bassi and voice. (a) and (b), the latter altered, form an interlude, and the text from 'Ach' is repeated, but the singer begins with a version of (b) and a long bassi descent is answered by a corresponding vocal ascent at the close—the impetuous joy at the knowledge that the blood of Christ will redeem from all misdeeds.

Bach departs from his common practice in the beautifully harmonized closing chorale by adding both oboes to the soprano line. The old folk-tune, 'Venus du und dein Kind' ('Venus, thou and thy child'), surely was transfigured spiritually when it was transformed into the chorale melody, 'Auf meinen lieben Gott', which is associated with J. Heermann's Lenten hymn, 'Wo soll ich fliehen hin', of which stanza 7 is used: 'To me lacks indeed very much, Yet, what I wish to have Is all for me to the good, Acquired with Thy blood, Wherewith I overcome Death, devil, hell, and sin.' During the last line the bassi remember their descent in the aria and sink to the lowest depths.

81 and 154. Two A.T.B. cantatas can be placed definitely at the beginning of 1724, for the First and Fourth Sundays after Epiphany, 9 and 30 January, respectively: No. 154, 'Mein liebster Jesus ist verloren' ('My dearest Jesus is lost'), and No. 81, 'Jesus schläft, was soll ich hoffen?' ('Jesus sleeps, vain all my hopes' B., 'Jesus sleeps, what hope remaineth?' N.). They have certain points in common: the librettist of both is probably the same, Christian Weiss, Senr.; each is based upon incidents in the life of Christ narrated in the specified Gospels: in the first the disappearance of the child and His being found in the temple discussing with the doctors (St. Luke ii. 41–52), in the second Christ's quelling of the tempest (St. Matt. viii. 23–27). In both, sayings of Christ are set in arioso style for bass with continuo, and, indeed, there is a similarity of idea in the two numbers.

154. The fine tenor aria (see P. 12) which opens No. 154 resembles in character No. 19 in the *St. John Passion*, the agony of Peter at his denial, though musically it is more mature and less extravagantly expressed. The opening ritornello is a wild, passionate melody for violin I, significant of the distraction of the seeker after Christ, accompanied by strong chords in the lower strings:

A comparison of this theme with the number in the *St. John Passion* shows how Bach's mind ran in certain directions when similar emotional schemes were concerned. When the singer repeats this to 'Mein liebster Jesus ist verloren, o Wort, das mir Verzweiflung bringt!' ('My dearest Jesus is lost, oh word, that to me despair brings!'), violin I plays four times a short cry of lamentation:

The repetitions of the text are broken into short groups, indicative of increasing distress of mind, and a passage of distraction comes in violin I:

With the words 'O Schwert, das durch die Seele dringt' ('O sword, that through the soul pierces') to the same time-pattern as that of the initial melody, but with a different contour, the upper strings rush upwards through the chord of C♯ major, almost the identical 'sword' motive of Wagner's 'Ring'. At 'o Donnerwort, in meinen Ohren'

('O thunder-word, in my ears') the strings vibrate in repeated semi-quavers, a motive which always accompanies 'Donnerwort' in other cantatas. The latter part of the aria states the complete text without repetition, the same melodic outlines being employed, and there are two short tremblings for upper strings.

A short tenor recitativo secco, 'Where find I my Jesus, Who points to me the road, where my soul's fervent longing, My Saviour, (has) passed? No misfortune can me so grievously move, than if I Jesus shall lose', leads to a simple four-part chorale, of which the orchestration is not stated. It is stanza 2 of M. Janus's (or Jahn) 'Jesu, meiner Seelen Wonne', a renewed cry for the Saviour, to J. Schop's melody 'Werde munter, mein Gemüthe', 'Jesu, my refuge and rescuer, Jesu, my confidence, Jesu, strong serpent-treader, Jesu, my life's light! How longs my heart, dear Jesu, after Thee with sorrow! Come, ah come, I await Thee, Come, O dearest Jesus!' ('Jesulein'—'little' or 'dear Jesus', a diminutive used as a term of endearment.)

In iv, alto aria (see P. 73 and S. & B. 'Angels pour their blessing', the latter not a translation) the singer searches for Jesus: 'Jesu, laß dich finden, laß doch meine Sünden keine dicke Wolken sein! Wo du dich zum Schrecken willst für mich verstecken, stelle dich bald wieder ein!' ('Jesus, let (me) Thee find, let therefore my sins no thick clouds be! Where Thou Thyself to (my) fear wilt from me hide, appear Thou soon again!'). There are parts for two oboes d'amore, violins and violas play in unison, often rising above the reeds. The latter play much in parallel motion:

Ex.612 (a)

and:

Ex.613 (b)

Does this signify Joseph and Mary seeking for Jesus? We find a similar imagery in Wolf's Spanish religious Lieder. There are long, wandering phrases in imitation:

Ex.614 (c)

The string line is mostly either a rocking phrase,

or repeated notes. There are no bassi, but a part exists for figured cembalo, playing an octave below the strings—a unique feature. This may have been a later addition, to rectify the thinness of the original scoring. It is given in small type in the *BGS*. The vocal line of this lovely number is very melodious and is chiefly based on (*a*); these passages are generally accompanied by similar motives in one or both oboes d'amore. During (*c*) it moves independently and there are runs on 'Wolken'. (*b*) is sometimes used for interludes and sometimes to accompany the voice. Oboe d'amore II frequently borrows (*d*) from the strings.

The reply of the Child to His Mother—'Wisset ihr nicht, daß ich sein muß in dem, das meines Vaters ist?' ('Know ye not, that I be must in that, which my Father's is?' St. Luke ii. 49)—is spun out to a twenty-two-bar arioso secco. The vocal theme,

is used persistently in both voice and bassi, and the impression is of powerful determination. It is sung by a bass, not logically correct so far as the incident is concerned, as Jesus was a child of twelve. The interpretation, no doubt, is that the story is merely a general foundation for the libretto, which is not the Biblical narrative but the search of the anxious Christian for the Redeemer. The colouring is unwontedly sombre, the vocal part often lying below the continuo, so far as the 8-ft. tone is concerned. It is scarcely the treatment of the words that one would expect from Bach.

A very long tenor recitativo secco follows: 'This is the voice of my Friend' (see Song of Sol. ii. 8), 'to God be praise and thanks! My Jesus, my faithful refuge, lets through His word Himself again comfortingly be heard; I was from afflictions ill, the lamentation would in me the marrow in my bones almost consume; now, however, grows my faith again strong, now am I highly rejoiced, for I behold my soul's bliss, the Saviour, my sun, who after (a) troubled mourning-night through His splendour my heart joyful makes. Up, soul, make thee ready! Thou must to Him in His Father's house, into the temple go; there lets He Himself in His word be seen, there will He thee in the sacrament refresh; yet, willst thou worthily His flesh and blood (to) enjoy, so must thou Jesus also in penitence and faith kiss.'

The orchestration of the lively A.T. duet, vii, is not stated, but presumably employs the complete forces. The voices move much in blissful thirds and sixths:

The opening two bars of violin I (possibly plus oboe d'amore I) are a decorated form of this. The voices cause the movement to be brilliant by trilling simultaneously; they use a dropping figure, in sequence, with shakes:

which is almost identical with a theme in a similar duet in No. 32. The continuo figure (a) resembles that used by the unison strings in iv. A delightful derivative is heard against Ex. 618 in the strings:

A charming feature is sustained 'wohl's' against the bustling movement. Similar themes are employed for 'Der, den meine Seele liebt, zeigt sich mir zur frohen Stunden' ('He, Whom my soul loves, shows Himself to me at the glad hour'). The section is almost wholly with continuo, the upper instruments play brief interludes based on the two chief themes, the bassi gallop down semiquaver scales and shake with laughter:

and the excitement is so high that 'meine' is broken by a rest. A $\frac{3}{8}$ section, mostly with continuo, interrupts the $\frac{4}{4}$: 'Ich will dich, mein Jesu, nun nimmermehr laßen, ich will dich im Glauben beständig um- faßen' ('I will Thee, my Jesus, now nevermore leave, I will Thee in the faith constantly embrace'). The first clause imitates with:

It will be seen that the latter part of this is a reminiscence, inten- tional or unintentional, of (c) in iv, another connexion with that aria. A similar figure is employed in the canons in the second clause. At the end of this section comes a rare 'transformation of themes', the first vocal idea in the new time:

The upper instruments enter here, also with their original matter adapted, while the bassi, as will be seen, dance about almost de- liriously on a decorated pedal. The first ritornello is repeated to close the movement, and a touchingly harmonized chorale, with a finely rolling bass line, concludes the stanza of C. Keimann's 'Meinen Jesum laß' ich nicht', which is translated for No. 157, page 387, to the same melody.

81. The flûte à bec, written for with the so-called violin clef, G on the first line, makes its reappearance in the fine opening aria of No. 81. (See P. 43.) Two are employed, playing mostly an octave above violins I and II respectively. They are also used without the upper strings, in detached phrases in sixths, where the alto singer, viewing the abyss of death, says 'Seh' ich nicht mit erblaßtem Angesicht schon des Todes Abgrund offen?' ('See I not with paled face already the death's abyss open?'), the hollow colour in the upper register being as appropriate as Handel's choice of bassoons for the Witch of Endor scene in *Saul*. The doubling at the octave is designed to produce an 8 plus 4 ft. effect, and where there is a series of $^6_3$ chords on a descending bass, the score shows parallel fifths in abundance between violin I and flute II. It is a mere paper effect, of course, but it reveals how Bach understood orchestral effect. The sleeping of Christ is suggested by the opening waving figure:

Ex. 623

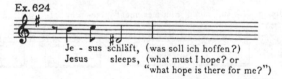

by a pulsating and long descent for the bassi, by a drop from the second to the third note of the vocal line:

Ex. 624

Je - sus schläft, (was soll ich hoffen?)
Jesus   sleeps, (what must I hope? or
                  "what hope is there for me?")

and a long-sustained low note to 'schläft'. There is a series of cries to the second clause, the last ending on a dissonance. A fine effect is produced when after a descent to 'schon des Todes Abgrund' the voice flings up on a decorative phrase, as if shuddering and recoiling at the sight of the yawning chasm.

The mood is sustained in a tenor recitativo secco. Chromatic harmonies,

Ex. 625

support 'Lord! why remainest Thou so distant? Why hidest Thou Thyself in time of need, when everything to me a mournful end threatens?' Dissonances are also numerous in 'Ah, will Thine eye not through my need stir, that otherwise never to slumber tends? Thou directedst yea with a star formerly the newly converted Wise Men, the right way to travel'. Then a like guidance is prayed for, 'Ah, lead me through Thine eyes' light', and on the verb a downward streaming run suggests a beam from heaven. A chord of the augmented sixth divides 'because this road nothing but danger' from 'promises', as if the Christian found himself unable to speak from terror.

As in the case of the previous cantata, the librettist is free in his treatment of the Biblical narrative. Though it deals with Christ on the ship, i refers to the abyss of death, an imagery of the earth, ii speaks of Christ being distant, and employs terms suitable to a land journey. In the tenor aria (see P. 13), however, we are at sea: 'Die schäumenden Wellen von Belial's Bächen verdoppeln die Wuth' ('The foaming waves of Belial's rivers redouble their fury'), 'doch suchet die stürmende Fluth die Kräfte des Glaubens zu schwächen' ('yet seeks the stormy flood the strength of faith to weaken'). Bach had seen the Baltic at Lübeck in his youth, his visit to Hamburg in his maturity would surely provide opportunity for a trip down the Elbe to the wild North Sea. He was able to limn a magnificent seascape from personal knowledge. Violin I dashes furiously up and down, rolling in billows of sound, the lower strings are the mutterings of the storm:

Ex. 626

Sometimes the bassi represent dashing waves and the inner strings toss spray over the decks. The voice surges in arpeggio leaps:

Ex. 627

and at 'verdoppeln' scurries in whirling demisemiquavers. Suddenly an adagio, piano bar, with sustained upper strings and bassi pulsating in repeated quavers, stems the turmoil and the soloist sings, 'Ein Christ soll zwar wie Wellen' ('A Christian shall indeed like waves'), but on the next word, 'steh'n' ('stand'), the fury of the tempest bursts again for three bars, while the singer sustains, as if breasting the storm. The treatment is repeated to 'wenn Trübsalswinde um ihn gehn' ('when trouble's-winds round him go'). The two clauses are repeated in two bars of adagio and then the great tempest returns. The vocal material of the opening is modified for the remainder of the text.

'Ihr Kleingläubigen, warum seid ihr so furchtsam?' ('Ye little-faithed, why are ye so fearful?' St. Matthew viii. 26) is set in the same manner, with the same voice and accompaniment, as the Biblical quotation of No. 154, and, as has already been pointed out, there is a similarity of musical material. It is not, however, so dark in colour. Christ in wonder frequently asks 'Warum?', and the initial 'Ihr' is always stressed. Repeated quavers in voice and continuo make the Saviour's admonition stern and inflexible. It ends on a half-close, which assumes that the next number is to be taken segue. It is another storm scene (see P. 44), in which the rebuke to the winds and the sea —'Schweig', schweig', aufgethürmtes Meer!' ('Be still, be still, towering ocean!')—is not obeyed; the 'great calm' of the Scripture narrative is delayed in order that Bach may paint another canvas of tempest. The strings rush furiously,

Ex. 628

often in tutti octaves, two oboes d'amore maintain independent passages above,

Ex. 629

suggestive of lashing waves, and

Ex. 630

only occasionally borrowing 'wave' themes from the strings. The solo line is splendid in its declamation,

Ex. 631

hurling out 'verstumme' ('verstumme, Sturm und Wind!' 'be dumb, storm and wind!'), rolling out billowy semiquavers borrowed from (a), and ranging over nearly two octaves, from the troughs to the crests of the mighty waves. In the middle section Christ further admonishes the storm: 'Dir sei dein Ziel gesetzet, damit mein auserwähltes Kind kein Unfall je verletzet' ('To thee be thy boundary set, so that my chosen child no mishap ever harms'). The orchestral material is as before, the storm continues, though raging less furiously; 'auserwähltes' rises in semiquavers and we see the Saviour stretching forth His hand to raise the apostle of little faith as he is sinking in the waters. Five bars before the Da Capo the upper strings cease for a while and the voice falls as if Peter were being immersed in the sea, and then it rises triumphantly as the strings resume. A singer of commanding voice and great dramatic power is needed to do justice to this superb aria.

A short alto recitativo secco does not follow very logically: 'Well for me! my Jesus speaks a word, my Helper is awakened; so must the waves' storm, misfortune's night and all trouble away.'

Stanza 2 of J. Franck's 'Jesu, meine Freude', with J. Crüger's associated melody, beautifully set, is well fitted to close the work: 'Under Thy shelters Am I from the storms Of all enemies free. Let the Satan find me' ('wittern', in the sense of an animal scenting out or smelling), 'Let the enemy be provoked, Me stands Jesus by. Although it now even roars and flashes, although sin and hell affright: Jesus will me cover.' In the manuscript full score this is followed by a sketch of the first chorus of No. 65, 'Sie werden aus Saba'.

153. The libretto of 'Schau, lieber Gott, wie meine Feind'', possibly by the composer, is indifferently designed; there is no clear progression from one mood to another, it sways backward and forward without definite aim. The opening chorale, stanza i of D. Denicke's hymn of the above title, to the anonymous tune 'Ach

Gott, vom Himmel sieh' darein', is a cry of despair: 'Behold, dear
God, how mine enemies, With whom I continually must battle, So
cunning and so mighty are, That they me easily extinguish! Lord,
where me Thy mercy (does) not hold, so can the devil, flesh and world
Me easily into misfortune cast.' ii, alto recitativo secco, continues to
despair: 'My dearest God, ah let Thee of it take pity, ah help then,
help me poor man! I dwell here with only lions and with dragons, and
these will for me through fury and rage in (a) short time utter ruin
completely make.'

iii, a simple bass aria with continuo, quotes Isaiah xli. 10, the
familiar 'Fürchte dich nicht, ich bin mit dir. Weiche nicht, ich bin
dein Gott, ich stärke dich, ich helfe dir auch durch die rechte Hand
meiner Gerechtigkeit' ('Fear thou not, I am with thee. Yield not, I
am thy God, I strengthen thee, I help thee even with the right hand
of my righteousness').

iv, tenor recitativo secco, commences happily enough—'Thou
speakest even, dear God, for my soul's rest to me a comfort in my
sorrow'—but soon falls back on despair. A diminished third appears
in the continuo during 'Ah, but my torment increases itself from
day to day, for mine enemies are so many, my life is their target'.
A run occurs to 'Bogen' ('bow') in 'their bow is against me
stretched', the voice shoots up on 'they aim their arrows to destruction'. 'Sterben', the last word of 'I shall by their hands die',
concludes a brief arioso by sinking chromatically above detached
continuo quavers. There is an agonized section in recitative, 'God!
my need is to Thee known, the whole world becomes for me a torture-
chamber', and a chromatic Andante arioso, 'help, Helper, help!
save my soul!', is so tense that the bassi play two diminished fourths
and a diminished third, and it ends vocally unfinished. (See Ex. 1280.)

The next chorale, v, is confident in the succour of the Almighty
and the defeat of Satan. It is stanza 5 of P. Gerhardt's 'Befiehl du
deine Wege', which is an acrostic upon Luther's version of Psalm
xxxvii. 5: 'Commit thy way unto the Lord; trust also in Him; and
He shall bring it to pass.' H. L. Hassler's 'Herzlich thut mich verlangen', known in this country as the Passion chorale, is the tune:
'And although all devils Thee would withstand, So will yet without
doubt God not backward go; What He to Himself has taken And
what he have will, That must then finally come To its purpose and
goal.'

In spite of all this avowal of confidence, the tenor, in vi, sings:

'Stürmt nur, stürmt, ihr Trübsalswetter, wallt, ihr Fluthen, auf mich los! Schlagt, ihr Unglücksflammen, über mich zusammen, stört, ihr Feinde, meine Ruh', spricht mir doch Gott tröstlich zu: ich bin dein Hort und Erretter' ('Storm only, storm, ye trouble-tempest, rush, ye floods, on me freely! Strike, ye misfortune's-flames, over me together, disturb, ye enemies, my repose, speaks to me yet God comfortingly: I am thy refuge and deliverer').

Even the bass recitativo secco, vii, begins with an admonition to tolerate tears—'Be comforted, my heart, bear thy pain, let thee thy cross not down weigh!'—but even then striking harmonies depict unhappiness:

Ex. 632

The next sentences contrast the fortunate state of the believer with that of the Infant Christ: 'God will thee certainly at the right time refresh; must yet His dear Son, thy Jesus, in still tender years much greater affliction undergo, when Him the tyrant Herod the outward danger of death with murderous fists threatens!' 'Flüchtling' ('fugitive') is allotted a demisemiquaver run in 'Scarcely comes He on the earth, so must He already a fugitive become!' A peaceful 'Well then, with Jesus comfort thyself, and believe steadfastly;' brings an andante arioso with confident melodic movement: 'to those who here with Christ suffer, will He the heavenly kingdom award.'

Only in the penultimate number, alto aria with strings, is Bach content to cease looking on the darker side of things: 'Soll ich meinen Lebenslauf unter Kreuz und Trübsal führen, hört es doch im Himmel auf. Da ist lauter Jubiliren, daselbsten verwechselt mein Jesus das Leiden mit seliger Wonne, mit ewigen Freuden' ('Shall I my life's-path under cross and trouble lead, ceases it yet in heaven. There is loud jubilation, in that very place exchanges my Jesus pain with blissful rapture, with everlasting joy'). Having at long last reached this desirable state of mind, the concluding chorale maintains it. Stanzas 11 and 12 of M. Moller's (?) 'Ach Gott, wie manches Herzeleid', arranged as three verses, are set unwontedly simply. The tune is the anonymous one known under that name and also as 'Herr Jesu Christ, mein's Lebens Licht', 'Therefore will I, because I live still, The cross Thee joyfully bear after; My God makes me thereto ready, It serves for the best always! Help me my affairs rightly to undertake, That I my journey accomplish can, Help me also to constrain flesh and blood, Against sin and shame me protect! Preserve my heart in faith pure, So live and die I To Thee alone; Jesus, my comfort, hear my desire, Oh my Saviour, were I with Thee!'

The only reference to the Gospel for the Sunday after the Circumcision, St. Matthew ii. 13–15, the flight into Egypt, is in vii. The introduction of three chorales, the overshadowing of everything else by the tenor aria and the condition of the libretto, almost suggest that it is a composite work. The fact that the two arias are both scored for strings (which also double in the chorales), confirms this speculation. Spitta places it chronologically with the two cantatas just discussed, but Terry points out that the Sunday concerned, that after the Circumcision, fell during Bach's early Leipzig years in 1727 and 1728 only, and that in the latter year mourning for the Queen precluded cantatas, leaving 1727 as a likely date.

iii is simply set, almost like an arioso, and is pitched rather high; more than once a drop of a ninth is accomplished by two fifths, an unusual melodic progression:

Ex. 633

and a similar fall, C–F♯–B, is troublesome to the singer. Bach's reticence in this number is surprising when one recalls the splendid motet on the same text. The foundational continuo idea, sung afterwards with the initial clause:

Ex. 634

is singularly undescriptive. On the other hand, the mood is one of gentle comfort, allowing the weight of the drama to be particularly effective two numbers later, and there are many subtleties which one may easily overlook in one's expectation of more vivid treatment, the thrusting up of the detached 'ich', an invitation to complete confidence in the Almighty, the wavering figure to 'weiche nicht', the unusual unison of voice and continuo in bars 22 and 23, indicative of union between God and man, the throwing of 'dich' and 'dir' on the culmination of the short phrases 'ich stärke dich' and 'ich helfe dir', the upward arpeggio 'rechte Hand', while the quoted ninths give a sense of calm omnipotence. Bach packs much subtle significance into this apparently simple arioso; he is as great in small things as he is superb in great ones. There are several cases of three bars of duple time thrown across two bars of triple, thus avoiding what might have been monotonous owing to the placidly moving continuo.

The tenor aria, like its counterpart in the last cantata described, is a vivid and crowded canvas, with wild leaping figures,

Ex. 635

and

Ex. 636

(in both of these and throughout the number ♩. ♪ must be played in the traditional manner as [figure] and ♪. ♪ as [figure] ; the vehemence of the orchestral score is much increased thereby), tearing instrumental runs,

Ex. 637   Vl. I

(played as — [figure])

and

Ex. 638

Cont.
8ve lower   6
             4
             2

a disjunct vocal line,

Ex.639

with furious demisemiquaver runs on 'wallt', 'flammen', and even
to 'Erretter'. 'Ruh'' is sustained, the rushing and leaping of the
upper strings are marked 'piano', the bassi sink gently down in
repeated quavers. Except for 'Erretter' the vocal line from 'spricht
mir' to this word is less agitated, but bassi and violin I continue their
raging and tossing, apart from the first two bars, where a calmer
mood prevails.

The alto aria is based on a charming melody of comfort,

Ex.640

and the reference to 'Lebenslauf' calls up many peaceful quaver
passages, foreshadowed in the continuo of Ex. 640, one ascending
slowly heavenwards while the bassi pulsate on a pedal. The introduction begins with the above melody; it is repeated slightly elaborated with voice added, the latter partly doubling violin I and partly
making a fifth strand to the texture. The twelve-bar introduction is
expanded instrumentally into twenty-four, the melody of bar 1 being
inverted, and the quaver passage described *supra* forms an important
portion. Eight bars of the interlude are repeated with a fresh melody
for the singer. At bar 8 of this violin I poises on an E and the voice
climbs upwards with the quaver idea. 'Da ist lauter Jubiliren'
begins with bar 1 of the chief melody for voice alone, in bar 2 the
continuo imitates, and with bar 3 bars 9–16 of the interlude reappear, with an altered bassi line and a new vocal one:

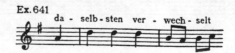

Ex.641

The quaver idea, though altered in outline, is much heard in violin I
and continuo, the inner strings play mostly detached chords; there is
an eleven-bar passage to 'Freuden', during the first part of which
violin I climbs in quavers, and during the latter part, above a pulsating continuo, the voice does likewise, but with leaps of abounding
delight.

60. The latest cantata of the group possibly belongs to 1732, for
the Twenty-Fourth Sunday after Trinity, 23 November. It bears the
same title as No. 20 and begins with the same hymn-verse: 'O Ewigkeit, du Donnerwort', and Bach's autograph describes it as a
'Dialogus zwischen Furcht und Hoffnung' ('Dialogue between Fear
and Hope'). The incident of the daughter of Jairus, St. Matthew ix.
18–26, gives rise to the discussion of death, and the quotation from
Psalm cxix. 166, 'Herr, ich warte auf dein Heil' ('Lord, I wait on
Thy Salvation'), has direct bearing on the Epistle, Colossians i.
9–14. The two states of mind, Mr. Fearful and Mr. Hopeful, as
Bunyan would have visualized them, are interpreted respectively by
alto and tenor. Except for the final chorale all the numbers are duets.
    i is a fine chorale fantasia, the outstanding number of the cantata.
The canto is sustained by alto and corno, stanza 1 of J. Rist's hymn:
'O eternity, thou thunderword, O sword, that through the soul
bores, O beginning without ending! O eternity, time without
time, I know from great affliction Not, whither I myself may turn:
My completely affrighted heart quakes, that to me the tongue to my
gums cleaves.' J. Schop's melody, 'Wach auf, mein Geist', was reconstructed by J. Crüger for this hymn. The trembling of the terrified
heart is heard at the very opening, semiquaver repeated notes in the
upper strings, above a long 'tasto solo' pedal, symbolic of eternity,
first A in unison, then the strong dissonance, three adjacent notes,
B, A, and G, all sounding together:

Ex.642

This striking motive permeates almost every bar, sometimes broken
into fragments, sometimes prolonged. Two oboes d'amore have
intertwining duet ideas expressive of Hope, generally independent
of the strings:

Ex. 643
(b) Ob. d'am. I, II

but motives are occasionally interchanged. To the upper strings are often assigned syncopations and groups of arpeggio quavers:

Ex.644 (c)

with the oboe d'amore duet intermingled and continuo tremblings below, (a) in part or complete. With line 7—'mein ganz erschrocknes Herze bebt'—the pulsating bassi move by semitones and drop a diminished third. The text of the tenor is restricted to the Psalm verse quoted. It does not begin until line 4 of the canto is reached, so that a new and persistent feature is added to the four groups of ideas. The first long note to 'warte' coincides with 'O Ewigkeit'; later the word has many sustained notes and lengthy passages. (b) is incorporated into some of the latter, at other times there is new material, always in a consolatory mood. (b) also is found elsewhere in the vocal line. (c) is heard in the oboes d'amore and upper strings only. The continuo part is almost wholly confined to pedal notes, (a) in fragments or complete, or ascending semiquaver scales. It is interesting to compare this fantasia with that in No. 20, where greater forces are employed, and to see how infinitely resourceful Bach was when dealing with the identical material.

The recitatives, ii and iv, are secchi. It is only to be expected that Bach, dealing with such a congenial subject, should provide us in ii with moments of great beauty. The drops in the melody to 'Die Todesangst, der letzte Schmerz' ('The death-anguish, the last pain') are exquisitely lovely, and there is an extraordinarily chromatic sentence in the Andante Arioso to the word 'martert':

Ex. 645

tortures
mar - - - - - - - - - - - - tert

The closing arioso depicts the enduring ('tragen') of the earthly burden to a twisting run, while the bassi struggle upwards and fall again, but the ending is triumphant. The text of this fine number is: *Fear*. 'Oh heavy going to the last combat and struggle!' *Hope*. 'My help is already there, my Saviour stands with me, yea, with comfort at my side!' *Fear*. 'The death-anguish, the last pain overtakes and attacks my heart, and' (andante) 'tortures these limbs.' (Recitative) *Hope*. 'I lay this body before God as an offering down. Is already trouble's fire hot, enough, it purifies also to God's praise.' *Fear*. 'Yet, now will itself sins' great guilt before my visage place!' *Hope*. 'God will therefore yet no death-judgement pronounce. He grants an end to temptation's tortures, that' (arioso) 'one them can endure.'

The unknown librettist propounded a problem to the composer by his text for iii. Fear and Hope are allotted line and line about, expressing in each case exactly opposite sentiments: *Fear*. 'Mein letztes Lager will mich schrecken' ('My last halting-place will me frighten'). *Hope*. 'Mich wird des Heilands Hand bedecken' ('Me will the Saviour's hand cover'). *Fear*. 'des Glaubens Schwachheit sinket fast' ('the faith's weakness sinks almost.'). *Hope*. 'mein Jesus trägt mit mir die Last' ('my Jesus bears with me the burden'). *Fear*. 'Das off'ne Grab sieht gräulich aus' ('The open grave appears grim'). *Hope*. 'Es wird mir doch ein Friedenshaus' ('It will be for me yet a peace-house'). It is beyond the powers of music to cope with such a situation, so Bach forsakes his customary meticulous interpretation of his texts and merely writes charming music of no particular significance for most of this Duetto. The oboe d'amore theme,

Ex.646

Cont.

clearly expresses, by its halting dotted notes and its contour, the state of mind of Fear. In addition to the oboe d'amore there is a violin, and its chief idea, heard also in inversion,

Ex.647

may be considered as depicting the restlessness of the afflicted soul.

In the last section only does the violin introduce anything but this. The alto has a tortuous and broken run on 'schrecken'. 'Sinket fast', naturally, falls step by step; 'trägt' is treated similarly. The assurances of Hope are without avail; he makes way for a greater power. At the end, while the tenor is singing bar after bar of florid runs, the alto sweeps up a diminished seventh on 'gräulich' and ends before the other soloist with an upward querying augmented fourth. Twice, against 'gräulich', the obbligato instruments descend,

as if the doubter were tottering on the brink of the grave; later, they turn to the confident one and play leaping phrases.

In iv, Fear speaks always in recitatives; after each a bass replies in arioso. *Fear.* 'The death remains yet to the human nature hateful, and drags almost the hope completely to earth.' The bass, with a confidently moving continuo, intones part of Revelation xiv. 13: 'Blessed are the dead.' But in dramatic manner Fear raves again: 'Ah! but ah, how much danger presents itself to the soul, the death-road to go! Perhaps will it hell's-jaws, death, frightful make, when it it' (i.e. the soul) 'to devour seeks; perhaps is it already cursed to eternal damnation.' The bass, employing the phrases of the first arioso, extends the Scriptural quotation, 'Blessed are the dead who in the Lord die'. Fear is somewhat consoled, though still distressed: 'If I in the Lord die, is then the blessedness my portion and inheritance? The body becomes indeed the worm's food! Yea, become my limbs dust and earth again, as I a child of death am called, so seem I, verily, in the grave to decay.' The bass now completes the quotation by adding 'von nun an' ('from henceforth') and extends its arioso to fourteen bars, a passage of intense beauty, the final 'sterben' ('die') being most beautifully set:

Fear is now, at last, convinced: 'Well then! shall I from henceforth blessed be: so appear thou, oh hope! again. My body may without fear in sleep rest, the spirit can a vision in that joy have.' The *BGS* marks the bass line 'The voice of the Holy Ghost.' in brackets; Schering points out that this is not in accordance with the theology of Bach's time, and that it is intended to be the voice of Christ.

The harmonization of the closing chorale is positively startling, and six bars before the end begins a series of chromatic harmonies ('mein grosser Jammer', 'my great lamentation') almost unparalleled in Bach's works. The melody itself commences surprisingly:

Ex.650

Es · ist ge - nug:

unlike most of the hymn-tunes used, it was, in a sense, modern, dating twenty-three years only before Bach's birth. Bach does not use it elsewhere. It was written by J. R. Ahle for F. J. Burmeister's 'Es ist genug; so nimm, Herr, meinen Geist', stanza 5 of which is heard here: 'It is enough; Lord, if it Thee pleases, so set me then free. My Jesus comes: now good-night, oh world! I journey into heaven's house, I journey safely thither with peace, My great lamentation remains here below. It is enough.' Here, as in so many cases, especially if there is reference to sorrow in any form, Bach prefers to illustrate one aspect of the text even though the general trend is in the directly opposite direction.

For Four Voices

(27), (42), 86, 88, (156), 159, (164), 165, (166), 167,
(168), (188)

No. 27 closes with a five-part chorale, all the others with four-part chorales, that of 167 being extended.

Order of Discussion: 165, 86, 167, 159, 88

165. It is strange that about 1724 Bach should revert to a Salomo Franck libretto which was published in 1715 (unless it be a reconstructed cantata), and still more strange that after the intervening years and contact with other writers he should be attracted by a text beginning in such a bald manner: 'O heil'ges Geist- und Wasserbad' ('Oh holy spirit- and waterbath'). In spite of this No. 165 is most attractive. It may be performed with strings only, as the bassoon, included in the score of i, iv, and vi, merely doubles the continuo save for an occasional note. In form, i, soprano aria, is a fugue, and it is called 'Concerto', presumably because the strings are on an equality with the voice, though not more so than in dozens of other instances. The fugue moves along placidly, beautiful in idea and in texture. The exposition is confined to strings and bassoon. After a full close the voice enters with subject and countersubject,

Ex. 651

beginning a counterexposition and continuing: 'das Gottes Reich uns einverleibet' ('that God's kingdom in us incarnates'). When the vocal section ends there are violin, viola, and bassi entries of the subject. Then the voice again leads off, this time with the theme in inversion: 'und uns in's Buch des Lebens schreibet' ('and us into the book of life writes'). 'Lebens' begins with a decorated inversion of the countersubject and pursues its flowing movement for another three bars. Violin I enters with the direct subject during this, and after an episode comes an instrumental stretto, original and inverted forms being used. With 'O Fluth, die alle Missethat durch ihre Wunderkraft ertränket' ('Oh flood, that all misdoings through its magicalstrength drowns'), a theme with a new idea, but merging into semiquavers akin to the countersubject, comes in close imitation between voice and violin I:

Ex. 652

It is afterwards used as a second countersubject, and then both it and the subject come together inverted, 'und uns das neue Leben schenket' ('and to us the new life gives'). The fugue, therefore, is full of scientific devices. Naturally, Bach cannot resist assigning copious vocal runs to 'Wasser', 'Lebens', and 'alles'. His genius once more rises superior to his text.

A bass recitativo secco discusses the sinful birth of man (a reference to the Gospel, St. John iii. 1–15, Christ's declaration to the inquiring and puzzled Nicodemus that he must be born again), and there is picturesque treatment of 'Gottes Zorn', 'Tod', and 'Verderben' ('God's anger', 'death', and 'destruction'). The text is: 'The sinful birth of the condemned Adam's-heirs, brings forth God's anger, the death and the destruction. For what of flesh born is, is nothing but flesh, by sin infected, poisoned and polluted. How blessed is a Christian! He becomes in the spirit- and waterbath a child of blessedness and grace, he puts on Christ and His innocence's white silk, he is with Christ's blood the honour-purple-garment, in the baptism-bath clothed.'

The librettist is constant in his versification, even though imagination fail him, for water and baptism recur in the short alto aria secca, where voice and continuo move in a graceful slow gigue:

Ex.653

Each clause of the text is sung twice. 'Jesu, der aus großer Liebe in der Taufe mir verschriebe Leben, Heil und Seligkeit' ('Jesus, Who from great love in the baptism to me prescribed life, salvation and blessedness') decorates the continuo phrase delightfully, and the first time, in swaying passages, brings 'Leben', 'Heil', and 'Seligkeit' in a syncopated manner on the weaker parts of the bars, thus stressing their importance, 'hilf, daß ich mich deßen freue und den Lebensbund erneue in der ganzen Lebenszeit' ('help, that I myself therein rejoice and the life-covenant renew in the whole lifetime') uses on its first appearance another form of the continuo melody, but with 'hilf' thrown on a high note, and on its second introduces a decorated trilling phrase on 'freue', which rises above a continuo pedal with falling decorations. Syncopations, throwing bars of $\frac{9}{8}$ across $\frac{12}{8}$, are also a charming feature of the settings of this clause.

There are many points of interest in a long and beautifully rich recitative for bass with strings and bassoon. It abounds in chromaticisms and is extraordinarily flexible. The singer is at first content with the blessed condition of the new birth and sings a lovely decorative passage, with a corresponding part for violin I, on 'heil'ges' ('holy'). But now thoughts of his unworthy retrogressions crowd upon him. Christ had spoken to Nicodemus of the serpent which Moses lifted up in the wilderness (verse 14), and twice the writhing of the snake is pictured vividly in the vocal line:

The lifting of the cross ('an dem Kreuz erhöhet') brings a poignant rising violin passage:

Christ restores him 'wenn alle Kraft vergehet' ('when all strength passes away') but Bach deals less with regained confidence than with the fading away of strength; in the penultimate bar the voice sinks to the depths and the strings have an exquisite piano passage which combines rising with falling. The continuo is marked 'senza accomp.' (without chords), the strings melt away at the end of the bar, and the final note is heard only in continuo, bassi, and bassoon. (There is a similar effect at the end of the 'Esurientes' of the Latin Magnificat, where the rich are sent empty away.) The complete text is: 'I have indeed, my soul's-bridegroom, when Thou me newly created, to Thee everlastingly faithful to be sworn' (adagio) hail holy God's Lamb! (See Ex. 1324.) (Recitative) 'Yet have I, alas! the baptism-covenant oft broken, and not fulfilled, what I promised, pity Thou in grace me! Forgive me the committed sin, Thou knowest, my God, how painfully I feel the old snake-sting; the sin-poison pollutes me body and soul, help, that I believingly Thee choose, blood-red snake-image, that on the cross is raised, that all pains soothes and me refreshes when all strength passes.'

In the tenor aria—'Jesu, meines Todes Tod' ('my death's death', a fantastic phrase for salvation)—Christ is again spoken of as the serpent-symbol: 'laß in meinem Leben und in meiner letzten Noth mir für Augen schweben, daß du mein Heilschlänglein sei'st vor das Gift der Sünde' ('let in my life and in my last need before my eyes hover, that Thou my salvation-snakelet (redeemer) art against the poison of sin'). The whole of the obbligato for violins in unison is constructed out of the image of the bending, writhing, twisting reptile, usually a symbol of horror, but in Bach's musical speech a thing of pellucid beauty:

Ex.656

Cont.

The emotional intensity of the joy of the new birth is so great that the singer, on the word 'Leben'—('Heile, Jesu, Seel' und Geist, daß ich Leben finde', 'Save, Jesu, soul and spirit, that I life (may) find')—must needs leap upwards twice to the extent of a ninth. The closing chorale is very simple, of heavenly peace and contentment: 'His word, His baptism, His communion Serves against all misfortune, The Holy Ghost in faith Teaches us thereon to trust.' It is stanza 5 of L. Helmbold's Grace after Meat, 'Nun laßt uns Gott dem Herren' with its anonymous melody.

86. Nos. 166 and 86 appeared at a week's distance from each other, on the Fourth and Fifth Sundays after Easter, possibly 1725. Their libretti, both conjectured to be by Christian Weiss, Senr., are on the same lines, beginning with a bass aria to a verse taken from the Gospel, containing a solo chorale as iii, the sole recitative being iv and a four-part chorale, vi. No. 166 has already been discussed; the opening aria of 'Wahrlich, wahrlich, ich sage euch' ('Verily, verily, I say unto you'), St. John xvi. 23 (the Gospel is 23–30), shows the same reticent, reverent style. The utterance of Christ is in terms of calm and dignified beauty, strings and voice pursuing a fugal form in which there is little incident, but where everything is serene. Each of the clauses has usually its own especial theme:

Ex.657

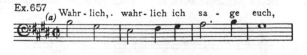

(a) Wahr-lich,. wahr-lich ich sa - ge euch,

Ex.658

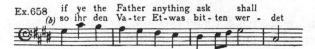

(b) if ye the Father anything ask   shall
so ihr den Va-ter Et-was bit-ten wer - det

in   mei-nem Na - - men,
in   My   name,

and

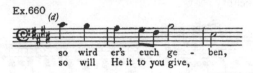

so   wird   er's   euch ge - ben,
so   will   He it to you give,

(*a*), (*b*), and (*c*) are heard simultaneously at the opening, the subjects of a triple fugue. (*b*) is always found in the continuo when (*a*) is sung, indicative of the unity of the Father and the Son. (*d*) is an interlude; violins I and II imitate with quavers above it, a suggestion of the plenteousness of the Father's gifts; a fragment of (*b*) is heard below, the cross-accentuation caused by the throwing of the first syllable of 'geben' on the half-bar (as also with 'werdet') adding to the quiet charm of the dignified vocal line.

Incident there is in plenty in the violin obbligato to the alto aria, ii—luxuriant runs,

and many bars of arpeggi in semiquavers, the chords only being indicated:

The text begins unusually—'Ich will doch wohl Rosen brechen' ('I shall then forsooth roses gather')—and this accounts for the florescence of the obbligato. 'Brechen' is set to a disjointed passage:

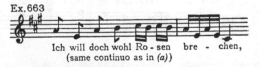

Ich will doch wohl Ro - sen bre - chen,
(same continuo as in (*a*))

and an unexpected chromatic note comes at the reference to the 'stechen' of the thorns—'wenn mich gleich die Dornen stechen' ('if me immediately the thorns prick')—in a long run at the close of the first vocal section. The second vocal section, like the first, begins with detached phrases—'Denn ich bin der Zuversicht' ('For I am of the confidence')—but it continues with a more lengthy idea: 'daß mein Bitten und mein Flehen Gott gewiß zu Herzen gehen, weil es mir sein Wort verspricht' ('that my prayer and my supplication (to) God certainly to the heart go, because it to me His word promises'). From 'Bitten' there are five bars of successive dissonances, richly rainbowed in violin arpeggi, and 'Flehen' is made expressive by the tearmotive. With the repetition of the words the short phrases are modified melodically, though the time-pattern is retained, 'Flehen' is shorter and the same phrase is used to 'gehen' to signify the sure upward flight of supplication; the whole section indicates increased confidence.

To the soprano is given the middle chorale, with an uninteresting duet for two oboes as accompaniment. The anonymous melody is that associated with G. Grünwald's 'Kommt her zu mir, spricht Gottes Sohn', and the text stanza 16: 'And what the everlastingly good God In His word promised has, Sworn by His name, That holds and gives He certainly in truth. He helps us to the angel host Through Jesus Christ, Amen!' The waving counterpoint of the oboes suggests the swaying of throngs of angels. Bach's merciless attitude towards his players is shown here; in fifty-one oboe I bars of $\frac{6}{8}$, six beats in a bar, there are only three opportunities for breath-taking, one of one quaver and two of two, and in one passage seventy-two semiquavers come in succession with no break whatsoever! His vocalists were treated no less sternly; in the short tenor recitativo secco, iv, a piece of delightful declamation demands the following intervals in succession: augmented fourth, minor second, diminished fifth, diminished fourth. The text is: 'God does it not even as the world, which much promises and little keeps: for, what He says, must happen, that one therein can his delight and joy see.'

The short tenor aria, a splendidly tuneful, almost Handelian number, is accompanied by strings. The opening five notes of the violin melody,

Ex. 664

are the motto, associated with 'Gott hilft gewiß' ('God helps certainly'), and are not only delivered in detached groups by the singer and heard in various forms in the upper instrumental lines, but are used largely by the continuo, hammering out the dominant idea of the verse. The melodies associated with the remaining words—'wird gleich die Hülfe aufgeschoben, wird sie doch drum nicht aufgehoben. Denn Gottes Wort bezeuget dies: Gott hilft gewiß!' ('is immediately the help deferred, is it therefore not abandoned. For God's word shows this: God helps certainly!')—are finely vigorous. The chief impression made by the aria is the joyful reiteration of the motto. Contrary to Bach's normal practice the introduction is heard afterwards fragmentarily only, a bar and a half accompany the first 'wird gleich', &c., there is a brief interlude before the second part of the text, two bars come later, and the portion quoted above accompanies the last section, in which the singer, abandoning himself to his exuberance, flings up to high B. The orchestration of the concluding chorale is not stated. It is the anonymous melody of P. Speratus's 'Es ist das Heil uns kommen her', with stanza 11—'The hope awaits the right time, which God's word assures: When that happen shall for our joy, Sets God no certain day. He knows well when it best is, And requires from us no deceitful craft, Therefore shall we Him trust.'

167. Another cantata, 'Ihr Menschen, rühmet Gottes Liebe' ('Ye mortals, extol the love of the Father' B.), for St. John's Day, belongs probably to the same year. When we remember what Handel did with the Epistle for the Day, Isaiah xl. 1–5, which begins with 'Comfort ye' and ends with 'And the glory', we realize how much the futility of some of Bach's authors has lost to us. The prophecy is referred to but not quoted, and a string of insipid reflections on the Gospel, St. Luke i. 57–80 (the birth of John the Baptist, the unloosening of Zacharias's tongue and his Benedictus), was all that the composer had provided for him. Yet there is not a dull number. The sole aria, i, tenor with strings, suggests the flowing Jordan by its gracious undulating phrases, although there is no mention of waters in the text: 'Ihr Menschen, rühmet Gottes Liebe und preiset seine Gütigkeit. Lobt ihn aus reinem Herzenstriebe, daß er uns zu bestimmter Zeit das Horn des Heils, den Weg zum Leben an Jesu, seinem Sohn, gegeben' ('Ye men, extol God's love and praise His goodness. Laud him out of pure heart's-impulse, that He us at the appointed time the horn of salvation, the way of life to Jesus, His Son, (has) given').

The animated semiquaver runs to 'preiset' indicate a moderate tempo. A particularly lovely effect comes in bars 9 and 10, where violin I swings up and down over a single chord:

(The inner parts will be played as .)
This comes five times again in the aria and there are four distinct methods of presentation of the same idea, perhaps the most fascinating being where the singer leaps from height to height:

with pulsating inner strings, the bassi merely stressing the first beat of the bar. The vocal melody here is also a skeleton of the main theme, announced by violin I and afterwards divided between violin and voice:

The alto recitativo secco—'Praised be the Lord God of Israel, Who Himself in mercy to us turns and His Son from high heaven's-throne as world-redeemer sends. First appeared John and had to (the) way and path for the Saviour prepare, afterwards came Jesus Himself, the poor human children and the lost sinners'—ends with a very beautiful arioso: 'With mercy and love to rejoice, and then to the heavenly kingdom in true penitence to lead.' A swaying semiquaver continuo envisages the bliss of the future life.

A S.A. duet, with oboe da caccia obbligato, is on a generous scale. The affirmation that God's word is ever reliable—'Gottes Wort, das trüget nicht' ('God's word, that deceives not')—is always sung simultaneously by the two voices, and the succeeding words—'es geschieht was er verspricht' ('it happens as He promises')—are treated in free canon, with leaps, runs, and trills, joyfulness in the inevitable following of what has been pre-ordained. There is the same subtle connexion between instrumental and vocal material that we find in innumerable instances, an underlying secret of unity of thought to which Bach alone possessed the clue:

Ex.668
Andante
Ob. da cacc.

and

Ex.669
Got-tes Wort, das trü-get nicht,

Throughout the fifty-seven bars of this section the continuo rarely departs from its initial idea. At 'Was er in dem Paradies und vor so viel hundert Jahren denen Vätern schon verhieß' ('What He in the Paradise and before so many hundred years to the fathers already promised') the time changes to $\frac{4}{4}$, there is an eight-bar canon for the voices and the many hundred years are suggested by interminable runs, while oboe da caccia and continuo doggedly [reiterate] the opening vocal theme of this section,

Ex.670
Was er in dem Pa-ra-dies

emphasizing the promise of the Father. We return to $\frac{3}{4}$—'haben wir gottlob! erfahren' ('have we, God be praised! proved')—and a very animated section culminates in repeated and dovetailed cries of 'gottlob'. The oboe da caccia fashions most of its phrases from a theme of its own:

Ex.671

the continuo maintains the time-patterns ♫ ♫♫♫ | ♪ and

♫ ♫♫ ♫ | ♪, sometimes borrowing octaves from the obbligato.

The bass recitativo secco is noble in character: 'Of woman's seed came, after which the time fulfilled (was); the blessing, which God to Abraham, the faith-hero, (had) promised, has as the splendour of the sun dawned, and our sorrow is soothed.'

There is an impressive break between the last two words. (See Ex. 1274.) 'A dumb Zacharias praises with loud voice God for his wonder-deed, which He To the people has shown. Remember, ye Christians, also, what God in you has done.' The conclusion is arioso and line 1 of J. Kugelmann's (?) 'Nun lob', mein Seel', den Herren' is sung to 'and strike up to Him a song of praise'.

Stanza 5 of J. Graumann's hymn of that name serves for an extended chorale, in which oboe and violin I in unison pursue many lively runs, the running of Jordan. (See B.E.C., No. 15, O.) The translation is: 'Be glory and praise with honour (To) God Father, Son, Holy Spirit. Who will in us increase, what He to us from grace promised. That we to Him firmly trust, wholly rely on Him, from hearts on Him build; that our heart, spirit and mind on Him firmly hang: therefore sing we at all times. Amen, we will it obtain, believe we from heart's depth.' This number makes the cantata uncertain in its classification; it may be considered either as solo or choral, but the simple vocal lines incline one to the former. A clarino doubles the soprano; middle strings and often the continuo maintain the time-pattern— ♪ ♫♫ | ♫ . Trumpet and oboe may be omitted, and the obbligato to the duet may be played on a viola if it is desired to give the cantata with strings only.

159. There are four cantatas for Quinquagesima. In all cases the Epistle, 1 Corinthians xiii, the apotheosis of charity, is neglected in favour of the Gospel, St. Luke xviii. 31–43, the chief incident of which is Christ's announcement that He must go up to Jerusalem and that there the prophecies concerning His sufferings and death will be fulfilled. This episode made the strongest impression on the librettists, and three of these cantatas deserve to be studied together as they have so much emotionally in common. No. 22, which was performed at Leipzig for Bach's Probe, begins with Christ's announcement. No. 23 does not refer directly to this, but foreshadows the agony and dwells upon the incident of the curing of the blind man, which falls in the last part of the Gospel. Both of these have been discussed.

No. 159 came five years later: 'Sehet, wir geh'n hinauf gen Jerusalem' ('Behold, we go up to Jerusalem'). Picander's libretto makes of the opening recitativ-arioso a number with two characters; Christ, in the arioso sections, repeats the Biblical text, an alto is pictured as an onlooker, lamenting the labour of the journey, seeing the Cross already prepared, yet helpless and unable to accompany the Saviour. Wustmann thinks that as No. 23 was a prelude to the *St. John Passion* this cantata was a prelude to the *St. Matthew Passion*. If that be the case it is curious that in the opening number Bach should reverse the well-known procedure of the later *Passion*, accompanying the bass voice with continuo only, except in one short phrase, and allotting strings to the onlooker. The ariosi have a peculiar flavour, because the six-note continuo figure first proceeds upwards by the step-motive and then drops a seventh,

Ex.672

a plan which produces some interesting harmonies. The figure is afterwards inverted, a falsifying of its implication. Once only during the ariosi is this motto departed from, when 'gen Jerusalem' is sung for the first time, and this fragment is accompanied by all the strings, thus emphasizing the object of the journey and all that by it was signified. The commentatory recitative is expressive and chromatic. The bass opening confines itself to 'Sehet', and the alto replies: 'Come, behold then my mind, whither goes thy Jesus?' The bass now completes his clause, beginning with the drop of the seventh. With poignant supporting harmonies the alto cries: 'Oh hard road! up?' (quoting the Saviour's 'hinauf'). 'Oh monstrous mountain, which my sins show! How painfully wilt Thou have to climb!' Christ answers, 'to Jerusalem', and the complete clause is expanded, the final 'geh'n hinauf gen' picturing the ascent of the steep by rising through an arpeggio of a diminished seventh. Passing from A♭ through B♭ minor, E♭ minor, F minor, G minor, and F minor to C minor, the alto passionately exclaims: 'Ah, go not! Thy cross is for Thee already erected, where Thou shalt to death bleed; here seeks one whips, there binds one rods, the bonds await Thee, ah, go Thyself not thither! Yet, remainest Thou behind, then must I myself not to Jerusalem, ah, alas, to hell go!'

Although the onlooker at first declares his inability to accompany

Christ to Jerusalem, courage is gained and a fresh resolution announced in a duet—*Arie mit Choral* (see S. & B. 'I follow Thee') —'Ich folge dir nach durch Speichel und Schmach; am Kreuz will ich dich noch umfangen. Dich laß' ich nicht aus meiner Brust, und wenn du endlich scheiden mußt, sollst du dein Grab in mir erlangen' ('I follow Thee after through spittle and shame; on the cross will I Thee yet embrace. Thee let I not (go) out of my heart, and if Thou finally depart must, shalt Thou Thy grave in me attain'). A swinging $\frac{6}{8}$ movement, with step-motives in the continuo (plus bassoon) and voice,

Ex.673

combining with a chorale in the soprano, doubled by an oboe, makes a beautifully intimate number. It will be noticed that the imitations are similar to those in the first soprano aria of the *St. John Passion*, which has a like text. We know the melody (originally a secular song by H. L. Hassler) in Britain as the ' Passion Chorale', associated with a translation of P. Gerhardt's 'O Haupt voll Blut und Wunden' as 'O Sacred Head once wounded'. Stanza 6 of the hymn is used here: 'I will here with Thee stand, Despise me then not! From Thee will I not go, Even till Thy heart breaks. When thy head becomes pale In the last death-stroke, Then will I Thee hold In my arm and bosom.' There are many beautiful incidents in the alto line, the elaborate third 'folge' in which a leap to a high E♭ suggests victory in scaling the 'monstrous mountain', the almost wholly unaccompanied chromatic passage to 'Speichel und Schmach' (later employed in the continuo, which otherwise is mostly concerned with the 'folge' motive), the unexpected sustained D♭ on 'Kreuz', the broken sobs in bars 78–80—'und wenn du — endlich — scheiden mußt', a drop of a seventh to 'Grab' and the slow descent when the clause containing this word is sung for the last time, and the high-pitched, agonized 'und wenn du endlich scheiden mußt', even though the soprano is comfortingly singing the last line of the hymn-stanza.

The next three numbers carry the story farther; the tenor, in a recitativo secco, is a spectator of the Crucifixion and the Resurrection:

'Now will I myself, my Jesu, over Thee in my hiding-place grieve; the world may ever the poison of pleasure to itself take, I lave myself in my tears' (these two clauses are strongly contrasted in pitch), 'and will not after one joy yearn, till Thee my countenance shall in glory perceive, till I by Thee redeemed am; there will I myself with Thee be refreshed'.

The remarkable bass aria (see P. 53) opens with an oboe playing against sustained strings. The solo instrument gives out a short six-note idea,

which is repeated inverted immediately. This theme we see afterwards to be associated with the opening three words, 'Es ist vollbracht' ('It is fulfilled'). Then comes a rising syncopated idea,

which the voice uses later in a different form,

illustrating the grief which the text declares to have departed. The continual stressing of the subdominant key produces a wonderful feeling of solemnity; the Christian, though rejoicing at deliverance, is awed by the sight of the suffering Saviour on the cross. The first half of the aria, which continues 'wir sind von unser'm Sündenfalle in Gott gerecht gemacht' ('we are from our sin-fall in God right made'), is constructed out of these three fragments, together with sighings for oboe and violin I and a lovely vocal line. 'Nun will ich eilen und meinem Jesu Dank ertheilen' ('Now will I hasten and to my Jesus thanks give') introduces rapid passages in close imitation, the inner strings ceasing and violin I joining in the imitations. When the bassi take up the 'eilen' theme, the voice sings in a stately manner, 'Welt, gute Nacht' ('World, good night' or 'farewell'), and on 'Nacht' the bustle ceases, upper strings sustain, the continuo pulsates downward, and the oboe delivers (a) in its two forms. The 'eilen' theme is resumed modified, oboe and violin I dovetailing three-note quaver groups and not participating in the vocal theme till the second clause is sung. The continuo, too, is different; instead of leaping it pulsates slowly in semitones in grave confidence. The 'Welt, gute Nacht' idea is repeated and the bustling runs are heard no more. The oboe falls nearly two octaves with (a) inverted thrice, the voice declaims: 'Welt, welt, gute Nacht.' A four-bar subdominant pedal precedes the final tonic chord of the vocal section, an unusual harmonic feature, and even the subdominant of the subdominant is touched. Above the pedal violin I rises slowly, the two versions of (a) are heard in the oboe. (a) and (b) are now heard surprisingly in combination, 'es ist vollbracht' twice for the voice, and (b) on the oboe.

The ante-penultimate line of the closing chorale contains wonderfully beautiful chromatic harmonies. Stanza 33 of P. Stockmann's 'Jesu Leiden, Pein und Tod', translated in the discussion on No. 182, p. 154, is used, with the same melody.

88. The remaining solo cantata of the period, 'Siehe, ich will viel Fischer aussenden', dates possibly as late as 13 July 1732. There is an indefinable quality about it which marks it off from the others; what it is is difficult to say, it may be a certain spaciousness which is created in i. It is not one of the most popular solo cantatas, yet it has a fascination which increases on acquaintance. The unknown librettist was at once fortunate and unfortunate in his text. The Gospel for the Fifth Sunday after Trinity, St. Luke v. 1–11, contains Christ's remark to Peter, 'Fear not, from henceforth thou shalt catch men'. The poet begins Part II with this and ingeniously makes Part I an Old Testament parallel by opening with Jeremiah xvi. 16: 'Behold, I will send for many fishers.' As the quotation from Jeremiah refers to the children of Israel, who had been scattered by the angry Jehovah for having 'filled mine inheritance with the carcasses of their detestable and abominable things', but who are now being pardoned, there is a vast difference of mood from the more humane and tender attitude of Christ on the ship. The poet takes insufficient advantage of his opportunities; nevertheless, there is sufficient contrast between the two parts of the libretto to make the division anything but an arbitrary one, as is so often the case.

The noble opening bass aria falls into two portions, and Bach happily does not mark a Da Capo, freeing himself in this instance from a mechanical habit of mind which so often nullifies his dramatic conceptions. For a hundred bars strings, doubled by two oboes d'amore and taille, are not granted a single rest. There is no mistaking the zeal of the missionaries who are summoned: 'Siehe! ich will viel Fischer aussenden, spricht der Herr, die sollen sie fischen' ('Behold! I will many fishers send out, saith the Lord, them shall they fish'). The usual wave-motives, rippling in quaver steps, rising and falling in quaver arpeggi:

rolling in semiquavers, and lengthy swaying pedal-points, cover the whole of the instrumental sea. The voice has a splendid and commanding line:

The power of Jehovah's declaration is shown by the placing of 'will' on the strong beats. There is no suggestion of interludes, the material is merely repeated in ever-varied form. One interesting point is that 'Siehe!' is always separated from what follows; after one or two hearings one expects the usual course to be followed. Bach, however, does not intend to allow his listeners' minds to accept the formula lazily, and at the beginning of one section decorates the usual phrase to the word and then adds another 'Siehe!', which begins arrestingly on high E. Soon after comes a magnificently rolling sequence of eighty-four semiquavers to 'aussenden', the great multitude of missionaries pouring over the land. 'Fischen' is also set to rolling runs; it is not difficult to see the nets being cast. The orchestra is always marked 'pianissimo' when the voice enters. The imagery of Jeremiah changes: 'Und darnach will ich viel Jäger aussenden, die sollen sie fahen auf allen Bergen, und auf allen Hügeln, und in allen Steinritzen' ('And thereafter will I many hunters send out, them shall they catch on all mountains, on all hills, and in all rock-gorges'). The time changes to $\frac{2}{2}$; above an animated continuo the singer leads off with the new words, and during a long run on 'Jäger' comes a kind of hallooing which assumes great importance afterwards:

Ex.679

Two horns enter at the halloo, first with repeated notes, later becoming contrapuntal. The upper strings are silent for fifteen bars. The second clause introduces another long run on 'fahen' and this brings another important figure, a kind of horn call,

Ex.680

demanding a break between the two groups, a realistic device. The horns halloo at the same moment. Then upper strings and oboes d'amore enter with the first vocal theme, while the horns add to the polyphony with the 'fahen' idea, the repeated notes and the opening quaver passage of the continuo. It is a joyous movement, full of exciting adventure. Sometimes the upper strings and oboes d'amore halloo against the combination of the other two motives in the horns; Bach's faculty for presenting his ideas in infinitely varied forms stimulates one's attention during the whole of this lengthy portion. 'Bergen' and 'Hügeln' are always sung to crag-like falls of minim sevenths and octaves. 'Fahen' is frequently spread over seven and more bars, at one place the singer begins on low G and mounts gradually for an eleventh. Most of the vocal sections are in seven-part counterpoint.

A tenor recitativo secco meditates on the forgiveness of the Almighty in spite of our gross misdeeds: 'How easily could then the Highest with us dispense, and His mercy from us turn, if the perverted sense itself evilly from Him separates' (here a continuo E♯, which one expects to resolve on F♯, turns back to E♮) 'and with obstinate mind into its destruction runs. What, however, does His

Fatherly-true mind? Steps He with His goodness from us, even as we from Him, back? And yields He us to the enemy's cunning and malice?' It ends with a half-cadence, as the question demands. The answer is given in the tenor aria: 'Nein, nein! Gott ist allezeit geflißen, uns auf gutem Weg zu wißen' ('No, no! God is always anxious, us on the good road to know'). The second clause wanders upwards by wavering steps, the Christian believing yet dogged by fear; at 'unter seiner Gnaden Schein' ('under His mercy's-light') the melody rises blissfully scalewise for an octave and a fourth. These three ideas are sung with continuo only (without introduction):

and then an oboe d'amore takes up the tale, modifying the vocal phrase:

Soon, however, it introduces a new motive, another wavering, halting idea, more acutely suggestive of the believer's indecision:

This is explained when the voice exclaims 'Ja, ja! wenn wir verirret sein, und die rechte Bahn verlaßen, will er uns gar suchen laßen' ('Yea, yea! if we erring are, and the right road forsake, will He us indeed to be sought cause'), and the vocal line stumbles unsteadily downwards in the first clause. There are fine climbing phrases to the last clause. It is a fascinating picture of mingled doubt and confidence. When the voice ceases the oboe d'amore recapitulates all the motives, accompanied by violin I doubled by oboe d'amore II, violin II, viola

and continuo; the holding back of all the orchestra except obbligato
and continuo until the final ritornello is a most unusual procedure.
The recitative proceeding without break into the aria which answers
its questions produces a fine dramatic scene.

Part II opens with the quotation from the Gospel: 'Jesus sprach
zu Simon: Fürchte dich nicht; denn von nun an wirst du Menschen
fahen' ('Jesus said to Simon: Fear thou not; for from henceforth
wilt thou men catch'). The first four words are sung by a tenor, with
a comforting accompaniment for strings. Christ's assurance is developed into a long arioso secco for bass. The continuo line consists
almost wholly of repetitions of a one-bar figure, the lowering of the
nets, derived from the opening notes of violin I:

Ex. 684

'Fahen' is always expanded in ample runs. There is a further connexion between the violin phrase of the recitative:

Ex. 685 *piano*

and the recitative:

Ex. 686   fürch - te   dich nicht

A S.A. duet admonishes the believer to call upon God, Who will
bless him and drive away sorrow, but it also warns him the Giver
of the talent expects that it will not be buried, but put out to interest.
The number is unusual in character. A graceful melody is announced
by all violins and both oboes d'amore in unison (violas are tacet):

Ex. 687   Ob. d'am.I.II. Vl.I.II

Cont.

(a) is developed by the upper instruments, punctuated by continuo chords. It is the chief theme of the movement, associated with the command to call upon God, the believer being admonished time and time again with all the reiteration of a fanatical preacher. The text of Part I is 'Beruft Gott selbst, so muß der Segen auf allem unsern Thun im Übermaaße ruh'n, stünd' uns gleich Furcht und Sorg' entgegen' ('Calls God Himself, then must the blessing on all our doings in plenteousness rest, should stand us even fear and sorrow against'). The unison melody is modified to serve the first clause as far as 'Thun'. The alto delivers it, the soprano follows, and then the obbligato line, the latter continuing so as to repeat $7\frac{1}{2}$ bars of the introduction. Then comes a fine idea, a slowly descending step passage for the unison instruments, while the voices sink with wavering figures on 'entgegen' and the continuo reiterates the motto, a reminder of God's promise even though we are succumbing to the ills of human trials. 'Gleich Furcht und Sorg'' is set to (a) in thirds, broken by rests, while the descending idea of the obbligato instruments accompanies it, pitched low to add to its warning solemnity. The librettist's unfortunate introduction of the buried talent brings the poetic side of the duet to a low level, a hindrance to musical inspiration: 'Das Pfund, so er uns ausgethan, will er mit Wucher wieder haben, wenn wir es nur nicht selbst vergraben, so hilft er gern damit es fruchten kann' ('The pound (talent), which He to us (has) given, will He with interest again have, if we it only not itself bury, then helps He willingly that it fructify can'). Bach was evidently nonplussed by this lapse, and merely used the same music over again, with, naturally, much variation, the only way of keeping up interest even at the expense of negativing the significance of the association between verse and sound. At one point he even uses a fourfold repetition of (a), broken by rests, to 'so — hilft — er — gern', a nonsensical treatment of the words, particularly odd after the appropriateness of the figure to 'Furcht und Sorg''.

A fine soprano recitativo secco seizes the opportunity of 'kommt Mühe, Überlast, Neid, Plag' und Falschheit her' ('comes weariness, trouble, envy, torment and falsehood here') for a dramatic episode. Before it is 'What can thee then in thy conduct affright, if to thee, my heart, God Himself the hands reaches? before Whose mere beckoning already all misfortune yields, and Who thee mightily can protect and cover'. Afterwards: 'and strives what thou doest, to disturb and to hinder, let deceit and adversity the purpose not diminish, the work, which He determines, will for no one ever (be) too heavy. Go always joyfully onwards, thou wilt at the end see, that, what thee formerly (has) afflicted, to thee has for thy good happened.'

There is a lovely chorale of confidence and rejoicing, with oboes d'amore, taille, and strings: 'Sing, pray and go in God's ways, Perform thy part only faithfully, And trust in heaven's rich blessing, So will He to thee become new: For who his confidence On God places, him forsakes He not.' It is stanza 7 of G. Neumark's 'Wer nur den lieben Gott läßt walten' with its associated melody. To the inadequacy of the librettist must be laid the blame that this cantata does not reach to the level of No. 56; in spite of this we are grateful for a work of outstanding significance.

In studying these solo cantatas, in which there is no chorus or large orchestra to create an externally imposing effect, one may be forgiven for fearing that the wonders of the church cantatas will never be revealed to the general musical public. Even the vast majority of professional musicians know no more than a handful and have little idea of the immense treasures which lie waiting to be discovered. Routine has so strong a hold over most conductors that there is little effort to make these works known. Even with considerably more public enterprise than is found today, they must remain a closed book to the average music-lover. For one thing, the area they cover is so immense. Were one to attempt to make a selection of the finest the total would be forbidding. For another, many are scarcely suitable for the concert-room, unless there is a choice body of listeners gathered together in a suitable frame of mind. The beauty of a Haydn quartet, a Mozart symphony, a Beethoven sonata, can be appreciated without further acquaintance than a concert performance. It is not so with the cantatas, for the best atmosphere is undoubtedly the church; one is less concerned there with external aspects, one is prepared to accept the moralizings and the homilies as part of a service, the recitatives acquire their rightful significance.

Yet we cannot recapture the spirit of St. Thomas's; the beliefs of eighteenth-century Lutherans are not our beliefs; the seasons of the church years do not mean to the modern world what they did to a people whose life was centred in their church, surrounded by nations holding a faith which they considered detestable; the hymns do not carry the associations now that they did 200 years ago. Germany had no literature save religious; it moulded the mind of every thinking man.

Practical considerations limit the number of performances in churches—we cannot hope for more than occasional hearings under such conditions. Even so, the cantata can only be an additional number, little related or related not at all, to the rest. In Bach's time the Hauptmusik was the central musical event of a long service which was grouped round certain Biblical events or theological discussions. It was prepared for in the hearts of the worshippers, it was followed by relevant matter. We give a cantata side by side with other music, or as one of a group. The effect cannot now be the same. If we try to create the right atmosphere and devote an evening to cantatas, what is to be the proper procedure? If we choose them from the same period of the Church year, variety is lacking. If we vary them in character, then it is impossible to approach each one appropriately. A Christmas cantata needs one outlook, a Whitsun another, and the various incidents in the many Sundays after Trinity have their own significance. We cannot recapture the thrill of trumpets and drums in Easter cantatas after the period of Lent, when there was no concerted music.

Moreover, practical considerations again intervene; Bach used so many different orchestral groups that few concert-giving bodies can arrange a recital of cantatas without weighing carefully the cost of production and deciding selection rather on this ground than for reasons more abstract. Singers who are suitable for one cantata are often not suitable for another; Bach wrote for the special voices at hand at the moment. While first-rate performances of sonatas, quartets, and symphonies are fairly common, the production of a Bach cantata in the right manner and in the right surroundings, with conductor and singers of understanding, is almost an experience of a lifetime. It is not to be wondered at that they are misunderstood; the marvel is that in spite of all these contrary influences they are more performed than ever before. In their own day they were disregarded; Bach poured out treasures of pearls before unheeding and indifferent burghers, and then they passed into complete oblivion. Now, times and conditions and outlook are so much changed that we cannot reincarnate what might, on hundreds of Sundays, have been felt by some few appreciative worshippers.

The intimate connexion between the cantata and the Order of Service for the Day is insisted on frequently in these pages; indeed,

discussion is impossible otherwise. Yet it is only recently that these
details have been available for anyone not a German theologian;
interpreters have been working mostly in the dark. These points cannot be brought home to a general audience, so that only a tithe of the
significance of the music can be grasped. To those who wish to get
to know these priceless works in bulk, Schweitzer's advice is invaluable—to gather a few friends together round a pianoforte and
sing them through. The inadequacies of performance are com-
pensated for by the intimacy of common music-making. Let all the
sopranos sing in unison the recitatives and arias for that voice, and
so on. A previous reading together of the commentaries in this book
and in *Fugitive Notes* will help to get at the kernel of each work.
Afterwards the student, in the solitude of his sanctum (for whom this
book is chiefly written), with the great score in his lap and the
memory of the actual sound of the great music in his mind's ear,
can attune himself to the spirit of the noblest master of all time.

(*b*) CHORAL CANTATAS

Terry's article on the librettists of the cantatas, together with
subsequent alterations given in his *Bach's Cantata Texts*, brings
together all that is known or conjectured up to date. With that subject I do not deal; it would be mere repetition. As an aid, however,
towards classification of the cantatas yet to be discussed under this
heading, a greater bulk than in any previous section, a grouping
under type of libretto may be helpful. The whole of the first Leipzig
period is surveyed; where a cantata has been dealt with already, its
number is given in parentheses. The numbers are given in the order of
the BGS, but in the subsequent discussion of each number in the
group the supposed chronological order will be followed. The texts
of the middle period fall under eight heads:

(i) Unaltered hymns without any extraneous matter: (4), 97,
112, 117, 129, 137, 177, 192.

(ii) Complete and unaltered hymns plus original matter: (80),
140.

(iii) Complete (or almost complete) hymns, but with some verses
paraphrased: 8, 9, 20, 93, 99.

(iv) Biblical text—(191). This is the adaptation from the 'Gloria'
of the B Minor Mass, the Latin scripture version being
employed.

(v) Biblical text plus original matter—'O ewiges Feuer'—unnumbered and incomplete Wedding Cantata.

(vi) Hymn verses plus original matter: 16, 19, (23), (27), (36), (49), (51), (52), (55), (56), (58), 66, 72, 73, (84), 95, 98, 105, 119, (153), (156), (164), (165), (167), (168), (169), (174), (184), (186), (188), (194).

(vii) Biblical (and Apochryphal) quotations plus hymn verses plus original matter: (12), (22), 24, 25, (29), 37, 39, 40, (42), 44, 46, (60), 64, 65, 67, 69, (75), (76), 77, (81), (83), (86), (88), (89), 102, 104, 109, (120), (136), (144), 145, 148, (149), (154), (157), (159), (166), (171), 172, 179, 187, 190, (195), and the incomplete and unnumbered 'Ehre sei Gott'.

(viii) Wholly original matter: (35), (53), (54), 63, (82), (170), 181.

(i) Unaltered Hymns without any Extraneous Matter
97, 112, 117, 129, 137, 177, 192

Order of discussion: 112, 129, 177, 137, 192, 117, 97

It is quite easy to understand why Bach in his middle and late life, as Terry points out, turned more and more to hymns for his libretti. His literary library consisted chiefly of chorale books;[1] his detailed knowledge of their contents and the deep impression they made on his life are revealed over and over again. The best hymns were constructed upon some attractive and logical scheme; their literary merits were of a higher order than was to be expected from the purveyors of cantata texts on whom he otherwise was forced to rely. The hymns were household words with his congregation, who would recognize the original verses even when in the form of paraphrases, and would know the general trend of thought of the entire scheme. The melodies could bind his structures together, they provided splendid opportunities for varied treatment, they were familiar to his people, and called up in their minds associations with particular hymns and seasons. In some cases, such as 'Ein' feste Burg', they were historical documents of their struggles for religious freedom and watchwords in their perilous political circumstances.

It is difficult for us today and in this country to realize how large a part the Bible and the hymns of the church played in the lives of

---

[1] It is not generally known that one of these, a Moravian hymn-book, is in the possession of the Library of Glasgow University. It is the only complete copy of the book in existence, and was presented to Burney by Carl Philipp Emanuel in the latter's study. Burney recorded the gift in his History and inscribed particulars on a fly-leaf of the interesting treasure.

the people and in their common speech. The citizens of Leipzig were nurtured in the church and reared on its services: it was not only the visible symbol of the right to worship in their own way, won by many years of bloody suffering, but it was the token of the civic and national unity of Saxons in a world of relentless enemies. France, Austria, and Spain were inveterate Catholic foes, the Calvinists of Switzerland and Holland were as bitterly opposed to Lutherans as were the Romanists. German states were perpetually at war with one another. This is the explanation of many of Bach's texts and of many of his methods. It must not be forgotten that despite complexity of texture, beyond the intellectual grasp of the majority of his congregation, despite frequently startling harmonic language, far in advance of anything in his day (often, indeed, startling to us), his church music was an appeal to the man in the pew, popular religious music in the best sense of the word. We sometimes think of the master as an introspective composer, interpreting his own feelings only, caring little for the worshippers in the great side-galleries and down in the body of the church, for his obtuse municipal superiors, or for the outside world. Yet that, in a way, is a false impression. His church music faithfully served his congregation, and those members who were not intelligent enough to follow his loftier flights were ever and anon brought face to face with music that was their own music, with texts that were the language of their everyday life, their familiar speech, and their common heritage.

While the use of complete unaltered hymns was attractive in many ways, it brought in its train serious difficulties. The various types of composition found in a cantata, chorus, aria, duet, recitative, arioso, provide a scheme which unites diverse qualities, and they must needs have different rhythmical plans. The unvarying scansion of a number of hymn-verses, sometimes running to twelve, defeats this end. A chorale-stanza is not always cast in a mould suitable for recitative or aria, and problems present themselves which the composer did not always solve satisfactorily. The hymns used, for example, in Nos. 97 and 117, have nine long verses each; a lengthy stanza gives rise to an uncommonly protracted aria. The aria type of his day demanded compact verses, the lines of which were separable, and of which the second part would afford thought and imagery different from what had gone before and lead conclusively to the Da Capo. We often see in the cantatas how recitatives are contrasted with each other— short and long, dramatic and reflective, and contrasted again with choruses and arias. This is not possible in a hymn-cantata, as the text is of the same length in all numbers and there is not sufficient variety of subject-matter; there is generally a comma or a full stop at the end of each line. Moreover, hymns are written for continuous legato singing, a recitative needs more possibilities of broken groups. The magnificent result of his first hymn-cantata, No. 4, was another factor, no doubt, which weighed Bach's inclination towards this type of libretto. The poem of 'Christ lag in Todesbanden', however, is exceptionally varied and dramatic, a series of scenes lending themselves admirably to a succession of contrasted numbers; no other hymn chosen proved as suitable.

112. So far as can be ascertained, it appears that this group of works was written at the close of the middle period, one in 1731, four the following year, and one each in 1733 and 1734. The first of this class to follow No. 4 is one of three (the others are Nos. 85 and 104) inspired by the Epistle (1 Pet. ii. 21–25, ending 'For ye are as sheep going astray') and Gospel (St. John x. 11–16, beginning 'I am the good shepherd') for the Second Sunday after Easter, 8 April. The date is fixed because the text was printed in the *Leipziger Kirchen-Musik* for the year. Wolfgang Meusel's (Musculus) versification of the Twenty-Third Psalm—'Der Herr ist mein getreuer Hirt' ('The Lord is my faithful Shepherd')—would better have been replaced by the Psalm itself, but in spite of unavoidable comparison with the original it is an excellent text for the purpose. There are only five stanzas, and its association with the much-used melody 'Allein Gott in der Höh' sei Ehr'', N. Decius's (Hovesch) adaptation of the 'Gloria in excelsis' plain chant, provides a splendid canto fermo. Nearly all hymn-cantatas open, as one would expect, with a chorale fantasia, though in the case of No. 177 there is merely an extended chorale. In this case the texture of the choral sections is unwontedly simple, and the first line only—d r m f s—is utilized in the lower parts, so that almost all vocal melodic progressions are scale-wise. Two horns begin unaccompanied, I playing a diminished version of line 1, II a repeated note idea which, curiously enough, is never heard again. Corno I doubles the soprano canto fermo throughout, but is not silent in the ritornelli: indeed, it is never granted a single rest. This is one of the most exacting tasks ever set a brass player. Corno II is less continuously employed and is mainly independent, working out a leaping three-crotchet figure— ♩ | ♩ ♩ ♩ —although it occasionally doubles a string line. Two oboes d'amore double the violins, I refraining from playing some of the low string passages only. A gently swaying and falling figure is the chief feature of the upper string lines,

violin I always acting independently of the chorus, but II and viola frequently strengthening the altos and tenors. The continuo mostly occupies itself with a diminished version of the five notes, though from time to time it takes over (*a*). The text paraphrases verses 1 and 2: 'The Lord is my faithful Shepherd, Holds me in His keeping, Therein to me at all nothing lack will at any time for good. He pastures me without ceasing, Whereon grows the well-tasting grass Of His holy word.' The fantasia is one of the most miraculously beautiful things Bach ever wrote; its beatific peace, the fascinating texture produced by the calm scale-wise movement of the voices, the decorative figure and the reiterated calls of corno II, the picture of the Good Shepherd moving serenely at the head of His contented flock, hold one spellbound as if by a vision. It is not easy to secure a perfect performance, simple though most of the writing is; the utmost reticence, delicacy, and subtlety are required from the orchestra.

A longish alto aria, not of the most spontaneous character, with oboe d'amore obbligato, is a scene of the countryside, waters running through green pastures. The initial line of the chorale, inverted, is apparent in the opening oboe d'amore phrase:

and, exact or modified, it is associated with the beginning of four vocal clauses: 'Zum reinen Wasser er mich weist, das mich erquicken thue' ('To pure water He me directs, that me refresh may'); 'Das ist sein fronheiliger Geist, der macht mich wohlgemuthe' ('It is His holy Spirit, which makes me joyous'); 'Er führet mich auf rechter Straß' seiner Geboten ohn' Ablaß' ('He guides me on the right road of His commandments without ceasing'). The last clause is treated fully: 'von wegen seines Namens willen' ('on account of His name's sake'). The voice borrows trickling streams of semiquavers from the introduction for 'fronheiliger' and 'Geist', and fragments of the opening notes of the chorale are frequently heard in the continuo. The continuo accompanies the bass in the first part of an arioso-recitative, verse 4 of the Psalm, the chief figure portraying the descent into the valley of darkness:

Ex. 690

The voice thrice sings 'Und ob ich wandert' im finstern Thal, fürcht' ich kein Ungelücke' ('And though I wander in the dark valley, fear I no misfortune'), alternating with the bassi the chief part of the theme quoted. (See Ex. 1260.) The second section is an adagio arioso —'in persecution, sorrow, trouble, and this world's wiles'—with beautifully expressive chromatic harmonies. It modulates from A♭, stepping there suddenly from G minor, to F minor. With 'for Thou art with me constantly' it moves from a chord of F minor through a brief dissonance to the comforting chord of E major. (See Ex. 1317.) From this to the end it modulates through A minor to G major, a message of peace and confidence: 'Thy rod and staff comfort me, on Thy word I me rely.'

A joyous feast-song follows, verse 5 of the Psalm; a bright, strongly rhythmic string melody:

Ex. 691   Vl. I
Va.
Cont.

and leaping bassi arpeggi tell of the delight of the delivered when assembled at a table 'in presence of mine enemies'. The anointing with oil is suggested by many triplet runs, and a short triplet figure in violin I,

Ex. 692

adds cries of intense happiness. The S.T. lines of the duet are pitched somewhat uncomfortably high at times, but the tessitura produces a feeling of almost unrestrained exhilaration. Tenor and soprano sing in turn, 'Du bereitest für (? vor) mir einen Tisch vor mein'n Feinden allenthalben' ('Thou preparest for (? before) me a table before mine enemies everywhere'), and then each sings shortened and altered versions. After a repetition of the introduction the vocal section comes again to 'machst mein Herze unverzagt und frisch, mein Haupt thust du mir salben' ('makest my heart undismayed and fresh, my head dost Thou for me anoint'), with the voice parts reversed. The triplet runs connect with the next clause: 'mit deinem Geist, der Freuden Oel' ('with Thy spirit, the joy oil'). The vocal lines begin with a modification of the opening melody, but 'Freuden' departs from it, running along in triplets. This ornate section dovetails into the last: 'und schenkest voll ein meiner Seel' deiner geistlichen Freuden' ('and pourest out fully in my soul Thy spiritual joy'). Again the chief melody is fitted to the words, in subdominant and tonic, and an animated development leads to a Da Capo of the introduction. It will be seen that both in aria and duet Bach departs from the customary aria form in order to accommodate them to the hymn-verses.

Interesting features of the final chorale, verse 6 of the Psalm, are slightly independent oboe d'amore passages and a chuckling little corno II fragment on the two last chords. The paraphrase runs: 'Goodness and mercy Follow me after in life, And I shall remain everlastingly In the house of the Lord assuredly: On earth in the Christian community; And after the death there shall I be With Christ, my Lord.' Strongly contrasted though Nos. 4 and 112 are, they stand at the head of all the pure hymn-cantatas.

129. The four that may be placed in 1732, the first definitely, the others conjecturally, are Nos. 129, 177, 137, and 192, for Trinity Sunday, the Fourth and Twelfth Sundays after, and the Reformation Festival respectively. J. Olearius's 'Gelobet sei der Herr' ('Praised be the Lord') is one of the hymns set for Trinity. The obstructions lurking in a text not designed for cantata purposes reveal themselves at once. The entire hymn is one of praise, little change of mood is possible, although verses 1–3 refer to the members of the Trinity in turn. Of the five stanzas 1–4 begin with the same words, and the initial lines of 1–3 are identical. Variety is thus negatived. i and v, in which

the anonymous melody, 'O Gott, du frommer Gott', is used, the latter
being an extended chorale (see B.E.C. No. 12, O.) are splendidly
orchestrated—three trumpets, timpani, flauto traverso, two oboes,
and strings—used with striking resilience. In the fantasia the brilliant
violin I part, with its vigorous passage work,

and its far-flung leaps,

is doubled nearly all the way by flute and violin II. The trumpets
often burst in with short, crackling fanfares:

The lower voice parts are very animated and never sing any themes
derived from the canto. The chorale is confined solely to the sopranos:
'Praised be the Lord, my God, my light, my life; My Creator, Who
to me has My body and soul given; My Father, Who me protects
From the womb onwards, Who every instant Much good for me
(has) done.' It is a stirring number and the pioneer of many great and
magnificent chorale fantasias with independent orchestra. No. 112,
though surpassing it in beauty, almost seems a miniature by its side.

The extended chorale, v, mates it on terms of equality: 'To Whom
we the "Holy" now With joy cause to resound, And with the angel
host The Holy, Holy sing; Him heartily praises and lauds The whole
Christendom: Praised be my God In all eternity!' The flute doubles
the canto at the octave above, but the other instruments are mostly
independent; brass and percussion, oboes, upper strings are treated
as three groups answering one another. The reference to the 'angel

host' explains the presence in the orchestra of the two-note angel-motive:

The chief instrumental theme,

embodying the joy-motive, is announced by tromba I and is also used by oboes and upper strings. There are impulsive shouts from the angel hosts and the redeemed:

Bach evidently considered stanzas 2–4 unsuitable for recitative, so we find a succession of arias, B., S., and A., a weakness in construction. ii, dealing with the Son, is with continuo only, which, after a graceful descent,

based on notes 1–4 of the canto fermo (the significance is obvious), indulges in many wild leaps of joy:

The appoggiature given at the beginning of bars 2 and 4 are often absent subsequently. This is frequently the case in the cantatas, graces differ between instrument and voice, between one instrument and another. Must one assume that the first-written appoggiature were intended as an example and that singer and player were expected to introduce similar ones at identical places? As an appoggiatura gives a special character to melody and harmony one must assume that this is an unwritten law. The voice begins with a modification of the continuo theme,

Ex 701

during which, as will be seen, the bassi keep the principal figure in prominence. Even Bach's prodigious basses could not be expected to negotiate Ex. 700, so a long run on 'gelobet' outlines the passage and introduces many allusions to the joy-motive. The leaps are prominent in the continuo during the early part of 'des Vaters liebster Sohn, der sich für mich gegeben' ('the Father's dearest Son, Who Himself for me (has) given'). After an interlude based on both ideas a more tender phrase comes to 'der mich erlöset hat mit seinem theuren Blut' ('Who me redeemed has with His precious blood'), with a joyous run on the last 'erlöset' and references to both themes by the continuo, the second forming the next interlude. A gracious winding melody comes to 'der mir in Glauben schenkt sich selbst' ('Who to me in faith bestows Himself'), and with that marvellous resourcefulness which perpetually astonishes one, there is a new form of (a) in the bassi. A long run on 'höchste' ('das höchste Gut', 'the highest good') is supported by (a) entire. Almost the whole of the 'gelobet' run is set to 'Glauben'; splendid drops of sevenths occur to 'sich selbst' above the wild leaps.

Line 1 is s m r d s s l, dwelling on the submediant. iii also begins with a phrase which reaches upward to the sixth note and stresses it:

Ex.702 Fl.tr.

Although the progression is merely scalewise, the resemblance can
scarcely be accidental, and the same outline is to be found in iv, proceeding from the lower dominant:

Ex.703

The soprano aria, speaking of the Holy Ghost, has an obbligato
for flauto traverso and violin solo, and a prominent feature is the
little group (*a*), evidently indicating the quickening of the mortal
spirit by the divine Third Person of the Trinity. The introduction,
after a four-bar melody, develops (*a*). The ritornello is reconstructed
for the first vocal section—'Gelobet sei der Herr, mein Gott, mein
Trost, mein Leben, des Vaters werther Geist, den mir der Sohn gegeben' ('Praised be the Lord, my God, my comfort, my life, the
Father's worthy Spirit, Who to me the Son (has) given')—and there is
a lengthy trilled flourish on 'Leben'. After an interlude based on (*a*),
there is another vocal section, based on the first, with the same words
and ending on the dominant. The introduction is repeated in this
key, but, in keeping with Bach's meticulous care, the obbligato parts
are interchanged. 'Der mir mein Herz erquickt, der mir giebt neue
Kraft, der mir in aller Noth Rath, Trost und Hülfe schafft' ('Who in
me my heart quickens, Who to me gives new strength, Who for me in
all need, counsel, comfort and help provides') brings a new melody
and, appropriately, (*a*) predominates in the orchestra. A shortened
form of the introduction stresses again the necessity to praise the
Almighty and a longer vocal section to the same words follows. It
opens with yet another melody, but the rising scalic sixth is sung to
'der mir giebt neue Kraft'. To six bars on the (*a*) part of the introduction are added bold leaping passages on the two first clauses and
then 'schafft' is sung to the trilling 'Leben' run. The command to
praise is reinforced by a repetition of the introduction. A curious
structural feature is that when the voice enters after the first ritornello, it does not repeat the initial theme at once, but for two bars
sings a flourish on 'Gelobet', a prolongation of the theme before
proceeding on its way.

The alto aria (see P. 63) is a lengthy and tender pastoral. The oboe
d'amore obbligato begins with a lovely melody of twenty-four bars
(see Ex. 703); this comes again in the middle of the aria, commencing

in the dominant and leading to the tonic, and then again at the end in its original form. Thus, counting another ritornello, there are no fewer than eighty-two bars without the voice. Probably Bach was already growing restive under the circumscribed conditions imposed by hymn-verses, and decided to cut the Gordian knot by concentrating on the instrumental side of the number. 'Gelobet sei der Herr, mein Gott, der ewig lebet' ('Praised be the Lord, my God, Who ever lives') is sung to the quoted theme, into which the oboe d'amore neatly fits an imitation. The answering clause follows, instrumentally. The Scarlattian repetition brings the whole of the introduction, with interesting modifications; there is a new counterpoint to the theme, as the oboe d'amore continues the melody the voice sings a free inversion of the first figure: at 'den Alles lobet' ('Whom everything praises') the obbligato ceases and the singer flourishes on 'Alles' and 'lobet', the oboe d'amore resuming its line part-way through the latter. In the continuation the word 'schwebet' ('was in allen Lüften schwebet', 'that in all heavens hovers') is allotted a run, and the original sentence is elongated in order to permit of a further and lengthier run on this word. In the remainder the motto-line of the text always associated with the chorale line—'deß Name heilig heißt, Gott Vater, Gott der Sohn, und Gott der heil'ge Geist' ('Whose name holy is called, God Father, God the Son, and God the Holy Ghost')—is generally sung to material fashioned from earlier ideas, but it once receives picturesque treatment.

177. No. 177, for the Fourth Sunday after Trinity, 6 July, has also five verses and the three middle numbers are again arias. One distinctive feature is the high degree of elaboration of the orchestral texture in all numbers except v, which is a plain chorale. The Gospel, St. Luke vi. 36–42, begins, 'Be ye therefore merciful, as your Father also is merciful. Judge not, and ye shall not be judged', and the appointed hymn selected, J. Agricola's (Schneider) 'Ich ruf' zu dir, Herr Jesu Christ', is a plea for mercy and consolation, affording an excellent opportunity for the composer. The fantasia employs, in addition to two oboes and strings, a violino concertante, which has many florid passages, recalling the style of the slow movement of a violin concerto. The oboes double the canto fermo and are much occupied when that is silent. The first suggests the agonized cry of the sufferer by many lengthily sustained notes. Frequently the continuo is silent and from time to time are the unusual directions 'senza Organo' and 'con Organo'. Except where there is doubling, the canto is only employed at one point in the orchestra, although the falling third which opens it,

Ex.704

may perhaps be considered the source of notes 1–3 of oboe II, and of accompaniment figures often found in the lower strings and continuo. The exception is before the final line; the oboes anticipate the coming melody, inverted in repeated quavers, and then the continuo takes it up, also in its original form. All the chorale lines except the last two are prefaced by long passages for the lower voices, the motives of the first four being a rising fifth or sixth, a cry to the Almighty. In order to avoid the mechanical effect of nine isolated lines, each with pre-liminary matter, 5, 6, and 7 are continuous vocally. In the two latter the lower voices utilize the canto line in anticipation, otherwise their material is independent. Lines 8 and 9 begin without vocal prelude. At the end of the canto the sopranos continue for four bars with fresh matter, and Bach meticulously refrains from adding the oboes to this deviation from the strict letter of the law. It is a powerful and emo-tional chorus, on an immense scale, nearly 300 bars of slow tempo. The melody is that associated with the hymn, and the text from line 2 onwards is: 'I beg: hear my complaint, Bestow on me grace at this time, Let me then not despair; The right faith, Lord, I believe, It wilt Thou me grant, To Thee to live, To my neighbour helpful to be, Thy word to hold exactly.'

A nine-line stanza is not suitable for aria form, no Da Capo is possible and opportunities for repetition are limited. Bach treats his lines almost as if they were sung to a chorale melody, though much more floridly; as clauses 1 and 2 of the hymn-tune are repeated for lines 3 and 4 of the stanza, so in the alto aria (with continuo) the music is repeated in varied form, even though appropriateness to the text disappears. For example, 'geben' in line 2 ('du kannst es mir wohl geben', 'Thou canst it to me well give') is set to a lovely run of over four bars, which is meaningless the second time to 'dar-neben' ('die Hoffnung gieb darneben', 'the hope give besides'). The opening of the verse—'Ich bitt' noch mehr, noch mehr, O Herre Gott' ('I ask yet more, yet more, O Lord God'—the repetition is the composer's) gives rise to the two chief continuo ideas, which are never heard vocally—a five-note figure, repeated over and over again, separated by short rests,

Ex.705 (a)

significant of incessant praying (the connexion with Ex. 704 is obvious), and a semiquaver phrase of nearly two bars, in which the outline rises by semitones,

Ex.706 (b)

—the ascent of prayer. These are of no particular significance when lines 3 and 4 are sung (the former 'daß ich werd' nimmermehr zu Spott', 'that I shall nevermore (be delivered) to mockery'), but they are appropriate to the mood of the verse as a whole.· Line 1 of the chorale is elaborated into:

Ex.707

Ich bitt' noch mehr, noch mehr, o Her - re Gott,
((a) in the continuo)

The vocal melody of line 2 is changed in an interesting way in line 4 in order to stress 'Hoffnung'. With line 5—'Voraus, wenn ich muß hier davon' ('Before, when I must here from (go)')—a new continuo figure is introduced, the only departure from (a) and (b). With 6— 'daß ich dir mög' vertrauen' ('that I Thee may trust')—(b) is expanded and the singer has an expressive phrase to 'vertrauen'. 'Und nicht bauen' ('And not build') allots a meaningless passage to 'bauen'; 'auf alles mein Thun' ('on all my doings') is appropriately florid on 'alles'. It is difficult to see any meaning in a long ascending passage on 'reuen' ('sonst wird mich's ewig reuen', 'else shall I of it eternally repent'), nor in the rising sequence on (a). It is not often that Bach reveals himself to be so much baffled by his text.

    The whole canto fermo is not heard in the arias, although in all three the initial vocal notes are the dropping third of the chorale melody, disguised in the second aria by an appoggiatura, in which form it is found in the closing simple chorale. The plan of ii is not followed in iii, which is for soprano, with a very elaborate obbligato for oboe da caccia, the instrument being possibly chosen to secure a sombre colour, as the verse speaks of the enemies of the believer. The introduction tells of a beatific peace despite the opposition of the outside world, and the opening melody, which is echoed immediately, is modified for the beginning of the vocal line:

Line 3—'verzeih' mir auch zu dieser Stund'' ('pardon me also in this hour')—is set to a dominant modification of this vocal and instrumental section, with the upper parts reversed, and later a portion of the second half of the introduction is heard on the oboe da caccia,

which is never found in the vocal line. 'Gieb mir ein neues Leben' ('Give me a new life') rounds off the section, introducing new material and a run on 'Leben' which had been foreshadowed at the close of the introduction. The opening theme and this run constitute a brief interlude. The remainder of the verse—'dein Wort mein'

Speis' laß allweg sein, damit mein' Seel' zu nähren, mich zu wehren, wenn Unglück geht daher, das mich bald möcht' abkehren' ('Thy word my food let always be, wherewith my soul to nourish, me to defend, when misfortune comes along, which me soon might turn away')—is twice heard complete, in two sections. The initial theme of the earlier begins with a fresh melody, but 'allweg sein' reproduces that of 'Herzens Grund', only slightly amended. 'Nähren' and 'wehren' are allotted runs and the coming along of misfortune is portrayed by a long succession of continuo semiquavers, during the latter part of which the mental distress of the believer and the possibility of his turning from the true path are indicated by syncopations. A fine passage occurs to a subsequent setting of 'wenn Unglück', the bassi climbing slowly by semitones through a stretch of a seventh. At the close of the section 'abkehren' is broken in twain by a rest. A brief interlude recapitulates part of the opening melody and a new melody opens the second division of the text. There are hints at previous material, though the whole treatment is different and there are more syncopations for the voice. The rising bassi passage recurs, but not till the end does the original material reappear. These are numbers which can never achieve their full effect in a concert-room, they need the atmosphere of the church. This is so often the case with Bach's arias, especially those which have no accompaniment but continuo. In concert-rooms the public looks for more colour, listeners are not so ready to accept an intimate meditation, to be willing to join in introspective communings with one's own soul. In preparing performances one is often deeply impressed with some number which, when the time comes, fails to make its expected effect. The music is too true to its own purpose, too truly church music and nothing else, it shrinks sensitively when exposed to the glare of a concert-room. It is the same with Palestrina and with the Masses and Great Service of Byrd.

The tenor aria is more externally attractive. The lines 'Laß mich kein' Lust noch Furcht von dir in dieser Welt abwenden' ('Let me no desire nor fear from Thee in this world turn away') are summarized in the opening bars. The continuo boldly repeats a note, an idea which is afterwards emphasized by octave leaps:

Ex.710 (a)

Cont.

and

We see the full significance of this when the words 'Beständigsein an's End' gieb mir, du hast's allein in Händen' ('Steadfastness to the end grant me, Thou hast it solely in (Thy) hands') are repeated. The hammered note, in both forms, is allotted to the first clause and the leaps are heard in the concertante line. Violino concertante and fagotto obbligato play passages which seem to turn and hesitate before proceeding on their way:

and:

Combined with (e) is a figure which becomes important in the last vocal section:

and a violin sequence formed from the initial four notes is accompanied by swirling bassoon scales and ♪ ♩ leaps for the continuo. The vocal line begins with a reference to the chorale (Ex. 716). The instrumental portion of this is entirely new; part of the introduction is repeated, the voice being free. 'Welt abwenden' is set to (d), with (b) in the concertante. While the obbligato instruments play (d) in tenths, the voice leaps determinedly, incorporating an octave jump from (b). During further florid passages to 'Welt

Ex.716

abwenden' the sequence on (f) is heard in the bassoon. The whole of the introduction and this section are now repeated, an unusual procedure, dictated, no doubt, by the problems of writing an aria to a hymn-verse. The new text is set to (g); after that there are differences in the vocal line, the chief being the use of (a) and (b). Runs are inappropriate to 'hast's', 'allein', and 'Händen', though the spaciousness of the music causes one to overlook this pouring of new wine into old bottles. The twelve-bar introduction is condensed into an eight-bar interlude, the latter portion with reversed obbligati parts. The remainder of the verse—'und wem du's giebst, der hat's umsonst; es kann Niemand ererben, noch erwerben durch Werke deine Gnad', die uns erret't vom Sterben' ('and to whom Thou it bestowest, he has it free; it can no one inherit, nor acquire through works Thy mercy, Which us delivers from death')—enables the composer to provide a strong contrast to the earlier vocal sections, even though much of the instrumental material is utilized. The singer pursues a fresh melody, (f), and fragments of (e) are heard in the obbligati instruments, and hints at (c) in all orchestral lines. With 'Sterben' come a sudden pianissimo hush and slower movement; the last 'die uns erett't' introduces the tear-motive. The (f) sequence is played by the bassi as an interlude, violin and bassoon add lively counterpoints. The vocal section is repeated modified and then 'Sterben' is allotted a beautiful chromatic melisma, the continuo pulsating and the obbligati sustaining. A forte delivery of the last clause, voice and continuo only, with unrelated material, leads to a reprise of the introduction. The fagotto obbligato is one of the finest for that instrument in the cantatas.

The final chorale is 'I lie in strife and resist, Help, Oh Lord Christ, the weak one! To Thy grace alone I cling, Thou canst me stronger make. Comes now temptation, Lord, so defend That it me not subverts,

Thou canst judge That to me it (may) not bring danger; I know Thou wilt it not allow.' While every number is notable in itself, the scheme of the cantata is not satisfactory; the immense opening chorus followed by three long arias, all requiring close concentration, demands too much from the listener.

137. No. 137 has no special connexion with the Twelfth Sunday after Trinity (in this case 31 August 1732), nor is the hymn one of those appointed. This Sunday, however, came near the Town Council Election service, and, as in the case of No. 69, production at both was intended, so that the needs of municipal celebrations were in mind when the text was selected. J. Neander's hymn 'Lobe den Herren, den mächtigen König der Ehren' has certain points in common with the libretto of No. 129; there are five stanzas, all of praise, and all begin alike. Bach, in the light of his recent experiments, is beginning to learn how to outwit the unyielding character of such a hymn, and here provides a splendid work of unflagging interest. For the first time since No. 4 the canto fermo, the anonymous 'Hast du denn, Liebster, dein Angesicht' is introduced into every number; in some similar instances later the method proves slightly mechanical, but here it is spontaneous. The fantasia employs three trumpets and timpani, two oboes and strings. The open key of C major adds to the festal character of the whole. Lines 1 and 2 are: 'Praise the Lord, the mighty King of honours, My beloved soul, that is my desire' ('meine geliebte Seele, das ist mein Begehren'). Two motives appear simultaneously, a leaping syncopated figure in the oboes and one in unison for the upper strings:

The rest of the material of the ritornello is based mainly on the joy-motive:

the climax being (a) in trumpets I and II, combined with (b) in violas and bassi and fragments of (c) alternating between violins and oboes,

followed by (c) in all the upper instruments. A figure in the middle
of the introduction,

against (c) and a syncopated arpeggio, is heard often in the remainder
of the number. The canto fermo is delivered by the sopranos, though
not in long notes as is usually the case. (b) never appears in the choral
lines, but acts as instrumental counterpoint. The lower voices utilize
no fragments of the canto, but preface lines 1 and 2, leading off
fugally with a form of (a), the upward thrust of a sixth producing
an effect unsuspected when it is first heard in the oboes,

followed by (c) accompanied by (b) and (d), the latter in another form.
With the entry of the canto brass and percussion reappear, the oboes
doubling the melody. The introduction is repeated and the music of
line 1 serves for line 2. In the introduction the upper trumpets
reiterate quavers, in the ritornello (b) is now played by upper strings
in this way, trombe I and II deliver (a), the oboes alternate (c); then
(d) with its companion ideas and brilliant reiterated quavers for the
trumpets, leads into lines 3 and 4: 'Kommet zu Hauf', Psalter und
Harfen, wacht auf!' ('Come in multitudes, psaltery and harps,
awake!'). These are set block-wise, with no preliminary matter and
with only one orchestral bar between. Line 3 is accompanied in the
foregoing manner, during 4 all the trumpets play (d), an overwhelming peal of rejoicing, oboes and upper strings leap through
arpeggi. It is a stirring interlude between the two contrapuntal choral
sections. There is now a 15-bar interlude, with (a), (b), (c), and (d),
the last being heard for the first time in the bassi. The final line—
'Laßet die Musicam Hören' ('Let the music (be) heard')—is pre-

luded vocally by (*e*), and (*a*) rings out in the highest notes of tromba I
as the line concludes.

The alto chorale (see O.C.S. 'Praise to the Highest') is familiar to
all as No. 6 of the Schübler organ preludes, albeit in that form the
violin solo obbligato lies awkwardly on the keyboard, and there is
no clue for those who do not know the cantata to the fact that its
lovely fluttering and soaring passages are due to a reference in the
hymn-verse to eagles' wings:

Ex.721

and

Ex.722

Ex.723

The chorale is written in $\frac{3}{4}$ and much elaborated. The text is 'Praise
the Lord, Who all things so gloriously governs, Who thee on eagles'
wings securely guided (has), Who thee holds, As it thee thyself
pleases; Hast thou not this perceived?'

Verse 3, a S.B. duet with two oboes, is based mainly on four ideas,
or, rather, on two pairs of twin themes. Line 1 of the canto is transformed into

Ex.724 Ob.I.
(a)

and:

Ex.725
(b)

Lo - be den Her - ren, der künst - lich und fein (dich bereitet,)
Praise the Lord,   who skilfully   and beautifully (thee prepares,)

While oboe I plays graceful phrases oboe II adds a counterpoint embodying the joy-motive:

its counterpart is vocal:

The arpeggio of (a) appears in the oboes during line 1, the remainder is with continuo only, mostly occupied with the arpeggio, direct and inverted. (d) occurs thrice in the soprano, as a rising sequence, above a long-sustained 'lobe' for the bass. The introduction is repeated. Line 2—'der dir Gesundheit verliehen, dich freundlich geleitet' ('Who to thee health granted (has), thee kindly led (has)'),—is the same musically as line 1, with oboe and voice parts reversed and the sequence allotted to one word only—'geleitet'. The next interlude reproduces the introduction in the dominant, with obbligato parts reversed. Line 3, 'in wieviel Noth' ('in how much need'), is a canon at the fourth, the corresponding line of the canto being transformed into two expressive chromatic versions, the continuo moving in sequential crotchet passages, and the oboes imitating each other with falling stepwise quavers. In the last bar the arpeggio in both oboes dovetails into lines 4 and 5: 'hat nicht der gnädige Gott über dir Flügel gebreitet!' ('has not the merciful God over thee wings spread!'). These are set to the same music as lines 1 and 2, the oboes being more active, a canonical figure suggests the spreading of wings and they join in the joy-motive. It was noticed in the last cantata discussed that the first group of lines was repeated with altered treatment. The same plan is adopted here with the later ones. After a ritornello, the introduction in the subdominant minor, 'in wieviel Noth' comes in another guise, the voices beginning together, instead of separately, the chromatics extended, and the arpeggio figure for the oboes instead of descending scales. The remainder is as before, with voices reversed and oboes also in the opposite order. During

the last few bars 'gütige' ('good') is substituted for 'gnädige',
possibly a slip of the pen.

Extravagant joy is indicated in the continuo motive of iv, a two-
bar idea beginning with a flying scale, either up or down, followed
by downward arpeggi involving such leaps as tenths and twelfths:

Ex.728

It is heard no fewer than thirty-four times, and with no other material
save for a single bar! A trumpet peals out the canto fermo, the solo
voice is tenor. Line 1—'Lobe den Herren, der deinen Stand sichtbar
gesegnet' ('Praise the Lord, Who thy state visibly blessed (has)') is
ornate, with runs on 'lobe' and 'gesegnet'. Here as in the previous
number Bach makes use of the appoggiatura sign ↘. At certain
periods he favoured this notation instead of a written grace-note.
Two bars of the continuo figure suffice here and on the next occasion
for interludes. The bassi for line 2—'der aus dem Himmel mit
Strömen der Liebe geregnet' ('Who from the heaven with streams
of love rained (has)') is the same as for line 1. The vocal part, however, is mostly different, the streaming down of love being vividly
depicted. After a short interlude comes a reflective section—'denke
d'ran, was der Allmächtige kann' ('think thereon, what the Almighty
can (do)')—though the continuo pursues its motive unceasingly.
After the tromba delivers line 4 there is a great flourish on 'Allmächtige'. At the third bar of the interlude the trumpet enters with the
last line, and two bars later the voice imitates—'der dir mit Liebe
begegnet' ('Who thee with love meets')—the only vocal quotation
from the canto fermo. Freed from the superimposition of the hymn-
melody, the singer indulges in a seven-bar flourish on the verb,
derived from the 'gesegnet' run of line 1.

Oboes and strings double the voices in the closing chorale; brass
and percussion are independent, tromba I concluding brilliantly on
high C, befitting an exultant stanza—'Praise the Lord, what in me
is, praise His name! All that breath has, praise with Abraham's seed!
He is thy light, Soul, forget it never; Ye praising one, Close with
Amen!' The setting was transferred to the incomplete wedding
cantata, 'Herr Gott, Beherrscher aller Dinge.' The more amenable
text, the splendour of the opening chorus, the haunting beauty of the

alto chorale, the loveliness of the duet and the compelling vigour of the tenor aria combine to make a much more attractive cantata than the preceding one.

192. No. 192 is unlike the other hymn-cantatas of the period and raises conjectural points. The date can only be guessed and the Reformation Festival is assumed. It is vastly different in style from the other two known to have been written for those occasions, Nos. 79 and 80. These are resplendent with brass and percussion; No. 192 has only two transverse flutes, two oboes and strings. It does not rise to the heights of its fellows in inspiration and the conclusion seems singularly unsuitable for such a day of triumphant national rejoicing. M. Rinkart's well-known 'Nun danket Alle Gott' ('Now thank we all our God' in the English version) has three verses only. The ritornello to stanza 1 commences with a three-part passage which is afterwards combined with line 2 of the canto fermo, a semiquaver idea for unison violin I and flauto I,

Ex.729 (a)

a repeated note theme in unison violin II and viola, almost identical with the fugal subject in No. 21, ii, and sustained notes for the oboes:

Ex.730
(c) Ob I.II.
VI.II.
Va.   (b)

(a) and (b) are developed considerably. A duet phrase for oboes,

Ex.731 (d)

answered by flutes and clenched by two fuller bars in upper strings, with figures inverted, all accompanied by detached notes on every beat in the continuo (a device much used afterwards), serves as relief from the tutti. The plan of the choral parts is unusual. The soprano intones J. Crüger's melody, but sometimes joins in the prologues to the lines. The tenor part of the entire cantata is missing from the manuscript; it has been skilfully supplied by Breitkopf's editor, thus enabling the work to be put into use. This voice, accompanied by S.A.B., leads off with a double theme, a sustained melodic phrase,

Ex.732

Now thank all God,
Nun dan - - ket Al - - le Gott,

then a leaping one to line 2:

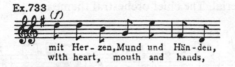

Ex.733

mit Her- zen,Mund und Hän-den,
with heart, mouth and hands,

These are repeated by the alto but (*f*) only is developed subsequently. The orchestra punctuates with a chord on every beat. The soprano sings one line of the hymn only, although the lower voices are using two. (*a*), (*b*), and (*c*) are heard in the orchestra. The duet episodes are repeated and lead to line 2 of the foundational melody, which enters without vocal prologue and which is accompanied by (*a*), (*b*), and (*c*) in the orchestra, and by (*b*) in the lower voices. The last six bars of the introduction herald lines 3 and 4—'der große Dinge thut an uns und allen Enden' ('Who great things does in us and all places') —which receive identical treatment. After (*d*), (*a*), and (*b*) line 5 is prefaced by a long development of a fresh version of (*e*), this time coming in all the lower voices, associated with 'der uns von Mutterleib' ('Who us from (the) mother-womb'), sounding much more tender than in its original setting, and accompanied by a portion of the orchestra only, with short semiquaver tremblings for the flutes, a realistic reference to the movements of the unborn child—a piece of naïve imagery also found elsewhere. Lines 5 and 6 are practically continuous in the canto, only two bars separating them, while the lower voices maintain their movement. Lines 6—'und Kindesbeinen an' ('and (from) infancy on'), 7—'unzählig viel zu gut' ('inestimably much for good'), and 8—'und noch jetzund gethan' ('and still now (has) done')—are sung by the lower voices after the version of (*e*), beginning with a variant of (*b*). Bars 1–4 of the introduction, in the dominant and with (*b*) in the bassi instead of violin II and viola,

(e) in A minor and E minor, and the string version in the subdominant, C, join the chief entries of lines 6 and 7. The variant of
(b) dominates the lower voices. The final ritornello begins in C, with
the combination (a), (b), and (c) twice, and an elongation of (b) in
the continuo. A bar after the return to the tonic the composer springs
a surprise—the choir thunders out 'Nun danket Alle Gott, nun, nun
danket Alle Gott' to conclude. It is a curious scheme and nothing
akin to it is found in any other chorale fantasia.

Stanza 2 is set as a S.B. duet with strings, flauto I and oboe I
doubling violin I throughout. The vocal part is cast in two sections,
with an instrumental interlude, four lines in each, with identical
thematic material. The chief orchestral theme is,

Ex.734
(a)   Fl.I. Ob.I. Vl.I.

and a figure emerges later:

Ex.735 (b)

It is always interesting to see how Bach deals in solo numbers with
the problems imposed by hymn-verses. The bass begins,

Ex.736

(we pray that)   Der   e - wig   rei - che   Gott
                 the   ever   rich   God

accompanied by (a), and continues 'woll' uns bei unserm Leben
ein immer fröhlich' Herz und edlen Frieden geben' ('wished (to) us in
our lifetime an ever joyful heart and noble peace to give'), in
animated melody, accompanied by ♫ | ♩ in the upper strings.
The soprano now takes up the long theme, the orchestral portion is
repeated, and the bass adds a counterpoint. Then the first portion of
the second part of the subject is developed and added to, the whole
text being employed; there are runs on 'fröhlich'. Except for the
♫ | ♩ figure the orchestral matter is new until (a) clenches the
close of the section. The portion of the introduction beginning with

(*b*) forms the ritornello. The soprano leads off with (*c*)—'und uns in seiner Gnad'' ('and us in His mercy')—and continues with a modification of the succeeding melody to 'erhalten fort und fort, und uns aus aller Noth erlösen hier und dort' ('sustain continually, and us out of all need redeem here and there'). The bass follows and the music of section I is pursued till the end, with reversed parts, the soprano sometimes deviating from the former bass line. A break occurs to emphasize the final 'und uns aus aller Noth erlösen hier und dort', in which there is the only departure from the previous orchestral accompaniment—(*a*) is shortened in order to allow the voices to conclude in the conventional way, with continuo only. The runs on 'fröhlich' fit, appropriately, to 'aller'. While bright and effective, the duet is not particularly notable.

Stanza 3 is set as a $\frac{12}{8}$ pastoral, the most charming number of the cantata, producing a quiet and meditative conclusion where the nature of the hymn would lead one to expect something more vigorous, especially as the verse is a resounding doxology: 'Laud, honour and praise be to God, To the Father and to the Son, And to Him, Who to both equal (is) In high heaven's throne, To the three-in-one God, As Who first was, And is and remain will, Now and always.' Possibly Bach's meaning was that peace had been won by the struggles of Luther, and that the Good Shepherd had led His flock into green pastures. The two upper lines of the strings are each doubled by a flute and an oboe, adding to the pastoral character. The chief orchestral theme is

Ex.737 Fl.I.Ob.I.Vl.I.

and the last five notes are beautifully developed in this manner:

Ex.738

The lower voices do not quote the foundational melody, but sweep along almost incessantly in triplets. It may be that Bach, as elsewhere, intended the triplets to be symbolical of the Trinity.

117. One wonders why Bach chose for the next two cantatas hymns running to nine stanzas each, with seven and six lines respectively. As both are for unspecified occasions we do not know if some circumstances dictated the selection of the poems. He deals somewhat summarily with J. J. Schütz's 'Sei Lob und Ehr' dem höchsten Gut' to form No. 117. Stanzas 4 and 9 are sung to the same four-part setting. It is strange that he who was so meticulous in his chorale settings should allow the same harmonization to stand for lines 1–4 of stanza 4, 'I cry to the Lord in my need: Ah God, hear my crying! Then assisted my helper me from death And let to me comfort increase', and the corresponding lines of 9, 'So come before His countenance With exultant leaping; Pay the vowed allegiance, And let us joyfully sing'. This illustrates his rather casual attitude to the text of this cantata; perhaps it was prepared in desperate haste. The orchestration of these two numbers is not even indicated. The rest of the stanzas mate. 4 is 'Therefore thank, ah God, therefore thank I Thee; ah thank, thank God with me! Give to our God the honour!' —and 9—'God has it all well thought And all, all well wrought! Give to our God the honour!' The first part of verse 2 is a brief bass recitativo secco—'There thank Thee the heavenly hosts; Oh Lord of all thrones, and those (who) on earth, air and sea in Thy shadow dwell; they praise Thy creator-might, Which all so well thought has'. There is an expansion afterwards, an arioso treatment of 'Gebt unserm Gott die Ehre!' ('Give to our God the honour!'), which seems unnecessary in view of the fact that every stanza concludes with this line, and that it receives considerable prominence elsewhere. It comes thrice in the seven lines of stanza 8, which are set rapidly in ten bars of tenor recitativo secco: 'Ye, who your Christ's name name, Give to our God the honour! Ye, who our God's might recognize, Give to our God the honour! The false idols commit to mockery, The Lord is God, the Lord is God! Give to our God the honour!'

Even i is an extended chorale and not a fantasia. The soprano entries of the canto fermo, the anonymous 'Es ist das Heil uns kommen her', are quite plain with relatively little independent movement for the lower voices, though the last line is extended. There is much doubling of the violins by two transverse flutes and two oboes, but a semiquaver figure,

Ex.739

is sometimes tossed about among the three groups. The initial theme anticipates the repeated notes of the canto:

Ex.740

The bassi, as will be seen, are very active and this contributes towards making the movement bustling and vigorous. The text is: 'Be praise and honour to the highest good, To the Father of all goodness, To God, Who all wonders does, To God, Who my spirit With His rich comfort fills, To God, Who all lamentation stills. Give to our God the honour!'

Stanza 3 is a not particularly interesting tenor aria with two oboes d'amore. 'Was unser Gott geschaffen hat, das will er auch erhalten' ('What our God created has, that will He also maintain') begins with a modification of the theme of the introduction:

Ex.741

The ritornello develops (a) and the above is modified in another way for 'darüber will er früh und spat mit seiner Gnade walten' ('thereover will He early and late with His mercy govern'). The remainder of this section differs from the earlier; there are joyful breaks between 'er', 'früh', and 'und'. The next ritornello is the second half of the introduction. The repeated notes of the canto fermo are recalled at the beginning of 'In seinem ganzen Königreich ist Alles recht und Alles gleich' ('In His whole kingdom is all right and all equal'), which is delivered once only. (a) curls above the repeated note and forms the basis of a flourish on 'Königreich'. Four bars of the introduction recur and the voice starts off with a fragment of it to the ubiquitous 'Gebt unserm Gott die Ehre!', and elongates the 'Königreich' run to 3½ bars on 'Ehre!'

The repeated notes are further developed in the alto recitative with strings, verse 5. After a few bars—'The Lord is now and ever not from His people separated, He remains their confidence, their blessing, salvation and peace. With mother-hands leads He His own continually hither and thither'—the upper strings cease and 'Gebt unserm Gott die Ehre!' is developed in a longish arioso, with the repeated notes and the joy-motive:

The same two ideas dominate the last third of the bass aria with violin obbligato, stanza 6. The joy-motive is also important in the preceding sections, which move with a quiet beauty. The continuo line is more important than the violin melody,

and is developed in various ways,

and

'Wenn Trost und Hülf ermangeln muß' ('When comfort and help

fail must') modifies (a); 'die alle Welt erzeiget' (which all (the) world manifests') forms a counterpoint to its violin continuation and later takes over the continuation itself. 'So kommt, so hilft der Überfluß' ('So comes, so helps the abundance',) is at first broken up by joyful leaps, with (c) above, and then a run tells of the speedy coming of the Lord's great bounty. Part of the introduction is now repeated. 'Der Schöpfer selbst, und neiget die Vatersaugen denen zu' ('The Creator Himself, and inclines the Father's-eyes those to') introduces a new melody, with (c) direct in the continuo and inverted in the violin. 'Die sonsten nirgend finden Ruh'' ('Who otherwise nowhere find rest') is treated in a delightful manner, 'nirgend' is repeated and the rest between filled by an imitation of its falling second. 'Ruh'' is sustained, while the violin plays (b), low-lying, and the continuo part of (a); the words are sung again, but the first 'nirgend' rises instead of falling, the obbligato drops a sixth, the voice repeats 'nirgend', to the same interval, and then softly sinks to a sustained 'Ruh'', during which the continuo waves blissfully and the violin plays (c). A brief interlude, (d) and (a), brings the coda already spoken of, at the end of which the introduction is repeated. The scheme is unique.

The only aria on a grand scale is stanza 7, for alto. Flute and [strings] have expansive phrases written in $\frac{3}{4}$ but virtually in $\frac{9}{8}$, and the voice swings along, singing its praises in leisurely confidence. The form is akin to rondo; there is a principal subject,

Ex.746 Fl.tr.
Vl.I. 8ve lower
(a)
Cont. 8ve lower

Ex.747 (b)
Cont. 8ve lower

(repeated a tone higher) and:

Ex.748
(c)
Cont.
8ve lower

These comprise the introduction. (*a*) is fitted to 'Ich will dich all mein Leben lang, O Gott, von nun an ehren' ('I will Thee all my life long, O Lord, from now on honour'), (*b*), with an alteration at the end, follows with the same words, (*c*) is deleted, but the three themes, with a change at the close of (*c*), are given in succession to the voice, fitted to 'man soll, O Gott, dein'n Lobgesang an allen Orten hören' ('one shall, O God, Thy praise-song in all places hear'). The flute mainly doubles violin I at the octave above all through the ritornelli, departing only occasionally from the chief line; in the vocal sections it plays mostly an independent line, accompanied fragmentarily by the upper strings, which make much of the figure:

Ex.749 (*d*)

After the vocal section (*a*) and (*c*) come in the dominant. The tonic returns, and a modified version of (*a*) to 'Mein ganzes Herz ermuntre sich, mein Geist und Leib erfreue sich' ('(Let) my whole heart enliven itself, my spirit and body rejoice itself') modulates to B minor and the motto line reproduces an altered form of (*b*). There are sweeping phrases to 'Geist und Leib' and to 'Ehre', and the upper strings confine themselves to detached entries of (*d*). A ritornello follows; the inner strings sustain, the rising sixth of (*b*) forms a prominent feature of the unceasing flow of triplets for the flute, and the continuo pursues its chief motive, taken from the introduction:

Ex.750

A swift modulation from B minor to D repeats the last group of lines to (*a*) and (*b*), both extended, and there is a modulation to the dominant at the end of (*a*). (*d*) is introduced in the upper strings and flute with diversified treatment. The introduction is heard again, modulating from D to A; for the final ritornello it is altered, the subdominant and dominant being touched upon before the cadence and (*b*) lengthened at the expense of (*c*). Because of the lack of variety of mood in the hymn and the frequent appearances of the last line, the cantata does not attain to the greatest heights. Nevertheless it contains much that is beautiful, and Bach's unfailing resourcefulness in coping with the motto is astonishing; not only does he not shrink from dealing with the burden of all the verses, he actually expands it, as we have seen, in v and vi.

97. There is no compromise in the setting of Paul Flemming's 'In allen meinen Thaten', although verses 3 and 5 are condensed into eight-bar recitatives, contrast being obtained by using continuo in one case and strings in the other. The other stanzas are fully developed and a cantata of unusual length results. The fantasia is in the form of the introduction and vivace of a French overture, without a reprise of the slow portion. The *grave*, for two oboes (both independent), fagotti (the plural is indicated; they are always in unison), upper strings, and separate lines for organo and *violoncello e violone* (which in this portion are identical) is solely instrumental. Flemming's hymn was written prior to setting out on a journey, the *grave* may represent the solemn meditation of the traveller before departure. In the vivace section the oboes play with the violins during the tutti sections. There are episodes marked 'trio' for oboes and fagotti, the organ doubling the latter. Piano and forte marks are abundant and even *tutti e piano*. One figure is used persistently throughout,

both for instruments and lower voices. The canto fermo is intoned in long notes by the sopranos. When it is concluded all four voices sing four bars which bear no thematic relation to the rest of the number. The lower voice parts are mostly based on (*a*), and there is no connexion with the canto except a rising fourth at times. Spitta is of opinion, from evidence of different periods in the manuscript paper, that this fantasia belonged originally to another cantata. The melody served four successive purposes. H. Isaak's tune was originally for a secular song: 'Innspruck, ich muß dich laßen' ('Innsbruck, I must thee leave'). It became attached to J. Hesse's hymn 'O Welt, ich muß dich laßen' ('O world, I must thee leave'), then to P. Gerhardt's 'Nun ruhen alle Wälder' ('Now rest all woods') and then to Flemming's hymn. The third title is given in the score. The text is: 'In all my doings Let I the Highest counsel Who all things can (do) and has, He must in all things, shall it otherwise well succeed, Himself give advice and help.' There is no clause on which the composer could seize for pictorial illustration, no mood to invite treatment; that is probably why an instrumental form is commandeered and why no particular quality is emphasized.

The bass aria begins with a tuneful theme for continuo (the only accompaniment), the first part consisting of graceful curves:

the second a line:

which, returning ever and anon to a dominant pedal, eventually climbs upwards, the struggling referred to in the text. Bach's bowing is worth studying; the whole number is carefully marked. The voice takes up (*a*) to 'Nichts ist es spat und frühe um alle meine Mühe, mein Sorgen ist umsonst' ('Nothing is there late and early for all my trouble; my anxiety is vain'), with a modification of (*b*) in the bassi. Over (*b*) the voice repeats the last clause to a phrase climbing wearily upwards. The complete sentence is sung again to (*a*), the continuo being mostly an octave lower than before, the darker colour producing an intriguing change, and then comes a long twisting and syncopated passage to 'Sorgen', formed from the quavers of (*a*). The bassi repeat the introduction beginning a third higher and modulating to B♭, the singer adds a new melody above, but while (*b*) is in progress introduces the first phrase of (*a*). (*b*) serves for interlude. A modification of (*a*) is sung to 'Er mag's mit meinen Sachen nach seinem Willen machen' ('He may it with my affairs after His will do') and, with (*b*) in the continuo, continues 'ich stell's in seine Gunst' ('I place it in His goodwill'). An elegant version of (*a*), modulating every two bars, provides an interlude and support for the first clause, with (*b*) the voice sustains 'stell's' on high D, and during the remainder of the vocal section (*a*) mounts confidently.

One of the most elaborate and most meticulously bowed of all violin obbligati, resembling a movement from the solo sonatas, is provided for the tenor aria, stanza 4. (See P. 18.) The chief theme is:

There are many double-note passages, such as:

(which is a variant of (a), above the same continuo), three- and four-part chords, lengthy demisemiquaver runs and intricate syncopations. The chords are tremendously effective where the voice declaims 'nichts, nichts! wird mich verletzen, nichts, nichts! nichts wird mir fehlen, was mir nützt' ('nothing, nothing! will me injure, nothing, nothing! nothing will me lack, that I need'). 'Ich traue seiner Gnaden' ('I trust His mercy') modifies (a), and (b) accompanies. The 'allem' of 'die mich vo rallem Schaden' ('which me from all hurt') is set to a marvellous coloratura and the violin splashes with four-note chords. 'Vor allem Übel schützt' (from all evil protects') produces a tortuous phrase on 'Übel'. The lines are repeated with another modification of part of (a), a despairing cry on 'schaden' and sinking chromatics on 'Übel'. (a) for the obbligato, in the dominant, is followed by two long-sweeping successions of demi-semiquavers, the second with alternations of forte and piano. The 'Ich traue' form of (a) begins with a long note, decorated at one point. A further modification serves for 'Leb' ich nach seinen Gesetzen' ('Live I according to His commandments'), the sustained note being undecorated. The phrase is altered for 'So wird mich nichts ver-letzen'; the long notes are accompanied by a version of (b) and the conclusion of each phrase is dovetailed into semiquavers derived from the interlude. During the 'nichts' portion the tear-motive is prominent in the bassi. Present suffering is emphasized rather than trust in the Almighty's protection. Fragments from the middle and end of the introduction join this vocal section with a third, in which the same words are provided with even more elaborate treatment.

Both of the first phrases are altered, 'leb' ich nach seinen Gesetzen' is repeated, with an impulsive flourish on 'leb'', the tear-motive below and swaying, swinging syncopations above. It is curious that Bach, with his love of economy of material, does not let us hear again a three-bar decorative passage in demisemiquavers which occurs in the introduction. While one must admire the technique of a singer who can negotiate the many difficulties of this fine aria, one must concede the honours to the violinist.

The most externally interesting aria is verse 6, alto with richly worked strings. The singer is confident of the protection of the Almighty when weak in bonds, whether lying down to rest or rising in the morning. The thematic material is deliberately connected with 'Leg' ich mich späte nieder ('Lay I myself late down') and 'erwache frühe wieder' ('awaken early again'); the first violin phrase sinks:

Ex.756 (a)

then haltingly moves upwards, with the bassi moving steadily down:

Ex.757 (b)

Another rising violin idea is accompanied by continuo drops of ninths:

Ex.758 (c)

There is yet another 'erwache' phrase:

Ex.759 (d)

Each of the two verbal clauses is sung once to appropriate melodies, (*a*) and (*b*) being separated in the orchestra to allow for the second. 'Lieg' oder ziehe fort' ('Lie or move forth') is extended considerably. A version of the close of (*a*):

heard both vocally and instrumentally, the latter in rising sequence, illustrates the going forth into the world. The first two clauses come again, with (*c*) and (*d*) in the orchestra, and the third is elaborated, over continuo only, (*d*) appearing in the latter. The delightful introduction is now played in the dominant. An ingenious transformation of (*a*) serves for 'in Schwachheit und in Banden' ('in weakness and in bonds') and 'und was mir stößt zu Handen' (or 'zu handen') ('and what to me falls to the hands'), with pathetic appoggiature on 'Schwachheit' and 'was', and with (*a*) in its original form alternating in violin I. 'So tröstet mich sein Wort' ('then comforts me His word') ascends triumphantly on 'tröstet' with the time-pattern, though not the melody, of (*c*), violin I and bassi playing it, altered in outline and with reversed accents. A fine interlude is formed from (*c*) and its continuo dropping ninths. As in the other arias there is a completely transformed version of this vocal section. 'In Schwachheit' is less despairing; and though calm repeated quavers for the upper strings diminish the stress of 'und was mir stößt', and the continuo repeats a connecting figure from the introduction:

which is frequently heard in this line and in no other, 'stößt' stumbles down and struggles up and (*e*) reappears above 'Handen'. 'Tröstet' begins with a sustained note and then convolutes, with the previous 'tröstet' modification of (*c*) in violin I and continuo and (*f*) also in the latter. The last 'Schwachheit' is again agonized, with soaring syncopations for violin I and (*f*) for the continuo, 'Banden' is sustained against (*e*) and (*f*), 'stößt' ascends in a phrase similar to (*d*). Despite momentary lapses of spirit the aria is expressive of abounding confidence in the care and watchfulness of the Almighty.

Both here and in verse 7, a S.B. duet with continuo, is the bowing full and instructive, showing how fond Bach is of phrasing contrary to the beat. The sternness of God's decrees is indicated by a firm and steadily moving upward figure:

used by both continuo and voices, each of the two opening clauses— 'Hat er es denn beschlossen, so will ich unverdrossen' ('Has He it then ordained, then will I undaunted') —being sung to it. 'Verhängniß' ('an mein Verhängniß gehn' ('to my fate go')) is sung to a syncopated falling scale, the antithesis of (a), while the continuo plays the second portion of the introduction, a series of falls to the depths:

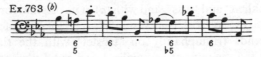

The vocal form of (a) decorates bar 2, introducing an upward appoggiatura; this version is never found in the continuo. The bass entry of the nine-bar theme dovetails with the close of that of the soprano, which then makes a four-bar canon at the distance of a bar. A slowly ascending 'Verhängniß' follows for the soprano, with syncopations, the bass moving freely and the bassi introducing a compound of (a) and (b). Another canon on (a), this time at a distance of a beat, concludes the vocal section, which is succeeded by the introduction in the dominant, dovetailing into 'Kein Unfall unter allen soll mir zu harte fallen, ich will ihn überstehn' ('No mischance among all will on me too hard fall, I shall it overcome'). The bass leads off and incorporates the rising steps of (a) to 'soll mir zu harte', the soprano follows, (a) is used with both clauses later. 'Fallen' and 'Unfall' frequently drop, with a leaning tone on the second syllable; the continuo part is at first fashioned out of (a), direct and inverted (the latter illustrative of 'fallen'), and during the latter portion of the section there is extended treatment of (b). A short interlude, based on (a) and (b), brings a reconstruction of the initial vocal section, moving from F minor to the tonic.

The soprano aria, stanza 8, with two oboes, is pleasant enough but of no particular significance, though not without points of interest. The antithesis of 'Ihm hab' ich mich ergeben zu sterben und zu leben' ('To Him have I myself surrendered to die and to live') and 'Es sei heut' oder morgen' ('It be today or tomorrow') explains the contours of the oboe I theme:

which is modified for both sets of words, and the short contrasting groups, placed alternately in different parts of the compass, are the chief feature of the aria. The figure:

is adapted to various purposes, it sounds upsoaring with 'so bald er mir gebeut' ('so soon (as) He me bids'), with 'so' and 'bald' thrown into relief; it is solemnly impressive when played pianissimo above a sustained 'sterben'; it is joyous on 'leben' and confident on 'er weiß die rechte Zeit' ('He knows the right time'). When oboe II takes over the chief theme in the introduction, oboe I adds a charming counterpoint, Schubertian in the change from E to Eb:

It accompanies 'ihm hab' ich mich ergeben zu sterben oder leben' and is sung to 'sorgen' in 'dafür laß' ich ihn sorgen' ('for that let I Him care'), with the syncopation elongated, and (a) and (b) in oboe I.

The texts of the recitatives are—iii, 'There can to me nothing happen, but what He has ordained, and what for me blessed is: I take it, as He it gives; what He from me desires, that have I also chosen.' v, 'May He (be willing) from my sins in mercy me (to) release, cancel my guilt! He will on my evil-doing not immediately the judgement pronounce, and have yet patience.' The final chorale is marked 'Siebenstimmig' (seven-voiced), the upper strings being independent, soaring aloft in illustration of line 5. The text is 'So be now, soul, His, And trust on Him alone, Who thee created has; (May) it happen, as it (may) happen, My Father in the heights Knows all things best.'

The occasion of the cantata is not known. Schweitzer surmises a wedding, but the care and elaboration shown throughout this long work scarcely suggests an occasional composition. A note at the end of the score fixed the date as 1734, but the parts were not copied till the following year. Fine as much of the music is, one cannot regard the cantata as a satisfactory whole. In actual performance there is an uncomfortable feeling of ponderousness, of lack of flexibility. This does not mean that it should not be performed, but only an audience familiar with the cantatas and ready to overlook certain inequalities for the sake of much fine music is suitable. Bach himself must have been dissatisfied with the results obtainable from a pure hymn-libretto, for in his later Leipzig period he reverted to this type of text twice only.

(ii) *Complete and Unaltered Hymn plus Original Matter* (80), 140

140. This type, naturally, is possible only when the hymn is short. Both examples are outstanding specimens of Bach's genius, No. 80 in his earlier style, or styles, No. 140 in the glorious ripeness of his maturity. It is a cantata without weaknesses, without a dull bar, technically, emotionally and spiritually of the highest order, its sheer perfection and its boundless imagination rouse one's wonder time and time again. We do not know the year when Leipzigers first heard this, another of those masterpieces which they heeded not, but 1731 (25 November) or a later year seems likely. The day was the Twenty-Seventh after Trinity, the Gospel being the parable of the Ten Virgins, St. Matthew xxv. 1–13, the hymn and tune P. Nicolai's 'Wachet auf, ruft uns die Stimme' ('Sleepers, wake' N., and Boosey, 'Sleepers wake, loud sounds the warning' B. For iv and vii see 'Wake, O wake!' O.). The three verses are the great pillars of the cantata, i, iv, and vii. Stanza 1 combines a reference to verse 1 of the Gospel with Revelation xxi. 2, 'the new Jerusalem, coming down from God out of heaven, prepared as a bride adorned for her husband' and the third is based on verse 21 of the same chapter: 'And the twelve gates were twelve pearls.' Verse 1 is 'Wake up! cries to us the voice Of the watchers very high on the battlements: Wake up, thou city Jerusalem! Midnight is this hour: They call us with ringing mouth: Where be ye wise virgins? Prepare! the Bridegroom comes, Arise! the lamps seize. Alleluja! Make you ready For the marriage, Ye must Him to meet go.' There are few dramatic scenes in the whole range of music so vivid, so compelling, so completely satisfying musically after the first sensations are past, as the opening chorus. And yet how simple the forces! A four-part choir, the soprano chorale doubled by a horn, a reed group—two oboes and taille, strings, with violin I doubled by violino piccolo, and continuo. And how simple and economical the orchestral material! Groups of chords are tossed from upper strings to reeds:

(this idea must always be played as ♩♪♪♩ according to the custom of the day, it sounds tame otherwise), the short, impulsive figure:

the syncopated note of which should be strongly emphasized, the rushing string scales, the semiquaver figures in which the melodic outline leaps from point to point:

the staccato quavers, that is all. The clamorous lower voices, with their short, sharp cries, their accents opposed to the normal, the climbing scale to 'der Wächter sehr hoch' ('the watchmen very high'), their reiterated minor sevenths from the tonic in some of the cadences, contribute to an amazing scene of excitement and confusion, people rushing to and fro, sounds of voices coming from all quarters of the streets, while the serene and divine announcement of the coming of the Bridegroom peals above the melée. In the Allelujah section, where the lower voices develop a theme incorporating the syncopated idea from the strings, there is a momentary change. The repeated note time-pattern is heard cumulatively instead of in antiphonal chords, the steady movement of the bassi suggests the tramp of armed men. After the temporary hush in the excitement forces gather and roll and mount until we are again in the midst of the seething multitude. It is well to begin this section a little slower, and to regain the original tempo in the ritornello.

The choral portions invite the effect that can be made with a big choir, but involves one in orchestral difficulties. To answer a large mass of strings by two oboes and cor anglais is to produce an almost comic effect. To quadruple the reed forces is not a practical proposition. Once the choir enters, oboes and cor anglais are completely obliterated, so are the passages for a single oboe. Thus quite half the orchestral colouring is washed out. The matter may be improved by doubling the orchestral reed passages by powerful organ reeds; this is a makeshift, but better than nothing. Many concert-givers never think of these things: Bach to them is a choral composer and little else. The writer will never forget his bitter disappointment on hearing his first complete Festival performance of *St. Matthew Passion*. What had been read with delight and anticipation in the score was simply not there. In the closing chorus of Part I, six oboes and six flutes played the lovely two-note passages in the introduction. Then in came the steam roller of the chorus. The wood-wind disappeared entirely, to reappear when the choir was kind enough to cease for a while. So it went on throughout, for all the world like those figures on some continental public clocks, which revolve on a disk, disappear into their hole and come out again after a while from the opposite aperture. The full effect of it can be realized only with a string orchestra of one or two desks of violin I, the same of violin II, one desk each of violas and 'celli, and a single contrabass, harpsichord or organ, two oboes, cor anglais, a trumpet muted in the manner described

elsewhere, and an efficient choir of twenty to thirty voices. It is not
the mere mass of choral tone that counts, but the alertness, intelligence, and diction of the singers.

Stanza 2, iv—'Zion hears the watchmen sing, The heart does in her
for joy spring'—is another supreme manifestation of Bach's genius.
Against the tenor chorale (the singing of the watchmen sounding
from one of the turrets), comes one of the finest melodies ever conceived by man, the mystic, swaying dance of the Bridesmaids. (See
O.C.S. 'Wake, O Wake!' in which both this and vii are contained.)
In a sense it is a mere counterpoint to a canto fermo, yet unfettered
imagination could invent no more glorious tune. In order to ensure
a broadly sonorous tone, rich but not bright, the violino piccolo is instructed to refrain from joining the melody of tutti violins and violas:

Ex.770

which is repeated piano immediately, the broad sweeping:

Ex.771

the fragmentary:

Ex.772

which is related to Ex. 768, and the tremendously intense conclusion:

Ex.773

The remainder of the stanza is 'She wakes, and rises hurriedly. Her

Friend comes from heaven gloriously, In mercy strong, in truth mighty, Her light becomes bright, her star ascends. Now come, Thou worthy Crown, Lord Jesus, God's Son, Hosianna! We follow all To the joy-hall, And partake of the Lord's supper.' One wonders why the composer arranged this number to be the first of the Schübler chorale preludes; its glowing warmth and compelling rhythm disappear when transferred to the rather cold tones of the organ, and even if one departs, legitimately, from the strict trio-writing of the Schübler set and fills in harmonies, the effect is a mere shadow of the original. Schering's interpretations of i and iv are at variance with those commonly accepted.

It is strange that Bach never harmonized the chorale in four parts except for vii, although it may have happened in his lost works. It is the plainest of all chorale settings and extraordinarily powerful, the twelve gates of pearl stand four-square to the winds of heaven. The violino piccolo is directed to play the melody an octave higher, a rare indication. The intense rapture of the verse evaporates in a literal translation: 'Gloria be to Thee sung With men's and angels' tongues, With harps and cymbals besides. Of twelve pearls are the gates Of Thy city; we are consorts Of angels high about Thy throne. No eye has ever traced, No ear has ever heard Such joy. Of that are we glad, Io! Io! Eternally in dulci jubilo.'

Between each two stanzas are placed a recitative and a duet, the texts being possibly by Picander. The tenor recitativo secco addresses the Bride, calling her to come forth to greet her Lord: 'He comes, He comes, the Bridegroom comes! Ye daughters of Zion, come out, His procession hastens from the heights into your mother's house. The Bridegroom comes, Who to a roe and young stag like, on these hills leaps, and to you the feast of the marriage brings. Wake up, rouse yourselves! the Bridegroom to receive! there! see! comes He hitherward.'

Soprano and bass, typifying Bride and Bridegroom, now sing one of the most exquisite of all duets. The chief melodic theme is yet one further variant of the 'Have mercy, Lord' alto aria in the *St. Matthew Passion*:

Ex.774 *Adagio*

and the obbligato, violino piccolo, is embellished with many lovely arabesques, the flowing of the anointing oil. There is another violin phrase of melting beauty:

Ex.775

There are long sustained notes for the soprano on 'ich warte'; the singers address each other in the tenderest of phrases, the Bride queries, the Bridegroom answers. As in so many duets of this character, the singers have almost identical lines, changed to suit the person:

S.	B.
'Wann kommst du, mein Heil?	'Ich komme, dein Theil,
('When comest Thou, my salvation?)	('I come, thy portion,)
ich warte mit brennendem Öle.	
(I await with burning oil.)	
Eröffne den Saal zum himmlischen Mahl,	Ich öffne den Saal zum himmli- schen Mahl,
(Open the chamber for the heavenly feast,)	(I open the chamber for the hea- venly feast,)
komm, Jesu!'	ich komme;
(come, Jesu!')	(I come;)
	komm', liebliche Seele!'
	(come, lovely soul!')

A vocal phrase of much loveliness is derived from (a):

Ex.776   Ich   öff - ne den Saal,

It goes without saying that all appoggiature must be long. The duets in this cantata are the only ones in the series which should be sung by solo voices.

After the watchmen's stanza the Bridegroom addresses the Bride

with words of comfort; the accompaniment to the recitative is for
all strings and there is a beautiful chromatic change at 'dein be-
trübtes Aug'' ('thy troubled eye'). (See Ex. 1312.) The text is: 'So
come within to me, thou by me chosen Bride! I have myself with thee
for eternity wedded. Thee will I on My heart, on Mine arm even as
a seal set, and thy troubled eye delight. Forget, O soul, now the
anguish, the pain, which thou suffer must; on My left (hand) shalt
thou rest, and My right (hand) shalt thou kiss.' The second duet is
of pure bliss, one of the most engaging Bach ever wrote. The opening
melody of the oboe obbligato, with its tender two-note groups and
its ecstatic semiquavers, is allotted to the voices as follows:

and its running semiquavers:

subsequently wind their way through the vocal lines like a gay
rippling streamlet among clover-bespangled meadows. Notes 3–6 of
'Und ich bin dein' are detached for the obbligato, a little chuckle of
laughter, and become important after the Fine pause. The bassi
frequently join in the general delight with descending semiquaver
scales. The portion from the oboe run to the end of the quoted vocal
portion is repeated, the voices answer each other with an arpeggio
version of the dialogue, imitate the first clause by contrary motion
and then sing a new melody in canon with cross accents, while the
oboe streamlet pursues its course and the continuo plays detached
quavers. A development of previous ideas rounds off the section and
the introduction is repeated. The text of Part II is:

S.	B.
'Ich will mit dir	'Du sollst mit mir
('I will with Thee)	('Thou shalt with Me)
in Himmels Rosen weiden,'	in Himmels Rosen weiden,'
(in heaven's roses pasture,')	(in heaven's roses pasture,')

and, together, 'da Freude die Fülle, da Wonne wird sein' ('there (of) joy the fullness, there bliss shall be'. See Ps. xvi. 11). The first quoted phrase is associated with both the lines above, the answering group and the soprano idea of the last bar of the quotation are heard, the oboe figure is incessant for four bars and is then transferred to the bassi, which otherwise leap widely in detached quavers or ripple down their scales. A combined flourish on 'weiden' leads to the final clause, which is delivered simultaneously. A decorated version of the arpeggio ensues:

Ex.779

da Freu - de   die Fül - le,   da Won - ne   wird sein,

the initial oboe melody reappears, the voices imitate on a new melodic version of the time-pattern of Ex. 779, and the soprano cascades down on 'Wonne'. Picander rarely served the master so well as in his interludes to Nicolai's stanzas. (See *Fugitive Notes*.)

(iii) *Complete (or almost complete) Hymns, but with some Verses Paraphrased*
8, 9, 20, 93, 99
Order of Discussion: 20, 8, 93, 9, 99

The value of this type of text is shown by the fine character of most of the cantatas in the group, and will be proved even more decidedly when those of the last period are considered. That Bach was slow to realize the superiority of the partially paraphrased hymn over the unaltered version is revealed by an examination of numbers and dates. Although up to 1731 he had set four amended texts, he began in that year the series of seven just considered, while only two were written during the composition of these to the more flexible type of libretto.

20. J. Rist's 'O Ewigkeit, du Donnerwort' ('O eternity, thou

thunderword') runs to sixteen verses and is reduced to a convenient
length by the omission of stanzas 4, 5, 7, and 8. The only original
verses retained are 1, 11, and 16 for i, vii, and xi respectively, the last
two being four-part chorales. J. Schop's 'Wach auf, mein Geist'
reconstructed for this hymn by J. Crüger, is used. Stanza 1 is translated for Cantata 60, see p. 407. The chorale fantasia is again blended
with the French Overture; here the choir participates in all sections;
the opening Grave is more important than the Vivace, which is quite
brief, and although the return of the Grave is shortened, its significance is heightened by new treatment. Lines 1–3 of the canto fermo
appear in the first Grave, their repetition in the Vivace and the last
two in the second Grave. The solemn time-patterns of the opening:

and:

(to be played in the traditional manner)

with its rich reed tone (three oboes and strings), and a note of sternness added to the soprano canto fermo by the doubling of a *tromba
da tirarsi*, accord with the sombre opening lines of the hymn. The
lower voices are mostly slow-moving, though in line 1 the basses
flourish on 'Donnerwort' and they all clench the end with a simultaneous shout. With the introduction of the canto is heard in the
oboes a figure suggestive of trembling:

which is also found in the treatment of this stanza in the later solo
cantata of the same title, No. 60. In the Vivace the oboes cease for

the time being to be independent and double the upper strings. A dual theme is heard perpetually:

Ex.783

The lower voices are dramatic, a huge sweep for basses on 'Traurig-keit' ('mourning'), repetitions of 'nicht' ('not') on the unaccented part of the bar, and several powerful cross-rhythms. After a pause the Grave resumes and one of the most remarkable passages in all the cantatas comes with arresting suddenness. 'Mein ganz erschrocknes Herz' ('my completely affrighted heart') is heralded by strong dis-sonances tossed in short fragments from oboes to strings, and when the canto is solemnly intoned the lower voices quiver on broken phrases to the word 'erschrocknes', an extraordinary transmutation of previous material. It is one of those strokes of genius that produce a feeling of awe.

A mournful tenor recitativo secco, ii, stanza 2, is chromatic and consists almost wholly of dissonances—'No misfortune is in all the world to be found, that eternally enduring is; it must yet finally with the time once disappear. Ah! but ah! the pain of eternity has only no limit' (see Ex. 1298) 'it carries on ever and ever its martyr-sport, yea, as Himself Jesus says, from it is no redemption.' (See Matt. xxiii. 33.)

The same voice, in an aria with strings, iii, stanza 3, sings of eternity, anxiety, of life being no jest, of flames eternally burning, the trembling and quaking of heart, of pain, of hell. The thematic material is exceedingly varied, long notes and gently undulating quavers to suggest eternity ('Ewigkeit')—

Ex.784

(Key C minor, with signature of 2 flats.)

tortuous groups anxiety:

Ex. 785
(Thou makest me) anxious:
(du machst mir) ban

wild runs for flames and burning:

Ex.786

syncopated chromatic passages interpreting the quaking of the heart:

Ex.787

and an agonized passage, akin to that on 'bange', telling of pain: 'wenn ich diese Pein bedenke, und den Sinn zur Höllen lenke' ('when I this pain remember, and the mind to hell direct'). Yet all are welded almost incredibly into a perfect whole. A pleading figure is often heard in violin I and continuo:

Ex.788

During 'ewig ist zu lange!' ('eternally is too long!') it is played above the sustained note on 'ewig', the 'bange' motive comes in the bassi in the middle of the clause and is repeated by violin I while the voice sustains 'lange'. 'Ach, hier gilt fürwahr kein Scherz' ('Ah, here prevails in truth no jest') is sung thrice to agitated phrases, with continuo only.

A longish bass recitativo secco, vi, stanza 10, exploits with theological grimness the terrors of hell: 'Granted, it lasted the damned's torment as many years, as in the number on earth (of blades of) grass, in heaven the stars were; granted were pain so long continued, as men in the world from the beginning (have) been, so would be yet at last to the same an end and measure placed, so must it indeed finally cease. Now, therefore, when thou the danger, thou damned one, a thousand million years with all devils endured, so is yet never the ending at hand;' (see Ex. 1304) 'the time, which no one reckon can, begins each moment to thy soul's eternal misfortune always anew.'

From this harrowing contemplation we turn with relief to a charming bass aria, v, stanza 9, in which three oboes above a staccato continuo beguile us with lovely tripping tunes:

The Christian has lost all his terror at the thought:

(b) is the opening continuo notes, a delightful linking-up of instrumental and vocal material. Fragments of (a) are tossed between voice and oboes, and the singer continues—'in seinen Werken' ('in His works'). The voice leaps to (b) while the oboes answer and the continuo takes up the melody of (a). (a) is now developed by the singer and oboe I adds a counterpoint. Part II begins 'Auf kurze Sünden dieser Welt hat Er so lange Pein bestellt; ach, wollte doch die Welt dieß merken!' ('For short sins of this world has He such long pain ordained; ah, would then the world this mark!'). The initial figure of (a) is incorporated into the vocal line, there is momentary agony at 'so lange Pein', but a passage for oboes I and II formed from (a), and (b) in the bassi, cause us to look beyond the pain to be endured. On 'merken', unison oboes proclaim emphatically 'Gott ist gerecht'. A new working of (a) forms an interlude, and the singer calls out 'Kurz ist die Zeit' ('short is the time'), an inversion of (b), and 'der Tod geschwind' ('the death quick'), to a fragment of (a); the first phrase of (a), with (b) below, punctuates these, 'bedenke dieß, o Menschenkind' ('remember this, oh mortal child') also introduces the fragment. From 'kurz' to 'geschwind' the vocal line zigzags down as if the universe were tottering, 'bedenke' is expanded in rising sixths and falling sevenths and the comforting oboe melody comes more fully. The three bars before the Da Capo, the last one adagio, are with continuo only, and the (*a*) fragment is heard.

In an alto aria with strings, vi, stanza 10, we are bidden to save our souls and to fly from the slavery of Satan. The prevailing rhythm is a $\frac{3}{2}$ bar cast into two bars of $\frac{3}{4}$, an intriguing device:

There is a momentary departure from the time-pattern to introduce a run on 'entfliehe':

and the melody continues in the same vein until the last word of 'damit in jener Schwefelhöhle der Tod, so die Verdammten plagt' ('so that in that sulphur-hole the death, which the damned torments'). 'Plagt' is set to a passage full of pathos, the continuo sinking by semitones. The comforting thought—'nicht deine Seele ewig nagt' ('not thy soul eternally gnaws')—is set soaringly, with the cross-rhythm on 'ewig'. The first sentence is resumed, altered in the latter half. The construction of the aria is singular; the introduction lasts ten bars and the vocal section, which is without break, for thirty-two. Then the section beginning at 'damit', over twenty bars, is repeated by the strings to form a coda.

The three extant cantatas for the First Sunday after Trinity are in two sections, the sermon coming between. Part I of No. 20 closes with the pessimistic eleventh stanza, which is a retrograde outlook after v and vi: 'so long as a God in heaven lives And over all the clouds soars, Will such martyrdom endure; Will them torment cold and heat, Anguish, hunger, terror, fire and lightning And them yet not consume. For will end this pain When God no more eternal is.'

If the sermon dwelt on this verse, it must have been truly harrowing, and the call to the lost sheep to awaken and throw off the sleep of sin, which is the subject of the magnificent trumpet aria for bass, viii, stanza 13 (see P. 49) must have been electrifying. Ringing tromba calls:

and florid triplets:

pierce through the mass of sound created by strings with oboes doubling the three upper lines, with strong rhythms, wild, upward rushes and brilliant flourishes:

while the bassi emulate their fury with such phrases as (b) and pound away as in (a). The opening of the introduction is repeated while the singer calls 'Wacht auf, wacht auf' ('wake up, wake up') to mounting arpeggi, covering a range of a thirteenth. A pathetic flattened seventh singles out the adjective of 'verlorne Schaafe', ('lost sheep') and the soloist sweeps down a twelfth on 'ermuntert euch vom Sündenschlafe' ('arouse ye from sin-sleep'). The whirling violin figure and the bassi phrase accompany. 'Ermuntert euch' is twice sung as a rousing trumpet call, with orchestral bursts after each. The second

'Sündenschlafe' struggles upwards like a slumberer just awaking to consciousness and the strings are hushed to piano. The concluding clause is 'und bessert euer Leben bald' ('and amend thy life soon'). After 2½ bars of the introduction in the dominant, the singer again cries 'Wacht auf' and then extends in a magnificent passage:

Ex.796

repeating both, with an expansion of 'schallt', even finer, while the orchestra accompanies with its motives and flings ♪♪ between the tromba and the remainder of the forces. In less than three bars the trumpet covers two octaves and a fourth. Short phrases follow, with similar accompaniment, and with drops of sevenths for the voice 'die euch mit Schrecken', ('which you with fear'), 'mit Schrecken aus der Gruft' ('with fear out of the grave'), and 'zum Richter aller Welt' ('to the judge of all the world'). A solemn passage, modulating through the subdominant minor to the tonic minor, with the whirling figure falling and the bassi octave leaps descending step by step, brings the last summons before our eyes—'vor das Gerichte ruft' ('before the tribunal calls')—with a chromatic syncopated passage on the noun. The major introduction bursts in and we visualize the end of the world. A powerful voice of great range (low G to high E), fine vocal technique and dramatic ability are needed to do justice to the leaping arpeggi, the glorious runs on 'schallt' and the grim passage on 'Gerichte'.

There are also wild rushings up and down of the continuo during the recitativo secco, ix, stanza 14, at the words, 'Pracht, Hoffahrt, Reichtum, Ehr' und Geld' ('splendour, pomp, riches, honour and wealth'), the attributes of the carnal world which the Christian must forswear: 'Forsake, Oh man, the delights of this world.' The continuo settles down to normal recitative procedure in the remainder: 'remember then in this time while yet, for thee the tree of life blossoms, what for thee to thy peace serves. Perhaps is this the last day, no man knows when he die may; how easily, how soon is many a one dead and cold, one may yet this night the coffin to thy door bring! Therefore be before all things thy soul's salvation heeded.'

There are many remarkable features in the A.T. duet with continuo, x, stanza 15. 'O Menschenkind' is set tenderly in parallel thirds and sixths:

followed by 'hör' auf geschwind, die Sünd' und Welt zu lieben' ('cease quickly, the sin and world to love') in parallel motion, in imitative and answering phrases, and with flowing runs on 'lieben'. There are two continuo figures, (*b*) and—

which accompany this section throughout. The text continues— 'daß nicht die Pein' ('that not the pain')—and the next words bring an extraordinary chromatic passage:

The conclusion of the sentence—'dich ewig mag betrüben' ('thee eternally may trouble')—reverses the parts of (*d*). The Gospel is the story of Dives and Lazarus, St. Luke xvi. 19–31, and the Christian is admonished to remember the fate of Dives: 'Ach spiegle dich am reichem Mann, der in der Qual auch nicht einmal ein Tröpflein Wasser haben kann' ('Ah see thyself in the rich man, who in torment even not once a little-drop (of) water have can'). 'Ach spiegle dich am reichen Mann' is sung twice, the parts reversing; 'der in der Qual' is set canonically and the bassi fall to a pulsating pedal, almost the only place where they depart from (*b*) and (*c*). 'Auch nicht einmal ein Tröpflein' is again canonical, using (*c*), 'Wasser' flows in semi-quavers, the bubbling stream which is forbidden the parched Dives. The text is repeated with a beautiful chromatic extension, supported by an equally chromatic version of (*c*):

Ex.800

A bar of parallel motion brings momentary comfort, two bars of the answering 'hör' auf geschwind' are quoted, with the new words, and a double cascade on 'Wasser' follows. (*a*) is never referred to after its twofold appearance at the beginning of the duet.

Stanza 16 duplicates lines 1–4 of i and proceeds: 'I know for great sadness not, Where I myself may turn away. Take Thou me, when it Thee pleases, Lord Jesus, into Thy joy-tabernacle.' It is set simply, albeit not without further chromaticisms, and worthily concludes this splendid, if grim, cantata. The work was probably written about 1725 and revised ten years later.

8. 'Liebster Gott, wann werd' ich sterben?' ('When will God recall my spirit?' N., 'Gracious God, when call Thou me?' B.) also deals with the summons of death, but how differently! In No. 20 death is a terrifying ordeal, medieval visions of damnation and torture fill the heart with dread, one is reminded of those Dutch and Flemish paintings in which the artist delights in obscene monsters rending and devouring the evil-doers, crooked devils with prongs, cauldrons of boiling oil and furnaces at white heat. The church tried to secure its adherents through fear and not through love. In No. 8 is to be found the true Christian doctrine, Christ the all-merciful One, death a release and call to a life of bliss. There is fear, to be sure, but it is more at the thought of the penitent's unworthiness than any anticipation of relentless persecution beyond the vale. It is strange that Bach should have given us two such totally different conceptions of death (No. 8 is possibly *c.* 1725), as contrasted as are the conceptions of Berlioz and Franck.

The Gospel for the Sixteenth Sunday after Trinity is St. Luke vii. 11–17, the incident of the raising of the widow's son, and while Caspar Neumann's hymn makes no direct reference to the miracle, the mood of the libretto is appropriate. There are five stanzas only, 1 and 5 are retained in their original form while the others are paraphrased for ii–v. Stanza 1 is 'Beloved God, when shall I die? My time runs ever hence, And old Adam's heirs, Among whom I also am, Have this for patrimony, That they a little while Poor and wretched are on earth, And then themselves earth become.' The design of the fantasia is unique. It is virtually a duet for two oboes d'amore, tender and mournful, an example of 'endless melody' long before Wagner coined the term:

Ex. 801

For nearly seventy long, slow bars this haunting lament continues, almost oblivious of time and space. The upper strings are pizzicato throughout, always in quaver arpeggi descending through each beat. Only four times do they cease for a moment from this gentle ringing of mourning bells. The continuo is nearly always silent on the second and fourth beats of the bar, so leaving the upper six-part instrumental structure in suspense above the earth. This formula is employed even through most of the choral entries. A flauto traverso has an extraordinarily individual line. It is pitched high all the time so that it stands out clearly. Every now and then it plays a note twenty-four times in semiquavers, the trembling of the departing soul. For the rest it plays semiquaver arpeggi, the chime of small bells.

The movement is more akin to an extended chorale than a chorale fantasia, for not only is there no expansion of the melody, but it plays a relatively humble role in the scheme. The canto fermo is different in style from most of those employed by Bach; it is more florid, with more contrasts of lengths of notes. It was indeed at the time a modern hymn-tune rather than a chorale, as it was composed in 1695 for a well-known and much admired libretto of Neumann, by Daniel Vetter, who was organist of St. Nicholas, Leipzig, from 1679 till his death, and it was published twelve years only (1713) before the conjectured date of the cantata. Bach uses it nowhere else. The melody is unsuitable for augmentation in the customary manner; it is here sung at about its normal speed, doubled by a horn, with changes necessitated by $^{12}_8$ time and a certain amount of ornamentation. Once only does a line occupy more than three bars. The canto begins before the accompanying voices except in one case, when it is joined by the tenor. It will be seen, therefore, how different from the procedure of the normal fantasia is that which the nature of the tune has imposed. At the end is a curious effect. The strings, of course, are pizzicato, the wood-wind have a quaver, the continuo has a crotchet. It is a difficult point to manage satisfactorily. An extant set of parts is in D, instead of E, with the oboes d'amore replaced by two violins concertante. As the reed parts, owing to length and lack of opportunities for breath, impose an excessive strain on the players, Bach may have been obliged to make this change. The number occupies a special niche in one's affections; it is wholly unlike any other expansion of a chorale. One may think of it as a solemn funeral procession which is watched by someone who is himself about to depart, and who, from time to time, breathes to himself this hymn.

Bach again treats the melody differently from his wont in the final number, on account of its modernistic approximation to the aria type found in the Schemelli Chorale Book. The lower lines generally begin at different times from the melody. There are mournful harmonies to the word 'Schanden' ('shame') at the conclusion, and the basses have a splendid phrase sinking from upper C to low E. The flute is instructed to double the melody *ottava*. The text is 'Lord over death and life, Make once for all my ending good, Teach me my spirit to yield up With right well-held courage. Help, that I an honourable grave Near pious Christians may have And also finally in the earth Nevermore to shame come.'

The other numbers are of fine quality. In the tenor aria, ii, stanza 2, the watcher turns his thoughts to himself, he is no longer a mere spectator: 'Was willst du dich mein Geist entsetzen, wenn meine letzte Stunde schlägt?' ('Why wilt thou, my soul, be terrified, when

my last hour strikes?'). The pizzicato bassi figure is the unmistakable
and insistent peal of funeral bells. Above it is a lovely oboe d'amore
obbligato. Here again is the 'Have mercy' theme from the *St.
Matthew Passion*; bars 1 and 2 are melodically exact, though the
phrasing is altered:

Ex.802

One encounters this idea time and time again in other works where
the idea of pity is spoken of; it is almost a leitmotiv. Here it is followed by a long procession of semiquavers, the significance of which
is revealed later. In spite of the lyric nature of the aria the dramatic
situation is not overlooked. In the vocal line there is a curious treatment of the seventh word:

Ex.803   ent - set - zen,

there are repeated notes—the strokes of a single bell; there is a passage of three bars of staccato notes:

Ex.804   schlägt?

and there are copious semiquavers to 'tausend'. The remainder of
the text is 'Mein Leib neigt täglich sich zur Erden, und da muß seine
Ruh'statt werden, wohin man so viel tausend trägt' ('My body bends
daily itself to the earth, and there must its resting-place be, whither
one so many thousands carries'). 'Mein Leib' begins with an inversion of (*a*), 'sich zur Erden' sinks step by step, and inversion

comes again with 'und da muß seine'. The second presentation of this portion of the text is extended. 'Ruh'' is sustained while an altered form of (a) is heard above. These are reversed, the motive being again subjected to change.

An alto recitative with strings, iii, stanza 3, complaining of worldly sufferings and loss, is beautifully romantic in feeling. 'Indeed feels my weak heart fear, sorrow, pain: where will my body the rest find? Who will my soul then from the over-laid sins'-yoke free and release?' (Here violin I moves uneasily, as if the soul were trying to raise its load.) 'My belongings become scattered, and whither will my loved ones in their sadness be scattered and dispersed?'

Complete confidence and an entire change of outlook come in the bass aria, iv, part of stanza 4. (See P. 51.) It is a delightful gigue, a piece of unabashed dance music made to serve the purpose of the church;

and its sequels:

and:

are as irresponsible as anything in the suites or Brandenburg concertos. The flute, which was an instrument of mourning in i, is here merry and laughing. Although the strings have much of interest, to the traverso fall equal honours with the singer. It may have been adapted from an instrumental work, for the second, fourth, and sixth of the opening words—'Doch weichet ihr tollen vergeblichen Sorgen' ('Then vanish your mad fruitless cares')—after the first statement to a modification of (*a*), are allotted identical flourishes, none of which have any particular significance, though they help to carry the rollicking tune along. It is contrary to Bach's methods. A delicious idea accompanies the first vocal clause:

accompanied by little sighings; that the Christian regards his sorrows as of no consequence is indicated by (*c*) being twittered above a long holding note to 'Sorgen'. 'Mich rufet mein Jesus: wer sollte nicht gehn?' ('Me calls my Jesus: who would not go?') is developed extensively, its brief clauses permitting of much variety of detail. The brilliant runs of (*b*) accompany the first deliveries, which are to a gay tune. From here a few bars of the introduction follow. The second clause is shortened by the omission of 'gehn', (*d*) is extended, rising higher and higher and breaking off abruptly on a top A, a note of interrogation which permits of no answer to the oft-repeated question. The whole sentence is now sung to (*d*). Another rollicking tune comes to 'Nichts, was mir gefällt, besitzet die Welt!' ('Nothing, that me pleases, belongs to the world!'), with fragments of (*a*) and (*b*) interpolated in the orchestra, 6½ bars of decorative flute semiquavers follow, 'nichts' is thrown about in leaps. A modification of (*a*) is set to the clause, and 'Erscheine mir seliger fröhlicher Morgen' ('Appear to me (thou) blessed joyous morning') brings yet another captivating melody from Bach's endless stores, with a turn on 'Morgen'. The latter is developed in an ascending sequence on the initial word of 'verkläret und herrlich vor Jesu zu stehn' ('transfigured and glorious before Jesus to stand'), the soul rising buoyantly from the world. A cascade of traverso semiquavers prefaces a sustained 'verkläret', during which (a) is played and the violins return to their brief sighings. The introduction and the whole of the first section are repeated, the latter to end in the tonic instead of the dominant, the final 'wer sollte nicht gehn?' leaping up to the third of the chord to ask the already answered question for the last time.

The remainder of stanza 4 is paraphrased for a soprano recitativo secco: 'Retain only O world my belongings! Thou takest indeed even my flesh and my bones, so take also my poverty away; enough, that to me out of God's abundance the highest possession yet come must, enough, that I there rich and blessed am. What however is by me to inherit, but my God's Father-faithfulness? This becomes indeed every morning new and cannot die.' In spite of the happiness of the mood Bach cannot resist falsifying the meaning of the sentence by painting 'die' with a melisma including a diminished third. Few cantatas are so wholly attractive and so individual as this lovely work.

93. The Gospel is more often favoured as a subject for a cantata than the Epistle, but the latter for the Fifth Sunday after Trinity, 1 Peter iii. 8–15, advice as to righteous conduct in life, even though it bring false accusation and suffering, is the basis of G. Neumark's hymn 'Wer nur den lieben Gott läßt walten' ('If thou but sufferest God to guide thee', N. 'He who relies on God's compassion', B.) which is one of the appointed hymns. It was possibly set for 27 June 1728. Picander (?) adopted a new plan; stanzas 1, 4, 5, and 7 are retained and original lines remain in the paraphrases of 2, 3, and 6. Two of these verses present a previously untried method, which we find in later hymn-paraphrased cantatas. In ii, four lines of 2 are quoted and each is followed by a sermonette on the text, in v all six lines of 5 are introduced, with sermonettes on the first five. These are for bass and tenor respectively, in both cases with continuo only. The chorale line, the hymn-writer's own melody, is sung plain or embellished in tempo, adagio, with generally a moving bass, while the reflections are in recitative, with a plain or a commentary bassi line. They are always named *Recitativ und Choral*. ii begins 'What avail us the heavy cares?' and the continuo weightily drops by leaps of fourths and fifths. The corollary is, 'They oppress only the heart with a hundredweight of pain, with a thousand anguishes and pains'. In

this translation of the remainder the hymn lines are printed in ordinary type, the commentaries in italics. The chorale lines are always accompanied by the fourths-and-fifths bass. 'What avails us our woe and Ah? *It brings only bitter discomfort.* What avails it that we every morning *with sighs from the sleep arise, and with tearful countenance by night to bed go*? We make our cross and suffering *through anxious mourning only greater. Therefore does a Christian much better, he carries his cross with Christ-like calmness.*' There is a pathos-laden melisma on 'Kreuz und Leid' ('cross and sorrow') and '*Gelassenheit*' ('*calmness*') rocks blissfully.

v is more elaborate—'Think not in thy oppression-heat *when lightning and thunder crack*' (this is allegro, continuo demisemiquavers leap and then rumble down). Andante, '*and thee sultry tempest anxious makes*' (the bassi pulsate in semiquavers) 'that thou by God forsaken art' (the continuo throbs on G, A♭, D♭.) '*God remains also in the greatest need, yea even till in the death with His mercy by His own. Thou mayest not suppose* that this God in the lap (of luxury) lives' (here the continuo solemnly and comfortingly descends the scale of B♭ minor) '*Who daily, like the rich man, in pleasure and delight live can.* Who himself with constant good-fortune feasts *on nothing but good days, must often finally, after he himself with vain pleasures satiates*; "*death in the pots*" *say*.' (See 2 Kings iv. 40.) Line 5—'the posterity changes much!', which is accompanied by minims, is ingeniously followed, accompanied by long notes, by a lengthy meditation on the incident of the fruitless toiling of Simon overnight and the miraculous draught of fishes in the morning, which occurs in the Gospel, St. Luke v. 1–11: '*Has Peter even the whole night with empty work spent, and nothing caught: on Jesu's word can he yet a shoal obtain. Therefore rely only in poverty, suffering and pain, on thy Jesu's goodness with believing mind. After rain gives He sunshine.*' In the final line—'and sets to everyone his goal.' the continuo sways happily. In spite of Bach's boundless ingenuity and illimitable invention, such recitatives with chorale are rarely satisfactory. The poetaster has to force his muse, the sermonettes are often far-fetched and the language involved frequently chaotic. From the musical point of view they are too patchy; the alternations of strict tempo with free, of sustained phrases with recitative style, do not cohere. One can imagine the master dealing with them in despair, throwing into their composition all his wealth of idea and resource, but groaning under the burden of an uncongenial task.

The canto fermo is found in every number. The tenor aria (see P. 18) with strings, iii, introduces lines 1 and 3 of stanza 3—'Man halte nur ein wenig stille' ('(Let) one endure only a little quietly') and 'denn unsres Gottes Gnaden-Wille' ('for our God's mercy-will'). The paraphrase of line 2 is '*wenn sich die Kreuzes-Stunde naht*' ('*when the cross's-hour approaches*') and lines 4 and 5: '*verläßt uns nie mit Rath und That. Gott, der die Auserwählten kennt, Gott, der sich uns ein Vater nennt, wird endlich allen Kummer wenden, und seinen Kindern Hülfe senden*' ('*forsakes us never with counsel and deed. God, Who the chosen knows, God Who Himself to us a Father calls, will finally all trouble turn away, and to His children help send*'). The introduction is singularly simple and homophonic, six two-bar phrases followed by one of four. The melody is almost identical with Miecke's song in 'town-style' (viii) in the Coffee Cantata, and a startling anticipation of the slow movement of Beethoven's second symphony. When the soloist takes it up, slightly decorated:

the upper strings sustain a B♭, to illustrate 'halte'. The introduction is modified so as to end in the dominant, the voice moving independently, with a happily tender phrase on 'denn unsres Gottes', &c. Eight instrumental bars follow and the section is marked to be repeated, an unusual procedure, decided, no doubt, by the fact that the aria is looked upon as an expansion of the chorale, in which lines 1 and 2 are sung again to lines 3 and 4. A variant of bars 7 and 8 of the opening melody:

is the chief accompaniment figure of Part II; notes 4–6 come four times, three of these with alterations, in violin I, while the middle strings are silent. At first the voice pursues a new melody, but, beginning with 'wird endlich', the 'denn unsres Gottes' melody is repeated. As if the composer grew impatient of short and simple melodic phrases, there is at the close a tremendously long run, of eleven bars, to the verb 'senden', the overflowing of God's gracious aid, at first accompanied by (*a*) and then left alone with the continuo.

Bach indicates that the soprano aria, vi, with oboe obbligato, is *Mit stellenweiser Benutzung der Choral-Melodie*. ('With occasional use of the chorale melody.') Line 3 of the original stanza is retained, the others are paraphrases. A delicious melody for the oboe is not unconnected with line 1 of the canto, which runs—m l t d¹ t l t se m:

Ex. 813

later there are gleeful laughs:

Ex. 814

while the continuo skips down the chord of the diminished seventh staccato, and:

Ex. 815

The voice sings '*Ich will auf den Herren schau'n*' ('*I shall on the Lord look*'), the upward-turning of the eyes being indicated by a modi-fication of (*a*), the oboe replying with (*b*). The vocal (*a*) is repeated, the oboe playing a version above, and then the voice simplifies (*b*) to '*und stets meinem Gott vertrau'n* ('*and ever on my Lord trust*'). Other forms of (*a*) and (*b*) are used for repetitions of the clauses, (*c*) and a figure compounded of (*c*) and (*d*) contribute to the gaiety; a sustained '*vertrau'n*' is accompanied by (*a*). (*d*) in the oboe and part of (*a*) in the bassi lead to a quotation from the canto, line 5, 'er ist der rechte Wundersmann,' ('He is the true magician'), with (*a*) for the oboe and the fragment for the continuo. '*Der die Reichen arm und bloß*' ('*Who the rich poor and naked*') and '*und die Armen reich und groß*' ('*and the poor rich and great*') are both set to alterations of the vocal (*a*), while the oboe thrice repeats the initial form. It is unusual for Bach to associate a chorale-melody with any text not quoted exactly from a hymn, but he does so twice, using the last line of the tune, with '*nach seinem Willen machen kann*' ('*according to His will make can*'), (*c*) leaping above before the voice is left impressively alone with the continuo. When the last three lines of the text are repeated, there are partial quotations from the canto; 'er ist', &c., is set to a condensed form of line 5 of the canto, 'der die', &c., to one of line 6; (*b*) is above and there is a fall of a seventh to a sustained 'bloß', during which the oboe begins (*a*), (*b*), and (*c*) in succession. 'Und die Armen' again ascends and the final line follows as before. Again one stands amazed at Bach's miraculous deftness with his material.

There is nothing in stanza 1 to stimulate ideas of musical imagery: 'Who only the loving God allows to govern And hopes on Him at all times, Him will He wonderfully uphold In all suffering and mourning. Who on God, the All-Highest, trusts, He has on no sand built.' Bach therefore constructs his large fantasia on a purely thematic basis. The chief theme, accompanied by chords for the strings, is a canon for two oboes:

Ex.816

(Key C minor, signature of 2 flats)

The oboes in unison, after:

Ex.817

modify (*a*), while the violins transform the semiquavers of (*a*) into a blissful duet:

Ex.818

The canto fermo is given to the sopranos and thrown into $\frac{12}{8}$ time, which with Bach always means spaciousness of treatment. The sopranos, however, are not permitted to confine themselves to the canto. Each line is prefaced by a fugato:

for 1 and 3, and modified for 5—t d¹ r¹ m¹ m¹ r¹ r¹ d¹—that for 2 and 4—s s f m l l t se l:

and for 6—m¹ r¹ d¹ t l t d¹ t l:

Except in the case of line 6 the fugato is separated by a rest from the chorale line in block harmony. The final note of each chorale line is prolonged, the lower voices moving freely. To save wordiness the fugato is indicated by (1) in the following analysis, the chorale line by (2) and the prolongation by (3). Line 1—(1), S.A. concluding with (d) on 'walten'; (2), (a) in canon in the oboes; (3), figures from (c) in the voices, (a) in canon for the oboes. This theme, unison oboes, with (c) in the violins, dovetails into the line 2 section—(1), (f) for

S.A., (d) tossed from upper strings to oboes and (a) in oboe canon near the end; (2), (b) in the orchestra; (3), (a) in canon between violin I and II, the oboes (c) and (d), the voices concluding with (c) and (d). The staccato mark and the trill in (f) are purely musical devices, not called for by any particular point in the text, as is shown by the different words of line 4, to be referred to later. The introduction comes again. Line 3—an exact repetition of the treatment of line 1, except that (1) is for T.B. Line 4—as in line 2, but again (1) is transferred to T.B.; the staccato note on 'Kreuz' ('suffering') and the trill on 'Traurigkeit' ('mourning') are quite out of keeping—this is one of the few cases where Bach has sacrificed interpretation of the text for the sake of musical unity; (2), by way of compensation the lower voices are more ornate and expressive than before. A long ritornello introduces (a) in canon in the oboes and in the violins, and then violas and bassi play it in octaves, an unusual device, with (c) and part of (d) in the other instruments. Line 5—(1), the fugal theme (e) is modified so as to conform with the canto, the whole choir is employed, the upper instruments are silent, the continuo develops a portion of (c); (2), canon (a) in the oboes, the violins prolong (c) and (d) till (3) is finished, and during the latter the altos sing the fugato theme. Violins and violas play (a) in unison during the interlude, the oboes adding (c) and (d) above. Line 6—(1) as (g) enters in all voices, the bassi roll down in semiquavers, (h) indicating the fate of the house not built on a rock, and the upper strings and oboes toss to each other ♪♩ in leaps, the same figure which is used earlier in the accompaniment, (see Exs. 816, 819, and 820), though heretofore it has mostly moved stepwise. The new form intensifies the animation of the closing section, the sopranos climb gradually to high G, and as it is reached the tenors and altos enter in close imitation with (g); (2), (a) in free imitation in the oboes, (d) in the violins; (3), violins and oboes reverse and at the end the basses leap upwards step by step in a final assurance: 'der hat auf keinen Sand gebaut.' It is a splendid and fascinating chorus.

Bach thought sufficiently well of the setting of stanza 4 to include it in the Schübler chorale preludes, in which form it is one of the most effective. The verse runs: 'Er kennt die rechten Freudenstunden, Er weiß wohl, wenn es nützlich sei. Wenn er uns nur hat treu erfunden Und merket keine Heuchelei; So kommt Gott, eh' wir's uns versehn, Und lässet uns viel Gut's geschehn' ('He knows the right joy-hours, He knows well when it profitable is. If He us only has faithful found and observes no hypocrisy; So comes God, before we it expect, And permits to us much goodness to happen'). The canto fermo is heard instrumentally only, violins and violas in unison, in crotchets. The vocal parts of the S.A. duet sing line 1 in diminution and fragments of 2 and 6. A new theme enters after the double bar—

Ex. 822

(the connexion with line 5 of the canto is apparent), and it is the most important vocal idea in the second part. The continuo, which has been exploiting a time-pattern which is really a diminution of the diminution of line 1:

Ex. 823

takes up this new theme belatedly, on the very last note of the chorale. The four-part concluding chorale is plain; it has been trans- lated for No. 88, p. 431. Spitta thinks the cantata conceived more as domestic music than for the church, which scarcely seems a justifiable theory.

9. Neither Gospel nor Epistle for the Sixth Sunday after Trinity has much connexion with the hymn set, P. Speratus's 'Es ist das Heil uns kommen her', save that all three are in the nature of theological discussions. The anonymous melody is that commonly associated with the hymn. The date is possibly about 1731; Wustmann is in- clined to place it later and some of the qualities of the music support this view. The twelve stanzas are rendered suitable for the text of the cantata by the omission of 10 and severe compression; 1 and 12 are left in their original form and the remaining nine are condensed to serve five numbers. The chief burden of the hymn is justification by faith rather than by works, the Lutheran doctrine which, ardent theologian as Bach was, is an insufficient stimulus to musical imagina- tion. Once only in the cantata does the flame become white-hot, and that is when doctrinal argument gives place to human emotion. One is fascinated by the fine handling of the material of the chorale

fantasia, the development of the three ideas announced in the opening
two bars by flauto traverso, oboe d'amore, and strings:

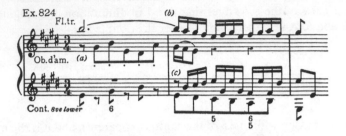

Ex.824

which appear in so many ever-new forms, the canto fermo in whole-
bar notes, the skilful lower parts. Yet it lacks warmth, it is cold
reasoning, reasoning about faith instead of the glow of enthusiasm
of faith itself. In the penultimate line some feeling manifests itself;
'der hat g'nug für uns all' gethan' is set in all lower voices to detached quavers, the curious effect continuing for about six bars. It is
difficult to sing 'g'nug' on a detached quaver; one feels that the composer was making an abortive effort to get away from the icy statement of doctrine. The text is, 'It is the salvation to us come hither'
(or 'Salvation has come to us here') 'Through grace and pure goodness; The works they help nevermore, They may not protect; The
faith regards Jesus Christ, Who has sufficient for us all done, He has
the Mediator become.' Lines 1–4 are accompanied in the lower voices
by a variant of (a) and by runs derived sometimes from (b). (c), being
purely instrumental in type, is not found in the vocal parts. Line 5
contains leaps of fourths and fifths indicative of the firm faith of the
Christian. There are similar significant leaps in line 7.

It is unusual to assign three recitatives, all with continuo, to one
voice, in this case a bass. Perhaps they are intended to represent the
preacher elaborating his theories. ii is a paraphrase of stanzas 2, 3,
and part of 4: 'God gave us a law yet were we too weak, that we it
had to hold been able;' (see Ex. 1322) 'we went only the sins after,
no man was devout to be called; the spirit remained to the flesh
clinging and dared not resist. We should in the law walk, and there
as in a mirror see, how our nature displeasing is: and yet remain we
therein; by his own strength was no-one able sin's wrongdoing to
relinquish, should he even all strength together exert.' It goes without
saying that with such a text the number is without incident.

iv paraphrases 5, 6, and 7: 'Yet must the law fulfilled be; therefore came the salvation of the world, the Highest's Son, Who has it Himself fulfilled and His Father's anger calmed; through His guiltless dying' (here Bach warms the cold body of theological logic by a melismatic 'unschuldig' ('guiltless')) 'allowed He us help to acquire. Who now on the same relies, who on His suffering builds, he goes not lost: the heaven is for him chosen, who true faith with himself brings and firmly round Jesus (his) arms entwines.' The last clause is a lovely arioso in which the continuo descends in a long series of thirds, as if the believer were nestling into the bosom of his Redeemer.

vi compounds 9 and 11, and is very long—'When we the sin through the law recognize, then strikes it the conscience down; yet is that our comfort to be called, that we in the Gospel even again glad and joyful become: this only strengthens our faith again. Therefore hope we (for) the time, that God's goodness to us promised has, yet therefore also through wise counsel the hour from us has hidden. Nevertheless, we let ourselves be contented: He knows it when it necessary is, and requires no craft in us; we may on Him build and on Him alone rely.' There is little in these recitative-texts to stimulate the unfortunate composer.

v, stanza 8 paraphrased, is an uncompromising statement of the doctrine that faith of heart is more important than good works. Bach views this as law and not as doctrine and writes according to the severest musical laws. There are two pairs of canonical lines, S. and A., flute and oboe d'amore, the majority of the passages being strict. In the first part the two pairs work out different forms of the same theme. The instrumental canon begins:

the vocal:

and the latter continues in the same way as did (a):

Ex.827

Dovetailing with this, the obbligati instruments begin to work out a fresh canon on (a) while the voices make it a 4-in-2 with a new theme:

Ex.828

After a prolongation and a close, (a) occurs in the obbligati, the voices begin a fifteen-bar canon, varying (a) and adding a form of (b), and there is a semiquaver passage:

Ex.829

borrowed from the latter part of the introduction. Fragmentary entries of (a) appear in the upper instruments. The 4-in-2 canon comes again with a free continuation and the introduction is repeated. The whole of Part II, some thirty bars, is a single two-part canon, beginning:

Ex.830

and continuing 'als daß es uns helfen kann' ('than that it us to help is able'), in which part of (c) appears. The obbligati double the voices, decorating some of the plainer passages. Intellectually the number is interesting but it is crystal cold.

The one real glow of the cantata is to be found in the tenor aria with violin obbligato, iii, a paraphrase of part of stanza 4: 'Wir waren schon zu tief gesunken, der Abgrund schluckt' uns völlig ein, die Tiefe drohte schon den Tod, und dennoch konnt' in solcher Noth uns keine Hand behülflich sein' ('We were already too deeply sunk, the abyss swallowed us completely, the depths threatened already the death, and yet could in such distress to us no hand helpful be'). Triplets staggering downwards begin the obbligato and are modified for the chief vocal phrase:

We see the wild throwing-up of despairing hands:

precipitation into the abyss:

and the continuo struggles and falls. 'Abgrund' descends ominously, 'schluckt' uns völlig ein' sways in terror. 'völlig' is thrust on an upper note. Part II is even more chaotic; the agonized struggle for life is indicated by:

while (b) and later (a) come in the obbligato, and the bassi roll into the depths, 'keine Hand behülflich sein' struggles desperately upwards, but (c) indicates the futility of the cry for the helping hand which comes not. In the recapitulation (*a*) is extended and then the voice leaps in terror a diminished twelfth, to high A on 'der Abgrund'. The tortuous vocal line is of immense difficulty yet a dramatic singer of ability finds in it superb opportunities. Stanza 12, the final chorale, has been translated for No. 155, p. 103.

It always has been, and possibly always will be, a problem for church composers to decide how far music may be a personal document and how far it should sink its individuality in the greater issues of God, the church, and humanity. Palestrina and Vittoria attained the highest sublimity in impersonality; even so we often [find] the man speaking and not the priest. A hyper-personal type of church music never survives beyond its epoch. Only the greatest men can guide their vessel along the middle course, and even then they are prone to error at times. Bach ventured on both sides of the channel in this cantata and there is no mistaking which appeals to later generations.

99. 'Was Gott thut, das ist wohlgethan' is the title of three cantatas. As far as conjecture can tell, they lie near each other. No. 98 ('What God doth, surely that is right' O.) employs stanza 1 only, though probably another was sung in a four-part version to conclude. The date is possibly 1732. It will be discussed under section (v). For the Fifteenth Sunday after Trinity, possibly 1733 and 1735, came 99 and 100, the former to an adapted version of Samuel Rodigast's hymn, stanzas 2–5 being paraphrased for the corresponding numbers of the cantata, while, curiously enough, No. 100 reverts to the unaltered hymn type. The melody is that commonly attached to the hymn. The fantasia of No. 99 is on a generous scale, the chief feature being the orchestral writing. The ritornelli are disproportionately long. For example, the introduction lasts nineteen bars, the first choral entry 4½. This in no wise interferes with the beauty of the movement. The orchestral score, flauto traverso, oboe d'amore, and strings, is a fine study in the art of the development of themes. The material is sparse; the rising two-note idea of the opening, with the firm bass indicative of God's unassailable acts:

Ex.835 (*a*)
Str.
bis
Cont.
8ve lower

subsequent variants:

and:

that is almost all, and it suffices for 116 bars! A charming variant of
(*a*) is where violin II and viola are silent and violin I and oboe
d'amore play it in tenths while the flute trips in semiquavers above.
There are fine sequences above dropping fifths in the bassi:

(*b*) of which is copiously developed from the middle of the last line of
the verse, the latter being heralded by the bassi descending stepwise
with the two-note idea for nearly two octaves. (*a*) is also heard in the
continuo. The movement is a beautiful piece of chamber music. The
choral sections are plain, the soprano, doubled by corno, always
enters before the lower voices and the lines are never extended. The
text is: 'What God does, that is well done, There remains righteous
His will: However He manages my affairs, Will I to Him hold quietly.
He is my God, Who in the distress Me well knows (how) to sustain:
Therefore let I Him only govern.'

The bass recitativo secco, ii, indulges in a lengthy passage to
'wenden' ('turn away') at the end, after a long spell of plain and
rapid movement: 'His word of truth stands fast and will me not de-
ceive, because it the believers neither to fall nor to be destroyed permits. Yea, because it me (along) the way to life guides, so composes
my heart itself, and lets itself be contented in God's Father-faithfulness and favour, and has patience, if me a misfortune touches, God
can with His Almighty hands my misfortune turn away.'

The tenor aria, iii, admonishes the despondent spirit not to shudder when the 'Kreuzes Kelch' tastes too bitterly. The obbligato flute soon slides down chromatically:

a foretaste of similar passages, both direct and inverted, and flutters like a wounded bird for many bars at a time:

It is a beautiful and effective number. The voice begins: 'Erschütt're dich nur nicht, verzagte Seele' ('Shatter thee only not, despondent soul') with (a); (c) follows, incorporating (b) in contrary motion. (b) comes in all three lines during 'wenn dir der Kreuzes-Kelch so bitter schmeckt' ('when to thee the suffering-cup so bitter tastes'), and later to 'verzagte'. Variants occupy the remainder of Part I. 'Gott ist dein weiser Arzt und Wundermann' ('God is thy wise physician and miracle-worker') begins diatonically and straight-forwardly with continuo only, which plays part of (a); on the repetition of the clause the flute enters, and (a) is heard in both instrumental lines. 'So dir kein tödlich' Gift' ('So into thee no deadly poison') ascends gradually with (a) and (b) above, the latter coinciding with 'Gift'. A long run follows on 'einschenken kann' ('be poured can') with the shuddering (c) for the flute. (c) is present during the most of 'obgleich die Süßigkeit verborgen steckt' ('although the sweetness hidden lies'), which is set to a new melody with a nine-bar passage on 'verborgen', emphasizing the presence of concealed virtue in the cup. At the close 'obgleich die Süßigkeit' soars aloft, but Bach negates the comfort of the assurance by a flute reference to (b) and a sinking low to 'verborgen steckt'.

A short alto recitativo secco, iv, ends, like its predecessor, with an arioso on the final word: 'Now, the from-eternity-made covenant remains my faith's-ground. It speaks with confidence in life and death: God is my light, to Him will I myself surrender. And (should) have all days likewise their own trouble, yet after the endured suffering, when one enough (has) wept, comes finally the deliverance-time, when God's true meaning appears.'

There is an elaborate S.A. duet, v, with flute and oboe d'amore, the same scoring as ix in No. 9, but vastly different in emotional outlook. The bitterness of the cross and the weakness of the spirit are spoken of in stubborn melodic phrases:

'Streiten' struggles and bends:

The wavering on 'Schwachheit' will be noticed. The obbligati add (b) and phrases constructed from (a). A ritornello is formed out of canonical treatment of (a) and the 'Schwachheit' idea, rising higher and higher, the struggling upwards of the spirit. A lengthier section deals with the same themes, the voices running in parallel semiquavers to 'streiten' and ending with continuo to a homophonic passage on 'ist es dennoch wohlgethan' ('is it nevertheless well-done'), the burden of the hymn. Here the bassi, almost for the only time in the duet, depart from their detached quavers on the beats and race joyfully upwards. A new theme appears:

(continuo similar to other examples)

in voices and obbligati, and later 'unerträglich' suggests the body writhing under an unendurable burden. 'Wird auch künftig nicht' ('will even in the future not') is set to (*a*) and followed on 'ergötzet' ('be rejoiced') to the 'streiten' semiquavers, more appropriate to the first word than to the second. The upper instruments toss phrases to each other:

as if the Christian were being flung hither and thither. When flute and oboe d'amore take up the canonical movement the voices alternate in groups akin to the above, and the obbligati reply to each other with yet a third form as the singers pursue the 'ergötzet' run. The close of the vocal section unexpectedly introduces new ideas with ascending groups for the obbligati.

The closing four-part chorale is bold and forceful, atoning for its previous neglect. Lines 1 and 8 of stanza 6 are the same as the corresponding ones in 1; the intermediate lines are 'Thereon shall I rest; There may me on the rough road, Distress, death and misery drive, Yet will God me All fatherlike In His arms hold'. Oboe d'amore, corno, and violin I double the sopranos at the unison and the flute plays *ottava*.

(iv) *Biblical Text*

(191)

(v) *Biblical Quotations plus Original Matter*

'*O ewiges Feuer*' Unnumbered and incomplete

'*O ewiges Feuer.*' Of the five wedding cantatas that have been preserved, one only, which was written for a family ceremony, is wholly original. Three of them, Nos. 195, 197 and the incomplete 'Herr Gott, Beherrscher aller Dinge' are mostly quarried from material already in existence, probably hurriedly compiled for the occasions. The remaining one, the incomplete and unnumbered 'O ewiges Feuer', written sometime after 1734, contains one number only that was possibly borrowed, but the remainder seems original, and, by a converse process, it and two other numbers loaned themselves for the cantata of the same title, No. 34, about 1740 or 1741. It must, therefore, have come into being for some marriage in which Bach took a particular interest, and the anonymous libretto suggests that it was 'for the wedding of a clerical dignitary, probably one of the Leipzig clergy'. Terry, from whom this quotation is made, asks, 'May it have been Christian Weiss the younger?', as Bach was friendly with both father and son, and a number of cantata libretti may be speculatively assigned to them. The splendid opening chorus, with three trumpets, timpani, two oboes and strings, became i in the well-known Whit-Sunday cantata, and it is well for us that it is so, as all the instrumental lines of the source, except violin I, viola, and unfigured continuo have been lost. The borrowed numbers will be dealt with when No. 34 is discussed.

ii is a bass recitativo secco:—'How is it that love's great might in men's souls a heavenly kingdom on earth creates? What draws Thee, Oh Highest Being, love's effect to choose? a heart as dwelling to choose?' This begins almost as in No. 34, G instead of B minor, and then deviates.

A long Arie, A.T. dialogue, follows. To the alto are given recitatives, which are accompanied by strings (it need not be repeated that violin II line is missing, that is the case throughout the cantata), and the other portions are for tenor, with continuo only. These consist mostly of short phrases speaking of the blessings promised by the Almighty on man and his children; five quotations from Psalm cxxviii. 4–6, form the text. There is a nine-bar introduction and then the chief continuo idea accompanies the first tenor entry:

Ex.845

The remainder of the verse—'der den Herren fürchtet' ('who the Lord fears')—is reserved till the close of the long opening section. (a) functions in all the tenor arioso portions. The remainder of the text is —A. 'Whither penetrates the spirit with faith's eyes? Where seeks it the blessings' sources, which the true soul's wedlock as a blessed, promised land, may represent?' T. 'Der Herr wird dich segnen aus Zion,' ('The Lord shall thee bless out of Zion'), A. 'What, however, has Thy God for thee designed, for thee, whose diligence in God's house watches? What will the service of the holy dwellings on thee for blessing scatter?' T. 'daß du sehest das Glück Jerusalems dein Leben lang' ('that thou seest the happiness of Jerusalem thy life long'), A. 'Because Zion's well-being first thy heart moves, will itself even earthly pleasure after thy heart's desire direct, that God a chosen child to thee leads, that thou in unnumbered years renewed well-being mayest experience.' (See Ex. 1282.) T. 'und sehest deiner Kinder Kinder' ('and seest thy children's children'), A. 'So call we at the blessings-hour from hearts with united mouth.' The last words of verse 6 of the Psalm 'Friede über Israel!' ('Peace upon Israel!') are omitted from the duet and act as an Adagio prelude to the next number, an unusual plan, meaningless when the chorus was transferred to the Whitsun cantata to serve as finale.

After the ceremony (*Post copulationem*) comes the lovely alto aria with which we are familiar as the only example of this form in No. 34. The text is 'Wohl euch, ihr auserwählten Schafe, die ein getreuer Jacob liebt. Sein Lohn wird dort am größten werden, den ihn der Herr bereit auf Erden durch seiner Rahel Anmuth giebt' ('Well for you, you chosen sheep, whom a faithful Jacob loves. His reward will there the greatest be, which to him the Lord already on earth through his Rachel grace gives'). Was the allusion a personal one? Had the clerical bridegroom waited long for his lady-love? The character of the music is that of a slumber-song over the Infant Christ, with waving of angels' wings; it may have been borrowed from some lost Christmas cantata. On the other hand Jacob's ladder may have been in Bach's mind.

A soprano addresses the bridegroom in a recitativo secco: 'That is for thee, oh honour-worthy man, the noblest reward that thee delight can. (May) God, Who from eternity the love itself was called and through a virtuous child thy heart to be touched caused, fill now with blessing thy dwelling, that it as Obed-Edom's may be, and add might to the blessings-word.' The reference to Obed-Edom, the Gittite in whose house the ark sheltered for three months, and who with his household was blessed by God in consequence (2 Sam. vi), is further confirmation of the supposition that the bridegroom was a cleric; a layman would scarcely be likely to be familiar with the incident.

The text of the concluding chorus is much the same in construction as that of the duet, except that two free lines come before the first Biblical quotation. Numbers vi. 24, 25, and 26 are interleaved by original matter. The Scripture passages are set to the associated intonation of the Blessing, evidently in choral unison (A. and T. lines are missing throughout), and only in these are the full strings employed. The plan is (1) continuo, four bars:

Chorus: 'Gieb, höchster Gott, auch hier dem Worte Kraft, das so viel Heil bei deinem Volke schafft' ('Grant, Highest God, even here to the word might, that so much salvation with Thy people produces'):

(*aa*) occurs in nearly every bar of the continuo. After two bars of interlude, (*a*), there are eleven bars of vocal matter. There is some confusion of text here, the bass line substitutes 'sonst' for the soprano 'so', but the sense of the verb agrees with the latter. There are now four bars of (*a*), and the upper strings enter for the first time. (2) Intonation—'The Lord bless thee and keep thee!' v. 24, above the original four bars of (*a*). Violin I introduces a new theme:

(3) 'Es müsse ja auf Den zurücke fallen, der Solches läßt an heil'ger Stätte schallen' ('It must yea on him back fall, who the same causes in the holy place to resound'). From this point the continuo part is lost. The vocal material is new, except that part of (*c*) is incorporated into the bass 'fallen'. There are six choral bars, then four instrumental, with a new figure in violin I:

(4) Intonation—'(May) the Lord let shine His countenance upon thee and be to thee gracious', v. 25, five bars, (*c*) and the time-pattern of

(d) in violin I. (5) 'Sein Dienst, so stets am Heiligthume baut, macht daß der Herr mit Gnaden auf ihn schaut' ('His service, (which) so constantly on the holy-work builds, causes that the Lord with mercy on him looks'), six bars, (b) is modified, (c) is used in a soprano run on 'baut' and a fresh idea is introduced:

Ex.850

four bars interlude, (d) and part of (e) in violin I. (6) Intonation— 'The Lord lift up His countenance upon thee, and give thee peace!' Eight bars, (c) in violin I and (d) over the sustained choral note, suggestions of (a) in viola. Four bars ritornello, (d), with several repetitions of (aa). (7) 'Der Herr, von dem die keuschen Flammen kamen, erhalte sie und spreche kräftig Amen' ('The Lord, from Whom the pure flames came, maintain them and say mightily Amen'). Eleven bars, beginning with the opening of (b), bursting into florid passages on the last two words, incorporating (c) and ending with (e) to Amen. After a bar rest there are three bars of interlude. (8) Coda on Amen, ten bars. S. & B. run in tenths to (c); after some monotoned Amens violin I sweeps upward on (c) and the S. trills the theme in its highest register. It is an interesting scheme, a worthy conclusion to a splendid cantata. Its brilliance and the reference to divine flames link it up with i. The gaps in the score indicate that there must have been many passages for brass and percussion. A reconstruction of the cantata is published in the Breitkopf Edition, numbered 34A.

(vi) *Hymn-Stanzas plus Original Matter*
16, 19, 66, 72, 73, 95, 98

Order of discussion: 16, 73, 72, 19, 66, 95, 98

16. The interest of 'Herr Gott, dich loben wir' centres in its choruses. The occasion, possibly Bach's first New Year's Day in Leipzig, did not, for some reason or other, cause the libretto, which may be by the composer, to be particularly attractive. The two recitativi secchi are pleasant enough, but of no especial value. The single aria, for tenor, is humdrum. Its obbligato is for oboe da caccia or violetta, a separate part existing for the latter. What exactly this instrument was is still a matter for speculation; and that Bach, though acquainted with it from the time of his Arnstadt soprano Magnificat, did not put it to any characteristic use, implies that we lose nothing through its very identity being now a matter of doubt. In spite of the comparative lack of interest in the chief theme of the aria:

Ex. 851.

Cont.

Bach develops it for sixteen bars. 'Geliebter Jesu, du allein sollst meiner Seelen Reichthum sein!' ('Beloved Jesus, Thou alone shalt my soul's kingdom be') is set to independent material, the obbligato fashioning its line from the introduction and occasionally borrowing from the voice. Lack of inspiration did not prevent Bach from spinning out the opening section to nearly forty bars and then repeating the introduction. Part II begins with a more interesting idea, ascending groups sandwiched in between repeated notes—'Wir wollen dich vor allen Schätzen in unser treues Herze setzen' ('We shall Thee before all treasures in our faithful heart set')—but it does not come again, the repetition of the clause being to new material. The obbligato is partly old and partly new. With continuo only comes 'ja, wenn das Lebensband zerreißt, stimmt unser gottvergnügter Geist noch mit den Lippen sehnlich ein' ('yea, when the life-band tears, joins our divinely-contented spirit again with the lips ardently in'). The composer evidently did not realize that *his* spirit had not been moved with divine ardour, for he marks the whole of the fifty-four bars of Part I to be repeated. It was not often that he lapsed so. Spitta thinks the aria to be related to those of Keiser and Telemann.

The alto recitative, iv, contains some of his characteristic felicities, the slight melisma to 'beliebte Ruh' ('beloved rest'), the dropping series of thirds to 'fällt lauter Wohlsein' ('falls (to our lot) nothing but well-being'), and the speech-like 'Wohl uns' ('Well for us'). Though without striking incident the number is grateful and pleasing, coming happily after the tumultuous second chorus. The text is: 'Ah faithful refuge, protect even further Thy worthy word, protect church and school, so is Thy kingdom increased, and Satan's wicked cunning disturbed; maintain only the peace and the blessed rest, so is to us already enough granted and to us falls nothing but well-being. Ah! God! Thou wilt the land yet further water, Thou wilt it continually improve, Thou wilt it Thyself with Thine hand and Thy blessing cultivate. Well for us, when we Thee ever and ever, my Jesus and my Salvation, trust.'

The bass recitative, ii, is not so interesting: 'So sing we in this glad time with warm devotion, and lay to Thee, Oh God, on this New Year the first heart's offerings down. What hast Thou not from eternity for salvation to us done, and what must our breast even now of love and truth perceive? Thy Zion sees complete rest, it falls on it happiness and blessings; the temple resounds with psalteries and with harps, and our soul swells, when we only devotion's-glow in heart and mouth express. Oh! Should therefore not a new song resound and we in warm love sing?'

Two clauses of Luther's versified form of the Te Deum in the vernacular are set in i. The plainsong adaptation associated with it is sung by the sopranos doubled with a Corno di caccia: 'Lord God Thee praise we, Lord God we thank Thee! Thee, God the father in eternity, Honours the world wide and broad.' The introduction begins with continuo only, the rhythm of joy:

Ex.852

from which it rarely departs and which permeates the lower vocal lines. It is derived from the plainchant: m s l d' l l. Bass, tenor, and alto in close imitation support line 1 by a figure which begins with the third and then merges into semiquavers. This forms the vocal interlude and continues through line 2. Violin II plus oboe II and viola enter with the theme in bar 10, violin I plus oboe I in the next. The oboes double the violins throughout. A similar treatment of the upper instruments occurs when lines 3 and 4 are intoned. In these the lower voices sing one theme resembling line 3 of the canto, the alto has another version of it, but otherwise they are thematically independent. The chorus is full of vigorous animation.

The second chorus, iii, called 'Aria', almost suggests a secular origin: 'Laßt uns jauchzen, laßt uns freuen' ('Let us exult, let us rejoice') gives rise to choral trills, and almost extravagant semi-quaver leaping passages:

Ex.853

The *corno di caccia* sometimes doubles the sopranos, sometimes plays independent counterpoint, and once adds a long trill to the brilliant mass of tone. As in i, the oboes double the violins. (*a*) is delivered unaccompanied; on (*b*) the rest of the forces are added, (*a*) being in the upper voices. (*c*) is for basses and continuo and is repeated by the sopranos in another short tutti. In a ritornello violin I plays another joyous leaping figure:

Ex.854

and then:

Ex.855

All voices re-enter, (*a*) above and (*b*) below, and (*b*) is treated fugally, the sopranos having a glorious run beginning with (*c*), the structure being overwhelming in its brilliance. The upper voices now sing 'Gottes Güt' und Treu'' ('God's goodness and truth') to a modification of (*d*), the bassi leaping octaves and with (*d*) in violin I and II, and continue 'bleibet alle Morgen neu' ('remains every morning new'); the basses take up 'Gottes Güt'' with (*e*) in violin I and a florid passage for the corno. A middle section ensues. A bass soloist sings floridly: 'Krönt und segnet seine Hand, ach so glaubt daß unser Stand ewig glücklich sei' ('Crowns and blesses His hand, ah so believe that our state eternally fortunate is'). It begins with a melody based on (*e*), and violin I plays another version while the voice repeats 'ach so glaubt'. There is a long note on 'ewig', with (*d*) in the upper strings and leaping octaves for the continuo. The tutti burst in for two bars, in A minor, with (*a*), (*b*), and (*c*), the corno trilling throughout. The previous solo section is now modified, (*d*) this time accompanying a series of dropping thirds (the falling of blessings), (*e*) comes above 'ewig'. An instrumental fugato on (*a*), with contrapuntal references to (*c*) and (*e*), leads to the final tutti. No doubt it would be understood that the oboes are silent during the solo portions. The tutti section is a reconstruction of the opening, ending in the tonic instead of in the dominant; the fugato begins accompanied with continuo only and entries are in the reverse order. Spitta sees in this brilliant chorus the influence of Telemann.

In the final four-part chorale the viola, most unusually, is added to violin II and oboe II to double the alto, the tenor is unassisted. The melody is W. Figulus's 'Helft mir Gott's Güte preisen', which is also associated with L. Hembold's 'Von Gott will ich nicht lassen'. The text is stanza 6 of P. Eber's New Year hymn of the first title above: 'All such of Thy goodness we praise, Father on heaven's throne, That Thou to us dost show Through Jesus Thy Son And beg moreover of Thee, Give us a peaceful year, From all sorrow preserve And cherish us generously.'

73. The Gospel for the Third Sunday after the Epiphany, St. Matt. viii. 1–13, the cleansing of the leper and the healing of the centurion's servant, has less influence on the libretto of the beautiful cantata No. 73 (possibly 1725) than the hymn on which i is based, C. Bienemann's (Melissander) 'Herr, wie du willt, so schick's mit mir'. Some of the lamentations in the text may be traced to Christ's prophecy of the weeping and gnashing of teeth by the children of the kingdom. The unknown librettist has preached a sermon on the hymn, which was not set for the day, even though stanza 1 only is actually used. A stanza of another hymn closes the work appropriately; we have thus two chorale melodies. The first is developed into a very extended fantasia, which contains some unique features. The use of the organ is exceptional. It may be that when the cantata was composed a corno was available, but at its production (or a later rehearing) the horn, for some reason or other, was not possible, and the composer gave the line to a manual—*Corno, ossia Organo obligato*—(corno staccato for the ritornelli and corno legato where it doubles the

chorale), and indicated *Rück-Positiv* and *Brust-Positiv* at various points, the former beginning. The pedals are the ordinary continuo. The horn always doubles the soprano chorale, but in the interludes often reiterates the notes 1–4 of the melody in a diminished form, a leitmotiv employed elsewhere, thus driving home the motto of the hymn: 'Lord, as Thou willst.' At the close of the introduction the corno introduces part of the chorale. In the longish post-chorale coda and just before the double bar, it is released from its dual task of motto and chorale, and indulges in a little free movement. (1) The introduction is constructed in an interesting way. The chief theme:

is clenched by the diminution of notes 1–4 of the canto in strings and horn, a message of comfort:

(*a*) and (*b*) are repeated a third higher, (*a*) again a tone lower, but not answered exactly by (*b*). (*aa*) is then developed in imitation while the corno anticipates line 1 of the canto. (2) Line 1—'Lord, as Thou willst, so ordain it with me' in block harmony, (*aa*) in the upper strings; interlude of a little more than a bar, Ex. 856 in B♭; line 2: 'In living and in dying!' with flowing lower parts, indicative of 'life', (*a*) in bass and all strings. (3) Interlude. Ex. 856 concluding with motto. Tenor recitative—'Ah! but Ah! how much lets me Thy will suffer! My life is the misfortune's limit where lamentation and vexation me living torture must, and scarcely will my distress in dying from me separate.' Poignant harmonies predominate; (*a*), in thirds in the oboes, comes once in each of five bars, the first and fifth times followed by the motto for upper strings and corno, the latter marked *Brust-positiv*. To conclude is (*aa*) imitated in the oboes. (4) Line 3— 'But on Thee stays my desire,'—almost as in 1, anticipated by the line, forte, diminished to staccato quavers, strings and horn. Line 4—'Lord, let me not be destroyed', as in line 2. (5) First comes Ex. 856. Bass recitative: 'Thou art my helper, comfort and refuge,

Who the troubled ones' tears counts, and their confidence the weak
reed dost not wholly break; and because Thou me choosest to speak
a comfort and joy-word.' A duet for oboes based on (*aa*) accompanies the opening words, then (*aa*) comes in sixths and thirds in
each of three successive bars, the first two answered by (*b*), strings
and corno. At the end (*a*) in imitation in the oboes. (6) Line 5—
'Maintain me only in Thy favour'—a rolling quaver bass, semiquavers in the inner strings. Interlude, Ex. 856 in F. Line 6—'Otherwise, as Thou willst, grant me patience'—(*aa*) in all strings. Interlude,
Ex. 856 in D minor. Line 7—'For Thy will is the best'—animated
upper strings. (7) Ex. 856 in G minor, clenched with (*b*). Soprano
recitative—'Thy will indeed is a sealed book, there man's wisdom
nothing perceives. The blessing appears to us often a curse, the
chastisement furious punishment, the rest, which Thou in the deaths'
sleep for us once determines, an entrance into the hell. Yet makes
Thy spirit us of this error free, and shows that to us Thy will healing
is.' The accompaniment is in the manner of those of the other
recitatives, but freer, there being extended oboe duets. (8) A twelve-
bar coda. Ex. 856 begins, it is clenched not only by horn, *Rück-
Positiv*, but by the chorus crying out in quavers 'Herr, wie du willt,'.
This is all repeated in B♭. After Ex. 856 in C minor, strings and oboes
work out four bars on (*aa*), during which the corno first plays a free
repeated-note version of line 7 and then, corno legato, the line in its
normal form. Two bars follow, in the first of which the chorus again
cries 'Herr, wie du willt!' This diversified scheme results in a very
lovely scena, a dramatic picture of the varying moods of the Christian troubled by his own unworthiness, dreading the possibility of
being cast into outer darkness, yet comforted by the thought of the
tempering of God's stern judgement by divine mercy.

The tenor aria, ii, is a request that the spirit of joy be sown in
the heart, and the obbligato oboe gives out a delightful tune prefaced
by a confident upward step-movement of the continuo—

Ex.858 *(a)*

Cont.
8ve lower

The melody is modified for 'Ach, senke doch den Geist der Freuden
dem Herzen ein' ('Ah, plant then the spirit of joy the heart in') and
the oboe repeats it with most of the falling ideas inverted, as if to

declare that the seed was already sending forth a shoot. With the repetition of the text (*a*) is the chief factor, set appropriately at times to 'den Geist der Freuden'. A charming picture of the variable spirit of the believer is presented, the voice ascends merrily on 'Es will oft bei mir geistlich Kranken' ('It will often with me the spiritually ailing') with a trembling figure on 'Kranken' and (*a*) in bassi and oboe; 'die Freudigkeit' ('the joy') is sung to (*a*), 'und Hoffnung' ('and hope') sustains against (*a*), 'wanken' ('vacillate') is clearly indicated, and 'und zaghaft sein' ('and timid be') seems to suggest a shrinking down, though (*a*), trebled in length, accompanies it. (*a*) in the continuo and the ascending figure, transferred from voice to oboe, join with a swift repetition of the words from 'es' to 'geistlich', 'Kranken' is set to a low-placed chromatic run, 'Freudigkeit' to a high-placed leaping one, while bassi and oboe toss to each other detached quavers, 'wanken' hovers in a bar of undulating semi-quavers with the oboe in sixths above, and then, as if freed from vacillation, the singer plunges into an extension of (*a*).

A bass recitativo secco (see P. 48, Recit. & Aria) contains bold chromatic harmonies: 'Ah, our will remains perverted, now obstinate, now timid', with appropriate gestures for the voice, and laments that 'of death will it never think!' Plainer harmonies support 'But a Christian, in God's spirit instructed, learns himself in God's will to sink'. 'Und sagt' ('and says') leads attacca to one of the finest of all arias for that voice. It begins with the initial words of the hymn:

Ex. 859 Herr, so du willt
(*a*)
Cont.
(C minor, signature of 2 flats)

and again its associated phrase is a tender and pleading motto for the number. It is answered immediately by a one-bar melody in the strings, an instrumental counterpart:

Ex. 860
(*b*)
Cont.

which is developed for a while before the voice re-enters. Thrice the singer delivers (*a*), varied each time, and thrice the strings reply with (*b*). Although these themes are used largely, there is much fresh material later, more than is customary. The aria is in free rondo form, the chief subjects, (*a*) and (*b*), being subjected to infinite variety, and once the other portions of the text are dealt with, they are not reverted to. The number is almost a dramatic scena. 'So preßt, ihr Todesschmerzen, die Seufzer aus dem Herzen, wenn mein Gebet nur vor dir gilt' ('So draw, ye death-pains, the sighs from the heart, if my prayer only before Thee prevails') does not depict the happy release pleaded for, but the present condition of woe, expressed by broken, laboured vocal phrases, accompanied by sighings for violin I:

Ex. 861

The ritornello which succeeds is a rich working-out of (*a*) and (*b*). Three vocal forms of (*a*) follow, all new. 'So lege meine Glieder in Staub und Asche nieder, dies höchst verderbte Sündenbild' ('So lay my limbs in dust and ashes low, this most corrupt sins-picture') naturally brings descending scales, but is followed by a passionate interlude for strings, with tense imitative passages for the violins. After the motto yet another interlude speaks of the tolling of funeral bells—'so schlagt, ihr Leichenglocken' ('so strike, ye funeral bells') with despairing, falling phrases; and pizzicato strings ring a solemn knell. With only one sharp chord added to the continuo, the singer asserts, to the step-motive, 'Ich folge unerschrocken' ('I follow unaffrighted'), and there is a picture of blissful peace: 'mein Jammer ist nunmehr gestillt' ('my lamentation is henceforth stilled'). A return of the bells indicates that peace is attained in the grave. The final return of the rondo-theme is remarkable for the changes to which it is subjected. Bach often constructs an aria out of one or two short phrases, economy of material is carried to its most logical conclusion and is productive of the most beautiful results; here he exhibits consummate skill in another way, not only presenting old material in ever-fresh ways and with cumulative effect, but uniting it with wholly different matter in such a manner that the aria is an indivisible whole. The vocal line, too, attains the utmost freedom and perfect appositeness.

The final chorale is stanza 9 of L. Helmhold's hymn 'Von Gott will ich nicht lassen' with its anonymous melody—'That is the Father's will, Who us created has; His Son has good in abundance Earned for us out of goodwill; Also God, the Holy Ghost, In faith over us reigns, To the kingdom of heaven leads; To Him be laud, honour and praise.'

72. For the same Sunday, possibly a year later, with the same underlying thought throughout, using frequently a slightly different expression—'Herr, so du willst'—(though not employing the hymn of the last), comes 'Alles nur nach Gottes Willen'. As Bach harks back to Salomo Franck for a libretto published in 1715, Wustmann suggests a pre-Leipzig date, and the unequal character of the cantata may be due to a reconstruction. The octave drop suggesting the swing of a pendulum, which was heard in No. 73, i, reappears here, but, instead of being subsidiary, it dominates the whole of the splendid opening chorus, often supporting detached chords. Oboes, violas, and continuo hammer it out on beats 1 and 2 of the bar (though not always in the octave form), at the beginning, while the violins have brilliant passage work:

and:

Sometimes the whole orchestra accompanies the choir with (aa), the voices often sing it to 'Alles'. It gives the sense of great power. On account of the line-by-line character of Franck's verse, the choral parts are mostly in short sections, almost as if each group were endeavouring breathlessly to out-bid the others in gladness. In line 1 —'All only according to God's will'—the voices enter successively with:

Ex.865

with the (*aa*) chords orchestrally and chorally, oboes and violins leaping in quavers. (*a*) and (*aa*) accompany a phrase:

Ex.866

which is bandied about between pairs of voices. Shouts of 'Alles', sometimes on beats 2 and 3 of the bar, instead of on 1 and 2, are accompanied by (*d*). Lines 2 and 3 of the verse—'So bei Lust als Traurigkeit, so bei gut als böser Zeit' ('So in pleasure as (in) mourning, so in good as (in) evil time')—are sung by the sopranos, 'Lust' on a high note, 'Traurigkeit' to a wailing figure, while the other voices continue to reiterate line 1 in simultaneous quavers, with (*a*) and (*aa*) in the orchestra. A four-fold shout of 'Alles', (*a*) being in the violins, brings lines 1–3 in all voices, at first in simultaneous quavers, with (*a*), (*b*), and (*c*) in the orchestra, afterwards with flowing passages against (*a*), (*d*), and the leaping quavers. The section is clenched by lines 1 and 3, the former in repeated notes, (*a*) in the bassi, the 'Traurigkeit' figure in upper strings and oboes, the latter in chords, accented as three bars of $\frac{2}{4}$ across two bars of $\frac{3}{4}$. All the themes of the introduction reappear in a ritornello. 'Gottes Wille soll mich stillen' ('God's will will me quiet'), brings an entire change of character, although for fifteen bars the orchestra reiterates (*aa*). The voices work out a new theme:

Ex.867

'Bei Gewölk und Sonnenschein' ('In clouds and sunshine') begins successively in the voices with a tumultuous climbing theme on 'Gewölk', (*aa*) and the leaping quavers in the orchestra. Line 1 is resumed to (*f*) and quaver chords, with accompaniment as before, and holds the field for eleven bars. The altos then deliver line 4 to a sustained melody, aptly introducing the 'Traurigkeit' figure to 'bei Gewölk' and the other voices repeat line 1 in quaver groups; (*a*) and (*aa*) are present in the orchestra. The whole of the section beginning with the four-fold 'Alles' and concluding with the cadential cross-accents comes now in the tonic instead of the subdominant, introducing the final line: 'dies soll meine Losung sein' ('this shall my watchword be'). Bach later turned this splendid chorus into the 'Gloria' of the Short Mass in G minor.

An extremely long number for alto follows—Recitativo, Arioso ed Aria—the first two with continuo. The text of the Arioso is plebeian; Franck can think of nothing better to do than begin nine successive lines with 'Herr, so du willt'. Even though the latter parts of the lines contain contrasts, the verse is not attractive. Bach contrives to maintain some interest in the Arioso by a series of five-bar phrases and by some attempts at word-painting, but not wholly successfully. The text of the preliminary recitative is 'Oh blessed Christian, Who always His will in God's will sinks, let it go, as it may in weal and woe'. There are melismata to open and close. It is typical of Bach's ingenuity that all nine entries of 'Herr, so du willt' are different. The intermediate lines of the arioso are—(1) 'so must themselves all things dispose!'; (2) 'so canst Thou me content!'; (3) 'disappears my pain!'; (4) 'shall I become healthy and clean!'; (5) 'will mourning (turn) to joy'; (6) 'find I on thorns pasture'; (7) 'shall I one day blessed be!'; (8) ('let me this word in faith hold and my soul calm'); (9) 'so die I not'. A three-bar recitative—'if body and life me leave, when to me Thy spirit this word into the heart speaks'—leads to the aria. It begins with continuo, 'Mit Allem, was ich hab' und bin, will ich mich Jesu lassen!' ('With all that I have and am, will I myself to Jesus leave!'), the first phrase:

Ex. 868

being repeated immediately in a freely inverted form, (aa), with trills on 'hab'' and 'und'. This is followed by:

Two violins are now added, and there is a twelve-bar ritornello based chiefly upon a semiquaver figure related to (a):

There is another dual theme:

and after a reversal of (c) and (d) a new figure, which ascends as well as descends:

The 'hab' und' trills round off the interlude. The text is repeated, (a), (aa) slightly different, (d) in imitation between the violins and to 'will ich mich Jesu', and a new version of (b) to this clause complete, (c) successively in the violin lines, with (d). (e) accompanies an extension of the vocal line. (c), (d), and (f) form an interlude. 'kann gleich mein schwacher Geist und Sinn des Höchsten Rath nicht fassen' ('can even my weak spirit and sense the Highest's counsel not comprehend'), is with continuo, (a), (aa), again altered, and (b). The whole of the first part from the beginning of the long ritornello to this point comes again with the new words. 'Er führe mich nur immerhin auf Dorn- und Rosen-Straßen' ('(Whether) He guides me only in the future on thorn and rose-paths') introduces a new melody, with a drop on 'Dorn', and twice on this word forms of (f); a new version of the semiquaver theme of (e) is passed from violin to violin, and there are swaying quavers in voice and bassi, as if the Saviour were gently leading the Christian. Yet another section comes to the first part of the text, corresponding with the longer treatment of these words, but altered, a long note and pause to 'lassen', another sustained note to 'Allem', both with (f) above and an ecstatic rushing up and down on the final 'Jesu'. There is a lengthy concluding ritornello, at first the swaying quavers in the continuo, much extended, and the 'Er führe' violin (a) semiquavers, and then the last part of the first interlude. Bach seems to be seeking compensation for being forced to set the unattractive text of the arioso.

The fine bass recitativo secco, iii, runs: 'So believe now! Thy Saviour says: I will it do! He is wont the grace-hand yet willingly out to reach, when suffering and pain thee affright. He knows thy need, and loosens thy sufferings-band! He strengthens, what is weak! and will the lowly roof of the poor hearts not disdain, among them graciously in to go.'

A lovely soprano aria with oboe and strings follows. The message is that Jesus will sweeten all suffering, and the oboe trips a merry melody:

Ex. 873

In the second four bars, while the oboe continues, the violins chase each other in upward runs:

Ex. 874

and then the oboe modifies (a) into a form which we shall call (c). At the close of the introduction two bars of (a) are heard in the bassi, accompanied above by gently repeated chords—(d). Schweitzer draws an interesting comparison between this and the aria 'Wirf, mein Herze', from No. 155, and considers that it interprets later lines of the verse: 'Obgleich dein Herze liegt in viel' Bekümmernissen, soll es doch sanft und still in seinen Armen ruh'n' ('Although thy heart lies in great afflictions, shall it yet soft and quiet in His arms rest'). The whole of the aria is practically a series of repetitions of the introduction with changed key-schemes and modifications, an unusual structure. For the sake of clearness the remaining sections will be numbered. (1) The initial phrase of (a) is sung to 'Mein Jesus will es thun' ('My Jesus will it do', or 'accomplish') doubled by violin I. The oboe takes up the second phrase and the voice continues: 'er will dein Kreuz versüßen' ('He will thy suffering sweeten'). The remainder is instrumental. (2) During (a) the voice sustains, runs up to high G and then joins the oboe, during (b) it has sustained notes and syncopations on 'Kreuz versüßen', during (c) it pursues an independent line, and in the latter part the strings are tacet. (d) is instrumental. (3) (c) begins, there is a new section to 'Obgleich dein Herze liegt in viel' Bekümmernissen'. (a) is now shortened to two bars, with (b) the singer repeats this text to sinking phrases, (c) is also shortened, the melody being transferred to violin I; the voice monotones to 'soll es doch sanft und still' and sinks down on 'in seinen Armen ruh'n', sustaining the final word during (d), in which the melody is allotted to the oboe. A coda is added—the singer borrows the oboe melody which was accompanied by (b)—'wenn es der Glaube faßt' ('if it the faith comprehends'), the violins being the same as before, oboe and violas alternating a dropping syncopated figure which the latter had used previously. A version of (a) occurs in oboe and voice, and the singer ends with the initial phrase to 'Mein Jesus will es thun!' (4) (a), (b), and (c), the oboe line of the last ornamented, are instrumental. With (d) comes a masterly touch of exquisite beauty; one had expected the normal repetition, but the bassi theme is replaced by quaver pulsations on low C, and the voice re-enters—'Mein Jesus will es thun!'—to a falling phrase, which is followed by a modification of the opening of (a):

Ex. 875

Mein Je - sus will es thun, mein Je - sus will es thun!

Cont. 8   ♭7   6
2 8ves lower   4   5 3

The dreamy recollection of Christ's promise and the confidence expressed by the high-placed 'will' make a unique ending to a most beautiful aria.

The only hymn-verse of the text ends the cantata, stanza 1 of Markgraf Albrecht of Brandenburg-Culmbach's 'Was mein Gott will, das g'scheh' allzeit', translated for No. 111, pp. 403–4, Vol. II, with its anonymous melody.

19. In 1725 Picander published, in a collection, a libretto for Michaelmas. This was revised and expanded by someone, it may have been Bach himself, and was set by the composer possibly in the next year. The text starts off well, i and ii treat of the [casting out of the] Dragon by St. Michael and his angels (the Epistle is Revelation xii. 7–12), but the theme is not pursued, and the centre is shifted from St. Michael to the angels as guardians and protectors, so that the character of the cantata undergoes a sudden change and the magnificent opening is not adequately supported by what follows. In spite of references to the divine beings in connexion with Jacob, Elijah, and Lazarus, or perhaps because of them, learning exhibited at the expense of continuity, the major part of the libretto is somewhat purposeless.

Bach was always roused by texts about Satan, the Dragon, the Serpent, and the like, and in the first chorus he revelled in the picture of the great combat. It opens uncompromisingly, without ritornello, without even a preliminary chord, basses and continuo plunge into the fugal subject with hammered repeated notes and an octave leap:

Ex. 876

The immense vigour of the voice parts, with much wild leaping and many twisting, writhing runs (one 'Streit' extends to no fewer than 120 semiquavers!) and the thrusts of the spear represented by detached chords for the three trumpets and timpani, produce a musical counterpart of scenes in *Paradise Lost*. The other voices follow the basses at a distance of a bar, doubled by upper strings, which are reinforced by two oboes and a taille, and after the soprano entry brass and percussion add to the tumult. The voices in reverse order repeat the exposition and then bass and tenor have the theme to themselves, followed by soprano and alto, the violins now leaping in quavers. In the next development of the subject the upper strings also develop their quaver leapings. The trumpets take up in succession the octave leaps and Part I roars along to its conclusion. After the pause comes 'Die rasende Schlange und höllische Drache stürmt wider den Himmel mit wüthender Rache' ('The blustering serpent and hellish dragon storm against the heaven with raging vengeance') and the voices move in fierce quaver chords, a low unison of the trumpets being almost terrifying. The octave leaps are still there, the semiquavers of the fugue subject, altered, enable the basses to bluster for 3½ bars, and, following this, all voices seethe and bubble like a veritable cauldron in hell. It is one of the most exciting passages in Bach's works. During most of this the reeds and upper strings double the choral lines. There is a tutti orchestral interlude compounded of the repeated quavers and the swirling semiquavers. All instruments except the continuo cease when the chorus thunders out the glad news of victory, 'Aber Michael bezwingt' ('But Michael conquers'), and it is noteworthy that the only time all the voices move together in semiquavers is on 'Schaar' ('und die Schaar, die ihn umringt' 'and the host, who him surrounds') with the trumpets playing a new rhythmic figure above, thus placing the company of angels in the foreground of the canvas. 'Stürzt des Satans Grausamkeit' ('overthrows Satan's ferocity') brings bounding passages in all parts, descending chromatic movement and another immense series of semiquavers for the basses. The dramatic scene would be perfect but for one amazing error. Bach forgets that the Archangel has won the days in the second section, that the Monster has been thrust tumbling into the mire of the abyss and that victory has been proclaimed, and he absent-mindedly writes Da Capo! The great strife arises again and the *Fine* arrives in the middle of it! One can rectify this falsification of dramatic verity by making a Dal Segno from the last instrumental bar before the return of the chorus to four bars before the *Fine* pause.

Johann Sebastian was roused to vehemence in this chorus not only by this text but, doubtless, by a tremendous choral cantata of the same title by the uncle whose musicianship he so much revered and whose works he included in the Leipzig repertoire, Johann Christoph. The text of the older composition had the advantage of being wholly Biblical; Picander took the first clause only and related the story in his own words. The score is formidable, *à 22 Vocum*, two lines of violins, four of violas (used by Johann Sebastian to such different purposes in No. 18), bassi, bassoon, four trumpets, timpani, continuo and two five-part choirs, one *Concertae*, S.A.T.B.B., the other

Cappella, S.A.T.T.B. The fight is most realistically depicted, at first by two lines of basses following each other at a bar distance, with all the trumpets blaring violently, and then by the two choruses in like manner. The energy is amazing and the effect extraordinarily exciting. Whereas the nephew's treatment is contrapuntal, the uncle's is mostly chordal, the triad of C hammering away for many bars with scarcely any harmonic variation and with almost maddening persistence. Johann Christoph is elemental, though less crude than Strauss in the battlefield scene of *Ein Heldenleben*; one feels more in the presence of a great war in remote aeons of time than one does even in the superbly writhing polyphony of Sebastian. The earlier work is often referred to in histories, but publishers have never been enterprising enough to make it known to the public. The present writer has had opportunity to perform the work (without orchestra, alas!) and found it positively overwhelming. It would suit great festival conditions, where powerful forces would provide a great surprise to music lovers. We honour the lesser masters in word but not in deed.

A bass recitativo secco continues the tale of No. 19 in lurid language but ends with the comforting thought that body and soul are protected by the angels. A mighty passage begins in bar 2, after 'God be praised! the dragon lies'. 'The uncreated Michael' ascends to high E, 'und seiner Engel Schaar hat ihn besiegt' ('and his angels' host has him defeated') drops by a major seventh to low G. The remainder is 'there lies he in the darkness with chains bound, and his abode will no more in the heavenly kingdom be found. We stand safe and sure, and when us even his roaring terrifies, so becomes yet our body and soul by angels covered.'

The soprano aria, iii, begins with the statement that 'Gott schickt uns Mahanaim zu' ('God sends us Mahanaim to'); the editor of the Breitkopf vocal score, wisely realizing that in these days few listeners will have sufficient Biblical knowledge to remember that Mahanaim is the place where Jacob was met by angels prior to his encounter with Esau, alters the line to 'Gott schickt uns seine Heere zu' ('God sends us His host to'). The original line is retained in the Peters edition. An obbligato for two oboes d'amore introduces a tender note:

Ex. 877

welcome after the turbulence of the opening of the cantata. (*a*) is fitted to the opening words. 'Wir stehen oder gehen' ('(Whether) we stand or move') contrasts long notes with runs based on (*b*). 'So können wir in sichrer Ruh für unsern Feinden stehen' ('So can we in sure calmness before our enemies stand') utilizes a longer portion of the melody, 'stehen' is generally sustained, 'Feinden' is allotted various runs. When 'Gott schickt uns' returns, 4½ bars of bassi semiquavers indicate our hurrying to the place of the angels, the 'gehen' run is extended, 'Ruh' is sustained twice, first with oboes d'amore gracefully winging upwards with (*b*), and second with (*a*) in close canon. Throughout all this (*a*) occurs frequently in the oboes d'amore, sometimes in single line, sometimes canonically, and once in the continuo. The introduction is repeated in the mediant minor, an unusual choice of key. In Part II the oboes d'amore suggest peace and happiness by moving frequently in thirds and sixths, often to (*b*), while 'Feuer, Roß und Wagen', an anticipation of the reference in the concluding hymn-stanza to the translation of Elijah, not only brings runs on the first word, but a surprising series of forty semiquavers on the last, the heavenly journey of the Prophet. During the last 'Feuer' the oboes d'amore climb in staccato arpeggio quavers, the crackling of flames. The text of Part II is 'Es lagert sich, so nah, als fern, um uns der Engel unsers Herrn mit Feuer, Roß und Wagen' ('Encamps himself, so near as (well as) far, round us the angel of our Lord with fire, horse and chariot'). (*a*) is modified for the opening words and the complete sentence is heard later, (*b*) running into the lengthy 'Wagen'. 'So nah', 'als fern', are generally separated, with picturesque effect. (*a*) is employed fragmentarily and complete in the obbligati.

The tenor, in a recitative with strings, contrasts the lowly state of man with the condition which is to be: 'What is the worthless man, the earth-child? A worm, a poor sinner. See, how him Himself the Lord so loves, that He him not too lowly estimates and for him the heaven's children, the seraphim host for his guard and resistance, for his protection sets.' The same voice sings an aria which is a prayer that angels may guide him and teach him to sing praises to the Holiest: 'Bleibt, ihr Engel, bleibt bei mir!' ('Bide, ye angels, bide with me!'). The prevailing movement in the strings and voice is of the type so often associated with angels, for instance in the Pastoral Symphony of the Christmas Oratorio:

Ex. 878

Unfortunately Bach decided to comment on this by giving the tromba the anonymous melody associated with one of the hymns for the day, M. Schalling's 'Herzlich lieb hab' ich dich, o Herr', referring, as Terry points out, to stanza 3, 'Lord, let Thy blessed angels come At my last end.' (The verse is translated for No. 149, see p. 318). The introduction of the twelve-line melody, with interludes, protracts the aria to an inordinate length. The swinging character of the chief ideas, and the number of runs for the voice, prevent the adoption of a quick tempo, and consequently, in spite of the beauty of much of the music, the aria becomes wearisome. It is well to omit bars 30–61 inclusive. The persistence of the bassi figure—| ♩. ♫ ♩ ᭼ |—is unique, even for Bach; occasionally there is—| ♩. ♫ ♩. ♫ |. At one place 'gleiten' is set realistically, and the 'führet' runs suggest the *need* for guidance rather than guidance itself. The text after the quoted clause is: 'Führet mich auf beiden Seiten, daß mein Fuß nicht möge gleiten, aber lernt mich auch allhier euer großes Heilig singen, und dem Höchsten Dank zu bringen!' ('Guide me on both sides, that my foot not may slip, but teach me even here your great holiness to sing, and to the Highest thanks to bring!').

There is a short soprano recitativo secco: 'Let us the presence of the holy angels love, and them with our sins not drive away, or even trouble, for are they, when the Lord bids to the world farewell to say, for our blessedness and also our heavenly chariot.'

The conclusion of the cantata is a brilliant and plainly harmonized version of L. Bourgeois's 'Ainsi qu'on oit le cerf bruire' set to stanza 9 of the anonymous funerary hymn 'Freu' dich sehr, o meine Seele'. Brass and percussion are independent, the prophet's chariot wings its way to heaven in resplendent glory; upper strings, oboes and taille double the voices. The text is: 'Let Thine angels with me journey On Elijah's chariot red, And my soul well keep As Lazarus's after his death. Let it rest in Thy bosom, Fill it with joy and comfort, Till the body comes from the earth, And with it united becomes.'

66. There is much that is puzzling in the attractive cantata 'Erfreut euch, ihr Herzen'. Bach often joins his first and second violins in unison for the sake of brilliance, but to find them in this way for the major portion of a long and powerful chorus is unusual, especially as violin II is thus taken to the unwonted height of the second A above the stave. One can see no reason for this departure from the magnificent polyphony of this period of maturity; it would have been quite easy to have added another line, part-writing for a relatively small orchestra of trumpet, two oboes, bassoon and strings was child's play. That the fagotto is often independent does not complicate matters. The second section, andante, as a contrast to the (unindicated) allegro of the opening, is mostly an A.B. duet, with a short burst for all voices in the middle and a few tutti bars at the end. There is nothing to justify the exclusive use of the pair of voices for this portion of the text, although the entry of the full chorus on 'der Heiland erquicket sein geistliches Reich' ('the Saviour invigorates His spiritual Kingdom') produces a fine contrast. These considerations lead one to surmise that it may be an adaptation, and the fact that the author is un-named in the printed libretto (Leipzig church music 1731), makes it possible that the composer wrote the words, as he did for so many adaptations. It may be argued contra that the musical ideas are apposite to the text; in the first part the abundant use of the joy-motive, the rushing demisemiquaver scales, appropriate to a chorus on the subject of the Resurrection (the cantata is for Easter Monday); in the duet section the chromatic realism of 'Trauern' ('mourning'), the wailing passages to 'ängstliche Zagen' ('anxious tremblings') (the music is a negative interpretation of the clause, for the text says that the Saviour can drive these away), the continual use of orchestral motives from the allegro, the instruments pointing the message of the Resurrection while the voices are regarding the necessities of mankind, and the brilliant coloratura to 'verjagen' ('drive away'). In many other cases, however, Bach has shown aptness in doctoring a secular text so skilfully that the same general ideas remain and carry on the union of words and music from the one to the other. The introduction is superb. The bassi are silent for three bars:

(tromba and oboe II are omitted from this quotation)

and dash down in the fourth:

They now take up (*b*) and the violins invert (*c*), mounting two octaves and a fourth. The joy-motive appears in the oboes:

and is answered by a swirling figure:

These alternate, (*e*) is extended and (*d*) is elongated to five exhilarating bars, the tromba joining with oboe I. (*a*) is modified for the choral entries, with (*d*) linking them up:

and the full chorus utilizes it for 'es lebet der Heiland und herrschet in euch' ('lives the Saviour and governs in you'). These ideas are developed, and the introduction, with alterations, comes in the dominant. Altos and basses introduce a long choral section, the tutti (*a*) passage being altered. A condensed form of the introduction ensues, the basses sustain and the other voices fling groups of quaver chords, on 'herrschet', during (*a*). While (*d*) and (*e*) are alternated altos and basses imitate on the (*a*) derivative, the trumpet mounting exultantly, and all voices gradually join in with 'es lebet', the alto line decorated with trills. The sopranos cry 'herrschet' on high A and F♯ entirely unaccompanied, a moment of tense excitement. (*b*) in the bassi supports a six-bar soprano note on 'herrschet', which is doubled by the tromba, upper strings and oboes throw to each other the two-note figure associated with the word, and the lower voices join in with it. The fourteen bars which concluded the first vocal section come now in the tonic instead of in the dominant. Bach is not content to end here. He wishes to stress more and more the word 'herrschet', and before the final phrase, which tallies with the initial vocal tutti, he sandwiches in the group of bars in which the word was sustained by sopranos and trumpet. But here the basses also sustain, trilling, the trumpet breaks up its note with repetitions (as at the beginning of the introduction), the upper strings chords are on a different part of the bar, the bassi play quaver arpeggi instead of (*b*), and the middle voices, in lieu of the detached 'herrschet's, repeat their earliest commands—'erfreut euch, ihr Herzen!' and 'erweichet, ihr Schmerzen!' —to (*f*). Enamoured of his resilient introduction Bach lets us hear it again, and we now see the meaning of the tromba two-quaver leaps, for they are fixed in our minds with 'herrschet'. Most of Part II is for A.B. duet. For twenty-four bars the upper strings play | ♪ ⌐ ♪ | *piano e andante*, the continuo (*b*) on repeated semiquavers, while the singers wail in descending semitones and in syncopations: 'Ihr könnet verjagen das Trauern, das Fürchten, das ängstliche Zagen' ('You can drive away the mourning, the fear, the anxious trembling'). Unison upper strings play (*b*) while the voices twist and turn on 'ängstliche', and again, several times, during a long 'Zagen', first a sustained note, then with a picturesque figure:

Ex.884

When the basses have finished with (*g*) the voices move more happily, and (*d*) reappears in bassoon and oboes. The whole choir shouts briefly 'der Heiland erquicket sein geistliches Reich!' ('the Saviour refreshes His spiritual Kingdom!'). Not content with having elaborated the earlier clauses for forty-four bars, Bach devotes to them another twenty-nine. The chromatics disappear from 'ihr könnet

verjagen', though the melody begins as before, and the putting to
flight of the cares of the world is indicated by whirling demisemiquavers (in No. 107, there is a like treatment of a similar verb,
'erjagen', 'to drive away' as in hunting), and trilling for the basses.
The upper strings transform:

Ex.885

from bar 5 of the introduction, never introduced otherwise till this
point, into:

Ex.886

(g) is reintroduced to 'Fürchten' and 'ängstliche', and both words,
heard simultaneously, quake and leap:

Ex. 887

while the bassi jump about, the upper strings play (b) and the oboes
add a short new melody. For a few bars, at first with bassoon and
bassi only, with a figure borrowed from the introduction—

Ex.888
(h)

then with continuo only, the voices combine (g) and the demisemiquavers; there are then a new form of (a) for the voices and (b) for
the upper strings, to conclude this section. Bach now makes amends
for his scant treatment of the 'der Heiland' clause and allots to it
twenty-four bars, at first separate entries leaping to sustained notes,
then homophonic passages, and finally a brief fugato. (b) and (h) are
in the orchestra, the former persisting almost to the end. Bach certainly did not waste any of the thematic material of the introduction!
   The sustained strings of the bass recitative afford contrast to the
brilliance of the chorus and the lively aria, iii: 'Broken is the grave

and therewith our need, the mouth proclaims God's doings, the
Saviour lives: so is in need and death to the faithful completely well
prospered.' The last two bars bring an interesting point; 'vollkommen
wohl gerathen' ('completely well prospered') is set to (*h*) in quavers,
and dovetailed into it the upper strings play the figure in the original
manner. Such quotations from movement to movement are rare.

The usual scoring of the strings in i recurs in the splendid bass aria.
Here, however, the oboes are seldom independent of the line of
violins, the fagotto part is almost identical with the continuo, the
viola alone forms the middle of the three-part score. It looks as if
Bach had utilized some previously written music and neglected to
strengthen the overpowered viola line. 'Leben' ('live') is appropriately accommodated to lively passages; the word may have been
there in the original text. 'Jesus erscheinet' ('Jesus appears') is set
to a downward arpeggio, (*h*) in i, imitated in diminution by upper
strings and oboes. Would not a rising figure be expected in a cantata
dealing with the Resurrection? The same passage is heard to 'Jesus
berufet' ('Jesus calls'), thus betokening no special meaning. If the
aria is borrowed, the recitative may have been written later and the
passage introduced there, but one fails to see the connexion. The
introduction is long, another point of contact with i, and contains
three principal ideas:

Ex. 889
Ob. I. II. Vl. I. II.
Cont.

Ex. 890
(*b*)
Cont.
8ve lower

and:

Ex. 891
(*c*)

which is continued in ascending sequence. When the voice enters
violin I plays (*a*) and (*b*), the other instruments being silent, (*a*) is

modified to 'Lasset dem Höchsten ein Danklied erschallen' ('Let to the Highest a thanks-song resound') and 'für sein Erbarmen und ewige Treu'' ('for His pity and everlasting faithfulness') runs in counterpoint against (*b*). A long 'ewige' follows, the orchestra tutti, (*a*) against a sustained note, (*b*) against syncopated vocal movement. Another sustained 'ewige' is accompanied by (*c*) for the violins, with new leaps for the other instruments. Fragmentary entries of (*c*) ensue and the second clause slowly climbs with turn-like ideas, while the orchestra invents a fresh figure from (*c*). Vocal counterpoint is added to (*c*) tutti. After the recapitulation of the introduction comes the 'Jesus erscheinet' passage referred to, the voice continues 'uns Frieden zu geben' ('to us peace to give') in counterpoint to a twofold (*a*), and 'Frieden' is treated as was 'ewige' with (*c*). A fragment of (*b*) heralds the 'Jesus berufet' passage which agrees with 'Jesus erscheinet'. There is a lengthy treatment of 'uns mit ihm zu leben, täglich wird seine Barmherzigkeit neu' ('us with Him to live, daily becomes his compassion new'), at first violin I, bassoon and continuo only, the former developing a fresh melody from (*a*), afterwards tutti with (*c*), and then three bars with fagotto and bassi only. Now both the Jesus clauses are sung, violin I and oboe I being the only upper instruments ((*a*) and (*b*) are present), except for a tutti of one bar to 'leben'. The concluding ritornello before the Da Capo also omits oboe II, violin II and viola and utilizes (*a*) and (*b*). At the close the violin drops out and the voice enters for four bars. The whole construction is curious and not in agreement with Bach's methods at the date of the cantata.

A Dialogus between Fear (alto) and Hope (tenor) is also problematic. Its introduction into the libretto after the rejoicing in the risen Lord is justified by the Gospel, St. Luke xxiv. 13–35, where Christ, during the walk to Emmaus, comforted the two disappointed and sorrowing men. The entire scena consists of the Dialogus proper, secco, and a duet with violin solo obbligato. The former is in five sections. (1) A curiously worded recitative for Hope—'In Jesu's life joyful to be, is in our breast a bright sunshine. With comfort filled on his Saviour to look, and in himself a heavenly kingdom to build, is of true Christians (the) possession. Yet! because I here a heavenly refreshment have, so seeks my spirit here its delight and rest. My Saviour calls to me mightily'. (2) The supposed words of the Saviour —'My grave and death bring you life, my Resurrection is your comfort'—is a three-bar arioso with pulsating continuo. (3) Hope resumes in recitative: 'My mouth will indeed an offering give, my Saviour! yet how little, how small, how so very trifling will it before Thee, Oh great conqueror, be, if I for Thee a victory and thanks-song bring.' An animated bassi passage, based on the coming theme, leads into (4), a florid arioso or aria duet. Hope announces a freely canonical subject:

Ex. 892

My   eye   sees   the   Saviour   arisen,
Mein Au-ge sieht   den   Hei-land auf-er-weckt,

Cont.

Fear answers, one note only being different and 'Mein' replaced by 'Kein' ('No'). 'Weckt' is developed into long runs, each voice enters again with the subject, and before Fear finishes her semiquavers Hope enters with a new theme—'es hält ihn nicht der Tod in Banden!' ('it holds Him not the death in bonds!'), with an extremely long run on 'Banden'. Fear substitutes 'noch' ('yet') for 'nicht'. The two themes are reviewed, with their florid parts curtailed, at the end. The section is false dramatically, as Hope and Fear would not express their opposite view-points in identical music. (5) Recitative is resumed. Hope—'How! may then fear in a heart arise?' Fear—'Lets well the grave the dead escape?' Hope—'When God in a grave lies, then hold grave and death Him not.' Fear—'Ah God! Thou Who the death conquers, for Thee yields the grave's stone, the seal breaks. I believe, but help me weak one, Thou canst also stronger make. Conquer me and my irresoluteness! The God, Who wonders does, has my spirit through comfort's might strengthened, that it the arisen Jesus perceives.'

In Part I of the florid duet the two characters, which are not named, although the connexion with the previous number is obvious, discuss their past state, Hope—'Ich fürchte zwar des Grabes Finsternissen, und klagete, mein Heil sei nun entrissen' ('I fear indeed the grave's darkness, and mourned, (that) my Salvation be now torn away'; Hope replaces 'zwar' by 'nicht' ('not') and 'klagete' by 'hoffete' ('hoped'). Fear declares her now-found complete assurance by a fourfold repetition of her initial note. Otherwise the general mood only is considered, as 'klagete' and 'hoffete' are set to the same idea, which inclines one to think that the music existed in some other form. The figuration of the violin obbligato is worthy of a concerto movement, further suggesting adaptation, even though the process is carried through with considerable aptness. The opening bars:

are modified in a subtle manner for Hope:

and the first figure gives rise to the idea used for 'des Grabes Finster-nissen'. Arpeggi are followed by:

and this by:

both of which are extensively employed in the vocal sections, al-though (c) is not heard in Part I. The trilling portion of (c) appears in various ways, sometimes an octave upwards, and twice in a splen-did passage it is formed into a decorated inverted pedal while a reiterated pedal note is heard underneath:

Two of the introduction passages, (e), a bar of semiquaver arpeggi gradually descending for a full two octaves, and:

Ex. 898

followed by a modification for the bassi, are reserved for use in Part II, but the figuration:

Ex. 899

continuing for two bars, and not found in the introduction, precedes (d), twice in Part I and once in Part II. A rolling series of semi-quavers often used to 'entrissen' is not found in the violin line. Part II opens with new vocal themes: 'Nun ist mein Herze voller Trost, und wenn sich auch ein Feind erbost, will ich in Gott zu siegen wissen' ('Now is my heart full (of) comfort, and if himself even an enemy angers, will I in God (how) to conquer know'). Fragments from (a) flit above, during a very long 'siegen' (e) appears for the first time against the voices, a paean for victory, three bars of (c) culminating in a crashing chord and (f) fragmentarily in the continuo. (f) in the obbligato and a splendid descent on it in the bassi form an inter-lude. Hope now delivers the first two clauses of this part of the text to hammered notes, akin to the alto's initial entry, Fear swings and bounds with a more rapid use of the words, (e) thrice plunges down-wards. A few bars of animated vocal lines with continuo only bring us to a repetition of (e) and the three-bar (c), Fear's 'siegen' lasting 7½ bars. The passage in Part I in which there are two bars of (g) fol-lowed by (d) is adapted to the new text, the vocal lines being reversed. The Da Capo adds the first thirty-nine long bars to this tremendous duet.

The orchestration of the closing four-part chorale is not stated in the score. The melody is a medieval Easter hymn—'Christ ist erstan-den' and the words the third stanza—'Allelujah, Allelujah, Allelu-jah! Of this shall we all glad be: Christ will our comfort be, Kyrie eleis!' It is not found elsewhere in the church works, but the three verses are treated individually in an organ prelude. One is prepared to overlook the problems raised by this cantata for the sake of the very fine music. As one cannot be certain that it is not original, it has not been classified definitely with cantatas containing borrowed material.

95. Probably to the next year, 1732, belong Nos. 95 and 98, for the Sixteenth and Twenty-First Sundays after Trinity respectively, 28 September and 2 November. The scheme of 95, 'Christus, der ist mein Leben' ('O Christ, my all in living' N. 'Since Christ is all my being' B.), provided by an unknown librettist, is unique in that it contains four different chorales, the only cantata with so many. All the hymns are 'Sterbe-Lieder' ('death-songs'), as the Gospel, St. Luke vii. 11–17, narrates the story of the raising of the widow's son, and these were prescribed for the day; but no conductor need hesitate to present the work on that account, as it is of rich beauty, easily grasped and extremely attractive to an audience. The choir sings chorales only, an easy task; there is only one hindrance in the way of many performances, the extraordinarily [high] tessitura of the solitary aria. (See P. 23.) It must have been written for some kind of light tenor, or what used to be called in this country a 'counter-tenor', for top B's are frequent and there are many passages which impose strain on the ordinary singer, to say nothing of the listeners. It is rarely wrong to replace a tenor soloist by a soprano, providing the balance of soloists in the complete cantata is not disturbed thereby. Satisfactory tenors are not so commonly found as good sopranos and many fine cantatas are made suitable by such a substitution. The composer himself was often forced to change arias from one voice to another and we need not hesitate to do the same. A high-lying female voice is more easily secured than the exceptional type for which Bach wrote here.

The theme of the aria, iv, is the frequent one of the knell striking the last [hour], and, as in all cases with this subject, the music is of great beauty. The strings are pizzicato throughout, the bassi toll the larger bells, the violas move mostly in octave leaps, recalling, though in more solemn tones, the violin passages at the end of No. 4, i; violin I moves generally in semiquavers, alternating the notes of a quaver melody with a repeated upper pedal note, the most rapid pizzicato in all Bach's works, while Violin II reinforces the melodic line and is rarely independent. The almost naked consecutive fourths for the oboes d'amore:

Ex. 900
Ob. d'am. I. II.

is a daring innovation for those days. Many composers of modern times have tried to imitate the strange combinations of notes heard from bells, but Bach anticipated them by more than a hundred years. The violin pizzicato line scarcely fills in the thirds of the triads, and the fourths are left stark. The echo in bar 4 is a poignant effect and is frequently heard. A closing passage commences:

Ex. 901
Ob. d'am. I. II.

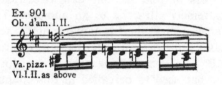

With oboe d'amore I circling above and II echoing at the end, and with octave leaps for the violas and tollings of larger bells by the bassi, the singer begins:

Ex. 902

and (a) follows, short cries of 'schlage doch' being fitted to it, and a sustained phrase on 'sel'ge Stunde' ('blessed hour'). Repetition of this material, with the addition of 'den allerletzten Glockenschlag!' ('the final bell-clang!'), the voice often left unaccompanied, continues till the end of the first vocal section. Seven bars from the introduction, a reconstruction of the vocal portion containing two lovely pathos-laden bars for the oboes d'amore during one 'sel'ge Stunde', and the introduction again entire, complete Part I. Part II opens with a melisma on 'Komm!' ('Come!') and continues 'ich reiche dir die Hände, komm, mache meiner Noth ein Ende' ('I stretch out to Thee

the hands, come, make of my distress an end'). Bars 1 and 2 of (*a*)
accompany thrice, the first time strings only. There is a change at 'du
längst erseufzter Sterbenstag' ('thou long sighed-for death-day')—
the oboes d'amore pass from sostenuto to a sighing phrase, the upper
strings pulsate in crotchets and the bassi toll:

Ex. 903

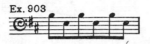

the lower note descending step by step for four bars. (*a*) comes in the
supertonic minor, and when the first two clauses are sung again the
violin portion of (*a*) takes a new form and the oboes d'amore move
in close canon, as if faltering hands were being raised in petition.
The 'du längst' passage is much altered, the bassi reverse the position
of the notes in Ex. 903, and in the last four bars 'längst' is sustained
against (*b*). Dynamic indications are surprisingly frequent, not only
are piano, pianissimo, and forte common, but the rarely found più
piano occurs. The vocal line of this unique aria is of profound
impressiveness and the general impression is that of a happy though
thoughtful welcome to death. The Da Capo of seventy-five bars is
better omitted out of consideration for the soloist. A repetition of the
introduction is ample, as it is in the majority of arias.

There is one interesting feature of the three recitatives, all with
continuo, for S.T. and B. Except at the end of the last, which breaks
into a brief arioso, where the continuo ascends scalewise in illustration of 'mein selig' Aufersteh'n' ('my blessed resurrection') while the
voice sinks slowly on the last word of 'auf meinen Heiland gründen'
('on my Saviour establish'), the voices are not supported by sustained
chords. The continuo plays detached notes only and the singers are
for the most part unaccompanied. The soprano recitative, ii, is 'Now,
false world, now have I further nothing with thee to do! My house
is already prepared, I can far softer rest, than when I formerly in thee,
by thy Babylon's waters the lust-salt to swallow had' (here is one of
the rare cases in Bach in which the continuo cadence must come after
the closing notes of the voice) 'when I in thy lust-region only Sodom's
apples could pluck. No, no!—now can I with composed spirit speak'.
This leads without break to stanza 1 of V. Herberger's familiar
funerary hymn, 'Valet will ich dir geben' with M. Teschner's melody:
'Farewell will I to Thee give, Thou wicked, false world, Thy sinful
evil life By no means me pleases. In heaven is it good to dwell,

Thitherward stands my desire, There will God ever reward Him who serves Him here.' Three instrumental figures persist throughout this exquisite number (see S. & B. 'Dear Angels'—not a translation) in the continuo:

Ex. 904

also used in inversion, in the obbligato unison oboes d'amore:

Ex. 905

(the last two notes sometimes rise, indicative of pleading) and:

Ex. 906

As these figures are short and separated by quaver and semiquaver rests, the effect is one of intense eagerness to leave detestable earth. There is no indication as to whether it is to be sung solo or tutti, but the doubling of the oboes d'amore in the obbligato line suggest that Bach employed all his boys. Otherwise one instrument would have been enough.

The tenor recitative, iii, continues the mood, though less beautifully expressive: 'Ah! could (it) to me then soon so well happen, that I the death, the end of all distress, in my limbs could see: I would it for my dower choose, and all hours towards it count.' That for bass, v, is—'For I know this, and believe it quite certainly, that I from my grave quite a sure way to the Father have. My death is but a sleep, through it the body, which here from cares taken away (is), to rest comes. Seeks now a Shepherd His lost sheep, how should Jesus me not again find, when He my head and I His limb am? So can I now with glad thoughts'—and the aforementioned arioso concludes.

The first number is of an unusual design and falls into four sections. In (1) and (2) two oboes d'amore and violins employ as their chief motive a gently swaying syncopated figure in thirds and sixths, the principal idea being four beats in length:

Ex. 907

It is the pulsating of life caused by the benignity of the Christ. Sometimes violin I soars gently upwards in lengthy scales, the ascent of the believer's aspirations, violin II and viola have figures of their own akin to the bassi motto of the soprano chorale. The chorale is stanza 1 of an anonymous hymn, the melody by M. Vulpius. Line 1—'Christ, Who is my life'—is delivered simply. 2—'To die is my gain'—is heard in a wonderful transformation; the voices, beginning with the sopranos, enter in succession and sustain with the following notes— E, F, G♯ (the sopranos falling meanwhile to D), C, a passage of extra-ordinary expressiveness. The remaining lines—'Thereto I yield myself, With joy journey I thither' —are sung simply. All the while the pulsating phrases appear against the voices and in the interludes. A horn doubles the soprano melody. (2) The tenor (not marked solo, but undoubtedly so) rejoices at the thought that soon the world will be left: 'Mit Freuden, ja, ja! mit Herzenslust will ich von hinnen scheiden' ('With joy, yea, yea! with heart's-delight will I from here depart'). 'Freuden' is florid, 'scheiden', in spite of the assertion of joy, vacillates and then plunges headlong downwards. The pulsating ideas are heard in the orchestra. (3) is a remarkable experiment in free rhythm. The tenor sings a recitative, accompanied, as are ii, iii, and v, by detached chords only. Recitatives of the period were always in common time; here each fragment is separated from its neighbour by an orchestral bar of $\frac{3}{4}$, during which the pulsating motives are heard. The succession of bars which results is—$\frac{4}{4}+\frac{3}{4}$ four times, $\frac{4}{4}$, $\frac{2}{4}$, $\frac{3}{4}$, $\frac{4}{4}$, $\frac{4}{4}$, $\frac{2}{4}$, $\frac{3}{4}$, an astonishing sequence. It is mostly virtually in $\frac{7}{4}$ time, a counterpart of Handel's $\frac{5}{8}$ in *Orlando*. The separated portions of text are—'And were it today even: "thou must!"'—'so am I willing and prepared',—'the poor body, the consumed limbs',—'the garment of mortality',—'to the earth again in its bosom to bring'.— 'My death-song is already composed; ah, might I it, ah, might I it today sing!' The last $\frac{3}{4}$ bar leads without break into (4), $\frac{2}{2}$ Allegro. Here a second chorale is introduced, the well-known hymn (stanza 1) and tune of Luther's free versification of the Nunc Dimittis: 'Mit Fried' und Freud' ich fahr' dahin.' The text is 'With peace and joy I journey thither According to God's will, Comforted is in me my heart and being, Soft and calm. As God to me promised has; the death is my sleep become.' The librettist made an apt choice of hymns in this number, for the last line of the first and the first of the second are almost identical. The oboes d'amore are replaced by *Oboe ordinaria* I and II. With the exception of a crotchet in bar 6 and a pause-bar at the end of line 4 the continuo proceeds wholly in quavers, the steady march of the journey. The lines of the chorale, which are plainly harmonized in minims, are introduced by ritornelli in which corno and oboes only are heard above the continuo. The former announces each coming line of the canto in crotchets (with decorations at times) and unison oboes make a canon at the distance of a minim; then two or three bars of derivatives lead to the vocal entry. Except for the last three bars horn and oboes double the vocal canto fermo, violin II and viola the altos and tenors respectively, while violin I is free. The line 'sanft und stille' is marked piano and forte is resumed immediately. The inference is that lines 1–3 must also be loud; the march to the grave is a joyous one. During the last line violin I soars ecstatically, and while solemn minor harmonies support the elongated final note of the chorale, the horn reminds us of line 1 by playing the associated phrase in crotchets.

vi is stanza 4 of N. Herman's 'Wenn mein Stündlein vorhanden ist' with his own melody. The choral lines are simple, but violin I is free, it wings aloft, the soul hovering over the body, ready to begin its ascension. The stanza is translated for No. 15, see p. 22.

98. No. 98, for the Twenty-First Sunday after Trinity, possibly 2 November 1732, is the first of three cantatas with the title 'Was Gott thut, das ist wohlgethan', the others being conveniently numbered 99 and 100. The last two are related; 98 has nothing in common with either except for the chorale. Three of the cantatas for this Sunday begin with an expression of confidence in the Almighty will, while the fourth, No. 38, is based on one of the appointed hymns, a versification of Psalm cxxx, 'Out of the depths have I cried unto Thee'. That such different emotions are suitable to the same Sunday is explained by the fact that the Epistle is Paul's command to 'Put on the whole armour of God', Ephesians vi. 10–17, while the Gospel, St. John iv. 46–54, relates the appeal of the nobleman whose son was sick. Both states of mind are shown in No. 98 ('What God doth, surely that is right' O.) because after the confidence of the verse that opens, stanza 1 of S. Rodigast's hymn, the tenor pleads for rescue from misery, the soprano bids her eyes cease from weeping, since God the Father lives, the alto breathes a message of solace and the bass declares that he will never leave Jesus. The librettist thus provides a well-graded scheme. The text of i is translated for cantata No. 99, see p. 507. It is a much-extended chorale; some of the ritornelli are lengthy compared with the choral entries. The latter begin simply, the fine anonymous canto fermo not in long notes; the penultimate line is a little more ornate, the final one—'drum laß' ich ihn nur walten' ('therefore let I Him only govern')—is extended, there are animated runs on 'walten', in the basses the word is once broken by a rest and once by phrasing indicated by the grouping of the quavers. Two oboes and taille strengthen the upper voices. The continuo moves in strong passages denoting confidence and violin I rejoices in rapid movement:

Ex.908

There are also:

Ex.909

and:

Ex.910

The inner strings play detached phrases, reinforcing the significance of the bassi.

The tenor recitativo secco is finely expressive—'Ah, God! when wilt Thou me once from my sorrow's torment, from my anxiety free? How long shall I day and night for help cry? And is no deliverer there? The Lord is to all those near, who His might and His favour trust. Therefore shall I my confidence on God alone build, for He forsakes His own not.'

An oboe obbligato graces the soprano aria (see O.S.B.A. No. 10) and paints weeping by the familiar two-note groups:

Ex.911
Ob. (a)
Cont.
8ve lower   (Key C minor, signature of 2 flats)

which are also heard thrice from the soloist:

Ex.912 wei - - - - - nen,
(b)
Cont.
8ve lower

the last time followed by five bars consisting mostly of chromatics:

Ex.913
(c)

borrowed from the introduction. 'Hört, ihr Augen, auf zu weinen' ('Cease, ye eyes, to weep') is set to (a) minus the two-note idea, and is answered by a phrase from the introduction:

Ex.914
(d)   tr
Cont.
8ve lower

in which the happy trill and the chirruping of bar 4 would indicate that the command is already obeyed. That, however, would render the remainder of the aria unnecessary, so (c) weeps in the oboe when the voice repeats (a). The vacillating mind of the Christian is further shown by the superimposition over (b) of yet another happy phrase from the introduction:

Ex.915
(e)
Cont.
8ve lower

'Trag' ich doch mit Geduld mein schweres Joch' ('Carry I yet with patience my heavy yoke') borrows abundantly from the oboe melody, the beginning of (d), without the trill, the beginning of (e) and even part of (b); the obbligato suggests smiles shining through tears by the use of (c), the opening and closing bars of (a) and the chirruping of (d). 'Gott, der Vater, lebet noch' ('God, the Father, lives yet') employs the initial vocal phrase modified, and 'lebet' flourishes in triplets while the oboe plays (a). 'Von den Seinen, läßt er Keinen' ('Of His own, leaves He none') is at variance with the obbligato two-note figure. Combinations of (b) and (a) round off this part of the text and from 'Gott, der Vater' is repeated with the extension spoken of. 'Weeping' is so much in the mind of the composer that he must needs link up the closing vocal note with the Da Capo by yet another (c).

The alto recitativo secco leaves tears behind—'God has a heart, that (is) pity's abundance! And if the mouth to His ears cries, and to Him of suffering's pain in faith and confidence tells, then breaks in Him the heart, so that He on us compassion must (have). He keeps His word; He says: knock, so will to you be opened!' (See St. Matt. vii. 7.) 'Therefore let us then away, if we in highest need hover, the heart to God alone to raise.'

It seems singular that the chief vocal idea of the vigorous bass aria (see O.S.B.A. No. 11) should never be found on the continuo or in the line for all violins in unison, the only accompaniment, until one realizes that, as Terry points out, the phrase:

Ex. 916   My   Jesus   leave   I not,
          Mei - nen Je - sum   lass'   ich nicht,

Cont.

resembles line 1 of Hammerschmidt's melody to the hymn beginning with these words:

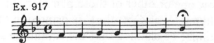

Ex. 917

It is therefore a quotation, to be considered apart from the thematic material proper. The violins and bassi indulge in powerful, imitative leaps:

the former play spacious scales:

(*b*) gives rise to an ever-recurring idea:

(*a*) is the motto which comes over and over again, once with continuo
only, the other times associated with (*b*) 'bis mich erst sein Angesicht' ('till me first His presence') is set to cross-grouping of quavers
across the beat—| ♪ ♫ ♪ ♫ |: 'wird erhören, oder segnen'
('will hear, or bless') climbs to a syncopated phrase, with (*d*) in the
violins. Part II begins 'Er allein soll mein Schutz in Allem sein' ('He
alone will my protection in all be'), again the cross-groupings, the
continuo the sole support, with (*b*); 'was mir Übels kann begegnen.'
('which me of evil may befall') reproduces the 'erhören' passage.
There is a splendid upsoaring passage on 'begegnen', related to (*c*),
unobscured by the violins. Part III is an altered form of Part I.

Here the score ends, unsatisfactorily. Bach's usual addition at the
close of a work—*Fine S.D.G.*—is absent, so it must be assumed that
he considered it unfinished and that either a hymn-verse is to be
added, or, as in other cases, i is to be repeated. For concert purposes
it is well to follow one or other of these plans. In the English edition
stanza 6 of the hymn 'Was Gott thut' is printed in the setting found
in No. 100. It cannot be claimed that the cantata is outstanding, but
it is attractive and useful. i is bold and easy to sing, the soprano aria
is full of pathos and the bass one attractive. The oboes and taille in i
merely double; where an oboe is not available a violin solo can play
the obbligato of ii, so that the modest forces of strings and organ can

be employed in church, or a pianoforte for continuo in a concert-room where there is no organ. By exercising a little patience in in-vestigation, conductors can find many cantatas which may be per-formed with inexpensive accompaniment; the tables at the end of *Fugitive Notes* indicate what possibilities exist in that direction. One is often surprised to find so little thought given to this consideration; one of the first points to be decided in choosing cantatas is that of orchestra, and the choice is wide even where instrumental possi-bilities are severely limited. One has heard of cases in which the orchestration is not discovered until the work is in progress of choral rehearsal, and of such absurd makeshifts as a pianoforte representing three trumpets and timpani against a large chorus and body of strings.

(vii) *Biblical and Apocryphal Quotations plus*
Hymn-Stanzas plus Original Matter
24, 25, 37, 39, 40, 44, 46, 64, 65, 67, 69, 77, 102, 104, 105, 109, 119, 145, 148, 172, 179, 187, 190, '*Ehre sei Gott*' (*Un-numbered and incomplete*)

Order of discussion: 24, 119, 40, 64, 65, 172, 179, 69, 190, 67, 104, 44, 105, 46, 77, 148. 37, 'Ehre sei Gott', 145, 102, 25, 109, 39, 187

24. Bach was unwise in his choice when he decided to set Neu-meister's 'Ein ungefärbt' Gemüthe', possibly for 20 June of 1723, his first year in Leipzig. The Gospel for the Fourth Sunday after Trinity is St. Luke vi. 36–42, and Christ's preaching on the virtues of mercy, forgiveness, and generosity stirred the pastor to nothing more than dry, didactic statements and crude denunciations of the failings of mankind. The bass recitative, iv, begins uncompromisingly—'The hypocrisy is a spawn, which Belial breeds' accompanied by three crashes on the strings separated by a bar. The chords come at closer quarters during 'who himself into this mask puts, he wears the devil's livery.[1] How, permit themselves then Christians the like even to lust after? To God be it complained! The integrity is precious. Many a devilish monster appears like an angel' (grimness is mitigated momentarily by a melisma on 'Engel' ('angel')), 'one turps the wolf within, the sheepskin turns one without: how could it worse be? Calumny, slander and judgement, condemnation and annihilation

[1] The Breitkopf vocal score has a different text at this point: the translation is 'who in his slavery bends, he counts among Satan's servants'.

is everywhere common'. With 'So geht es dort' ('So goes it there') the voice dashes up in semiquavers, followed by upper strings, 'so geht es hier' ('so goes it here') does the opposite. There is now an Arioso Andante of comfort—'der liebe Gott behüte mich dafür!' ('(may) the beloved God protect me therefrom!'). Even Bach's vigorous setting and his fine declamation cannot make this number palatable to modern taste.

i, alto aria, upper strings in unison, is one of the most sterile things Bach ever wrote; even the energetic unison figure and the leaping bass:

Ex. 921

cannot galvanize it into life. They promise well, and so does a later figure:

Ex. 922

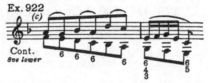

but the expectation is not realized. 'Ein ungefärbt Gemüthe von deutscher Treu' und Güte' ('An unstained mind of German truth and goodness') is set to an independent melody, and 'macht uns vor Gott und Menschen schön' ('makes us before God and men fair') to (a), the latter occurring in both instrumental lines and (b) in the bassi only. The text of Part II is appallingly dry: 'Der Christen Thun und Handel, ihr ganzer Lebenswandel soll auf dergleichem Fuße stehn' ('The Christians' action and deeds, their whole life's-way shall on like footing stand'). (c) is heard several times, (a) both vocally and instrumentally, canonically between the latter lines; Bach tries to infuse some life by a long and meaningless run on 'Handel'. Part III recapitulates some of the material of Part I, but omits (a) from the vocal line.

v, tenor aria with two oboes d'amore, is more interesting, the obbligati parts are not without charm and there is a glow in the florid passages to 'Gott und Engeln'. The three instrumental lines enter canonically with:

Ex. 923

and oboe d'amore I continues with:

Ex. 924

The idea which is afterwards refashioned for 'Gott und Engeln' follows, in parallel motion for the obbligati:

Ex. 925

and then there are upward-sweeping runs, (d), against (a) in the bassi. 'Treu' und Wahrheit sei der Grund' ('Faithfulness and truth be the basis') is sung twice to (a), with a canonic treatment of a phrase resembling (b), with (a) in the continuo and triplet decorations the second time; 'aller deiner Sinnen' ('of all thy thoughts') is set to (b), and during the trilling (c) the voice joins in with simplified fragments. An interlude, based on (b), brings us to 'wie von außen Wort und Mund, sei das Herz von innen' ('as from without word and mouth, be the heart from within') to a new melody, save that part of (c) appears to 'Wort und Mund'. (d) and (a) accompany and (d) forms an interlude. 'Gütig sein und tugendreich, macht uns Gott und Engeln gleich' ('Good to be and virtuous, makes us (to) God and angels like') is exceedingly florid, and except for (c) new, both in voice and continuo. The oboes d'amore are silent till halfway through, when they enter with (a) in canon, to remind us that only faithfulness and truth can make us resemble divine beings, and then they solemnly sustain a long low A during the most ornate of the vocal passages. Bach frequently writes floridly when angels are mentioned, there are many instances; perhaps it is this that has dictated the style of much of the latter part of the aria.

The tenor recitativo secco, ii, is much more reasonable textually than that for bass, though it is dull—'The integrity is one of the God's-gifts; that it in our time so few men have, that means, they beg not God for it. For by nature associates our hearts' musings with only evil; shall it His way to anything good direct, so it God through His Spirit govern and on the path of virtue guide. Desirest thou God as friend, so make to thee the neighbour not an enemy: through falsehood, fraud and cunning.' (See Ex. 1293.) 'A Christian shall the doves'-way strive after, and without false trick live.' An arioso concludes: 'Mach' aus dir selbst ein solches Bild, wie du den Nächsten haben willt' ('Make of thyself such an image as thou the neighbour to have wilt').

This prepares for the chorus, a setting of St. Matthew vii. 12, all too short for a number of importance, but hailed by the composer as an oasis in a dreary wordy desert. The German version begins with 'Alles' ('All') and this, as always, gives rise to passages of much animation. The antiphonal character of the verse—'Therefore all things whatsoever ye would that men should do to you, do ye even so to them'—is interpreted in anticipation. The first choral entry:

and the second, a variant, the shorter 'Alles nun' ('All now') only three beats in length, and its variant are accompanied by continuo only and answered immediately by clarino, violin I plus oboe I, violin II plus oboe II, and viola, the phrases overlapping, thus increasing the excitement rapidly. 'das ihr wollet, das euch die Leute thun sollen' ('that ye will, that to you the people do shall') flows strongly with the clarino trilling in semiquavers. 'Das thut ihr ihnen' is set to a vigorous phrase:

imitated by the other three voices in succession at the distance of a crotchet, bringing an accented 'thut' on every beat for five bars. It goes without saying that accentuation must be according to words, not bar-lines. Similar treatment of other phrases, though with a varying number of voices, keeps up the cross rhythms, while the orchestra pursues elaborate polyphony in semiquavers, a tumultuous crowd of men. Sometimes (*a*) appears in the orchestra against different vocal material. After two shouts of 'Alles, alles nun, das ihr wollet', each followed by an orchestral version of (*a*), a double fugue begins, commencing with solo voices and gradually bringing in all the singers, the continuo accompanying until the first vocal tutti:

At bar 44 the second subject is discarded for a time, and a continuous stretto for sopranos and basses utilizes the first part of subject I with an octave drop on 'wollet'. From bar 56 to the end subject II, in a maze of cross rhythms, holds the field; (*a*) reappears in the orchestra, with semiquavers tearing down and a vigorous figure for the bassi— ♪♪♪ | ♫ —the final quavers being an octave leap. The clarino climbs up with the 'das thut' idea, and then breaks into brilliant passage work. The last section boils with tumultuous excitement.

The closing extended chorale (B.E.C. No. 3, O.) is likewise one of the redeeming features of the cantata. Stanza 1 of J. Heermann's 'O Gott, du frommer Gott', with its anonymous melody, is used: 'O God, Thou upright God, Thou source of all gifts, Without Whom nothing is that is, From Whom we all things have: Healthy body give to me, And that in such a body An inviolate soul And clean conscience (may) remain!' Line 2 gives opportunity for musical imagery, and unison oboes and upper strings imitate the lapping of waters. The clarino doubles the canto in the choral sections and in the interludes repeats notes in the lowest part of its compass, producing a feeling of solemn peace. The last line is slightly extended and the cantata concludes with a few tender notes from the orchestra. The work is seldom performed on account of the dryness of the arias and the crudity of the text of the bass recitative; the fine choruses could be salvaged if some editor would construct a cantata embodying these and adding attractive arias from elsewhere.

119. It is interesting to compare the two first cantatas for the Inauguration of the Town Council, No. 71, produced at Mühlhausen on 4 February 1708, and No. 119, 20 August 1723, fifteen-and-a-half years later at Leipzig. It is true that the increase in technical mastery shown in the latter makes the earlier one look rather tentative. The tremendous sweep and assured command of the choruses in No. 119 are not found in the rather restless and patchy ones of No. 71. But there are qualities in the youthful composition which attract one, its freshness, its ingenuousness; there are numbers which are unforgettable, the touching lament of Samuel, with the lovely tones of the chorale twining in and out, the exquisite 'turtle-dove' chorus, the bright and kaleidoscopic finale. One may admire much that is in 'Preise, Jerusalem, den Herrn' ('Praise thou the Lord, Jerusalem' N.) but one's heart goes out to 'Gott ist mein König'. There are three reasons for this difference. Bach as a young composer wrote as his emotions dictated, but his years in official capacities taught him to write whatever the occasion and whatever the text. He could generally produce something that served the purpose and impressed the listeners, even though his heart was not in the task. The second reason is that the earlier libretto is superior to the later; there are four Biblical quotations in No. 71, there is much poetic thought, the work is mostly in praise of God, with a personal reference to an honoured old Bürgermeister, and the amount of space granted to Town Council and state is but little. Contrastingly, six out of nine numbers of No. 119 are purely local in purport, praise of Leipzig, satisfaction with its rulers, exhortation in favour of loyalty to municipal powers, argument as to divine authority manifest in the elected council—not subjects suitable to artistic and emotional ecstasy. The third reason is that while Bach in Mühlhausen was merely a young, enthusiastic organist of a church, rejoicing in new opportunities, anxious to please his new-found friends and to make a stir in the musical world, in Leipzig he was the chief musical servant of the Town Council, their official composer and director of the church music of the city. In his first year there he was out to make an impression on his employers and to show them how he appreciated their temporal greatness. That the cantatas for his initial two Sundays, Nos. 75 and 76, fell flat is evident, for he forsook their splendour and spaciousness in the

immediately subsequent ones. Time came when his stubborn ways, his undoubted defects as a choirmaster and the lack of understanding of the worthy but artistically circumscribed Bürgermeisters had set up strife which embittered him. That he could as a private individual praise Leipzig with ardour is shown in some of his secular cantatas, but, however generously his powers rose to the occasion of providing music of external impressiveness for a municipal ceremony, his heart-springs were not tapped. Who wrote the libretto of No. 119 is not known; if it was Picander, as is conjectured, he thought more of the local event than of providing a text which would stir a creative artist. Yet much of the music has splendid qualities. It is one of the most externally brilliant works the master ever wrote.

The text of i, Psalm cxlvii. 12, stimulated him to put forth his powers. The orchestra is regally magnificent, 4 trumpets, timpani, 2 flutes, 3 oboes, and strings. The number is cast appropriately in French Overture form. The chorus does not appear in the slow sections. In the first, brass and percussion are used for fanfares only against the sustained chords of the rest of the orchestra. Wood-wind and strings are allotted a very long and splendid movement of great dignity:

Ex. 929
Fl.I.II.Ob. I. VI.I.
Ob. II.VI.II.
Ob.III. Va.
Cont.

and the fanfares over the chords in bars 4 and 8:

Ex. 930
Tb. I. II.
Tb. III.IV.

Timp. on C

produce a stirring effect. (*a*) and (*b*) are developed in bars 9–20 minus brass and percussion, and these enter in bar 21. The whole of the material is now repeated, except that the final bar is deleted. The section after the $\frac{12}{8}$ movement is a shortened version of the first, with a different key-scheme, and during the last six bars trumpets and drums join hands with the other forces, massively playing (*a*), which has not previously been heard in that department of the orchestra. The middle movement is exceedingly florid. During bars 1–3 the trumpets are used severally for the only time, I and II anticipate the chief vocal theme, entering in close imitation, followed at bar 2 by the basses. Tromba III plays a fanfare and at bar 3 all forces make a mighty noise:

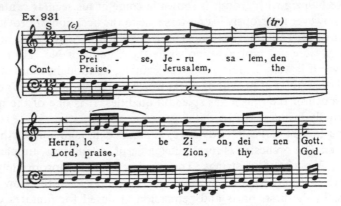

Ex. 931

Prei - se, Je - ru - sa - lem, den
Praise, Jerusalem, the

Herrn, lo - - be Zi - on, dei - nen Gott.
Lord, praise, Zion, thy God.

Particularly fine are the rolling semiquavers which support (c):

Ex. 932

Herrn,

which are used later for 'lobe' and 'segnet' ('und segnet deiner Kinder drinnen' 'and bless thy children within'), and which form the groundwork of numerous bassi passages. After (c) and (d) are developed the voices enter above (d) in pairs: 'Denn er maçhet fest die Riegel deiner Thore' ('For He makes fast the bolts of thy portals'). After a short tutti (except for trumpets and drums), there is an interlude based on (c) and (d), the trills of the former being multiplied. 'Er schaffet deinen Grenzen Frieden' ('He procures for thy borders peace') is vouchsafed four bars only, a simplified version of 'Denn er machet'. Brass and percussion are silent until the recapitulation of the chief subject-matter, when they enter simultaneously; in the last bar of the $\frac{12}{8}$ the trumpets play in pairs. There are some bars of splendid ten-part writing; the movement is a magnificent combination of massiveness and of Gothic intricacy of complicated detail. Never before had any Town Council been honoured with such gorgeous splendour.

On account of the nature of the texts the three recitatives with continuo, T. (ii), S. (vi), and A. (viii), are straightforward and without subtlety, although ii contains an expressive portion where Psalm lxxxv. 10, 'Mercy and truth are met together, righteousness and peace have kissed each other' is paraphrased. ii—'Blessed land! fortune-favoured town! where even the Lord His hearth and fire has. How can God better reward, than where He honour allows in a land to dwell? How can He a town with richer vigour bless, than where He goodness and faithfulness one another allows to meet, where He justice and peace to kiss, never weary, not weary, never satiated to become (has) firmly promised, even indeed fulfilled has? This is the ending effected; Blessed land! fortune-favoured town!' At the opening is a melisma on 'fortune-favoured town!', at the close this is allotted to 'Blessed land!', a little point of detail which shows how meticulously careful was Bach in setting even these platitudinous texts.

vi—'Now! now we acknowledge it and bring to Thee, Oh highest God, an offering of our thanks for it. Chiefly, after the present day, the day, which to us the Lord (has) made, you, dear fathers, partly from your burden released, partly also on your sleepless worry-hours to a new choice brought (has), so sighs a faithful people with heart and mouth together:' and the second great chorus follows attacca.

viii—'Finally! As Thou us, Lord, to Thy people (hast) taken, so let from Thy pious ones yet but a poor prayer before Thine ears come: And hear! yea hear! The mouth, the heart and soul sighs profoundly.'

Another recitative, iv, for bass, vaunts the magnificence of the city, and something more than bare continuo is needed, so splendid fanfares are heard on trumpets and drums; two flutes and two oboes da caccia sustain through most of the delivery of the text. The suppression of the upper strings produces the effect of an out-of-doors municipal function, when the wind and brass of the town musicians would accompany the bürgermeisters. A fanfare on the chord of C major (Wagner chose the same key for his mastersingers) is replied to by an arpeggio of the same chord—'So gloriously standest thou, beloved town,', two chords punctuate 'du Volk' ('thou people') and an unaccompanied 'that God for inheritance to Himself chosen has!' brings a briefer military fanfare. Then with wood-wind and bassi comes a long extolation of Leipzig, its people and its rulers—'Yet well and again well' (see Ex. 1266) 'when one it to the heart hold and rightly acknowledge will, through whom the Lord the blessing to grow permits! Yea, what requires it much! The testimony is already there: heart and conscience will us convince, that what we of goodness in us see, next to God, through clever authority and through your wise government happens. Therefore be, beloved people, for faithful thanks prepared! Otherwise would even thereof not thy walls be silent.' The opening fanfare is repeated without continuo.

There are two arias, iii and v. The tenor reflects on the blessings of God upon the people of the lindens. (Leipzig was very proud of these trees, there are references in every text concerning the city.) Though it is not music of the highest order it is not devoid of interest; the swaying of branches is indicated by dotted-note time-patterns:

Ex. 933

and the richness of blessings by florid runs, while two oboes da caccia obbligato bestow on it a befitting solemnity. 'Wohl dir' ('Well for thee') begins with a long note and a melisma; 'du Volk der Linden, du hast es gut! Wie viel an Gottes Segen und seiner Huld gelegen, die überschwenglich thut, kannst du an dir befinden' ('thou people of the lindens, thou art fortunate! How much on God's blessing and His grace depending, which boundlessly does, canst thou within thee find') is mostly in the dotted-note time-pattern, though 'Segen' has a passage akin to 'Wohl dir' and triplets enter on 'befinden'. Later, variety from the prevailing time-pattern is secured by a run of triplets and sextuplets on 'Segen', by a flourish on 'überschwenglich' and by casting a long 'Volk' in triplets and syncopations.

The alto reasons that 'Die Obrigkeit ist Gottes Gabe' ('The authority is God's gift'), 'ja selber Gottes Ebenbild' ('even itself God's image') and that he who will not recognize this 'divine right of kings' as applied to a municipal council must also be guilty of forgetting God. (Yet a certain writer on Bach argues that his works reveal him to be a communist!) The composer must have been puzzled as to how to deal with this tribute to the sacrosanctity of the assembled elected; he cut the Gordian knot by not attempting any interpretation of the text, and just wrote charming tunes and an obbligato for two unison flutes, scarcely instruments one would associate with such a disquisition on the law and its administrators!

Indeed, the twelve staccato quaver B flats in bars 18 and 19 are more suggestive of impudence than of dignity. The charming effect of the syncopation in bar 2 of the obbligato:

Ex.934

Cont.
8ve lower

(G minor, with signature of 1 flat)

is not reproduced in the vocal phrase:

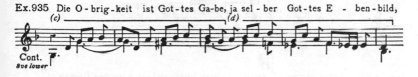

Ex.935 Die O - brig - keit ist Got - tes Ga - be, ja sel - ber Got - tes E - ben - bild,

Cont.
8ve lower

nor can the staccato quavers of:

Ex.936

Cont.
8ve lower

be legitimately employed by the singer, even in such a light-hearted aria as this, but the semiquavers find their way into the solo line. During a sequential treatment of (e) the voice fashions a flowing passage from (f), the graciousness of the Almighty. (a) and (b) as an interlude introduce 'Wer ihre Macht nicht will ermessen' ('Who its power (not) will measure') which is sung to (c) and then to (d), with (a) between, and the flowing phrase accompanies (d). During 'der muß auch Gottes gar vergessen: wie würde sonst sein Wort erfüllt?' ('he must also God quite forget: how would be otherwise His word fulfilled?'), (e) is exploited in the top line and (f) in the bottom. (e) persists in the last sentence until the voice is left alone with the continuo.

Trumpets, drums, and continuo announce the massive chorus, vii, which occupies eighteen pages of the *BGS* score and then repeats eleven of them. A waving figure in tromba I is indicative of joy, tromba II accompanies the first bar of I with quaver arpeggi, and then joins his fellow in parallel motion, trumpets III and IV taking up the quavers in unison:

Ex.937

The upper strings, doubled by the three oboes, enter with rushing semiquavers:

Ex. 938

while the flutes dovetail into each other with a quaver figure:

Ex. 939

Violins I and II conclude the six bars with:

Ex. 940

toss passages to each other for two bars, and then for other two bars two trumpets and drums enter with part of (a) and (b), oboes I and II play (c) and then trumpets I and II take up the upper line of (e). A fugue begins, the subject probably derived from the chorale 'Nun danket alle Gott' ('Now thank all God'):

Ex.941

the countersubject being:

Ex.942

At bar 8 flutes and oboe I enter with (*f*), slightly ornamented, and continue with (*g*), while sopranos, oboe II, and violin I deliver (*f*). The remaining wind and strings double successive entries and there are brilliant runs on 'fröhlich'. At bar 14 trumpets I and II ring out a stretto on (*f*), III, IV, and timpani add a short fanfare. 'Deß sind wir alle fröhlich' is now sung to (*e*), brass and percussion crashing in, and during the penultimate bar of the fugue tromba I and flutes trill on a passage akin to (*c*). The introduction is repeated. After the *Fine* bar comes a series of short passages—(1) 'Er seh' die theuren Väter an' ('(May) He regard the beloved fathers'), choir, almost homophonic, and continuo; (2) orchestra, two bars, without brass or percussion, two bars of (*a*) in oboes, a fanfare for unison upper strings, a new laughing figure for the flutes:

Ex.943

(3) 'und halte auf unzählig' und späte lange Jahre 'naus' ('and hold to innumerable and late long years beyond') beginning with imitations, strings double the voices. (4) A brief 'in ihrem Regimente Haus' ('in their government house'). A four-bar ritornello includes (*e*) and both limbs of (*a*). With continuo only, the chorus repeats the words, plainly set. On a sustained chord (*a*) and (*b*) accompany and there comes a surprising pause, a $\frac{4}{2}$ chord on F, with the soprano flinging up to high G, following a dominant seventh on D. It is almost as if some far-reaching and splendid vista of years were suddenly revealed to us. 'So wollen wir ihn preisen' ('So shall we Him praise'), concludes.

The twenty-second and twenty-third clauses of Luther's version of the Te Deum, very plainly set to the traditional plainchant, end the cantata: 'Help Thy people, Lord Jesus Christ, And bless that (which) Thine inheritance is. Serve and tend Thine to all time And exalt them high in eternity. Amen.' The orchestration is not stated; no doubt all forces would be employed. The cantata was first heard after Bach's death on a historic occasion in the story of the gathering appreciation of the composer; Mendelssohn conducted it at the opening of the Bach memorial at Leipzig, 23 April 1843, 120 years after its first production.

40. Nos. 40 and 64, for Christmas Monday and Tuesday respectively, probably represent the closing labours of this memorable year (1723), and in both cases the libretto is possibly by the composer. The first, 'Dazu ist erschienen der Sohn Gottes' ('To this end appeared the Son of God' B.), is one of the most perfect cantatas, every number being of superb quality, and is truly representative both of the composer's religious outlook and of his supreme inventive and imaginative powers, not the Cantor in his official position, but the real man, passionate in his spiritual fervour, believing in the personal activity of the Evil One and in the all-conquering might of the Saviour. There are few choruses in the whole range of the cantatas which can equal in dramatic power and vivid representation the opening number of No. 40, 1 John iii. 8. Every detail has its inevitable place in the scheme, diverse elements are melted together into a mighty structure, orchestral and vocal effects stir listeners as potently as anything in the immensely widened range of musical language of subsequent times. In addition to two oboes and strings, two horns are included in the score, the instruments of regal dignity, welcoming the appearance of the Holy One. They give out a short phrase which is answered by the rest of the orchestra:

Then a longer phrase:

is answered by (a) and (b). Now comes a swirling figure:

then taken up by Corno I and oboes, and a short figure:

in close imitation, which dashes up and down above a tumultuous
continuo:

There are four elements in the choral portions. The world hails the
appearance of the Christ in brief cries of exultation:

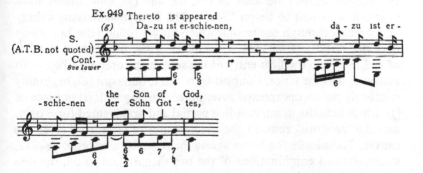

This fits in with a repetition of the opening instrumental material.
During the restatement of (d) comes a vocal motive which becomes of
supreme importance later, a rapid repetition of a single note:

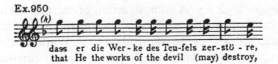

sometimes hurled out by the whole choir. Its vital rhythm and its vehement force are the hammer-blows of the powers of evil. It also explains the significance of (d), which is heard against it. Surging semiquaver ideas, (f) for the basses, a form of (e) for the altos, a modification of (f) in parallel motion for sopranos and altos, with (h) in the basses, part of the treatment of 'zerstöre', add to the description of the confusion among the forces of evil. It stops suddenly and a plain fugue begins with continuo only, subject:

countersubject:

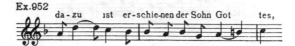

The accentuation of 'der Sohn' is peculiar, but it is consistent throughout, as will be seen in (g), (i), and (j). One would have expected the stress to be on 'Sohn'. The Saviour is moving calmly and serenely through the tumult which ranges round Him but which does not disturb Him. One is reminded of the incident on the Sea of Galilee. With the fifth entry of the subject the orchestra begins to reappear, and the tenor, doubled by corno I, hurls out (h), beginning startlingly on an unexpected seventh, combining with (i) in place of (j), which henceforth appears in a partial and ornamented form only, and the 'zerstöre' runs to the modification of (f) spread over the canvas. Technically the fugue shows the common scholastic devices, stretti, various combinations of the two themes, and so on, but one never thinks of this. It is the tremendous conflict which occupies our attention, the noble figure of the Christ, the vehemence of the actions of the devil (for it is these which Bach paints, rather than their destruction), the bewildering tumult and the mighty strength of the combatants. One of the most thrilling moments is where the altos ring out (h) on high E♭. A reconstruction of the first section closes this remarkable chorus. It was a strange idea to adapt it later as the 'Cum Sancto Spiritu' of the Short Mass in F. While all the imagery is lost there, it sounds astonishingly well in its new surroundings.

A fine tenor recitativo secco contains an upward semiquaver run in both voice and continuo to illustrate 'bestrahlt' ('illuminates') and a thoughtful passage of the bassi, dropping to F♯ at 'Bedenkt doch diesen Tausch' ('Remember then this exchange'), Christ becoming man in order that man may become a child of heaven. The excellent text is: 'The Word became flesh and dwells in the world, the light of the world illuminates the round of earth, the great God's Son leaves the heaven's throne, and to His majesty pleases a little men's-child to become. Remember then this exchange, who only remember can: the King becomes a subject, the Lord appears as a servant and becomes of man's race—oh sweet word in all ears! for comfort and salvation born.'

The first of three chorales, iii, is richly endowed with chromatic harmonies. The melody is by Caspar Fuger, Jnr., and the text stanza 3 of the senior Caspar Fuger's Christmas hymn, 'Wir Christenleut'' —'The sin makes sorrow, the sin makes sorrow; Christ brings joy, because He for comfort in this world (is) come. With us is God now in the distress: who is (there), who us as Christians can condemn?' Lines 1 and 2 are awe-inspiring; the chromatically ascending bass at the beginning of the last line answers the question while it is being asked, by indicating the maliciousness of the Evil One.

The next three numbers are dominated by the representation of Satan as a serpent. In the bass aria an almost unbroken succession of semiquavers in violins or bassi shows us the writhing of the 'Wurm':

Ex. 953

(Continuo as in Ex. 954.)

The chief melodic figure, announced against (a) by unison oboes, and repeated many times by the soloist, its time-pattern outlined by the lower strings:

Ex. 954

Hellish serpent, becomes to thee not fear?
Höl - li-sche Schlan-ge, wird dir nicht ban - ge?

suggests the twisting upwards of the monster and the smiting of it

down. The introduction with voice added is repeated in an extended
form, to emphasize its salient features. At one place bars 1 and 2 of
(b) come five times, imitated by oboe I, the first three rising from low
A to high E. For thirty-four bars, spreading over the ritornello, (a),
except for a solitary semiquaver rest, writhes and twists. During 'Der
dir den Kopf als ein Sieger zerknickt' ('Who to thee the head as a
victor lops off'), (a) is in the bassi, (b) in oboe I, reinforced in alternate
bars by the remainder of the upper instruments, and the last two notes
thrice appear inverted with nothing underneath save voice and continuo. The second syllable of 'zerknickt' is twice flung up picturesquely, the phrases being clipped off abruptly. 'Ist nun geboren, und
die verloren' ('is now born, and those (who were) lost') is sung to
(b), oboe I in imitation, oboe II stressing the wailing two-note figure,
(a) in violin I and the remainder of the strings stressing the time-
pattern of (b); 'werden mit ewigem Frieden beglückt' ('are with
eternal peace rejoiced') brings scale runs. After an interlude, (a) and
(b), the text is repeated with diversified treatment. The bassi begin a
new version of (a), the upper strings reiterate the time-pattern of (b),
which does not appear melodically till the end of 'geboren', the oboes
punctuate the beginnings of the bars, the voice leaps even more
energetically than before, dropping a seventh instead of rising on
'verknickt', 'ist nun geboren' runs up and down. One expects the
fragment with continuo to lead into a recapitulation of the introduction, but this is delayed, 'ewigem' is sustained against (a) and
(b), 'Frieden' is given a blissful high note. The vocal writing of this
splendid aria is finely declamatory, the singer is called upon to negotiate many sevenths, major, minor, and diminished, and to deal with
such passages as:

Ex. 955

Picturesque writing is also found in the succeeding alto accompanied recitative. The upper strings bend and twist throughout:

Ex. 956.

and, as the continuo puts in a note only occasionally, we feel that
the creature is suspended in mid-air. As the text speaks of the serpent
no longer exciting fear, because the coming of the Saviour has
brought salvation to the seed of woman, it is evident that Bach had
in his mind St. John iii. 14, 'And as Moses lifted up the serpent in
the wilderness, even so must the Son of man be lifted up.' The vocal
line is beautifully expressive and superbly declaimed. Particularly
lovely is the close, in which the upper strings move in the same
manner as above:

The remainder of the text is 'The serpent, which in Paradise on all
Adam's children the poison of the souls to fall let, brings us no more
danger; the woman's seed appears, the Saviour is into the flesh come
and has from it all poison taken. Therefore be comforted!' Choir
and orchestra now burst into a magnificently harmonized chorale—
stanza 2 of P. Gerhardt's 'Schwing' dich auf zu deinem Gott', to
F. Funcke's (?) melody 'Bleiches Antlitz, sei gegrüßet'—'Shake thy
head and say: Away, thou old serpent! Why renewest thou thy sting,
(why) makest me troubled and anxious? Is to thee then the head
lopped off, And I am through the suffering Of my Saviour from thee
snatched Into the hall of the joys.' Again Bach demonstrates his uncanny power of moulding a hymn-tune to serve any purpose he
desires.

Victory is now assured and the tenor aria calls upon all Christians
to rejoice. It is one of the most extraordinary arias the composer ever
wrote. When one reads the score one doubts whether the number will
'come off'. Two horns and two oboes, without upper strings, are
given most elaborate parts against which it seems impossible for the
singer to struggle, especially as his line is the most difficult in all the
cantatas. Yet the result is magical; voice and orchestra blend perfectly, the instrumental colour is masterly and splendidly effective.
The Saviour is depicted as conqueror, and the group of instruments
is chosen because of their association with military music of that day.
The middle section—'Wüthet schon das Höllenreich, will euch Satans

Grimm erschrecken: Jesus, der erretten kann, nimmt sich seiner
Küchlein an und will sie mit Flügeln decken' ('Rages already the
hell-kingdom, will you Satan's fury affright: Jesus, who save can,
gathers to Himself His chickens and will them with wings cover')—
provides ample opportunities for word-painting, the chief example
being a wildly broken passage on 'erschrecken':

Ex. 958

The whole of the instrumental material and much of the vocal is
derived from the four-bar introduction. The continuo leads off:

Ex. 959
(a)

Corno I dovetails into this:

Ex. 960
(b) ——— (c) ——— (d) ———

It will be seen that (c) and (d) are derived from (a). Corno II and
unison oboes enter on successive beats with (b). In bar 2 the upper
groups are antiphonal:

Ex. 961
Cor. I. II.   (e)——— Cor. I. II.

In bars 3–5 comes a wonderful passage:

Ex. 962 (tr)   (tr)
Ob. I. (f)

with corno II repeating C seventeen times and breaking into a semiquaver fanfare at the end, oboe II pursuing a line akin to (*f*) and the
bassi playing a derivative of (*b*). The voice begins:

Ex. 963

Christian   children,   rejoice   yourselves,
Chri - sten - kin - der, freu - et   euch,   ▪ freu - et   euch,

Cont.

which is compounded of (*a*) and (*g*). With part of (*f*) (*g*) the voice
begins a two-bar flourish based on (*g*). The (*f*) (*g*) group forms an
interlude, the voice repeats its first phrase, more fully accompanied,
but without continuo, and follows with a three-bar roulade on
'freuet' embodying (*a*) and (*g*), with (*d*) and (*e*) above in single
instruments and then the (*b*) derivative for the oboes, while the continuo utilizes (*b*) and beat 2 of (*f*). At the end the answering (*d*) and
(*e*), with reversed instruments, carry over into another vocal section,
which begins with (*b*) and continues with (*g*), during which the (*f*)
(*g*) group appears as before, except that corno I, being released from
other duties, joins the reiterated note of corno II. The (*f*) (*g*) section
links up with the middle portion. Both bassi and voice, the latter to
'Wüthet', use the (*g*) group and the continuo plunges headlong down
a semiquaver scale during 'schon das Höllenreich'. The (*g*) group is
heard in a new way, a descending sequence, horns and bassi reiterating an awesome diminished fifth. 'Satans Grimm' and 'erschrecken' borrow ideas from (*f*) and (*g*), the material of the previous
ritornello accompanies 'erschrecken' and the continuo rumbles to
an altered form of (*g*), while the voice, otherwise unaccompanied,
finishes the text, flourishing on 'Flügeln'. The (*f*) (*g*) group comes
again and then there are seven bars of voice and continuo on the lines
of the first portion of the section, in which the broken 'erschrecken'
reappears, and new melodies for 'Jesus—decken', the last word being
set to a roulade. Terror finally gives way to joy, and during the concluding pages of this notable aria, a reconstruction of the first section,
there are immensely long runs to 'freuet'.

Terry thinks the final chorale, stanza 4 of C. Keimann's Christmas
hymn, 'Freuet euch, ihr Christen alle', with A. Hammerschmidt's (?)
tune, was chosen because of the opening of the Peace Congresses at
Münster and Osnabrück which concluded the Thirty Years War:

'Jesus, take Thee Thy members Further in mercy; Bestow what one may pray for, To refresh Thy brothers: give to the whole Christian host Peace and a blessed year! Joy, joy beyond joy! Christ protects from all sorrow, Bliss, bliss beyond bliss! He is the mercy-sun.' Corno II is omitted from the ensemble. A fine feature of this noble setting is a magnificent rolling bass.

64. While the closing cantata of this richly fruitful year—'Sehet, welch' eine Liebe hat uns der Vater erzeiget' ('See now' O.)—is not as striking as its immediate predecessor, it is one of much beauty. It can be performed by moderate forces, for the choruses are not difficult and it may be given with strings and continuo only. The alto aria has an obbligato for oboe d'amore, which can be replaced by a solo violin if need be. The bass recitative is not essential; by its omission two soloists only, soprano and alto, are required. Cornetto and three trombones double the voice parts in i and in the three chorales; we do not need brass to pull our choristers through their lines nowadays, and modern trombones would obliterate any chorus except one of festival proportions. It almost seems as if the grouping of Nos. 40 and 64 together at the end of 1723 is incorrect, for the choral demands of the former are great, of the latter relatively little, and even then helped by brass and strings. It may be that the production of cantatas on successive days prevented adequate rehearsal and that the composer trusted to his orchestra for choral safety. Moreover, there is a large number of cautionary, though otherwise unnecessary, accidentals in No. 64, betokening a want of trust in his singers.

Although the quotation from the Scriptures for the chorus, 1 John iii. 1—'Behold, what manner of love the Father hath bestowed upon us, that we should be called the sons of God'—is appropriate to the Festival, the first chorale one of the hymns set for the Day, and the third akin to another, the original matter, possibly by Bach, has but little bearing on the season or relation to Epistle or Gospel, save for one reference. From ii to the end the burden is weariness of the world and anticipation of heavenly joys, not the mood one would expect in the 'Hauptmusik' for the third day of the Christmas Festival. The numbers other than the choral ones may possibly have been borrowed, for lack of time, from some other work.

i is in plain motet style, the continuo being in places independent, the rest of the orchestra merely doubling the voices. It is extremely beautiful, sheer musical joy from start to finish. The single 'Sehet' of the opening, with its drop of a fifth, comes in a fascinating form later, the word repeated, the four-note phrase leaping to the second word and tossed from voice to voice to emphasize the wonder of the Christian at the love of God:

Ex. 964

There are some very lengthy runs on 'erzeiget', in one case fifteen bars of quavers interrupted by only one crotchet, a delightful contrast to the accompanying series of plain minims and crotchets. The form is that of a fugue, with several two-part stretti. The subject, in which all voices join for the first two notes, is:

Ex. 905

the countersubject a continuation of the 'erzeiget' run with an addendum:

Ex. 966

Stanza 7 of Luther's 'Gelobet seist du, Jesu Christ' with its anonymous melody, follows immediately. It begins plainly, and increases in animation where the joy and thanks of Christendom are spoken of. It is translated for No. 91, p. 391, Vol. II.

The alto recitativo secco is notable for many semiquaver passages, both ascending and descending, in the continuo. This is the identical figure heard in the *St. Matthew Passion*, where Jesus and His disciples set forth for Gethsemane. The text speaks of the worthlessness of the things of the world and the continuo no doubt expresses their transitoriness. If the scales are played in a mysterious shadowy manner the effect of the recitative is greatly heightened. (The author confesses that when he edited the English version tabulated *supra* he had not understood their significance and that he, in consequence, marked them otherwise. It is only after several performances of a cantata that one begins to realize all that it means.) The text is 'Go, world! retain only thine own, I will and desire nothing from thee to have, the heaven is now mine, on this shall itself my soul refresh. Thy gold is a perishable possession, thy wealth is borrowed, who this possesses, he is indeed badly provided for.' Then with 'Therefore say I with comforted courage' it runs attacca into the first stanza of G. M. Pfefferkorn's hymn 'Was frag' ich nach der Welt', translated for No. 94, p. 334, Vol. II, to the anonymous tune 'Die Wollust dieser Welt', or 'O Gott, du frommer Gott'. The continuo marches in almost unbroken quavers from start to finish, the pilgrim is firmly treading the road to his goal.

The soprano aria (see O.S.B.A. No. 8), with strings, states that what the world contains must vanish like smoke, and that only what Jesus gives remains eternally. Violin I has many fleeting runs, some of them scale passages identical with those of the continuo in the alto recitative, a rare case of linked-up material. A restful waving quaver figure is heard frequently in the bassi (see the continuo of Ex. 967), and sometimes in the upper strings, the lulling of the believer to his last happy sleep. At one place the voice sings a much broken passage to 'vergehen', also the scale passages, but in quavers, and there are the inevitable long notes to 'fest' and 'stehen'. The singer borrows from the violin melody:

Ex. 967

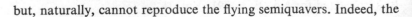

but, naturally, cannot reproduce the flying semiquavers. Indeed, the vocal line is unwontedly simple and even the middle strings do little but reiterate notes, possibly to indicate the clinging to the things of this world, and occasionally play (*a*). After (*b*) is repeated the voice sings 'muß als wie ein Rauch vergehen' ('must as like a smoke disperse') and violin I threads up and down. Later the soloist, to the second clause, modifies the violin passages, in quavers. The broken 'vergehen' upward scale runs are accompanied by violin I only, which takes a passage from the introduction, and continuo, which falls solemnly:

Ex.968

Cont.
8ve lower

and which afterwards reproduces the scales, in inverse direction and in quavers. At the beginning of Part II the continuo is silent for fourteen bars. The upper strings sometimes move in unison quavers, significant of bliss—'Aber was mir Jesus giebt, und was meine Seele liebt' ('But what to me Jesus gives, and what my soul loves')—and sometimes play in delicate three-part harmony, introducing (*a*) and (*b*), either complete or fragmentarily. The beginning of (*b*) is heard, modified, in the vocal line; 'bleibet fest und ewig stehen' ('remains firmly and eternally standing') sustains 'fest' and 'stehen' against moving strings; an ascending scale rounds off the section. The bassi re-enter in a short ritornello, (*a*) and (*b*) with a bar of semiquavers from the end of the introduction. The voice now proceeds continuously, with melodies which incorporate the first fragment of (*b*), the orchestra using the material of Part I, the violin flying passages indicating the contrast between the eternal gifts of the Saviour and the transitoriness of earthly possessions. The last 'und was meine Seele liebt' is accompanied by continuo only, which gracefully descends to the quavers of (*a*). While the voice slowly and dreamily intones 'bleibet fest und ewig stehen' on a C♯ the upper strings enter successively with a canon on a descending (*a*), and then the bassi murmur it, a waving F♯ E♯ for 2½ bars, with (*b*) above.

The bass recitativo with continuo contains the only reference to one of the Gospel lessons (two are indicated as alternatives), St. John xxi. 15–24. Peter asked the risen Lord what would happen to His betrayer, and the answer was 'If I will that he tarry till I come, what is that to thee?', and the singer speaks of remaining long on earth, until the divine summons is heard: 'The heaven remains to me assured, and it possess I already in faith. The death, the world and sin, yea even the whole hell-host can me, as one of God's children, the same now and nevermore out of my soul steal. Only this, only solely this makes for me still sorrow, that I even longer shall in this world remain; for Jesus will the heaven with me share, and thereto has He me chosen, on that account is the Man born.' There is a curious treatment of words at the close; 'Mensch' ('Man') is a trilled quaver and is separated from 'geboren' ('born') by a rest.

The alto in her aria (see O.S.B.A. No. 9) longs for nothing temporal seeing that the inheritance of heaven is promised. The connexion between the obbligato melody and the vocal line is fascinating. The oboe d'amore begins:

Ex. 969

and the singer opens:

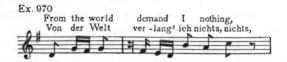

Ex. 970
From the world   demand I   nothing,
Von der Welt   ver -lang' ich nichts, nichts,

the rests and the repeated 'nichts' transforming the character of (a). The voice continues for a bar-and-a-half in the same vein, with (a) in the obbligato, and then repeats its initial idea shorn of its final note. Then comes 'wenn ich nur den Himmel erbe' ('if I only the heaven inherit') to (b), with a rest instead of the tied semiquaver. The second clause is continued while the oboe d'amore borrows another idea from the introduction:

Ex. 971
Ob. d'am.

Cont.
8ve lower

The two forms of (*a*) now alternate and during a variant of (*b*) the oboe d'amore exploits a soaring phrase which came near the end of the introduction. Later 'Himmel' is sustained against a variant of (*a*) and the soaring phrase is heard again while the voice climbs, trilling, on 'erbe'. The final vocal phrase, with continuo, is also derived from (*a*). Part II begins 'Alles, Alles geb' ich hin' ('All, all give I away') and thrice we have the gesture of throwing aside the things of the world, indicated by an upward leap of a major seventh. 'Weil ich genug versichert bin, daß ich ewig nicht verderbe' ('Because I sufficiently assured am, that I eternally not destroyed (be)') is set in a manner akin to Part I, a long note on 'ewig', short rests and repetitions of 'nicht'. The oboe d'amore is busy, moulding its previous themes, but ceases for twelve bars during which the vocal line is animated, and the continuo, which, so far, has played an almost incessant succession of quavers, breaks into lively runs. At the end the singer begins on high D and descends with a syncopated figure derived from notes 2–4 of (*a*), pitting $\frac{3}{4}$ against $\frac{6}{8}$ in the bassi during the penultimate bar. The loveliness of the tunes and the many cross accents in the vocal and obbligato lines make this number one of great charm.

Stanza 5 of J. Franck's favourite hymn, 'Jesu, meine Freude', with J. Crüger's melody, ends the cantata in blissful euphony—'Good-night (or "Farewell") oh existence, That the world (has) chosen! Me pleasest thou not. Good-night, ye sins, Remain far behind, Come not more into the light! Good-night, thou pride and pomp! To thee be completely, oh vice-life, Good-night given!' The beautiful hymn was actually modelled on a 1641 secular song—'Flora meine Freude; meiner Seele Weide' ('Flora my joy; My soul-pasture'). Both worldly tunes and verses were transformed into declarations of contempt for earthly things!

65. If the conjectured date for the Epiphany cantata 'Sie werden aus Saba alle kommen' ('The Sages of Sheba' N.), 6 January 1724, be correct, another masterpiece followed quickly on the heels of No. 40, and one so different that one wonders that they could have come from the same pen. When one thinks of a symphony of Beethoven a distinct personality arises before one's mind immediately, the symphonies can never be confused; the same is the case with many of Bach's church cantatas, the name or the number is sufficient to call up a distinct image, an impression of something uniquely expressed,

something which could be conveyed in no other terms. That is so
with No. 65, although one unconsciously links it up with the later
No. 1. The Gospel narrates the visit of the Magi to the stable, St.
Matthew ii. 1–12; the Epistle, Isaiah lx. 1–6, is its prophecy, and part
of the last verse was chosen by the librettist (perhaps the composer)
to form the first chorus. The opening words—'The multitude of
camels shall cover thee, the dromedaries of Midian and Ephah;'—
are not set, but Bach's imagination seized upon them and we have a
panorama of the leisurely procession of the caravan, the swinging of
the ships of the desert along the road, the opulence of their burdens,
the majesty and dignity of kings and slaves. No painter could bring
before our eyes a clearer picture or a more definitely oriental scene.
Regal horns lead their van, their phrase:

is echoed immediately by two transverse flutes, two solemn oboes da
caccia and upper strings, the chief melody, (a), appearing simultaneously in three octaves, an unusual orchestral device for Bach.
Bar 3 brings another lovely melody for the horns:

which is answered in the same way and followed by a short group
passed from corni to reeds and then to violins I and II and to flutes:

The introduction is short, but it is magnificent; after a sonorous
piece of ten-part writing, with leisurely suspensions moving in
thirds:

and the continuo descending in genuflexions based on a fragment
from (*a*):

(*a*) is heard in a tremendous unison spread over five octaves. The
voices enter in stately succession over a C pedal, the coming out from
Sheba:

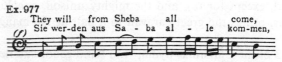

the variation from the (*a*) form on 'Alle' suggesting a great host
taking part in the mighty procession. Dovetailing with this come bars
1–4 of the introduction, with voices added. With bar 3 the basses
sweep down on 'Gold und Weihrauch bringen' ('Gold and incense
bring'). The voices sing (*f*) again, in reversed order, followed by
oboes da caccia, then strings and flutes. A new idea in close imitation
follows, with (*b*) in the orchestra. Then unrolls a splendid and dignified fugue, subject:

countersubject:

The connexion with (*a*) is obvious. There is a second countersubject:

Ex. 980

and   the Lord's   praise proclaim,
und des Her - ren Lob ver - kün _ - - - di - gen, ver-kün-di-gen,

At first the voices are accompanied by continuo only, wood-wind
and upper strings gradually join the procession and, after a lengthy
development, the corni add (*a*) to sweeping phrases, the introduction
is repeated, except for (*b*), and the mighty unison, concluded by a
few chords, brings the great caravan to a halt at the manger of the
Babe.

Stanza 3 of the Christmas hymn, 'Ein Kind geborn zu Bethlehem'
(an anonymous translation of the Latin 'Puer natus in Bethlehem')
follows, with simple, but rich harmonies. Flutes, oboes da caccia,
and continuo only accompany, an unmistakable suggestion of out-of-
doors singing of 'Weihnacht' hymns. The flutes double the melody
at the octave, the clear shining of stars above the heads of the celebrants of the Festival. There is a remarkable false relation between
basses and altos in the last line. The simplicity of the words—'The
Kings from Sheba came there, Came there, Gold, incense, myrrh
brought they there, Allelujah, Allelujah!'—and of the melody, which
originally was the descant of the Latin hymn, produces an effect
quite different from most chorale harmonizations and is a fine contrast to the elaborate chorus which has just been heard. There we
thought of the kings and their magnificence, now our minds are
turned to the Babe in the manger and the simple, sincere worship
which Christendom to this day offers to the Child. It would be even
more effective in St. Thomas's, as the hymn was sung by the choir at
the opening of the service.

A bass recitativo secco speaks of the fulfilment of Isaiah's prophecy
and of the gifts to the Child. It has a marvellously beautiful vocal
line and rich chromatic harmonies, rising augmented fourths and
fifths and twice a diminished third in the bassi, in the first case C♯
to E♭ and back immediately to C♯, a most unusual progression.
(See Ex. 1,290.) It occurs on 'Stall' ('manger') indicative of Christ's
loneliness, and the second comes to 'Erlöser' ('Redeemer'). The text
is 'What there Isaiah foresaw, that has at Bethlehem happened.
Here place themselves the Wise Men by Jesu's manger, and will Him
as their King praise, Gold, incense, myrrh are the costly gifts where-

with they this Jesus-child at Bethlehem in the manger honour. My Jesus, when I now on my duty think, must I myself also to Thy manger turn, and likewise thankful be: for this day is to me a day of joy, as Thou, oh life's-prince, the light of the heathen, and their Redeemer becomest. What however bring I indeed, Thou heaven's-King? Is to Thee my heart not too little', and it breaks into an ecstatic arioso—'so accept it graciously, because I nothing nobler bring can'.

The bass aria is somewhat unusual. The offerings at the cradle are still the subject of discourse; most of the instrumental phrases suggest the bowing of the Magi, and the grave solemnity of their genuflexions is indicated by the deep shades of two oboes da caccia. Gold, incense, and myrrh are symbolized in a triple canon:

Ex. 981
Ob. da C. I. II.

and for nearly thirty bars (a) forms a quasi-ostinato continuo, varying in pitch, the last leap frequently altered, but the figure as a whole rarely departed from. It is also heard in the vocal line, sometimes complete, sometimes fragmentarily. In bar 3 begins a rich oboe da caccia duet above (a):

Ex. 982

A two-part canon with the continuo—'Gold aus Ophir ist zu schlecht' ('Gold from Ophir is too base')—is answered by the close of the introduction; (a) comes in four-part canon. 'Weg, nur weg mit eitlen Gaben!' ('Away, only away with vain gifts!') brings a run on 'Gaben' modelled on (b), and later, after 'weg, nur weg mit eitlen', is set to (a); a three-bar run is yet more closely allied to (b). The introduction is repeated in the relative major; the next clause introduces 'die ihr aus der Erde brecht' ('which ye from the earth break'), which is at first a two-bar canon on (*a*) with the continuo, with a version of (*b*) above. There is a fine upward run on 'Erde', the singer rising step by step in a single bar from low F♮ to high D. Voice and continuo end the section: 'Jesus will das Herze haben!' ('Jesus wishes the heart to have!'). After three bars of ritornello Bach again adopts the device of opening a new vocal section with the final clause of the previous one, and continues: 'schenke dies, o Christenschaar, Jesu zu dem neuen Jahr' ('give this, oh Christian host, to Jesus for the New Year'). Epiphany was celebrated as the 'Hoheneujahr' ('High New Year'). The flowing line is accompanied by continuo only, which repeats the time-pattern of notes 1–5 of (*a*) five times in unbroken succession, there being only one deviation from the original melodic contour. (*b*), with instruments reversed, is played over a threefold repetition of (*a*) to the new words, with two brief references by the bassi, 'schaar' and 'Jahr' being approached from a seventh above. (*a*) here becomes a theme of rejoicing.

The tenor recitativo secco is less rich harmonically than that for bass but is full of charm—'Disdain not, Thou, my soul's light, my heart, that I in humility to Thee bring. It encloses yea such things in itself together, which Thy spirit's fruits are. Faith's gold, the incense of prayer, the myrrh of patience are my gifts, these shalt Thou, Jesus, ever and ever as possession and present have. Give but Thee also Thyself to me, then makest Thou me into the richest on the earth; for, have I Thee, so must the greatest wealth's abundance for me sometimes in heaven be.'

'Reichthums Überfluß' ('wealth's abundance') is the explanation of the exceptionally sonorous scoring of the tenor aria (see P. 10), in which the orchestra of i reappears, an unusual procedure. The main tune, tutti, is fascinating:

Ex. 983
Vl.I. Fl.I.II. *8ve higher*
(*a*)
Cont.
8ve lower

it is followed by four bars of a lilt:

Ex.984
Fl.I.II.
(*b*)
Cor.I.II.unis.

(one is reminded irresistibly of Handel's pifferari), with the upper strings, minus continuo, playing:

Ex. 985

(*a*) is extended to seven bars, tutti, the flute part of bar 1 of (*b*) joined to (*a*) is flung from group to group, flutes, oboes da caccia, corni, flutes, oboes da caccia, violins I, II—the last three, after Beethoven's manner, being shortened by the omission of (*c*)—and a compound of (*a*) and (*b*), tutti, concludes the introduction. As a contrast to this rich mass of sound, voice and continuo lead off to (*a*)—'Nimm mich dir zu eigen hin' ('Take me to Thyself as Thine own away')—and (*b*) replies, oboes da caccia taking over the repeated notes of the corni, the latter swinging in sixths, strings and continuo tacet. (*a*), tutti, with voice, is followed by 'nimm mein Herze zum Geschenke' ('take my heart as the gift') with the shortened antiphonal (*b*) in the orchestra; the eight-bar (*a*), voice plus orchestra, ends the section. The first three groups of the vocal section come again with a new clause—'Alles, Alles, was ich bin' ('All, all, that I am') but the ritornello is restored, the horns taking the florid part, the oboes da caccia the repeated notes, upper strings with (*c*), the flutes piping a quaver at the beginning of each bar, bassi silent. Violas are silent during 'was ich rede, thu' und denke' ('what I say, do and think') and each of the four groups of upper instruments enters in alternate bars with (*b*) or flying figures; the vocal melody and that of 'soll, mein Heiland, nur allein dir zum Dienst gewidmet sein!' ('shall, my Saviour, only alone to Thee as service dedicated be!') are new, lilting and care-free, but the continuo line is that which supported (*a*). The four bars, founded on (*b*), which formed the ritornello in the initial vocal section, are heard again, with flutes and corni interchanged and the eight-bar (*a*) in the relative minor. The singer now grows more excited, 'Alles' is allotted runs with demisemiquavers, bar 1 being a florid form of the (*b*) figure, the second time with the curious device of bars 1 and 2 reversed, the upper strings take over the flute pipings, each of the three wind groups plays a descending arpeggio for a bar, a new idea, and bar 4 unites the (*b*) figure in direct and contrary motion. Another new feature follows, sustained notes for flutes and horns, while violins and then violins and violas let us hear the (*b*) figure in alternate bars.

Repeated notes for unison oboes da caccia and for bassi, giving way in the latter to a semiquaver ascent, accompany the final vocal bars. One factor in the brightness of the scoring is that the flutes are kept continually in their upper registers, the second rarely descending as far as B, third line.

A second chorale, orchestration not stated, closes this engaging cantata—'Yea now, my God, so sink I to Thee, Comforted into Thy hands, Take me, and make it so with me Till my last end: As Thou well knowest, that to my spirit By that means its way may be directed, And Thine honour yea more and more Itself in myself be exalted'— stanza 10 of P. Gerhardt's 'Ich hab' in Gottes Herz und Sinn' to its anonymous melody.

172. The year of the Whit-Sunday cantata, 'Erschallet, ihr Lieder' ('Ring out, ye songs'), cannot be ascertained, but a libretto in the style of Salomo Franck and the employment of a double viola line point to an early date. Bach's first Whitsun in Leipzig was in 1724; that or the next year is probable. The cantata was certainly performed again in 1731, according to the printed book of words for these services, and it was no doubt then that the violin and 'cello obbligati in the duet were replaced by the organ, as that was the year of the organ obbligato series. The cantata is singular in being without treble wood-wind (unless an oboe is intended to be added to the duet), though bassoon, three trumpets, and timpani are found in the score, and in including one recitative only, ii, and that to a Biblical text, the first verse of the Gospel, St. John xiv. 23–31. It is the same verse which is used for the opening duet of No. 59, and it is paraphrased for the chorus in No. 74, both Whit-Sunday cantatas.

The first part of the bass recitativo secco is simple, 'Who Me loves, he will My word hold, and My Father will him love, and we shall to him come', but the last clause—'und Wohnung bei ihm machen' ('and dwelling with him make') and the preceding one are developed into an arioso longer than the recitative portion proper. Thrice the bassi curve downwards, the descent of the Holy Ghost, not mentioned in the text but appropriate for the Day. The final note for the singer is low C below the stave, a semibreve with a pause! Nowhere else in the cantatas is this depth encountered.

The last line of the text of the opening Da Capo chorus refers to this Biblical verse: 'Gott will sich die Seelen zu Tempeln bereiten' ('God will for Himself the souls as temples prepare'). The Festival

is alluded to only as 'O seligste Zeiten!' ('Oh blessedest times!'),
there is no other mention of the particular occasion, nor does the
music make any suggestion of it. Indeed, the style is so much that of
the kind of joyful chorus one finds in secular cantatas that one is
inclined to think that it may have served some previous purpose.
There is much antiphonal work between brass, percussion, and continuo on the one hand and strings and fagotto on the other, short
phrases or single chords hurled against each other. The introduction
is brief. In the chief theme:

upper strings and bassoon fill up the rests and join in the conclusion.
The remainder is developed from:

(a) is expanded:

with basses leaping octaves and bassi plunging down in semiquaver
scales for two octaves. 'Erklinget, ihr Saiten' ('Resound, ye strings')
is set to (b), (c) follows with all voices in animated polyphony, while
three-note groups are tossed between trumpets plus drums and upper
strings plus fagotto. (a) and (b) in the orchestra bring an exhilarating
tune for the choir (Ex. 989): the bassi continuous, upper strings and
bassoon joining in at times. (d) and the vocal (c), the latter with
the voices differently disposed, are repeated. The 'seligste' of 'o
seligste Zeiten!' is sustained twice by the chorus, with (a), slightly

Ex. 989

altered, in brass and percussion, the string parts being different each time. Brass and percussion are tacet in Part II, a fugue subject:

Ex. 990

There is no real countersubject; (f) is employed freely. The periods of entry are irregular, 3, 2, 3, and 2 bars, then, at 2 bars, a two-part stretto at a bar. After the seventh entry there is a glorious maze of sound caused by a derivative of (f) in cross accents. A halt is called and (e) comes in fourfold stretto, at 1, 2, 1, and 1 bars, (f) being absent, bassi and fagotto plunging down in semiquavers as in the first vocal section. Another (f) maze brings us to the Da Capo. Throughout the fugue the upper strings double the voices and great brilliance is produced by the unison of both violin lines and sopranos.

Bach's exceptional bass soloist was provided with a glorious opportunity in a non-Da-Capo aria (see P. 46) of thirty-one bars only, scored for three trumpets, timpani, and bassoon with continuo, no upper strings. 'Heiligste Dreieinigkeit, großer Gott der Ehren' ('Holiest Trinity, great God of the honours') calls up majestic fanfares on the common chord of C:

Ex. 991

and roulades:

Ex. 992
Tpts. I. II. III.

The repeated-note arpeggio of (*a*) is practically the sole occupation of the continuo, and (*a*) is the foundation of:

Ex. 993
Hei-lig-ste Drei-ei - nig - keit,   gro-sser Gott,

Cont.

and of 'komm doch in der Gnadenzeit' ('come then in the mercy-time'), which is followed by a passage—'bei uns einzukehren' ('with us to dwell')—which is a free inversion of 'großer Gott zu Ehren'. The unimportant syllables 'der' and 'zu' are, curiously, allotted groups of five demisemiquavers. (*b*) is predominant during 'komm doch in die Herzens-Hütten, sind sie gleich gering und klein' ('come then into the heart's-dwellings, be they even mean and small'), the demisemiquaver flourishes and (*a*) and (*b*) during 'komm und laß dich doch erbitten, komm und $\begin{Bmatrix} \text{kehre} \\ \text{ziehe} \end{Bmatrix}$ bei uns ein' ('come and let Thyself then implored (be), come and $\begin{Bmatrix} \text{turn} \\ \text{enter} \end{Bmatrix}$ into us'). Demands upon the performers are relentless. Tromba I has long and astonishingly virtuosic roulades in demisemiquavers, difficult enough today with valved instruments, but incredibly more so on the old natural trumpet. At one place there are nearly fifty successive tromba notes without an opportunity to take breath; the singer is called upon to negotiate:

Ex. 994
tr

uns   ein!

With a voice of right calibre and strength and discreetly used instruments, this splendid aria 'comes off' magnificently, a perfect balance being achievable, despite the forbidding appearance of the score.

The first distinct textual allusion to Pentecost comes in the tenor aria (see P. 14)—'O Seelen-Paradies, das Gottes Geist durchwehet' ('Oh soul's-paradise, which God's spirit through-breathes')—in which violins and violas in unison blissfully descend and ascend in quietly moving quavers, supported by a continuo which sways gently upwards in crotchet arpeggi:

Ex. 995

Another phrase of soft ecstasy is:

Ex. 996

Two bars of (a) are heard in the bassi at the close of the introduction. After two bars from the singer, derived from (a)—

Ex. 997

the whole of the introduction is repeated while the voice adds a third strand. The breathing of the Spirit of God is expressed by a waving passage:

Ex. 998

which at the end of the repetition of the introduction, with the portion beginning with (b) coming yet again, is extended to nine bars. Part II —'der bei der Schöpfung blies, der Geist, der nie vergehet' ('which

at the Creation breathed, the Spirit, Who never passes away')—
again begins with voice and continuo, this time for four bars, before
(*b*) and parts of (*a*) appear in the obbligato line. The continuo commences differently, but afterwards returns to its original figure and
uses part of (*a*). The vocal line is mostly new, though there are passages framed on (*a*). In Part III there are five bars, an increasing
number, before the upper strings commence a modified recapitulation of the introduction; 'auf, auf, bereite dich!' ('up, up, prepare
thyself!') is, naturally, less flowing than the preceding vocal lines;
'der Tröster nahet sich' ('the Comforter approaches') twice sinks
arpeggio-wise, and 'nahet' incorporates portions of (*a*). The aria is
of much delicate beauty, a delightful contrast to the splendour of the
preceding number. If Bach's bass at that time was of unwonted compass, his tenor must have been restricted in range, for it is very rare
in his arias for this voice to find G as the upper limit.

The S.A. duet is a dialogue between the soul and the Holy Spirit.
The text falls into three divisions. The soul, S., cries 'Komm, laß
mich nicht länger warten, komm, du sanfter Himmelswind, wehe
durch den Herzensgarten!' ('Come, let me not longer wait, come,
Thou soft heaven's-wind, blow through the heart's-garden!'), and
the alto replies 'Ich erquicke dich, mein Kind' ('I refresh thee, my
child'). The soul now addresses the Holy Spirit thus—'Liebste Liebe,
die so süße, aller Wollust Überfluß, ich vergeh', wenn ich dich misse,
sei im Glauben mir willkommen!' ('Dearest love, Thou so sweet, of
all delight abundance, I fail, when I Thee lack, be in the faith to me
welcome!')—and is answered by 'Nimm von mir den Gnadenkuß'
('Take from me the mercy-kiss'). Then the soul cries 'Höchste
Liebe, komm herein! Du hast mir das Herz genommen, sei im Glauben mir willkommen!' ('Highest love, come within! Thou hast from
me the heart taken, be in faith to me welcome!') and the Divine
Being reiterates over and over again the familiar 'Ich bin dein und
du bist mein!' ('I am thine and thou art Mine!'). Although there are
occasional similar phrases, the two characters are kept distinct
throughout, the lines being nearly always different. Particularly
beautiful are the long notes on the weak parts of the bar to 'I',
'thine', 'thou', and 'mine'. There is an infinite number of subtle
points in the vocal parts; pages might be written about these alone.
Both lines are highly ornate, the soprano particularly so; there is a
lovely flowing passage on 'wehe', for instance, there are trills, slides,
and appoggiature.

Two short quotations must suffice to give some idea of the delicate nature of the tracery:

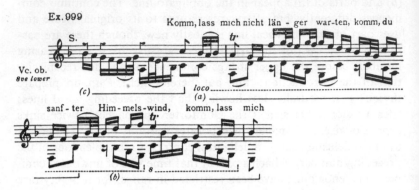

Ex. 999

and:

Ex. 1000

Again we find Bach using arabesques to express great spiritual ecstasy. In the original score the lowest part is allotted to violoncello obbligato, without 16-ft. tone, without figuring. The marvellous resource of Bach's technique is shown by the restriction of this line to three motives, delivered in the opening ritornello (lettered in Ex. 999 in order of appearance), there being no other material in this very lengthy movement. They are all illustrative of the 'soft wind of heaven'. The zephyr of divine grace pervades the whole number, the penetrating essence of the Holy Ghost, no longer the tongues of fire stimulating man to spread the Gospel, but consoling balm to the anxious and needy soul.

These three strands are not all; Bach adds a commentary of his own—the chief Whitsun chorale, 'Komm, heiliger Geist, Herre Gott' ('Come, Holy Ghost, Lord God') is heard in a most ornate form, decorated by the loveliest fioriture, twining in and out of the voices like the tendrils of a delicate and luxurious plant, penetrating, as it were, the innermost corners of the heart offered to the Spirit. The introduction of the chorale is one of those subtleties appreciated

only by a study of the score, for the canto fermo is so much transfigured by the richness of Bach's soaring invention, that even the most
devout worshipper at St. Thomas's, however familiar with the hymns
of the Festival, could scarcely have recognized it. The temptation to
quote several of these exquisite transformations must be resisted, one
must suffice; the last line:

Ex. 1001

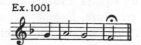

becomes:

Ex. 1002

To what instrument is allotted this exquisite line remains a matter
of doubt. The original violin part states tacet for the number; the
editor of the *BGS* volume, in the course of an argument too long to
be quoted here, decides, nevertheless, in favour of that instrument.
Schweitzer is of opinion that an oboe is more suitable and makes the
foundational melody more prominent. For the 1731 reconstruction
the composer negatived much of its beauty by transferring the instrumental lines to the organ; but the unemotional tone and inability
to shade with infinite subtleties cannot adequately replace violin or
oboe and 'cello, and the personal warmth of the ensemble is reduced
to an impersonal coldness. The duet is one of the most elaborate
numbers in all the church works, the endless convolutions of the
three upper lines, the intricate weaving of parts, the numerous
appoggiature, producing a marvellous texture and an ecstatic feeling
of bliss which no other composer has ever expressed. In i and iii we
are on earth, gazing wonderingly upwards at the might and glory of
the Highest; in iv and v we are dwelling in Christian Elysian fields,
transported from the world into the blissful realm of blest souls, in
full communion with the Spirit of God.

Reverting to technical matters—there is a peculiar effect at the
beginning of bar 23 of the duet (counting the quaver opening as
bar 1), produced by daring consecutive fifths; the number affords a
fascinating study of the methods by which Bach, through his
counterpoint, free, daring, regardless of momentary clashes, carried
the older harmonic system to a point almost unbelievable in its

plasticity and its prophecies of the yet distant future. The upper
obbligato line of the *BGS* score, p. 65, bottom line, bar 1, contains an
error. The sixth note is D, whereas the organ version has B (A in the
transposed part, for the organ was written a tone lower than the
orchestra). It is obvious that B is correct.

In the closing chorale, violin II, violas I and II, and bassoon
double the voices; violin I plays a lovely obbligato, mostly soaring
above the rest of the structure. Except for the first close and the
cadence at the repeat double bar, the obbligato is continuous;
the conventional chorale pauses must be disregarded. The meaning of the obbligato is to be found in the title of the hymn and
line 1 of the stanza (No. 4 of P. Nicolai's 'Wie schön leuchtet der
Morgenstern' ('How beautifully shines the Morning Star') with
its accustomed tune)—'From God comes to me a joy-light, When
Thou with Thy dear eyes' ('Äugelein', diminutive of 'Augen'
('eyes'), indicative of endearment) 'Me friendly dost behold. O,
Lord Jesus, my dearest possession, Thy word, Thy Spirit, Thy body
and blood Me inwardly quicken. Take me lovingly In Thine
arms, that I warm shall be through grace: To Thy word come I
laden down.'

[The cantata ends with a repetition of its first chorus.]

179. The Gospel for the Eleventh Sunday after Trinity is St. Luke
xviii. 9–14, the parable of the Pharisee and the publican. The libretto
of No. 179, possibly by Christian Weiss, Snr., and possibly for the
year 1724 (the English edition of Spitta states the Second Sunday after
Trinity, 18 June, obviously one of the countless egregious errors of
the translators), fiercely condemns the congregation of St. Thomas's
as hypocrites and indulges in violent language arraigning their foul
wickedness. Thrice only in the libretti is the Apocrypha drawn upon
for quotations, in No. 106 and the unnumbered 'Herr Gott, Beherrscher aller Dinge' and in the opening chorus of this work—'Siehe
zu, daß deine Gottesfurcht nicht Heuchelei sei, und diene Gott nicht
mit falschem Herzen' ('See to it, that thy God-fearing not hypocrisy
be, and serve God not with false heart' (Ecclus. i. 28). Bach adopts
the apparently incongruous form of a fugue, styled Concerto, packed
with recondite devices, upper strings doubling S.A.T., a frequently
independent continuo; and yet with his unerring skill the text is
interpreted with marvellous directness. Clause 1 provides the subject,
a vigorously declamatory theme:

Ex. 1003

It is answered by inversion, the perversity of the sinner; the next two voices follow the same procedure. The countersubject, to clause 2, flings 'nicht' into prominence and 'falschem' moves in stern chromatic crotchets:

Ex. 1004

Stretti at various distances pit original and inverted themes against each other, besides the original form in stretti. Half-way through, a new theme to clause 2 appears, in close imitation, but embodying the crotchet descent to 'falschem', stressing it in minims:

Ex. 1005

and introducing simultaneous semitonal passages in pairs of voices. Towards the end the subject and the new theme are heard together, and the latter concludes over a tonic pedal, in all the splendour of boldly developed chromaticism. It is one of the strangest facts in the wide field of Bach's adaptations that he should have turned this wild, fierce, and vehemently denunciatory chorus, so splendidly effective as an interpretation of its text, into the Kyrie of the Short Mass in G. Was it a gesture of contempt when he was forced to provide service music in which he had no interest?

A tenor recitativo secco continues the harangue: 'The present Christendom is unfortunately badly ordered: the most Christians in the world are tepid Laodiceans' (see Rev. iii. 16) 'and puffed-up Pharisees, who themselves outwardly pious show, and as a reed the head to earth bend; in the heart however sticks a proud self-glory; they go indeed into God's house and perform there the outward observances: makes however this really a Christian? No! Hypocrites can it also perform.' Needless to say the declamation is energetic. The text of the aria for the same voice may be arresting preaching but it is not conducive to musical inspiration. The false appearance of hypocrites can be likened to the apples of Sodom, fair of exterior, filled with filth, hypocrites may be outwardly of good semblance but are unable to stand before God. Except for some rather tortuous vocal phrases, Bach writes an interesting and not-too-fierce aria, the decorative line for violin plus two oboes in unison being most important, the lower parts rather subsidiary. The opening idea:

Ex. 1006

is the basis of:

Ex. 1007

the high-lying 'Falscher' creating a feeling of tenseness; (b) is answered by the stern second idea of the introduction:

Ex. 1008
VI.I. Ob.I.II.

(a) and (b) now appear together, modified, and (c) is heard against 'die mit Unflath angefüllt' ('which with filth filled') and 'und von außen herrlich gleißen' ('and from without splendidly shine') is left alone with continuo, 'herrlich gleißen' being brilliantly florid at the top of the singer's voice. 'Heuchler, die von außen schön, können nicht vor Gott besteh'n' ('Hypocrites, who (are) from without fair, cannot before God stand') is at first with continuo, the latter rising and plunging down, as if the pretended Christian were attempting to ascend to heaven and were thrust below; (*a*) twice accompanies sustained notes on 'besteh'n'. (*b*) is now transformed:

Ex. 1009

with the original form in violin I. 'Besteh'n' is treated as before, and at the close of three final bars for voice and continuo, the singer sinks down on 'können nicht vor' and flings 'Gott' on high A. The bassi imitate the run in contrary motion, but after climbing an octave are hurled down a twelfth into the depths. In spite of its inappropriateness the aria was incorporated into the Short Mass in G as the 'Quoniam'.

The Pharisee having been the theme of the first recitative, mankind in relation to the publican is the thesis of the second, for bass with continuo. It is a great contrast to the other and an interesting study of Bach's resourcefulness and his ceaseless seeking after intimate connexion between words and music. Recitative—'Who then from within as from without is'; arioso—'He is called a true Christian', the continuo moves confidently in quavers; recitative—'So was the publican in the temple; he smote in humility on his breast, he ascribed not to himself a holy nature; and this one, place before you, oh mankind, as a praiseworthy example'; arioso—'in thy penitence', a melisma on 'deiner' ('thy') and the customary repeated 'prayer' quavers in the continuo; recitative—'art thou no robber, adulterer, no unjust honour-seducer, ah! picture to thyself then indeed not'; arioso—'thou art therefore angel-pure', the continuo storms up in righteous indignation; recitative—'Confess to God in humility thy sins'; arioso—'so canst thou mercy and help find', a florid passage for the voice, quavers for the bassi resembling those of the first arioso.

Denouncement now ends and the remaining two numbers represent the penitent sinner before the Saviour. The soprano aria pleads for mercy; 'Liebster Gott, erbarme dich' ('Beloved God, have Thou pity'). The text, however, cannot cleanse itself from lurid similes, sin afflicts the singer 'als ein Eiter in Gebeinen' ('as an abscess in bones') and help is implored to prevent sinking in deep mire ('tiefen Schlamm'). The harmonies here are most beautiful, richly emotional with a solemn bass, while the voice descends step by step for nearly two octaves. The aria is deeply felt despite the repellent verse. There is much pathos in the answering phrase of the two sonorous oboes da caccia at the opening, with the bassi moving up the scale, each note solemnly sounded thrice:

Ex. 1010 (a)

Ob.da C. I.
Ob.da C. II.
Cont.
8ve lower

There is a pleading theme:

Ex. 1011
Ob. da C. I.
(b)

Ob. da C. II.

during which the continuo moves agitatedly, and it is made even more intense:

Ex. 1012
(c)

the pathos-laden wailing being senza bassi till the last three notes. When the voice begins it adds another contrapuntal part to (a):

Ex. 1013
Lieb - ster   Gott,   er - bar - me - dich,

and then the idea begins a third time, with a different voice part. The bassi, however, move steadily upwards through a greater space, the octave scale of A minor, but with a C♯ introduced after the minor third, a most lovely harmonic progression, the key fluctuating between A minor and D minor. Against (b), (c) and its conclusion the singer pleads—'laß mir Trost und Gnad' erscheinen' ('let to me

comfort and mercy appear'). She twice bewails, in broken phrases—
'Meine Sünden kränken mich' ('My sins afflict me')—the oboes da
caccia pursue (a), the continuo motive sinks—r t₁ se₁ l₁. With the
original bassi idea and development of (a) in the obbligati, there are
two brief phrases to 'als ein Eiter in Gebeinen' ('as an abscess in
bones') and these words are repeated with (b) and (c) in the orchestra.
There is an agonized cry—'hilf mir, Jesu, Gottes Lamm' ('help me,
Jesus, God's Lamb')—the oboes da caccia modify (a) and (b), the
bassi for the first time take up the quavers of (a), continuing them for
eight bars, at the end dropping from E to F♯. Now begins a most
beautiful passage, the voice descends—'ich versink' in tiefen
Schlamm' ('I sink in deep mire'); part of (a) is heard in oboe da
caccia II, the continuo motive falls by semitones, and on 'Schlamm'
the obbligati sustain pianissimo. There is a further sinking for the
voice, from high A♭ to low B, the continuo moves by a diminished
third, and the close is one of profound despair:

Ex. 1014

The reprise is a shortened version of the first part; the slowly ascending bass scale occurs again, but with an unexpected alteration, the
upper tetrachord includes the sharpened sixth and seventh, the key
being A minor with a mere passing reference to the subdominant.
Bach returned to this quarry for the third time to dig out material
for his short masses, and the aria forms the *Qui tollis peccata* of that
in A, not an inappropriate change. It is made more tender by the
transference of the oboe da caccia parts to flutes, and by giving the
bass part to violins and violas in unison, with no continuo.

An entrancingly lovely harmonization of a chorale closes the cantata. The last line is highly chromatic, almost baffling to us even
today; there are few choirs which could sing the final bar unaccompanied and in perfect intonation. (This does not imply that chorales
should be sung a cappella; such procedure is contrary to Bach's practice.) The chromaticism is explained by the agonized cry of the
text, stanza 1 of C. Tietze's (Titius) 'Ich armer Mensch, ich armer

Sünder', set here not to its customary tune 'Wohl dem, der weit von hohen Dingen' but to G. Neumark's 'Wer nur den lieben Gott läßt walten'—'I poor man, I poor sinner, Stand here before God's countenance. Ah God, ah God, proceed gently And go not with me into the judgement. Have mercy, have mercy, God my compassionate One, on me!' No doubt Bach's choice of the more familiar melody was to drive home its message: 'Who suffers God only to guide.' Oboes and continuo only are instructed to assist the voices; the upper strings would join in without being told to.

69. Three performances are recorded of No. 69, the first of two cantatas bearing the title of 'Lobe den Herrn, meine Seele'. It was twice used in 1724, on the Twelfth Sunday after Trinity, 27 August, and for the Inauguration of the Town Council, the next day. The text was probably designed for the latter rather than for the former. It was revised, in the present form, for a like municipal celebration about 1730. The original work is printed in the appendix to the *BGS* volume; i and two arias remain, though one of them is rescored and altered, the recitatives are new, except for one phrase, the closing chorale is different. The original librettist is unknown; one may assume that alterations in the verbal text were made by the composer. The magnificent opening chorus, which occupies nearly thirty pages of the score, is based, as nearly always, on a few motives, the complete structure showing infinite resource in their development. It begins with massive chords for strings, three oboes, bassoon (always used for doubling), timpani and tromba III. Trumpets I and II announce a brilliant trilling motive, mostly in thirds:

in bar 3 unison oboes play a one-bar descending figure against it:

These are repeated in oboes I and II and upper strings respectively, and a series of vigorous arpeggio leaps leads into a new semiquaver idea:

Ex.1017

and a chain of suspensions. A modification of (a):

Ex.1018

against (c) and clanging of trumpets and drums usher in the choir: 'Praise the Lord, my soul' (the text is Psalm ciii. 2). They sing (a) and (b) in pairs of voices to 'Lobe den Herrn' with (c) in the continuo, and a modification of the (d) (e) section for combined forces rounds off the first choral section. A double fugue now begins. Subject I is based on (d):

Ex.1019

(c) is present in the form:

Ex.1020

There is a long double exposition. Entries are numerous, 1 to 4 above continuo only, S., A., T., B., then oboe II, oboe I, oboe III, bassi plus bassoon. The second exposition is—B., T. plus viola, A. plus violin II plus oboe III, S. plus violin I plus oboe II. The climax comes with the subject in oboe I plus trumpet I, trumpets II and III and timpani clenching it with hammered chords. These three instruments are the only ones denied the subject, on account of their restrictions. A new exposition leads off with subject II, more slow-moving, derived from the suspensions of the introduction:

Ex.1021

und   ver - giss nicht, ver - giss nicht
and   forget   not,

with a countersubject related to (e):

Ex.1022

was   er dir Gu - tes ge - than   (hat,)
what He to thee of good done   (has,)

It promises to develop on the same lines as the other, but at the eighth entry (f) reappears, combined with (g). There are now numerous simultaneous entries of the subjects, tromba I plays part of (f) and after a few bars' rest takes it up again, timpani and lower trumpets adding homophonic passages as before. A reconstructed version of part of the first ritornello, (a), (b), (c), (d), and (e), with voices added, leads to the Dal Segno. It is curious that the leaping arpeggio figure, which promised to be fruitful, does not appear elsewhere. With the exception of very short, almost passing, modulations, the whole of this exuberant chorus is confined to tonic and dominant keys.

The first phrase only of the original soprano recitative, with continuo and bassoon, is borrowed for the later version and the whole text is new: 'How great is God's goodness then! He brought us to the light, and He upholds us still! Where finds one even one creature which support lacks? Consider then, my spirit, the Almighty's unconcealed token, which even in the smallest thing itself right great proves. Ah, might it to me, oh Highest, then succeed, a worthy thanks-song to Thee to bring! Yet, should it to me thereby in strength fail, so will I then, Lord, Thy glory tell.'

The earlier cantata contained a tenor aria in C with flute and oboe da caccia obbligati above unison fagotto and continuo. This is transposed into G, the voice changed to alto and the upper instruments to oboe and violin, no doubt solo. The last clause of the text is altered; the allocation of the words is improved at times and one note is different. There are a few changes in the obbligati lines, though none in the continuo, and from time to time bowing and tonguing are revised.

The trills are not always the same. One curious point concerning alterations where numbers are rewritten is in the matter of appoggiature. It is odd to find new dissonances introduced by leaning tones, and even more odd to find old ones replaced by plainer progressions. Often there seems to be no reason for these changes, here and in other cases. These harmonic alterations appear important to us, to Bach apparently they were not. One cannot see any solution to the puzzling question of his attitude towards these changes. A strange manner of writing for the original oboe da caccia and for the oboe which replaces the flute, is a series of close arpeggi, of the Alberti bass type, so different from the usual style of melodic lines associated with these instruments:

Ex.1023

(b) is heard in the ritornello only. There are subsidiary themes:

Ex.1024

and:

Ex.1025

'Meine Seele, auf! erzähle' ('My soul, arise! tell') is twice set to (a) with a tail-piece, different in the two cases. (a) accompanies the first extension and (a) and (b) form an interlude of a bar. A rhythmically involved line is formed from beat 3 of (c):

Ex.1026

and there are elaborate trillings to 'erzähle' with (a) above. After an interlude a free form of (a), followed by further runs on 'erzähle' and entries of the modified (a), carry one to the end of Part I. 'Rühme seine Wunderthat' ('praise His wonder-deeds') introduces further flowing passages. The original 'laßt ein gottgefällig' Singen durch die frohen Lippen dringen' ('let a God-pleasing singing through the joyful lips push') is replaced by 'laß dem Höchsten zu gefallen ihm ein frohes Danklied schallen' ('let the Highest to please to Him a joyous thanks-song resound'); a waving passage is often heard in the orchestra, and near the close part of (c) appears. The thematic construction is more loose than is customary at the period.

The second recitative of the original cantata was for alto, with unison bassoon and continuo. It is replaced by an elaborate one for tenor, with a fresh text. There are three sections. (1) is with continuo and fagotto, the latter punctuating instead of sustaining and once departing from the bassi line—'The Lord has great things to us done. For He supplies and maintains, protects and governs the world. He does more than one say can. However, only of one thing to remember.' (2) Upper strings now enter with long-sustained chords to tell of the peace brought by the magistrates; the bassoons join the continuo permanently—'what could to us God right better give, than that He to our government the spirit of the wisdom gives, which then at every time the evil punishes, the good loves? Yea, which by day and night for our welfare watches?' An instrumental flourish indicates the contentment of the Leipzigers. 'Let us therefore the Highest praise; arise! cry to Him, that He Himself even yet further'. With 'so merciful will prove' comes a short arioso, violin I playing pleading phrases. (3) is remarkable; the voice is in recitative: 'What our land harm can wilt Thou, oh Highest, from us turn, and to us wished-for help send. Yea, yea, Thou wilt in suffering and distress us chastise, yet not kill.' The upper strings paint the lamentations of the people in three simultaneous motives; violin I has large sighing leaps:

Ex.1027

violin II sinks down:

Ex.1028

and struggles upward in inversion, the viola sways in crotchets:

The splendid bass aria, with oboe d'amore, strings, and fagotto doubling the continuo, is borrowed entire from the earlier version. The tender melody announced by violin I and oboe d'amore in unison is modified for the voice:

with an independent oboe d'amore melody above; the second clause begins in the upper instruments on the sustained note. After a repetition of (a) the words are repeated to a modification of the second clause, and the driving away of the evil things, referred to in the recitative, is shown vividly by three bars of:

Sustained notes for 'Wacht' and for the continuo indicate confidence in the Protector, the ♩♪ idea of 'nimm mich' is heard in the orchestra, pianissimo upper strings intone repeated chords, and the oboe d'amore plays short tender figures. One feature of the aria is the brevity of the introduction, eight bars, and of the intermediate ritornelli, two, two and four bars, all founded on (a). 'Steh' mir bei in Kreuz und Leiden' ('Stand me by in suffering and sorrow') is treated in a remarkable way. There is a long and beautiful passage to 'Leiden', the bassi descend in semitones bar by bar, the upper instruments sustain; viola, violin II, violin I, viola and violin II in turn play (b) poco forte, each dropping to piano in the next bar. 'Alsdann

singt mein Mund mit Freuden' ('then sings my mouth with joys')
begins with continuo and a long run with sextuplets is developed on
'Freuden'. The continuo is poco forte, the oboe d'amore enters with
flourishes of sextuplets piano and continues with a version of (a), still
piano, the upper strings play (b) poco forte. At the close of 'Freuden'
violin I and oboe d'amore swirl up in sextuplets and the singer
announces 'Gott hat Alles wohl gemacht' ('God has all (things) well
done') while (b) comes in imitation in the orchestra. In the final vocal
section the first two clauses of this part of the text are treated more
briefly. The bassi ascend semitonally instead of descending, in
repeated crotchets, during 'Steh'—Leiden', (b) is omitted and the
new version is one of assurance instead of sorrow. 'Freuden' is given
a different passage from before, though one or two fragments are
the same, and (b) is alternated between oboe d'amore and massed
strings. As 'Freuden' ends the oboe d'amore plunges down in sextuplets, and 'Gott—gemacht' is extended to thirteen bars. A turn from
'Freuden' is incorporated and the ♩♪ scale of (a) is inverted; and,
beginning with a long note on 'gemacht', the orchestra repeats the
introduction, the melody remaining intact, the lower parts altered and
voice added. During all the latter part of the aria (a) is never alluded
to by the singer. The elaborate dynamic markings are surely an indication that we may introduce varying degrees of strength in the orchestral parts of many other numbers, instead of permitting the dead
level of tone which so often stultifies performances of Bach's works.

The early cantata ended with a simple chorale; here it is replaced
by one more elaborate, a joyful song of praise. The vocal lines move
normally, strengthened by the three oboes, bassoon, and strings,
while trumpets and drums are independent. These enter at the ends
of lines 1–4—'May thank, God, and praise Thee The folk in good
deeds. The land brings fruit and enriches itself, Thy word has well
prospered.' During 5 and 6—'Us bless Father and the Son, us bless
God the Holy Spirit'—trumpets I and II are continuous, III and
timpani are likewise except for a brief halt before clenching the pause
chord of 6. In 7—'To Whom all the world the honour does'—they
change their manner, first hammering out ♫ | ♫ ♫ ♩,
resting for two beats, and then blazing in with the last two chords.
At the end of 8—'Before Him be afraid especially,' the trumpets in a
dread unison on a low note repeat the above time-pattern. Brass and
percussion rest for four beats of line 9—'And say from the heart:
Amen!'—and then add four independent parts, including the joy-

motive and with tromba I mounting to high D, a magnificent close to this exultant cantata. The stanza is the third of Luther's versification of Psalm lxvii, 'Es woll' uns Gott genädig sein' with its anonymous melody. The original ending was stanza 6 of S. Rodigast's 'Was Gott thut, das ist wohlgethan'.

190. The difficulty of affixing dates is indicated by the fact that Terry places nearly twenty cantatas within the year 1725, but marks all as problematical. Their composition and the copying out of band and chorus parts, which Bach often did himself, in part or in whole, would almost seem an impossible task, even allowing for the preparation of the New Year No. 190, 'Singet dem Herrn ein neues Lied' ('Sing to the Lord a glad new song' B.) during the preceding weeks. There must, however, have been torrential spates of church cantatas at certain periods, for at other times extraneous compositions would interfere with the regular supply for the Leipzig churches. Nine belonging to this abundant year have already been discussed, 20, 73, 86, 136, 144, 166, 167, and 168; eight others fall into the group we are at present surveying, 190, 76, 104, 44, 105, 46, 77, and 148, all containing splendid music and at least three of them masterpieces. Terry points out that the revision of the text of No. 190 for the Jubilee of the Augsburg Confession, 25 June 1730, was undertaken by Picander; this does not necessarily mean that he was the author of the 1725 libretto. If he were, then this was his first connexion with the master. The work as we know it is incomplete, iii–vii only being intact. They indicate a healthy and bright style, they are delightful music, even though they show us nothing new or arresting.

The alto aria of praise, iii, with strings, demands nothing more than bold straightforward singing. The introduction alternates forte and piano sections. The vigorous bassi figure:

Ex.1032

endows the aria with commanding strength. Doubtless the syncopations first heard in the second piano section:

Ex.1033

were designed as a comment on the last line of the stanza, a reference to the green pastures of Psalm xxiii. The opening melody of the introduction, with its joy-rhythm, serves for the first clause:

The inner strings are silent, but the repetition is tutti. Similar phrases are used for 'auf! erzähle dessen Ruhm' ('arise! tell of His glory') and (a) begins 'der in seinem Heiligthum fernerhin dich als dein Hirt will auf grüner Auen weiden' ('Who in His Holy place henceforward thee as thy Shepherd will in green meadows pasture'). All the text is repeated with a condensation of former material.

The imagery of Shepherd and sheep is continued in iv, a long bass recitativo secco—'Let wish to itself the world, what flesh and blood well pleases; only one thing, one thing beg I from the Lord, this one thing would I have gladly: that Jesus, my joy, my faithful Shepherd, my comfort and salvation, and my soul's best part, me as a lambkin of His flock also this year with His protection embrace (may), and nevermore from His arms let. His good Spirit, Which to me the way to life shows.' In an andante arioso—'govern and guide me on even path: so begin I this year in Jesu's name'—the firm movement of the continuo shows the Christian stepping out manfully on his road.

A charming T.B. duet, v, with unspecified, but possibly oboe d'amore, obbligato, somehow retains the pastoral feeling, although no conventional ideas are employed and the text does not suggest it. Descending continuo scale passages support the chief obbligato and vocal phrase:

The instrumental version is more attractive by reason of a drop of a

seventh across the bar-line, a form never used by the singer. A second
limb of the introduction:

and a third:

form the sole material of the obbligato line. 'Jesus soll mein Anfang
bleiben' ('Jesus shall my beginning remain'), a reference to the close
of iv, utilizes part of (*a*), with the bassi inverting their scales, and so
do 'Jesus ist mein Freudenschein' ('Jesus is my joy-light') and 'Jesu
will ich mich verschreiben' ('to Jesus will I myself ascribe'). There is
a passing shadow at the repetition of 'durch sein Blut':

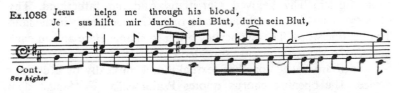

a touch of solemnity on 'Ende':

The seven bars containing these are expanded into eleven, with voices
reversed, the faint clouds over the sun dim the brightness of the pastoral scene even less than before.

The tenor recitative, with strings, speaks of blessings on church and
school during the year. It is without incident, save a tender 'Jesus'—
'Now, Jesus grant, that with the New Year also His anointed may
live; may He bless both, stem and branches, so that their happiness

to the clouds may ascend. (May) bless Jesus church and school, He may bless all faithful teachers, He may bless His word's hearers; he may bless council and judgement-seat; He may pour out also over each house in our city the blessings'-spring; He may grant that anew each other peace and truth in our boundaries kiss may.' (See Ps. lxxxv. 11.) 'So live we this whole year in blessing.' All of which, no doubt, is morally edifying, but not productive of interesting recitative.

The closing chorale, vii, adopts the same device that we find in two other New Year's Day cantatas, a blaring of trumpets and beating of drums at the close of the lines. In this case 1 and 3, with their repetition, are not clenched in this manner; it is obvious that to have released this mass of resplendent tone in every case would have lessened the total effect. The restricted scope of tromba III and timpani necessitates silence during the antepenultimate and penultimate lines, but that only increases the glory of the final outburst. The choral harmonization is exceedingly plain, and doubled by the rest of the forces. The text is stanza 2 of J. Hermann's New Year hymn 'Jesu, nun sei gepreiset', with its anonymous tune: 'Let us the year fulfil In the praise of Thy name, That we to the same sing In the Christian-community; (Thou) wilt to us the life ordain Through Thy Almighty hand, Sustain Thy beloved Christians And our fatherland. Thy blessings to us turn, Give peace to all time; Give genuinely in the land Thy beatific word. The hypocrites bring to shame Here and in each place.' The last two lines are repeated.

i and ii are linked together textually and musically by a curious device. The opening chorus quotes Psalm cxlix. 1—'Singet dem Herrn ein neues Lied, die Gemeine der Heiligen soll ihn loben!' ('Sing to the Lord a new song, the congregation of the Saints shall Him praise!'), Psalm cl. 4—'Lobet ihn mit Pauken und Reigen, lobet ihn mit Saiten und Pfeifen!' ('Praise Him with drums and dance, praise Him with strings and pipes!'), and Psalm cl. 6—'Alles, was Odem hat, lobe den Herrn! Allelujah!' ('Everything, that breath has, praise the Lord! Hallelujah!'). Between the second and third verses comes a line from Luther's vernacular version of the Te Deum —'Herr Gott, dich loben wir!' ('Lord God, Thee praise we!')—and another is added after the third—'Herr Gott, wir danken dir!' ('Lord God, we thank Thee!'). Luther's lines are thundered out in long notes by the choir in octaves, to the traditional plain-chant.

In ii, which is termed Choral, the first of Luther's clauses begins chorally, and a bass sings in recitative: 'that Thou with this New Year to us new good-fortune and new blessing sendest, and still in mercy on us thinkest.' The second clause (all these are choral) is followed by a tenor recitative—'that Thy goodness in the past time the whole land and our worthy town from famine, pestilence and war sheltered has'. The first clause was in D, it now begins in F♯ minor, with the second note sharpened, and moves rapidly through B minor to E major. An alto recitative succeeds: 'for Thy father-faithfulness has yet no end; it becomes with us still every morning new. Therefore fold we, merciful God, for this, in humility our hands, and declare life-long with mouth and hearts praise and thanks.' The second clause concludes. The choral blocks are short, each less than two bars.

The scoring of i, and probably of the choral portions of ii also, the recitatives being with continuo, is no doubt identical with that of vii, but the only orchestral parts which remain are the violin lines. In the introduction the parts which remain to us speak of brilliant orchestral texture. There are four chief figures:

and:

Vacant bars, 1 and 2, 5 and 6, were probably filled with brass and percussion fanfares. The choral portions which precede the first Te Deum clause are mostly short outbursts, partly polyphonic, based on the joy-motive which appears first near the end of the introduction,

partly homophonic, there being an exhilarating close to the first
choral entry:

accompanied by (*b*). This may have been the fanfares, repeated
orchestrally after (*b*) with (*a*) joining in. Two sets of choral block
chords, with (*b*) and (*c*), the first four choral bars again, two of (*b*)
and (*c*) and the block chords, bring us to 'Die Gemeine', at first
homophonic, and then a tremendously exultant 'loben', (*e*) for three
bars in sopranos and tenors, the upper part of (*d*) in the altos and
(*b*) in the basses, with a new figure for violin I and fragments of (*c*)
for violin II, as if the singers were unwilling to cede all brilliant passage-work to the orchestra. There are two bars of the joy-motive for
the sopranos and part of (*a*) for the altos, still to 'loben'. Then come
four further homophonic bars with (*b*) against the first. There would
doubtless be fanfares before:

(which is based on the first choral entry, with the lower voices moving
in a similarly lively fashion) and another before the second clause of
the verse. The joy-motive and the lower part of (*d*) join a modification
of (*f*), ((*e*) above for a bar) in which exhilaration is increased:

A bar of the joy-motive follows the second clause, and the mighty
unison Te Deum line is accompanied by (*e*), till the last bar brings
in the joy-motive. (*e*) and the motive accompany a fugal exposition
and episode, subject:

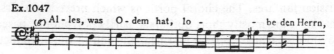

(the identity of the second limb with (*f*) and (*g*) will be noticed), countersubject:

Ex.1048

Here again is similarity of thematic matter. The episode is tumultuous, the joy-motive and 'Allelujah' sung by the sopranos to (*e*). A second exposition follows, the voices proceeding from high to low, the opposite of the first entries. (*h*) is replaced by:

Ex.1049

and there is an even more brilliant trilling second countersubject. Part of this, with bar 1 of (*i*) and (*c*), leads to the thundering-out of line 2 of the Te Deum. Against the plain-chant violin I plays (*g*) and violin II (*e*). The final sustained note was possibly accompanied by the fanfare; (*b*) enters in the last bar and leads to a series of Allelujahs, sopranos alone with the joy-motive, the whole chorus with S.A.T. singing (*c*). Then there are shouts to block chords, with (*b*) and (*c*) in the violins. 'Odem' has an exciting passage, the upper part of (*d*) in octaves for sopranos and violin I, the lower part for violin II, (*e*) for altos and tenors, (*b*) for basses, a modification of the 'loben' in the 'Die Gemeine' section, the latter part of which is fitted to the new words. Possibly the fanfare heralded the four concluding bars, (*b*), to 'Alles', for S.A.T. doubled by violins, (*b*) in the basses in the next bar, with (*a*) in the strings and a final shout of 'Allelujah!'. The Breitkopf edition cleverly reconstructs the missing orchestral parts, and so provides opportunity for performance of a cantata which, while possessing no deeper qualities, and in the first chorus of which we cannot help remembering the later and greater setting of the text, in the motet 'Singet dem Herrn', is outwardly attractive and brilliantly effective.

67. We now leap from New Year's Day to the First Sunday after Easter, for which Christian Weiss, Senr. (?), provided a skilful libretto offering splendid possibilities for the composer. 'Halt' im

Gedächtniß Jesum Christ' ('Hold in affection Jesus Christ', N. 'Hold in remembrance Jesu Christ' B.) is one of the finest of the series. The text of the opening chorus, II Timothy ii. 8, is an allusion to the Gospel, St. John xx. 19–31, the appearance of the risen Lord to the disciples closeted through fear of the Jews, and His admonition of Thomas eight days later. The *corno da tirarsi* announces the chief theme:

Ex.1050

the first note significant of 'Halt'', and (*aa*) afterwards associated with the title of the cantata, 'Hold in remembrance Jesus Christ'. The corno is supported by flauto traverso, two oboes d'amore, and strings. The minim chords of the latter come afterwards to the repeated cries of 'Halt''. After the chief theme flute and violin I maintain a long series of syncopations, later heard to 'Gedächtniß'. The oboes d'amore at the same time develop a quaver motive, the meaning of which is revealed subsequently. The inner strings play cross syncopations and the continuo firm, confident crotchets, (*aaa*). This combination of motives we shall call (*b*). The bassi repeat (*aa*) and a modification of (*b*) follows. The choir twice sings the first phrase of six bars, (*a*) in the sopranos and then in the basses. Against the long 'Halt'' the other voices cry out the word thrice, on minim chords, a command which is varied during the number with the utmost ingenuity. The upper strings in unison (except at two points where the composer hesitates to take his violas above high E and causes them to diverge from the main line) pit the quaver theme against the choral mass, the horn intones a long note and between the choral entries and after them repeats (*a*). It is notable that throughout the number, with the exception of the bassi entry mentioned *supra*, this is never announced independently of the voices except by the corno, a ringing command to bear the Saviour in remembrance. Now, with continuo only, the voices sing (*a*) thrice, and as counterpoint come the climbing quavers from the oboes d'amore of bars 3–5:

Ex.1051

The preliminary crotchets did not occur in the introduction, but are important in the development. 'Von den Todten' ('from the dead') falls precipitately, a particularization at variance with the general meaning of the text. The remainder of the orchestra re-enters and the now familiar material is developed with splendid virility and with amazing variety. The single cries of 'Halt'' frequently come on the second half of the bar. A brilliant and triumphant conclusion is produced by the ascension of the corno to (c), as if on mighty wings, to the highest notes of its compass, thus adding a new feature to the final (b).

Two contrasting motives dominate the splendid tenor aria (see P. 16) with oboe d'amore and strings. An upward run, heard numberless times:

Ex.1052

is indicative of the resurrection, and a short nervous figure:

Ex.1053

The two ideas present side by side the conflicting emotions of the followers of Christ in those days of perplexity and persecution after the apparent shattering of all their hopes. The introduction consists of these motives only and (b) is heard five times in the continuo, two being inverted, a musical device at variance with the significance of the passage. When the soloist sings (a) for the first time, (b) is tossed from unison upper strings to oboe d'amore, and on the second appearance it is dovetailed in close canon; then (c) is pursued for three bars, with (b) in the bassi. After a ritornello (a) is modified and against it violin I and oboe d'amore ingeniously reverse (b) and the preceding notes of (a):

Ex.1054

My   faith knows the Saviour's   victory, yet feels my heart   strife and war,
Mein Glau-be kennt des Heilands Sieg, doch fühlt mein Her-ze Streit und Krieg,

The uncertain mental condition of the early Christian is further shown when 'mein Heil! erscheine doch' ('my salvation! appear then') is sung to short panting phrases and the oboe d'amore gives vent to anxious sighings during the vocal rests. But he gathers confidence in a semiquaver swell on 'erscheine', while (a) comforts him momentarily, only to be confronted with (c) in the next bar. (d) is now modified, upper strings are silent, oboe d'amore and bassi alternate with (b), the former direct, the latter inverted. (c) is elongated in an interlude and a new melody appears to 'mein Glaube— Krieg', oboe d'amore and strings coming in with (b), at once direct and inverted, in the second halves of the bars. In the 'mein Heil' section, the oboe d'amore sighings are even more despondent, falling in all nearly two octaves. The second version of (d) comes as before and the singer flings up to high A on 'erscheine'.

The doubt of Thomas alternating with faith is again depicted in the succeeding three numbers, iii and v alto recitatives with continuo, iv a tutti chorale, attacca being indicated after iii and iv. iii, after 'My Jesus', refers to Hosea xiii. 14—'Called art Thou death's poison and a pestilence of hell' yet these still frighten the doubter—'ah, that me then danger and terror strike! Thou laidest Thyself on our tongues a praise-song, which we sung (have)'. iv is a plain setting, with a fine and stately bass, of N. Herman's melody 'Erschienen ist der herrlich' Tag' to stanza 1 of his hymn—'Appeared is the glorious day, Whereon himself no man sufficiently rejoice may: Christ, our Lord, today triumphs, All His enemies He captive leads. Hallelujah!' Even after this the singer knows no calm and prays for victory over self—'Yet appears almost, that me the enemies' dregs' (evidently referring to those who are battling with the individual Christian and not with the Saviour) 'whom I too great and all-too-terrifying find, do not peacefully leave alone. Yet, when Thou for me the victory acquired hast, so strive Thyself with me, with Thy child. Yea! we perceive already in faith, that Thou, oh Peace-Prince, Thy word and work in us fulfil wilt.' It is evident from iii that the chorale, though not one of those appointed for the day, must have been sung by the congregation before the cantata, no doubt by Bach's wish.

vi is one of the most remarkable numbers in the cantatas. It is termed 'Aria' but is a scena for bass (whether solo voice or chorus is not stated) with S.A.T. chorus, flute, two oboes d'amore and strings. It opens with world-tumult in the strings, whirling scales, vigorous leaping arpeggi, octave jumps in the bassi:

and:

On the last beat of the section the wood-wind enter piano and sustain into the next portion:

Upper strings are silent, the beatific wood-wind theme is the appearance of Christ, stilling the tumult of the world. When Jesus came to the disciples who had hidden themselves through fear of persecution, He twice said 'Peace be unto you' (St. John xx. 19), and eight days

afterwards He used the same sentence to Thomas. Thrice, then, in
arioso-like phrases, the bass sings 'Peace be with you', the final word
being sustained lengthily and comfortingly against the gently-moving
flute and oboes d'amore. The same three-fold repetition of the sentence is found in the first recitative of No. 158; there it is addressed
to the 'anguished conscience', here, not so much to the disciples as
to the whole world. In the last bar the upper voices enter:

Ex.1058

Wohl   uns!
Well   for us!

and, with the common time, the tumult bursts out again. The string
parts are identical with the introduction, S.A.T. are added. (*d*), heard
twice, is distinctive from the uproar, as if the believers were standing
calm and undisturbed. But they are drawn into the conflict:

Ex.1059   Jesus   helps us   to   fight,
 (*e*) Wohl uns, Je-sus hilft uns käm -   -   -   -   -   - pfen,

Cont.
8ve lower   *piano*
                    6   6   6

and:

Ex.1060

S.
A.
T.

käm -   -   -   - pfen,

It will be seen that both are derived from (*a*). After 'und die Wuth
der Feinde dämpfen' ('and the rage of the enemies to quench') the
voices shout 'Hölle, Satan, weich', weich', weich', weich'!' ('Hell,
Satan, yield!'). The last three detached chords on 'weich" rise
defiantly and the strings sink. The $\frac{3}{4}$ section comes again, the same
veiled wood-wind movement, the same threefold benediction of
Christ, only the course of keys is changed so that when the tumult
bursts in again it may commence in the relative minor. While identical
motives are now employed, groupings and chord progressions are

different. The choral ideas too are in the main fresh, though 'Jesus holet uns zum Frieden' ('Jesus draws us to peace') begins with (e) modified and 'dämpfen' ideas are partially reproduced to 'Frieden'; 'und erquicket in uns Müden' ('and refreshes in us tired ones') commences with a modification of (e), 'Müden' is sustained and the 'Hölle' section is condensed for 'Geist und Leib zugleich' ('(in) spirit and body equally'). The tumult is raging outside but in the chamber a new spirit is possessing the hearts of the concealed disciples. The peace section comes a third time. It is followed by (d), but this time to 'O Herr!' After this is heard thrice the voices sing 'O Herr, hilf und laß gelingen' ('Oh Lord, help and let us succeed'). It begins with bar 1 of (e), the semiquavers and (f) being omitted; 'durch den Tod hindurch zu dringen' ('through the death throughout to press') is almost identical with 'und die Wuth—dämpfen' and 'in dein Ehrenreich!' ('into Thy honour-kingdom!') ascends in quavers. For the first time the voice of Christ is heard in the tumult sections, the risen Lord is now in the midst of the world; the injunction, however, is sung twice only. This beautiful scena ends with a fourth presentation of the peace section. The benediction again comes thrice, and just before the second entry the upper strings join the wood-wind in (c); all tumult is stilled and the whole world is at peace. It is to be noted that in the second and third warring sections piano is indicated for the strings at bar 3 and at bar 1 of the fourth section. The correct way of performing the number is evidently with a solo bass and a small group of upper voices. The assembly of stricken disciples demands more than three singers; moreover, the effect would be thin. A large choir would obliterate the strings. It would seem inconceivable that Bach should turn this number into the 'Gloria' of the Short Mass in A; yet it sounds exceedingly well to the new text.

A very simple tutti chorale closes the work, stanza 1 of J. Ebert's 'Du Friedefürst, Herr Jesu Christ' to B. Gesius's melody. It is translated for No. 116, pp. 479–80, Vol. II.

104. The Gospel for the Second Sunday after Easter, St. John x. 11–16, begins 'I am the good shepherd', and the Epistle, 1 Peter ii. 21–25, concludes 'For ye were as sheep going astray; but are now returned unto the Shepherd and Bishop of your souls'. The three cantatas for this Sunday which remain to us, Nos. 85, 104, and 112, are chiefly concerned with this metaphor. 'Du Hirte Israel, höre'

('Thou Guide of Israel' N.) is one of the truly perfect cantatas, flawless in every detail. The libretto, possibly by Christian Weiss, Snr., is excellently designed, the sequence of ideas is admirable and it affords convenient opportunities for musical imagery. The whole score is meticulously marked with bowing and tonguing, giving us an insight into Bach's methods.

i is a choral setting of Psalm lxxx. i—'Give ear, O Shepherd of Israel, Thou that leadest Joseph like a flock; Thou that dwellest between the cherubims, shine forth'. The Lutheran version, as will be seen, inverts the first two groups of words. Pastoral colour is obtained by the use of two oboes and taille in addition to the strings, by long repeated pedal notes and by ambling $\frac{9}{8}$ passages (though the movement is written in $\frac{3}{4}$):

Ex.1061

Ex.1062

and:

Ex.1063

which is derived from bar 1 of (a). Sometimes the reeds are independent, sometimes they outline the melodies of the strings in staccato crotchets. A feature of the ritornello is a series of strong crotchet chords accompanying the leisurely melodies. Bach pictured not a flock of sheep following the Master, but the whole world crying after Him. After two mighty calls of 'Du Hirte Israel' ('Thou Shepherd of Israel'), incorporating part of bar 1 of (a), come two sharp shouts of 'höre!' ('hear!'), the two crotchets set to this word being used almost always on its appearance. After the voices sing in pairs, with (b) in the orchestra, comes a more sustained passage which suggests wavering, hesitating, turning hither and thither (Ex. 1064). The figure from bar 1 of (a) is again the foundation. It is an intriguing and charming device, which is again used later. After a varied repeti-

Ex.1064

tion of the opening material a fugal section begins, 'Schafe' being again set to long ambling runs:

Ex.1065

It goes without saying that throughout ♪♪ must be treated as ♪♪. It is unfortunate that the translator of the Novello edition did not understand the relation between text and music. 'Guide' does not indicate to an audience that the chorus is pastoral in character. The word 'shepherd' does not occur until the wandering passages on 'Schafe', thereby suggesting that it is the Shepherd who is uncertain of his movements, not the sheep! The whole imagery is destroyed. After a fugal exposition, in which (b) is passed from one violin line to another, the first material is heard again and there comes a second exposition, with voices in a different order, this time accompanied by shouts of 'höre!' and of 'erscheine' ('appear'), with (b) and (c) in the orchestra. When the second exposition is finished the shouts of 'erscheine' continue, there is a modification of (d), and the splendid number, one of the finest of Bach's choruses, ends with a magnificent climax on 'der du sitzest über Cherubim' ('Thou Who sittest above (the) Cherubim').

In a tiny recitativo secco and arioso the tenor betrays conflicting emotions; despite the knowledge of the Shepherd's care his heart is troubled: 'The highest Herdsman cares for me, what avail my cares? It becomes yea every morning the Shepherd's goodness new. My heart, so compose thyself, God is faithful.' The aria still finds occasion for brooding; it begins with weary upward steps for two oboes d'amore:

Ex.1066

This is succeeded by vaguely wandering passages:

Ex.1067

and anxious sighings accompanied by eager hurrying in the bassi:

Ex.1068

The singer complains that 'Verbirgt mein Hirte sich zu lange' ('Conceals my Shepherd Himself too long'), beginning with (a) imitated by the continuo, and with 'lange' set to long wailing passages. With 'macht mir die Wüste allzu bange' ('makes me the wilderness all too afraid') we have a striking picture of the dread of the lost traveller in the desert, strange chromatic passages for the voice, weary steps in the oboes d'amore and stumblings in the bassi. 'Mein schwacher Schritt eilt dennoch fort' ('My feeble step hurries yet onward') brings further use of the step-motive. 'Mein Mund schreit nach dir' ('My mouth cries after Thee') is declamatory, with the step-motive and wandering themes in the instruments. 'Und du' ('and Thou') is a pathetic little wail, 'mein Hirte' ('my Shepherd') a solitary cry, but 'wirkst in mir ein gläubig' Abba durch dein Wort' ('producest in me a believing Abba through Thy word'—see Romans viii. 15;

Gal. iv. 6) is more consoling, though (*a*) descends in the continuo and the wailings continue. Part I is modified and near the close a brave effort to hasten ('eilt'), indicated by a long upward run, is negatived by a descending scale in the bassi; the heart is brave, but the distressed body can scarcely be dragged along. The aria is marvellously faithful to the vision conjured up by the poet. It is important in performance that the first of each two notes in the step-motive should be heavily stressed and the second made lighter and broken off; otherwise the feeling of excessive weariness will not be obtained. The Novello edition nullifies all this imagery by placing 'His face my Shepherd' on the weary step-motive, 'hiding' where 'lange' should be, and 'guiding' on the strange passage associated with 'bange'. The middle section fits better.

The bass, in a recitativo secco, has found refreshment, green pastures and a foretaste of heaven in the word of God—'Yes, this word is my soul's food, a refreshment of my breast, the pasture which I my desire, heaven's foretaste, yea, my all call. Ah! gather together only, Oh Good Shepherd, us poor and erring ones; ah! let the way only soon ended be, and guide us into Thy sheepfold.' He then sings one of the loveliest of all Bach's many pastoral arias (see P. 47), a swinging, happy gigue. Strings, with violin I doubled throughout by one oboe d'amore, open with a lovely undulating melody, supported by a rhythmic pedal:

and a later phrase matches it in perfection of line:

'Beglückte Heerde, Jesu Schafe, die Welt ist euch ein Himmelreich' ('Fortunate flock, Jesu's sheep, the world is to you a heavenly-kingdom') begins with a countermelody, swinging its joyous way along, with flourishes and intriguing syncopations on 'Himmelreich' and during (*b*) a delicious twist of a lamb's tail on 'Schafe'. After an instrumental interlude comes a fascinating variant of the counter-melody to (*a*), the chord of the tonic seventh above the swaying pedal D, melting into the subdominant key and returning by a domi-nant seventh above a tonic pedal, producing a marvellous feeling of quiet, ecstatic bliss. The lulling melodic repetitions contribute largely to the effect:

Ex.1071

The remainder of the first vocal section is repeated in an altered form, and four bars of ritornello lead to the *Fine* chord. A subtle point of construction in both sections is a threefold free inversion of the first notes of (*a*) for the continuo, in the portion when the upper instru-ments cease. In Part II there is another lulling countermelody to (*a*):

Ex.1072

'hoffet' is twice sustained below a duet version of (*a*) in 'und hoffet noch des Glaubens Lohn' ('and hope still for faith's reward'). There is a miraculously beautiful passage to 'nach einem sanften Todes-schlafe' ('after a soft death-sleep'); the voice sinks to an unexpected C♮ on 'Tod', the two upper instrumental lines play (*a*) pianissimo, the viola has been silent for five bars and now adds solemnity by entering with a gently rocking phrase, 'Tod' sways up and down, as if the slumberer were moving gently in his sleep, to a long low B on 'schlafe', accompanied above by (*a*), and at the close the word swings softly upwards, the anticipation of the soul's resurrection. A subtle point is that 'Glaubens Lohn' has the same figure as 'ein Himmelreich'. From (*c*) onwards is now repeated, much modified;

the second 'hoffet' and 'Glaubens Lohn' are placed higher, signifying increased confidence, 'sanften Tod' sinks to low G, 'schlafen'
is on the F♯ above and elongated, again telling of growing hope, and
'nach einem sanften Todesschlafe' at the end begins with the opening
on (b) and falls solemnly to low F♯. Few arias of Bach are of such
engaging loveliness as this, every section is perfect and the character-
ization of the believing and trusting Christian is one of the supreme
miracles of even his miraculous art. The English text has devastating
misfits, 'number' to the merry 'sheep' idea, and worst of all, placing
'wake' on the awe-inspiring C♮ and on the deep G where Bach
intends 'death'! What must early singers and audiences in this
country have thought of the composer? A certain fine vocalist, an
artist of rare distinction, rebuked some competitors at a festival for
singing this aria allegretto; he told them emphatically that as it was
sacred music it must be taken slowly, twelve beats in a bar!

Stanza 1 of C. Becker's versification of Psalm xxiii. set to N.
Decius's melody 'Allein Gott in der Höh' sei Ehr' concludes. The
translation is: 'The Lord is my true Shepherd, To Whom I myself
completely trust; To the pasture He me, His lamb, leads, In (the)
beautiful, green meadow; To the fresh water leads He me, My soul to
refresh powerfully Through the blessed word of grace.' One cannot tell
how Bach endows this chorale with a pastoral feeling. It is true that
the melody is familiar, it is associated with the song of the angels—
'Glory to God in the Highest'—which the shepherds heard on the
night of the Birth; one cannot point to any device which contributes, yet in some extraordinary and inexplicable way it possesses
the character of the opening chorus and the bass aria. (See Fugitive
Notes, which gives suggestions for an emended text to the cantata.)

44. Possibly ten years separate the two cantatas, Nos. 44 and 183,
which bear the title 'Sie werden euch in den Bann thun', and both
are for the Sunday after Ascension. The earlier ('You will they put
under ban' B.) is not among the most interesting cantatas, though it
contains points worthy of attention. The Gospel is St. John xv. 26–
xvi. 4, and the gloomy prophecy of Christ which it contains—'They
shall put you out of the synagogues: yea, the time cometh, that whosoever killeth you will think that he doeth God a service'—is set in i.
The opening clause serves for a T.B. duet with two oboes (fagotto e
continuo is specified throughout the cantata). The music is uncompromisingly grim, Bach makes no attempt at external attractiveness,

the colour is never lightened, the fanatical stamping down of the
bassi, through common chord after common chord, is sinister:

The voices open with a stern eleven-bar canon, borrowed from the
introduction, with freely imitative oboe lines above:

and merge into similar motion with the quavers of (a). Two bars of the
upper parts of (a), reversed, bring the canon again, voices in opposite order. Again two bars of (a) and the canon as at first, but with
the upper parts of (a) and derivatives, bring one to the complete (a),
oboe II and bassi adding fresh parts, the tenor maintaining the
syncopations. A free continuation of the vocal lines, and a ritornello,
in which the continuo suggests the opening of (b) and the quaver
movement of (a) is heard, lead without break to a chorus. Strings are
added, the upper lines doubled by the oboes. The text is scarcely
suitable for musical treatment, but Bach makes it tensely dramatic.
While the bassi roll in fury the voices twice shout 'Es kommt aber
die Zeit' ('There comes but the time') answered by the upper instruments; 'daß' ('that') is flung on an isolated chord on the second beat
of the bar, answered by the orchestral group, and 'wer euch tödtet'
('who you kills') is piano, with descending semitones in basses and
bassi, the latter in repeated quavers, the upper voices sinking
tremblingly; 'wird meinen' ('will suppose') is set to three forte tutti
chords. The continuo resumes its rolling, upper strings toss phrases in
a way which adds confusion to the scene of persecution, and 'er thue
Gott einen Dienst daran' ('he does God a service thereby') is a canon
between sopranos and basses, the suggestion being that the servant
follows the intentions of the master. All this material is repeated, the
shouts beginning with upper strings instead of voices, thus bringing

the cry of 'daß' immediately after 'Zeit', instead of being separated from it by five beats, a change heightening the dramatic fierceness of the exclamation. The order of the canon is reversed. The solemn hush at the thought of the death of the martyrs is now forgotten in the spectacle of the cruelty of the persecutors, and, above the rolling bass, comes a wild four-part canon at two beats:

Ex.1075

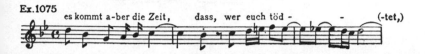

The emphasis on 'wer', a word that was formerly on a weak beat, still further turns one's thoughts to the fiendishness of the tormentors. More chromatics follow, 'der meinen' is set as before, but this time the 'er thue Gott' canon dovetails into it, hurrying on the action relentlessly.

An exhortation to be patient on earth and to await martyrdom, proscription and heavy pain, is set to uninteresting music, an alto aria with oboe obbligato. The oboe melody is promising enough:

Ex.1076

(C minor, signature of 2 flats)

the wandering triplets are undoubtedly significant of 'Christen müssen auf der Erden Christi wahre Jünger sein' ('Christians must on the earth Christ's true disciples be'), as the singer, after beginning with a new melody, employs them almost incessantly. Part II is 'auf sie warten alle Stunden, bis sie selig überwunden Marter, Bann und schwere Pein' ('for them wait all hours, till they (have) blessedly overcome martyrdom, ban and heavy pain'). Again triplets are frequent, thrice the oboe melody accompanies the final words, comforting the wandering disciples in the midst of persecution, the first time with an ominous scalic descent of the bassi for more than two octaves; 'schwere' generally struggles upwards.

The librettist (possibly Christian Weiss, Snr.) was helpful in inserting next a chorale speaking of pain of heart and the narrow way to heaven, part of stanza 1 of M. Moller's (?) 'Ach Gott, wie manches

Herzeleid.' to its anonymous melody. For translation see No. 3, p. 346, Vol. II. It is given to the tenor; and the continuo, the only accompaniment, evolves a quasi-ostinato theme from line 1 of the canto:

Ex.1077

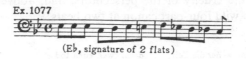

(E♭, signature of 2 flats)

its chromaticism expressing weariness and despair.

A description of the fearfulness of the Antichrist fails to rouse the composer to his customary eloquence in a short bass recitativo secco: 'There seeks the Antichrist, the great monster, with sword and fire, the members of Christ to persecute, because their teaching to him hateful is. He imagines himself thereby probably, it must his doings to God pleasing be. But there resemble Christians those palm-branches which through the burden only so much higher climb.'

The most interesting number musically is a soprano aria with the same scoring as the chorus. Schweitzer points out that the 'jubilant triplets' of the introduction:

Ex.1078
Ob.I Vl.I
(a)

Cont.
8ve lower

do not tally with the opening words—'Es ist und bleibt der Christen Trost' ('It is and continues the Christian's consolation')—but that they are explained by an expression which comes later—'die Freuden-Sonne bald gelacht' ('the joy-sun soon laughed') as 'gelacht' is set to twinkling triplets. (a) is developed from bar 1:

Ex.1079
Ob.I Vl.I
(b)

Cont.
8ve lower

Bar 6 is similar to (a) but the two lines reverse the falling intervals, the upper dropping sevenths, the lower fifths, an ingenious alteration. An important figure comes in bar 5:

Ex.1080
Ob.I Vl.I
(c)
Cont.

The opening clause, a new melody, is with continuo only, the triplet figure appearing in the latter. (a) dovetails into the last note, 'daß Gott für seine Kirche wacht' ('that God for His church watches') dovetails in turn into the tutti, the triplets come again in the bassi and 'wacht' is a splendid semiquaver run of 3½ bars, during which we hear (b) and (a). The ritornello combines (a) and (c) and the vocal section begins as before, but 'der Christen Trost' is happily set to part of (c). Against a prolongation of the last note of (b), 'Gott für seine' climbs to (c) inverted and there is another fine run on 'wacht', ascending confidently this time, while the orchestra plays (a). Two bassi triplet laughs join the vocal section with a repetition of the introduction. Part II begins 'Denn wenn sich gleich die Wetter thürmen' ('For although themselves immediately the storms pile up'), with a tossing and whirling passage on the last two words; the Christian, represented by the melody of (a), in the dropping seventh form, laughs boisterously at the impotent fury of the elements. Over a repeated pedal D, the rumbling of thunder, voice and upper instruments climb up on (c). As the words are repeated the violins are merry with the triplet and follow with (c), while the bassi ascend for an eleventh on the inverted motive, partially chromatically. 'Thürmen' is set to an even wilder passage, with demisemiquavers, thunder mutters in violin II, viola and bassi, and (a) is heard in violin I in another form, the quavers coming always on the open G string, the triplets ascending in sequence. While the voice hurls out defiantly 'die Wetter thürmen' against a repeated pedal, the upper instruments ascend to (c) in a succession of ⁶₃ chords. The remainder of the section is with continuo only—'so hat doch nach den Trübsals-Stürmen die Freuden-Sonne bald gelacht' ('so has yet after the trouble-storms the joy-sun soon laughed'); the bassi modify the melody of (a), the vocal line is joyous and there is a delightful ripple of triumphant laughter:

Ex.1081

(d)ge - lacht,-

After a ritornello, (b) and (a), Part II of the text is repeated with almost entirely different treatment. (c) comes twice in the violins, both times with the triplet figure tacked on, 'thürmen' joins in the motive, the terror of the storm has vanished entirely. Against (a) the voice swings down buoyantly. The upper instruments cease as an extended version of (d) is heard, with the melody of (a) in the violin form which accompanied the most florid 'thürmen' for continuo, and the singer ascends on the twinkling triplets to 'Freuden' to a high G on 'Sonne'. A simple chorale concludes—stanza 15 of P. Flemming's 'In allen meinen Thaten' to H. Isaak's secular tune 'O Welt, ich muß dich lassen'. The translation is: 'So be now, soul, thine, And trust Him alone, Who thee created has. (Let) it go, as it may go: Thy Father in the height, He knows for all things counsel.'

105. The unknown librettist of 'Herr, gehe nicht in's Gericht' ('Lord, enter not into wrath', O.) skilfully provided Bach with a text which satisfied his needs, spiritually, emotionally, and pictorially, and became the unrecognized partner in the production of a masterpiece. He combined ideas from the parable of the unjust steward (Gospel— St. Luke xvi. 1–9) and St. Paul's warning to the Corinthians (Epistle —1 Cor. x. 6–13) against idolatry, discontent, and pride (particularly v. 12 of the latter—'Wherefore let him that thinketh he standeth take heed lest he fall') and opened the cantata with Psalm cxliii. 2: 'And enter not into judgement with thy servant: for in thy sight shall no man living be justified.' The two clauses serve for an Adagio and an Allegro, a prelude and fugue. The chorus is so masterly that even a close analysis can only do scant justice to it. The orchestration is simple, strings, violin I with *Corno ed Oboe I all' unisono*, and oboe II doubling violin II. The opening ritornello establishes the mood of the trembling penitent; the bassi pulsate in repeated quavers, bowed in twos, the two highest lines sing a solemn canon with rapid modulations:

Ex.1082

At the end of bar 4 begins a plaintive idea:

Ex.1083
Cor. Ob. I. Vl. I

On the full close the voices enter and continue with the pulsating bassi only. 'Herr' is detached from 'gehe nicht in's Gericht', the rest producing a sensation of breathless suspense. Imitations follow closely upon each other, there are entries on every beat of the bar:

Ex.1084

On the closing chord of 'mit deinem Knecht' ('with Thy servant') the upper instruments re-enter, repeating the introduction a fifth higher, with the lines of the canon reversed. The choir now repeats its first bars, in the dominant, the voices being in a different order and the instruments exploiting a figure derived from the vocal lines:

Ex.1085

making seven- and eight-part counterpoint. A short orchestral interlude, with a variant of (d) in canon, leads to a long tutti section during which (a) and (b) join hands with vocal entries of (c), the viola developing (d), the bassi never ceasing from their solemn pulsations. After this an instrumental ritornello, a two-part canon on another form of (d) over a dominant pedal, leads to the fugue. Concerning this Schweitzer says: 'We might place at the head, as an appropriate motto, "I, the Lord thy God, am a jealous God"; the treatment of the resolute theme leads in many places to passages which rage and roll like angry billows.' The subject commences with another declamatory break (Ex. 1086). In the later part of the fugue the theme is sometimes used without notes 1 or 1–3, and the 'Lebendiger' portion is frequently heard in close canon. The countersubject

Ex.1086

is a stern descent of minims and where the continuo is independent it has many leaps of great power:

Ex.1087

There is a second countersubject:

Ex.1088

the source of many quaver passages. After five vocal entries the upper instruments gradually participate, generally doubling the voices. At the fifty-sixth bar 'piano' is marked, followed a few bars later by 'pianissimo', a dread hush comes over the multitude assembled before their Judge. A few forte bars conclude this magnificent and dramatic fugue.

An alto, in a fine recitativo secco, confesses guilt and throws herself on the mercy of God: 'My God, cast me not away, whilst I myself in humility before Thee bend, before Thy countenance. I know, how great Thine anger and my transgression is, that Thou at the same time, a swift witness and a righteous Judge art. I lay before Thee free confession, and fall myself not into danger, to Thee errors of my soul to deny, to conceal!'

Violins I and II tremble throughout the soprano aria (see O.S.B.A. No. 12) in repeated semiquavers; there is no continuo or bassi, the violas support the structure with incessant repeated quavers. In the introduction the vocal theme is heralded by an unnamed instrument, doubtless the oboe, plaintive, anguished phrases, betokening the deepest distress of soul—

Ex. 1089

(Violins bowed in fours, violas in sixes.)

with the oboe dovetailing the figure, beginning on the second half of each first beat. A wailing theme from the introduction, never used by the singer, forms an interlude:

Ex. 1090

after which (a) comes again. 'Indem sie sich unter einander verklagen, und wiederum sich zu entschuldigen wagen' ('While they themselves among one another accuse, and anew themselves to excuse dare') brings a remarkable vocal line. The first words of each clause are set to nervous, hurried, downward figures, 'verklagen' and 'wagen' are given wild, tortuous runs. The violin tremblings are broken into fragments, the oboe imitates the descent, and, borrowing part of the first 'verklagen', adds wild, jagged passages indicative of uttermost despair. (a) and (b) form a ritornello and the section is repeated with some alterations, one being a shortened interlude. After (b) as ritornello a new melody appears: 'So wird ein geängstigt' Gewissen durch eigene Folter zerrissen' ('So is an anguished conscience through own torture torn'). There is an agonized break between 'ein' and 'geängstigt', the vocal line is tortuous, the oboe adds (a). Even Bach himself has rarely crowded so many and such astonishing dissonances into a single number. One bar of quotation must suffice:

Spitta points out a striking resemblance between the melody in bars 78–81 and a passage in a soprano aria in Handel's early *Passion*, part of which work Bach had copied out.

The mood changes suddenly and completely in the succeeding bass recitative with strings. 'Wohl aber dem, der seinen Bürgen weiß, der alle Schuld ersetzet' ('Well however to him, who his Surety knows, Who all guilt indemnifies') speaks of the passing of the consciousness of unpardonable sins. A superbly rich vocal line faultlessly interprets every phase of the text, comfort, judgement, carrying of guilt to the grave, and at the end an ecstatic vision of an eternal habitation: 'so is the handwriting erased when Jesus it with blood sprinkles. He affixes it on the Cross Himself, He will of thy possessions, body and life, when thy death-hour strikes, to the Father Himself the account deliver. So may one thy body, which one to the grave carries, with sand and dust cover, thy Saviour opens for thee the eternal mansions.' Upper strings move in curving phrases expressive of blissful content, the bassi are pizzicato throughout in incessant octave leaps, the stroke of the death bell:

At 'Sterbestunde schlägt' ('death-hour strikes') 'piano' is indicated for the orchestra, at 'den man zu Grabe trägt' ('which man to (the) grave carries') the inner strings cease from the chief figure and move slowly as if in a solemn procession to the churchyard.

The scoring of the tenor aria (see O.S.B.A. No. 13) is curious; it is for strings plus horn, and the title of the number is 'Aria col Corno

in unisono'. The unisono means that the horn part is in the main a
modified form of violin I line. Sometimes the corno is silent when
violin I is playing; in one case this procedure is reversed. The opening
words are 'Kann ich nur Jesum mir zum Freunde machen' ('Can I
only Jesus to me to a friend make') and the first three are set to a
repeated note: ♪ ♪ ♩ . The horn plays this frequently, we may
almost call it the 'Kann ich nur' motive. It is heard in all the other
parts except the continuo. Violin I indulges in wild, almost un-
controllable flights of demisemiquavers, the unbounded exuberance
of the man whose sense of the oppression of sin has totally disappeared. Particularly exciting is the vocal line in bars 20–21, where
'so gilt der Mammon nichts bei mir' ('so is worth the Mammon
nothing to me') is pattered out quickly thrice, with 'nichts' thrown
higher each time. In Part II—'Ich finde kein Vergnügen hier bei
dieser eitlen Welt in irdischen Sachen' ('I find no pleasure here in this
vain world in earthly things')—the vocal line is new, but the 'Kann
ich nur' motive, the splendid opening tune:

Ex. 1093

and the scattering semiquavers are heard in the strings. The corno
is silent. The aria must move at a brisk pace, confident, bright and
rhythmic.

The conventional breaks between the lines of hymn-melody (the
normal pauses are to be disregarded in the closing number (No. 10,
B.E.C., O.) for the instrumental score does not allow for them) produce an awkward verbal gap, 'Now I know Thou wilt to me calm'—
three beats choral rest—'my conscience, which me tortures'. This is
not uncommon in hymn-settings; if the chorale is plain, pauses may
be disregarded at times to counteract it, but in fantasias and extended
chorales it cannot be remedied. Bach evidently saw no harm in it,
but modern taste is offended. The stanza is 11 of J. Rist's Lenten
'Jesu, der du meine Seele' with its anonymous melody 'Wachet,
doch, erwacht, ihr Schläfer'. The stanza speaks wholly of confidence
except for a reference in line 2 to the torments of conscience. The

tenor aria had been triumphant over the affairs of the world. Bach apparently falsifies his dramatic picture by harking back to fear of judgement and terror before the throne. Yet he is delineating truly the character of mankind; despite confident words on the lips of the departing, there may well be a return of the consciousness of sin and a dread that there may have been too many sins committed to be certain that complete divine pardon will be obtained. It is an unusual attitude for Bach, but it is a justifiable one. The upper string lines added to the simply harmonized chorale are extraordinary, and unique in his works. They begin by shuddering in repeated semiquavers. Bar 3 contains an extreme dissonance, left startlingly prominent through the silence of the continuo:

Ex. 1094

The same clash comes at the beginning of bar 9. In the second half of bar 6 the time of the upper strings changes to $\frac{12}{8}$, and the shuddering becomes less acute, triplet quavers against the $\frac{4}{4}$ chorale instead of semiquavers. At bar 12 the terror of the penitent is still further allayed, common time is resumed and triplets slow down to normal quavers. At bar 18 yet another change comes, the agony is past and the upper strings, again in $\frac{12}{8}$, mount high, and for four bars they move as follows:

Ex. 1095

In the string $\frac{12}{8}$ sections the voices and continuo maintain their common time, with frequent division into quavers, producing, especially in the last two chorale lines, a bewildering rhythmic conflict. On the last note of the chorale the upper strings slow down even further to crotchets. The continuo ceases and the cantata ends:

Ex.1096

The spirit is set free and the last vestiges of earth crumble away. The translation of lines 3–8 is: 'It will Thy truth fulfil, What Thou Thyself hast said: That on this wide earth None shall lost be, But ever live shall, If he only is trustful.'

46. It is not known who provided the libretto of 'Schauet doch und sehet' but it must have been a man of knowledge and imagination to have conceived a cantata based on the prophecy and the tale of the terrible calamity that overcame Jerusalem at the hands of Titus in the days after Christ. The references in the first recitative to enemies within the gates indicate that the writer must have been familiar with Josephus's monumental description of the causes which led to the total destruction of the city, and point to some scholar among the clergy of Leipzig. Unfortunately his literary abilities were not commensurate with his learning and vision. Josephus was in Bach's own library and we must assume that his muse was fired in an extraordinary way by the immortal story, for the cantata is unique among the two hundred for grim power and tense drama. It grips the hearer from start to finish by an uncanny power, some parts are almost savage in their wild vehemence, brutal dissonances and poignant false relations abound. Personal accounts had acquainted him with the horrors of warfare, for strife and destruction and misery were seldom absent from Germanic Europe during his life-time; the miseries of the thirty-years war were still vivid among his people, Vienna was besieged by the Turks two years before he was born, the thirteen years of the war of the Spanish succession ended just eleven years before this cantata was written. The siege and annihilation of the city on which his thoughts dwelt perpetually would stand vividly before him as a forerunner of the battling of opposing religions and principalities of his own time.

The Gospel for the Tenth Sunday after Trinity, St. Luke xix. 41–48, relates how Christ wept over Jerusalem, how He prophesied its total downfall and how He scoured the temple 'of them that sold therein'. The text begins with Lamentations i. 12: 'Behold and see if there be any sorrow like to my sorrow, which is done unto me, wherewith the Lord hath afflicted me in the day of His fierce anger.' Technically the chorus falls into the familiar divisions of prelude and fugue, a form which serves Bach for so many different purposes. The 'Qui tollis' of the B minor Mass has touched the heart of countless multitudes, but few music-lovers know it in its original form, the first part of this chorus. The Latin text is peculiarly apposite to the spirit of the German: 'Schauet doch und sehet, ob irgend ein Schmerz sei, wie mein Schmerz, der mich troffen hat' ('Behold then and see, if any sorrow be, as My sorrow, which me befallen has'); no injustice is done by the adaptation. Except for the reduction of the first two crotchets to quavers, alterations of length demanded by a different allocation of syllables, added grace or passing notes (the change, for example, from 'wie mein Schmerz' to 'miserere nobis') and transposition a minor third lower, the vocal parts are identical. In the Mass the 'celli *coll' arco e staccato* play a crotchet on each beat, an addition to the first score, where string bassi and continuo are the same. Beak flutes, not often used by Bach at that period, are changed into the transverse variety in the new version, and *Lento* is added. In the cantata *Tromba o Corno da tirarsi* and two oboes da caccia double the voices, beginning at fourteenth, fifteenth, and sixteenth bars of the vocal section respectively. These are omitted in the Mass. The chief difference is that the cantata version begins with an instrumental introduction, opening with the material of bars 21–29 of the chorus and then diverging. The flute lines, with their canons and imitations, are the same, the violas have a similar, though not identical, figure, the bassi tally, but the violins imitate against the chief theme for the flutes in passages which are not found in either chorus:

Ex.1097

Canonical devices are prolific in the vocal lines; bars 17–24, A.T. at the fifth below; 23–30, S.B. at the fifth below, with free imitation in A. and T.; 30–48, S.A. at the fifth below, with T. and B. employing a slightly different version answering at the same interval; 44–52, all four voices at the fourth above, the beginning of B. varied, the S. altered in intervals.

Clause 2 of the text is reserved for the fugue. Over a running continuo the altos lead off with a remarkably vigorous subject:

Ex. 1098

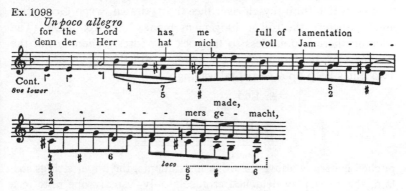

The countersubject has a realistic twist on 'Zorns' ('anger'):

Ex.1099

The fourth entry, S., is joined by violin I. The other upper instruments enter subsequently. The fifth entry is for flutes; during the fugue these instruments are in unison and independent, frequently playing mocking passages akin to those in the 'crowd' choruses in the *Passions*. Trumpet and corno da caccia are never independent, the upper strings rarely so, though there is sometimes nine-part counterpoint; the continuo often pursues a line of its own. The harmonic scheme and contrapuntal freedom are almost unbelievably harsh, false relations and extraordinary clashes are numerous; the effect is one of terrific power and terrible grimness. It is chorally the most difficult work ever written by Bach.

The tenor recitative is a lament over Jerusalem, which is compared to Gomorra: 'So mourn thou, destroyed God's city, thou poor stone and ash heap! Let whole streams of tears flow, because thee befallen has an irreparable loss of All-Highest favour, which thou lack must through thine iniquity. Thou wert as Gomorra judged, however not completely annihilated. Oh better! wert thou thoroughly destroyed, than that one Christ's enemy now in thee blasphemy hears. Thou regardest Jesu's tears not, so regard now the fury of the water-billows, which thou thyself over thee (hast) drawn, when God, after much patience, the rod in judgement breaks.' See Ex. 1296. (The reference here is doubtless to the rock of Moses.) There is not the fierceness of the chorus; it is the weeping, not the anger, of Christ. Two flutes keep up a perpetual wailing:

Ex. 1100

pitched generally above the other instruments, the upper strings sustain, the bassi play detached crotchets only, usually one note in a bar, never more than two. The rhetorical vocal line united with these three strands of colour is marvellously flexible, Bach has seen past the flatness of the text. For nine bars before the final one there is not a common chord, the chain of dissonances moves on and on. There are many emotional breaks in the words—'because to thee befallen has—an irreparable loss—of All-Highest favour'; 'as—Gomorra', a gap not in the *BGS* but restored according to the manuscript by Schering; 'the rod—to judgement breaks'. 'Streams of tears' cascades down and then leaps up a major seventh; 'an irreparable' jumps up a minor tenth; the disjunct line contains four upward augmented fourths and five upward sevenths, three of them diminished and two major. (See Ex. 1296.)

A tremendous aria for bass follows, one of the finest in the cantatas, with *Tromba o Corno da tirarsi* and strings. It is a scene of tempest—'Dein Wetter zog sich auf von Weitem, doch dessen Strahl bricht endlich ein!' ('Thy storm drew itself up from afar, yet its flash breaks at last in!'). The trumpet rings out the vocal theme, the strings depict thunder in vibrating chords:

Ex. 1101

and lightning in swiftly descending scales and arpeggi, or ascend
♩♪♩ through the tromba arpeggio. The trumpet throws quivering
light over the scene, the voice sings a stream of semiquavers lasting
eight bars, afterwards extended to nine, to 'Strahl'. With 'Und muß
dir unerträglich sein' ('And must to thee insufferable be') the voice
reverses the tromba arpeggio, the strings drop to pianissimo, the
bassi menacingly creep up by semitones, the trumpet is piano; the
balance indicated is curious, especially as the tromba has a series of
high-pitched brilliant semiquavers. 'Unerträglich' always receives
special treatment, in one case including a diminished third, fifth, and
seventh. The text of the latter part of the middle section is 'da überhäufte Sünden der Rache Blitz entzünden, und dir den Untergang
bereiten' ('there piled-up sins the vengeance's lightning kindle, and
for thee the destruction prepare'). 'Da überhäufte' twice climbs scale-
wise, the upper strings enter one after the other with sustained notes
as if burden after burden were being added. At 'der Rache Blitz',
which is declamatory, the upper strings burst in forte with the
familiar 'world-tumult' motive, 'Untergang' sinks, while violin I
depicts sighing. On the repetition of the words the upper strings
thrice play the ♩♪♩ trumpet arpeggio and there is a leap of a
diminished octave from 'Untergang' to 'bereiten'. An interlude with
(a) heralds the return of the earlier part of the text, which is prefaced
and partly accompanied by strings in octaves plunging down in
repeated semiquavers. Five notes of the tromba theme accompany
'auf von Weitem' and with a very long 'Strahl' the strings leap the
arpeggio and reiterate quavers in the first five bars, the trumpet
glittering above. In bar 6 the tromba begins three bars of ascending
quaver arpeggi, in the seventh the continuo ceases, in the eighth all the
strings reiterate a $\frac{7}{2}$ chord in semiquavers, in the ninth the voice tears
up, breaking off abruptly, and the trumpet streams down like a vivid
lightning flash. There are interesting variants in the final ritornello—
in bar 2 the tromba trills upwards with a derived figure, the strings
play the figure and then the bassi plunge headlong into the depths
with repeated semiquavers, the last going-down of the sun for the
unhappy city of Jerusalem.

A short alto recitativo secco runs: 'Then imagine to yourselves,
oh sinners, yea not there has Jerusalem alone before others (of) sins
full been. One can already for you this judgement read; because you
yourself do not improve, and daily (the) sins increase, so must you
all so terribly perish.' (See St. Luke xiii. 5.)

A complete change of emotional state is found in the next number, a remarkable alto aria, so much so that Schering speculates that a number of the libretto is omitted. The text is based on St. Matthew xxiii. 37, 'O Jerusalem, Jerusalem, thou that killest the prophets, and stonest them which are sent unto thee, how often would I have gathered thy children together, even as a hen gathereth her chickens under her wings, and ye would not!' The movement is a quartet for voices, two flutes and the unison of two oboes da caccia. The absence of bassi adds to the tenderness of the lovely melodies which are given to every part; one sees the mother bird drawing her 'Küchlein' under her protection. Three main ideas occur in the opening four bars of the introduction, (c), with its quotations from (b) being carried on sequentially:

Ex. 1102

The final bar is formed from (b). (a) is expanded into two bars: 'Doch Jesus will auch bei der Strafe' ('Then Jesus will even by the chastisement'); against (b) the soloist sings 'der Frommen Schild und Beistand sein' ('of the godly shield and helper be'). (c) and its sequel are repeated, with slight changes. (a) is again lengthened to two bars, the flute parts are reversed, the oboes da caccia line altered and the voice more ornate—'er sammelt sie als seine Schafe' ('He gathers them as His sheep')—with the same instrumental variants in (b) the voice adds 'als seine Küchlein liebreich ein' ('as His chickens lovingly in') and the first words are repeated against the sequential (c), 'Strafe'

climbing in semiquavers, leading to two bars with voice and lowest line only. Such passages as the latter, in which no continuo chords are possible, add a peculiar flavour of gentleness to the aria. (c) comes again as a ritornello and the text is repeated, the treatment being entirely new. The flutes enter fragmentarily only, the upper figures of (b) are the chief factor, (a) and (c) are absent. The first 'Schafe' has a playful little figure often in Bach's mind when the imagery of Shepherd and sheep is indulged in by his poets:

Ex. 1103

Scha - - fe

The introduction begins again *per arsin et thesin*, but rights itself by the insertion of an extra half-bar. An extraordinary passage, all the more extraordinary in effectiveness considering the limited orchestral forces, now bursts into the picture:

Ex. 1104

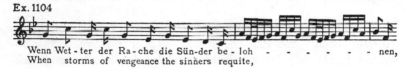

Wenn Wet - ter der Ra - che die Sün-der be - loh - - - - - - nen,
When   storms of vengeance the sinners requite,

This idea comes twice in succession, in the second the instruments enter forte, the oboes da caccia muttering ominous repeated quavers, the lowering of the darkened sky, the flutes spitting like hailstones and whirling like rain tossed by a violent wind. At bar 5 the voice ascends in a surge; at the same moment the flutes play (a) piano, the benign figure of the Christ appearing above the brief tempest. At the end of the bar the oboes da caccia rush up like the voice, not marked 'piano' till the next bar. The voice commences 'hilft er, daß Fromme sicher wohnen' ('helps He, that (the) godly secure live') with the 'er sammelt sie' phrase, and sustains on 'wohnen', the orchestral score being formed out of (b) and (c). The flutes are silent while the singer soars upwards on a semiquaver 'wohnen' and ends in a phrase of supreme confidence. On its last note flauto II anticipates the repetition of the introduction by half a bar of (a). It is advisable, in performance, to limit the lowest line to one oboe da caccia during the vocal sections, except during the tempest music, otherwise the doubling is apt to be too strong for the singer.

According to the score the oboes da caccia do not partake in the closing chorale (B.E.C. No. 5, O.) which is a prayer for mercy, stanza 9 of J. M. Meyfart's (?) 'O großer Gott von Macht' to M. Franck's (?) melody: 'Oh great God of truth, Since before Thee no man is worthy As Thy Son Jesus Christ, Who Thine anger calmed (has): So look then on His wounds, His martyrdom, anguish and heavy pain. For His sake, spare, And not according to sins requite.' The strings double the simple voice parts, but where the vocal lines have crotchets, the strings divide each note into quavers, bowed together; the tromba aids the sopranos. To the flutes (each line doubled—the direction 'a due' is unique and nowhere else do we find four flutes employed) are given most interesting parts. During the chorale lines they add a fifth and sixth strand; during the rests, unsupported by bassi, they cross and recross in legato semiquavers in strict canon at a quaver distance. Did the composer visualize doves of mercy appearing in the skies before the upturned eyes of the petitioners, bending and rising in graceful, floating curves, a sign from heaven that the wrath which descended upon Jerusalem would never again bring destruction and annihilation?

77. There is an affinity between Nos. 77—'Du sollst Gott, deinen Herren, lieben'—and 105. The libretti are probably by the same unknown hand; they are admirable models of connected and well-reasoned matter. The general scheme and development are similar, the orchestration of the opening choruses shows a like measure of independence, support of the voices, and freedom from high elaboration. The Gospel for the Thirteenth Sunday after Trinity is St. Luke x. 23–37, the question of 'a certain lawyer' and Christ's commendation of the querist's answer to his own question—'Thou shalt love the Lord thy God with all thy heart, and with all thy soul, and with all thy strength, and with all thy mind; and thy neighbour as thyself'—and the parable of the Good Samaritan. The dual theme of the libretto is law and love. The text of i is the verse quoted and Bach preaches on it a sermon of his own. He takes as his musical and didactic basis the chorale 'Dies sind die heil'gen zehn Gebot" ('These are the holy ten commandments'). In the twelve stanzas of Luther's hymn, associated with its anonymous melody, the commandments are paraphrased. At first it may seem as if this were not apposite, but no doubt Bach had in his mind the question of the Pharisees in St. Matthew xxii: 'which is the great commandment in the law?' and Christ's explanation of the two commandments on which 'hang all the law and the prophets'. The canto fermo is heard

in its entirety in the *Tromba da tirarsi* and continuo, but in a manner entirely different from any other chorale fantasia. The complete melody is delivered in imitation and canon at the fifth below by augmentation between trumpet and continuo. The orchestration throughout the cantata is not fully stated, so it may be that the tromba is strengthened by oboes, as in No. 80, though there they play an octave lower, which would not be effective here. The trumpet also drives home the decree by further quotations. The scheme is as follows—line 1, tromba and continuo, the latter entering at the fourth note: at the close of the bassi entry the tromba repeats 1 a second lower; this emphasis of the first statement of the hymn would be understood thoroughly by Bach's congregation; line 2, the continuo does not enter until half-way through the last trumpet note, over the long-sustained final note of the continuo line 1 is again played by the trumpet a fifth lower than the original entry; line 3, the continuo enters on the last note, during the third and subsequent bars of the continuo theme the tromba plays line 1 an octave lower than the original pitch, a solemn injunction to the listener, and then leaps up an octave to play line 2; line 4, a short one of four notes, the continuo enters on the last note, on the sustained final bassi note the trumpet rings out line 1 a fourth higher than the original pitch, ascending to top C; line 5, the continuo enters on the third note, and over a pedal which lasts ten bars the trumpet plays through the entire canto without break, at the original pitch, beginning on the antepenultimate note of the bassi line. The melody, a version of an old pilgrim song, is modal, commencing on G, ranging from the F below to the E above, B being flattened once; the number begins in C and ends in G. The violone, as in the chorale fantasia at the beginning of No. 80, is tacet except for the entries of the chorale line. This is not expressly stated in the score, but, with the exception of four notes, the continuo is written in the tenor clef during the ritornelli and the choral interludes between the canonical entries; it is understood by this procedure that the violone plays only when the F clef is used. The introduction begins with a quaver version of part of line 1 in close canon, rounded off by a figure containing two semiquavers. These ideas serve not only for the orchestral material (apart from tromba and violone) but for the choral as well. Line 1 of the canto is:

Ex. 1105

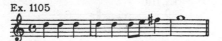

the instrumental derivative:

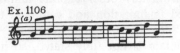

and the vocal:

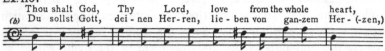

The ingenious transference of the initial repeated note of the canto to the middle of the derivative, and the inversion of the shorter notes, will be observed. Between the bassi line 2 and the trumpet line 3 part of the remainder of the text is introduced—'von ganzer Seele, von allen Kräften, und von ganzem Gemüthe' ('from whole soul, from all might, and from whole mind')—in lively movement, there being canonical entries of (b), T.B. in the middle, and tromba line 3 accompanying the latter part of the section. (b) enters again with bassi line 3 and holds sway till it finishes. The interlude between 3 and 4 begins with (a) in canon in the violins, S. and A. modify this for 'von ganzer Seele, von allen Kräften', with flourishes on 'Kräften', and the remainder is occupied with:

in S.A. canon, and:

in four-part canon, both themes being inversions of line 4:

(*a*) comes in the choir and upper strings during continuo line 4; its close entries are accompanied by a new counterpoint, also in canon:

Ex. 1111

von gan-zer See - - - le

heard only once so. After a bar of interlude the ubiquitous (*a*) appears once and with line 5 becomes chief subsidiary. When the trumpet begins the recapitulation of the entire canto a new theme, derived from the last note of 4 and the first note of 5, occurs against (*a*) in violin 1:

Ex. 1112

und dei-nen Näch-sten (als dich selbst,)
and thy   neighbour   (as   thyself,)

sometimes in free imitation, sometimes in canon. All four voices enter in imitation with these words to a form of (*a*) and then in the reverse order to a fresh form of the above, the basses finishing in a delightful manner:

Ex. 1113

und dei-nen Näch-sten als dich selbst.

Cont.

Practically all the upper string lines are based on (*a*) and (*b*), and all the vocal lines until two bars after line 3 is finished are formed from (*b*); the quaver canto is thus heard incessantly, sometimes as a canon at the distance of a crotchet, sometimes at a minim, sometimes two voices moving in parallel motion, perpetually driving home line 1 of Luther's text. It is a magnificent chorus; Bach's emphasis of the 'law' by the strictest of all musical devices, the canon, by augmentation, at the third, fourth, fifth, seventh, and octave, and the more genial corollary of 'love', as symbolized by the idea containing semiquavers, are blended into a movement in which beauty and technical skill, sympathy and preaching are marvellously combined, and which is superbly thrilling in performance.

A short bass recitativo secco begins 'So muß es sein!' ('So must it be!' or 'Such is the law!'; one thinks of Beethoven's use of the same clause!) and meditates on the necessity for obedience to the decrees of the Almighty: 'God will the heart for Himself alone have! One must the Lord from whole soul for one's desire choose, and oneself not more rejoice, than when He the mind through His Spirit enkindles, because we only of His grace and goodness then first rightly assured are.' The idea of the unalterableness of the law is stressed by the initial notes of the continuo, C, D, E, F♯, G♯, dropping to C♯.

The character of the two upper lines of the soprano aria, moving mostly in parallel thirds and sixths, significant of blissful content, suggests that oboes are intended. Law is here mentioned for the last time in the cantata—'Laß mich doch dein Gebot erkennen, und in Liebe so entbrennen, daß ich dich ewig lieben kann' ('Let me then Thy law know, and in love so burn, that I Thee ever love can'), the second portion of the text. The obbligati theme runs over a happily undulating continuo:

which, curiously, is never used except in ritornelli, possibly because it is so closely related to:

which is heard, in one form or another, four bars in succession, with (a), (b), (a), (b) dovetailing into the phrases. 'Mein ganzes Leben hangt dir an' ('My whole life hangs Thee on') is a passage of rejoicing. When the two clauses are repeated, the oboes play (a) and (b)

per arsin et thesin, (c) is heard vocally and later in the bassi. After
the introduction again with reversed oboes 'Laß — erkennen' begins
with continuo, *(a)* and *(b)* enter, and all the obbligati lines until the
final recapitulation of the introduction are fragmentary and are made
up of these and continuous semiquavers, allied to *(b)* from bar 7.
(c) is heard to open 'und — entbrennen', and, in addition to the bar 7
idea, in the ardent 4-bar run on 'entbrennen'. There is another sustained note on 'ewig' ('daß ich — kann.') and a form of the semiquavers of *(b)* ripples above. The repetition of the text employs the
same material, but practically every detail is altered and the 'ewig'
long note is followed by a 2½-bar flourish of semiquavers. The whole
aria is evolved from *(a)*.

The libretto now dwells on the parable, and a tenor recitative with
strings begs that the singer may always act as did the Samaritan:
'Give me thereby, my God! a Samaritan-heart, that I at the same time
the neighbour love may, and myself in his pain also over him grieve,
that I not past him go, and him in his distress not leave. Grant, that
I self-love hate may, then wilt Thou to me in future the joy-life,
according to my wish, yet in mercy give.' Expressive upper string
passages colour the penultimate bar.

It is difficult to see why Bach chose the tromba as obbligato for the
alto aria. Its melodic line is not of the usual trumpet order, it is
scarcely distinguishable from a violin or oboe countermelody, there
is nothing to demand it in the text, a complaint that the believer's
love is too feeble to be worthy of his Lord. The construction is
peculiar. The whole of the introductory tromba melody is repeated,
slightly altered in the second half, by the voice. The first sentence is:

Ex.1116

(Key D minor, without signature)

The text is repeated to the second sentence. A tender figure, (b), notes 2–6 of bar 4 of Ex. 1116, is heard frequently in the bassi line, and, with variants, in the trumpet counterpoint. An eight-bar ritornello leads to the *Fine* pause. Bars 1 and 3 of (a) are floridly decorated, bar 2 is as before, bars 14–16 become 8–10. The middle portion is a semi-quaver passage evolved from the new version of bar 3. It is an unusual procedure. 'Hab' ich oftmals gleich den Willen, was Gott saget, zu erfüllen, fehlt mir's doch an Möglichkeit' ('Have I often even the will, what God says, to fulfil, fails me it then the possibility') is sung over a continuo line of unceasing quavers, built freely on (b), and the tromba is silent. The melody is new, but bar 2 of (a) occurs thrice, once inverted. A ritornello of eight bars is heralded by an upward run which began the first interlude, but, with the exception of bar 2 of (a) twice, it is different from either instrumental section. (b) comes once in the bassi. The words are repeated, beginning two bars as before and the next two altered, but the remainder of the vocal melody, save for the last three bars, which agree with the first trumpet melody, is unrelated to what has gone before. The trumpet adds counterpoint, again new matter, except for (b) twice and two bars at the close which are the same as at the end of the 'Ach, es bleibt' section. (b) occurs several times in the continuo. When one compares this loosely constructed number with the closely knit soprano aria, one sees how infinitely varied are Bach's methods. With the right type of trumpeter and singer the aria 'comes off' much better than it promises on paper. The manuscript of the concluding chorale lacks both words and indication of instruments. The melody is the anonymous 'Ach Gott, vom Himmel sieh' darein' and Zelter fitted to it stanza 8 of D. Denicke's (?) 'Wenn einer alle Ding' verstünd'

148. Bach's long association with Picander began, so far as we can be certain, with the last of this series belonging to 1725, 'Bringet dem Herrn Ehre seines Namens', which opens with Psalm xcvi. 8. There is no connexion between the libretto and the appointed readings for the Seventeenth Sunday after Trinity, unless the references to the Sabbath in both recitatives are called for by the discussion between Christ and the Pharisees on the question of its observance, St. Luke xiv. 1–11. Bach amended Picander's text, as he did many others. His incessant literary activity is an astonishing feature of the colossal production of this truly amazing man. The opening *Concerto*, as it is termed, is a brilliant chorus with strings and trumpet. The tromba

announces an eight-bar theme, accompanied by the three lowest
strings:

Ex. 1117

It is repeated by violin I in the dominant, with the trumpet curvetting
above. Now comes an imitation of two bars between violin I and
tromba, neither instrument adhering to it further. The bassi, after a
falling sequence on the initial notes, give out the subject and lead to
the entry of the choir, which sings a modification of the theme above
continuo only: 'Bringet dem Herrn Ehre seines Namens, bctet an
den Herrn in heiligem Schmuck' ('Bring to the Lord honour of His
name, pray to the Lord in holy adornment'). Into this is dovetailed
a ritornello, phrase 1 of (a) for the trumpet, and a long descending
sequence for violin I, based on these two bars. When the choir re-
enters, the soprano, accompanied by the lower voices, announces a
four-bar fugal theme derived from the opening of (a). Entries occur
in regular order, but the bass extends the subject to resemble (b).
A tromba entry of four bars completes this section. Another fugue
subject is propounded—founded on (b):

Ex. 1118

strings double, the trumpet asserts its right to be a fifth voice.
Anticipating and joining with the soprano entry is a modification of
the initial notes of (c):

Ex. 1119

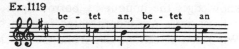

which is carried farther by the trumpet after the sixth (bass) entry. A ritornello employs fragments of (*a*). The choir re-enters in B minor with a modification of its first clause. This is repeated with the soprano a third higher and the lower parts altered. The two fugal themes carry on to the double bar, though they are never combined— A. (*c*), S. (*a*), violin I, part of (*a*), A. doubled at the octave by the tromba, part of (*c*), B. a modification of three bars of (*a*), the altos singing a long exultant flourish on 'Namens', B. (*c*), altered at the end. This brilliant chorus, resplendent with its independent trumpet, is yet one more of the many free fugal forms in which Bach's imagination luxuriated.

An exacting tenor aria, lasting about 150 bars, seizes on the opening sentence, 'Ich eile die Lehre des Lebens zu hören, und suche mit Freuden das heilige Haus' ('I hasten the teaching of life to hear, and seek with joy the holy house'), and exploits its suggestions with lively eagerness. An animated violin obbligato with hurrying runs:

Ex. 1120

and delightful melodic ideas alternating with a repeated note:

Ex. 1121

a dancing figure:

Ex. 1122

gay leaping passages in the continuo and vocal displays of semi-quavers to 'eilen' and 'Freuden' produce a scene of infectious exaltation. The violin borrows ideas from the continuo, and the continuo acknowledges the honour by borrowing from the violin. The repeated bassi notes are incorporated into an otherwise new melody to 'Wie rufen so schöne das frohe Getöne zum Lobe des

Höchsten die Seligen aus' ('How cry so beautifully the glad sound in the praise of the Highest the blessed out'). One would gladly hear it again, but as after it the obbligato develops its previous figures the voice must needs surrender its independence and content itself with brilliant counterpoints. That these are always attractive goes without saying. One particularly fine one is 'wie rufen', &c., against the first quotation *supra*, with a new bassi figure. 'Wie rufen so schöne' is sung five times, each to a different melody. With the exception of the omission of the Scarlattian false start, the reprise is unaltered till the eighteenth bar.

The alto aria, iv (see P. 45), is accompanied by three oboes, the lowest written for in the alto clef, possibly oboe da caccia is intended. The combination appears formidable, but proves most effective. The opening sentence is one heard in many variants in the libretti— 'Mund und Herze steht dir offen, Höchster, senke dich hinein' ('Mouth and heart stands to Thee open, Highest, sink Thyself therein') and a tender phrase rises and falls gently:

Ex. 1123
A. Ob. I.

Ob. II. III.

while 'Höchster' thrusts eagerly upwards:

Ex. 1124

Cont.

The construction up to this point is ingenious. The introduction consists of (*a*), with continuo, which is not heard in Ex. 1123, (*b*), slightly different, (*a*) a tone higher, and an idea which becomes important later on:

Ex. 1125 (*c*)

Cont.
8ve lower

The vocal sentence is of seven bars, not eight, (*a*) as above, (*c*), orchestra only, (*a*) harmonized afresh, (*c*), the inner instruments altered in the first bar. (*d*), original or inverted, occurs in each of the next four bars, voice and continuo alternating. These portions without bassi are peculiarly tender. There is a tutti in A minor, (*a*), but the voice breaks into (*d*) in the second bar, (*c*) follows, (*d*) is sung twice in the next bar, the two-bar phrase being otherwise new; another version of (*b*) leads to a recapitulation of the introduction. Another familiar expression—'Ich in dich und du in mich' ('I in Thee and Thou in me') is sung to a variant of (*a*), and 'Glaube, Liebe, Duldung, Hoffen soll mein Ruhebette sein' ('Faith, love, endurance, hope shall my repose-bed be') brings a most lovely idea, (*e*), the continuo rocks in quavers, A B C B, five times, oboes I and II repeat canonically a scale-wise lulling descent, E to F$\sharp$, based on (*d*)—

♩ | ♫♫♫ ♫ ♩ —oboe III reiterates D$\sharp$ E— ♪ ♩ ♫ ♩|♫

♩ ♫ ♩ —and the singer has soothing phrases. Over a pedal B comes another exquisite lulling idea, which is (*d*) in quavers:

Ex. 1126
Ob. I. II. III.

piano

followed by two free bars. The 'ich in dich' idea is sung, with three breaks instead of the previous one, oboe I gently descends in a passage formed from (*d*). (*a*) follows as an interlude, with yet another harmonization, the 'ich in dich' idea with two breaks this time and without continuo, the oboe parts different. (*a*) is repeated in B minor, the oboes reversing. 'Soll mein', &c., is repeated to close, the pedal note is transferred to 'Ruhe', (*f*) appears in another way, the general progression being downward instead of upward, and while the oboes sustain the voice undulates gently.

To the alto is assigned a beautiful recitative with strings, iii. It begins with a paraphrase of Psalm xlii. 1, 'As the hart panteth after the water-brooks', and extols the delight of earthly Sabbaths: 'Even as the hart after fresh water cries, so cry I, God, to Thee. For all my rest is none but Thou. How holy and how precious is, Highest, Thy Sabbath-celebration! There praise I Thy might in the community of the righteous. Oh, if the children of this night the lovingness would remember, then God dwells Himself in me.'

v, a tenor recitativo secco, looks forward to an eternity of Sabbaths: 'Remain also, my God, in me, and give me Thy Spirit, which me according to Thy word may govern, that I such a way of living may lead, which to Thee pleasing is, so that I in after time in Thy glory, my beloved God, with Thee the great Sabbath may hold.' No verse is attached to the simple chorale, the anonymous melody 'Auf meinen lieben Gott.' Spitta suggests stanza 11 of J. Heermann's Lenten 'Wo soll ich fliehen hin', the hymn generally associated with the tune.

37. No cantatas in this group are speculatively assigned to 1726 and one only to 1727, 'Wer da glaubet und getauft wird'. It is for Ascension Day, and while the other three works for the Festival, Nos. 11, 43, and 128, deal with Christ's translation, No. 37 entirely ignores it except in the opening lines of the bass aria, which speak of the soul winging heavenward. The librettist instead begins with St. Mark xvi. 16 (the Gospel is 14–20)—'He that believeth and is baptized shall be saved'—and develops the Lutheran thesis, that good works are of less importance than faith and baptism. It would seem likely therefore that it is from the pen of a clergyman, and Christian Weiss, Snr., is probable. Dogmatic assertion generally stirs Bach to action, but a line of argument such as this, though no doubt it was firmly believed in, merely places the cantata in the category of lesser works, interesting though much of it undoubtedly is. The orchestra of i consists of two oboes d'amore and strings, all lines being generally independent. The character of the music is rather unusual, one cannot recollect anything similar elsewhere. There are four main thematic ideas. Two are complementary to each other, two firm minims which rise to a long holding note, the firmness and the holding fast of faith, and against it a placidly moving theme in minims, the contentment of the believer:

Ex.1127
Ob. d'am. I. II.

The third is virtually a variant of the opening notes of (a):

Ex. 1128

and its corollary:

Ex. 1129

These quavers take an important place in the development of the three ideas, and in the nineteenth bar come in the form of a descending scale:

Ex. 1130

(the lapping of the baptismal stream), which acts as counterpoint to (c). The introduction is in six parts throughout, (a), (b), with (c) and (d) against them; a three-bar interlude; (a) and (b) in the dominant, also with (c) and (d); five bars similar to the other interlude; nine bars of development of (c) and (e) in which the rising third of (b) is heard. 'Wer da glaubet' ('Who there believes') is with continuo, (a) is sung by the basses, the other voices enter in close imitation with (b), the effect is one of calm faith. Nine bars of the introduction accompany these words and their continuation: 'und getauft wird, der wird selig werden' ('and baptized is, he will blessed become'). The dominant repetition comes again, but prefaced by (a) and (b) in voices and strings. The closing part of the introduction is now extended, (c), a preliminary note and a minim octave drop replacing the last note, is fitted to 'wer da — wird'. (e) is at first confined to the orchestra, later the voices participate. (a), (b) (always in the oboes d'amore, strings never touch the dual theme) in the dominant, is treated in a new way, piano. Unison upper strings play two bars of (c), one each of (d) and (e), and sopranos and altos sing a graceful duet. The interlude occurs again, tutti and forte. The new treatment of (a), (b) is repeated, again piano, in the supertonic minor, oboes d'amore reversed, the duet this time for tenors and basses, the upper part becoming the lower. The closing section of the introduction, with slight changes at the beginning in order to allow the oboes d'amore to reverse their parts for a few bars, and with voices added, ends this grateful and lovely chorus, which is too long for its brief text, but none too long in its gracious beauty.

The tenor aria with continuo is pleasant, though ordinary.

Although Bach's inspiration failed him at times, his technique and ingenuity never faltered. For example, the bassi theme is made up of quaver passages and semiquaver decoration. It opens:

Ex. 1131

The semiquaver group is heard often, but once only do the first eleven notes accompany the voice, once the second half remains intact, where the elaborated 'hegt' to be spoken of later is sung; the concluding two bars come in the first ritornello. Except for the final ritornello the remainder of the continuo line is derived from, but not coincident with, the quaver passages of the introduction. The warmly glowing groups (b) and (c) in:

Ex. 1132

are always associated with 'Glaube', 'Liebe', and 'Jesus', the key-words of the assertion. At the close of the repetition of (a), 'hegt' soars upwards and cascades down in loving groups of two notes. As fresh melodies unfold to the text (b) constantly finds a place in them. Part II is 'D'rum hat er bloß aus Liebestriebe, da er in's Lebensbuch mich schriebe, mir dieses Kleinod beigelegt' ('Therefore has He purely from love-impulse, when He in the life-book me (my name) wrote, on me this jewel conferred'). The melodies are similar in character, (b) is associated with 'Buch' and 'Kleinod', and (c) with 'triebe'.

The aria is overshadowed by a S.A. duetto secco based on P. Nicolai's melody 'Wie schön leuchtet der Morgenstern' ('How

beautifully shines the Morning Star') with stanza 5 of his hymn—
'Lord God Father, my strong hero! Thou hast me ever before the
world In Thy Son loved. Thy Son has to me Himself entrusted, He
is my treasure, I am His bride, Very highly in Him rejoicing. Eya,
eya! Heavenly life Will He give to me there above; Eternally shall
my heart Him praise.' Doctrine is now forgotten, faith is now not
reasoned about but is productive of complete joy in Christ. The tune
is cast into $\frac{12}{8}$ and much ingenious device is shown in its presentation.
It is highly ornamented, lines are lengthened, there is much imitative
and canonical treatment. On lines 1, 2, and 3 the soprano bears the
melody. When they are repeated, the alto is responsible, the continuo
is different and the soprano sings fresh counterpoints. In the remainder the lines are divided between the voices, there are flourishes
on repeated Eya's and long brilliant runs to 'loben' ('praise'). The
bassi move vigorously throughout:

Ex. 1133

which is an ornamental version of line 1—d s m d s l l s. During the
expansion of line 3 the alto counterpoint borrows (a), in the counterpoints to the 'Eya' lines (b) appears, and later (a) is set to 'Leben'
('life') and is incorporated into the 'loben' flourishes, once direct
and twice inverted.

The bass, in a recitative with strings, propounds the doctrine of
the supreme value of faith: 'Ye mortals, desire you with me the
countenance of God to contemplate? so may you not on good work
build; for if himself well a Christian must in the good works exercise,
because it the stern will of God is, so makes the faith then alone, that
we before God righteous and blessed (may) be.'

One is rewarded musically for this theological speculation in the
next number, a bass aria with one oboe d'amore (never independent)
and strings. Bach seizes on the opening sentence—'Der Glaube
schafft der Seele Flügel, daß sie sich in den Himmel schwingt' ('The
faith creates the soul's wings, that it itself into the heaven swings')—
and does not concern himself about the remainder. A joyous melody
(Ex. 1134) is accompanied homophonically, the middle strings reiterating chords (the fluttering of wings) at the same time as the bassi.
As the result of this method of treatment, unusual in Bach, the con-

Ex. 1134
Ob. d'am. I. Vl. I.

fident aria is more easily grasped than are most. The first clause is set to a modification of the above, the bassi alternate (d) with the rest of the orchestra. The introduction is repeated, moving from D to F♯ minor, the voice adding counterpoint, with runs on 'Seele Flügel' and 'Himmel'. The oboe d'amore is now silent for five bars, (a) forms an interlude, 'die Taufe ist das Gnadensiegel' ('the baptism is the mercy-seal') modifies (a), and 'Segen' in 'das uns den Segen Gottes bringt' ('that to us the blessing of God brings') flourishes joyously. The words are repeated, first with (a) and a sustained note for inner strings, and then with continuo only, 'Segen' being expanded to bring in a group of semiquavers sung to the first 'Flügel'. An interlude alters the order of the chief motives—(c), (b), (c), and a bar of (a). 'Und daher heißt ein sel'ger Christ, wer glaubet und getaufet ist' ('And therefore is called a blessed Christian, who believes and baptized is') is a theological dictum which might well have baffled a lesser composer, but the ingenious use of previous motives prevents any lag. 'Daher' and 'glaubet' reproduce the opening notes of (a), stressing the former connexion with 'Glaube', (b) and (c) twice accompany the voice, they are followed by (a) from violin I, the voice flourishes over the continuo and expresses firm faith by a sustained note to 'glaubet', with (a) above. The final 'getaufet' is expanded into a long run based on (c).

A tutti chorale concludes, stanza 4 of J. Kolross's (Rhodanthracius) morning hymn, 'Ich dank' dir, lieber Herre' to a melody which was originally a secular song, 'Entlaubt ist uns die Walde'— 'The faith to me lend In Thy Son, Jesus Christ, My sins to me also forgive Here at Thy appointed time, Thou wilt to me it not deny, What Thou promised hast, That He my sin dost carry And frees me from the burden.'

'**Ehre sei Gott.**' Judging by the fragments that remain of the only work in this class that can be attributed to 1728, we have lost a fine cantata for Christmas Day. Picander's libretto, published that year, shows the text of the opening chorus—'Ehre sei Gott in der Höhe' ('Glory to God in the highest, and on earth peace, goodwill towards men', St. Luke ii. 14)—to be one that has been set in the vernacular in the Christmas oratorio and as a S.A. duet in No. 110, and in Latin in the various Masses, in No. 191 (taken from the Mass in B Minor), and in an extra number to the first, E♭, version of the Latin Magnificat. It would have been interesting to be able to compare yet another setting with these; not a note is preserved. An aria and a recitative have also completely disappeared. Of iv, an alto aria, with two flauti traversi, separate lines for 'cello and continuo, only the concluding nineteen bars remain. The complete aria, however, is preserved in No. 197. A gentle bass recitativo secco and a bass aria with oboe d'amore obbligato, are intact. This aria, in an adapted version, also appears in No. 197. These borrowed numbers are dealt with under the heading of the cantata concerned. The concluding chorale is without indicated orchestration. (See Terry's edition of the Four-Part Chorales, No. 284, O.) It is stanza 4 of C. Ziegler's Christmas hymn 'Ich freue mich in dir' to the melody 'O Gott, du frommer Gott' or 'Die Wollust dieser Welt'. For translation see No. 133, p. 340, Vol. II.

145. One of the texts published by Picander in 1728 is for Easter Tuesday, and begins 'Ich lebe, mein Herze' ('I live, my heart'). Line 3 —'Du lebest, mein Jesu' ('Thou livest, my Jesus'), and line 5—'Die klagende Handschrift ist völlig zerrissen' ('The complaining handwriting is completely torn up')—refer to the Gospel, St. Luke xxiv. 36–47, the appearance of the risen Lord to the disciples in Jerusalem. Bach set this as a S.T. duet, but was evidently dissatisfied with a text which made no provision for a chorus on such a jubilant feast as the Third Day of Easter, prefaced the duet by a choral setting of Romans x. 9: 'That if thou shalt confess with thy mouth the Lord Jesus, and shalt believe in thine heart that God hath raised Him from the dead, thou shalt be saved'—and prefaced that again with a four-part setting of stanza 1 of C. Neumann's Easter hymn 'Auf, mein Herz! Des Herren Tag' ('Up, my heart! The Lord's day Has the night of fear driven away: Christ, Who in the grave lay, Has in death not remained. From henceforth am I wholly comforted, Jesus has the world redeemed'). The melody is J. Crüger's 'Jesus, meine Zuver-

sicht'. The result is that No. 145, belonging no doubt to 1729 or 1730, is confusedly known under all three titles.

It is one of the most engaging of the cantatas; every number is fresh and tuneful. The instrumentation of the opening and closing chorales is not stated. The latter is from another Easter hymn, words and melody by N. Herman: 'Erschienen ist der herrlich' Tag.' Stanza 14 is employed: 'Therefore we also justly joyful are, sing the Hallelujah well, and praise Thee, Lord Jesus Christ; as comfort Thou for us arisen art, Hallelujah!' The two recitatives, tenor and soprano, both with continuo, are delightful specimens of his art. The former, iv, comments on the 'klagende Handschrift' referred to in iii—('all things must be fulfilled, which were written in the law of Moses,—concerning me', v. 44 of the Gospel)—'Now claim, Moses, as thou wilt, the threatening decree to exercise, I have my receipt here with Jesu's blood and wounds signed. This same valid, I am redeemed, I am freed, and live now with God in peace and unity, the accuser becomes in me to shame, Thy God is arisen.', then a short adagio arioso: 'My heart, that mark to thee.' vi is 'My Jesus lives, that shall from me no one take, therefore die I without sorrow, and am certain and have the confidence that me the grave's darkness to heaven's glory raises; my Jesus lives, I have now enough, my heart and mind will today still to heaven go, even the Saviour to behold.' (See Ex. 1265.) A chorus, a duet and two arias complete a varied and well-balanced scheme; Bach's additions supply a need overlooked by the librettist.

Spitta doubts the validity of ii, thinking it to be by Wilhelm Friedemann, and points out that the manner of working-out is more that of Telemann than of Bach. Knowing Bach's passion for copying the methods of every composer who could teach him anything, we need not be suprised if he essayed a number in the style of his popular and fertile contemporary. The plan of the opening is certainly unusual. The male voices do not enter for a long while, and during the lengthy S.A. duet there is no support but the continuo. The sopranos lead off with a lilting three-bar theme:

Ex. 1135

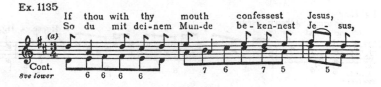

which is answered by the altos in the dominant. A charming effect is produced by a repeated 'Herr' in the countersubject on unaccented beats:

Ex. 1136

The sopranos now repeat their theme a tone higher than before, followed by the altos acting similarly. The total result is a thirteen-bar canon with a modulatory scheme different from the customary fugal entries. (a) and (b) are not heard again, a proceeding certainly not Bachian. A delicious figure:

Ex.1137

is tossed lightly from voice to voice and is dovetailed into and partially accompanies another important theme:

Ex. 1138

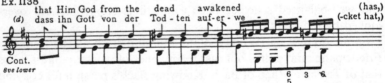

The naïve imagery of the last two bassi bars will not escape notice. The soprano run continues for another three bars, (c) is again tossed from voice to voice and (d) dovetails, this time the altos leading, who scintillate in semiquavers for eight bars, the last five with the sopranos above, chiefly in parallel motion. Four free bars conclude this section and a fugue for all voices begins, subject:

Ex. 1139

countersubject:

Ex. 1140

Throughout the fugue the initial three words are seldom heard, with
the result that 'selig' resounds from every voice. Close imitations of
the dropping sequence of the joy-motive, notes 3–8 of (*f*), produce a
brilliant effect. The upper strings enter one by one in the fugue, the
trumpet is at first independent, mostly formulating the joy-motive.
After an exciting passage for S.A.T. without continuo, in which (*e*)
and (*f*) are combined against a sustained 'selig', the tromba re-
iterating | ♩ ♪ ♩ | the latter doubles ottava an alto entry of (*e*).
The chorus ends with a longish plagal cadence, again an unusual
thing in Bach.

The S.T. duet, which begins Picander's libretto, has two instrumental lines only, the upper not being specified, though it is doubtless
for violins. One is struck immediately by the four upward rushes in
the opening bars:

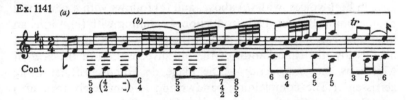

Ex. 1141

and there is much fragmentary use of them afterwards. Although the
words 'Die klagende Handschrift ist völlig zerrissen' do not come
till later in the aria, the orchestral symbolism keeps them in mind
throughout. Another fine idea of the introduction is:

Ex. 1142

(*b*) comes in other forms. The opening vocal melody, based on (*a*),
is unusual in style, almost like a folk-song:

Ex. 1143

(b) swings above. When the soprano takes up (d) the impulsive urge
of life is delineated by the tenor:

Ex. 1144

and when (c) is transferred to the soprano, the tenor leaps exultant
octaves, derived from the continuo motive of (a); the bassi also leap
octaves and a passage formed from (c) is heard in the obbligato. The
folk-song character of (d) is emphasized by its simultaneous appearance in both voices, with (b) above, and (e) follows with a new vocal
counterpoint. Part of the introduction, beginning with (c), forms an
interlude. Not until the next part of the text is revealed the cause of
all this joy, the cancellation of the old dispensation of the laws of
Moses by the resurrection—'Die klagende Handschrift ist völlig
zerrissen' ('The complaining handwriting is completely torn up')
(see Colossians ii. 14)—which is sung in parallel motion to another
folk-song-like tune, with continuo. It is curious that although these
words are heard twice, (b) is not played against them, though dovetailing with 'der Friede verschaffet ein ruhig' Gewissen' ('the peace
secures a quiet conscience') come six notes of (a). This sentence is
also without obbligato; the voices move in imitation and introduce
the joy-motive. (c) and octave continuo leaps enter with 'und öffnet
den Sündern das himmlische Thor' ('and opens to the sinners the
heavenly gate'), which is richly syncopated. Part of the introduction,
with swirling upward passages, brings a repetition of Part II of the
text, 'die klagende', &c., is now sung to imitations, the remainder is as
before, with voices reversed, and the obbligato line is as previously.
(a) introduces a modification of the first vocal section.

The bass aria (see P. 52) is splendid and direct. There are deliveries of the bold chief theme in octaves by the whole orchestra, tromba, flauto traverso, two oboes d'amore, violin I, II and continuo (why are violas omitted?):

Ex. 1145

or by the upper instruments above a firmly moving continuo, there are exhilarating sweeps for wood-wind and strings:

Ex. 1146
Ob. d'am. I. II. unis.

Vl. I. II. unis.

there are fine dropping arpeggi, derived from the chief theme, for violins in unison:

Ex. 1147

and semiquaver trillings for wood-wind and trumpet. Against a sustained note for violins, continuo octave leaps and brilliant flute arpeggi, the voice sings to a modification of (a)—'Merke, mein Herze, beständig nur dies' ('Mark, my heart, constantly only this') and an upward demisemiquaver swirl of the violins brings a short interlude:

Ex. 1148
Vls. W.-W. unis.

Cont.
8ve lower

Another swirl brings (a) in a vocal and orchestral octave tutti, dropping into a run on 'beständig', (c) and a flute figure derived from (a) accompanying. The flute develops (b), the tromba sustains; oboes d'amore in unison, violins and bassi take up successively an octave drop modelled on bar 1 of (a) and the voice swings along cheerfully on a melody derived from (b):

which is repeated a tone higher to 'daß dein Heiland lebend ist' ('that thy Saviour living is'). The singer joins the continuo, with powerful leaps, in a reprise of the last part of the introduction. 'Lasse dieses dienem Glauben einen Grund und Veste bleiben' ('Let this for thy faith a base and stronghold remain') is with continuo, and, as so often in Bach's methods, the melody is not entirely new, as bar 2 of (e) appears in it. Part I of the text, omitting 'beständig', comes again, the first part as an independent melody to (a) (wood-wind and strings) and the second free, with continuo. The latter part of the introduction, without tromba, as the key is the relative minor, brings twelve bars with continuo—'lasse dieses', &c., with 'auf solche besteht er gewiß' ('on such stands it safe'); long notes on 'besteht' are accompanied by (d) and by repetitions of bar 2 of (a), the upper note rising A♯, B, C♯, D, both ideas by wood-wind and violins in unison. In the reprise of the first vocal section (e) is replaced by another melody; one almost regrets that Bach's mind is so fertile, he so often denies one the delight of hearing attractive themes again. There is an imposing bigness about this aria; it is akin to the solo for the same voice in Part I of the Christmas Oratorio.

102. Three cantatas may be assigned to 1731, 102 definitely, 25 and 109 supposedly. All are fine specimens of Bach's genius and all contain choruses of superb quality. The cantata written for the Tenth Sunday after Trinity a few years before, dealing with the Gospel, St. Luke xix. 41–48, the weeping of Christ over Jerusalem (No. 46), is notable for its fierce, terrible anger. Its successor for the same day, 29 July (No. 102), while not so stupendous, is none the less stern; it deals with the fate of the stubborn sinner. No. 46 turned, in its last two numbers, from the scene of destruction and punishment to the figure of Christ as Shepherd; No. 102, on the other hand, allows no relief at all from the warnings to the 'impenitent heart', although in the penultimate number, an alto recitative, with two oboes playing short phrases in thirds, Bach writes more tender music than the words would imply. Even the heart of the stern preacher is moved to pity. The final chorale has two verses; the first, stanza 6 of J. Heermann's Lenten hymn, 'So wahr ich lebe, spricht dein Gott', 'Today livest thou, today convert thyself, Before tomorrow comes, can it alter itself for thee; Who today is well, healthy and ruddy, Is tomorrow ill, yea, even already dead. If thou now diest without penitence, Thy body and soul there burn must', is grim. With stanza 7, 'Help, Oh Lord Jesus, help Thou me, That I still today may come to Thee And penance do at this moment, Before me the quick death moves towards: In that today and at all time For my homeward-journey may be prepared', we have the first personal expression in the cantata. The prayer for help is all the more appealing because the melody is the anonymous one belonging to the versification of the Lord's Prayer, 'Vater unser in Himmelreich'. Few cantatas maintain a stern mood so consistently as this; it was more to Bach's liking to turn away from the wickedness of the world and its necessary punishment in the future to contemplation of the loving and merciful Saviour.

The unknown librettist selected two quotations from the Scriptures, neither of them from the appointed readings, but both appropriate to the Gospel for the Day. The opening chorus is a setting of Jeremiah v. 3 (the clauses are here numbered for convenience of reference), (1) 'Herr, deine Augen sehen nach dem Glauben!' ('Lord, Thine eyes look towards the faith!'); (2) 'du schlägest sie' ('Thou smitest them'); (3) 'aber sie fühlen's nicht' ('but they feel it not'); (4) 'du plagest sie' ('Thou tormentest them'); (5) 'aber sie bessern sich nicht' ('but they amend themselves not'); (6) 'Sie haben ein härter Angesicht denn ein Fels' ('They have a harder face than a rock'); (7) 'und wollen sich nicht bekehren' ('and will themselves not reform'). It will be seen that the Lutheran version differs considerably from that of the English Bible. The scoring is for two oboes and strings; the introduction is a network of themes, possibly more of musical importance than of symbolic significance. A dual one begins:

Ex. 1150

against:

A triple theme follows:

(it will be noted that the close coincides with that of (*a*)), combined with:

for violin I and (*c*) in the continuo. An oboe theme:

from (*c*), with (*c*) and (*g*) in violin I, is supported by a grim bassi figure:

(*i*) is often heard later, sometimes in stern repeated notes. (*c*), intro‧ duced by a tied crotchet and finished by leaps (called (*j*) hereafter) is played in imitation, with (*g*) in various parts. (*j*) is heard in thirds in the oboes, the violins stream down, (*c*) inverted, (*i*) is alternated in violas and bassi. Just before the entry of the choir there is a semi-quaver trill for the oboes, (*k*), against (*i*). The chorus ejaculates the word 'Herr' and the altos sing (1) to a recitative-like phrase, which embodies (*c*) and (*d*), and is accompanied by the staccato chords of

Ex. 1150. (A later cantata of the year, No. 109, introduces similar recitative-like phrases.) An orchestral interlude, (*j*), leads to a full choral statement of (1) twice over, the first akin to (*a*), with (*a*) in the violins, (*b*) in the oboes and bassi detached quavers; the second against (*e*) and (*f*), the instruments reversed, and (*c*) in the continuo. This is followed by the recitative idea in the sopranos. A restatement of the full choral section begins after (*k*) and (*i*) with different keys. (2), (3), and (4) are now set briefly, (2):

anticipates an extraordinary fugue subject which comes later. (*h*), (*c*), and (*i*) are heard against the three clauses. Four involved bars based on (*j*) and (*i*) return to (1). (*a*), (*b*) and the detached quavers lead to a fourteen-bar fugato with one of the strangest vocal subjects ever invented:

The countersubject is to (3):

and (4) adds another theme, 'plagest' writhing tortuously. Tenors and basses respectively lengthen (*l*) and (*m*), and until they are finished, only the oboes, with stinging groups—| r ♪♪ r ♪♪ |—and the continuo, the latter in detached quavers throughout the fugato, are the sole orchestral constituents. A threefold stretto of (*l*), with (*m*) in the tenors, is part of a piece of eight-part writing, oboes and violins akin to (*l*), and the violins leaping widely in detached quavers. During four bars of (*j*), (*d*) in its descending form and (*i*), the voices sing (2), (3), (4), and (5). The voices now cry out (1), 'Herr' being thrown on the fourth beat of the bar and detached, with (*d*) tossed between the treble instruments. With (*k*) and (*i*) in the oboes and the repeated-note (*i*) in the continuo, the basses cling firmly to 'Glauben', the upper voices enter in succession with (1), the 'Herr' being detached in each case, and there are direct and inverted imitations on 'deine Augen'. (*a*) and (*b*) lead to a full fugue, subject:

Ex.1159

(the augmented fourth leap to 'Fels' is splendidly descriptive), with (*d*), descending, and (*c*) appearing in the continuo. The countersubject (technically not so till half-way through, as it starts before the second entry) is:

Ex.1160

Beginning with the second entry the upper instruments gradually join in; oboe I and violin I have an extra entry of (*m*), (*c*) is frequently heard in the counterpoints. Against a soprano (*o*) the lower voices enter successively with (*m*); and while the basses sing their final (*o*), (*n*) is discarded and, instead, forms of (*c*) and (*a*) appear in the orchestra, heralding a reprise, altered at first, of the choral section from bar 34 to 44. An altered version of bars 60–69, with the isolated cry of 'Herr' thrown this time on the second beat of the bar, ends this mighty and powerful chorus. Can one imagine it as the 'Kyrie' of the Short Mass in G Minor? How the early English Bach enthusiasts who produced these borrowed works before the cantatas were known must have been puzzled, even though the staccato dots were deleted from (*l*) when it was adapted to 'Christe eleison'!

All three arias are striking and as diverse as the material of i. That for alto, iii, is a lament for the soul which loads itself with punishment. The oboe obbligato wails in desolate tones:

(F minor, with a signature of 3 flats.)

The continuo rarely departs from the tear-motive, moving heavily upward. 'Weh! der Seele' ('Woe! to the soul') modifies the above, and the first vocal section exploits this and other ideas from the introduction, voice and oboe interchanging. The tenseness of feeling may be shown by one bold passage:

The odd expression 'die den Schaden nicht mehr kennt!' ('which the harm no more knows!') is a reference to (2), (3), (4), and (5) of i. The beginning of Part II is diatonic, with continuo: 'und, die Straf' auf sich zu laden' ('and, the punishment upon itself to load'). The second 'laden' is expanded, and the oboe enters, playing (b) while there is a forceful passage to 'störrig rennt' ('stubbornly runs'); 'ja, von ihres Gottes Gnade selbst sich trennt' ('yea, from its God's grace itself separates') is sung against (a), and two interpolated cries of 'weh!' are flung against (b). The remainder of the vocal melody is new and (b) is heard persistently in the obbligato. (a) and (b), *per arsin et thesin*, bring the reprise, which is altered from the fifth bar onwards. The character of the number is a complete negation of its suitability to become the 'Qui tollis' of the Short Mass in F.

To the bass, iv, with strings, is given the second Biblical quotation, Romans ii. 4, 5. (See P. 56.) The number is termed 'Arioso' in the score, evidently only because the text is Scriptural, for it is not an arioso in the normal sense, but a fully developed aria. The stubbornness of the impenitent sinner is marvellously depicted. The sudden

repeated minor seventh sets the mood, and the holding note tells of
the obstinacy of the evil-doer:

Ex.1163   *Vivace*   *(b)*

While violin II sustains its B♭ violin I repeats (*a*) a fifth higher, and
then a passage, continuing two bars farther than the quotation, shows
us the relentless vengeance of the offended Almighty:

Ex.1164
(*d*)

'Verachtest du den Reichthum seiner Gnade, Geduld und Langmüthigkeit?' ('Despisest thou the riches of His grace, patience and
long-suffering?') is set to (*a*), with (*b*) during the first part, and the
leaps of (*d*), this time in octaves in violin II and viola; and during
the second, upward leaps for violin II and viola, based on a version
of (*a*):

Ex.1165   (*e*)

and then (*a*) itself in violin I. 'Verachtest du' is twice detached, a
third time it runs for three bars and dovetails into the complete (*a*).
The octave upward leap occurs in the violins. 'Langmüthigkeit'
breaks off, the violins resolve their dissonance on a pause, and
another pause, this time over a bar's rest, adds tremendous weight
to the question which ensues: 'Weißest du nicht, daß dich Gottes
Güte zur Buße locket?' ('Knowest thou not, that thee God's goodness to repentance calls?'). This is set to a modification of (*a*), violin
I entering thrice with the opening notes. As the vocal melody is
repeated in yet another form, (*c*) is exploited by the violins, together
with one hint of (*a*), (*e*) alternating in bassi and voices. (*d*), with a

different continuo, introduces a striking vocal passage, the angry summons to repentance:

The frantic, impotent battering of the evil-doers against the decrees of the Almighty is magnificently depicted:

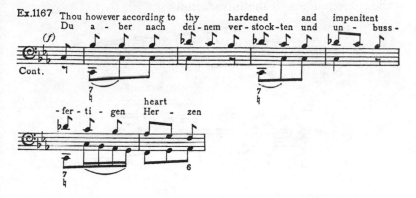

with sustained notes for violin II and viola. With the latter in the same vein violin I plays (*f*) and the singer dashes wildly, as if turning from this side to that—'häufest dir selbst den Zorn auf den Tag des Zorns' ('heapest for thyself the anger against the day of angers')— which we shall call (*g*). (*f*) is sung against (*g*) in violin I, (*g*) against (*f*), the lower strings continuing as before. The voice flings up on a splendid phrase, incorporating (*c*)—'und der Offenbarung' ('and the revelation')—answered by violin I, and again—'des gerechten Gerichts Gottes' ('of the righteous judgement of God')—also answered, with (*e*) in the continuo and fragments of (*d*) in the inner strings. The phrase begins a third time, there is a sustained note in the manner of (*b*), violin I imitates the initial figure during the prolongation, and the continuation of 'Offenbarung' is a syncopated run against (*b*). The reprise is singularly brief—(*a*) and (*b*) in the violins, in the subdominant, the low pitch of (*a*) producing an awesome effect of warning; the singer pits (*a*) against violin II (*b*), and (*a*) for violin I during part of the sustaining of the last syllable of

'Langmüthigkeit'. (c) heard once more, brings this great aria to a close and ends Part I of the cantata.

Part II opens with another aria. In Bach's day the sermon would separate iv from v, so the succession of two arias which occurs in modern performances would not happen. The solo voice is tenor; a very carefully tongued (or bowed) obbligato is for *flauto traverso solo* (*o violino piccolo*), a later addition to the manuscript—'violino spiccato'—suggests that the violin is more appropriate. 'Violoncello e violone piano sempre e staccato' is indicated in the continuo line. The self-satisfaction of the 'all-too-certain soul' is portrayed in various lovely ideas in the introduction:

and:

The voice pursues themes of its own and first paints the terror which the evil-doer should feel, but does not:

Beginning with the first 'doch', (a) is heard in the obbligato—the sinner is quite unmoved. These ideas are repeated and then (e) disappears altogether. Except for a Da Capo of the introduction the aria is an anticipation by nearly a century of the 'durchkomponirt' type of song. The voice continues: 'du allzu sich're Seele!' ('thou all-too-certain soul!'). (b) is heard for four bars while 'sich're' twice sways as if totally indifferent to the power of the righteous God. The admonition 'erschcrecke' is twice flung on upper notes, but (c) floats down unconcernedly. (a), (b), (c), and (d) inverted constitute a ritornello. 'Denk', was dich würdig zähle der Sünden Joch' ('Think, what (for) thee deservedly counts of the sin's yoke') is set calmly; the curious grouping of the words suggests that Bach found himself in difficulties with this odd clause. Most of the section is with continuo only, (d) comes against two sustained notes on 'Joch', and (c) and (d) when 'denk" is solemnly repeated, once to a high note and once to a low one. Another curious expression—'Die Gottes-Langmuth geht auf einem Fuß von Blei' ('God's long-suffering moves on a foot of lead') –cxtricates the composer from his difficulties; a long-drawn-out sequential descent is picturesque, during 'einem' the continuo drops through thirds, the first parts of (a) and (b) thrice ascend and descend. (d) leaps to the last clause, which is developed more than the others and is treated in no fewer than five different ways. (1) the spiccato semiquavers, a new figure, though notes 4, 5, and 6 of (h) are incorporated into it, an anticipation of Wagner's 'fire-motive', are heard above, and below the voice thrice sings an angry phrase:

Ex.1172

da - mit der Zorn her - nach dir de - sto schwe-rer sei,
that the anger hereafter for thee so much heavier may be,

followed in free imitation by the continuo. At the end (f) is sung twice rising from low D to high G, and the continuo sternly repeats (g). (2) 'Schwerer' is set to a long and tortuous passage, the continuo reiterates (h)—| ↲ ♫♫ ♫ |—and (a) and (b) are in the obbligato. (3) For two bars the clause is set to zigzagging semiquavers, as if the proud were being tumbled down, the continuo during (3) and (4) modifies (h) to— ♫♫ | ♫ —, there are fragments in the obbligato related to the close of (c) and the notes joining that with (d). (4) 'Desto schwerer' is set to heavy, slowly descending passages, an elongated (*c*) fills each bar. (5) The clause is set twice, syllable by syllable, to quavers, rising to high A and falling to low D. In the first two bars a new demisemiquaver figure suggests the licking of flames.

It is interesting to note how Bach, in the alto recitative with oboes, vi, creates a feeling of solemnity and fateful apprehension by dispensing with his bassi during the opening bars, when the sinner is warned that time is passing and that God's mercy may not endure: 'In the waiting is danger; wilt thou the time lose? the God, Who formerly merciful was.' After this the continuo plays isolated crotchets almost solely. The oboes maintain a wailing figure throughout:

Ex.1173

The remainder of the text is: 'can easily thee before His judgement-seat lead. Where remains then the atonement? There is a moment, which time and eternity, body and soul separates. Blinded sense, ah, turn then back, that thee this same hour not finds unprepared!'

ii is a bass recitativo secco: 'Where is the image, that God on us stamps, when the perverted will itself to Him contrary lies? Where is the strength of His word, when all improvement melts out of the heart away? The Highest seeks us through gentleness indeed to tame, if the erring spirit itself would yet be willing; yet, continues it in its hardened mind, so gives he it into the heart's darkness away.'

25. The Gospel of the Fourteenth Sunday after Trinity is St. Luke xvii. 11–19, the healing of ten lepers by Christ, and the Epistle is Galatians v. 16–24, in which St. Paul warns his readers against sins of the flesh. Picander (?) was not to be outdone by the Apostle's sinister list, 'Adultery, fornication, uncleanness, lasciviousness, idolatry, witchcraft, hatred, variance, emulations, wrath, strife, seditions, heresies, envyings, murders, drunkenness, revellings, and such like', and wallows in such expressions as 'The whole world is only a sick-house', 'The other lies ill with a loathsome stench on his honour' and 'No herb nor plaster can heal my leprosy, my boils, as does the balm from Gilead.' The translator of 'There is nought of soundness in all my body', N., the English version of 'Es ist nichts Gesundes an meinem Leibe', wisely avoids these nauseating lapses of taste. The splendid opening chorus takes as its text Psalm xxxviii. 3: 'There is no soundness in my flesh because of thine anger; neither is there any rest in my bones because of my sin.' The upper strings, violin I and II doubled respectively by oboe I and II (these are never independent), begin with a three-quaver wailing figure which is heard twice in each bar:

Ex.1174

This is maintained for forty-one bars.

Alto and soprano begin with a mournful, heavily laden figure:

Ex.1175

followed by a melody which includes those syncopated ideas so often found when God's wrath is spoken of:

Ex.1176

the whole a canon at two beats, lasting for eight bars. Before it ends bass and tenor begin a repeat of the canon, the other voices continuing contrapuntally, altos and sopranos dovetail the canonical (a) into (b). The sopranos continue with the ideas of (b), and during this the tenors sing (a), the basses follow two beats later, slightly altering the first phrase and freely inverting the second. The altos dovetail (a) into this and the choir ends on the dominant. After a ritornello, a repetition of the introduction, the whole of the material is heard afresh, the voices changing their order of entry, and the last few bars, before a second dominant close, being altered. The next section of thirteen bars is devoted to a new fugal theme, more animated than the other, with overlapping and irregular entries:

Ex.1177

Just accentuation of the words brings cross-rhythms, as shown by the dotted brackets. As in the first case, a pair of voices sings in canon at a distance of two beats, but that is not transferred to the other pair. The separate entries are at two beats and at six. With a close stretto for all four voices, at the distance of a beat, upper strings and oboes, which have been silent since (c) began, re-enter; for the remainder of the number they double the voices only. For most of this section the continuo moves in muttering semiquavers, betokening the troubled mind of the penitent. (c) now enters at distances of two, four, and four beats. Bach's consummate command of technical device is shown in the closing section. The canonical (a) is resumed, this time by the two middle voices, against it are worked (c) and an extra entry of (a). A free form of (c) comes in the basses during the (b) canon. As before, the next appearance of the (a) canon comes during (b), but between the outside voices, and there are two full entries of (a), two beats apart, while (b) is in progress. The canonical (a) comes in the middle voices, free versions of (b), sopranos and basses, join with it, and there is a canon, at two beats, on (c), for the middle voices. The prevailing mood is of gloom; there is something foreboding and austere which gives the chorus a special character. Bach, however, knew a consolation which the Psalmist wot not of, and in his own particular way adds a commentary which entirely changes the direction intended by the librettist. In bars 1–5, while the upper instruments carry on their ceaseless lament, we hear in the continuo line 1 of what the British people know as the 'Passion chorale'. Although H. L. Hassler's tune was also associated with 'Herzlich thut mir verlangen' it is stanza 1 of C. Schneegass's hymn on Psalm vi, 'Ach Herr, mich armen Sünder' ('Ah Lord, me poor sinner') which would be in Bach's mind. (See No. 135, pp. 121–2, Vol. II, for translation.) When bar 15 is reached a new orchestral group enters, three flutes à bec in unison, cornetto, and three trombones. The cornetto plays lines 1 and 2 of the chorale, the flutes double at the octave above, the trombones support. In the midst of the gloom this strong, confident prayer to the Saviour asserts that whatever ills betide, there is a rock on which to build, and hope of sure comfort. The remaining pairs of chorale lines enter in the same way: while the penultimate one is in progress the combination of the (a) canon with imitations of (c) is heard at the same time! Musically the effect of the number is magnificent, the chorale entries are a blaze of glory; technically it is an astounding feat. Nothing daunted his superb contrapuntal ingenuity. This is the

only case in Bach's known choral-orchestral works where trombones
are used for any purpose other than that of strengthening the voices.
Perhaps in the lost cantatas there may have been other examples
of this anticipation of the finale to Beethoven's Fifth Symphony
and Schubert's C Major.
The tenor recitative is that of the 'Hospital' and 'Gestank', and
a pretty picture of humanity is limned—'The whole world is only a
sick-house, where men, in uncountably great number, and also the
children in cradles, in illness cruel low lie. The one torments in the
breast a heated fever of evil desire; the other lies ill of his own honour
a hateful stench; the third wastes the avarice away and precipitates
him before his time into the grave. The first fall has everyone polluted
and with the sin's-leprosy infected. Ah! this poison penetrates even
my limbs. Where find I poor man healing? Who stands me in my
misery by? Who is my physician, who helps me anew?' (See Ex.
1263.) It leads to the bass aria, with continuo, which contains the
other expressions quoted. The number is of moderate interest only,
as might be expected from the unsavoury text—Part I, 'Ach, wo hol'
ich Armer Rath? Meinen Aussatz, meine Beulen kann kein Kraut,
noch Pflaster heilen, als die Salb' aus Gilead' ('Ah, where obtain I
poor man advice? My leprosy, my boils can no herb, nor plaster
heal, except the balm of Gilead'). (See Jer. viii. 22.) Part II, 'Du,
mein Arzt, Herr Jesu nur weißt die beste Seelenkur' ('Thou, my
physician, Lord Jesus only knowest the best soul-cure'). The continuo indicates the perplexed condition of the sufferer:

Ex.1178

(Key D minor, no signature.)

(a) (b) is stated thrice in succession, once without voice, and twice
with different vocal melodies. Beginning with 'Meinen Aussatz' (a)
is used several times and only with the final 'kein Kraut' does (b)
reappear. There is less variety than one might have expected. It is
true that the continuo moves placidly in quavers for four bars, that
'Du, mein Arzt' is set to a tender flourish, but afterwards (a) and
(b) persist to the end. There is a happy transformation of the

time-pattern of (*a*) to 'beste' and a long meaningless run to 'Arzt', but there is otherwise little or no attempt at distinctiveness.

The soprano recitativo secco is more reasonable textually. The singer turns to the Saviour, the healer of all sufferers—'Oh Jesu, beloved Master, to Thee fly I; ah, strengthen the weakened life's-spirits. Have mercy, Thou physician and helper of all sick ones, cast me not from Thy countenance. My Saviour! make me from sin's-leprosy clean: then will I to Thee my whole heart therefore as a constant offering dedicate, and life-long for Thy help thank.' In contrast to the arid 'Hospital' recitative, there are characteristic touches, a flourish on 'flieh'' and melismata on 'Erbarme' ('Pity') and 'lebens-lang' ('life-long').

After this long spell of continuo it is refreshing to encounter a fully scored number a soprano aria. Strings and doubling oboes are as in i, the three flutes form an independent group, never doubling strings and playing together almost always, in three parts. There are antiphonal passages between flutes and upper strings, and during the tutti sections the two groups are generally contrasted, holding or repeated notes in the one being balanced by movement in the others. The use of the flutes is explained by the lines 'Wenn ich dort im höhern Chor werde mit den Engeln singen' ('When I there in the higher choir shall with the angels sing'). The aria is very lovely in quality. Economy of material is notable in the long introduction, for:

Ex.1179

with 'gebunden' repeated quavers pitted by one group against (*b*) in the other, constitute the sole themes. At one point (*b*) descends in a fivefold sequence in the continuo while the upper strings sustain and the flutes divide (*b*) and the quavers among them. The orchestral tutti ceases while the voice outlines (*a*):

Ex.1180

The violins join in the last bar of this with (b). The flutes act similarly with 'Jesu, dein Genaden-Ohr!' ('Jesu, Thy grace-ear!').

Ex.1181

is answered by a bar in which (b) is played by violin I and (c) by violin II simultaneously:

Ex.1182

is imitated by the flutes and the four bars are repeated in a different key. Bach economically bases both these vocal fragments on (b). (a) is played by violin I and then by the flutes, in a tutti, while the singer invents a new melody and continues with bassi only. The introduction in the dominant, with the groups reversed, forms an interlude. 'Wenn ich dort im höhern Chor' is, like the opening phrase, with continuo and punctuated by (a). (b) occurs in the bassi and a form of (d) in the voice. With (a) in the strings the singer breaks up the clause, a rest, curiously, separating 'im' from 'höhern'; with (a) in the flutes a counterpoint is added. Another repetition extends with 'werde — singen', and (b) is dovetailed, strings, flutes, strings. To (c), with instrumental groups reversed, is sung 'soll mein Danklied besser klingen' ('shall my thanks-song better ring'). The section is now condensed, with new melodies for the first eight bars, though (d) clenches each phrase; the groups are reversed.

All instruments take part in the final chorale, L. Bourgeois's secular melody, 'Ainsi qu'on oit le cerf bruire' sung to stanza 12 of J. Heermann's 'Treuer Gott, ich muß dir klagen'—'I shall all my days Extol Thy strong hand, That Thou my misery and complaining Hast so sympathetically averted. Not only in the mortality Shall Thy praise be spread abroad; I shall it also hereafter demonstrate, And there eternally Thee praise.'

109. Another unusual chorus, and one which bears a certain resemblance to that in No. 102, opens No. 109. Although very lengthy it is based on two clauses only: 'Ich glaube, lieber Herr, hilf meinem Unglauben' ('I believe, Lord; help Thou my unbelief'),

St. Mark ix. 24. These are contrasted time and time again. The
scoring is for strings, with violin I part sometimes marked 'Solo',
sometimes 'Tutti', two oboes and corno da caccia. The opening
four-note figure:

Ex.1183
(a)

is of great importance, though it is never found in the vocal lines.
Given out by oboe I and violins in unison, continuo, and then the
initial instruments, it leads to a tutti in which is heard the phrase
which comes later in various guises to 'hilf meinem Unglauben':

Ex.1184 Cor. da C. Ob.I. Vl.I.
(b)
Cont.

Then it comes in turn in oboe I, oboe II, violin I, continuo, oboe II
plus violins plus corno. It forms the basis of a short duet between
oboe I and violin I, punctuated by a ♪ chord, an idea which
comes frequently later. The crotchet chord is always decorated by
one or more appoggiature, indicated by the sign ⌣, of which the
number contains very many. (The copyist of the orchestral parts
once supplied to the writer mistook this sign for a slur throughout!)
As always, the leaning notes must be long and stressed. They create
a feeling of pathetic pleading, the petition of the father with the child
possessed of a dumb spirit, from the narration of which the text is
taken. The choral section opens with a recitative-like phrase for the
sopranos:

Ex.1185   Ich   glau -   -   - be,lie - ber Herr,
(c)
Cont.
8ve lower

an imitative figure in oboe I and then (a) accompanying. After a short
portion for full choir, part of (c), the sopranos extend the recitative

idea, again accompanied by oboe I, this time joined by solo violin with suggestions of (a). Then comes a characteristic passage, a wandering group of semiquavers for two voices, turning hither and thither as if bewildered by conflicting states of mind:

Ex.1186.

The horn leaps octaves, again a picture of indecision. The two-chord group, marked 'forte', bursts in upon (d) and the sopranos cry out 'hilf, hilf' on short notes, and follow with a version of (b) against (a) in violin I. (a) in oboe I, oboe II, and violin I bring (d) and the cries of 'hilf' again, and (b) in the sopranos leads to four bars of choral tutti with continuo. Before it ends there are close imitations of (a), oboe I and violin I, and the introduction is then repeated. The choral section up to the end of the first (d), *per arsin et thesin*, with the altos as leaders, is repeated. (a), the leap enlarged to a seventh, enters successively in A.T.S. and B. to 'hilf meinem Unglauben', the noun extended in runs embodying the wanderings of (d), A. and T. in strict canon, S. and B. in free imitation. During this, (a), the leap sometimes further enlarged to an octave, is heard seven times in oboes and violins. The (d) section comes again, the principal idea for S. and A. and the second preceded by (a) with the seventh leap for the tenors. The choral tutti which followed its first appearance comes again, with S. and T. reversed. The dovetailing, with instruments reversed, and a shortened ritornello come as before. The basses deliver the text in quasi-recitative style, but to a new melody, (a) entering in oboe I, violin I, oboe II, and violin II, horn leaps clenching the close. Bars 1–4 of the opening vocal section, with tenors as leaders, begin what may be looked upon as a recapitulation, though two bars of dovetailing passages for tenors and basses, with an ambling oboe I, are quite new. (d) for S.A. and the fourfold section with the enlarged (a) leap, the voices reversed, and (d) again bring the final section, (a), with the seventh, quickly in all voices in succession, with new runs for 'Unglauben', and a concluding tutti. Oboes and upper strings play the ♪ ♪ chords twelve times, the corno punctuating the half-bars, and in the penultimate bar (a) is delivered by violin I and then by oboe I and horn in unison. This fascinating chorus needs the utmost flexibility of treatment; every voice and instrument must be considered a soloist.

The cantata is for the Twenty-first Sunday after Trinity. The Gospel, St. John iv. 46–54, relates the healing of the sick son of the nobleman and the confident faith of the father. The Epistle is Ephesians vi. 10–17; verse 16 is, 'Above all, taking the shield of faith, wherewith ye shall be able to quench all the fiery darts of the wicked'. The unknown librettist contrasts with the noblemen the hapless Christian who cannot believe as he; the verse from St. Mark expresses in brief the conflicting states of mind which are depicted throughout the cantata. Indecision continues in the fine tenor recitativo secco. Thrice the singer declares confidence, but after each assertion doubt possesses him. Bach adopts the unusual expedient of marking these contrasting sections forte and piano;—'The Lord's hand is indeed yet not shortened, I can helped be. Ah no! I sink already to the earth, from care, that it me to the ground smites. The Highest desires, His Father-heart breaks; ah no! He hears the sinners not. He will, He must thee soon to help hasten, in order thy distress to heal. Ah no! remain I for comfort very anxious.' The short arioso at the end—'Ah Lord! how long?'—is also marked forte.

A remarkable tenor aria with strings, which is akin to Peter's aria in the *St. John Passion*, begins, 'Wie zweifelhaftig ist mein Hoffen, wie wanket mein geängstigt Herz!' ('How doubting is my hope, how totters my anguished heart!'). The harmonic tissue is of great complexity; to the many fundamental dissonances are added numerous appoggiature, bewildering the hearer. The chief melody tosses from side to side:

'wanket' is interpreted vocally by long triplet runs and instrumentally by figures which stumble down and down:

The voice now modifies (*a*) and then swirls below in triplets. After (*a*), notes 1–3 replaced by the dotted-note figure, and (*b*) in violin I, the singer's twirling figures are supported only by (*b*) and the continuo. After the introduction is repeated, the voice alters its first phrase, with (*b*) in the continuo; while it gives vent to short cries, (*a*) and (*b*) in violin I add to the expression of dismay. The former passage with continuo and the introduction conclude Part I. 'Des Glaubens Docht glimmt kaum hervor' ('The faith's wick gleams scarcely forth') brings the one melodic idea of confidence, though (*b*) is in the bassi and (*a*) bursts in again immediately; 'es bricht dies fast zerstoß'ne Rohr' ('there breaks this almost bruised reed,' see St. Matthew xii. 20) and 'die Furcht macht stetig neuen Schmerz' ('the fear makes constantly new pain') are both wildly agitated and with continuo (*b*) only. (*a*) comes between and over a sustained 'Schmerz' with detached chords, as if the reed were indeed already broken. The last clause is repeated, there is a ritornello, (*a*), and the voice repeats the text of Part II with a scurrying triplet passage on 'Schmerz'. The upper strings are silent and a fourfold (*b*) comes in the bassi. The aria needs a first-rate singer with much dramatic power and the accompaniment must be played with much vehemence, with heavy stresses on the appoggiature and the dotted-note figures broken off at the dot, the shorter note being halved in value.

It is an emotional relief to pass from this state of distraction to the quiet little alto recitativo secco, which breathes sweet words of comfort: 'Oh contain thyself, thou doubting mind, because Jesus now still wonders does. The faith-eyes shall behold the salvation of the Lord; seems the fulfilment all-too distant, so canst thou yet on the promise build.'

'Der Heiland kennet ja die Seinen, wenn ihre Hoffnung hülflos liegt' ('The Saviour knows yea His own, when their hope helpless lies') is the message of the aria for the same voice. Two oboes and continuo begin a pastoral minuet, if such a contradiction of terms may be permitted:

Ex.1189

and:

The vocal line of Part I is unusually straightforward. The text is sung thrice, twice to an almost exact reproduction of (a) and its corollary, and again to a modification. The first and third 'liegt' are sustained while the oboes blissfully wander above to (c). The corollary, (c) and in particular (d) form the oboe counterpoints and the slide of (b) is heard in the continuo. At the close the last 'wenn — liegt', (d) in oboe I, and part of bar 1 of (c) in oboe II herald a repetition of the introduction. 'Wenn Fleisch und Geist in ihnen streiten, so steht er ihnen selbst zur Seiten, damit zuletzt der Glaube siegt' ('When flesh and spirit in them wrangle, so stands He to them Himself at their sides, so that at last the faith conquers') is a new melody, except that 'streiten' borrows an oboe II run from bar 5 of the first vocal section, a curious use of previous material, and that 'Glaube' is almost identical with the last 'hülflos'. The oboes play (a) in bars 2 and 6, and three staccato crotchets in bars 4 and 8, the remainder being with continuo. One can see no significance in the staccato crotchets, unless one thinks of them as the stinging pangs of inner conflict; they accompany both 'streiten' and 'Seiten'. 'Siegt' is sustained; the passage from (c) to the end of the introduction begins above it. The eight bars of vocal melody are presented in another form, though the 'streiten' run is retained. (a) is incorporated, bars 3 and 11; the same type of accompaniment is present, oboe I being altered in bar 2. 'Siegt' is a minim only; with it begins (c), elongated, and with the oboes reversed in bar 2 and corresponding bars. Its peaceful wandering is disturbed by a dramatic incident. The singer suddenly becomes animated (Ex. 1191). The semiquavers continue for another two bars, the bassi twice stamp downwards and then cease for three bars. 'Damit — siegt' comes as the first time, with the sustained note and (c). The voice ends 'damit zuletzt, zuletzt der Glaube siegt', 'letzt' being staccato, 'der Glaube siegt' adagio with a trill, and without continuo for two bars. It is interesting to observe how frequently Bach

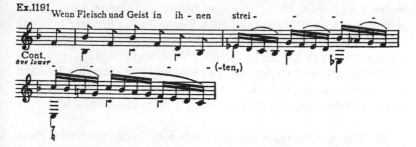

Ex.1191

indicates detached notes and groups of notes for his voices; people with a superficial knowledge of his vocal music are not aware that devices such as this are used freely for dramatic purposes. The writer has been severely reprimanded, more than once, by press critics, for allowing his choirs to sing certain choruses non-legato! The old legend of Bach as a severe and mechanical organ composer dies hard. In this number Bach again shows his temporary obsession for the curved sign indicating appoggiature.

A splendid large-scale extended chorale (B.E.C. No. 20, O.) ends this fine cantata. The *corno da caccia* doubles the canto, oboes and strings are independent. Line 3 speaks of building on a rock; the upper strings sustain an A while the oboes announce a short detached figure:

Ex.1192

(D minor, without signature.)

and this combination of ideas is heard in several forms. The continuo figure is much in evidence; it accompanies:

Ex.1193

There is also a quaver arpeggio figure ♪♪♪♩ which comes in all instrumental parts except corno and bassi. A dramatic incident occurs in the last line, where the lower voices shout 'er hilft' ('He helps') and wait for a moment before continuing with 'sein'n Gläub'gen allen' ('His faithful all'). Stanza 7 of L. Spenger's 'Durch Adams Fall ist ganz verderbt' furnishes the text and its associated anonymous tune the canto fermo: 'Who hopes in God and Him trusts He will never be shamed: For who on this rock builds, If to him even befall Many trials, have I yet never the man seen fall, Who himself throws upon God's comfort; He helps His faithful all.'

39. The circumstances which brought into being 'Brich dem Hungrigen dein Brod' ('Bring the hungry man thy bread' N.) are known. On the First Sunday after Trinity, 1732, 1,800 out of the 30,000 Protestants exiled from Salzburg, where an intensive and thorough campaign of prosecution was being carried through by the Archbishop, were received in St. Nicholas's. They had arrived on 13 and 14 June, had been warmly welcomed by their co-religionists and fed by the municipal authorities. Bach's heart was touched to the core by the sight of the forlorn and suffering people. By a happy coincidence the Gospel was St. Luke xvi. 19–31, the story of Dives and Lazarus, and the Epistle 1 John iv. 16–21, the love of God and the necessity for love among mankind. Part I opens with Isaiah lviii. 7 and 8, and continues to reflect upon the example of the Almighty and the blessings which fall upon believers if His commands to love one's fellow creatures are obeyed Part II opens with Hebrews xiii. 16; recitative and aria affirm determination to follow these precepts, and the final chorale is an expansion of the beatitude 'Blessed are the merciful'. The unknown librettist evolved an appropriate and well-constructed scheme.

The crowning glory of the cantata is the opening chorus, varied, flexible, imaginative, every phase of the text mirrored in music of superb quality. It is another miracle of the master's, for it must have been conceived and written in desperate haste. The German version differs from the English; the former is 'Break for the hungry thy bread', the latter 'Is it not to deal thy bread to the hungry, and that thou bring the poor that are cast out to thy house?' Two flutes à bec begin with two repeated quavers, weak to strong, two oboes follow, then upper strings:

Spitta (who misdates the cantata) and Schering see in this the breaking of bread, Schweitzer the tottering of the weak. This otherwise inexplicable idea, supported throughout by continuo detached quavers, occupies the first thirteen bars. Then the flutes in thirds, imitated by the oboes, play short semiquaver groups, the upper strings taking over the detached quavers from the bassi, while the continuo gives out a new version of the repeated two-note figure:

The significance of the latter is shown later, as it accompanies the choir when it sings 'führe in's Haus' ('take into the house'). The wood-wind now sustain, violin I repeats (c), violin II and viola keep up the detached quavers and the bassi bear the most important idea, an upward rush growing more and more intense:

We see later what it means, for the first form is associated with the word 'hungry', the despairing appeal of the starving refugees. Two bars of (d) in the upper strata of the orchestra and a form of (b) conclude the ritornello. When the chorus enters the (a) part of the introduction is repeated by the orchestra, extended by two bars. Sopranos and altos sing an infinitely tender theme, pathetically broken by rests after the first and third words, imitated by tenors and basses; emotion chokes the voices of the merciful:

The idea comes again immediately, with voices reversed. We now have sustained phrases to 'und die, so in Elend sind' ('and those, that in misery are', again the two versions of the Bible differ slightly), with a sorrowful chromatic progression for the sopranos and a tender rise of a minor sixth for the tenors, on the word 'Elend', and a beautifully touching phrase for the basses, the central point being a falling diminished fifth. The stressing of 'die' is a direct comment on the sufferers present in the church. Now comes the choral passage accompanied by (*b*), the sopranos and altos wandering vaguely in quavers and semiquavers:

Ex.1198

the tenors moving with uncertain steps over quaver leaps, the basses lagging in syncopated crotchets:

Ex.1199

One wonders more and more at the infinite loveliness of this picture of the homeless sufferers. (*d*) supports an impassioned choral section in which the voices enter successively with an upward leap, as if an agitated crowd were pressing forward for relief, and three bars at once close this modified repetition of the introduction and herald a new section, for a fugal subject begins in the tenors during the antepenultimate bar:

Ex.1200

It embodies the ascent of (*d*) on 'Hungrigen', 'Elend' recalls the
previous chromatic wailing, 'führe in's Haus' suggests the hurrying
of the weary wayfarers into the homes of the compassionate citizens.
Could more be condensed into a few bars? The subject is used for
nothing more than an exposition; as it proceeds we hear on 'Elend'
the familiar tear-motive, (*a*) is in the orchestra. The exposition ends
with the antepenultimate bar of the introduction, the ascent to
'führe'. The first fifteen bars of combined choral and orchestral
material are repeated, centred round the dominant instead of the
tonic, with the entries of the voices reversed. The next movement
sets first 'So du Einen nackend siehst, so kleide ihn' ('When
thou one naked seest, then clothe him') and the seven bars are
packed with interesting matter. The opening clause is delivered
unaccompanied:

Ex.1201

So du Ein-en nack-end sieh - est,

replied to by all voices in the second clause, with (*h*) for unison flutes.
Against a florid passage for sopranos the altos sing (*h*) and during
the answering tutti the oboes play this theme. The tenors now sing (*h*),
the florid passage is transferred to the altos, the sopranos add a
counterpoint, and when tenors and basses sing 'so kleide ihn', (*h*)
is given to unison upper strings. The remaining seven bars of $\frac{4}{4}$ are
no less crowded with things of moment and exhibit eleven-part
writing. Sopranos, altos, and tenors sing in short and almost homophonic phrases 'und entzeuch dich nicht von deinem Fleisch' ('and
withdraw thyself not from thy flesh'), the basses dovetailing, mostly
with:

Ex.1202

und ent - zeuch

which gives rise to incessant imitation for the flutes:

Ex.1203

The oboes wail in a motive of compassion:

Ex.1204

violin II and viola play (a) and violin I decorates it:

Ex.1205

In form the rapid final section consists of two fugal expositions, separated by an interlude, with a coda. The splendid subject is:

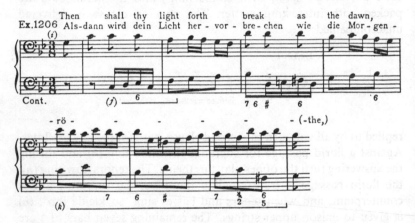

(It is evident that Bach intended an elision of the strong accent on 'die' and the stress of the bar to be transferred to the first syllable of 'Morgen'. 'Morgenröthe' is literally 'morning-redness' meaning 'dawn'.) 'Röthe' continues for another seven bars, mostly in semi-quavers, as a countersubject, and part of it is a figure:

Ex.1207

which becomes important later as:

Ex.1208

and in other forms, and the sequential continuo figure (*k*) produces an especially fine effect. Entries 1–3 of (*i*) are with bassi only; the remainder of the orchestra bursts in upon the fourth, the flutes being independent, hinting half-way through at (*k*). The choir now sings in short sharp phrases—'und deine Besserung wird schnell wachsen' ('and thy betterment will rapidly increase'). (*k*) is heard in the basses, 'wachsen', by its florid runs, suggests the budding of a powerful life. Oboes double, upper strings toss about to (*n*)—| ♩ ♫ |—unison flutes develop (*m*), the brilliance of the rosy rays of the dawn. In an interlude the flutes play (*m*) in thirds and the strings dovetail (*o*)— | ♫ ♩ |—with (*n*) in the oboes. There are now fourteen bars of 'Und deine Gerechtigkeit wird vor dir hergehen' ('And thy righteousness shall before thee go'), (*j*), direct and inverted, and (*m*) in the voices, (*m*) running in the unison flutes and a syncopated passage of great excitement at the end. A ritornello, a derivative of (*l*) for unison oboes, (*o*) in the strings against (*n*) in the flutes, dovetails into the second exposition. (*i*), with the opening altered, is the subject— 'und die Herrlichkeit des Herrn wird dich zu sich nehmen' ('and the glory of the Lord will thee to itself take'). The voices enter from basses upwards, but before the sopranos take up the theme there is a long codetta based on the countersubject for the tenors and (*e*) for the basses. The orchestral treatment is different, for fifteen bars the flutes utilize (*n*) or sustain, and as the alto entry ends, dovetail a passage compounded of the altered form of the opening of (*i*), and replace the sopranos by playing the complete subject. Then the sopranos are allowed their rightful entry, while the flutes play the countersubject. Oboes and upper strings strengthen tenors, altos, and sopranos. The interlude again disposes the thematic material differently, (*m*) in sixths in violins, (*n*) in the flutes and (*o*) in the strings. A short tutti outburst, in which the flutes anticipate the altered opening of (*i*) in the sopranos, with a final reminder of (*j*) in the basses, closes this superb chorus in a blaze of 'Herrlichkeit'.

A long bass recitativo secco speaks of the endless bountifulness of the Almighty as an example to ourselves. Where 'was jener nöthig ist' ('what to each necessary is') is sung, the continuo leaps up from E♮ to E♭ and then down to F♯; near the end, where mercy to one's neighbour is preached, it descends through five semitones, and the piercing of the heart is expressed by a lovely unaccompanied phrase. The accentuation of the words, like that of the chorus, lays special stress on the obligations of the occasion. The number begins in B♭

and after passing through many keys finally reposes in A minor. The text is: 'The great God throws His abundance on us, who without Him even not breath have. His is it, what we are; He gives us the enjoyment, yet not, that us alone only His treasures comfort. They are the touch-stone, whereby He makes known, that He to the poverty even the necessities of life dispenses, such as He with gentle hand, what to each necessary is, to us abundantly gives. We shall to Him for His loaned good the interest not in His barns bring; pity, which on the neighbour rests, can more than all gifts Him to the heart penetrate.'

The alto aria, which speaks of imitating the goodness of the Creator and of scattering the seeds of blessing, is dry, and one is inclined to think that Bach, in his haste to produce this cantata, borrowed a number from some existing work, perhaps modifying it in some particulars. There are tender two-note figures suggestive of mercy, (c), and 'streuet' ('scatters') is set to a scattering run during which the obbligato violin solo and oboe play imitative leaps, the flinging out of the sower's arm, but the number never glows with the warmth of the inner sun. Characteristic figures are:

and:

(a) is imitated, (b) developed, derivatives simultaneously ascend and descend, and (c) is hidden away at the close of the introduction. The setting of Part I of the text—'Seinem Schöpfer noch auf Erden nur im Schatten ähnlich werden, ist im Vorschmack selig sein' ('To his Creator yet on earth only in shadow similar to become, is in the foretaste blessed to be')—is at first a vocal form of (a), and then new melodic lines, with fragments of (a) and (b) in the obbligati and bassi, suggest that is not the original verse. In Part II—'Sein Erbarmen nachzuahmen, streuet hier des Segens Saamen, den wir dorten bringen ein' ('His pity to imitate, scatters here the blessings' seeds, which we yonder bring in')—is more verisimilitude of verse and music. It begins with one bar of Part I, but 'ahmen' comes to (c), there is then the scattering run described, based partially on (b); with 'dorten' the voice soars upwards, fragments of (a) being heard in the obbligati. On a long 'ein' (which is quite meaningless) the contrary movement and the two-note figure occur. The remainder continues to repeat in varied form these ideas, though (c) is completely neglected until it introduces the coda.

The Biblical extract which opens the 'Seconda Parte' is 'Wohl-zuthun und mitzutheilen vergesset nicht, denn solche Opfer gefallen Gott wohl' ('Well to do and to share forget not, for such offerings please God well'). It is set as a bass solo with continuo, and while not of the highest quality it contains interesting points. The continuo line is a series of varied repetitions of the opening bar-and-a-half:

Ex.1212

and of:

Ex.1213

the latter frequently expanded by the bassi but never used by the voice. (a) is always set to the first three words of the text, 'Vergesset nicht' is oratorically repeated in detached phrases, the second clause is generally in plain quavers, with much leaping, and at the end has a crowning run in the upper part of the compass. Bach drives home the crux of the verse—'solche Opfer gefallen Gott wohl'—by stressing each of the five words at different times.

The soprano aria, v, is the best of the three. Obbligato unison flutes in undulating figures:

Ex.1214

Cont.
8ve lower

trillings, sequentially ascending figures:

and an idea much in evidence for purposes of accompaniment:

tell of blissful content and anticipation. The voice utilizes none of
these motives but pursues a graceful line of its own—'Höchster, was
ich habe, ist nur deine Gabe!' ('Highest, what I have is only Thy
gift!'), and at the fifth bar the complete introduction commences
again as counterpoint. Fresh vocal melodies come to 'Wenn vor
deinem Angesicht ich schon mit dem Meinen dankbar wollt'
erscheinen, willst du doch kein Opfer nicht' ('When before Thy
countenance I already with mine ('my gift') thankfully would appear,
desirest Thou then no offering'). (c) is the chief accompaniment at
first, it serves as interlude, fragments of (a) and (b) are incorporated
into the obbligato of the remainder.

A fine alto recitative with strings thanks the Almighty for His love
and declares humbly that such lowly offerings as are possible are
brought—'How shall I to Thee, oh Lord, then sufficiently requite,
what Thou in body and soul to me hast for good done? yea, what I
still receive, and such even not seldom, because I myself every hour
still to Thee give praise can? I have nothing but the spirit, to Thee
of mine own to deliver, to my neighbour the eager desire, that I to
him serviceable may be, to the poverty, what Thou to me (hast)
granted in this life, and, when it Thee pleases, the weak body to the
earth. I bring, what I can, Lord! let it Thee please, that I, what Thou
promisest, yet one day from it may have.' It leads to a simple tutti
chorale, stanza 6 of D. Denicke's paraphrase of the beatitudes—
'Kommt, laßt euch den Herren lehren'—to L. Bourgeois's 'Ainsi
qu'on oit le cerf bruire'—'Blessed are (they) who from pity To themselves take others' needs, Are compassionate with the poor, Plead

faithfully for them to God. Who helpful are with counsel, Likewise, where possible, with deed, Will again help receive And pity acquire.'

187. The only other cantata of this class which may possibly be assigned to the same year is 'Es wartet alles auf dich' for the Seventh Sunday after Trinity. The text is probably by the same anonymous librettist as that of No. 39, because the plan is the same. It is in two parts and each opens with a Biblical quotation, neither taken from the readings for the day, and the first, as before, from the Psalms. The grouping is identical—Part I, chorus, recitative, aria; Part II, aria, aria, recitative, chorale. It is different in one way, it is wholly personal. All the numbers except the recitatives were pressed into service for the Short Mass in G minor, becoming respectively the 'Cum sancto spiritu', 'Domine Fili unigenite', 'Gratias agimus', and 'Qui tollis'. The basis of the text is the Gospel, the story of the feeding of the four thousand, related in St. Mark viii. 1–9, and i is a harvest song, Psalm civ. 27, 28.

It is constructed with amazing cunning. The chief choral theme is in canon:

The opening of the introduction heralds this, but violin I continues differently after the upward leap of the fourth:

This instrumental version of 'Es wartet' plays an important part in the working out. In bar 2 the two oboes suggest the waving of corn in the breeze, while the upper strings, the continuo being silent, illustrate the movement of a sickle:

A pastoral atmosphere is created by the almost exclusive use of the oboes for (*c*). That the interpretation of (*d*) is not too fanciful will be shown later. The introduction is long and there is copious development of all themes. In bars 3–5, (*a*), foreshortened, is heard canonically, oboes and violin I, and the continuo is based upon:

which assumes great importance later. Bar 6 is (*c*) and (*d*), bars 7–9 (*b*), slightly altered, in canon for the oboes, and (*e*), 10–12 are based on semiquavers (oboe II and violin II) against syncopations and leaps for the other upper instruments and a continuo in quavers incorporating two forms of (*e*). During bars 14 and 15 another form of (*b*):

is pitted against a unison variant of (*d*) for the upper strings. A sequential and canonical (*b*) at two beats, for the oboes, occupies bars 16–19 against another canon 2 in 1, a waving idea for violin I and viola:

a canon 2 in 1 at two beats, but almost made 3 in 1 by violin II, which, however, slightly varies the melodic progression, though not the time-pattern. A form of (*e*) is in the bassi. Bar 20 is (*c*) and (*d*), bars 21–23 a development of the semiquavers of (a), in thirds, with another canon (though not entirely strict) for the oboes, on a variant of (g), and a form of (d) in the continuo. Bars 24 and 25 vary the semiquavers, oboe I and violin I, and fragments of (c) occupy the next two bars, with an (e) in the bassi. We have now reached the choral portion, and rich development of this material is in store. There are seven bars, (a) for A.S. against (b) in canon for the violins and an (e) in the continuo; before (a) is completed the canon comes for B. and T., the latter with (b) for the viola, followed by the same idea for violin II and viola in unison, then (b) for the sopranos. (c) and (d) lead to a new treatment, (a) in canon for T. and A., but at the distance of a bar, linked with a counterpoint incorporating (e):

Ex.1223 that Thou to them food   givest   in   its   time,
         dass du ih-nen Spei-se   ge - best zu sei - ner   Zeit,

the one-bar canon in the oboes, joined partially by A. and S., and (h); and, as the semiquavers are continued by the sopranos, (b) for unison oboes and violin I. Again (c) and (d) form a brief ritornello, and bars 7 to the beginning of 12 of the introduction are found in chorus and orchestra, the canon of the variant of (b) for S. and A., doubled by the oboes, and splendid leaps for the upper strings. There is now a long ritornello, bars 1–6 of the introduction, four bars of (f) alternating between violins and oboes, with the variant of (d) alternating between bassi and upper unison strings, bars 19–27 of the introduction with the higher lines reversed. A fugue begins:

Ex.1224   When   Thou   to them givest,   so gather
          Wenn   du   ih-nen gie - best, so samm -

they,
- len sie,

countersubject:

'gesättiget' being expanded into a glorious four-bar roulade with trills and leaps, the abundance of good things. The connexion between (d) and bar 3 of (j) is clear. During the exposition and extra B. & T. entries strings only accompany. At the close (b) enters in oboes and violin I, (c) and (d) without violas and continuo dovetail into a counter-exposition, S.A.T.B.S. without (j) and with new treatment. During the soprano entry the tenors sing (d):

against (c) in the oboes, and 'sammlen' is accompanied by a variant for violin I, definitely establishing it as an interpretation of the movement of a sickle. The oboes continue to add (c). A third exposition follows, (i) in A.T.B. and then unison oboes, (j) once, in the sopranos, against the A. entry. The oboes are especially favoured in this section, (c), (d), (c), (i), (a), and (c), with (d) for the basses against the last. Bars 14–23 of the introduction recur, the choir joining in at bar 16; in the concluding three bars are fragments of (c). The whole world is in a state of supreme exaltation at the thought of the prolific bounty of the All-Merciful.

A bass recitativo secco reflects on the ample provision for all living things: 'What creatures contains the great sphere of the world! Look then the mountains on, where they in thousands move. What witnesses not the flood? Crowded are streams and seas. The birds' great host flies through the air to the field. Who nourishes such numbers, and who is able to it then the necessities to deliver? Can any monarch after such glory strive? Pays all earth's gold for it indeed a single meal?'

The three arias are better in quality than those of No. 39; all are interesting, each has its distinctive individuality. That for alto (see O.C.S. 'Thou, Lord, dost crown alone', & P. 68) is unusually direct and tuneful, a popular harvest-song. One is inclined to doubt whether its present form is the original. The introduction, strings with oboe doubling violin I throughout, begins with a homophonic three-bar phrase:

Ex.1227

which is repeated immediately, marked 'piano'. These six bars are associated with 'Du Herr, du krönst allein das Jahr mit deinem Gut' ('Thou Lord, Thou crownest alone the year with Thy goodness'). The quaver rest between the two sets of instrumental bars divides 'allein' and 'das', an awkward break, very unlike Bach's methods. The first phrase is marked 'piano', the second 'pianissimo', a meaningless differentiation. The chief musical idea therefore did not spring from the text; that is contrary to his practice. There are three other ideas in the ritornello, a two-bar sequential passage:

Ex.1228

a five-bar decorative passage for violin I and oboe, with quaver groups in the inner strings and a 'tasto solo' pedal:

Ex.1229

then a sudden drop to piano, followed by a forte. Again, there is nothing in the text to call up the last idea. The voice begins with the first clause set as a new continuous melody, above continuo only. It is evidently counted as of little importance, for it gives rise to no developments and is heard only once again, in the recapitulation. (c) comes orchestrally, without voice. Instead of the customary re-statement of the first vocal phrase, the voice re-enters with (a), in the manner described. (b) follows, with a vocal line pitted against it, beginning with part of (a); after two free bars (a) comes orchestrally with vocal counterpoint, including a run on 'krönst', which over-flows into a section with continuo. Fragments resembling (a) now accompany the voice, and (c) follows with a fresh run on 'krönst'. The second section begins 'Es träufet Fett und Segen auf deines Fußes Wegen' ('There drops fatness and blessing on thy foot's paths'), 'träufet' falls like a shower of rain, 'Weg' moves upwards with the same time-pattern, the upper strings drop in staccato groups of two notes. Against the dropping quavers appears a new and picturesque figure in the continuo:

Ex. 1230

'Und deine Gnade ist's, die alles Gutes thut' ('And Thy mercy is it, which all good does') continues with bassi, one phrase of the latter recalling (a), and one entry of violin I plus oboe with the same theme. After (b) orchestrally, the first of these clauses is repeated to (a), with (d) in violin I. 'Alles' introduces a new vocal counterpoint against (c). The recapitulation is a condensation of Part I: (a) is heard in the orchestra, the opening vocal phrase, then there is a cut to bar 24, (b) comes with the melody given over to the singer, causing the awk-ward succession of words: 'du Herr, du krönst', quaver rest, 'du krönst allein'. There is yet a third counterpoint to (c), descending instead of ascending, but the fourth idea will not fit the text and so only part of its melody is heard, with the piano, forte eliminated.

St. Matthew vi. 31, 32, furnishes the text of the bass aria: 'Darum sollt ihr nicht sorgen noch sagen: was werden wir essen, was werden wir trinken? womit werden wir uns kleiden? Nach solchen Allen trachten die Heiden. Denn euer himmlischer Vater weiß, daß ihr dies Alles bedürfet' ('Therefore shall ye not sorrow nor say: what shall we eat, what shall we drink? wherewith shall we ourselves clothe? After such things strive the heathen. For your Heavenly Father knows, that ye all these things need'). (See P. 69.) It is a curious choice for an aria, more suitable for an arioso. As in most other cases where sayings of the Saviour are set, the music is simple and the style very different from the normal aria. The accompaniment is for violins in unison and continuo. The introduction announces three ideas, a sequential movement of crotchets and quavers:

Ex. 1231

syncopated minims, serving as counterpoint to (a), and a continuous passage of quavers:

Ex. 1232

Most of the vocal line is ingeniously derived from these motives with modifications, preserving flexibility and textual fitness to the many short verbal clauses. In the opening bars of the vocal portion cross accents are produced by 'sorgen' and 'sagen'; accent must be according to words and not bar-lines. The questions are usually set to (a). Interesting points in this effective aria are the threefold ascending sequence to 'womit', the solemn modulation at 'die Heiden' and the run, based on (a), to 'Heiden', and the way in which 'Denn', 'weiß', and 'daß' are thrust upwards in the latter part.

The soprano aria is as elaborate as that for bass is simple, a deeply felt song of thanksgiving. The sinner is touched by the goodness of the Almighty and pours out her heart in gratitude. In the first section, Adagio, both vocal line and oboe obbligato are ornate, the latter particularly abounding in tender arabesques. The chief melody serves for both obbligato and voice (Ex. 1233), and as the singer continues in short phrases to modifications of the opening—'was hienieden Odem hegt' ('that here below breath has')—the oboe carols its bountiful flourishes. 'Sollt' er mir allein nicht geben, was er allen zugesagt?' ('Should He to me alone not give, what He to all (has) promised?') develops ♩♪ both in voice and obbligato, and a

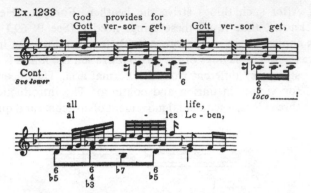

Ex. 1233

Ex.1234

staccato cry 'was, was' brings again oboe demisemiquavers. With the words 'Weicht, ihr Sorgen' ('Yield, ye sorrows') the time is changed to $\frac{3}{8}$ and the tempo to *un poco allegro*, and staccato oboe phrases indicate lightness of heart:

A scalic passage is heard to the repetition of these words, and also in continuo and voice, once inverted, during 'seine Treue ist auch mei-ner eingedenk und wird ob mir täglich neue durch manch' Vater-Liebsgeschenk' ('His faithfulness is also of me mindful and becomes for me daily new through many Father-love-gifts'). A modified ver-sion of bars 1–5 of the introduction, without voice, rounds off the aria. The same voice sings a recitative with strings, preaching faith and gratitude through the trials that are ordained of God—'Hold I only fast to Him with childlike faith, and take with gratitude, what He to me destined (has), so shall I me never without help see, and how He also for me the reckoning has made. The complaining profits not, the trouble is lost, which the faint heart for its need takes; the ever rich God has for Himself the sorrow chosen, so know I, that He for me also my portion ordains.'

Two verses of a tutti chorale of praise conclude. Both melody and hymn—'Singen wir aus Herzensgrund', a Grace after meat—are anonymous. Stanzas 4 and 6 are employed—'God has the earth beautifully arranged, Permits of nourishment to want not; Mountain and valley, these makes He wet, That for the cattle also grows its grass; From the earth wine and bread Creates God, and gives us plenty, So that the man his life has.' 'We thank greatly and beg Him, That He to us (may) give the spirit's sense, That we such rightly understand, Constantly after His laws walk, His name make great In Christ without intermission: So sing we the Gratias.'

(viii) *Wholly Original Libretti*
63, 181

63. Only two cantatas now remain to complete our study of the middle period. 'Christen, ätzet diesen Tag' ('Christians, grave ye this glad day', N.) for Christmas Day, possibly 1723, not only includes neither Biblical quotation nor chorale, but is without aria. Three contrasted recitatives, two duets, and two large choruses provide a well-varied musical scheme; the first chorus, the second duet and the third recitative call upon believers to rejoice, the first duet and second chorus are prayers, the first and second recitatives tell us of the change brought to the world through the birth of the Saviour. The librettist is unknown; perhaps the text is from the tireless pen of the composer and the work may have been intended as a companion to the Latin Magnificat. To take the recitatives first—that for alto, ii, with strings, is long, running to thirty-two bars, and blends arioso with declamation. It begins with an expressive flourish on the adjective of ('O sel'ger Tag!' ('O blessed day!'), an exclamation of delight, and continues—'Oh uncommon day, on which the salvation of the world, the Shiloh, which God already in Paradise to the human race promised, henceforth itself fully presented (has)', ('Shiloh' is a Hebraic word meaning 'Messiah'). A splendid passage terminates 'and seeks Israel from the imprisonment and slave-chains of Satan to deliver'. On 'Ketten' ('chains') adagio is indicated, the continuo struggles up and down as if striving to free itself from the shackles, 'erretten' ('deliver') is allotted a similar, but even more convoluting run, ending with a turn and a trill. 'Thou dearest God! what are we poor ones then?' is melismatic. At the close of 'A fallen people, who Thee forsake, And yet wilt Thou us not hate! For before we shall still after our deserts on the earth lie' (see Ex. 1286) the key changes startlingly from A minor to F major, the bassi moving by an awesome diminished third. The strings are low-lying during 'before must the Godhead deem it fitting human nature on Himself to take, and on the earth, in the ox-stall, a child to become'. The end of this magnificent number is extraordinarily fine. 'O unbegreifliches, doch seliges

Verfügen!' ('Oh inconceivable, yet blessed enactment!') is sung twice; the phrase to the first 'seliges Verfügen' is imitated by the continuo and comes twice in the ritornello; the final half-close leaves one in a state of expectancy.

The tenor recitativo secco, iv, is short, but full of variety. The chosen peoples acknowledge the new dispensation—'So turns itself now today the fearful suffering, with which Israel (was) distressed and laden'. An andante arioso repeats 'into pure praise and mercy' with imitations between voice and continuo. A steadfast note supports 'The lion from David's stem has appeared'. Upward rushing demisemiquavers and descending arpeggi illustrate the flight of mighty arrows in 'His bow is stretched, the sword is already whetted, wherewith He us in former freedom sets'.

The bass recitative, vi, is in yet another style. It is marked 'Achtstimmig' ('eight-part'), three oboes, strings and *fagotto, organo e continuo* contributing seven independent lines. Stroke after stroke of the orchestra drives home the injunction 'Redouble you therefore, ye hot devotion's-flames, and strike in humility ardently together'. 'Mount joyfully heavenwards' soars aloft, unaccompanied, and then, in an *andante e piano*, the continuo moves in a confident melodic line, the other instruments play detached quaver chords on all beats and the voice contentedly repeats 'und danket Gott für dies, was er gethan' ('and thank God for this, that He (has) done'). (See Ex. 1276.) Four forte chords end this splendid number.

The first duet, iii, is for S.B., adagio, with oboe obbligato. The text dwells upon the bounteousness of the Almighty; the oboe begins with a semiquaver phrase and then breaks into florid passages with many trills:

Ex. 1235

the overflowing benefactions of our Maker. (*a*) is frequently used as a motive by the bassi, the vocal lines are florid and canonical.

Ex. 1236

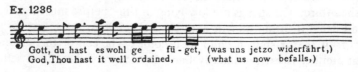

Gott, du hast es wohl ge - fü - get, (was uns jetzo widerfährt,)
God, Thou hast it well ordained,   (what us now befalls,)

is heard nine times, sometimes against (*a*) in the continuo; the oboe pours out its bountifully ornate melodies. After the *Fine* pause we are bidden to rely upon Him continually—'Drum laßt uns auf ihn stets trauen und auf seine Gnade bauen' ('Therefore let us on Him continually trust and on His mercy build')—and voices and continuo move in firm scales, the first four bars being a vocal canon. (*a*) is repeated sequentially in the continuo, while the voices imitate to 'denn er hat uns dies bescheert' ('for He has on us this bestowed'). A florid oboe passage brings us to 'was uns ewig nun vergnüget' ('what us ever now contents') in gracious canonical phrases for the voices, a placidly moving continuo, with (*a*) in the bassi during repetitions of 'vergnüget'.

The other voices, A. and T., are provided for in the second duet, v, with strings. It is bright and tuneful, with splendid descending arpeggi for violin I against upward springs for violin II and viola:

The bright opening serves for the chief vocal entries:

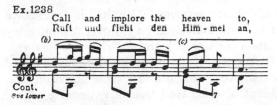

and the answering phrase in the introduction is delightfully apt:

There is a trilling motive:

which, as well as (*b*), is heard also in the continuo, which has in addition many octave leaps. Christians are called upon to come into the ranks, 'Kommt, ihr Christen, kommt zum Reihen' ('Come, ye Christians, come into the ranks', 'circle' or 'community'), and, as 'Reihen' may also mean a round dance, we have veritable dances on the word. (*b*) is used in abundance, both in the orchestral and vocal lines, (*c*) and (*d*) in violin I, and while the alto swings to 'Reihen' and the tenor sings a derivative of (*c*):

Ex.1241

Kommt, ihr Chri - sten,

(*a*) leaps and bounds. An instance of Bach's fertility in transforming his themes is an earlier derivative of (*c*):

Ex.1242

Kommt, ihr   Chri - sten,

'Ihr sollt euch ob dem erfreuen' ('Ye shall in that rejoice') is twice given short sections, imitations on (*b*) over continuo, separated by similar imitation for violins I and II. They are followed by a five-bar canon for the same instruments, based on (*b*) and (*c*), dovetailing into a new short vocal canon and a termination on 'was Gott hat anheut' gethan!' ('which God has today done!'). (*d*), (*e*), (*a*), and (*b*) form a ritornello, and 'Da uns seine Huld verpfleget und mit so viel Heil beleget, daß man nicht g'nug danken kann' ('When us His graciousness maintains and with so much prosperity loads, that one not enough thank can') is set as a thirteen-bar canon with continuo moving mostly by octave leaps. The last clause is repeated, the tenor beginning with a downward scale leading to a semiquaver trill and run, during which the alto reverses the scale and then joins in the florid movement, (*b*) joining this to the same ideas with voices reversed. The trill now comes in thirds with (*d*) in the orchestra and then the clause is broken by rests in joyous exaltation while fragments of (*b*) occur in the bassi. (*b*) and (*c*) herald a modification of the opening vocal section. The blend of canonical device, straightforward tunes and the circling movement provides a delightful picture of the

happy condition of believers swinging and swaying in a dance of unbounded joy.

Tremendous choruses open and close the cantata, employing four
trumpets, timpani, three oboes, bassoon (sometimes independent),
and strings. The first is of the type with which we are familiar in the
opening of the Christmas Oratorio and the 'Gloria' of the B Minor
Mass, $\frac{3}{8}$ time, allegro, ringing, and tuneful. Bars 1–10 of the introduction do not leave the chord of C major, a turn-like semiquaver
figure is thrown from group to group with big chords hurled against
it, bassi and bassoon leaping in octaves:

This is repeated in canon between the three trumpets and the upper
strings, and a second figure:

is developed by strings and trumpets. Fragments of (a) and the complete theme in canon between the upper strings and the oboes
terminate the introduction. The voices, sopranos followed at once
by the lower lines together, begin with strings only:

and after a short outburst of (aa) from brass and percussion,
strings, oboes, and fagotto are left for a while to accompany the
choir:

Ex.1246

A thirteen-bar florid canon between sopranos and basses, the other parts joining them in thirds or shouting short answering phrases, brings us to the end of the first choral section. (*aa*), tossed from upper strings to oboes and to trumpets, ushers in the next, where the previous material is presented in different ways, the position of the voices being reversed in the canon. After this the whole of the orchestral introduction is repeated; it concludes on the *Fine* pause and the choir enters again, with continuo:

Ex.1247

Again the sopranos enter before the other voices, the basses being for a while in canon. The passage reminds one of the first chorus of the Easter Oratorio, where the disciples hurry to the sepulchre. In the same broad style the choir continues: 'und erweist mit frohen Lippen euren Dank und eure Pflicht' ('and prove with glad lips your thanks and your duty'). An instrumental interlude, based on (*a*), is made brilliant by simultaneous trills for trumpets I and II. This is an anticipation of the next line of the text—'Denn der Strahl so da einbricht' ('For the ray which there in breaks') and in the choral section the voices stream gloriously up and down. After (*a*) comes the final choral section: 'zeigt sich euch zum Gnadenscheine' ('shows itself to you as the mercy-light'). Except for the 'Strahl' section, the unusual plan of beginning with one voice, soprano or bass, and answering by the other three, is adhered to for the opening of the choral portions, and all but one end with cadences throwing two bars of $\frac{3}{8}$ into three of $\frac{2}{8}$. The frequency of canons is a striking feature of the cantata.

The final chorus is a prayer, but that of a clamorous multitude. It opens with a brass and percussion fanfare:

Ex. 1248

and the oboes follow with a short idea:

Ex. 1249

This is repeated by violins and violas, and when reed and string groups unite this figure accompanies brilliant demisemiquaver rushes, (c), in oboe I and violin. Trumpets and drums resume with (b), and the rest of the ritornello, based on (b) and (c), concludes in a glorious blaze of sound. The choir begins with a modified form of the opening fanfare, accompanied by continuo only: 'Höchster, schau' in Gnaden an' ('Highest, contemplate in mercy'). It is answered by (b) and (c), strings and oboes, brass and percussion clenching the ritornello. Against (a) in tromba I, accompanied by all the other orchestral forces, the choir repeats the clause with the idea modified, and continues, without brass and percussion, fragments of (b) for the oboes being replied to by arpeggi in the upper strings: 'diese Gluth gebückter Seelen' ('this ardour of bowed souls' or 'souls making obeisance'). Twin fugue themes are announced, the lower afterwards proving the principal:

Ex. 1250

After five bars of unaccompanied singing, a most unusual procedure, these are worked out in the usual manner, at first with continuo only, then strings and oboes entering step by step. The soprano ceases for nearly six bars after the bass entry; when it reappears, with (d), trumpet I follows quickly in stretto. The latter follows with (c) against (d) in the basses. Timpani and lower trumpets now clench the final choral cadence, and an exact duplication of the introduction brings us to the *Fine* pause. A few straightforward bars for chorus—'Laß den Dank, den wir dir bringen, angenehme vor dir klingen, laß uns stets in Segen gehn' ('Let the thanks, which we to Thee bring, pleasingly before Thee sound, let us ever in blessing walk')—are at first accompanied by continuo and then by oboes, fagotto, and strings. Two bars of ritornello, based on (*b*) and (*c*), bring us to an Adagio—'aber niemals nicht geschehn' ('but never not happen,' the old-fashioned double negative), a momentary solemn remembrance of the period before Christ came to free the world. *Tempo primo* is restored when the sentence continues, though not so indicated. A triple subject is announced, the chief idea being descending semitones, the tormentings of Satan; another is in stubborn repeated quavers, and the third embodies the joy-motive, the assurance that by resistance the Evil One will be thwarted:

As these are developed oboes and strings gradually enter, and then tromba I and oboe I take up the quaver theme, extending it by a flourish on the joy-motive, carried further by oboe I alone. At the close of this choral section, trumpet I, beginning on high C, peals out the semitone idea. Oboes and tromba I and then violins and violas return to (*b*) and continue with it while the choir sings a few bars of fresh matter, leading to the Da Capo. One unusual feature in i and vii is the relative brevity of the choral sections; the orchestral ritornelli dominate both numbers.

181. The Gospel for Sexagesima is St. Luke viii. 4–15, the parable of the sower. An anonymous librettist, somewhere about 1725, provided the composer with a fine text in which almost every reference is to the parable. 'Leichtgesinnte Flattergeister' shows how keenly Bach realized its possibilities. The opening bass aria is most remarkable, unlike anything else in the cantatas. The fowls of the air devoured the seed; Christ explained that this was the devil, who

'taketh away the word out of their hearts, lest they should believe
and be saved'. 'Light-minded fickle persons' which 'rob themselves
of the word's strength' are imagined as devouring birds; the orchestra, flauto traverso, oboe and strings, begins with a short and
vehement staccato passage culminating in a trill, the fluttering of the
evil harpies and the flapping of their wings:

Ex.1252 *Vivace*

It is repeated and followed by two shorter ideas:

Ex.1253
(as before)

which suggest the nervous, eager movements of the hungry seekers
after seeds. (*a*) is first associated with 'Leichtgesinnte Flattergeister'
and then the upper strings repeat (*b*). 'Kraft' is elongated against
bar 5 of the introduction and 2½ bars of the introduction follow.
Upper strings and oboe accompany the repetition of the first part of
the vocal theme, the bassi being silent except for a reiterated (*b*).
'Rauben sich des Wortes Kraft' ('Rob themselves of the word's
strength') is without its florid ending, and (*c*) is heard in violin I,
the oboe joining each time for the last two notes, (*b*) in the middle
strings and isolated quaver octave leaps for the continuo; the voice
climbs tortuously to 'leichtgesinnte Flattergeister' and during the
rest of the clause the bassi plunge headlong down in a two-octave
semiquaver scale. This, reduced to one octave, is a feature of the
continuo line when the previous ritornello is repeated. It is the symbol
of Belial. Part II of the text begins: 'Belial mit seinen Kindern suchet
ohnedem zu hindern, daß es keinen Nutzen schafft' ('Belial with his
brood seeks besides to prevent, that it any profit procures'). 'Belial'
is solemnly intoned twice, the second time a tone higher, against (*a*)
and the scale, and then the complete sentence is sung to phrases
indicative of obstinacy, the upper strings dashing about and the bassi

rolling down their scale. (*a*) and (*c*) in violin I and oboe, with (*b*) in the middle strings, accompany 'daß es keinen Nutzen schafft'. The 'Belial' clause is repeated to (*a*), identifying the devouring fowls with Satan and his spawn, and fluttering phrases, with (*a*) in the orchestra. (*a*) and (*c*) lead to a repetition of the first vocal section, which is without the florid roulade. Normally Bach would not have returned to the second part of the text, but the imagery is too intriguing to be resisted, so after (*c*) for the strings the whole of its setting is repeated, modified, one ominous feature being the repetition of 'Belial' an augmented, instead of a major, second higher. There is an element of grimness which holds one spellbound during this extraordinary aria, the ravenous birds appear in devastating flocks, filling the air with their horrid clamour.

The alto recitativo secco is also remarkable and is crowded with long chains of dissonances. Bach thrice uses what is for him a remarkable device. After the exclamation 'Oh', 'unfortunate condition of perverted souls' is sung to a modification of (*a*) in i, 'which as it were by the wayside are' brings another form, and, after 'who will yet Satan's cunning tell' it comes to 'when he the word from the heart robs'. Four successive dissonances accompany 'which, of discernment blind, the mischief neither understands nor believes'. In andante arioso—'They become rocky hearts, who evilly resist, their own salvation trifle away, their own salvation trifle away and one day to the bottom go'—both voice and continuo hammer out repeated note ideas. A bar of recitative—'There operates yea Christ's last word'—leads to an Andante—'that rocks even burst in sunder; the angel's hand moves the grave's stone'—the bassi violently crash down for two octaves, like a boulder bounding down a hillside. (It is a pity that the Breitkopf vocal score overloads this with right-hand arpeggi.) Recitative is resumed: 'yea Moses' staff can there from a mountain water bring.' The number ends with a query—'Wilt thou, oh heart, yet harder be?' One cannot forbear quoting the remarkable final continuo bars:

Ex. 1254

A relief from this tenseness is provided by the introduction to the tenor aria. The continuo, the sole accompaniment, *piano e staccato per tutto*, treads steadily for thirty-four bars:

Ex.1255
(a)

and:

Ex.1256
(b)

the marching through life of the pilgrim. None of its motives are heard vocally, but, except for an occasional semiquaver run, the onward movement is maintained in the bassi throughout. The text grimly recounts the hindrances to the Christian life: 'Der schädlichen Dornen unendliche Zahl, die Sorgen der Wollust, die Schätze zu mehren, die werden das Feuer der höllischen Qual in Ewigkeit nähren' ('Of the dangerous thorns' countless number, the cares of desire, the treasures to multiply, they will the fire of hellish torment in eternity nourish'). The music skims over them lightly; runs on 'mehren' and 'Feuer', a chord of the minor ninth on 'Der schädlichen Dornen', a chord of the Neapolitan sixth above a low pulsating bass on 'höllischen Qual', are mere ripples on the surface of the water, over which the vessel of life moves as a ship in full sail with a gentle breeze behind her. Even 'Ewigkeit', though the fire of hellish torture is to be encountered there, is a calm sustained note against an unagitated continuo, (a). It is a curious type of treatment; one wonders what Bach meant by it. The time-pattern of the first complete bar of:

Ex.1257
Der schäd-li - chen Dor-nen un - end-li - che Zahl,

Cont.
8ve higher

is much heard in the vocal line, though once only in the bassi; it is incorporated into the first long run on 'nähren', which is a transformation of the ascending portion of (b).

The text of the soprano recitativo secco is possibly a reference to St. Paul's 'there was given to me a thorn in the flesh, the messenger of Satan to buffet me, lest I should be exalted above measure' in the Epistle, 2 Corinthians, xi. 19–xii. 9: 'By these is the strength choked, the noble seed lies fruitless. Whosoever himself not properly in spirit prepares, his heart betimes as good soil to prepare, that our heart the sweet things may taste, thus to us this word discloses the powers of this and of the future life.' (The *BGS* text is somewhat confused, Wustmann's emendation is followed here.)

The chorus is reserved till the final number, in which a trumpet is added to the orchestra. For five bars unison flute, oboe, and violin I pursue a semiquaver run, the tromba is independent, the continuo announces a syncopated octave figure, the other strings merely fill in. At bar 6 the trumpet takes up the semiquavers, in a different manner, and flute, oboe, and violin I trill a sustained note. The chorus begins with a prayer for the Holy word at all time as consolation. Sopranos and tenors lead off with a dual theme, the lower subject expressing perpetual faith in the continual fulfilment of the prayer:

Ex. 1258

When altos and basses take these up, tenors and sopranos borrow the tromba semiquavers and the held note from bars 6 and 7. A turn-like figure, ascending in sequence:

Ex. 1259

comes in all voices by way of episode. So far the chorus has been accompanied by continuo only. We have now four blocks of the dual idea, always accompanied by the two countersubjects, and these blocks are separated by the 'Herzens Trost' theme, with bassi only. It is characteristic of Bach's methods that the five entries of the four combined themes are always grouped differently, and that the four 'Herzens Trost' episodes show different orders of entries. The introduction is repeated to lead to the *Fine* pause. Sopranos, altos, and continuo only are heard in the next section: 'Du kannst nach deiner Allmachts-Hand allein ein fruchtbar gutes Land in unsern Herzen zubereiten' ('Thou canst with Thine Almighty-hand alone a fruitful good soil in our hearts prepare'). The vocal lines are richly florid, a parallel semiquaver run on 'Allmachts', imitative roulades on 'zubereiten', all suggestive of an overflowing abundance. In bars 11–13 and 17–18 the voices follow each other at the distance of a beat, producing that intriguing cross-accentuation with which we are familiar in Tudor choral music. The 'Höchster' syncopation of the upper theme is heard from time to time; the continuo indulges nearly all through in joyous leaping. Spitta thinks the number to be adapted from some lost secular cantata, a theory which the absence of male voices in the middle section supports.